Deploying Cisco
Voice over IP Solutions

Edited by: Jonathan Davidson and Tina Fox

Contributing Authors:

Phil Bailey

Rommel Bajamundi

Wayne Cheung

Thu Dao

Jonathan Davidson

Tina Fox

Sachin Gupta

Christina Hattingh

Ted Huff

Stephen Liu

Curt Mah

Greg Mercurio

Jeremy Pollock

Jim Rushton

Ravindar Shankar

Cisco Press

Cisco Press
201 W 103rd Street
Indianapolis, IN 46290 USA

Deploying Cisco Voice over IP Solutions

Jonathan Davidson, Tina Fox, et. al.

Copyright© 2002 Cisco Systems, Inc.

Published by:
Cisco Press
201 West 103rd Street
Indianapolis, IN 46290 USA

Printed in the United States of America 1 2 3 4 5 6 7 8 9 0

Library of Congress Cataloging-in-Publication Number: 2001086622

ISBN:1-58705-030-7

1st printing October 2001

Warning and Disclaimer

This book is designed to provide information about Voice over IP. Every effort has been made to make this book as complete and as accurate as possible, but no warranty or fitness is implied.

The information is provided on an "as is" basis. The authors, Cisco Press, and Cisco Systems, Inc., shall have neither liability nor responsibility to any person or entity with respect to any loss or damages arising from the information contained in this book.

The opinions expressed in this book belong to the authors and are not necessarily those of Cisco Systems, Inc.

Trademark Acknowledgments

All terms mentioned in this book that are known to be trademarks or service marks have been appropriately capitalized. Cisco Press or Cisco Systems, Inc., cannot attest to the accuracy of this information. Use of a term in this book should not be regarded as affecting the validity of any trademark or service mark.

Feedback Information

At Cisco Press, our goal is to create in-depth technical books of the highest quality and value. Each book is crafted with care and precision, undergoing rigorous development that involves the unique expertise of members from the professional technical community.

Readers' feedback is a natural continuation of this process. If you have any comments regarding how we could improve the quality of this book or otherwise alter it to better suit your needs, you can contact us through e-mail at feedback@ciscopress.com. Please make sure to include the book title and ISBN in your message.

We greatly appreciate your assistance.

Publisher	John Wait
Editor-In-Chief	John Kane
Cisco Systems Management	Michael Hakkert
	Tom Geitner
	William Warren
Production Manager	Patrick Kanouse
Development Editor	Andrew Cupp
Senior Editor	Sheri Cain
Copy Editor	Doug Lloyd
Technical Editor	Martin Walshaw
Team Coordinator	Tammi Ross
Cover Designer	Louisa Klucznik
Production Team	Argosy Publishing
Indexers	Tim Wright
	Larry Sweazy

CISCO SYSTEMS

Corporate Headquarters
Cisco Systems, Inc.
170 West Tasman Drive
San Jose, CA 95134-1706
USA
http://www.cisco.com
Tel: 408 526-4000
        800 553-NETS (6387)
Fax: 408 526-4100

European Headquarters
Cisco Systems Europe
11 Rue Camille Desmoulins
92782 Issy-les-Moulineaux
Cedex 9
France
http://www-europe.cisco.com
Tel: 33 1 58 04 60 00
Fax: 33 1 58 04 61 00

Americas Headquarters
Cisco Systems, Inc.
170 West Tasman Drive
San Jose, CA 95134-1706
USA
http://www.cisco.com
Tel: 408 526-7660
Fax: 408 527-0883

Asia Pacific Headquarters
Cisco Systems Australia, Pty.,
Ltd
Level 17, 99 Walker Street
North Sydney
NSW 2059 Australia
http://www.cisco.com
Tel: +61 2 8448 7100
Fax: +61 2 9957 4350

Cisco Systems has more than 200 offices in the following countries. Addresses, phone numbers, and fax numbers are listed on the Cisco Web site at www.cisco.com/go/offices

Argentina • Australia • Austria • Belgium • Brazil • Bulgaria • Canada • Chile • China • Colombia • Costa Rica • Croatia • Czech Republic • Denmark • Dubai, UAE • Finland • France • Germany • Greece • Hong Kong • Hungary • India • Indonesia • Ireland • Israel • Italy • Japan • Korea • Luxembourg • Malaysia • Mexico • The Netherlands • New Zealand • Norway • Peru • Philippines • Poland • Portugal • Puerto Rico • Romania • Russia • Saudi Arabia • Scotland • Singapore • Slovakia • Slovenia • South Africa • Spain • Sweden • Switzerland • Taiwan • Thailand • Turkey • Ukraine • United Kingdom • United States • Venezuela • Vietnam • Zimbabwe

About the Editors and Authors

Jonathan Davidson (CCIE #2560) is the Manager of Service Provider Technical Marketing for Packet Voice at Cisco Systems. He focuses on working with service provider and enterprise customers to develop solutions that are deployable in the new infrastructure of data and voice convergence. This includes designing customer networks and assisting with product direction.

Jonathan has been working on packet voice technologies for three years. During his seven years in the data-networking industry, he worked in various capacities, including network design, configuring, troubleshooting, and deploying data and voice networks.

Tina Fox is currently the Integration Solutions program manager for the Knowledge Management and Delivery group (IOS Technologies Division) at Cisco Systems and has been with Cisco Systems for 5 years. She attended the University of California at Los Angeles for both her undergraduate degree and graduate studies and completed a Certificate in Data and Telecommunications at the University of California at Irvine.

Phil Bailey is currently the technical documentation program manager for early deployment IOS releases for the Knowledge Management and Delivery group at Cisco Systems. He has a BSE in astronautical engineering, an M.Ed. in secondary education, and 15 years experience writing technical documentation for voice and data communications technologies, including Voice over IP, Voice over Frame Relay, and Voice over ATM.

Rommel Bajamundi is a Technical Marketing Engineer in Service Provider Technical Marketing at Cisco Systems. He has worked on various voice technologies at Cisco Systems for over 5 years and has focused on Voice over IP technologies for over three years.

Wayne Cheung is a manager in Service Provider Technical Marketing at Cisco Systems.

Thu Dao has been employed in the Voice over IP group at Cisco Systems for 4 years, mainly developing voice applications. She received her MS in computer science from Stanford University in December 1990.

Sachin Gupta (CCIE #3682) is currently the Manager of the Cisco IOS Technical Marketing group. Sachin worked in customer support at Cisco for the WAN and Multiservice teams for two years, and then as a Technical Marketing Engineer in Cisco IOS Technologies Division focusing on QoS and MPLS for two more years. Sachin holds a BS in electrical engineering from Purdue University and is completing his MS in electrical engineering at Stanford University.

Christina Hattingh is a member of the Technical Marketing organization at Cisco Systems. In this role, she works closely with product management and engineering, and focuses on assisting Cisco Sales Engineers, partners, and customers to design and tune enterprise and service provider Voice over X networks. Prior to this, she was a software engineer and engineering manager of PBX Call Center products at Nortel Networks. Earlier software development experience in X.25 and network management systems provide background to the issues involved today in migrating customers' traditional data and voice networks to packet-based technologies. Christina has a graduate degree in computer science and mathematical statistics.

Ted Huff has been Technical Marketing Engineer in the Service Provider TME group at Cisco Systems for almost 5 years. After graduating from California State University Chico in 1994 with a bachelor of science degree in computer engineering, Ted found his way to Cisco via Lockheed Martin.

All of Ted's time at Cisco has been in the same TME organization, where he has been involved in various aspects of Voice over IP technology including billing and accounting, interactive voice response programming, store and forward fax, and network management.

When not at his desk or in the lab, Ted enjoys working around the garden and spending time with his wife Catherine and his two lovely daughters, Anna and Jessi.

Stephen Liu is currently Manager of Service Provider Technical Marketing at Cisco Systems, where he has been employed for the past 6 years. He received his BSEE in Communications Systems from the University of California at San Diego and is CCIE certified (CCIE #2430). Stephen has served as Cisco's H.323 VoIP representative to IMTC/ETSI TIPHON and co-chaired the IMTC iNOW! H.323 Interoperability Forum. In his spare time, Stephen volunteers as a youth soccer coach.

Curt Mah (CCIE #3856) is a Technical Marketing Engineer for Cisco Systems, working on Voice over IP and wholesale voice networks for the service provider line of business. Curt joined Cisco Systems in 1996 and has worked assisting customers in various data networking capacities, including network design, training, implementation, and troubleshooting. Curt has a BSE in electronic engineering technology from Cal Poly, San Luis Obispo.

Greg Mercurio is a Senior Software Engineer at Cisco Systems. "Empowering the customer through advanced Internet media!"

Jeremy Pollock is a Technical Writer for Cisco Systems, working on Cisco IOS software documentation. He writes feature and solution documentation, specializing in VoIP and access VPDN documentation. He received a B.A. in physics from the University of California in 1997 and a Certificate in Technical Communications from San Jose State University in 1998.

Jim Rushton has worked with enterprise networking technology in various capacities for more than 15 years. He is currently a Cisco Systems Technical Writer in the Irvine, California office, assigned to the IOS Technologies Division.

Ravindar Shankar is a senior technical marketing engineer with a focus on voice solutions in service provider marketing. He has been with Cisco for 8 years and has served in the capacities of customer support, development engineering, and most recently in voice technical marketing. He has a master's degree, holds a patent in network management, is CCIE certified (CCIE #1303), and has a good understanding of both data and voice technologies.

About the Technical Reviewer

Martin Walshaw, (CCIE #5629), CCNP, CCDP, is a Systems Engineer working for Cisco Systems in the Enterprise Line of Business in South Africa. His areas of specialty include Convergence (voice and video) and security, which keeps him busy both night and day. During the last 12 years Martin has dabbled in many aspects of the IT industry, ranging from programming in RPG III and Cobol to PC sales. When Martin is not working, he likes to spend all of his available time with his expectant wife Val and his son Joshua. Without their patience, understanding, and support, projects such as this would not be possible. "To Infinity and beyond . . ."

Dedications

To Tina, whose dedication and determination made this project possible, and whose constant encouragement persuaded me to become a part of it.—Phil Bailey

Many thanks to my family for always being there. Thanks to all the folks on my team who help me on a daily basis: Jon Davidson, Stephen Liu, Brian Gracely, Wayne Cheung, Conrad Price, Ravi Shankhar, Anand Ramachandran, Edmund Lam, David Morgan, Oscar Thomas, Ted Huff, Shyam Kota, Curt Mah, Aseem Srivasta, and Wei Wang. Special thanks to my wife, Josie, who keeps me going.—Rommel Bajamundi

To my mother, Uma Gupta, for her strength, love, and support, always.—Sachin Gupta

My contribution to this book was made possible in large part by the technical guidance and mentorship of a number of Cisco colleagues—with particular thanks to Jonathan Davidson, Brian Gracely, Conrad Price, and Chris Spain. I dedicate this book to Robert Verkroost who never fails to support and encourage me in my various forays into the world of publishing.—Christina Hattingh

To Mom and Dad: Thanks for all of the wisdom and guidance over the years. To Tammy: Thanks for always providing love and encouragement to chase my dreams, and for reminding me of the power of "Hakuna Matata."—Curt Mah

To my family, for allowing me to spend the extra time to make a difference.—Greg Mercurio

To my parents for all of their love and support as I stumble along towards the life I'm trying to live. And to Tammy for keeping me in touch with life beyond networking and for showing me the power of the written word to make the real world a better place.—Jeremy Pollock

Acknowledgments

The writing of this book was a group effort and could not have been completed without the dedicated leadership and sacrifice of Tina Fox. She helped keep the book on track and quite literally was the brains and driving force behind this endeavor. A special thanks goes to her. I would also like to thank the writers who smoothed out the material submitted by the subject matter experts (SMEs) and created a single voice for the book. This includes Tina Fox, Phil Bailey, Jeremy Pollock, and Jim Rushton.

The SMEs wrote the initial draft of each of the chapters and provided expertise in specific areas. This book is truly a consolidation of some of the brightest minds in packet telephony today. These SMEs have real-world, in-depth knowledge of how the protocols work in live networks. Thus, the reader will receive up-to-date knowledge of the latest techniques and technologies in the packet voice arena. These SMEs include Christina Hattingh, Sachin Gupta, Rommel Bajamundi, Kevin Connor, Stephen Liu, Thu Dao, Curt Mah, Ted Huff, Wayne Cheung, Greg Mercurio, Ravi Shankar, and Massimiliano Caranza.

—Jonathan Davidson

Contents at a Glance

Contents

Introduction

This book is a sequel to *Voice over IP Fundamentals*, published by Cisco Press in 2000. Since the publication of that book, there has been a fundamental change in the assumptions made by those in the telecommunications industry. Instead of incumbent telecommunications service providers attempting to determine whether packet voice will be a viable technology, they are attempting to determine the right opportunity to begin deploying this technology. These providers are either actively researching the technology, conducting lab trials, or deploying it. In addition, existing TDM equipment providers have determined that they must provide packet voice equipment in addition to their TDM equipment. These equipment providers are forced down this path due to the fact that their customers want and need to purchase this type of equipment.

The next phase of packet voice will focus not just on lowering equipment costs (capital expenditures), but lowering operating expenditures. This phase will be completed over time by integrating voice technology into Network Management Systems (NMS) owned by incumbent carriers as well as integrating IP data NMS technology and packet voice network management systems.

Although service providers realize that there are many benefits to packet voice technology, they also recognize that there are potential downsides to this technology. The largest of the potential caveats is multi-vendor equipment interoperability. Although there are many standards defining how devices should communicate with each other, there are few standards defining how these independent standards should communicate with each other. One example is how many existing networks utilize H.323 to signal voice calls over IP. There are several newer protocols, however, that appear to have momentum in this space—MGCP, MEGACO, and SIP, for example.

The good news about *protocol interworking* is that there is much work being done in this space. Each major protocol has its own interoperability event at least yearly. There is a good analogy that can be drawn from the data networking industry. There are dozens of routing protocols currently in use across the world for routing IP across heterogeneous networks (OSPF, IS-IS, BGP, EIGRP, and so on), and all of these protocols must interoperate with one another in order for IP networks to be truly ubiquitous. This interoperability has, of course, been accomplished. Another comparison that can be drawn between packet voice signaling protocols and IP routing protocols is that there is a definite need for each of these protocols in certain types of networks, and one cannot expect to erase the need for another. In the packet voice space, a newer protocol such as MEGACO may be better for certain applications, but it doesn't solve the same problem that protocols such as H.323 solve. Therefore, they are both necessary, and interoperability between the two is required.

The interoperability between equipment vendors will be solved, and then the next level of interoperability will bubble to the surface—that of service interoperability, or how users can utilize a similar application across an entire service area in a similar manner.

Purpose of This Book

The purpose of this book is to provide you with a basic understanding of some of the advanced topics associated with designing and implementing a VoIP network. As such, this book is meant to accomplish the following goals:

- Provide an introduction to some of the more important preliminary design elements that need to be considered before implementing VoIP, such as echo and traffic analysis, quality of service (QoS), and call admission control (CAC).

- Introduce the basic tasks involved in designing an effective service provider-based VoIP network.

- Provide information on some of the more popular and widely requested VoIP services, such as prepaid services, fax services, and virtual private networks (VPNs).

Although this book contains plenty of technical information and suggestions for ways in which you can build a VoIP network, it is not meant to be used as a cookie cutter design and implementation guide. Examples shown in this book are included only to clarify concepts and design issues.

Audience

Although this book is written for anyone interested in understanding the design considerations and strategies necessary to deploy VoIP, its target audience is service provider voice and networking experts who are already familiar with VoIP and networking fundamentals. We strongly suggest that you first read *Voice over IP Fundamentals* before tackling the topics presented in this book.

Chapter Organization

Deploying Cisco Voice over IP Solutions is separated into four parts:

- Network Design Considerations

- Network Design Strategies

- Network Services

- Appendixes

Part I, "Network Design Considerations," discusses some of the preliminary topics you should take into account before designing a VoIP network:

- Chapter 1, "Understanding Traffic Analysis," describes different techniques to engineer and properly size traffic-sensitive voice networks, provides examples of several different kinds of traffic models, and explains how to use traffic probability (distribution) tables to engineer robust and efficient voice networks.

- Chapter 2, "Understanding Echo Analysis," describes basic concepts applicable to echo analysis, explains echo cancellation, and provides a method for locating and eliminating echoes.

- Chapter 3, "Understanding Quality of Service for Voice over IP," describes various QoS features applicable to voice and provides high-level examples showing how to deploy these features in different voice network environments.

- Chapter 4, "Understanding Call Admission Control," describes call admission control (CAC), when the CAC decision is made, how the information is gathered to support the CAC decision, what resources are needed for the voice call and how they are determined, and what happens to calls denied by CAC.

Part II, "Network Design Strategies," describes how to design a service provider-based voice network:

- Chapter 5, "Designing Static Dial Plans for Large VoIP Networks," describes dial plan configuration recommendations on Cisco H.323 gateways and gatekeepers used to support large dial plans.

- Chapter 6, "Designing a Long-Distance VoIP Network," describes the basic tasks of designing a long-distance VoIP network.

Part III, "Network Services" describes some of the more commonly requested services that service providers can offer through a voice network:

- Chapter 7, "Managed Multiservice Networks and Packet Voice VPNs," discusses two classes of hosted voice networks: Managed MultiService (MMS) networks and packet voice virtual private networks (VPNs).

- Chapter 8, "Fax Services," discusses store and forward and real-time relay fax services.

- Chapter 9, "Unified Messaging," discusses various unified messaging concepts and features that apply to Cisco's uOne unified messaging (UM) solution.

- Chapter 10, "Prepaid Services," discusses how to design and implement a prepaid services solution managed either through an internal network infrastructure or through an OSP clearinghouse.

The appendixes are as follows:

- Appendix A, "Erlang B Traffic Model," provides an explanation and example of an Erlang B Traffic Distribution Table. This information is supplementary to Chapter 1, "Understanding Traffic Analysis."

- Appendix B, "Extended Erlang B Traffic Model," provides an explanation and example of an Extended Erlang B Traffic Distribution Table. This information also is supplementary information for Chapter 1, "Understanding Traffic Analysis."

- Appendix C, "TCL IVR Scripts," provides an overview of Interactive Voice Response (IVR) Tool Command Language (TCL) scripts and examples of some of the more common IVR TCL scripts used with prepaid services. This information is supplementary information for Chapter 10, "Prepaid Services."

Features and Text Conventions

Text design and content features used in this book are intended to make the complexities of VoIP clearer and more accessible.

Key terms are italicized the first time they are used and defined. In addition, key terms are spelled out and followed with their acronym in parentheses, where applicable.

Chapter summaries provide a chance for you to review and reflect upon the information discussed in each chapter. You might also use these summaries to determine whether a particular chapter is appropriate for your situation.

Command Syntax Conventions

Command syntax in this book conforms to the following conventions:

- Commands, keywords, and actual values for arguments are **bold**.
- Arguments (which need to be supplied with an actual value) are *italic*.
- Optional keywords and arguments are in brackets [].
- A choice of mandatory keywords and arguments is in braces {}.

Note that these conventions are for syntax only.

Timeliness

As of the writing of this book, many new protocols concerning VoIP were still being designed and worked out by the standards bodies. Also, legal aspects of VoIP constantly arise in different parts of the world. Therefore, this book is meant as a guide in that it provides foundational voice network design information.

The Road Ahead . . .

Packet voice technology is here to stay. There are potential deployments of this technology in many applications, whether residential, transit, or managed service. The predominant consensus of potential migration paths is as follows:

- Migration for the Enterprise

    — Enterprise customers will follow the path of attaching voice gateways to their PBXs to allow inter-PBX communication via VoIP. Then they will replace their PBXs with IP PBXs that can offer greater efficiency and additional applications.

- Migration for the Service Provider

    — Service provider customers will use packet voice to replace or grow their services without having to grow their TDM networks. This will start with Tandem Class 4 type networking and interconnecting with other service providers via IP instead of TDM. It will then move to Business Local services and finally the consumer.

    — Wireless voice will follow a similar path as enterprise and service provider. It will start by having a separate data network and then move to having all of the services, including voice, run over the data network.

Network Design Considerations

## CHAPTER 1

Understanding Traffic Analysis

Networks, whether voice or data, are designed around many different variables. Two of the most important factors that you need to consider in network design are service and cost. Service is essential for maintaining customer satisfaction. Cost is always a factor in maintaining profitability. One way you can maintain quality service and rein in cost in network design is to optimize circuit utilization.

This chapter describes the different techniques you can use to engineer and properly size traffic-sensitive voice networks. You'll see several different traffic models and explanations of how to use traffic probability tables to help you engineer robust and efficient voice networks.

Traffic Theory Basics

Network designers need a way to properly size network capacity, especially as networks grow. Traffic theory enables network designers to make assumptions about their networks based on past experience.

Traffic is defined as either the amount of activity over a circuit or the number of messages handled by a communications switch during a given period of time. Traffic also includes the relationship between call attempts on traffic-sensitive equipment and the speed with which the calls are completed. Traffic analysis enables you to determine the amount of bandwidth you need in your circuits for both data and voice calls. Traffic engineering addresses service issues by enabling you to define a grade of service or blocking factor. A properly engineered network has low blocking and high circuit utilization, which means that service is increased and costs are reduced.

You need to take many different factors into account when analyzing traffic. The most important factors are the following:

- Traffic load
- Grade of service
- Traffic types
- Sampling methods

Of course, other factors might affect the results of traffic analysis calculations, but these are the main ones.

Traffic Load Measurement

In traffic theory, you measure traffic load. *Traffic load* is defined as the ratio of call arrivals in a specified period of time to the average amount of time it takes to service each call during that period. These measurement units are based on *Average Hold Time (AHT)*. AHT is defined as the total amount of time of all calls in a specified period divided by the number of calls in that period. For example:

3976 total call seconds / 23 calls = 172.87 sec per call = AHT of 172.87 seconds

The two main measurement units used today to measure traffic load are the following:

- Erlangs
- Centum Call Seconds (CCS)

In 1918, A.K. Erlang developed formulas that could be used to make predictions about randomly arriving telephone traffic. The Erlang—a measurement of telephone traffic—was named in honor of him. One Erlang is defined as 3600 seconds of calls on the same circuit, or enough traffic load to keep one circuit busy for 1 hour.

Traffic in Erlangs = (number of calls × AHT) / 3600
Example: (23 calls × 172.87 AHT) / 3600 = 1.104 Erlangs

CCS is based on 100 seconds of calls on the same circuit. Voice switches generally measure the amount of traffic in CCS.

Traffic in CCS = (number of calls × AHT) / 100
Example: (23 calls × 172.87 AHT) / 100 = 39.76 CCS

Which unit you use depends on the equipment you use and the unit of measurement it records in. Many switches use CCS because it is easier to work with increments of 100 rather than 3600. Both units are recognized standards in the field. The following is how the two relate:

1 Erlang = 36 CCS

Although you can take the total call seconds in an hour and divide that amount by 3600 seconds to determine traffic in Erlangs, you can also use averages of various time periods. These averages allow you to utilize more sample periods and determine the proper traffic.

Busy Hour Traffic

You commonly measure traffic load during your network's busiest hour because this represents the maximum traffic load that your network must support. The result gives you a traffic load measurement commonly referred to as the *Busy Hour Traffic* (BHT). Times can arise when you can't do a thorough sampling or you have only an estimate of how many calls you are handling daily. When that happens, you can usually make assumptions about your environment, such as the average number of calls per day and the AHT. In the standard business environment, the busy hour of any given day holds approximately 15 to 20 percent of that day's traffic. You generally use 17 percent of the day's traffic to represent the peak hour in your computations. In many business environments, an acceptable AHT is generally assumed to be 180 to 210 seconds. You can use these estimates if you ever need to determine trunking requirements without having more complete data.

Network Capacity Measurements

Many measurements can be used to discuss a network's capacity. For example:

- Busy Hour Call Attempts (BHCA)
- Busy Hour Call Completions (BHCC)
- Calls per second (CPS)

All these measurements are based on the number of calls. These measurements describe a network's capacity but they are fairly meaningless for traffic analysis because they do not consider the hold time of the call. You need to use these measurements in conjunction with an AHT to derive a BHT that you can use for traffic analysis.

Grade of Service

Grade of service (GoS) is defined as the probability that calls will be blocked while attempting to seize circuits. It is written as P.*xx* blocking factor or blockage, where *xx* is the percentage of calls that are blocked for a traffic system. For example, traffic facilities requiring P.01 GoS define a 1 percent probability of callers being blocked to the facilities. A GoS of P.00 is rarely requested and will seldom happen. This is because, to be 100 percent sure that there is no blocking, you would have to design a network where the caller-to-circuit ratio is 1:1. Also, most traffic formulas assume that an infinite number of callers exists.

Traffic Types

You can use the telecommunications equipment offering the traffic to record the previously mentioned data. Unfortunately, most of the samples received are based on the carried traffic on the system and not the offered traffic load.

Carried traffic is the traffic that is actually serviced by telecommunications equipment.

Offered traffic is the actual amount of traffic attempts on a system. The difference in the two can cause some inaccuracies in your calculations.

The greater the amount of blockage you have, the greater the difference between carried and offered load. You can use the following formula to calculate offered load from carried load:

Offered load = carried load / (1–blocking factor)

Unfortunately, this formula does not take into account any retries that might happen when a caller is blocked. You can use the following formula to take retry rate into account:

Offered load = carried load × Offered Load Adjustment Factors (OAF)
OAF = [1.0 – (x × blocking factor)] / (1.0 – blocking factor)
where x is defined as a percentage of retry probability (x = 0.6 for a 60% retry rate)

Sampling Methods

The accuracy of your traffic analysis will also depend on the accuracy of your sampling methods. The following parameters will change the represented traffic load:

- Weekdays versus weekends
- Holidays
- Type of traffic (modem versus traditional voice)
- Apparent versus offered load
- Sample period
- Total number of samples taken
- Stability of the sample period

Probability theory states that to accurately assess voice network traffic, you need to have at least 30 of the busiest hours of a voice network in the sampling period. Although this is a good starting point, other variables can skew the accuracy of this sample. You cannot take the top 30 out of 32 samples and expect that to be an accurate picture of the network's traffic. To get the most accurate results, you need to take as many samples of the offered load as possible. Alternatively, if you take samples throughout the year, your results can be skewed as your year-to-year traffic load increases or decreases. The ITU-T makes recommendations on how you can accurately sample a network to dimension it properly.

The ITU-T recommends that Public Switched Telephone Network (PSTN) connections measurement or read-out periods be 60 minutes and/or 15 minute intervals. These intervals are important because they let you summarize the traffic intensity over a period of time. If you take measurements throughout the day, you can find the peak hour of traffic in any given day. There are two recommendations on how to arrive at the peak daily traffic:

- **Daily Peak Period (DPP)**—Records the highest traffic volume measured during a day. This method requires continuous measurement and is typically used in environments where the peak hour might be different from day to day.

- **Fixed Daily Measurement Interval (FDMI)**—Used when traffic patterns are somewhat predictable and peak periods occur at regular intervals (i.e., business traffic usually peaks around 10:00 a.m. to 11:00 a.m. and 2:00 p.m. to 3:00 p.m.). FDMI requires measurements only during the predetermined peak periods.

In Table 1-1, by using FDMI sampling, you see that the hour with the highest total traffic load is 10 a.m., with a total traffic load of 60.6 Erlangs.

Table 1-1   *Daily Peak Period Measurement Table*

	Monday	Tuesday	Wednesday	Thursday	Friday	Total Load
9:00 a.m.	12.7	11.5	10.8	11.0	8.6	54.6
10:00 a.m.	12.6	11.8	12.5	12.2	11.5	60.6
11:00 a.m.	11.1	11.3	11.6	12.0	12.3	58.3
12:00 p.m.	9.2	8.4	8.9	9.3	9.4	45.2
1:00 p.m.	10.1	10.3	10.2	10.6	9.8	51.0
2:00 p.m.	12.4	12.2	11.7	11.9	11.0	59.2
3:00 p.m.	9.8	11.2	12.6	10.5	11.6	55.7
4:00 p.m.	10.1	11.1	10.8	10.5	10.2	52.7

The example in Table 1-2 uses DPP to calculate total traffic load.

Table 1-2   *Using DPP to Calculate Total Traffic Load*

	Monday	Tuesday	Wednesday	Thursday	Friday	Total Load
Peak Traffic	12.7	12.2	12.6	12.2	12.3	62.0
Peak Traffic Time	9 a.m.	2 p.m.	3 p.m.	10 a.m.	11 a.m.	

You also need to divide the daily measurements into groups that have the same statistical behavior. The ITU-T defines these groups as workdays, weekend days, and yearly exceptional days. Grouping measurements with the same statistical behavior becomes important because exceptional call volume days (such as Christmas Day and Mother's Day) might skew the results.

ITU-T Recommendation E.492 includes recommendations for determining the normal and high load traffic intensities for the month. Per ITU recommendation E.492, the normal load traffic intensity for the month is defined as the fourth highest daily peak traffic. If you select the second highest measurement for the month, it will result in the high load traffic intensity for the month. The result allows you to define the expected monthly traffic load.

Traffic Models

Now that you know what measurements are needed, you need to figure out how to use the measurements. You need to pick the appropriate model. The following are the key elements to picking the appropriate model:

- Call arrival patterns
- Blocked calls
- Number of sources
- Holding times

Call Arrival Patterns

Determining the call arrival pattern is the first step to designating the proper traffic model to choose. Call arrival patterns are important in choosing a model because arrival patterns affect traffic facilities differently.

The three main call arrival patterns are the following:

- Smooth
- Peaked
- Random

Smooth Call Arrival Pattern

A smooth or hypo-exponential traffic pattern occurs when there is not a large amount of variation in traffic. Call hold time and call inter-arrival times are predictable, which allows you to predict traffic in any given instance when a finite number of sources exist. For example, suppose you are designing a voice network for an outbound telemarketing company in which a few agents spend all day on the phone. Suppose that, in a 1-hour period, you expect 30 calls of 2 minutes each, with calls coming one after the other. You then need to allocate one trunk to handle the calls for the hour. Figure 1-1 provides a graph of what calls versus time might look like in a smooth call arrival pattern.

Figure 1-1   *Smooth call arrival pattern.*

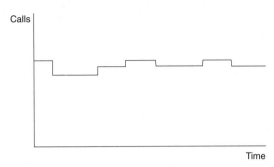

Peaked Call Arrival Pattern

A peaked traffic pattern has big spikes in traffic from the mean. This call arrival pattern is also known as a hyper-exponential arrival pattern. Peaked traffic patterns demonstrate why it might not be a good idea to include Mother's Day and Christmas Day in a traffic study. Times might arise when you would want to engineer rollover trunk groups to handle this kind of traffic pattern. In general, however, to handle this kind of traffic pattern, you need to allocate enough resources to handle the peak traffic. For example, to handle 30 calls all at once, you would need 30 trunks.

Figure 1-2 provides a graph of what calls versus time for a peaked call arrival pattern might look like.

Figure 1-2   *Peaked call arrival pattern.*

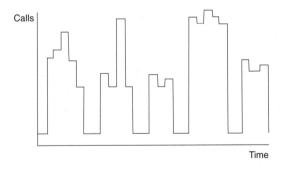

Random Call Arrival Pattern

Random traffic patterns are exactly that—random. They are also known as Poisson or exponential distribution. Poisson was the mathematician who originally defined this type of distribution. Random traffic patterns occur in instances where there are many callers, each one generating a little bit of traffic. You generally see this kind of random traffic pattern in PBX environments. The number of circuits that you would need in this situation would vary between 1 and 30.

Figure 1-3 illustrates what a graph of calls versus time for a random call arrival pattern might look like.

Figure 1-3   *Random call arrival pattern.*

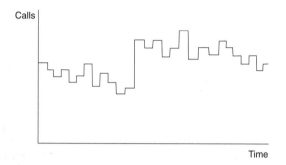

Blocked Calls

A *blocked call* is a call that is not serviced immediately. Calls are considered blocked if they are rerouted to another trunk group, placed in a queue, or played back a tone or announcement. The nature of the blocked call determines the model you select, because blocked calls result in differences in the traffic load.

The following are the main types of blocked calls:

- **Lost Calls Held (LCH)**—These blocked calls are lost, never to come back again. Originally, LCH was based on the theory that all calls introduced to a traffic system were held for a finite amount of time. All calls include any of the calls that were blocked, which meant the calls were still held until time ran out for the call.

- **Lost Calls Cleared (LCC)**—These blocked calls are cleared from the system— meaning that the call goes somewhere else (mainly to other traffic-sensitive facilities).

- **Lost Calls Delayed (LCD)**—These blocked calls remain on the system until facilities are available to service the call. This is used mainly in call center environments or with data circuits, since the key factors for LCD would be delay in conjunction with traffic load.

- **Lost Calls Retried (LCR)**—This assumes that once a call is blocked, a percentage of the blocked calls are lost and all other blocked calls retry until they are serviced. This is actually a derivative of the LCC model and is used in the Extended Erlang B model.

Number of Sources

The number of sources of calls also has bearing on what traffic model you choose. For example, if there is only one source and one trunk, the probability of blocking the call is zero. As the number of sources increases, the probability of blocking gets higher. The number of sources comes into play when sizing a small PBX or key system, where you can use a smaller number of trunks and still arrive at the designated GoS.

Holding Times

Some traffic models take into account the holding times of the call. Most models do not take holding time into account because call-holding times are assumed to be exponential. Generally, calls have short rather than long hold times, meaning that call-holding times will have a negative exponential distribution.

Selecting Traffic Models

After you determine the call arrival patterns and determine the blocked calls, number of sources, and holding times of the calls, you are ready to select the traffic model that most closely fits your environment. Although no traffic model can exactly match real-life situations, these models assume the average in each situation. Many different traffic models exist. The key is to find the model that best suits your environment. Table 1-3 compares some common traffic models.

Table 1-3   *Traffic Model Comparison*

Traffic Model	Sources	Arrival Pattern	Blocked Call Disposition	Holding Times
Poisson	Infinite	Random	Held	Exponential
Erlang B	Infinite	Random	Cleared	Exponential
Extended Erlang B	Infinite	Random	Retried	Exponential
Erlang C	Infinite	Random	Delayed	Exponential
Engset	Finite	Smooth	Cleared	Exponential
EART/EARC	Infinite	Peaked	Cleared	Exponential
Neal-Wilkerson	Infinite	Peaked	Held	Exponential
Crommelin	Infinite	Random	Delayed	Constant
Binomial	Finite	Random	Held	Exponential
Delay	Finite	Random	Delayed	Exponential

The traffic models that have the widest adoption are Erlang B, Extended Erlang B, and Erlang C. Other commonly adopted traffic models are Engset, Poisson, EART/EARC, and Neal-Wilkerson.

Erlang B Traffic Model

The Erlang B model is based on the following assumptions:

- An infinite number of sources
- Random traffic arrival pattern
- Blocked calls are cleared
- Hold times are exponentially distributed

The Erlang B model is used when blocked calls are rerouted, never to come back to the original trunk group. This model assumes a random call arrival pattern. The caller makes only one attempt and if the call is blocked, the call is then rerouted. The Erlang B model is commonly used for first-attempt trunk groups where you do not need to take into consideration the retry rate because calls are rerouted, or you expect to see very little blockage.

Equation 1-1 provides the formula used to derive the Erlang B traffic model.

Equation 1-1

$$B(c, a) \, 5 \, \frac{\dfrac{a^c}{c!}}{\displaystyle\bigwedge_{k \, 5 \, 0}^{c} \dfrac{a^k}{k!}}$$

where:

- B(c,a) is the probability of blocking the call.
- c is the number of circuits.
- a is the traffic load.

Example: Using the Erlang B Traffic Model

Problem: You need to redesign your outbound long-distance trunk groups, which are currently experiencing some blocking during the busy hour. The switch reports state that the trunk group is offered 17 Erlangs of traffic during the busy hour. You want to have low blockage so you want to design this for less than 1 percent blockage.

Solution: When you look at the Erlang B Tables (see Appendix A, "Erlang B Traffic Model"), you see that for 17 Erlangs of traffic with a Grade of Service of 0.64 percent, you need 27 circuits to handle this traffic load.

You can also check the blocking factor using the Erlang B equation, given the preceding information. Another way to check the blocking factor is to use Microsoft Excel's Poisson function in the following format:

=(POISSON(<circuits>,<traffic load>,FALSE)) / (POISSON(<circuits>,<traffic load>,TRUE))

There is a very handy Erlang B, Extended Erlang B, and Erlang C calculator at the following URL: www.erlang.com/calculator/index.htm.

Extended Erlang B Traffic Model

The Extended Erlang B model is based on the following assumptions:

- An infinite number of sources.
- Random traffic arrival pattern.
- Blocked calls are cleared.
- Hold times are exponentially distributed.

The Extended Erlang B model is designed to take into account calls that are retried at a certain rate. This model assumes a random call arrival pattern; blocked callers make multiple attempts to complete their calls and no overflow is allowed. The Extended Erlang B model is commonly used for standalone trunk groups with a retry probability (for example, a modem pool).

Example: Using the Extended Erlang B Traffic Model

Problem: You want to determine how many circuits you need for your dial access server. You know that you receive about 28 Erlangs of traffic during the busy hour and that 5 percent blocking during that period is acceptable. You also expect that 50 percent of the users will retry immediately.

Solution: When you look at the Extended Erlang B Tables (see Appendix B, "Extended Erlang B Traffic Model") you see that for 28 Erlangs of traffic with a retry probability of 50 percent and 4.05 percent blockage, you need 35 circuits to handle this traffic load.

Again, there is a handy Erlang B, Extended Erlang B, and Erlang C calculator at the following URL: www.erlang.com/calculator/index.htm.

Erlang C Traffic Model

The Erlang C model is based on the following assumptions:

- An infinite number of sources.
- Random traffic arrival pattern.
- Blocked calls are delayed.
- Hold times are exponentially distributed.

The Erlang C model is designed around queuing theory. This model assumes a random call arrival pattern; the caller makes one call and is held in a queue until the call is answered. The Erlang C model is more commonly used for conservative automatic call distributor (ACD) design to determine the number of agents needed. It can also be used for determining bandwidth on data transmission circuits, but it is not the best model to use for that purpose.

In the Erlang C model, you need to know the number of calls or packets in the busy hour, the average call length or packet size, and the expected amount of delay in seconds.

Equation 1-2 provides the formula used to derive the Erlang C traffic model.

Equation 1-2

$$C(c, a) = \frac{\dfrac{a^c c}{c!(c-a)}}{\displaystyle\sum_{k=0}^{c-1} \dfrac{a^k}{k!} + \dfrac{a^c c}{c!(c-a)}}$$

where:

- C(c,a) is the probability of delaying.
- c is the number of circuits.
- a is the traffic load.

Example: Using the Erlang C Traffic Model for Voice

Problem: You expect the call center to have approximately 600 calls lasting approximately 3 minutes each and that each agent has an after-call work time of 20 seconds. You would like the average time in the queue to be approximately 10 seconds.

Solution: Calculate the amount of expected traffic load. You know that you have approximately 600 calls of 3 minutes duration. To that number, you must add 20 seconds because each agent is not answering a call for approximately 20 seconds. The additional 20 seconds is part of the amount of time it takes to service a call:

(600 calls × 200 seconds AHT) / 3600 = 33.33 Erlangs of traffic

Compute the delay factor by dividing the expected delay time by AHT:

10 sec delay / 200 seconds = 0.05 delay factor

Example: Using the Erlang C Traffic Model for Data

Problem: You are designing your backbone connection between two routers. You know that you will generally see about 600 packets per second and 200 bytes per packet or 1600 bits per packet. Multiplying 600 pps by 1600 bits per packet gives the amount of bandwidth you will need to support—960,000 bps. You know that you can buy circuits in increments of 64,000 bps, the amount of data necessary to keep the circuit busy for 1 second. How many circuits will you need to keep the delay under 10 milliseconds?

Solution: Calculate the traffic load as follows:

960,000 bps / 64,000 bps = 15 Erlangs of traffic load

To get the average transmission time, you need to multiply the number of bytes per packet by 8 to get the number of bits per packet, then divide that by 64,000 bps (circuit speed) to get the average transmission time per packet:

200 bytes / packet × 8 bits = 1600 bits per packet / 64,000 bps =
0.025 seconds to transmit, or 25 milliseconds
Delay factor 10 ms / 25 ms = 0.4 delay factor

With a delay factor of 0.4 and a traffic load of 15.47 Erlangs, the number of circuits you need is 17. This calculation is based on the assumption that the circuits are clear of any packet loss.

Again, there is a handy Erlang B, Extended Erlang B, and Erlang C calculator at the following URL: www.erlang.com/calculator/index.htm.

Engset Traffic Model

The Engset model is based on the following assumptions:

- A finite number of sources.
- Smooth traffic arrival pattern.
- Blocked calls are cleared from the system.
- Hold times are exponentially distributed.

The Engset formula is generally used for environments where it is easy to assume that a finite number of sources are using a trunk group. By knowing the number of sources, you can maintain a high grade of service. You would use the Engset formula in applications such as global system for mobile communication (GSM) cells and subscriber loop concentrators. Because the Engset traffic model is covered in many books dedicated to traffic analysis, it is not covered here.

Poisson Traffic Model

The Poisson model is based on the following assumptions:

- An infinite number of sources.
- Random traffic arrival pattern.
- Blocked calls are held.
- Hold times are exponentially distributed.

In the Poisson model, blocked calls are held until a circuit becomes available. This model assumes a random call arrival pattern; the caller makes only one attempt to place the call and blocked calls are lost. The Poisson model is commonly used for over-engineering standalone trunk groups.

Equation 1-3 provides the formula used to derive the Poisson traffic model.

Equation 1-3

$$P(c, a) = \left(1 - e^{-a} \sum_{k=0}^{c-1} \frac{a^k}{k!} \right)$$

where:

- P(c,a) is the probability of blocking the call.
- e is the natural log base.
- c is the number of circuits.
- a is the traffic load.

Example: Using the Poisson Traffic Model

Problem: You are creating a new trunk group to be utilized only by your new office and you need to figure out how many lines are needed. You expect them to make and receive approximately 300 calls per day with an AHT of about 4 minutes or 240 seconds. The goal is a P.01 Grade of Service or a 1 percent blocking rate. To be conservative, assume that approximately 20 percent of the calls happen during the busy hour.

> 300 calls × 20% = 60 calls during the busy hour.
> (60 calls × 240 AHT) / 3600 = 4 Erlangs during the busy hour.

Solution: With 4 Erlangs of traffic and a blocking rate of 0.81 percent (close enough to 1 percent), you need 10 trunks to handle this traffic load. You can check this number by plugging the variables into the Poisson formula, as demonstrated in Equation 1-4.

Equation 1-4

$$P(10, 4) \; 5 \; 1 \; 2 \, e^{24} \, \bigwedge_{k \, 5 \, 0}^{10 \, 2 \, 1} \frac{4^{k}}{k!} \; 5 \; 1 \; 2 \, e^{24}\left(1 \; 1 \; 4 \; 1 \; \frac{16}{2} \; 1 \; \frac{64}{6} \; 1 \; \frac{256}{24} \; 1 \; \dots\right) \qquad \approx 0.00813$$

Another easy way to find blocking is by using Microsoft Excel's Poisson function with the following format:

> = 1 – POISSON(<circuits>–1,<traffic load>,TRUE)

EART/EARC and Neal-Wilkerson Traffic Model

These models are used for peaked traffic patterns. Most telephone companies use these models for rollover trunk groups that have peaked arrival patterns. The EART/EARC model treats blocked calls as cleared and the Neal-Wilkinson model treats them as held. Because the EART/EARC and Neal-Wilkerson traffic models are covered in many books dedicated to traffic analysis, they are not covered here.

Applying Traffic Analysis to VoIP Networks

Because Voice over IP (VoIP) traffic uses Real-Time Transport Protocol (RTP) to transport voice traffic, you can use the same principles to define your bandwidth on your WAN links.

Some challenges exist in defining the bandwidth. The following considerations will affect the bandwidth of voice networks:

- Voice codecs
- Samples
- Voice activity detection (VAD)
- RTP header compression
- Point-to-point versus point-to-multipoint

Voice Codecs

Many voice codecs are used in IP telephony today. These codecs all have different bit rates and complexities. Some of the standard voice codecs are G.711, G.729, G.726, G.723.1, and G.728. All Cisco voice-enabled routers and access servers support some or all of these codecs.

Codecs impact bandwidth because they determine the payload size of the packets transferred over the IP leg of a call. In Cisco voice gateways, you can configure the payload size to control bandwidth. By increasing payload size, you reduce the total number of packets sent, thus decreasing the bandwidth needed by reducing the number of headers required for the call.

Samples

The number of samples per packet is another factor in determining the bandwidth of a voice call. The codec defines the size of the sample, but the total number of samples placed in a packet affects how many packets are sent per second. Therefore, the number of samples included in a packet affects the overall bandwidth of a call.

For example, a G.711 10-ms sample is 80 bytes per sample. A call with only one sample per packet would yield the following:

80 bytes + 20 bytes IP + 12 UDP + 8 RTP = 120 bytes/packet
120 bytes/packet × 100 pps = 12,000 × 8 bits / 1000 = 96 kbps per call

The same call using two 10-ms samples per packet would yield the following:

(80 bytes × 2 samples) + 20 bytes IP + 12 UDP + 8 RTP = 200 bytes/packet
200 bytes/packet × 50 pps = 10,000 × 8 bits / 1000 = 80 kbps per call

Layer 2 headers are not included in the preceding calculations.

The results show that a 16-kbps difference exists between the two calls. By changing the number of samples per packet, you definitely can change the amount of bandwidth a call uses, but there is a trade-off. When you increase the number of samples per packet, you also increase the amount of delay on each call. DSP resources, which handle each call, must buffer the samples for a longer period of time. You should keep this in mind when you design a voice network.

Voice Activity Detection

Typical voice conversations can contain up to 50 percent silence. With traditional, circuit-based voice networks, all voice calls use a fixed bandwidth of 64 kbps, regardless of how much of the conversation is speech and how much is silence. With VoIP networks, all conversation and silence is packetized. Voice Activity Detection (VAD) enables you to send RTP packets only when voice is detected. For VoIP bandwidth planning, assume that VAD reduces bandwidth by 35 percent. Although this value might be less than the actual reduction, it provides a conservative estimate that takes into consideration different dialects and language patterns.

The G.729 Annex-B and G.723.1 Annex-A codecs include an integrated VAD function, but otherwise have identical performance to G.729 and G.723.1, respectively.

RTP Header Compression

All VoIP packets are made up of two components: voice samples and IP/UDP/RTP headers. Although the voice samples are compressed by the digital signal processor (DSP) and vary in size based on the codec used, the headers are always a constant 40 bytes. When compared to the 20 bytes of voice samples in a default G.729 call, these headers make up a considerable amount of overhead. Using RTP Header Compression (cRTP), which is used on a link-by-link basis, these headers can be compressed to 2 or 4 bytes. This compression can offer significant VoIP bandwidth savings. For example, a default G.729 VoIP call consumes 24 kbps without cRTP, but only 12 kbps with cRTP enabled. Codec type, samples per packet, VAD, and cRTP affect, in one way or another, the bandwidth of a call. In each case, there is a trade-off between voice quality and bandwidth. Table 1-4 shows the bandwidth utilization for various scenarios. VAD efficiency in the graph is assumed to be 50 percent.

Table 1-4 *Voice Codec Characteristics*

Algorithm	Voice BW (kbps)	FRAME SIZE (Bytes)	Cisco Payload (Bytes)	Packets Per Second (PPS)	IP/UDP/RTP Header (Bytes)	CRTP Header (Bytes)	L2	Layer2 header (Bytes)	Total Bandwidth (kbps) no VAD	Total Bandwidth (kbps) with VAD
G.711	64	80	160	50	40		Ether	14	85.6	42.8
G.711	64	80	160	50		2	Ether	14	70.4	35.2
G.711	64	80	160	50	40		PPP	6	82.4	41.2
G.711	64	80	160	50		2	PPP	6	67.2	33.6
G.711	64	80	160	50	40		FR	4	81.6	40.8
G.711	64	80	160	50		2	FR	4	66.4	33.2
G.711	64	80	80	100	40		Ether	14	107.2	53.6
G.711	64	80	80	100		2	Ether	14	76.8	38.4
G.711	64	80	80	100	40		PPP	6	100.8	50.4
G.711	64	80	80	100		2	PPP	6	70.4	35.2
G.711	64	80	80	100	40		FR	4	99.2	49.6
G.711	64	80	80	100		2	FR	4	68.8	34.4
G.729	8	10	20	50	40		Ether	14	29.6	14.8
G.729	8	10	20	50		2	Ether	14	14.4	7.2
G.729	8	10	20	50	40		PPP	6	26.4	13.2
G.729	8	10	20	50		2	PPP	6	11.2	5.6
G.729	8	10	20	50	40		FR	4	25.6	12.8
G.729	8	10	20	50		2	FR	4	10.4	5.2
G.729	8	10	30	33	40		Ether	14	22.4	11.2
G.729	8	10	30	33		2	Ether	14	12.3	6.1
G.729	8	10	30	33	40		PPP	6	20.3	10.1
G.729	8	10	30	33		2	PPP	6	10.1	5.1

Table 1-4   *Voice Codec Characteristics (Continued)*

Algorithm	Voice BW (kbps)	FRAME SIZE (Bytes)	Cisco Payload (Bytes)	Packets Per Second (PPS)	IP/UDP/RTP Header (Bytes)	CRTP Header (Bytes)	L2	Layer2 header (Bytes)	Total Bandwidth (kbps) no VAD	Total Bandwidth (kbps) with VAD
G.729	8	10	30	33	40		FR	4	19.7	9.9
G.729	8	10	30	33		2	FR	4	9.6	4.8
G.723.1	6.3	30	30	26	40		Ether	14	17.6	8.8
G.723.1	6.3	30	30	26		2	Ether	14	9.7	4.8
G.723.1	6.3	30	30	26	40		PPP	6	16.0	8.0
G.723.1	6.3	30	30	26		2	PPP	6	8.0	4.0
G.723.1	6.3	30	30	26	40		FR	4	15.5	7.8
G.723.1	6.3	30	30	26		2	FR	4	7.6	3.8
G.723.1	5.3	30	30	22	40		Ether	14	14.8	7.4
G.723.1	5.3	30	30	22		2	Ether	14	8.1	4.1
G.723.1	5.3	30	30	22	40		PPP	6	13.4	6.7
G.723.1	5.3	30	30	22		2	PPP	6	6.7	3.4
G.723.1	5.3	30	30	22	40		FR	4	13.1	6.5
G.723.1	5.3	30	30	22		2	FR	4	6.4	3.2

Point-to-Point Versus Point-to-Multipoint

Because PSTN circuits are built as point-to-point links, and VoIP networks are basically point-to-multipoint, you must take into account where your traffic is going and group it accordingly. This becomes more of a factor when deciding bandwidth on fail-over links. Figure 1-4 shows the topology of a properly functioning voice network.

Figure 1-4 *Properly functioning topology.*

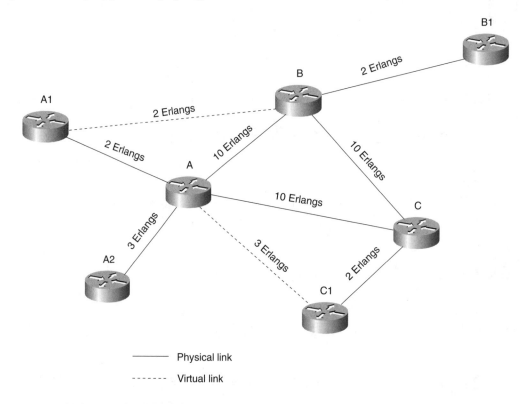

Point-to-point links will not need more bandwidth than the number of voice calls being introduced to and from the PSTN links, although as you approach link speed, voice quality may suffer. If one of those links is lost, you need to ensure that your fail-over links have the capacity to handle the increased traffic. In Figure 1-5, the WAN link between nodes A and B is down. Traffic would then increase between nodes A and C, and between C and B. This additional traffic would require that those links be engineered to handle the additional load.

Figure 1-5   *Topology with broken connection.*

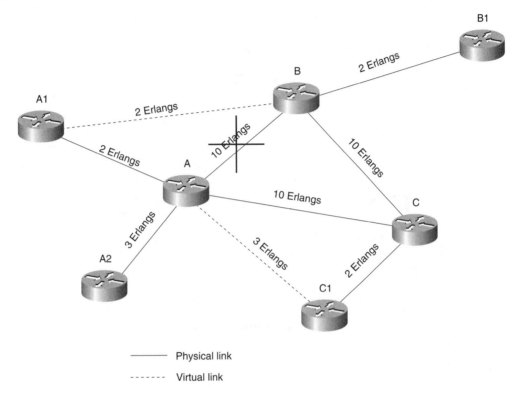

—————— Physical link

------- Virtual link

End-to-End Traffic Analysis Example

With the proper traffic tables, defining the number of circuits needed to handle calls becomes fairly simple. By defining the number of calls on the TDM side, you can also define the amount of bandwidth needed on the IP leg of the call. Unfortunately, putting them together can be an issue.

End-to-End Traffic Analysis: Problem

As illustrated in Figure 1-6, you have offices in the U.S., China, and the U.K. Because your main office is in the U.K., you will purchase leased lines from the U.K. to the U.S. and to China. Most of your traffic goes from the U.K. to the U.S. or China, with a little traffic going between China and the U.S. Your call detail records show:

- U.K. 36,000 minutes/day

- U.S. 12,882.4 minutes/day

- China 28,235.3 minutes/day

Figure 1-6 *End-to-end traffic analysis example topology.*

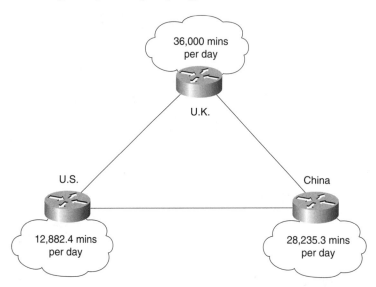

In this network, you are making the following assumptions:

- Each node's traffic has a random arrival pattern.
- Hold times are exponential.
- Blocked calls are cleared from the system.
- Infinite number of callers.

These assumptions tell you that you can use the Erlang B model for sizing your trunk groups to the PSTN. You want to have a GoS of P.01 on each of your trunk groups.

End-to-End Traffic Analysis: Solution

Compute the traffic load for the PSTN links at each node:

U.K. = 36,000 mins per day × 17% = 6120 mins per busy hour / 60 = 102 BHT
U.S. = 12,882.4 mins per day × 17% = 2190 mins per busy hour / 60 = 36.5 BHT
China = 28,235.3 mins per day × 17% = 4800 mins per busy hour / 60 = 80 BHT

These numbers will effectively give you the number of circuits needed for your PSTN connections in each of the nodes. Now that you have a usable traffic number, look in your tables to find the closest number that matches.

For the U.K., a 102 BHT with P.01 GoS indicates the need for a total of 120 DS-0s to support this load.

U.S. traffic shows that for P.01 blocking with a traffic load of 36.108, you need 48 circuits. Because your BHT is 36.5 Erlangs, you might experience a slightly higher rate of blocking than P.01. By using the Erlang B formula, you can see that you will experience a blocking rate of ~0.01139.

At 80 Erlangs of BHT with P.01 GoS, the Erlang B table (see Appendix A) shows you that you can use one of two numbers. At P.01 blocking you can see that 80.303 Erlangs of traffic requires 96 circuits. Because circuits are ordered in blocks of 24 or 30 when working with digital carriers, you must choose either 4 T1s or 96 DS-0s, or 4 E1s or 120 DS-0s. Four E1s is excessive for the amount of traffic you will be experiencing, but you know you will meet your blocking numbers. This gives you the number of circuits you will need.

Now that you know how many PSTN circuits you need, you must determine how much bandwidth you will have on your point-to-point circuits. Because the amount of traffic you need on the IP leg is determined by the amount of traffic you have on the TDM leg, you can directly relate DS-0s to the amount of bandwidth needed.

You must first choose a codec that you are going to use between PoPs. The G.729 codec is the most popular because it has high voice quality for the amount of compression it provides.

A G.729 call uses the following bandwidth:

- 26.4 kbps per call full rate with headers
- 11.2 kbps per call with VAD
- 9.6 kbps per call with cRTP
- 6.3 kbps per call with VAD and cRTP

Table 1-5 lists the bandwidth needed on the link between the U.K. and the U.S.

Table 1-5   *Bandwidth Requirements for U.K.–U.S. Link*

Bandwidth Consideration	Full Rate	VAD	cRTP	VAD/cRTP
Bandwidth Required	96 DS0s × 26.4 kbps = 2.534 Mbps	96 DS0s × 11.2 kbps = 1.075 Mbps	96 DS0s × 17.2 kbps = 1.651 Mbps	96 DS0s × 7.3 kbps = 700.8 Mbps

Table 1-6 lists the bandwidth needed on the link between the UK and China.

Table 1-6   *Bandwidth Requirements for U.K.–China Link*

Bandwidth Consideration	Full Rate	VAD	cRTP	VAD/cRTP
Bandwidth Required	72 DS0s × 26.4 kbps = 1.9 Mbps	72 DS0s × 11.2 kbps = 806.4 Mbps	72 DS0s × 17.2 kbps = 1.238 Mbps	72 DS0s × 7.3 kbps = 525.6 Mbps

As you can see, VAD and cRTP have a significant impact on the bandwidth needed on the WAN link.

Summary

This chapter covered the various traffic measurement techniques and sampling methods you can use to select the appropriate traffic model to help you engineer and properly size a traffic-sensitive voice network. The chapter explained how to calculate traffic load in Erlangs and in CCS. The chapter discussed the key voice network characteristics that determine which traffic model is appropriate for a particular network. Finally, you saw a description of the Erlang B, Extended Erlang B, Erlang C, and Poisson traffic models. This chapter included examples of specific network design problems that can be solved using these models.

For additional information about traffic analysis, see the following:

Martine, Roberta R., *Basic Traffic Analysis.* Englewood Cliffs, NJ: Prentice Hall, Inc.; 1994

Harder, J., Alan Wand, and Pat J. Richards, Jr. *The Complete Traffic Engineering Handbook.* New York, NY: Telecom Library, Inc.

Newton, H. *Newton's Telecom Directory.* New York, NY Miller Freeman, Inc.

Sizing Trunk Groups, Crawley, West Sussex RH10 7JR, United Kingdom: Westbay Engineers Ltd., 1999. http://www. erlang.com/link_traffic.html

## CHAPTER 2

Understanding Echo Analysis

In a voice call, an echo occurs when you hear your own voice repeated. An echo is the audible leak-through of your own voice into your own receive (return) path. This chapter discusses basic concepts applicable to echo analysis, explains echo cancellation, and provides a process for locating and eliminating echoes.

Echo Analysis Basics

Every voice conversation has at least two participants. From each participant's perspective, every call contains two voice paths:

- **Transmit path**—The transmit path is also called the send or Tx path. In a conversation, the transmit path is created when a person speaks. The sound is transmitted from the speaker's mouth to the listener's ear.

- **Receive path**—The receive path is also called the return or Rx path. In a conversation, the receive path is created when a person hears the conversation. The sound is received by the listener's ear from the speaker's mouth.

Figure 2-1 shows a simple voice call between Bob and Alice. From Bob's perspective, the transmit path carries his voice to Alice's ear, and the receive path carries Alice's voice to his ear. Naturally, from Alice's side these paths have the opposite naming convention: The transmit path carries her voice to Bob's ear, and the receive path carries Bob's voice to her ear.

Figure 2-1   *Simple telephone call.*

As previously mentioned, an echo is the audible leak-through of your own voice into your own receive (return) path. Figure 2-2 shows the same simple telephone call where Bob hears an echo.

Figure 2-2   *Simple telephone call with an echo.*

Bob hears a delayed and somewhat attenuated version of his own voice in the earpiece of his handset. Initially, the source and mechanism of the leak are undefined.

One of the key factors in echo analysis is the round-trip delay of the voice network. The round-trip delay of the network is the length of time it takes for an utterance to go from Bob's mouth, across the network on the transmit path to the source of the leak, and then back across the network on the receive path to Bob's ear.

Two basic characteristics of echo are the following:

- The louder the echo (the greater the echo amplitude), the more annoying it is.

- The later the echo (the longer the round-trip voice delay), the more annoying it is.

Locating an Echo

In Figure 2-2, Bob experiences the echo problem, which means that a signal is leaking from his transmit path into his receive path. This illustrates one of the basic properties of echo: Whenever you hear echo, the problem is at the other end. The problem that's producing the echo that Bob hears—the leakage source—is somewhere on Alice's side of the network (London). If Alice were the person experiencing the echo, the problem would be on Bob's side (Montreal).

The echo leak is always in the terminating side of the network because of the following:

- Leak-through happens only in analog circuits. Voice traffic in the digital portions of the network doesn't leak from one path into another.

  Analog signals can leak from one path to another, either electrically from one wire to another, or acoustically through the air from a loudspeaker to a microphone. When these analog signals have been converted to digital bits, they don't leak.

  It is true that all digital bits are represented by analog signals at the physical layer and these analog signals are subject to leakage. The analog signals that represent bits can tolerate a good deal of distortion before they become too distorted to be properly decoded. If such distortion occurred in the physical layer, the problem wouldn't be echo. If you had connectivity at all, you would hear digital noise instead of a voice echo.

- Echoes arriving after short delays (about 20 ms) are generally imperceptible because they're masked by the physical and electrical sidetone signal.

  This point is a corollary to the previous assertion that echoes become increasingly annoying with increasing mouth-to-ear delay. A certain minimum delay is needed for an echo to become perceptible. In almost every telephone device, some of the Tx signal is fed back into the earpiece so that you can hear yourself speaking. This is known as *sidetone*. The delay between the actual mouth signal and the sidetone signal is negligible, and sidetone is not perceived as an echo.

  Also, your skull resonates during speech (an acoustic sidetone source) and the human auditory system has a certain integration period that determines the minimum time difference between events that will be perceived as separate events rather than a single one. Together, these phenomena create a minimum mouth-to-ear delay of about 20 ms for an echo signal to be perceivable.

Given these two premises—that echoes must be delayed by at least 20 ms to be audible and that leaks occur only in the analog portion of the network—you can deduce much about the location of the echo source. Figure 2-3 shows possible sources of echo in a simple VoIP network.

Figure 2-3   *Potential echo paths in a network with both analog and digital segments.*

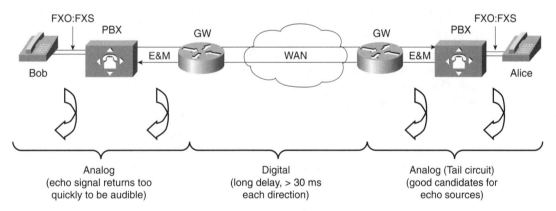

In this typical VoIP network, the digital packet portion of the network is sandwiched between two analog transmission segments. Bob in Montreal is connected by FXS (2-wire analog) to a local PBX, which is connected to a local VoIP gateway by E&M (4-wire analog). The Montreal gateway communicates with the London gateway through an IP network. As you will see later in this section, this packet transmission segment has an end-to-end latency greater than 30 ms. At the London end of the call, the gateway is connected in the same fashion to Alice's telephone (by E&M to the PBX and by FXS to the terminal).

The analog circuit in London is known as the *tail circuit*. It forms the tail or termination of the call from the user experiencing the echo, which in this case, is Bob.

Suppose that you want to locate potential sources of echo in the network in Figure 2-3. You know that bits don't leak, so you can disqualify the digital segment of the system. Therefore, the leak causing Bob's echo must be located in either the tail circuit in Montreal or the tail circuit in London. Any leak in the Montreal tail circuit would not have a long enough delay to be perceptible; echoes there would be masked by Bob's sidetone. So the source of the echo must be the London tail circuit, as shown in Figure 2-4.

Figure 2-4   *Simplified version of the VoIP network.*

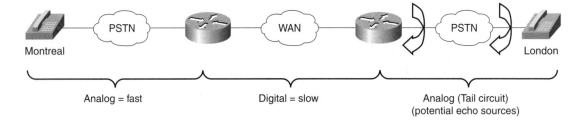

Remember that an echo problem has three ingredients:

- An analog leakage path between analog Tx and Rx paths
- Sufficient delay in echo return for echo to be perceived as annoying
- Sufficient echo amplitude to be perceived as annoying

The packet link in Figures 2-3 and 2-4 is called *slow* because it takes a relatively long time for analog signals entering this link to exit from the other side: the end-to-end delay of the link. This delay occurs because packet transmission fundamentally imposes a packetization and buffering delay of *at least* two to three packet sizes, and packet sizes of 20 ms are typical for VoIP. Assuming for the moment that the WAN link imposes an end-to-end delay of 50 ms, you can see that Bob's voice takes 50 ms to cross the transmit path to Alice in London. The echo that leaks from the transmit path to the receive path in the London tail circuit takes another 50 ms to make it back to Bob's ear. Therefore, the echo that Bob hears is delayed at least 100 ms, well into the range of audibility.

Tail Circuits

A packet voice gateway is a gateway between a digital packet network and a PSTN network. It can include both digital (TDM) and analog links. The tail circuit is everything connected to the PSTN side of a packet voice gateway—all the switches, multiplexers, cabling, PBXs—everything between the voice gateway and the telephone as demonstrated in Figure 2-5. The PSTN can contain many components and links, all of which are potential echo sources.

Figure 2-5   *Tail circuit in a VoIP network.*

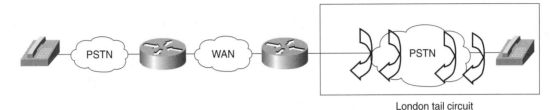

London tail circuit

Gateways have two types of PSTN interfaces: digital (ISDN BRI, T1/E1) or analog (E&M, FXO, FXS). Recalling that bits don't leak, further refine your search for echo sources to the analog elements of the tail circuit. You can extend the echo-free digital zone out from the gateway to the point of digital-to-analog (D/L) conversion in the PSTN, as shown in Figure 2-6.

Figure 2-6   *Tail circuit with both analog and digital links.*

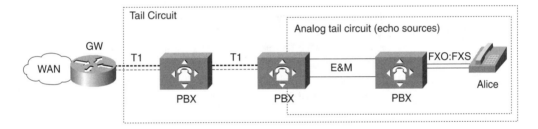

Effects of Network Elements on Echo

The following network elements in a VoIP network can have an effect on echo:

- Hybrid transformers
- Telephones
- Routers
- Quality of service (QoS)

Effect of Hybrid Transformers on Echo

Echo sources are points of signal leakage between analog transmit and receive paths. Hybrid transformers are often prime culprits for this signal leakage. Figure 2-7 shows an analog tail circuit with a hybrid transformer.

Figure 2-7   *Detail of analog tail circuit with a hybrid transformer.*

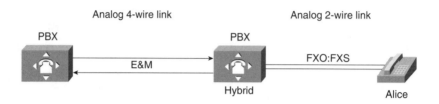

The analog telephone terminal is a 2-wire device, with a single pair of conductors used to carry both the Tx and Rx signals. For analog trunk connections, known as 4-wire transmission, two pairs of conductors carry separate Tx and Rx signals. Digital trunks (T1/E1) can be considered virtual 4-wire links because they also carry separate Tx and Rx signals.

A hybrid is a transformer that is used to interface 4-wire links to 2-wire links. It is a non-ideal physical device, and a certain fraction of the 4-wire incoming (Rx) signal will be reflected back into the 4-wire outgoing (Tx) signal. A typical fraction for a properly terminated hybrid is about –25 dB (ERL = +25 dB). This means that the reflected signal (the echo) will be a version of the Rx signal attenuated by about 25 dB. Remember, an echo must have both sufficient amplitude and sufficient delay to be perceived. Echo strength of –25 dB relative to the talker's speech level is generally quiet enough to not be annoying, even for relatively long delays of 100 ms.

Echo strength is expressed in decibels (dB) as a measurement called *echo return loss* (ERL). The relation between the original source and the ERL is as follows:

Original source amplitude = Echo amplitude + ERL

Therefore, an ERL of 0 dB indicates that the echo is the same amplitude as the original source. A large ERL indicates a negligible echo.

The ERL is not a property of the hybrid alone, however. It depends on the load presented by the terminating device, which might be a telephone or another PBX. The hybrid has a certain output impedance that must be balanced by the input impedance of the terminating device. If the impedances are not matched, the returning echo fraction will be larger (the ERL will be smaller) and the echo will be louder.

You can expect a certain amount of impedance mismatch (a few tens of ohms) because a normal hybrid connection will yield ERLs in the range of 20 to 30 dB. However, it is possible that one device could be provisioned for an output impedance of 900 ohms, and the terminating device provisioned with an input impedance of 600 ohms, which would yield a large echo, and would be expressed by a small ERL.

The main point to remember about hybrids is this: Ensure that output and input impedances are matched between the hybrid and the terminating device.

Effects of Telephones on Echo

Once again, the analog tail circuit is the portion of the PSTN circuit between the point of digital-to-analog conversion and the telephone terminal. By using digital telephones, this point of D/A conversion occurs inside the terminal itself. As a general rule, extending the digital transmission segments closer to the actual telephone will decrease the potential for echo.

The analog telephone terminal itself presents a load to the PBX. This load should be matched to the output impedance of the source device (FXS port). Some (inexpensive) telephones are not matched to the output impedance of the FXS port and are sources of echo. Headsets are particularly notorious for poor echo performance.

Acoustic echo is a major concern for hands-free speakerphone terminals. The air (and the terminal plastics) provide mechanical or acoustical coupling between the loudspeaker and the microphone. Speakerphone manufacturers combat this with good acoustic design of terminals, directional microphones, and acoustic echo cancellers/suppressors in the terminal. However, this is a very difficult problem, and speakerphones are inherently good echo sources. If you are hunting for an echo problem and the terminating tail circuit involves a speakerphone, eliminate the speakerphone.

Effects of Routers on Echo

The belief that adding routers to a voice network creates echoes is a common misconception. Digital segments of the network do not cause leaks; so technically, routers cannot be the source of echoes. Adding routers to the network, though, adds delays to the network—delays that can make a previously imperceptible echo perceptible. The gateway itself doesn't add echo unless you are using an analog interface to the PSTN and the output impedance is incorrectly provisioned with respect to the PBX. It is more likely that the echo was already in the analog tail circuit but was imperceptible because the round-trip delay was less than 20 ms.

For example, suppose that you are visiting London and you want to call a friend who lives on the other side of town. This call is echo free. But when you call the same friend (whose telephone is on the same tail circuit) from the U.S. over a satellite link with a round-trip delay of several hundred milliseconds, the echo is obvious and annoying. The only change has been the insertion of delay.

VoIP technologies impose a fundamental transmission delay due to packetization and the buffering of received packets before playout at the receiving endpoint. This delay is generally much smaller than the delay associated with satellite links, but it is usually sufficient to make a previously unnoticeable echo objectionable.

End-to-End Voice Call Delays

Analog transmission is very fast, limited only by the propagation speed of electrons in a wire (which is much lower than the speed of light, but still very fast) or photons in a fiber-optic link. TDM transmission is similarly very quick. A transcontinental PSTN call in the U.S. has a typical round-trip delay of about 10 to 20 ms. A local PSTN call has a typical round-trip delay of only a few milliseconds. Such short delays mean that even relatively loud echoes in the PSTN remain imperceptible as echo because they are masked by sidetone.

Imagine a call between Bob and Alice over a VoIP transmission link as in Figure 2-3. Consider the path Bob's voice takes from Montreal to London. Bob speaks into his mouthpiece and the analog signal arrives at the Montreal PBX within 1 ms. At the PBX, his analog voice signal is converted to a digital PCM stream and arrives at the Montreal IP gateway after only 1 ms more of delay. So it takes 2 ms for Bob's voice to go from his mouth to the voice gateway. The gateway sends out packets every 20 ms, which means each packet contains 20 ms of voice payload. Therefore, the voice gateway must wait to collect 20 ms of Bob's voice before it can fill the first packet. The first packet leaves the Montreal gateway 22 ms after Bob starts talking. Assuming that the WAN is very quick and uncongested, this packet arrives at the London voice gateway after only 5 ms of transit. So the London gateway gets the packet 27 ms after Bob starts speaking.

This packet is not played out from the London gateway to Alice immediately upon receipt, however. The Montreal gateway delivers new packets at 20 ms intervals, but the vagaries of packet transmission mean that packets arrive in London at non-constant intervals: Packet 2 might be 1 ms late, packet 3 might be 4 ms late, and so on. If the London gateway played out packet 1 immediately, it would be caught short 20 ms later when packet 2 was due but had not yet arrived—and Bob's voice would be interrupted.

The London gateway puts incoming packets into a buffer. The deeper the playout buffer, the longer packets wait before being played. The minimum buffer depth you can safely use is one packet, or 20 ms in this case. So packet 1 arrives at time 27 ms and is played out to the London PSTN tail 20 ms later at time 47 ms. It takes two more milliseconds to go from the London gateway across the PSTN to Alice's earpiece, for a total of 49 ms for Bob's words to go from Bob's mouth to Alice's ear. This is the end-to-end delay of the voice transmission system: 45 ms in the WAN and 4 ms in the PSTN.

You could increase the packet transmission rate to reduce the end-to-end delay, but this would increase the bandwidth necessary for the call because it would increase the ratio of header size (which is a constant) to payload size (which you would reduce).

As a general rule, the end-to-end latency for a packet transmission link has a fundamental minimum of about two to three packet sizes (in milliseconds). Even if the packet transit time was instantaneous, it still takes one packet size of time to fill the first packet. Even an unrealistically ideal, "fast-as-light" gateway and network face this fundamental, minimum delay.

If there is an echo source in the London tail circuit, it will go all the way back across the WAN, facing another 47 ms of delay. The echo will return to Bob's earpiece after a round trip—almost 100 ms of delay—which is quite enough to make an existing echo audible.

Therefore, the use of a packet transmission link imposes an extra delay of at least two to three packet sizes that was not present before. Echoes occur in the analog tail circuit, not the packet network, and existed before any routers were added. Adding the delay makes the existing, inaudible echo an audible echo. The delay of the packet network cannot be reduced below a fundamental limit. Cisco voice gateways already operate very close to this minimum delay (50–80 ms end-to-end is typical). Because of these long delays, all VoIP gateways employ echo cancellers to reduce the amplitude of returning echoes. However, the best solution to echo problems is always to remove the source of the echo.

In summary:

- Network delay increases user annoyance for an echo of equal strength.
- Adding routers doesn't cause echo; it exacerbates existing echo problems.

Effect of QoS on Echo

QoS might improve your end-to-end network delay for a given level of congestion; the shorter the delay, the less annoying a given echo becomes. However, you will never be able to reduce the delay below the "danger zone" for echo perception with any form of QoS because the minimum delay inherent in VoIP networks is long enough for echoes to be perceptible. QoS can help in other ways, but it cannot, by itself, eliminate echo.

Echo Canceller

An *echo canceller* is a component of a voice gateway that reduces the level of echoes that have leaked from the Rx path (from the gateway into the tail circuit) into the Tx path (from the tail circuit into the gateway) as demonstrated by the topology in Figure 2-8. Rx and Tx here are from the perspective of the voice gateway—London, in this case.

Figure 2-8   *Echo canceller in London eliminates Bob's echoes in London tail circuit.*

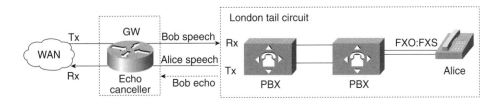

Echo cancellers have the following properties:

- Echo cancellers face into the PSTN tail circuit.
- An echo canceller eliminates echoes in the tail circuit on its side of the network.

Note that delay and jitter in the WAN do not affect the operation of the echo canceller because the tail circuit is static, and that's where the echo canceller operates.

From the perspective of the echo canceller in the London voice gateway, the Rx signal is Bob's voice coming across the packet network from Montreal. The Tx signal is a mixture of Alice's voice and the echo of Bob's voice, which comes from the London tail circuit and will be sent to Montreal.

The echo canceller in the London gateway looks out into the London tail circuit and is responsible for eliminating Bob's echo signal from the London Tx signal and allowing Alice's voice to go through unimpeded. If Alice were hearing an echo in London, the source of the problem would be in Montreal, and the echo canceller in Montreal would eliminate it.

Basics of Echo Canceller Operation

The role of the echo canceller is to strip out the echo portion of the signal coming out of the tail circuit and headed into the WAN. The echo canceller does this by learning the electrical characteristics of the tail circuit and forming its own model of the tail circuit in memory. Using this model, the echo canceller creates an estimated echo signal based on the current and past Rx signal (Bob's voice). Bob's voice is run through this functional model to come up with an estimate of what Bob's echo signal would sound like. This estimated "Bob echo" is then subtracted from the actual Tx signal that comes out of the tail circuit.

Mathematically, this means the following:

Tx signal sent from the gateway back to Bob
= Tx signal – estimated Bob's echo
= (Alice's voice + Bob's echo) – estimated Bob's echo
= Alice's voice + (Bob's echo – estimated Bob's echo)
= Alice's voice (if the estimation is accurate)

The quality of the estimation is continuously improved by monitoring the estimation error. Figure 2-9 shows a simplified version of the echo canceller operation.

Figure 2-9   *Echo canceller operation: training.*

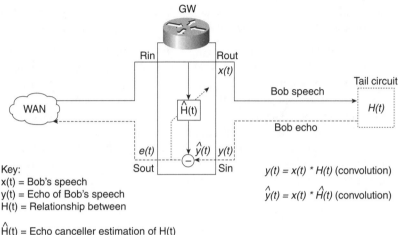

Key:
x(t) = Bob's speech
y(t) = Echo of Bob's speech
H(t) = Relationship between

$\hat{H}$(t) = Echo canceller estimation of H(t)
$\hat{y}$(t) = Echo canceller of estimation of y(t)
e(t) = Remaining echo after echo cancellation

The key to echo canceller operation is that the tail circuit can be functionally represented by a mathematical formula. For the moment, assume that Alice is not talking. The tail circuit is a black box with an input (Bob's speech) and an output (Bob's echo). A formula exists that describes the relationship between these two signals—a recipe for transforming the input signal into the output signal. If you knew what the formula was, you could simulate the black box in software. Then you could record the input signal and use the formula to predict what the output signal should sound like.

This is precisely what an echo canceller does. Bob's voice signal, x(t) enters the real tail circuit and emerges as the echo signal y(t). The input-output relationship (impulse response) of the real tail circuit is H(t). H(t) is a mathematical representation of the transformation applied to x(t) to obtain y(t).

The echo canceller stores an estimate of this impulse response, denoted Hhat(t). The echo canceller has access to the signal x(t), Bob's voice, and runs this signal through Hhat(t) to obtain a "virtual" echo signal yhat(t). This virtual echo is subtracted from the real echo, and the resulting signal e(t) (error signal) is ideally zero. The echo is cancelled.

How does the echo canceller obtain the formula for H(t)? The simple answer is through trial and error. The precise answer is the use of a gradient descent algorithm to drive the coefficients of an adaptive finite impulse response (FIR) filter.

The echo canceller starts out with an all-zeroes formula for Hhat(t). Naturally, this is a very poor guess and the error signal e(t) is large. A control method exists that allows the formula for Hhat(t) to *wiggle*, or adapt in a controlled fashion. If a wiggle causes the error to decrease, the formula keeps wiggling like that. If the wiggle causes the error to grow, the formula stops wiggling in that direction and starts wiggling in the opposite direction. Gradually the error decreases, the wiggles get smaller, and Hhat(t) becomes a better and better estimate of the true H(t). This period of wiggling is known as the *adaptation* or *convergence* period—Hhat(t) wiggles until its formula converges on the true formula H(t).

Alice is not talking in the previous example. If Alice is talking, the signal coming back from the tail circuit is a mixture of Alice's voice and Bob's echo. This condition is known as *double talk*. Double talk obscures the clean relationship of H(t) that the formula is trying to estimate; therefore, convergence occurs only when Alice is silent. This does not mean that echo canceling stops. The whole point of converging is to provide a method of estimating Bob's echo signal. When Alice talks, the formula continues to generate echo estimates and subtract these from the incoming signal. In this way, only the portion of the signal from Bob's echo is stripped out. Bob hears Alice's voice with no echo from his own speech. Figure 2-10 illustrates how echo cancellation works when there is double-talk.

Figure 2-10   *Echo canceller operation: double-talk.*

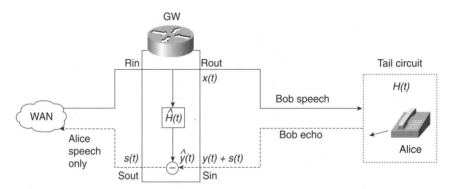

For a more detailed explanation of how echo cancellers operate, see the book *Digital Signal Processing in Telecommunications*, by K. Shenoi, Prentice Hall PTR, 1995.

Measuring Echo

The following list describes the primary measurements used by echo cancellers (expressed in dB), and Figure 2-11 illustrates where these measurements come into play during the echo-cancelling process:

- **Echo return loss (ERL)**—The reduction in the echo level produced by the tail circuit without the use of an echo canceller. Thus, if an Rx speech signal enters the tail circuit from the network at a level of X dB, the echo coming back from the tail circuit into the S in terminal of the echo canceller is X – ERL.

- **Echo Return Loss Enhancement (ERLE)**—The additional reduction in echo level accomplished by the echo canceller. An echo canceller is not a perfect device; the best it can do is lower the level of the returning echo. ERLE is a measure of this echo attenuation performed by the echo canceller. It's the difference between the echo level arriving from the tail circuit at the echo canceller and the level of the signal leaving the echo canceller.

- **Acombined (ACOM)**—The total echo return loss seen across the Rin and Sout terminals of the echo canceller. ACOM is the sum of ERL + ERLE, or the total echo return loss seen by the network.

Figure 2-11 *ERL, ERLE, and ACOM.*

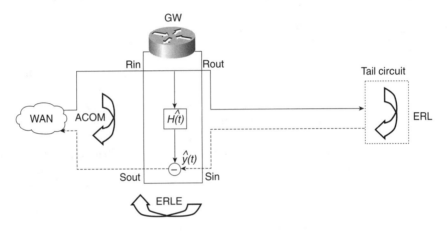

ERL = Echo Return Loss through Tail = Rout – Sin dB

ERLE = Echo Return Loss Enhancement through echo canceller = Sin – Sout dB

ACOM = Combined Echo Return Loss through system = Rin – Sout dB

Insufficient ERL

ERL is the amount of echo loss inherent in the tail circuit (illustrated in Figure 2-11) without the effect of the echo canceller included. ERL describes how loud the natural echoes are. Naturally, louder natural echoes (which have smaller ERLs) require the echo canceller to be more active in rendering the echoes inaudible. If every tail circuit gave infinite ERL, there would be no echoes.

Insufficient ERL means the ERL of the tail circuit (the amount of echo reduction inherent in the tail circuit) combined with the ERLE of the echo canceller is not enough to render echoes inaudible. It's "insufficient ERL" (as opposed to "insufficient ACOM") because the ERL is the variable that you attempt to minimize in the tail circuit, while the ERLE is a constant function of the echo canceller—typically 20 to 30 dB.

There are two main causes of insufficient ERL:

- Echo canceller operation is not sufficient to eliminate the echo.

  In this case, the echo canceller is operating properly but is unable to attenuate the echo signal enough to make it inaudible. Recall that ERL for a typical tail is about 20 dB. If this is the case, the echo canceller will provide an extra 20 to 30 dB of cancellation (ERLE), and the returning echo will be reduced 40 to 50 dB (ACOM), which is almost certainly inaudible.

  But if, for example, the ERL of the tail circuit is only 7 dB, the echo canceller will not be able to eliminate the echo. The same 20 to 30 dB of ERLE it provides will result in an ACOM of only 27 to 37 dB, which might still be an audible echo. A general rule of thumb is that if the ERL of the tail circuit is not at least 15 dB, you should attempt to find and eliminate the source of the echo.

- Echo canceller cannot operate because the echo is too strong.

  This second case is much more rare, but also more dangerous. Recall from the discussion of echo canceller operation that it stops improving its echo cancellation during periods of double-talk (when both parties are speaking at once). How does the echo canceller detect double-talk? Typically, the conditions for double-talk are when the Sin signal is within 6 dB of the Rout signal. That is, the combined Alice + echo signal is almost as loud or louder than Bob's voice. Therefore, if the ERL is less than 6 dB, the echo signal will be considered to be a proper part of the call and not an echo. So the echo is declared double-talk, and the echo canceller will never attempt to eliminate it.

To sum up, smaller ERL means louder natural echo. The louder the natural echo, the more likely it is that users will be annoyed by echoes with the same degree of cancellation. For extremely loud echoes, the echo canceller can be fooled into double-talk mode and will not converge.

Echo Canceller Coverage

Echo canceller coverage (also known as tail coverage or tail length) specifies the length of time that the echo canceller stores its approximation of an echo, Hhat(t), in memory. You can think of coverage as the echo canceller's cache. It's the maximum echo delay that an echo canceller will be able to eliminate.

Previously, it was noted that the echo canceller faces into a static tail circuit. The tail circuit has an input and an output. If a word enters a tail circuit (input signal x(t) in Figure 2-10), the echo (output signal y(t) in Figure 2-10) is a series of delayed and attenuated versions of that word, depending on the number of echo sources and the delays associated with them. After a certain period of time, no more signals will come out. This time period is known as the *ringing time* of the tail circuit.

Think of the original echo source as a pebble tossed in still water and the echoes as the series of attenuated ripples the pebble produces. The ringing time is the time required for all of the ripples to disperse.

Therefore, to fully eliminate all echoes, the coverage of the echo canceller must be as long as the ringing time of the tail circuit.

Figure 2-12 is an example of tail circuit impulse response. The peaks correspond to individual echoes in the tail circuit. We see that this system has three echoes: a strong one at about 3 ms and two weaker ones at about 7 ms and 9 ms. After about 12 ms, there is no significant energy in the impulse response. The amplitudes of the peaks correspond to the strength of the echo—the higher the peaks, the stronger the echo, and the smaller the ERL.

Figure 2-12 *Example of tail circuit impulse response H(t).*

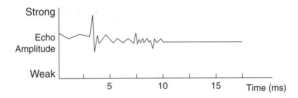

You should provision an echo canceller facing into such a tail circuit for at least 12 ms of tail coverage to cancel all three echoes. An echo canceller with 5 ms of coverage would perform fairly well with this circuit because the primary echo falls within the 5 ms window. The second two echos, though, would remain uncancelled because the echo canceller would discard its approximation of those echos from its memory.

It is important to stress again that the echo canceller faces into a static tail circuit—it eliminates echoes in its own tail circuit that are experienced by callers on the other end of the network. Echo cancellers are not aware of the rest of the network; therefore, tail coverage has nothing to do with the WAN, the round-trip delay, or whether the network delay is changing.

Many people assume incorrectly that the long delays associated with VoIP require that the echo cancellers have equally long tail coverage. However, only the tail determines the needed coverage. Remember that analog transmission is quick—almost all simple tails ring for only a few milliseconds. You see longer ringing times when the tail is very complex (for example, a large number of PSTN hops, multiple D/A conversions), or when it contains long-distance trunks. If the tail of your VoIP system contains another VoIP link, then your tail is going to be far too long to cover. In that case, the embedded VoIP link requires its own echo canceller on its own tail.

We recommend that you avoid such embedded VoIP links. We suggest that you provision all your echo cancellers to their maximum tail coverage all the time.

Uncancellable Echo

An uncancellable echo is an echo that is either of the following:

- Too loud to render inaudible
- Delayed beyond the time window of the echo canceller's coverage

If the echo is too loud, it can require more attenuation than an echo canceller can provide—meaning that either the echo canceller will be unable to make the echo imperceptible or that the echo will trigger the double-talk detector. Tail circuits that involve multiple PSTN hops, some long-distance trunks, and alternating series of digital and analog links can have ringing times that exceed the tail coverage window.

Verifying Echo Canceller Operation

The quickest way to tell if you have a working echo canceller in the circuit is to make a call and immediately begin to say something like, "Tah Tah Fish" repeatedly. The person on the other end of the line should be silent. If you are calling a voice-mail system, wait for the announcer to stop talking before starting the experiment.

If the terminating tail circuit has cancellable echoes and if the echo canceller is enabled, you will hear echo for the first few utterances and then it will die away. After a few seconds of speech, the echo should be gone or at least very quiet compared to the echo level at the beginning of the call. This is the signature of a working echo canceller. Recall that an echo canceller starts out with no knowledge of the tail circuit that it is looking into. It needs to observe a certain amount of speech and echo flowing through the tail circuit to form the virtual tail circuit model. This training period is known as the *convergence time* of the echo canceller. You should expect convergence within the first few seconds of active speech.

If you try this experiment and do not obtain echo reduction with time, there are two possibilities: The echo canceller is disabled or broken, or the echo is uncancellable (either too loud or delayed beyond the tail coverage of the canceller). Try making calls to other destinations and looking for the standard "echo die-away" behavior.

The surest way to determine if your echo canceller is working is to run the test described previously, first when the echo canceller is off, and then again when the echo canceller is on. If you don't find the standard "echo die-away" behavior, follow these steps to determine if your echo canceller is working:

Step 1   Telnet to the destination voice gateway and check the provisioning of the voice ports (for POTS). (Remember, the echo canceller you are interested in is the echo canceller in the destination voice gateway.)

Step 2   Disable the echo canceller by issuing the **no echo-cancel enable** voice-port command, then shut down and reopen the voice port by issuing the **shutdown** and **no shutdown** commands.

Step 3   Make a call to a destination telephone and listen for echo by saying something like "Tah Tah Fish." If you don't hear any echo, try different destination phones until you do. When you've found an echo that persists throughout the call, save the destination number.

Step 4   Re-enable the echo canceller by using the **echo-cancel enable** voice-port command, set coverage to maximum by using the **echo-cancel coverage** voice-port command, and shut down and reopen the voice port. You should hear the echo die away within the first few seconds of speech. If the echo persists, the problem is in your echo canceller.

If the echo diminishes but is still noticeable, try to locate the source of the echo path and eliminate the echo. Clearly, the echo canceller is working but it is unable to give sufficient ERLE. Occasionally, tiny bursts of echo might emerge during the conversation, especially if the talker makes a quick, loud, bursty sound. This is normal echo canceller behavior. If these types of echoes are loud enough to be unacceptable, you need to identify and eliminate the source of the echo in the tail circuit.

Customer Expectations About Echo

Because of the fundamental delays associated with VoIP technologies, existing echoes will be more annoying than with TDM, and even the normal operation of an echo canceller will be more apparent. Customers of VoIP networks need to be educated to expect the standard echo canceller operation described previously so that they do not confuse these types of echoes with abnormal echoes. Abnormal echoes persist throughout a call and do not fade.

Service Provider Expectations About Echo

Echo problems are relatively rare in the PSTN with its short delays; they are much more common over cellular and satellite long-distance calls. Interestingly, they are also much more readily tolerated in cellular and long-distance calls because customers have been educated to have lower expectations for such calls.

As long as VoIP calls continue to be terminated in analog tails, echo will be a problem. One of the major obstacles to widespread VoIP implementation is that many tail circuits have pre-existing delays that will become noticeable only when service providers introduce digital segments to the networks.

These problems will gradually be solved as digital networks extend toward homes and telephone endpoints. Until then, how much echo can you expect? One call in 50? 100? 1000? Even if customers are trained to complain only when an echo problem is persistent and repeatable, it is simply not possible for a service provider to hunt down and destroy every echo complaint. No one has sufficient resources to do this task, and hunting down an echo is a necessarily intrusive process.

The challenge is to determine when an echo complaint is both solvable and worth solving. You know that the echo source is in the destination tail circuit. To solve an echo problem, the tail circuit needs to be accessible.

In an enterprise application where the PBXs are in the basement, for example, it is relatively easy to solve echo problems by examining levels and impedances in the customer PBX. The things to look for are consistency and commonality in the echo problems. If every call going through a particular PBX or transmission link exhibits echo, then you can concentrate on that particular link. That is a problem worth solving. If you receive an isolated echo complaint for a particular destination phone number in the PSTN that doesn't share any links with other echo complaints, then you might find yourself hunting down a single telephone echo complaint, which is usually not worth the resources.

The goal of service providers in eliminating echoes, therefore, is to identify clusters of echo complaints, look for common links, and fix the echos. There are a lot of *dirty tails* out in the PSTN, and it's unrealistic to think that every echo can be eliminated. The best you can do is make sure that your own network and tails are clean, which requires care in installation and provisioning, especially when connecting gateways to analog equipment.

Configuring Gateways to Minimize Echo

As you've seen, echoes live in the analog tail circuit, not in the gateway. The gateway has an echo canceller that can attenuate manageable echoes, but gateways cannot affect the root causes of the echo problems. The following are all you can do on a gateway to fix an echo:

- Ensure that the echo canceller is enabled with maximum coverage.
- Match output impedances and levels with the analog telecom equipment attached to the gateway's analog voice ports.

You can adjust the audio levels of voice ports to help eliminate echoes, but you should consider this method more of a workaround than a solution. You can adjust the audio level of either the outputs or the inputs of a voice port on a gateway.

Lowering the Sin input audio level (also called *increasing the input attenuation* or *adding a loss pad*) correspondingly decreases the level of any echoes by increasing the ERL of the tail. However, lowering the Sin input audio level also decreases the audio level of the Tx speech signal for every call (Alice's voice in this example).

Similarly, lowering the R(out) output audio level correspondingly decreases the level of any echoes, but also decreases the audio level of the Rx speech signal for every call (Bob's voice in this example).

You can end up helping the echo canceller for calls to tails with poor ERL but hurting voice quality by reducing levels for *all* calls through that particular voice port. Again, you should adjust audio levels to alleviate echoes only as a temporary workaround while you attempt to eliminate the echo source in the tail circuit.

Process for Locating and Eliminating Echoes

Before you look at the process for eliminating echoes in the tail circuit, take note of the following summary of the process for dealing with echoes in general:

Step 1   Identify which tail circuit is causing the echo. Remember, the echo is caused by the tail circuit on the opposite side of the network from the caller hearing the echo.

Step 2   Check for speakerphones or headsets. If the destination telephone is a speakerphone or headset, this is probably the source of the echo. Try replacing the speakerphone or headset with a better quality handset and see if the echo dies away normally.

Step 3   Telnet to the destination voice gateway and check that the echo canceller is enabled and that the coverage is set to maximum.

Step 4   Test for normal echo canceller behavior as described in the "Verifying Echo Canceller Operation" section earlier.

  If the echo is still persistent and you have verified that the echo canceller is working properly, you can conclude that the echo canceller cannot fix the echo for one of the following two reasons:

  — The echo is too loud (called a *loud echo*).

  — The echo is too delayed (called a *long echo*).

Step 5   Identify which type of echo you are experiencing, either long or loud.

Step 6   Eliminate the echo source.

After you have verified that the echo canceller is working properly, you still need to determine the cause of the echo: Is the problem insufficient ERL in the tail, or is the echo delayed beyond the coverage of the echo canceller? Most persistent echoes are loud echoes. Delayed echoes are common, however, when the tail circuit involves a long-distance PSTN link, a series of alternating digital and analog links, or any other link with high latency.

Identifying a Loud Echo

You can use the voice gateway itself to measure the ERL of the tail circuit by using the gateway's echo canceller statistics reporting function. For a Cisco VoIP gateway, output from the **show call active voice** privileged EXEC command contains valuable statistics.

To generate these statistics, first establish a voice call over the gateway. Then type the **show call active voice** privileged EXEC command without pressing the Return key. Finally, make a loud continuous sound into the mouthpiece or hold down a button on your touch-tone keypad to generate a sound, and then press Return to display the call statistics.

TIP	You can also use commercial test devices (including handheld telecom level meters) to measure ERL for a particular destination circuit.

Remember, you need to look at the *destination* voice gateway. Looking at Figure 2-12, you see that the ERL is the difference in the reported Tx and Rx levels. Ideally, you would like your gateway to have an ERL of at least 15 dB. If your ERL is less than 10 dB, you probably have insufficient ERL in the tail circuit. Repeat the test outlined previously using louder and softer noises and verify that the ERL is consistent and that when you vary your volume, the levels vary accordingly. If these tests are consistent, you can be confident that the tail circuit is not providing enough echo loss for the echo canceller to be able to eliminate the echo.

Identifying a Long Echo

You can also identify a long echo problem with a technique similar to the one described previously for loud echoes. The signature of a loud echo problem is that the echo is somewhat attenuated but still noticeable. The echo is the same regardless of whether the echo canceller is enabled. If you determine that the ERL is reasonable (greater than 10 dB) but the echo is still persistent, then the problem might be a long echo.

If the problem is a long echo, there is not much that you can do to solve it. If the tail includes a long-distance hop, make sure that the PBX terminating the long-distance hop has its own echo canceller turned on. If possible, extend the digital portion of your network as close as possible to the endpoint.

Locating and Eliminating Echoes in the Tail Circuit

Because of the variety of possible network scenarios, it's difficult to give specific instructions for finding and eliminating an echo in a tail circuit. However, you can do a few general things to track down the source of an echo and eliminate it.

Draw a diagram of the tail circuit, including all the digital and analog links between the destination voice gateway and the destination telephone. This diagram will likely form a tree; from the voice gateway out, each device will have one or more potential destination branches. You need to identify the break point off the main branch for which calls give consistent echo.

For example, the gateway might be connected to a PBX with three output cards. If several of the calls through one of these ports exhibit echo, then you've narrowed the problem tail to the circuits attached to that voice port. Look for clusters of echo associated with common links. If you trace your tail out to the uncontrolled PSTN, then remember that there will always be a certain percentage of PSTN tails that do not provide sufficient ERL and you will be unable to correct them. When you find a link that's giving insufficient ERL, examine the levels and provisioning of the devices at both ends of the link.

Echo Analysis Case Study

The following case study describes how Cisco worked with an enterprise customer to eliminate echo in a VoIP network. The customer is a large manufacturing firm with headquarters in Reading, PA, and several plants in the United States and overseas. One of the plants, located in Belgium, previously used the PSTN for inter-site calling, which resulted in large toll charges. Because the customer already had a data network in place, the logical choice was to implement a combined voice/data network. Because traffic at the headquarters was required to cross the Ethernet backbone to the PBX, the customer decided to use IP for voice traffic. It was calculated that the customer would save $3000 a month by installing three voice trunks across the data infrastructure.

Figure 2-13 shows the network topology between the headquarters and the remote site in Belgium. The Belgium site has 4-wire E&M trunks connected from an Ericsson PBX to the Cisco 3640 router. In Reading, PA, a Cisco AS5300 access server is connected to a Lucent Definity GR3 PBX. All the proper QoS considerations and dial plan configurations were discussed and properly planned and will not be discussed here.

Figure 2-13 *Case study: customer topology.*

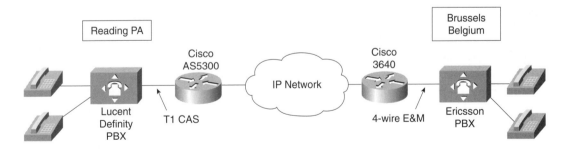

Echo Problem Description

When the voice and data network was first implemented, users experienced substantial echoes and reverted to the PSTN for calls between headquarters and the Belgium site. The customer initially believed that the Cisco routers were causing the echo, but we explained that our routers function like a 4-wire circuit and that it was not possible for leakage between the two voice paths to create echo.

After testing calls between headquarters and Belgium, we noticed large amounts of echo and determined that the echo was being heard only on the headquarters end of the calls; therefore, the source of the echo was in the Belgium tail circuit—between the Cisco 3640 and the telephone in Belgium.

Initially, we thought this might be a case of loud echo, which means an echo caused by insufficient ERL in the tail circuit. We ruled out the possibility of a long echo—an echo delay longer than the echo canceller's coverage. Because the Cisco 3640 had echo cancellers active on the Belgium tail circuit and the Belgium tail was connected only to the PBX, which wouldn't cause a delay long enough to cause long echo, long echo was not a possibility. If calls from headquarters were dropping off the Belgium PBX or being routed to a third destination, long echo could then have been a possibility.

Eventually we discovered that in the tail circuit, a hybrid was converting signals from 4-wire to 2-wire. Hybrids can be a common echo source. Figure 2-14 shows how the hybrid was deployed in the customer's network:

Figure 2-14 *Echo in customer topology.*

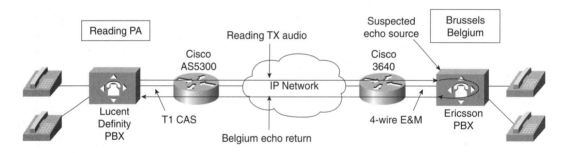

We explained to the customer that the echo problem probably existed before implementing VoIP but that it had not been perceivable because the PSTN delay was below the noticeable threshold. Packet-based networks create some small delays (as a result of packet encoding, queuing delays, and jitter buffers) that might unmask pre-existing echo problems. This is normal and is characteristic of a packet-based network.

We set out to resolve the echo issue by proving that the problem was the PBX in Belgium and by proposing a solution to eliminate the echo problem. We looked at the following issues:

- Source of the echo
- Audio levels of the PBX
- ERL of the PBX
- Impedance settings

To thoroughly check the network, we ordered a commercial test set for the Belgium site. Before the test set was delivered, we ran a simpler preliminary test. We had an FXS module shipped to the customer's site in Brussels from the local Cisco Technical Assistance Center (TAC). We instructed the customer's onsite personnel to install and configure the FXS module in the existing Cisco 3640 to allow calls from the FXS port on the Belgium 3640 to the PBX in Reading, PA. When we established calls between the Belgium 3640 and the PBX in Reading, there was no perceivable echo and the quality was very clear.

This test indicated that if the 4-wire to 2-wire conversion occurred on the router (as opposed to the Ericsson PBX), there was no echo present. Therefore, the Ericsson PBX was most likely causing the echo. The simplest solution to such an echo problem would be to connect only FXS ports from the Cisco 3640 into the PBX. This configuration would allow the router to perform the 4-wire to 2-wire conversion, and the FXS ports would appear as CO trunks to the Ericsson PBX. Although this wouldn't provide as much flexibility as the 4-wire E&M trunks, it wouldn't take away any functionality from the customers because they used an auto-attendant. Figure 2-15 shows this FXS test configuration.

Figure 2-15 *FXS test configuration.*

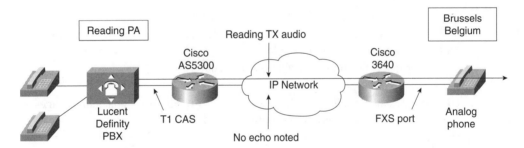

Eliminating the Echo

After our test generator arrived, we arranged to have a Cisco representative in PA and an Ericsson representative on site in Belgium. The following steps illustrate the process to eliminate the echo:

Step 1   Verify proper impedance levels on the Ericsson PBX in Belgium.

Step 2   Verify proper audio levels.

Step 3   Measure the ERL of the Ericsson PBX.

Verifying Proper Impedance Levels

The Ericsson representative verified that the impedance of the 4-wire E&M circuits was set for 600 ohms, which matched the configuration on the Cisco 3640.

Verifying Proper Audio Levels

Next, we verified proper audio level settings from the PA site to the Belgium site. The test set had the ability to connect to the Lucent PBX like any 2-wire analog phone; it also had a dial pad that allowed our test set to initiate a call to Belgium. After we established a call to Belgium, we injected a 1004 Hz tone at 0 dB into the Lucent PBX. We then measured the audio levels at various points along the voice path. These levels were verified in accordance with Cisco audio guidelines, which are available at the following URL: http://wwwin.cisco.com/servpro/msa/products/ReleaseInfo/docs/voice_level_adj.html.

We entered a **show call active voice** privileged EXEC command on the PA router to verify the audio levels. The level on the PA router measured –3 dB, which was the correct level according to the Cisco guidelines.

TIP

If the levels had needed to be adjusted, we would have entered the **input gain voice-port** configuration command. For example:

```
voice-port 1/0/0 (Cisco 3600 series router)
   input gain 3
```

This increases the level into the VoIP network by 3 dB. For these input gain changes to take effect, you need to hang up and re-establish the call.

After we verified the proper audio settings on the PA router, we entered a **show call active voice** privileged EXEC command on the Cisco 3640 in Belgium. This router displayed a –7 dB audio setting heading toward the Ericsson PBX. Even though the –7 dB level itself was acceptable, the optimal level is –12 dB at the phone on the PBX because different PBXs have different loss levels. Figure 2-16 and Example 2-1 depict the level adjustment configuration and the levels that were seen.

Figure 2-16 *Audio level and echo test setup.*

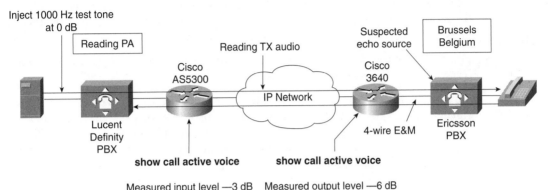

Inject 1000 Hz test tone
at 0 dB

Reading PA

Reading TX audio

Suspected echo source

Brussels Belgium

Cisco AS5300

Cisco 3640

IP Network

Lucent Definity PBX

4-wire E&M

Ericsson PBX

show call active voice   **show call active voice**

Measured input level —3 dB   Measured output level —6 dB
Measured ERL 7 dB

Example 2-1   **show call active voice** *Command Output*

```
Reading AS5300
Reading#show call active voice

CoderTypeRate=g729r8
NoiseLevel=0
ACOMLevel=0
OutSignalLevel=-79
!This is the input level
InSignalLevel=-3
```
```
Belgium 3640
Belgium#show call active voice

CoderTypeRate=g729r8
NoiseLevel=0
ACOMLevel=0
!This is the output level, R(out)
OutSignalLevel=-7
!This is the input level, S(in)
InSignalLevel=-14
InfoActivity=2
ERLLevel=7

!ERL = R(out) - S(in)
!ERL = (-7) - (-14) = 7 dB
!ERL should be > 15 dB
```

Measuring ERL

Because the audio levels were acceptable to the customer, we didn't adjust them. However, we did raise and lower the audio levels during the ERL test. We sourced a tone from PA and measured the echo on the Cisco 3640 router in Belgium.

You don't need an official test generator for echo testing. You can use DTMF tones or your own voice to get a rough idea of level mismatches.

We applied the same 1004 Hz tone at 0 dB into the PA PBX and again entered the **show call active voice** priveleged EXEC command to display the ERL level. The ERL represents the level of the echo coming out of the PBX in relation to the signal into the PBX. Notice in Example 2-1 that the ERL level is –14 dB, which means that, in relation to the signal going into the PBX, the echo is coming back at a level only 7 dB less than what was going in.

The ITU-T G.131 specification states that the ERL of a PBX should be greater than 15 dB. The ERL was way above what an echo canceller can effectively nullify; therefore, the echo problem was with the Belgium PBX. To further verify this, we adjusted the audio level into the PBX up and down. When we adjusted the audio level, the ERL remained constant.

We ran the same test with the FXS port plugged into the Ericsson PBX, as shown in Figure 2-17. Example 2-2 shows output from the **show caller active voice** priveleged EXEC command, which showed an acceptable ERL level of 19 dB. This call exhibited no echo.

Figure 2-17 *ERL test using the FXS port in Belgium.*

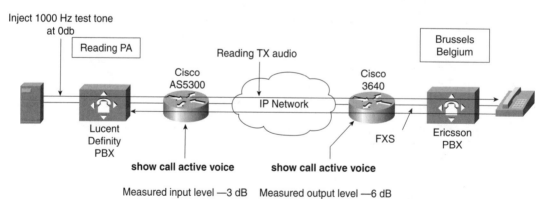

Example 2-2   **show call active voice** *Command Output for FXS Test*

```
Reading AS5300
Reading#show call active voice

CoderTypeRate=g729r8
NoiseLevel=0
ACOMLevel=0
OutSignalLevel=-79
!This is the input level
InSignalLevel=-3
```
```
Belgium 3640
Belgium#show call active voice

CoderTypeRate=g729r8
NoiseLevel=0
ACOMLevel=0
!This is the output level, R(out)
OutSignalLevel=-7
!This is the input level, S(in)
InSignalLevel=-27
InfoActivity=2
ERLLevel=20

!ERL = R(out) - S(in)
!ERL = (-7) - (-27) = 20 dB
!ERL is > 15 dB
```

Case Study Summary

The customer was satisfied with our testing results and decided to use our suggested
workaround of using FXS ports, which appeared as CO trunks to the Belgium PBX, out of
the Belgium Cisco 3640 router. This solution reduced some of the network's inward dialing
flexibility, but because all inbound calls were handled by an auto-attendant, no functionality
was lost.

This case study illustrates the importance of educating customers about the proper
expectations of packet-based networks. Specifically, you should stress that the normal
characteristics of packet-based networks may unmask pre-existing problems in TDM-
based voice infrastructures.

This particular kind of echo problem—where the echo is PBX-based—is the easiest to
solve. It is much more difficult to solve a case where the tail circuit is the PSTN and calls
to only some locations are being affected. Not only are such cases difficult to troubleshoot,
but you are faced with the challenge of convincing the customer that the problem is in the
PSTN, not the VoIP network. In reality, this type of echo problem isn't just related to VoIP.
It's essentially media-independent and can occur wherever added delays in the network
might exist.

Summary

This chapter explained what echo is and where it occurs in a voice network. This chapter examined the basics of echo analysis and described the effects of various network elements on echo. It also explained how echo is measured and how echo cancellers work to estimate and eliminate echo.

It also looked at customer and service provider expectations about echo, and explained how to configure routers and gateways to minimize echo. You saw that the normal characteristics of packet-based networks can unmask pre-existing problems in the TDM-based voice infrastructure.

Finally, the chapter outlined a process for locating and eliminating loud echoes and long echoes, and concluded with a real-life case study involving PBX-based echo in an international voice network.

## CHAPTER 3

Understanding Quality of Service for Voice over IP

Quality of Service Requirements

For VoIP to be a realistic replacement for standard PSTN telephony services, customers need to receive the same quality of voice transmission that they receive with basic telephone services: consistently high-quality voice transmissions. Like other real-time applications, VoIP is extremely bandwidth and delay sensitive. For VoIP transmissions to be intelligible to the receiver, voice packets should not be dropped or excessively delayed, or suffer varying delay (otherwise known as jitter). For example:

- The default G.729 codec requires packet loss far less than 1 percent to avoid audible errors. Ideally, there should be no packet loss for VoIP.

- ITU G.114 specification recommends less than 150 ms one-way end-to-end delay for high-quality real-time traffic, such as voice. (For international calls, one-way delay up to 300 ms is acceptable, especially for satellite transmission. This takes propagation delay into consideration—the time required for the signal to travel the distance.)

- Jitter buffers (used to compensate for varying delay) further add to the end-to-end delay, and are usually effective only on delay variations of less than 100 ms. Jitter must therefore be minimized.

VoIP can guarantee high-quality voice transmission only if the voice packets, for both the signaling and audio channels, are given priority over other kinds of non-critical network traffic. To deploy VoIP so that users receive an acceptable level of voice quality, VoIP traffic must be guaranteed certain compensating bandwidth, latency, and jitter requirements. Quality of service (QoS) ensures that VoIP voice packets receive the preferential treatment they require.

This chapter discusses various QoS concepts and features that are applicable to voice. This chapter also provides high-level examples showing how to deploy these features in different voice network environments.

Sufficient Bandwidth

Before you consider applying any of the QoS features discussed in this chapter, you must first provision sufficient network bandwidth to support real-time voice traffic. For example, an 80 kbps G.711 VoIP call (64 kbps payload + 16 kbps header) will sound poor over a

64 kbps link because at least 16 kbps of the packets (or 20 percent) will be dropped. Keep in mind that this example also assumes that no other traffic is flowing over the link (although link management and routing protocol traffic usually will exist). After you provision sufficient bandwidth for voice traffic, you can take further steps to guarantee that voice packets have a certain percentage of the total bandwidth and give voice packets priority.

Packet Classification

To guarantee bandwidth for VoIP packets, a network device must be able to identify VoIP packets in all the IP traffic flowing through it. Network devices use the source and destination IP address in the IP header or the source and destination UDP port numbers in the UDP header to identify VoIP packets. This identification and grouping process is called *classification* and it is the basis for providing any QoS. Besides the static classification methods involving Layer 3 or Layer 4 header information matching, you can use a mechanism such as Resource Reservation Protocol (RSVP) for dynamic classification. RSVP uses H.245 signaling packets to determine which UDP port the voice conversation will use. It then sets up dynamic access lists to identify VoIP traffic and places it into a reserved queue. We'll explain RSVP in the section, "RSVP—Dynamic Classification and Admission Control."

Packet classification can be processor intensive, so classification should be done as far out toward the edge of the network as possible. Because every hop still needs to make a determination on the treatment a packet should receive, you need to have a simpler, more efficient classification method in the network core. This simpler classification is achieved through *marking* or setting the type of service (ToS) byte in the IP header.

The three most significant bits of the ToS byte are called the *IP Precedence bits*. Most applications and vendors currently support setting and recognizing these three bits. Marking is evolving so that the six most significant bits of the ToS byte, called the Differentiated Services Code Point (DSCP), can be used to define differentiated services (DS) classes. We discuss DSCP in the section, "Differentiated Services for VoIP."

After every hop in the network is able to classify and identify the VoIP packets (either through port/address information or through the ToS byte), those hops can then provide each VoIP packet with the required QoS. At that point, you can configure special techniques to provide priority queuing to make sure that large data packets don't interfere with voice data transmission, and to reduce bandwidth requirements by compressing the 40-byte IP + UDP + RTP header down to 2 to 4 bytes—a technique known as Compressed Real-time Transport Protocol (cRTP). We discuss cRTP in the section, "IP RTP Header Compression."

Classification and Marking

Classification is the process of identifying what class or group a packet belongs to. Network devices use various *match* criteria to place traffic into a certain number of classes. Matches are based on the following criteria:

- The **dial-peer voice voip** global configuration command
- Access list (standard and extended)
- Protocol (such as URLs, stateful protocols, Layer 4 protocol, etc.)
- Input port
- IP Precedence or DSCP
- Ethernet 802.1p class of service (CoS)

It can be processor intensive if nodes must repeat classification based on access list matches. Therefore, nodes should mark packets as soon as they have identified and classified the VoIP packets. If a node can set the IP Precedence or DSCP bits in the ToS byte of the IP header as soon as it identifies traffic as being VoIP traffic, then all the other nodes in the network can classify based on these bits.

Marking is the process of the node setting one of the following:

- Three IP Precedence bits in the IP ToS byte
- Six DSCP bits in the IP ToS byte
- Three MPLS Experimental (EXP) bits
- Three Ethernet 802.1p CoS bits
- One ATM Cell Loss Probability (CLP) bit

In most IP network scenarios, it is sufficient to mark IP Precedence or DSCP.

Voice Dial Peers to Classify and Mark Packets

With Cisco VoIP gateways, you typically use voice dial peers to classify the VoIP packets and mark the IP Precedence bits. Example 3-1 shows how to mark the IP Precedence bits. (Highlighted commands are the specific commands used to configure the discussed QoS feature.)

Example 3-1 *Classification and Marking Using Dial Peers*

```
dial-peer voice 100 voip
 destination-pattern 100
 session target ipv4:10.10.10.2
 ip precedence 5
```

In Example 3-1, any VoIP call that matches dial peer 100 will have all its voice payload packets set with IP Precedence 5, meaning that the three most significant bits of the IP ToS byte are set to 101.

Committed Access Rate to Classify and Mark Packets

Committed Access Rate (CAR) is an older technique that involves rate-limiting or policing traffic that matches certain criteria to an upper bound. CAR supports most of the matching mechanisms and allows IP Precedence or DSCP bits to be set differently depending on whether packets conform to a specified rate or exceed the specified rate.

In general, CAR is more useful for data packets than for voice packets. For example, all data traffic coming in on an Ethernet interface at less than 1 Mbps can be placed into IP Precedence Class 3, and any traffic exceeding the 1-Mbps rate can go into Class 1 or be dropped. Other nodes in the network can then treat the exceeding or non-conforming traffic marked with lower IP Precedence differently. All voice traffic should conform to the specified rate if it has been provisioned correctly.

Example 3-2 shows how to use CAR to classify and mark VoIP packets.

Example 3-2   *Classification and Marking Using CAR*

```
access-list 100 permit udp any any range 16384 32767
access-list 100 permit tcp any any eq 1720
!
interface Ethernet0/0
 ip address 10.10.10.1 255.255.255.0
 rate-limit input access-group 100 1000000 8000 8000 conform-action
    set-prec-continue 5 exceed-action set-prec-continue 5
```

In Example 3-2, any traffic that matches access list 100 will be set with IP Precedence 5— meaning that the three most significant bits of the IP ToS byte are set to 101. Access list 100 here matches the common UDP ports used by VoIP and the H.323 signaling traffic to TCP port 1720. For more information about the **rate-limit** interface configuration command, refer to the "Cisco IOS Quality of Service Solutions Command Reference, Release 12.2."

Policy-Based Routing to Classify and Mark Packets

Policy-Based Routing (PBR) is another older feature that allows traffic to be routed based on a source port or access list. It can also be used to classify and mark packets. Example 3-3 shows a simple configuration.

Example 3-3   *Classification and Marking Using PBR*

```
access-list 100 permit udp any any range 16384 32767
access-list 100 permit tcp any any eq 1720
!
route-map classify_mark
```

Example 3-3   *Classification and Marking Using PBR (Continued)*

```
  match ip address 100
  set ip precedence 5
 !
interface Ethernet0/0
 ip address 10.10.10.1 255.255.255.0
 ip policy route-map classify_mark
```

In Example 3-3, any traffic that matches access list 100 will be set with IP Precedence 5, meaning that the three most significant bits of the IP ToS byte are set to 101. Access list 100 here matches the common UDP ports used by VoIP and H.323 signaling traffic to TCP port 1720.

Modular QoS Command Line Interface to Classify and Mark Packets

The recommended classification and marking method is Modular QoS Command Line Interface (Mod QoS CLI, or MQC). This is a template-based configuration method that separates the classification from the policy, allowing multiple QoS features to be configured together for multiple classes. You use a *class map* to classify traffic based on various match criteria and a *policy map* to determine what should happen to each class. Finally, you apply the policy to incoming or outgoing traffic on an interface using the **service-policy** interface configuration command. Example 3-4 shows how to use Modular QoS to classify and mark packets.

Example 3-4   *Classification and Marking Using MQC*

```
access-list 100 permit udp any any range 16384 32767
access-list 100 permit tcp any any eq 1720
 !
class-map voip
 match access-group 100
 !
policy-map mqc
 class voip
  set ip precedence 5
  <#various other QoS commands>
 class class-default
  set ip precedence 0
  <#various other QoS commands>
 !
interface Ethernet0/0
 service-policy input mqc
```

In Example 3-4, any traffic that matches access list 100 will be classified as **class voip** and set with IP Precedence 5, meaning that the three most significant bits of the IP ToS byte are set to 101. Access list 100 here matches the common UDP ports used by VoIP and H.323

signaling traffic to TCP port 1720. All other traffic is set with IP Precedence 0. The policy is called **mqc** and is applied to incoming traffic on Ethernet 0/0.

QoS Queuing Mechanisms

After all traffic has been placed into QoS classes based on their QoS requirements, you need to provide bandwidth guarantees and priority servicing through an intelligent output queuing mechanism. A priority queue is *required* for VoIP. You can use any queuing mechanism that effectively gives VoIP high priority, but we recommend low latency queuing (LLQ) because it is flexible and easy to configure.

Low Latency Queuing

The most flexible queuing method that satisfies VoIP requirements is LLQ. LLQ uses the MQC configuration method to provide priority to certain classes and to provide guaranteed minimum bandwidth for other classes. During periods of congestion, the priority queue is policed at the configured rate so that the priority traffic does not hog all the available bandwidth. (If the priority traffic monopolizes the bandwidth, it prevents bandwidth guarantees for other classes from being met.) If you provision LLQ correctly, the traffic going into the priority queue should never exceed the configured rate.

LLQ also allows queue depths to be specified to determine when the router should drop packets if too many packets are waiting in any particular class queue. A *class default* is also used to determine treatment of all traffic not classified by a configured class. The class default can be configured with *fair-queue*—which means that each unclassified flow will be given an approximately equal share of the remaining bandwidth. Figure 3-1 shows how LLQ works.

In Figure 3-1, all traffic going out of an interface or subinterface (for Frame Relay and ATM) is first classified using MQC. Four classes exist: one high-priority class, two guaranteed-bandwidth classes, and a default class. The priority class traffic is placed into a priority queue and the guaranteed bandwidth class traffic is placed into reserved queues. The default class traffic can be given a reserved queue or it can be placed in an unreserved default queue where each flow will get an approximately equal share of the unreserved and available bandwidth. The *scheduler* services the queues so the priority queue traffic is output first unless it exceeds a configured priority bandwidth and this bandwidth is needed by a reserved queue (for example, when there is congestion). The reserved queues are serviced according to their reserved bandwidth, which the schedule uses to calculate a *weight*. The weight is used to determine how often a reserved queue is serviced and how many bytes are serviced at a time. The scheduler services are based on the weighted fair queuing (WFQ) algorithm, a discussion of which is beyond the scope of this book.

Figure 3-1 *LLQ operation.*

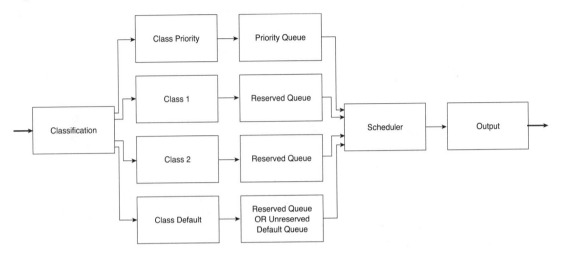

If the priority queue fills up because the transmission rate of priority traffic is higher than the configured priority bandwidth, the packets at the end of the priority queue will be dropped *only* if there's no more unreserved bandwidth available. None of the reserved queues are restricted to the configured bandwidth if there is bandwidth available. Packets violating the guaranteed bandwidth and priority are dropped only during periods of congestion. You must, therefore, provision the priority queue with enough bandwidth to handle all the VoIP traffic requiring priority servicing.

Example 3-5 shows how to configure LLQ.

Example 3-5 *LLQ*

```
access-list 100 permit udp any any range 16384 32000
access-list 100 permit tcp any any eq 1720
access-list 101 permit tcp any any eq 80
access-list 102 permit tcp any any eq 23
!
class-map voip
 match access-group 100
class-map data1
 match protocol
class-map data2
 match access-group 102
!
policy-map llq
 class voip
  priority 32
 class data1
  bandwidth 64
 class data2
  bandwidth 32
```

Example 3-5 *LLQ (Continued)*

```
class class-default
  fair-queue
!
interface Serial1/0
  bandwidth 256
  service-policy output llq
```

In Example 3-5, any traffic that matches access list 100 will be classified as **class voip** (meaning voice traffic) and given high priority up to 32 kbps. (This value is defined by the **priority 32** command.) Access list 100 matches the common UDP ports used by VoIP and H.323 signaling traffic to TCP port 1720. Class **data1** matches web traffic (TCP port 80 as seen in access list 101) and guarantees 64 kbps; class **data2** matches Telnet traffic (TCP port 23 as seen in access list 102) and guarantees 32 kbps. The default class is configured to give an equal share of the remaining bandwidth to unclassified flows. The policy is called **llq**, and is applied on outgoing traffic on Serial1/0, which has a total bandwidth of 256 kbps. (If no bandwidth is specified on the Serial1/0 interface, it will default to a speed of 1.544 Mbps.) Note that by default, the total guaranteed bandwidth and priority bandwidth for all classes should be less than 75 percent of the interface bandwidth. You can modify this percentage by using the **max-reserved bandwidth** interface configuration command.

Other QoS Queuing Mechanisms

Several other queuing methods are available. For example, Modified Deficit Round Robin (MDRR) is a queuing mechanism available on the Cisco 12000 Series Gigabit Switch Routers (GSR) that allows bandwidth guarantees and priority servicing based on IP Precedence, DSCP, and MPLS EXP classes. MDRR supports one priority queue, seven reserved queues, and one multicast queue.

Once again, VoIP requires priority, but several data applications cannot be starved and need bandwidth guarantees. You can use any queuing mechanism that effectively gives VoIP high priority, but we recommend LLQ.

Table 3-1 describes some of the available software queuing mechanisms.

Table 3-1 *Software Queuing Mechanisms*

Software Queuing Mechanism	Description	Benefits	Limitations
First-in, first-out (FIFO)	Packets arrive and leave the queue in exactly the same order.	Simple configuration and fast operation.	No priority servicing or bandwidth guarantees possible.

Table 3-1   *Software Queuing Mechanisms (Continued)*

Software Queuing Mechanism	Description	Benefits	Limitations
Weighted fair queuing (WFQ)	A hashing algorithm places flows into separate queues where weights are used to determine how many packets are serviced at a time. You define weights by setting IP Precedence and DSCP values.	Simple configuration. Default on links less than 2 Mbps.	No priority servicing or bandwidth guarantees possible.
Custom queuing (CQ)	Traffic is classified into multiple queues with configurable queue limits. The queue limits are calculated based on average packet size, MTU, and the percentage of bandwidth to be allocated. Queue limits (in number of bytes) are de-queued for each queue, therefore providing the allocated bandwidth statistically.	Has been available for a few years and allows approximate bandwidth allocation for different queues.	No priority servicing possible. Bandwidth guarantees are approximate and there are a limited number of queues. Configuration is relatively difficult.
Priority queuing (PQ)	Traffic is classified into high, medium, normal, and low priority queues. The high priority traffic is serviced first, then medium priority traffic, followed by normal and low priority traffic.	Has been available for a few years and provides priority servicing.	Higher priority traffic can starve the lower priority queues of bandwidth. No bandwidth guarantees possible.

continues

Table 3-1 *Software Queuing Mechanisms (Continued)*

Software Queuing Mechanism	Description	Benefits	Limitations
Class-based weighted fair queuing (CBWFQ)	MQC is used to classify traffic. Classified traffic is placed into reserved bandwidth queues or a default unreserved queue. A scheduler services the queues based on weights so that the bandwidth guarantees are honored.	Similar to LLQ except that there is no priority queue. Simple configuration and ability to provide bandwidth guarantees.	No priority servicing possible.
Priority queue— weighted fair queuing (PQ-WFQ, also called IP RTP Priority)	A single interface command is used to provide priority servicing to all UDP packets destined to even port numbers within a specified range.	Simple, one command configuration. Provides priority servicing to RTP packets.	All other traffic is treated with WFQ. RTCP traffic is not prioritized. No guaranteed bandwidth capability.
Low latency queuing (LLQ, previously called priority queue —class-based weighted fair queuing, or PQ-CBWFQ!)	MQC is used to classify traffic. Classified traffic is placed into a priority queue, reserved bandwidth queues, or a default unreserved queue. A scheduler services the queues based on weights so that the priority traffic is sent first (up to a certain policed limit during congestion) and the bandwidth guarantees are met.	Simple configuration. Ability to provide priority to multiple classes of traffic and give upper bounds on priority bandwidth utilization. You can also configure bandwidth guaranteed classes and a default class.	No mechanism for providing multiple levels of priority yet. All priority traffic is sent through the same priority queue. Separate priority classes can have separate upper priority bandwidth bounds during congestion, but sharing of priority queue between applications can introduce jitter.

Fragmentation and Interleaving

Even if queuing is working at its best and prioritizing voice traffic, times can arise when the priority queue is empty and a packet from another class is serviced. Packets from guaranteed bandwidth classes must be serviced according to their configured weight. If a priority voice packet arrives in the output queue while these packets are being serviced, the VoIP packet could wait a significant amount of time before being sent. If you assume that a VoIP packet will have to wait behind one data packet, and that the data packet can be, at most, equal in size to the Maximum Transmission Unit (MTU) (1500 bytes for serial and 4470 bytes for high-speed serial interfaces), you can calculate the wait time based on link speed.

For example, for a link speed of 64 kbps and an MTU size of 1500 bytes, you have:

Serialization delay = (1500 bytes × 8 bits/byte) / (64,000 bits/sec) = 187.5 ms

Therefore, a VoIP packet might have to wait up to 187.5 ms before it can be sent if it gets stuck behind a single 1500-byte packet on a 64 kbps link. VoIP packets are usually sent every 20 ms. With an end-to-end delay budget of 150 ms and strict jitter requirements, a gap of more than 180 ms is unacceptable.

You need a mechanism that ensures that the size of one transmission unit is less than 10 ms. Any packets that have more than 10 ms serialization delay need to be fragmented into 10 ms chunks. A 10 ms chunk or fragment is the number of bytes that can be sent over the link in 10 ms. You can calculate the size by using the link speed, as shown here:

Fragmentation size = (0.01 seconds × 64,000 bps) / (8 bits/byte) = 80 bytes

It takes 10 ms to send an 80-byte packet or fragment over a 64 kbps link.

On low speed links where a 10 ms packet is smaller than the MTU, fragmentation is required. But simple fragmentation is insufficient, because if the VoIP packet still has to wait behind all the fragments of a single large data packet, nothing has been accomplished. The VoIP packet must be interleaved or inserted between the data packet fragments. Figure 3-2 illustrates fragmentation and interleaving.

Figure 3-2 *VoIP packet fragmentation and interleaving.*

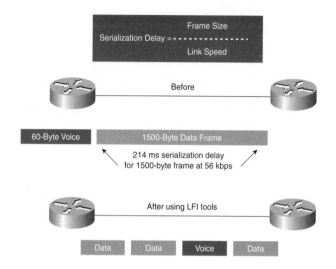

Table 3-2 shows recommended fragment sizes for various link speeds based on the 10 ms rule.

Table 3-2 *Link Speed and Fragmentation Size*

Link Speed (kbps)	Fragmentation Size (bytes)
56	70
64	80
128	160
256	320
512	640
768	960
1024	1280
1536	1920[1]

1. No fragmentation is required if the fragment size is larger than the link MTU size. For example, for a T1 link with a 1500-byte MTU, the fragment size is 1920 bytes; therefore, no fragmentation is required.

NOTE The packet fragmentation size should never be lower than the VoIP packet size. Also, you should never fragment VoIP packets because fragmenting causes numerous call setup and quality issues.

Currently, three link fragmentation and interleaving mechanisms are available. Table 3-3 lists their benefits and limitations.

Table 3-3   *Available Link Fragmentation and Interleaving Mechanisms*

Link Fragmentation and Interleaving (LFI) Mechanism	Description	Benefits	Limitations
MTU fragmentation with WFQ	Interface level command to change MTU size or IP MTU size. Used to fragment large IP packets to specified MTU size. LFI uses WFQ to interleave real-time packets between the fragments.	Simple configuration.	Fragments reassembled only by receiving application, an inefficient use of the network. Only IP packets with Don't Fragment (DF) bit not set can handle fragmentation well. Highly processor intensive. Not recommended.
Multilink Point-to-Point Protocol (MLPPP) Link Fragmentation and Interleaving (LFI)	On point-to-point serial links, Multilink PPP must first be configured, then a fragmentation size must be set in ms. Interleaving must also be enabled on the multilink interface.	Packets are fragmented on one end of a link and reassembled at the other. Several links can be combined to act as a large virtual pipe.	Available only on links configured for PPP. Solutions for PPP over Frame Relay or PPP over ATM also supported in Cisco IOS Release 12.1(5)T or later.
Frame Relay Fragmentation (FRF.12)	On Frame Relay PVCs, the **frame-relay traffic-shaping** interface configuration command must be enabled and a fragmentation size set under the map-class.	Packets are fragmented on one end of PVC and reassembled at the other.	Available only on Frame Relay PVCs with the **frame-relay traffic-shaping** interface configuration command enabled.

Examples 3-6 and 3-7 show how to configure fragmentation and interleaving using MLPPP
LFI and FRF.12.

Example 3-6 *MLPPP LFI*

```
interface Serial1/0
 bandwidth 256
 encapsulation ppp
 no fair-queue
 ppp multilink
 multilink-group 1
 !
interface Multilink1
 ip address 10.1.1.1 255.255.255.252
 bandwidth 256
 ppp multilink
 ppp multilink fragment-delay 10
 ppp multilink interleave
 multilink-group 1
```

In Example 3-6, MLPPP LFI is configured with a fragmentation size of 10 ms, which is
calculated based on the bandwidth configured for the multilink interface. Interface serial
1/0 is placed into multilink-group 1 and therefore inherits the multilink configuration in the
multilink 1 interface.

Example 3-7 *FRF.12*

```
interface Serial 0/1
 no ip address
 encapsulation frame-relay
 frame-relay traffic shaping
 !
interface Serial 0/1.64 point-to-point
 ip address 10.14.96.2 255.255.255.252
 frame-relay interface-dlci 128
  class voice
 !
map-class frame-relay voice
 frame-relay cir 256000
 frame-relay fragment 320
```

In Example 3-7, Frame Relay traffic shaping is enabled on DLCI 128, and FRF.12 is
configured with a fragmentation size of 320 bytes, which is 10 ms of the Committed
Information Rate (CIR). The fragmentation size should be 10 ms of the lower port speed at
the endpoints of the PVC; this example assumes that the CIR and the lower port speed are
the same: 256 kbps.

Traffic Shaping

Traffic shaping is a QoS mechanism used to send traffic in short bursts at a configured transmission rate. It is most commonly used in Frame Relay environments where the interface clock rate is not the same as the guaranteed bandwidth or CIR. Frame Relay traffic shaping is the most common traffic-shaping application in VoIP environments.

Frame Relay scenarios usually have a hub-and-spoke network where the hub link speed is higher than any of the remote link speeds. In some cases, the sum of the remote link speeds is higher than the hub link speed, causing over-subscription. Without Frame Relay traffic shaping, the hub might try to send at higher rates than the remotes can receive traffic, causing the Frame Relay network to arbitrarily drop traffic. On the other hand, the remotes could all send at an aggregate rate that is higher than the hub can receive, again causing the Frame Relay network to arbitrarily drop traffic. When we refer to the Frame Relay network, we mean the Service Provider network of WAN switches that provides the end-to-end PVC connectivity. Because the WAN SP cloud has no Layer 3 or above intelligence, it can drop VoIP traffic if contracts are violated. Therefore, you need to control transmission rates into a Frame Relay cloud so that you can control which packets get dropped and which packets receive priority servicing. Figure 3-3 shows an example of a typical Frame Relay network without traffic shaping.

Figure 3-3   *Frame Relay network.*

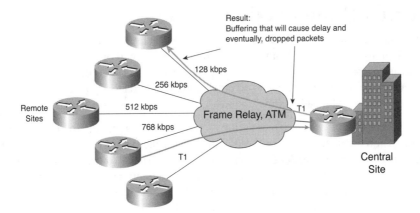

Example 3-8 shows how to configure Frame Relay traffic shaping.

Example 3-8   *Frame Relay Traffic Shaping*

```
interface Serial 0/1
 no ip address
 encapsulation frame-relay
 frame-relay traffic shaping
```

continues

Example 3-8 *Frame Relay Traffic Shaping (Continued)*

```
!
interface Serial 0/1.64 point-to-point
 ip address 10.14.96.2 255.255.255.252
 frame-relay interface-dlci 128
  class voice
!
map-class frame-relay voice
 no frame-relay adaptive-shaping
 frame-relay cir 256000
 frame-relay bc 2560
 frame-relay mincir 256000
```

In Example 3-8, Frame Relay traffic shaping is enabled on the main serial 0/1 interface and DLCI 128 is placed into a voice shaping class. The map-class **voice** sets up a CIR of 256,000 bps, and a **bc** of 2560 bits. This means that the router will send 2560 bits every 2560/256,000 seconds (10 ms) and queue any excess bursts. The minimum CIR is set to the same value as CIR, and adaptive-shaping is disabled. The **frame-relay be** value is not set and therefore defaults to 0, preventing any bursting over CIR. This is the recommended configuration for traffic shaping when carrying VoIP. This will be covered in more detail in the section, "VoIP QoS over Frame Relay Networks Example."

IP RTP Header Compression

IP RTP header compression reduces the 40 byte IP + RTP + UDP header down to 2 to 4 bytes, thereby reducing the bandwidth required per voice call on point-to-point links. The header is compressed at one end of the link and decompressed at the other end. Another standard name for this technique is cRTP, or compressed RTP. Figure 3-4 shows the functionality of RTP header compression.

To configure IP RTP header compression, you need to configure the **ip rtp header-compression** command under the serial interface, or the **frame-relay ip rtp header-compression** command under the Frame Relay subinterface. You can also configure the **ip rtp compression-connections** command to set a maximum number of flows that will be compressed. Because cRTP can be processor intensive, you need to limit the number of compressed flows to prevent router performance degradation. Compressed RTP is recommended on low-speed links where bandwidth is scarce and there are few VoIP calls. Generally speaking, a Cisco voice gateway can do cRTP on as many calls as it can originate, which is basically the number of digital voice or analog voice ports it has. For more specific platform information, refer to www.cisco.com.

Figure 3-4   *RTP Header compression.*

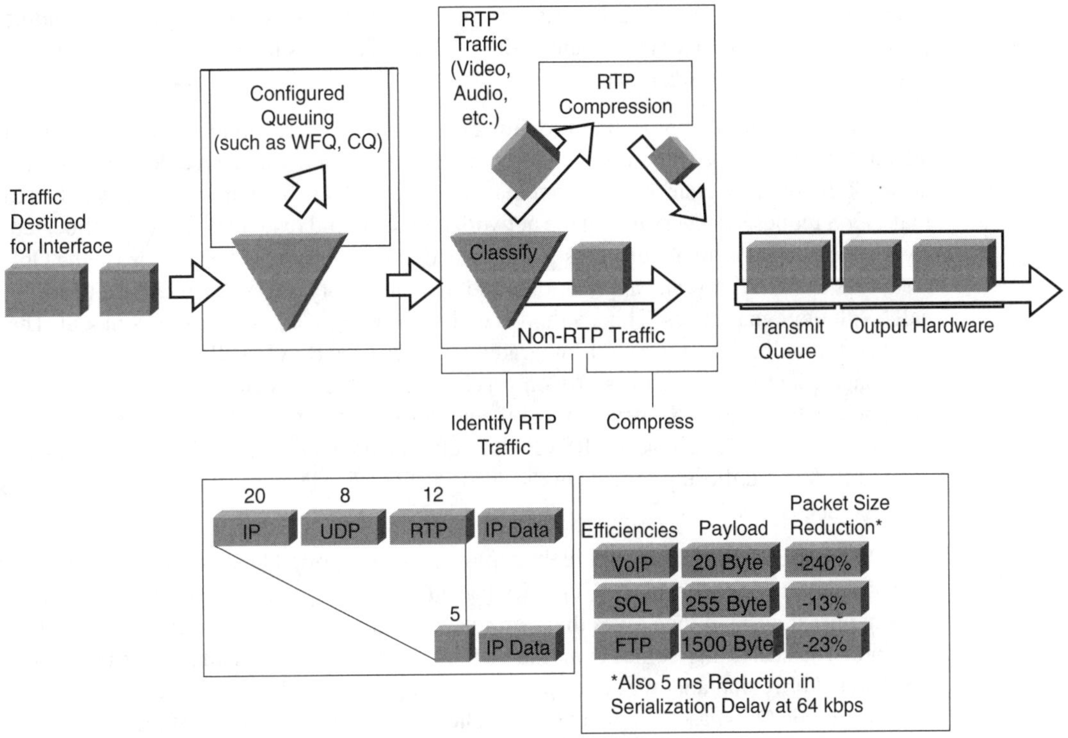

Differentiated Services for VoIP

Before you deploy a specific solution to provide QoS for VoIP, it helps to understand differentiated services (DS) and the way in which the DS architecture provides QoS.

This section covers the following:

- DS and the DS Code Point (RFC 2474, RFC 2475)
- Implementing DS for VoIP: Expedited Forwarding PHB (RFC 2598)

DS and the DS Code Point (RFC 2474, RFC 2475)

The first IP networks were based on the best-effort service model, which meant that delay, jitter, packet loss, and bandwidth allocation were unpredictable. Today, a large number of networks still follow this best-effort model and do not support enhanced applications that require a service guarantee.

Using the best-effort model, service providers have no means of offering service-level agreements (SLAs) to their customers other than over-provisioning their network to deal with the busiest traffic hours. Enterprise customers and end-users have no way of providing priority treatment or guaranteed bandwidth for VoIP. Traffic is treated on a simple FIFO basis with no QoS enforcement.

The first architectural approach to providing end-to-end QoS required that the application signal its QoS resource requirements (such as bandwidth and guaranteed delay) to the network. In a VoIP scenario, this meant that either the IP telephone or voice gateway had to make QoS requests to every hop in the network so end-to-end resources would be allocated. Every hop needed to maintain call state information to determine when to release the QoS resources for other calls and applications, and if enough resources were available, to accept calls with QoS guarantees. This method is called the Integrated Services QoS model. The most common implementation of Integrated Services uses RSVP. RSVP has some advantages, such as Call Admission Control (CAC), where a call can be rerouted by sending an appropriate signal to the originator if the network does not have the QoS resources available to support it. However, RSVP also suffers from some scalability problems; we discuss RSVP and those problems in the section, "RSVP—Dynamic Classification and Admission Control."

The DS architecture is the most widely deployed and supported QoS model today. It provides a scalable mechanism to classify packets into groups or classes that have similar QoS requirements and then gives these groups the required treatment at every hop in the network. The scalability comes from the fact that packets are classified at the edges of the DS "cloud" or region and marked appropriately so that the core routers in the cloud can simply provide QoS based on the DS class. The six most significant bits of the IP ToS byte are used to specify the DS class; the DSCP defines these 6 bits. The remaining two bits in the IP ToS byte are currently unused.

Figure 3-5 shows how the IP header defines the DS class.

Figure 3-5 *DS field definition.*

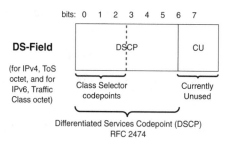

DS is described and defined in the following RFCs:

- RFC 2474: *Definition of the Differentiated Service Field (DS Field)*
- RFC 2475: *An Architecture for Differentiated Service*
- RFC 2597: *Assured Forwarding PHB Group*
- RFC 2598: *An Expedited Forwarding PHB*

RFC 2474 proposes a way of interpreting a field that has always been part of an IP packet. The ToS field describes one entire byte (eight bits) of an IP packet. Precedence refers to the three most significant bits of the ToS byte; that is, [012]34567. (Occasionally, the term ToS refers to the next three bits—012[345]67; however, to be consistent with the original RFC specification for the IP header (RFC 791), when we say ToS, we are referring to the entire set of 8 bits.)

The first three bits of the DSCP are used as *class selector* bits; this makes DSCP compatible with IP Precedence because IP Precedence uses the same three bits to determine class. Table 3-4 shows IP Precedence bit values mapped to DSCP.

Table 3-4   *IP Precedence to DSCP Mapping*

IP Precedence	IP Precedence Bit Values	DSCP Bits	DSCP Class
5	101	101000	Expedited Forwarding
4	100	100000	Assured Forwarding 4
3	011	011000	Assured Forwarding 3
2	010	010000	Assured Forwarding 2
1	001	001000	Assured Forwarding 1
0	000	000000	Best effort

The next two bits are used to define drop preference. For example, if the traffic in Class 4 (the first three bits are 100) exceeds a certain contracted rate, the excess packets could be re-marked so that the drop preference is raised instead of being dropped. If congestion were to occur in the DS cloud, the first packets to be dropped would be the "high drop preference" packets. This is similar to DE-bit marking in Frame Relay and CLP-bit marking in ATM. These mechanisms allow the Layer 2 network to make intelligent drop decisions for non-conforming traffic during periods of congestion. DS allows for similar operations over an IP network. The sixth bit must be set to 0 to indicate to the network devices that the classes have been set according to the DS standard.

The DS architecture defines a set of traffic conditioners that are used to limit traffic into a DS region and place it into appropriate DS classes. Meters, markers, shapers, and droppers are all traffic conditioners. Meters are basically policers, and Class-Based Policing (which you configure using the **police** QoS policy-map configuration command under a class in Modular

QoS CLI) is a DS-compliant implementation of a meter. You can use Class-Based Marking to set the DSCP and Class-Based Shaping as the shaper. Weighted Random Early Detect (WRED) is a dropper mechanism that is supported, but you should not invoke WRED on the VoIP class. A per-hop behavior (PHB) describes what a DS class should experience in terms of loss, delay, and jitter. A PHB determines how bandwidth is allocated, how traffic is restricted, and how packets are dropped during congestion.

The following are the three PHBs defined in DS based on the forwarding behavior required:

- **Best-Effort Class**—Class-selector bits set to 000
- **Assured Forwarding PHB**—Class-selector bits set to 001, 010, 011, or 100
- **Expedited Forwarding PHB**—Class-selector bits set to 101

The Assured Forwarding (AF) standard specifies four guaranteed bandwidth classes and describes the treatment each should receive. It also specifies drop preference levels, resulting in a total of 12 possible AF classes, as shown in Table 3-5.

Table 3-5   *Possible Assured Forwarding Classes*

Drop Precedence	Class AF1	Class AF2	Class AF3	Class AF4
Low Drop Precedence	001010	010010	011010	100010
Medium Drop Precedence	001100	010100	011100	100100
High Drop Precedence	001110	010110	011110	100110

You would most likely use AF classes for data traffic that does not require priority treatment and is largely TCP based. Expedited Forwarding more closely matches VoIP QoS requirements.

Implementing DS for VoIP: Expedited Forwarding PHB (RFC 2598)

Expedited Forwarding (EF) is intended for delay-sensitive applications that require guaranteed bandwidth. An EF marking guarantees priority service by reserving a certain minimum amount of bandwidth that can be used for high priority traffic. In EF, the egress rate (or configured priority bandwidth) *must* be greater than or equal to the sum of the ingress rates, so that there is no congestion for packets marked EF. You implement EF behavior by using the strict priority queue in LLQ. Constant bandwidth is guaranteed for traffic belonging to the EF class, but at the same time if there is congestion, non-conforming packets exceeding the specified priority rate are dropped to assure that packets in other queues belonging to different classes are not starved of bandwidth. The recommended DSCP value for EF is 101110 (46). The first three bits of this EF value correspond to IP

Precedence 5, which is the recommended IP Precedence setting for VoIP traffic. Therefore, if IP devices in the network can understand IP Precedence or DSCP for classification and marking purposes, you can provision end-to-end QoS.

The DS architecture specifies how to classify, mark, police, and shape traffic entering a DS region and how to treat different classes at every hop in the DS region. At the DS edge, all IP packets are marked with the appropriate DSCP so that QoS can be provided based on the DSCP inside the DS region. Example 3-9 shows how to configure DSCP marking at the edge using Class-Based Marking.

Example 3-9 *Class-Based Marking of DSCP*

```
access-list 100 permit udp any any range 16384 32000
access-list 100 permit tcp any any eq 1720
access-list 101 permit tcp any any eq 80
!
class-map voip
 match access-group 100
class-map webtraffic
 match access-group 101
!
policy-map dscp_marking
 class voip
  set ip dscp 46    #EF Class
 class webtraffic
  set ip dscp 26    #AF Class
!
interface Ethernet0/0
  service-policy input dscp_marking
```

In Example 3-9, all traffic coming in on Ethernet 0/0 is inspected and classified based on the **voip** and **webtraffic** class maps. The **dscp_marking** policy set the DSCP on the **voip** class traffic to 46 (101110 for EF) and the **webtraffic** class traffic to 26 (011010 for AF3).

All queuing and other QoS parameters can now be set to match on DSCP in the rest of the DS region.

In the remaining sections of this chapter, we will match IP Precedence 5 traffic as VoIP and IP Precedence 3 traffic as HTTP (web traffic), with all other traffic going into the default class. Similarly, DSCP 46 could be used for VoIP and DSCP 26 for HTTP. We could use several other classification and marking mechanisms, but to maintain consistency and simplicity, we will use IP Precedence.

VoIP QoS over Leased Lines (Using PPP) Example

A typical application of VoIP is for a large corporation to use its existing WAN infrastructure for data traffic to carry voice calls between its headquarters and its branch offices. The following example shows one method of configuring QoS for VoIP where both data and voice traffic are being transported via WAN links.

Scenario: VoIP QoS over Leased Lines

Figure 3-6 shows a typical VoIP network environment where low-speed WAN links are being used to carry both data and voice traffic.

Figure 3-6   *Typical VoIP network environment.*

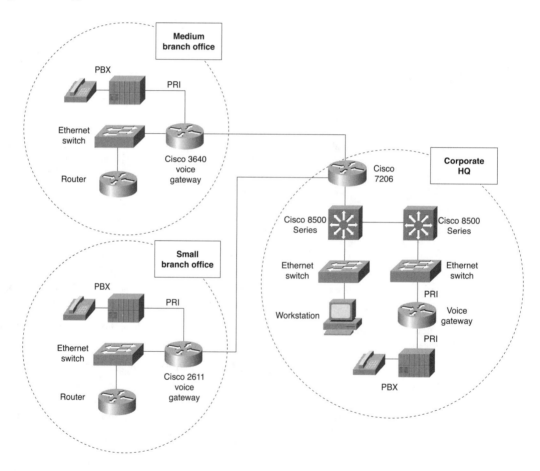

For low-speed WAN links that are not well-provisioned to serve voice traffic, problems such as delay, jitter, and loss become even more pronounced. In this particular network environment, the following factors can contribute to poor voice quality:

- Large data packets transmitted before voice packets introduce long delays.

- Variable length data packets transmitted before voice packets make delays unpredictable, resulting in jitter.

- Narrow bandwidth makes the 40-byte combined RTP, UDP, and IP header of a 20-byte VoIP packet especially wasteful.

- Narrow bandwidth causes severe delay and loss because the link is frequently congested.

- Many popular QoS techniques that serve data traffic very well, such as WFQ and random early detect (RED), are ineffective for voice applications.

  — If you apply WFQ to both voice and data, as the number of data and voice application flows increases across the link, flow-based WFQ will allocate less and less bandwidth for each flow. Unlike the elastic data traffic that adapts to available bandwidth, voice quality becomes unacceptable after too many drops and too much delay.

  — RED is specifically designed for TCP traffic. VoIP rides on top of UDP. Therefore, whenever possible, voice and data traffic should be classified into separate categories and RED should be applied to data but not voice.

In addition, each link and piece of equipment in the VoIP path adds delay to voice packet transmission. The possibility of voice packet loss also increases as voice traffic travels a longer distance and over more hops in the network. Low-speed WAN connections are usually the weakest links.

Recommended Solution: VoIP QoS over Leased Lines

Under normal conditions, network equipment and end stations cannot differentiate between the requirements of real-time voice packets and standard data traffic. This could result in serious speech degradation. To ensure voice quality, you must classify data and voice traffic into different categories and give voice traffic priority handling across a shared data network backbone. Giving voice traffic priority handling minimizes delays and drops and, whenever possible, gives voice traffic predictable transmission performance. For PPP links, we recommend the following QoS features:

- Packet Classification Through Modular QoS Command-Line Interface (MQC)

- Class-Based Marking (at the DS edge)

- Priority Handling through LLQ

- cRTP

  — Needed only on low-speed links with a low number of calls for bandwidth optimization.

- MP LFI

  — Needed only on low-speed links (below 1.2 Mbps) to ensure that one fragment transmission time is less than 10 ms.

Table 3-6 shows a complete configuration (including description) with all the preceding QoS features enabled.

Table 3-6 *QoS for VoIP over PPP WAN Links*

Configuration	Description
```class-map voip match ip precedence 5 !```	Creates the class **voip** for voice traffic that has been marked with IP Precedence 5 using one of the available marking methods.
```class-map webtraffic match ip precedence 3 !```	Creates the class **webtraffic** for web traffic that has been marked with IP Precedence 3 using one of the available marking methods.
```policy-map llq class voip priority 64 class webtraffic bandwidth 64 class class-default fair-queue !```	Defines the QoS policy-map llq: Class voip traffic gets priority and is limited to 64 kbps during congestion; class **webtraffic** packets are guaranteed 64 kbps. All other traffic shares the remaining bandwidth.
```interface Serial1/0 bandwidth 256 encapsulation ppp no fair-queue ppp multilink multilink-group 1 !```	Attaches the serial interface 1/0 to multilink interface in Group 1. (For link bandwidths over 1.2 Mbps, Multilink PPP LFI and cRTP are not needed. In that case, the IP address and service-policy statement would go under the serial interface configuration.)
```interface Multilink1 ip address 10.1.1.1 255.255.255.252 bandwidth 256 !```	Configures Multilink PPP LFI for links less than 1.2 Mbps.
```ip rtp header-compression iphc-format ip tcp header-compression iphc-format !```	Configures cRTP to reduce the bandwidth requirements of each voice call.
```ppp multilink ppp multilink fragment-delay 10```	Enables a fragmentation size of 10 ms.

Table 3-6   *QoS for VoIP over PPP WAN Links (Continued)*

Configuration	Description
`ppp multilink interleave`	Enables packet and fragment interleaving.

`multilink-group 1`
`service-policy output llq`
`!`
	Attaches the multilink interface to group 1.
	
	Attaches the llq QoS policy to outgoing traffic on the multilink interface.

In Table 3-6, Multilink PPP LFI prevents VoIP packets from getting stuck behind large data packets, cRTP reduces VoIP bandwidth requirements, and LLQ provides priority to VoIP traffic and guaranteed bandwidth to another class. Note that you will have to configure these features on both ends of the PPP link. Multilink PPP LFI is needed only for links less than 1.2 Mbps, and cRTP is recommended only on links with a low number of VoIP calls and if the CPU is not running too high.

VoIP QoS over Frame Relay Networks Example

Another typical VoIP application is for a large corporation to use its existing Frame Relay WAN data traffic infrastructure to carry voice calls between its headquarters and its branch offices. The following example shows one way to deploy VoIP QoS over Frame Relay WAN links.

Scenario: VoIP QoS over Frame Relay WAN Links

There are two options here: Carry the voice and data on separate permanent virtual circuits (PVCs), or use the same PVC for voice and data traffic. In the first scenario, you must still give the voice traffic priority by using a technique such as PVC Interface Priority Queue (PIPQ). PIPQ lets you assign different priorities for PVCs—high, medium, normal, or low. PIPQ also allows PVCs to be queued at the main physical interface so that high-priority traffic goes before medium, normal, and low-priority traffic. PIPQ, however, has the same problem as priority queuing—the high-priority traffic can starve the other traffic of bandwidth. However, if you use Frame Relay traffic shaping correctly, you can minimize this problem because each PVC will have a defined maximum transmission rate.

In the most common scenario, you use a single PVC to carry all the traffic between sites, as shown in Figure 3-7.

Figure 3-7 *VoIP QoS over low-speed Frame Relay links.*

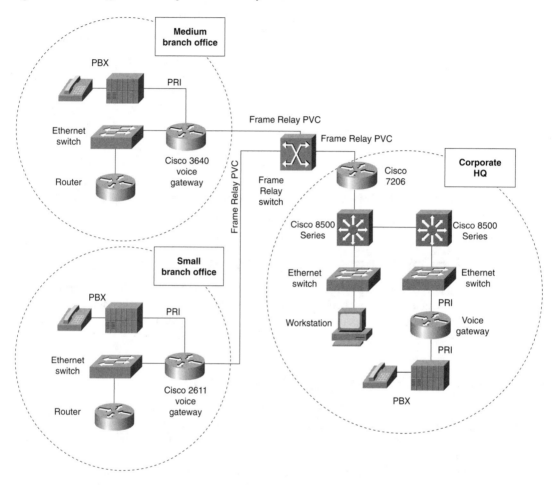

Recommended Solution: VoIP QoS over Frame Relay WAN Links

You need to configure Frame Relay traffic shaping to ensure that speed mismatches at the remote and hub sites are handled correctly. For example, if the hub site has a T1 connection into the Fame Relay network and the remote site has a 128 kbps access speed, the hub site has the capability to send at T1 speeds toward this single remote. The Frame Relay switches will buffer this traffic to a small extent, but then arbitrarily drop anything over 128 kbps. You need to decide what should be dropped and what should be prioritized at the endpoints of the PVC.

Frame Relay traffic shaping allows the routers to send traffic into the Frame Relay cloud below a preconfigured rate. Any traffic over this rate is queued, and a queuing algorithm such as LLQ can be used to make intelligent decisions on which packets should be sent. If the queues fill up, the packets are simply dropped. However, if VoIP is given priority, and the total VoIP traffic is below the traffic-shaping rate, VoIP packets will be serviced with low latency and will not be dropped.

For lower-speed links less than 1.2 Mbps, you need to configure packet fragmentation to ensure that a VoIP packet does not have to wait behind a large packet. Fragmenting larger data packets to 10 ms of the link speed can bind the maximum waiting period. You can use cRTP to efficiently use bandwidth, if the number of calls is not too large.

To provide high quality to VoIP over Frame Relay, you need to configure the following features:

- Frame Relay Traffic Shaping

  — Set the **frame-relay cir** map-class configuration command to the maximum transmit rate (it should be the negotiated guaranteed rate from the service provider).

  — Disable the **frame-relay adaptive-shaping** map-class configuration command and set **mincir** to **cir** for best quality voice.

  — Set the **frame-relay bc** map-class configuration command to 1/100 of CIR to allow traffic-shaping to service packets at least every 10 ms.

- FRF.12 Link Fragmentation and Interleaving

  — You need link fragmentation and interleaving only if the remote or hub end port speed is less than 1.2 Mbps; fragmentation size should be 10 ms, or 80 bytes multiplied by the number of DS-0s (For example, for $4 \times 64k$, fragmentation size would be $4 \times 80 = 320$ bytes)

- LLQ on Frame Relay PVC

  — LLQ is applied under the map-class for Frame Relay traffic shaping.

- cRTP

  — cRTP is applied under the Frame Relay subinterface; you should use cRTP only if the CPU utilization is low, and for a small number of calls depending on the platform.

Table 3-7 shows the preceding QoS features enabled, with explanations.

Table 3-7 *QoS of VoIP over Frame Relay WAN Links*

Configuration	Description
```class-map voip match ip precedence 5 !```	Creates the class **voip** for voice traffic that has been marked with IP Precedence 5 using one of the available marking methods.
```class-map webtraffic match ip precedence 3 !```	Creates the class **webtraffic** for web traffic that has been marked with IP Precedence 3 using one of the available marking methods.
```policy-map llq class voip priority 64 class webtraffic bandwidth 64 class class-default fair-queue !```	Defines the QoS policy-map **llq**: Class **voip** traffic gets priority and is limited to 64 kbps during congestion; class **webtraffic** packets are guaranteed 64 kbps. All other traffic shares the remaining bandwidth.
```interface Serial 0/1 no ip address encapsulation frame-relay frame-relay traffic shaping !```	Enables Frame Relay traffic shaping. You must enable Frame Relay traffic shaping to handle speed mismatches and over-subscription. (LLQ per Frame Relay PVC also requires Frame Relay traffic shaping.)
```interface Serial 0/1.64 point-to-point ip address 10.14.96.2 255.255.255.252 frame-relay interface-dlci 128 class voice```	Attaches traffic shaping **class voice** to this Frame Relay PVC.
``` frame-relay ip rtp header-compression !```	Configures cRTP to reduce the bandwidth requirements of each voice call.
```map-class frame-relay voice no frame-relay adaptive-shaping```	Disables adaptive shaping. We do not recommend adaptive shaping for VoIP.
``` frame-relay cir 256000```	Sets CIR or upper transmit rate at 256 kbps.
``` frame-relay bc 2560```	Sets committed burst rate to 1/100 of CIR.
``` frame-relay mincir 256000```	Sets the minimum acceptable CIR rate. The **mincir** value needs to be greater than total priority and bandwidth allocated.
```frame-relay fragment 320```	Enables FRF.12 fragmentation with fragment size of 320 bytes.
```service-policy output llq !```	Attaches the **llq** QoS policy to the defined map class.

In this example, Frame Relay traffic shaping handles speed mismatches, FRF.12 fragmentation prevents VoIP packets from getting stuck behind large data packets, cRTP reduces VoIP bandwidth requirements, and LLQ provides priority to VoIP traffic and guarantees bandwidth to another class. Note that you will have to configure these features on both ends of the Frame Relay link. FRF.12 is needed only for links of less than 1.2 Mbps, and cRTP is recommended only on links with a low number of VoIP calls and if the CPU is not running too high.

VoIP QoS over ATM Example

ATM technology has inherent advantages in handling VoIP traffic because of its small, fixed-size cells and class of service (CoS) mechanisms. These advantages don't ensure, however, that VoIP traffic will automatically obtain the QoS it needs from the ATM network carrying it. This is because QoS definitions at the IP layer, such as the IP Precedence settings in the packet header, do not automatically match ATM CoS settings, namely traffic class (CBR, VBR, ABR, UBR) and traffic parameters such as SCR, PCR, and burst size. Consequently, after data and voice packets are identified and sorted at the IP layer, it's up to the network operator to manually configure the ATM virtual circuits (VCs) to ensure QoS for voice packets across an ATM network. This manual provisioning is time consuming, labor intensive, error prone, and, above all, doesn't scale as more and more voice traffic is introduced into the network.

The following examples show how to deploy VoIP QoS over ATM.

Scenario: VoIP QoS over ATM

Two solutions are available for providing QoS to VoIP over an ATM network: one uses separate data and voice VCs and one uses shared data and voice VCs, as shown in Figure 3-8.

Figure 3-8 *VoIP QoS over ATM links.*

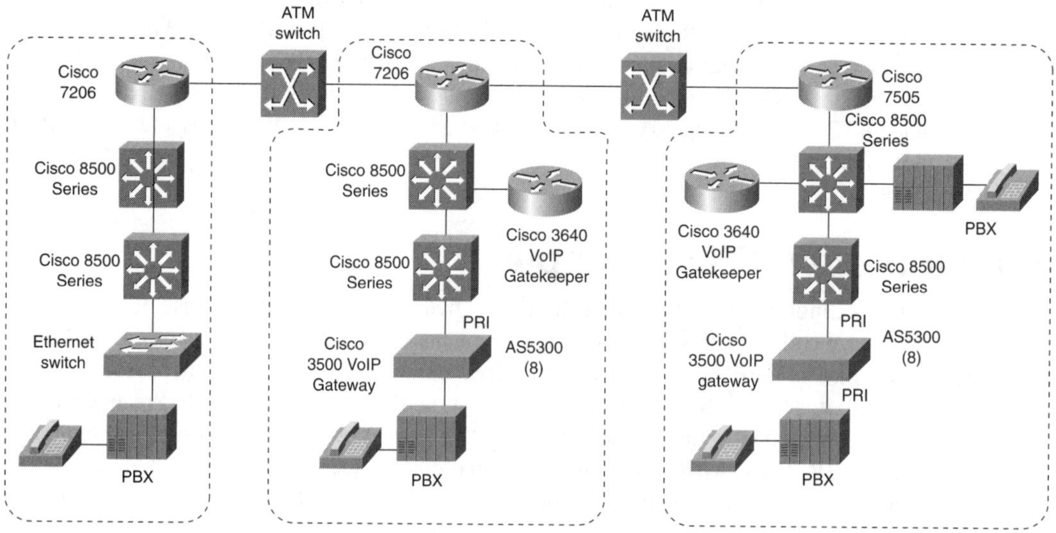

Recommended Solution: Separate Data and Voice ATM PVCs

For data and voice traffic sharing the same destination but requiring different QoS, you need to define groups of ATM VCs to form *PVC bundles*. In a PVC bundle, all the PVCs share the same source and destination, and each bundle is assigned to carry IP traffic with a specific IP Precedence level or range of levels. After you configure PVC bundles, you must then configure each PVC with its specific ATM QoS parameters. As voice and data traffic with different IP Precedence levels arrives at the router's ATM interface, Cisco IOS Software dynamically sends it out on the appropriate PVC, effectively mapping IP QoS classes to ATM CoSs.

The following are the key benefits of implementing VoIP QoS using this method:

- Automatic separation of voice and data traffic onto different PVCs
- Preservation of the IP network's DS through the ATM network

Table 3-8 shows how to configure VoIP over ATM using PVC bundles to separate voice and data PVCs.

Table 3-8   *QoS of VoIP over ATM with Separate Voice and Data PVCs*

Configuration	Description
`ip cef` `!`	Enables IP CEF switching. You must enable IP CEF switching for this solution to work.

`interface ATM 2/0/0`
` no ip address`
`!`
`interface ATM 2/0/0.1 point-to-point`
` ip address 10.1.1.2 255.255.255.252`
` bundle qosmap`
	Creates a PVC bundle group called **qosmap**.

`protocol ip 10.1.1.1 broadcast`
`  pvc-bundle control 1/100`
`  precedence 6-7`
	Maps IP Precedence 6 and 7 traffic to a VPI/VCI of 1/100.

`pvc-bundle voice 1/101`
`  vbr-rt 6000 5000 1000`
`  precedence 5`
	Maps IP Precedence 5 traffic (VoIP) to a VPI/VCI of 1/101 with an SCR of 5 Mbps and bursting capabilities.

`pvc-bundle web 1/102`
`  cbr 5000`
`  precedence 4`
	Maps IP Precedence 4 traffic (webtraffic is another example) to 1/102 with an SCR of 5 Mbps.

`pvc-bundle data 1/103` `  precedence 0-3`	Maps other precedence traffic to a PVC with a VPI/VCI of 1/103.

In the configuration in Table 3-8, four traffic classes based on IP Precedence are mapped to four separate ATM PVCs in a bundle. The voice PVC has a guaranteed bandwidth of 5 Mbps with some bursting capabilities and the web traffic PVC is also guaranteed 5 Mbps but with no bursting (constant bit rate). Control traffic and all other traffic flows are not given any ATM rate guarantees.

Recommended Solution: Shared Data and Voice ATM PVC

If you decide to use separate PVCs for voice and data, you must adjust the bandwidth allocation accordingly as voice traffic grows beyond the bandwidth configured on the voice PVC. This manual reprovisioning isn't necessary when voice and data share the same PVC, provided that voice always gets the priority it needs. You can configure VoIP traffic to have absolute priority over data traffic by configuring LLQ on the ATM PVC.

Table 3-9 shows how to configure VoIP over ATM using the same PVC for data and voice traffic.

Table 3-9   *QoS of VoIP over ATM Using a Shared Voice and Data PVC*

Configuration	Description
| ```
ip cef
!
``` | Enables IP CEF switching. You must enable IP CEF switching for this solution to work. |
| ```
class-map voip
 match ip precedence 5
!
``` | Creates class **voip** for voice traffic that has been marked with IP Precedence 5 using one of the available marking methods. |
| ```
class-map webtraffic
 match ip precedence 3
!
``` | Creates class **webtraffic** for web traffic that has been marked with IP Precedence 3 using one of the available marking methods. |
| ```
policy-map llq
 class voip
  priority 1000
 class webtraffic
  bandwidth 1000
 class class-default
  fair-queue
!
``` | Defines policy map **llq**, which defines the QoS policy: Class **voip** traffic gets priority and is limited to 1 Mbps during congestion; class **webtraffic** packets are guaranteed 1 Mbps. All other traffic shares the remaining bandwidth. |
| ```
interface ATM2/0/0
  no ip address
!
interface ATM2/0/0.1 point-to-point
  ip address 10.1.1.2 255.255.255.252
  pvc data+voice 1/101
   vbr-rt 6000 5000 1000
   encapsulation aal5snap
!
``` | Configures ATM shaping parameters. |
| ```
service-policy output llq
!
``` | Attaches the **llq** QoS policy map to the ATM PVC. |

In the configuration in Table 3-9, LLQ is used on a single ATM PVC carrying both VoIP and data. The LLQ policy is applied to an ATM subinterface for one PVC. Class **voip** traffic gets priority up to 1 Mbps and class **webtraffic** is guaranteed 1 Mbps but does not get priority treatment. ATM shaping also guarantees that the PVC gets a sustained rate of 5 Mbps.

RSVP—Dynamic Classification and Admission Control

RSVP is an implementation of the Integrated Services (IntServ) architecture for QoS (RFC 2205). When VoIP was first introduced, RSVP was immediately seen as a key component that would provide admission control and QoS for VoIP flows. However, the way RSVP and

H.323 were previously integrated provided neither admission control nor adequate QoS for voice flows. Several enhancements have now been made to address these limitations, and RSVP can now be used to implement Call Admission Control (CAC) and to signal a desired QoS that will provide good quality voice end-to-end, even in the presence of congestion. In this section, we discuss RSVP in general, focusing on a particular subset of platforms, topologies, and protocols. We assume that you are using H.323 as the session protocol for a VoIP gateway-based network. We thoroughly discuss CAC in Chapter 4, "Understanding Call Admission Control."

Introduction to RSVP

The initial implementation of RSVP for VoIP had two limitations. The first was that CAC could not be implemented with RSVP because the reservation process was not synchronized with the voice-call signaling. A call would proceed even if the RSVP reservation had failed or hadn't been completed. The second limitation was that a successful RSVP reservation might not provide good voice quality during periods of network congestion. RSVP created a reserved queue per traffic flow within the WFQ system and relied on that system to guarantee a bounded delay. However, WFQ was unable in some cases to provide an acceptable delay bound for voice. RSVP needed to be able to use the priority queue in LLQ to guarantee a bounded delay that wouldn't affect voice quality. In addition, RSVP wasn't supported on ATM or on shaped Frame Relay PVCs.

You should deploy RSVP to improve VoIP QoS only where it can really have a positive impact on quality and functionality. The benefits of using RSVP outweigh the costs (management, overhead, and performance impact) only where there is limited bandwidth and frequent network congestion. Some IP environments have enough bandwidth to guarantee the appropriate QoS without having to implement CAC for every call.

Using RSVP for Call Admission Control

The following four mechanisms were recently introduced in Cisco IOS Software to handle resource-based CAC:

- **PSTN fallback**—This method relies on network probing to measure delay, jitter, and loss to estimate the potential voice impairment that the call will experience. (The potential impairment is called the Calculated Planning Impairment Factor (CPIF) and is explained in ITU-T G.113.) With this mechanism, you can define several thresholds so that calls are rejected if an IP network is congested.

- **Defining CAC on local gateway resources such as CPU, memory, and number of calls**—With this method, you can configure thresholds that trigger different actions, such as hairpin call, reject call, or play a message.

- **Having the H.323 gatekeeper do bandwidth management**—In this method, you can configure a maximum amount of bandwidth that the gatekeeper then allocates to calls.

- **RSVP**—Covered in this section.

This chapter covers only the use of RSVP for CAC. The other CAC mechanisms are discussed in Chapter 4.

RSVP for CAC Overview

Using RSVP for VoIP CAC requires the synchronization of the call setup signaling and the RSVP signaling. This synchronization guarantees that the called-party phone rings only after the resources for the call have been reserved successfully. This synchronization also gives voice gateways the control of what action to take before the call setup moves to the alerting stage if the reservation fails or cannot be completed within a predefined period of time. A voice call will trigger two RSVP reservations because the reservation and admission control mechanisms provided by RSVP are unidirectional. Each voice gateway is responsible for initiating and maintaining one reservation toward the other voice gateway. CAC for a VoIP call fails if at least one of the reservations fails. Figure 3-9 shows the sequence of packets exchanged between the gateways during a successful call setup if RSVP is used for resource reservation.

In Figure 3-9, an originating gateway initiates a call toward a terminating gateway. The originating gateway sends an H.323 SETUP message to the terminating gateway to initiate the call. That SETUP message carries the QoS that the originating gateway considers acceptable for the call. The terminating gateway responds with an H.323 CALL PROCEEDING message. Both the originating gateway and the terminating gateway initiate a reservation request by sending an RSVP PATH message. The packet flows of both reservations are independent of each other unless one of them fails. The terminating gateway blocks the call setup process while waiting for the reservation results. The terminating gateway controls the admission decision for the call and needs to be notified that the reservations in both directions were successful. The terminating gateway discovers that its reservation was successful when it receives the RSVP RESV message. The terminating gateway detects that the originating gateway reservation was successful when it receives an RSVP RESV CONFIRMATION message from the originating gateway. At this point, the terminating gateway lets the call setup continue and sends an H.323 ALERTING message to the originating gateway once it is notified that the called side is in alerting state. A normal disconnect is initiated by sending an H.323 RELEASE COMPLETE message after the call is connected. At that point, the gateways tear down their reservations by sending RSVP PATH TEAR and RESV TEAR messages.

Figure 3-9   *Successful call setup with RSVP enabled.*

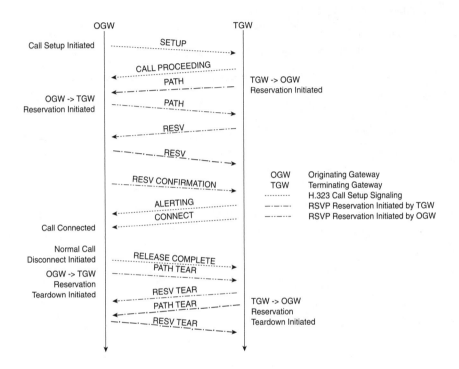

You can configure a voice gateway to take the following actions if at least one RSVP reservation fails:

- The voice gateway can report the call failure to the user or the switch that delivered the call.

- The call can be rerouted through another path.

- The call can be connected with best-effort QoS.

This last behavior is possible because the terminating gateway knows what QoS is acceptable for the call from its own configuration and the value included by the originating gateway in the H.323 SETUP message. If the terminating gateway and the originating gateway request a non best-effort QoS and at least one reservation fails, the call will proceed as best-effort only if the originating gateway and the terminating gateway are willing to accept best-effort service. Call release and call rerouting are possible if one of the two voice gateways will not accept best-effort service. If you configure the gateway to reject the call and report the failure, CAS trunks and analog lines generate a fast busy tone. On CCS Primary Rate Interface (PRI) trunks, a Q.931 DISCONNECT message with a cause "QoS unavailable" (49) is generated.

Figure 3-10 shows the details of a call that is rejected because the reservation initiated from the terminating gateway failed.

Figure 3-10 *Call failing RSVP CAC because of terminating gateway reservation failure.*

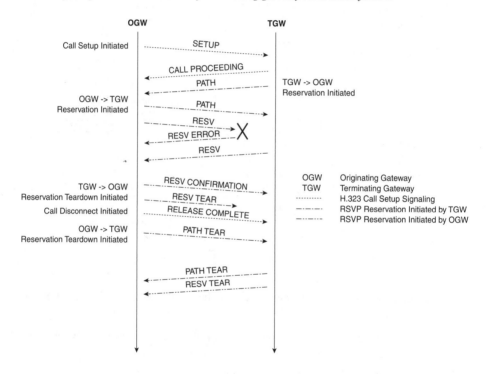

Deploying CAC Based on RSVP

You should deploy RSVP to improve VoIP QoS only where it can really have a positive impact on quality. The benefits of using RSVP outweigh the costs only where bandwidth is limited. We recommend using Cisco IOS Release 12.1(5)T or later if you wish to implement CAC for VoIP using RSVP.

You must complete three basic steps to configure CAC for VoIP calls using RSVP:

- Enable synchronization between RSVP and the call signaling. (This is enabled by default when Cisco IOS Release 12.1(5)T or later is running.)

- Configure the voice gateways on both sides of the VoIP dial peers to request a particular QoS via RSVP.

- Enable RSVP and specify the maximum bandwidth on all links that are traversed by voice packets where congestion is likely to occur.

Example 3-10 shows how to configure CAC for VoIP calls using RSVP.

Example 3-10 *Deploying CAC Using RSVP*

```
hostname LongBay
!
isdn switch-type primary-ni
call rsvp-sync
!
controller T1 1/0
 framing esf
 linecode b8zs
 pri-group timeslots 1-24
!
interface Ethernet0/0
 ip address 10.0.152.254 255.255.255.0
!
interface Serial0/0
 bandwidth 1536
 ip address 10.10.1.1 255.255.255.0
 encapsulation ppp
 ip tcp header-compression iphc-format
 ip rtp header-compression iphc-format
 ip rsvp bandwidth 1152 24
!
interface Serial1/0:23
 no ip address
 no logging event link-status
 isdn switch-type primary-ni
 isdn incoming-voice voice
 no cdp enable
!
ip route 0.0.0.0 0.0.0.0 10.10.1.2
!
voice-port 1/0:23
!
dial-peer voice 100 pots
 destination-pattern 2......
 no digit-strip
```

continues

Example 3-10 *Deploying CAC Using RSVP (Continued)*

```
 direct-inward-dial
 port 1/0:23
 !
dial-peer voice 300 voip
 destination-pattern 3......
 session target ipv4:10.77.39.129
 req-qos guaranteed-delay
 acc-qos guaranteed-delay
 !
line con 0
line aux 0
line vty 0 4
 !
end
```

Example 3-10 shows a complete voice gateway configuration that highlights the commands for configuring CAC using RSVP. The voice gateway can act as both an originating gateway and a terminating gateway with this configuration. We haven't prioritized voice signaling in this example.

The default dial-peer configuration requests and accepts best-effort QoS for VoIP calls. This translates to the gateway not initiating an RSVP reservation for the call because IP provides best-effort service by default. The other two service alternatives are controlled-load or guaranteed-delay QoS. These two services require RSVP signaling; they are requested using the **req-qos** dial-peer configuration command. The acceptable QoS controls how strict or loose the CAC criteria should be; you configure the acceptable QoS controls by using the **acc-qos** dial-peer configuration command. We recommend that you configure the originating gateway and the terminating gateway to request and accept guaranteed delay.

Sometimes, you can configure the implicit dial peer matched on a terminating gateway to request and accept best-effort QoS. This dial peer takes effect when there is not an explicit dial peer match.

Configuring Local Gateway Resources if CAC Fails

You can configure a voice gateway to take different actions if admission control fails. The first is to have the gateways signal the user or the switch that delivered the call with a fast busy signal or a disconnect cause. If the call was delivered to the gateway by an ISDN switch, you can tune the Q.931 disconnect cause to guarantee that the switch handles calls correctly, as shown in Example 3-11. A "QoS unavailable" (49) cause is returned by default when an ISDN call fails CAC because of the requested and acceptable QoS configured. You can modify this cause with the **isdn network-failure-cause** or **isdn disconnect-cause** interface configuration commands. The current implementation of **isdn network-failure-cause** overrides the value configured using **isdn disconnect-cause**.

Example 3-11 *Tuning the O.931 Disconnect Cause*

```
!
interface Serial1/0:23
 no ip address
 no logging event link-status
 isdn switch-type primary-ni
 isdn network-failure-cause 42
 isdn incoming-voice voice
 no cdp enable
!
```

In Example 3-11, the router sends a Q.931 DISCONNECT message with a cause "Switching Equipment Congestion" (42) when an ISDN call fails CAC on the VoIP leg.

A second option is to allow the gateway to reroute the call through another path, as shown in Example 3-12. If the dial peer matched by the call is part of a hunt group, other dial peers in that group are tried according to the **preference** dial-peer configuration command. This allows you to implement different types of call routing on the gateway that considers QoS across IP networks.

Example 3-12 *Call Rerouting on the Gateway*

```
dial-peer voice 100 pots
 destination-pattern 2......
 no digit-strip
 direct-inward-dial
 port 1/0:23
!
dial-peer voice 300 voip
 preference 0
 destination-pattern 3......
 session target ipv4:10.77.39.129
 req-qos guaranteed-delay
 acc-qos guaranteed-delay
!
dial-peer voice 400 voip
 preference 2
 destination-pattern 3......
 session target ipv4:10.23.45.2
 req-qos guaranteed-delay
 acc-qos guaranteed-delay
!
dial-peer voice 500 pots
 preference 5
 destination-pattern 3......
 no digit-strip
 direct-inward-dial
 port 1/1:23
!
```

Example 3-12 shows the implementation of call rerouting on the gateway. Calls to seven-digit numbers starting with digit 3 try two voice gateways first. Calls are routed through the PSTN via voice port 1/1:23 if the VoIP calls fail due to CAC or any other reason.

The third possibility, available in Cisco IOS releases later than 12.1(5)T, is to configure the gateways to proceed with the call even if RSVP reservations fail. This option, however, doesn't provide a major improvement over earlier Cisco IOS release functionality. The only benefit it provides is that in case of a successful RSVP reservation, the call doesn't proceed until the reservation is established.

A call can fail admission control if at least one of the two RSVP reservations needed for the call fails. For each RSVP reservation, admission control is performed on all interfaces where you have enabled RSVP by using the **ip rsvp bandwidth** interface configuration command. You can configure two values with the **ip rsvp bandwidth** command: the maximum total reserved bandwidth and the maximum bandwidth per reservation. The maximum total bandwidth is limited by default to no more than 75 percent of the total bandwidth of the interface. You can modify that limit with the **max-reserved-bandwidth** interface configuration command. Exceptions to the maximum total bandwidth limitation are Frame Relay and ATM PVCs. For Frame Relay PVCs, the maximum reservable bandwidth is the minimum CIR, or, if not configured, half of the CIR. For ATM PVCs, the maximum reservable bandwidth is 75 percent of the configured ABR **output-mcr**, **nrt-VBR output-scr**, or **rt-VBR average-rate**, whichever is configured. The total bandwidth available for RSVP reservations might be lower if you've reserved bandwidth using class-based weighted fair queuing (CBWFQ) or LLQ through the modular QoS command line interface (MQC). A bandwidth manager makes sure that the interface or the PVC bandwidth is not oversubscribed during the router operation. (Note that this check is not performed during router configuration.) You should configure the maximum bandwidth per reservation to be no lower than what the codec requires, plus all other protocol overhead except Layer 2 protocol overhead. Table 3-10 shows the lowest values you can use for different codecs. Keep in mind that these values do not account for the bandwidth savings introduced by cRTP or voice activity detection (VAD). The actual voice stream might use less bandwidth, but the system will use the worst-case bandwidth.

Table 3-10   *Bandwidth Reserved by RSVP per VoIP Call*

Codec	Reserved Bandwidth per VoIP Call (kbps)
G711alaw	80
G711ulaw	80
G723ar53	22
G723ar63	23
G723r53	22
G723r63	23
G726r16	32

Table 3-10 *Bandwidth Reserved by RSVP per VoIP Call (Continued)*

Codec	Reserved Bandwidth per VoIP Call (kbps)
G726r24	40
G726r32	48
G728	32
G729br8	24
G729r8	24
GSMEFR	29
GSMFR	30

One consideration when deploying RSVP for VoIP is the impact of resource reservation on the post-dial delay. Implementing VoIP CAC based on RSVP relies on a prompt confirmation or rejection of the requested reservation. The time it takes to reserve resources adds to the post-dial delay, which should be kept as low as possible in most cases. RSVP packets are carried inside IP datagrams and are unreliable by nature. If an RSVP packet is lost during the initial reservation setup, an RSVP refresh timer has to expire before the lost packet is retransmitted. Because this refresh timer is typically defined in tens of seconds, a scenario that might add a post-dial delay is unacceptable for the user. The **call rsvp-sync resv-timer** global configuration command lets you control the maximum amount of time that the terminating gateway waits for the result of RSVP reservation requests. The default value of this timer is 10 seconds; you can set it to a value between 1 and 60 seconds according to your expectation of post-dial delay.

Using RSVP with LLQ

Flows requesting a particular QoS via RSVP can take advantage of the queuing alternatives available in LLQ, which has two major components: a strict priority queue (PQ) and a CBWFQ system. Earlier implementations of RSVP relied on WFQ to meet the QoS requirements for delay-sensitive traffic. A reserved queue with a low weight was created when the RSVP reservation was installed. However, WFQ could not meet the delay requirements of voice traffic, and voice calls using RSVP were not able to take advantage of the PQ available throughout LLQ.

In Cisco IOS Release 12.1(3)T and later, a priority profile based on traffic characteristics exists so that certain flows can take advantage of the strict PQ in LLQ. When an RSVP reservation request is received on an interface where you have enabled WFQ, the flow traffic specification (Tspec) is compared against the profile to decide if that flow should take advantage of the PQ or if a queue should be reserved on the WFQ system. The TSpec is the traffic description carried in RSVP messages. This traffic description is made in terms of a token bucket (token rate r, plus a bucket size b) and some additional parameters (peak rate p, minimum policed unit m, and maximum packet size M). The PQ profile is defined in terms of token rate, bucket size, and an optional peak-rate to token-rate ratio. Flow reservations with a TSpec that do not exceed those defined in the PQ profile will use the PQ. Those flows with a TSpec that exceeds at least one parameter defined in the profile will get a reserved queue in the WFQ system. The priority profile allows you to classify priority flows based on their traffic characteristics—not just on the transport protocol and port. Figure 3-11 shows the LLQ structure for an interface where traffic is classified into different queues using several methods, including RSVP.

Figure 3-11 *RSVP support for LLQ on point-to-point interfaces.*

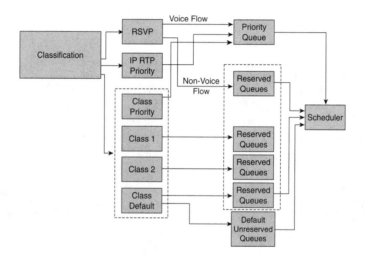

Cisco IOS Release 12.1(5)T introduced RSVP support for LLQ on Frame Relay PVCs. In this case, each PVC has its own queuing structure, with a PQ and a CBWFQ system. At the interface level, a FIFO queue is set up unless you have enabled FRF.12 fragmentation. In that case, a dual FIFO system is set up with a high-priority queue and a low-priority queue. The high-priority queue receives the PQ traffic from all PVCs plus Layer 2 control traffic. The low-priority queue receives all other traffic from all PVCs. Remember that Frame Relay traffic shaping (FRTS) is required for Frame Relay circuits whether FRF.12 fragmentation is enabled or not. FRTS provides the backpressure mechanism to detect congestion per PVC. Support for ATM PVCs is available in Cisco IOS Release 12.2(1)T.

Deploying RSVP Support for LLQ

You enable RSVP support for LLQ by default for voice flows on interfaces where RSVP and WFQ are enabled. You don't need to explicitly configure priority queues for voice packets. You can configure a custom priority queue profile using the **ip rsvp pq-profile** global configuration command. Configuring the profile as **ip rsvp pq-profile voice-like** restores the default behavior. The default priority queue profile uses a token rate of

12,288 bytes per second (approximately 98 kbps), a bucket size of 592 bytes, and a peak rate equal to 110 percent of the token rate (13,516 bytes per second or approximately 108 kbps). These parameter values support all possible codec configurations on voice gateways running Cisco IOS software. A Cisco voice gateway configured to reserve resources via RSVP will infer the correct TSpec exclusively from the codec used on the dial peer. You can't control TSpec values using the CLI, and no other bandwidth-saving features (such as VAD) are taken into consideration. Some revisions of Microsoft NetMeeting for Windows 98 and Windows 2000 (which use RSVP) signal a bucket size in the TSpec that is not compatible with these defaults. This problem affects Microsoft NetMeeting for calls using codecs that require 32 kbps or more. In those cases, you need to create a custom profile to match the parameters signaled by Microsoft Windows.

Example 3-13 shows how to configure RSVP support for LLQ on a Frame Relay circuit with two PVCs.

Example 3-13 *RSVP Support for LLQ on Frame Relay PVCs*

```
hostname LongBay
!
isdn switch-type primary-ni
call rsvp-sync
!
interface Serial0/0
 bandwidth 1536
 no ip address
 encapsulation frame-relay
 no fair-queue
 frame-relay traffic-shaping
!
interface Serial0/0.1 point-to-point
 ip address 10.10.1.2 255.255.255.0
 frame-relay interface-dlci 16
 class VoIPoFR
 ip rsvp bandwidth 48 24
!
interface Serial0/0.2 point-to-point
 ip address 10.10.2.2 255.255.255.0
 frame-relay interface-dlci 17
 class VoIPoFR
 ip rsvp bandwidth 48 24
!
ip rsvp pq-profile voice-like
!
map-class frame-relay VoIPoFR
no frame-relay adaptive-shaping
frame-relay cir 64000
frame-relay bc 640
frame-relay mincir 64000
frame-relay fair-queue
frame-relay fragment 80
!
```

In Example 3-13, WFQ is enabled on the PVCs and disabled on the physical interface. Each PVC has a priority queue for voice traffic, and the physical interface has the dual-FIFO queue structure. FRTS is enabled and its parameters are defined in the **VoIPoFR** map class.

One of the important implications of RSVP support for LLQ is that it lets you classify voice traffic based on its traffic characteristics rather than on the transport protocol (UDP) and port number (16,384 through 32,767). The proper operation of LLQ relies on the assumption that the priority queue is used only by well-behaved traffic (such as voice) that has a predictable rate and a very low burst size. Classification based on transport protocol and ports could allow bursty or noncritical traffic into the priority queue, which might affect the quality of existing voice calls and the performance of the traffic using the WFQ system. You need to take this into account when you are defining a custom PQ profile. You should understand all the implications on other types of traffic—in particular, when the PQ profile could let flows with some degree of burstiness into the priority queue. RSVP support for LLQ prioritizes voice packets but doesn't take care of the voice signaling. It might not be possible to initiate new calls during periods of heavy congestion due to loss of signaling packets. To address this situation, you can reserve a certain amount of bandwidth explicitly for signaling packets using the MQC. You can also mark RSVP messages for special treatment using the **ip rsvp signaling dscp** interface configuration command. In Example 3-14, voice packets are prioritized using RSVP, while the signaling is guaranteed a minimum bandwidth during periods of congestion through the MQC.

Example 3-14 *RSVP Support for LLQ + QoS for Signaling Traffic*

```
hostname LongBay
!
class-map h323
 match access-group 101
!
policy-map VOIP_SIG
 class h323
  set ip dscp 34
  bandwidth 96
 class class-default
  fair-queue
!
isdn switch-type primary-ni
call rsvp-sync
!
controller T1 1/0
 framing esf
 linecode b8zs
 pri-group timeslots 1-24
!
interface Ethernet0/0
 ip address 10.0.152.254 255.255.255.0
!
interface Serial0/0
 bandwidth 1536
 ip address 10.10.1.1 255.255.255.0
```

Example 3-14 *RSVP Support for LLQ + QoS for Signaling Traffic (Continued)*

```
 encapsulation ppp
 ip tcp header-compression iphc-format
 ip rtp header-compression iphc-format
 service-policy output VOIP_SIG
 ip rsvp bandwidth 1152 24
!
interface Serial1/0:23
 no ip address
 no logging event link-status
 isdn switch-type primary-ni
 isdn incoming-voice voice
 no cdp enable
!
ip route 0.0.0.0 0.0.0.0 10.10.1.2
!
access-list 101 permit tcp any eq 1720 any
access-list 101 permit tcp any any eq 1720
!
voice-port 1/0:23
!
dial-peer voice 100 pots
 destination-pattern 2......
 no digit-strip
 direct-inward-dial
 port 1/0:23
!
dial-peer voice 300 voip
 destination-pattern 3......
 session target ipv4:10.77.39.129
 req-qos guaranteed-delay
 acc-qos guaranteed-delay
!
line con 0
line aux 0
line vty 0 4
!
end
```

In Example 3-14, access list 101 matches H.323 signaling traffic to and from TCP port 1720. This traffic is placed into class **h323**, which is guaranteed 96 kbps of bandwidth using LLQ. Voice payload is given priority using the RSVP configuration.

Summary

QoS for VoIP begins with your having sufficient bandwidth in your network to support the demands associated with real-time voice traffic. After you've provisioned sufficient bandwidth, you can do a number of things to facilitate the priority of voice traffic:

- Classify voice traffic into priority groups and mark voice packets to reflect the classification. There are a number of ways to classify and mark voice packets, but we suggest using Modular QoS CLI.

- Provide some sort of queuing mechanism to guarantee bandwidth and priority servicing. There are a number of available queuing mechanisms, but we recommend LLQ because it's flexible and easy to configure compared with the other methods.

- Configure data packet fragmentation and voice traffic interleaving, where data packets can be broken into a series of smaller packets and the voice packets interleaved between them. This will prevent voice packets from being excessively delayed behind large data packets.

- Use IP RTP header compression to reduce the amount of bandwidth needed per call on point-to-point links. This reduces the 40-byte IP + RTP + UDP header down to two to four bytes.

DS architecture is a scalable mechanism for classifying packets into groups or classes that have similar QoS requirements and then giving these groups the required treatment at every hop in the network. Packets are classified at the edges of the DS cloud or region and marked appropriately so that the core routers in the cloud can simply provide QoS based on the DS class. In DS, a defined per-hop behavior determines how bandwidth is allocated, how traffic is restricted, and how packets are dropped during congestion.

Finally, RSVP can be used to implement CAC and to signal a desired QoS that will provide good quality voice end-to-end, even in the presence of congestion.

## CHAPTER 4

Understanding Call Admission Control

Call Admission Control

Call admission control (CAC) is not a concept that applies to data traffic. If an influx of data traffic oversubscribes a particular link in the network, queuing, buffering, and packet drop decisions resolve the congestion. The extra traffic is simply delayed until the interface becomes available to transmit the traffic, or, if traffic is dropped, the protocol or the end user initiates a timeout and requests a retransmission of the information.

Network congestion cannot be resolved in this manner when real-time traffic, sensitive to both latency and packet loss, is present, without jeopardizing the quality of service (QoS) expected by the users of that traffic. For real-time delay-sensitive traffic such as voice, it's better to deny network access under congestion conditions than to allow traffic onto the network to be dropped or delayed, causing intermittent impaired QoS and customer dissatisfaction.

CAC is, therefore, a deterministic and informed decision that is made before establishing a voice call and is based on whether the required network resources are available to provide suitable QoS for the new call. The following questions about CAC are discussed and answered in this chapter:

- When exactly is the CAC decision made, and by what network component?
- How is the information gathered to support the CAC decision?
- What exact resources are needed for the voice call, and how are these determined?
- What happens to the calls that are denied by CAC?

Call Admission Control and Other QoS Mechanisms

A variety of QoS mechanisms other than CAC exist in Cisco IOS for the purpose of designing and configuring packet networks to provide the necessary low latency and guaranteed delivery required for voice traffic. These QoS mechanisms include tools such as queuing, policing, traffic shaping, packet marking, and fragmentation and interleaving. These mechanisms differ from CAC in the following important ways:

- They are designed to protect voice traffic from data traffic competing for the same network resources.

- They are designed to deal with traffic that is already on the network.

CAC mechanisms extend the capabilities of the QoS tool suite to protect voice traffic from being negatively affected by other voice traffic, and to keep excess voice traffic off the network. Figure 4-1 shows why CAC is needed. If the WAN access link between the two PBXs has the bandwidth to carry only two VoIP calls, admitting the third call will impair the voice quality of all three calls.

Figure 4-1   *VoIP network without CAC.*

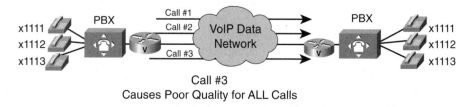

Call #3
Causes Poor Quality for ALL Calls

The reason for this impairment is that the queuing mechanisms provide policing, not CAC. This means that if packets exceeding the configured or allowable rate are received, these packets are simply tail-dropped from the queue. There is no capability in the queuing mechanisms to distinguish which IP packet belongs to which voice call. Any packet exceeding the given rate will be dropped as measured by arrival rate within a certain period of time. Thus, all three calls will experience packet loss, which is perceived as clips by the end users.

This problem is easier to solve for the Layer 2 voice transport mechanisms (VoFR and VoATM), but is particularly vexing for the predominant and far more attractive VoIP applications.

Call Rerouting Alternatives

Figure 4-2 illustrates the point at which a CAC decision is reached by the originating gateway (OGW) that insufficient network resources are available to allow a call to proceed.

Figure 4-2   *VoIP network with CAC.*

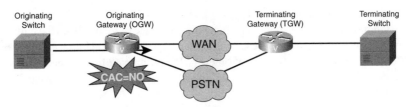

The outgoing gateway now has to find another means of handling the call. Several possibilities exist, most of which depend on the configuration of the gateway. In the absence of any specific configuration, the outgoing gateway will provide a reorder tone to the calling party. The reorder tone is called "fast-busy" in North America, and is known as "overflow tone" or "equipment busy" in other parts of the world. This tone is often intercepted by PSTN switches or PBXs with an announcement such as, "All circuits are busy, please try your call again later."

The outgoing gateway can be configured for the following rerouting scenarios:

- The call can be rerouted via an alternate packet network path if such a path exists. This will require the configuration of a second VoIP dial-peer of a lower preference than the original one chosen.

- The call can be rerouted via an alternate TDM network path if such a path exists. This will require the configuration of a POTS dial peer and a physical TDM interface to the PSTN or another PBX.

- The call can be returned to the originating TDM switch to leverage its rerouting capabilities.

  — If the connection between the originating switch and the outgoing gateway is a common channel signaling (CCS) trunk (for example, QSIG, PRI, or BRI), the call can be rejected with a cause code and the originating switch will tear down the trunk and resume handling of the call.

  — If the connection between the originating switch and the outgoing gateway is an analog or channel-associated signaling (CAS) trunk (for example, E&M, T1 CAS, T1 FGD), the call must be hairpinned (using a second trunk on the same interface) back to the switch.

CAC Mechanisms

As the many interesting aspects of CAC on packet networks have been considered, several different solutions have come into prominence. None of them solves the entire problem, but all of them are useful to address a particular aspect of CAC. Unlike circuit-based networks (looking for a free DS-0 timeslot on every leg of the path that the call will take), determining whether a packet network has the resources to carry a voice call is not a simple undertaking.

Categories of CAC Mechanisms

The remainder of this chapter discusses ten different CAC mechanisms available in current versions of Cisco IOS software. They are grouped into the following three categories:

- **Local mechanisms**—Local CAC mechanisms function on the outgoing gateway. The CAC decision is based on nodal information such as the state of the outgoing LAN/WAN link. Clearly, if the local packet network link is down, there is no point in executing complex decision logic based on the state of the rest of the network, because that network is unreachable. Other local mechanisms include configuration items to disallow more than a fixed number of calls. For example, if the network designer already knows that no more than five calls can fit across the outgoing WAN link because of bandwidth limitations, then it seems logical that it should be possible to configure the local node to allow no more than five calls.

- **Measurement-based mechanisms**—Measurement-based CAC techniques look ahead into the packet network to gauge the state of the network to determine whether to allow a new call. This implies sending probes to the destination IP address (usually the terminating gateway or terminating gatekeeper) that will return to the outgoing gateway with information on the conditions it found while traversing the network to the destination. Typically, loss and delay characteristics are the pertinent information elements for voice.

- **Resource-based mechanisms**—Two types of resource-based mechanisms exist: Those that calculate resources needed and/or available, and those reserving resources for the call. Resources of interest include link bandwidth, DSPs and DS-0 timeslots on the connecting TDM trunks, CPU power, and memory. Several of these resources could be constrained at any one or more of the nodes that the call will traverse to its destination.

There are two additional categories of CAC functionality, but they do not deal with network design or infrastructure issues and, therefore, are not discussed in this book. These two

CAC categories focus instead on the policy question of whether or not the call or the end user is allowed to use the network:

- **Security**—Is this a legitimate device or gateway on the network? Authentication mechanisms, including protocols such as H.235, cover this aspect of CAC.

- **User**—Is this end user authorized to use the network? There are CLID/ANI and PIN verification methods, typically done through Interactive Voice Response (IVR), to verify this.

Measurement-Based Versus Resource-Based CAC

Little overlap exists between local CAC mechanisms and those that look ahead to the rest of the network to determine non-local conditions. Thus, it is easy to understand why distinct local and cloud mechanisms are useful. However, there is considerable overlap between the measurement techniques and the resource reservation techniques of the two "cloud look-ahead" CAC mechanisms. For this reason, there is debate over which is the better method.

Table 4-1 compares the strengths and weaknesses of the measurement-based and resource-based CAC mechanisms. With this information, you can determine the best method for your individual network.

Table 4-1   *Comparison of Measurement-Based and Resource Reservation-Based CAC Features*

Criteria	Measurement-Based Techniques	Resource Reservation-Based Techniques
Network topology	Topology independent. The probe travels to a destination IP address. It has no knowledge of nodes, hops and bandwidth availability on individual links.	Topology aware. The bandwidth availability on every node and every link is taken into account.
Backbone transparency	Transparent. Probes are IP packets and can be sent over any network, including SP backbones and the Internet.	To be the truly end-to-end method that reservation techniques are intended to be, configuration of the feature is required on every interface along the path. This means the customer owns his WAN backbone, and all nodes run code that implements the feature. This is impractical in some cases, so hybrid topologies might be contemplated—with some compromise of the end-to-end nature of the method.

continues

Table 4-1 *Comparison of Measurement-Based and Resource Reservation-Based CAC Features (Continued)*

Criteria	Measurement-Based Techniques	Resource Reservation-Based Techniques
Post-dial delay	An increase in post-dial delay exists for the first call only; information on the destination is cached after that, and a periodic probe is sent to the IP destination. Subsequent calls are allowed or denied based on the latest cached information.	An increase in post-dial delay exists for every call, because the RSVP reservation must be established before the call setup can be completed.
Industry parity	Several vendors have "ping"-like CAC capabilities. For a customer familiar with this operation, measurement-based techniques are a good fit.	
CAC accuracy	The periodic sampling rate of probes can potentially admit calls when bandwidth is insufficient. Measurement-based techniques perform well in networks where traffic fluctuations are gradual.	When implemented on all nodes in the path, RSVP guarantees bandwidth for the call along the entire path for the entire duration of the call. This is the only technique that achieves this level of accuracy.
Protecting voice QoS after admission	The CAC decision is based on probe traffic statistics before the call is admitted. After admission, the call quality is determined by the effectiveness of other QoS mechanisms in the network.	A reservation is established per call before the call is admitted. The call's quality is therefore unaffected by changes in network traffic conditions.
Network traffic overhead	Periodic probe traffic overhead to a cached number of IP destinations. Both the interval and the cache size can be controlled by the configuration.	RSVP messaging traffic overhead for every call.

Table 4-1 *Comparison of Measurement-Based and Resource Reservation-Based CAC Features (Continued)*

Criteria	Measurement-Based Techniques	Resource Reservation-Based Techniques
Scalability	Sending probes to thousands of individual IP destinations might be impractical in a large network. However, probes can be sent to the WAN edge devices, which proxy on behalf of many more destinations on a high-bandwidth campus network behind it. This provides considerable scalability, because the WAN is much more likely to be congested than the campus LAN.	Individual flow reservation is key on the small-bandwidth links around the edge of the network. However, individual reservations per call flow might not make sense on large-bandwidth links in the backbone such as an OC-12. Hybrid network topologies can solve this need, while additional upcoming RSVP tools in this space will provide further scalability.

CAC Mechanism Summary

Table 4-2 summarizes the ten different voice CAC mechanisms that will be discussed in detail in this chapter. It also lists the first Cisco IOS release in which the feature became available.

Table 4-2 *CAC Features*

Type	CAC Feature	SW Release
Local		
	Physical DS-0 Limitation	SW independent
	Max Connections on the Dial Peer	11.3
	VoFR Voice Bandwidth	12.0(4)T
	Trunk Conditioning	12.1(2)T
	Local Voice Busyout (LVBO)	12.1(2)T
Measurement-based		
	Advanced Voice Busyout (AVBO)	12.1(3)T
	PSTN Fallback	12.1(3)T
Resource-based		
Resource Calculation	H.323 Resource Availability Indication (RAI)	12.0(5)T (AS5300) 12.1(3)T (2600/3600)

continues

Table 4-2 *CAC Features (Continued)*

	Gatekeeper Zone Bandwidth Limitations	11.3 (Local Zone)
		12.1(5)T (Inter-zone)
Resource Reservation	RSVP to ATM SVCs for H.323 Video[1]	12.1(5)T
	RSVP/H.323 for Voice	12.1(5)T

1. Translating an RSVP request to an ATM SVC setup is a video feature listed here for completeness only. This feature is not available for voice calls and is not discussed further in this chapter.

Technology Applicability of CAC Mechanisms

When considering the various features that are available to solve a particular design requirement such as CAC, it is helpful to immediately eliminate the mechanisms that do not apply to the network technology under consideration. Table 4-3 summarizes the voice technologies to which the various CAC features apply.

Table 4-3 *Voice Technologies Support of CAC Features*

Feature	VoIP H.323	VoIP SIP	VoIP MGCP	VoFR	VoATM	H.323 Video
DS-0 Limitation	Y	Y	Y	Y	Y	N
Max Connections	Y	Y	Y	Y	Y	N
Voice Bandwidth	N	N	N	Y	N	N
Trunk Conditioning	Y	Y	Y	Y	Y	N
LVBO	Y	Y	Y	Y	Y	N
AVBO	Y	Y	Y	N	N	N
PSTN Fallback	Y	Y	Y	N	N	N
H.323 RAI	Y	N	N	N	N	N[1]
Gatekeeper Zone Bandwidth	Y	N	N	N	N	Y
RSVP to ATM SVCs	N	N	N	N	N	Y
RSVP for H.323 Voice	Y	N	N	N	N	N

1. The H.323 RAI capability does in concept apply to H.323 video applications. However, it is listed here as "No" because the gateways under consideration in this chapter are Cisco IOS voice gateways and they will not generate RAI messages for video traffic.

Voice Bandwidth Determination

To successfully implement CAC mechanisms in your voice network, you should have a clear understanding of exactly how much bandwidth is required by each call so that you can provision the network for the required number of calls and adjust the CAC mechanisms to reject calls exceeding that number. Despite well-published bandwidth figures for each codec, there is no single answer to the amount of bandwidth required for a call. In addition to the codec used, several other network attributes determine the exact bandwidth requirements.

Although an exhaustive discussion of bandwidth calculations is beyond the scope of this book, some of the considerations to keep in mind are worth reviewing. At the physical interface, voice bandwidth used by a single voice call depends on the following factors:

- Voice technology used (VoIP, VoATM, VoFR)
- Layer 2 media used (Ethernet, serial/MLPPP, FR, ATM)
- Codec used
- Header compression techniques (applicable only to VoIP)
- Voice Activity Detection (VAD, also known as silence suppression)

For ATM networks, which use fixed-length cells, the overhead of the voice payload (IP packet for VoIPoATM, or codec payload for VoATM) fitting into ATM cells must be taken into account.

Table 4-4 summarizes some of the more common VoIP combinations of the preceding factors, and the resulting bandwidth of the call.

Table 4-4   *VoIP Bandwidth Requirements*

Codec	Codec Bandwidth (kbps)	Sample Length (ms)	Sample Size (bytes)	Samples per Packet	IP Header Size (bytes)	Layer 2 Technology	Layer 2 Header Size (bytes)	Voice Call Bandwidth Required (kbps)
G.711	64	10	80	2	40	Ethernet	14	85.6
G.711	64	10	80	2	40	MLPPP/FR	6	82.4
G.711	64	10	80	2	2 (cRTP)	MLPPP/FR	6	67.2
G.729	8	10	10	2	40	Ethernet	14	29.6
G.729	8	10	10	2	40	MLPPP/FR	6	26.4
G.729	8	10	10	2	2 (cRTP)	MLPPP/FR	6	11.2

The formula used to calculate the bandwidth for any other combination of factors is:

Voice bandwidth = (Payload + L3 + L2) x 8 x PPS
Payload = Payload in bytes generated by the codec

L3 = Layer 3 and higher layer header overhead in bytes (0 for VoFR and VoATM)
L2 = Link Layer header overhead in bytes (see Table 4-5)
8 = Number of bits per byte
PPS = Packets per second rate generated by the codec

Table 4-5 provides the header overheads of various Layer 2 transport technologies.

Table 4-5   *Layer 2 Header Sizes*

Layer 2 Media	Layer 2 Header Size (Bytes)
Ethernet	14
PPP/MLPPP	6
FR	6
ATM (AAL5)	5 (plus cell fill waste)
MLPPP over FR	14
MLPPP over ATM (AAL5)	5 bytes for every ATM cell + 20 bytes for the MLPPP and AAL5 encapsulation of the IP packet

Examples:

- G.729 / VoIP / MLPPP / no cRTP / no VAD: (20 + 40 + 6) x 8 x 50 = 26.4 k
- G.729 / MLPPP / cRTP / no VAD: (20 + 2 + 6) x 8 x 50 = 11.2 k
- G.729 / VoIPovFR / no cRTP / no VAD: (20 + 40 + 6) x 8 x 50 = 26.4 k
- G.729 / VoFR / no VAD: (20 + 6) x 8 x 50 = 10.4 k

CAC Mechanism Evaluation Criteria

As each CAC method is described in the remainder of this chapter, it will be evaluated against various factors and criteria that will help determine which is the best or most appropriate CAC mechanism for the network design under consideration.

Table 4-6 describes the criteria that will be used to evaluate the different CAC tools.

Table 4-6   *CAC Feature Evaluation Criteria*

Evaluation Criteria	Description
VoX supported	Which voice technologies does the method apply to? Some methods apply to a single technology, others apply across the board.
Trunking/IP telephony	Is the method usable only between voice gateways connected to the PSTN or a PBX, or can this method also be used with IP phone endpoints?

Table 4-6   *CAC Feature Evaluation Criteria (Continued)*

Evaluation Criteria	Description
Platform/Release	Which IOS platforms is this feature available on, and in which software release was it introduced?
PBX trunk types supported	Some CAC features depend on the PSTN/PBX trunk type used in the connection, or act differently with CCS trunks versus CAS trunks.
End-to-end/Local/IP cloud	The scope of visibility of the CAC feature. Some mechanisms work locally on the outgoing gateway only, others consider the cloud between the source and destination nodes, some consider the destination POTS interface, and some work end-to-end.
Per call/ interface/endpoint	Different mechanisms involve different elements of the network. Several CAC methods work per call, but some per interface and some per endpoint or IP destination.
Topology awareness	Does the CAC mechanism take into account the topology of the network, and therefore provide protection for the links and nodes in the topology?
Guarantees QoS for duration of call	Does the mechanism make a one-time decision before allowing the call, or does it also protect the QoS of the call for the duration of the call by reserving the required resources?
Post-dial delay	Does the mechanism impose an additional post-dial delay because it requires extra messaging or processing during call setup?
Messaging network overhead	Does the method use additional messaging that has to be provisioned in the network to gather the information necessary for the CAC decision?

Local CAC Mechanisms

The local mechanisms are the simplest CAC mechanisms to understand and implement. They work on the outgoing gateway and consider the local conditions of the node. They also tend to have low overhead, so if any of these mechanisms provide the desired functionality, there's little reason to implement any of the more complex features. However, it is likely that in a network of any reasonable size, satisfactory CAC functionality will require more than the use of a local mechanism.

In this section, the following five local CAC mechanisms are discussed:

- Physical DS-0 limitation
- Max connections
- Voice bandwidth
- Trunk conditioning
- Local voice busyout

Physical DS-0 Limitation

This is not a specific software feature, but rather a design methodology based on the physical limitations of the interfaces. Although simple when compared to some of the other features, this is nevertheless a key building block to many existing customer networks.

For example, if you desire to limit the number of calls from the originating PBX to the outgoing gateway to five, then configure or enable only five timeslots on the T1/E1 trunk between the switch and the outgoing gateway. Figure 4-3 illustrates this principle.

Figure 4-3 *Physical DS-0 limitation.*

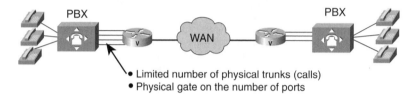

Because it is local, this CAC design method provides adequate protection for the egress WAN link from the outgoing gateway. It has the same limitation as the other local mechanisms: It provides no protection against the unavailability of bandwidth on any other link in the network. It works well in simple hub-and-spoke topologies and also reasonably well in more complex multi-layer hierarchical networks for the simple reason that the maximum number of possible calls (worst case) on any backbone link can be accurately estimated by a calculation based on the known number of calls that can come in from each edge location and the busy-hour traffic patterns of calls between locations.

Although this CAC method works well in trunking applications (gateway to gateway), it does not work for IP telephony as there is no physical TDM interface on which time slots can be restricted. As shown in Figure 4-4, when calls are originated by devices on LAN media, the bandwidth capacity of the physical media far outstrips that of the WAN egress interface. Without other software features at the aggregation point (typically the WAN edge router) to "gate" the arrival of new calls, there is no physical way of keeping new calls off the network.

In summary, the following are advantages of restricting the physical DS-0s entering the network:

- Adds no extra CPU or bandwidth overhead to the network
- Works well for many toll bypass applications
- Predominant CAC mechanism deployed in toll bypass networks today
- Protects the bandwidth on the egress WAN link of the local site
- Can provide predictive protection across the backbone based on busy-hour traffic patterns

Figure 4-4   *IP telephony applications.*

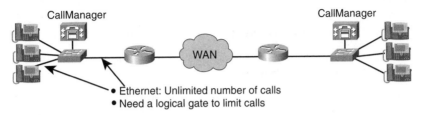

- Ethernet: Unlimited number of calls
- Need a logical gate to limit calls

The following are limitations of this CAC mechanism:

- Doesn't work for IP telephony applications
- Limited to relatively simple topologies
- Doesn't react to link failures or changing network conditions

Table 4-7 evaluates the physical DS-0 limitation mechanism against the CAC evaluation criteria described earlier in this chapter.

Table 4-7   *Summary of Physical DS-0 Limitation*

Evaluation Criteria	Value
VoX supported	Independent of the VoX technology used
Trunking/IP telephony	Trunking applications only
Platform/Release	All voice gateways and all IOS releases
PBX trunk types supported	All
End-to-end/Local/IP cloud	Local
Per call/ interface/endpoint	Per DS-0/trunk (per call)
Topology awareness	None
Guarantees QoS for duration of call	None
Post-dial delay	None
Messaging network overhead	None

Max Connections

The max connections CAC mechanism involves using the **max-conn** dial-peer configuration command on a dial peer of the outgoing gateway to restrict the number of concurrent connections (calls) that can be active on that dial peer at any one time.

This tool is easy to use but limited in the scope of the network design problems it can solve. Because it is applied per dial peer, it isn't possible to limit the total number of calls the outgoing gateway can have active simultaneously unless you have a limited number of dial peers and you use the **max-conn** dial-peer configuration command on each one.

With this limitation in mind, the **max-conn** dial-peer configuration command provides a viable CAC method in at least two scenarios:

- For a relatively small number of dial peers pointing calls onto an egress WAN link, the sum of the individual **max-conn** dial-peer configuration commands will provide the maximum number of calls that can be simultaneously active across the WAN link.

- If the design objective is to limit the maximum number of calls between sites (rather than protecting the bandwidth of the egress WAN link), this is a suitable feature to use, provided the dial peers are structured in such a way that each remote site has one dial peer pointing calls to it.

Figure 4-5 shows an example of this type of network: There are three remote sites, each with recognizable first digits in the dialing plan. The outgoing VoIP dial peers at the headquarters (HQ) site therefore match the remote sites one for one. The number of calls to remote sites 1, 2, and 3 will be limited to 4, 6, and 8 respectively. The egress WAN link can therefore have no more than 18 calls active at any one time. In this configuration, it would be prudent to provision the bandwidth of this link for that number of calls.

Figure 4-5 *Max-connections configured on the dial-peer.*

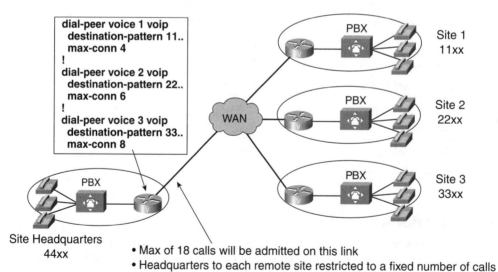

The max connections feature can also be used on the POTS dial peer to limit the number of calls that can be active on a T1/E1 to a PBX/PSTN if the desire is to provision all time slots on that connection, but limit the number of calls to a lesser number than the physical number of time slots.

In Example 4-1, no more than 24 VoIP calls will be allowed (dial peer 800) over the egress WAN link. Call 25 will be hairpinned back to the PBX to be redirected to the PSTN. (Note that the suitable digits are prepended to the dial string to direct the routing logic of the PBX.)

Example 4-1 *Maximum Connections*

```
dial-peer voice 800 voip
  preference 1
!Defines a rotary-group with 1st priority.
  max-conn 24
!Max connection is 24 (Active Admission Control).
destination-pattern 83123...
  ip precedence 5
  session target ipv4:172.17.251.28
!
dial-peer voice 600 pots
  preference 2
!Defines a rotary-group with 2nd priority.
  destination-pattern 83123...
  direct-inward-dial
  port 0:D
  prefix 9983123
!Prefix 99 in front of calling number to alert PBX to overflow to PSTN
```

Although useful in many scenarios, the drawbacks of this feature include the following:

- While providing some protection for the voice gateway egress WAN link, little or no protection is provided for links in the network backbone.
- Doesn't work for IP telephony applications that do not use dial peers.
- Limited to simple topologies.
- Doesn't react to link failures or changing network conditions.

Table 4-8 evaluates the max connections mechanism against the CAC evaluation criteria described earlier in this chapter.

Table 4-8 *Summary of Max Connections*

	Evaluation Criteria	Value
1	VoX supported	All VoX that use dial peers
2	Trunking/IP telephony	Trunking applications only

continues

Table 4-8 *Summary of Max Connections (Continued)*

	Evaluation Criteria	Value
3	Platform/Release	All voice gateways and all IOS releases
4	PBX Trunk types supported	All
5	End-to-end/Local/IP cloud	Local
6	Per call/ interface/endpoint	Per dial peer
7	Topology awareness	None
8	Guarantees QoS for duration of call	None
9	Post-dial delay	None
10	Messaging network overhead	None

Voice Bandwidth

In Voice over Frame Relay (VoFR) configurations, a **frame-relay voice-bandwidth** map class configuration command is used in the Frame Relay map class to set aside bandwidth for VoFR calls. This operates in a way similar to the way in which the IP Real-Time Transport Protocol (RTP) Priority and Low Latency Queueing (LLQ) features reserve bandwidth for general traffic flows. However, the **frame-relay voice-bandwidth** map class configuration command also provides CAC, which the general queuing features do not.

The **frame-relay voice-bandwidth** map class configuration command is able to provide CAC because VoFR is a Layer 2 technology. By looking at the FRF.11 (voice) or FRF.3.1 (data) headers, the Frame Relay software is able to determine which frames are voice frames and which are data frames. The software also knows which frames belong to which voice call as subsequent fields in the header carry Channel Identification (CID) and payload information. Because the **frame-relay voice-bandwidth** map class configuration command sets aside bandwidth for voice, it can also deny the next call if that additional call will cause the total bandwidth allocated to voice to be exceeded.

This CAC method is of use only if VoFR is a viable technology in your network. It should also be noted that the voice bandwidth size defaults to 0 so that if no bandwidth reservation is specified, no voice calls are allowed over the WAN link. Do not include signaling traffic in the bandwidth you specify with this command—just voice payload traffic.

Example 4-2 shows how voice bandwidth provides CAC in a VoFR configuration.

Example 4-2 *Voice Bandwidth*

```
interface Serial0/0
 encapsulation frame-relay
 no fair-queue
 frame-relay traffic-shaping
!
interface Serial0/0.1 point-to-point
```

Example 4-2   *Voice Bandwidth (Continued)*

```
   frame-relay interface-dlci 16
   class vofr
 !
 map-class frame vofr
   frame cir 60000
   frame bc 600
   frame frag 80
   frame fair-queue
   frame-relay voice-bandwidth 24000
 !24 kbps is enough for 2 G.729 calls at 10.4 kbps each.
```

Table 4-9 evaluates the voice-bandwidth mechanism against the CAC evaluation criteria described earlier in this chapter.

Table 4-9   *Summary of Voice Bandwidth*

	Evaluation Criteria	Value
1	VoX supported	VoFR
2	Trunking/IP telephony	Trunking applications only
3	Platform/Release	2600s, 3600s, 3810, 7200; Cisco IOS Release 12.0(4)T
4	PBX trunk types supported	All
5	End-to-end/Local/IP cloud	Local
6	Per call/ interface/endpoint	Per call, per PVC
7	Topology awareness	None
8	Guarantees QoS for duration of call	None
9	Post-dial delay	None
10	Messaging network overhead	None

Trunk Conditioning

Trunk conditioning provides more functionality than just CAC, but only the CAC aspects will be discussed here. It can be used in *connection trunk networks* (networks with nailed-up voice connections across the VoX portion of the network) to monitor the state of the VoX connection and busy back the trunk to the originating PBX if the VoX connection should fail.

This feature is limited in scope, as it applies to connection trunk networks only. On the other hand, most of the other CAC features apply only to switched networks.

Implementing CAC on a connection trunk configuration is a slightly different problem than implementing it for switched networks. This is because the VoX connections between the two gateways are nailed up, as shown in Figure 4-6. The bandwidth is, therefore, already established and allocated, and must be available, or the connection trunk connections will not be established properly.

Figure 4-6 *Trunk conditioning.*

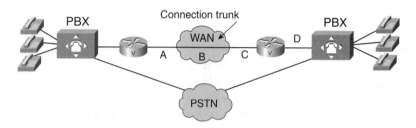

The unique attribute of trunk conditioning compared to other CAC features is that it has visibility not only into the condition of the WAN end-to-end, but also into the condition of the POTS connection on the terminating side of the network. In Figure 4-6, if any one of the A, B, C, or D legs should fail, the outgoing gateway will know this and can busy back the trunk to the originating PBX to trigger rerouting capability at the source. This information is carried as part of the keepalive messages that are generated on connection trunk configurations.

You can tune the precise bit pattern that will be generated to the originating PBX. The ABCD bits can be conditioned to specific busy or out-of-service (OOS) indications that the originating PBX will recognize and act upon.

Trunk conditioning is therefore not a call-by-call feature, as are those that we have discussed so far. It is a PBX trunk busy-back (or OOS) feature. If a failure occurs in the WAN, the trunk to the PBX is taken out of service so that no calls can be made across that trunk until the WAN connectivity is recovered.

Table 4-10 evaluates the trunk conditioning mechanism against the CAC evaluation criteria described earlier in this chapter.

Table 4-10 *Summary of Trunk Conditioning*

	Evaluation Criteria	Value
1	VoX supported	VoIP/H.323, VoFR, VoATM connection trunk configurations only
2	Trunking/IP telephony	Trunking applications only
3	Platform/Release	2600s, 3600s, MC3810; Cisco IOS Release 12.1(3)T
4	PBX trunk types supported	Analog and CAS
5	End-to-end/Local/IP cloud	Local
6	Per call/ interface/endpoint	Per telephony interface

Table 4-10   *Summary of Trunk Conditioning (Continued)*

	Evaluation Criteria	Value
7	Topology awareness	None
8	Guarantees QoS for duration of call	None
9	Post-dial delay	None
10	Messaging network overhead	None; uses pre-existing connection trunk keepalives

Local Voice Busyout

Several CAC mechanisms are called trunk busy-back features. The first one we encountered was trunk conditioning. That feature operates on connection trunk networks only. Similar functionality is needed for switched networks, and local voice busyout (LVBO) is the first of two features that achieve this.

LVBO allows you to take a PBX trunk connection to the attached gateway completely out of service in the event the WAN conditions are considered unsuitable to carry voice traffic. This technique has the following advantages:

- Not every call has to be rejected individually and incur a post-dial delay.

- Prevents the need for hairpinning rejected calls back to the originating PBX, using up multiple DS-0 slots for a single call.

- Works well to redirect rejected calls with PBXs that either do not have the intelligence or are not configured appropriately.

- Solves the hairpinning problem of the PBX putting the call right back onto a third DS-0 on the same T1/E1 to the gateway that has already rejected the call and hairpinned it (a condition called tromboning). This is usually easier to deal with on CCS trunk types where cause code information can be returned to the PBX that triggers rerouting logic, but on CAS trunks the PBX does not know what went wrong, and unless digits are manipulated in the gateway, it cannot easily make a decision to reroute the call over a different trunk group.

LVBO provides the outgoing gateway with the ability to monitor the state of various network interfaces, both LAN and WAN, and busy back the trunk to the PBX if any of the monitored links should fail. Up to 32 interfaces can be monitored; if any or all of them change state, the gateway can be configured to busy back the trunk to the PBX. The reason this feature is called local voice busyout is because only local links can be monitored. This feature does not have any visibility into the network beyond the local gateway's links.

LVBO in current software works on CAS and analog PBX/PSTN trunks only. On CCS trunks, the cause code functionality can be used to inform the PBX/CO switch to redirect a rejected call. LVBO can be configured in one of the following two ways:

- To force individual voice ports into the busyout state
- To force an entire T1/E1 trunk into the busyout state

Figure 4-7 illustrates the operation of the local voice busyout feature, including a CLI segment to show its configuration. In the example, the outgoing gateway is monitoring two interfaces, Ethernet interface E0/1 and WAN interface S0/1 on behalf of voice port 2/0:1, a T1 CAS trunk to a PBX. As shown in the example, this feature is applicable only if the origination device is a PBX/PSTN interface, although the destination device can be anything, including an IP-capable voice device.

Figure 4-7 *Local voice busyout functionality.*

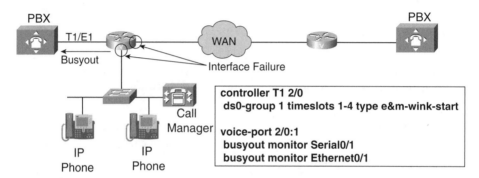

The following limitations apply to the LVBO feature:

- It has local visibility only in current software (Cisco IOS Release 12.2), and it monitors only Ethernet LAN interfaces (not FastEthernet).

- It only applies to analog and CAS trunk types.

Table 4-11 evaluates the LVBO mechanism against the CAC evaluation criteria described earlier in this chapter.

Table 4-11 *Summary of Local Voice Busyout*

	Evaluation Criteria	Value
1	VoX supported	All
2	Trunking/IP telephony	Trunking
		Calls originating from PBX and terminating to IP telephony destinations
3	Platform/Release	2600s, 3600s, MC3810; Cisco IOS Releases 12.0(7) XK, 12.1(2)T
4	PBX trunk types supported	Analog and CAS
5	End-to-end/Local/IP cloud	Local
6	Per call/ interface/endpoint	Per WAN, LAN, and telephony interface
7	Topology awareness	None
8	Guarantees QoS for duration of call	None

Table 4-11   *Summary of Local Voice Busyout (Continued)*

	Evaluation Criteria	Value
9	Post-dial delay	None
10	Messaging network overhead	None

Measurement-Based CAC Mechanisms

This section describes the following measurement-based CAC techniques:

- Advanced voice busyout
- PSTN fallback

These are the first of two types of CAC mechanisms that add visibility into the network itself in addition to providing local information on the outgoing gateway as discussed in the preceding sections.

Before covering the actual features within this category, some background information on Security Assurance Agent (SAA) probes is necessary, as this is the underlying technique employed by the measurement-based CAC methods. SAA probes traverse the network to a given IP destination and measure the loss and delay characteristics of the network along the path traveled. These values are returned to the outgoing gateway to use in making a decision on the condition of the network and its ability to carry a voice call.

The following attributes of measurement-based CAC mechanisms are derived from their use of SAA probes:

- Because an SAA probe is an IP packet traveling to an IP destination, all measurement-based CAC techniques apply to VoIP only (including VoFR and VoATM networks).

- As probes are sent into the network, there is a certain amount of overhead traffic produced in gathering the information needed for CAC.

- If the CAC decision for a call has to await a probe to be dispatched and returned, there is some small additional post-dial delay for the call. (This should be insignificant in a properly designed network.)

Security Assurance Agents

Security Assurance Agents (SAA) is a generic network management feature that provides a mechanism for network congestion analysis. It also underlies a multitude of other Cisco IOS features. It was not implemented for the purpose of accomplishing CAC, nor is it a part of the CAC suite. But its abilities to measure network delay and packet loss are tremendously useful as building blocks on which to base CAC features. The SAA feature was called Response Time Responder (RTR) in earlier releases of Cisco IOS Software.

SAA probes do not provide any bandwidth information, either configured or available. However, if bandwidth across a link anywhere in the path that the voice call will follow is oversubscribed, it is reasonable to assume that the packet delay and loss values that the probe returns will reflect this condition, even if indirectly.

SAA Probes Versus Pings

SAA probes are similar in concept to the popular ping IP connectivity mechanism, but far more sophisticated. SAA packets can be built and customized to mimic the type of traffic for which they are measuring the network—in this case, a voice packet. A ping packet is almost by definition a best-effort packet, and even if the IP Precedence is set, it does not resemble a voice packet in size or protocol. Nor will the QoS mechanisms deployed in the network classify and treat a ping packet as a voice packet. The delay and loss experienced by a ping is therefore a very crude worst-case measure of the treatment a voice packet might be subject to while traversing the very same network. With the penetration of sophisticated QoS mechanisms in network backbones, a ping becomes unusable as a practical indication of the capability of the network to carry voice.

SAA Protocol

The SAA protocol is a client-server protocol defined on UDP. The client builds and sends the probe, and the server (previously the RTR) returns the probe to the sender. The SAA probes used for CAC go out randomly on ports selected from within the top end of the audio UDP-defined port range (16384-32767); they use a packet size based on the codec the call will use. IP Precedence can be set if desired, and a full RTP/UDP/IP header is used. By default the SAA probe uses the RTCP port (the odd RTP port number), but it can also be configured to use the RTP media port (the even RTP port number) if desired.

SAA was first introduced on selected platforms in Cisco IOS Release 12.0(7)T. The higher-end Cisco router platforms tend to support it (for example, the Cisco 7200/7500 series), while the lower-end platforms tend not to support it (for example, the Cisco 1750). Neither the Cisco cable modems nor the IP phones currently support SAA probes or respond to SAA probes.

ICPIF

The ITU standardizes network Transmission Impairments in ITU G.113. This standard defines the term ICPIF (Calculated Planning Impairment Factor), which is a calculation based on network delay and packet loss figures. ICPIF yields a single value that can be used as a gauge of network impairment.

ITU G.113 provides the following interpretations of specific ICPIF values:

- 5: Very good
- 10: Good
- 20: Adequate
- 30: Limiting case
- 45: Exceptional limiting case
- 55: Customers likely to react strongly

SAA probe delay and loss information is used in calculating an ICPIF value that is then used as a threshold for CAC decisions, based on either the preceding ITU interpretation or on the requirements of an individual customer network.

Advanced Voice Busyout

Advanced voice busyout (AVBO) is an enhancement to local voice busyout. While LVBO provides for busyout based on local conditions of the outgoing gateway, AVBO adds the capability to trigger an SAA probe to one or more configured IP destinations. The information returned by the probe—either the explicit loss or delay values, or the ICPIF congestion threshold—can be used to trigger a busyout of the connection to the PBX.

AVBO therefore introduces the ability to busy out a PBX trunk, or individual voice ports, based on the current conditions of the IP network. This is illustrated in Figure 4-8.

Figure 4-8   *Advanced voice busyout.*

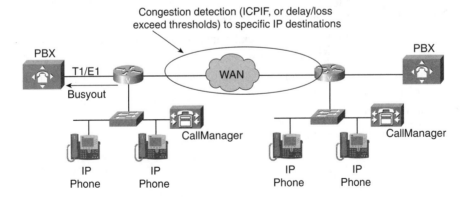

Example 4-3 shows a sample configuration of AVBO on a T1 CAS trunk to a PBX.

Example 4-3   *Advanced Voice Busyout*

```
controller T1 2/0
 ds0-group 1 timeslots 1-4 type e&m-immediate-start
!
voice-port 2/0:1
  voice-class busyout 4
!
voice class busyout 4
 busyout monitor Serial0/1
 busyout monitor Ethernet0/1
 busyout monitor probe  1.6.6.48 codec g729r8 icpif 10
```

When using AVBO, you should keep in mind the following restrictions and limitations:

- Busyout results based on probes (measurement-based) are not absolute. Conditions will arise where a *false positive* happens.

- The IP addresses monitored by the probes are statically configured. It is necessary to manually ensure that these IP addresses are indeed the destinations to which calls are being made. There is no automatic coordination between the probe configuration and the actual IP destinations to which VoIP dial peers or a gatekeeper can direct calls.

- The destination node (the device that owns the IP address to which the probe is sent) must support an SAA responder.

- This feature can not busy back the local PBX trunk based on the state of the telephony trunk on the remote node; it monitors IP network only.

- SAA probe-based features will not work well in networks where the traffic load fluctuates dramatically in a short period of time.

- As with LVBO, this feature can be applied only to analog and CAS trunks; CCS trunks are not yet supported.

Table 4-12 evaluates the AVBO mechanism against the CAC evaluation criteria described earlier in this chapter.

Table 4-12   *Summary of AVBO*

	Evaluation Criteria	Value
1	VoX supported	VoIP only
2	Trunking/IP telephony	Trunking
		Calls originating from PBX and terminating to IP telephony destinations
3	Platform/Release	2600s, 3600s, MC3810; Cisco IOS Release 12.1(3)T
4	PBX trunk types supported	Analog and CAS
5	End-to-end/Local/IP cloud	IP cloud

Table 4-12   *Summary of AVBO (Continued)*

	Evaluation Criteria	Value
6	Per call/ interface/endpoint	Per IP destination
7	Topology awareness	None
8	Guarantees QoS for duration of call	None
9	Post-dial delay	None
10	Messaging network overhead	Periodic SAA probes

PSTN Fallback

The name PSTN Fallback is, to some extent, a misnomer because a call can be redirected to any of the rerouting options discussed earlier, not simply the PSTN. And even if redirected to the PSTN, it can be done by the outgoing gateway or by the PBX attached to the outgoing gateway, depending on the configuration. For this reason, this feature is sometimes referred to as VoIP Fallback.

Unlike AVBO, PSTN Fallback is a per-call CAC mechanism: It does not busy out any trunks or provide any general indication to the attached PBX that the IP cloud is not capable of taking calls. The CAC decision is triggered only when a call setup is attempted.

As PSTN Fallback is an IOS feature based on SAA probes, it has all the benefits and drawbacks of a measurement-based technique. It is unusually flexible in that it can make CAC decisions based on any type of IP network, including the Internet. All IP networks will carry the SAA probe packet as just another IP packet. Therefore, it doesn't matter if the customer backbone network is comprised of one or more service provider (SP) networks, and/or the Internet, and/or any combination of these. The only requirement is that the destination device (the owner of the IP address to which the probe is sent) support SAA responder functionality.

This destination device is hopefully part of the customer network at the destination site, with an SP backbone in between. PSTN Fallback on an IOS voice gateway, therefore, cannot be used directly with IP phones and PC-based VoIP application destinations, but can be used indirectly if these destinations are behind a Cisco IOS router that can support the SAA responder. The destination device itself does not need to support the PSTN Fallback feature (it's an outgoing gateway feature only). Only the SAA probe responder is needed.

For CallManager and IP phone deployments, CallManager itself has call rerouting and admission capabilities that can be used. The discussion here is limited to the IOS voice gateway feature that allows the gateway to make CAC decisions.

SAA Probes Used for PSTN Fallback

As shown in Figure 4-9, when a call is attempted at the outgoing gateway, the network congestion values for the IP destination will be used to allow or reject the call. The network congestion values for delay, loss, or ICPIF are provided by sending an SAA probe to the IP destination the call is trying to reach. The threshold values for rejecting a call are configured at the outgoing gateway.

Figure 4-9 *PSTN Fallback.*

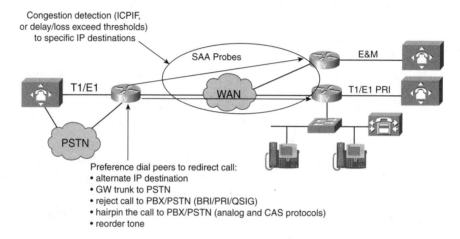

IP Destination Caching

Unlike AVBO, PSTN Fallback doesn't require the static configuration of the IP destinations. The software keeps a cache of configurable size that tracks the most recently used IP destinations to which calls were attempted. If the IP destination of a new call attempt is found in the cache, the CAC decision for the call can be made immediately (Examples 1 and 2 in Figure 4-10 illustrate "call allowed" and "call rejected" scenarios respectively). If the entry does not appear in the cache, a new probe is started and the call setup is suspended until the probe response arrives (Example 3 in Figure 4-10). Therefore, an extra post-dial delay is imposed for only the first call to a new IP destination.

Figure 4-10 *PSTN Fallback call setup.*

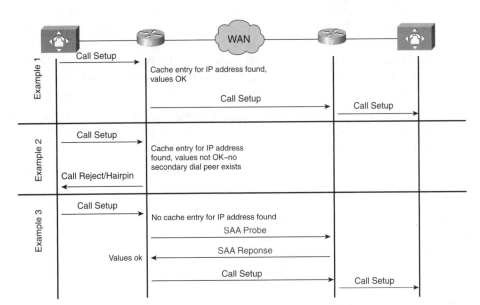

After an IP destination is entered into the cache, a periodic probe with a configurable timeout value will be sent to that destination to refresh the information in the cache. If no further calls are made to this IP destination, the entry will age out of the cache and probe traffic to that destination will be discontinued. PSTN Fallback thus dynamically adjusts the probe traffic to the IP destinations that are actively seeing call activity.

SAA Probe Format

Each probe consists of multiple packets, a configurable parameter of the feature. The delay, loss, and ICPIF values entered into the cache for the IP destination will be averaged from all the responses.

If the call uses the G.729 and G.711 codecs, the probe packet sizes will mimic those of a voice packet for that codec. Other codecs will use G.711-like probes. In Cisco IOS software releases later than Cisco IOS Release 12.1(3)T, other codec choices can also be supported with their own exact probes.

The IP Precedence of the probe packets can also be configured to mimic the priority of a voice packet more closely. This parameter should be set equal to the IP Precedence used for other voice media packets in the network.

PSTN Fallback Configuration

PSTN Fallback configuration applies only to calls initiated by the outgoing gateway; it has no bearing on calls received by the gateway. The destination node (often the terminating gateway, but not necessarily) should be configured with the SAA Responder feature. In most networks, gateways generate calls to each other, so that every gateway is both an outgoing gateway and a terminating gateway. But in some networks (for example, service provider networks), call traffic direction is one-sided, either outgoing or incoming.

PSTN Fallback configuration is done at the global level and therefore applies to all calls attempted by the gateway. You cannot selectively apply PSTN Fallback only to calls initiated by certain PSTN/PBX interfaces.

To turn on PSTN Fallback, enter the following global configuration commands:

- Outgoing gateway: the **call fallback** command

- Destination node: the **saa responder** command

A number of optional parameters can be tuned for PSTN Fallback using the **call fallback** global configuration command. Table 4-13 shows the different keywords for this commnd and their defaults in Cisco IOS Release 12.1.3T software. Consult the Cisco IOS feature documentation for a full discussion of what each variation of this command does.

Table 4-13   *Keywords for the* **call fallback** *command*

Parameter	Description	Default
cache-size	Configure cache size	128
cache-timeout	Configure cache timeout	600 s
instantaneous-value-weight	Configure the instantaneous value weight	66
jitter-probe num-packets	Configure the number of packets in the jitter probe	15
jitter-probe precedence	Configure the precedence of the packets in the jitter probe	2
jitter-probe priority-queue	Have the jitter probes sent through the voice PQ	off
key-chain	Configure MD5 key chain	none
map	Configure IP mapping	none
probe-timeout	Configure probe timeout	30 s
threshold delay n loss m	Configure delay threshold	none
threshold icpif n	Configure ICPIF threshold	10

PSTN Fallback Scalability

Customers with large networks are often concerned about PSTN Fallback causing a large amount of probe traffic on their networks. In smaller networks, the terminating gateways can be used as the probe destination nodes. In other words, the IP addresses kept in the outgoing gateway cache will be those of the terminating gateways to which call traffic is sent.

However, for large sites or campus sites that might have multiple terminating gateways; or for sites with IP phone or PC-based applications as destinations; or for sites that have a WAN edge router that is separate from the terminating gateway, the call traffic destination IP addresses can be mapped to a much smaller set of probe destinations that will be kept in the cache.

Consider an example based on Figure 4-11. A large number of IP phones are installed at Site 6, each one having a unique IP address. If Site 1 calls an IP phone at Site 6, it is not necessary for the cache at Site 1 to contain an entry for each separate IP destination at Site 6 and to send a separate probe for each IP address. All IP call destinations at Site 6 can be mapped to the IP address of the WAN edge router of Site 6 so that a single probe from Site 1 to Site 6 can probe CAC information for all calls destined to Site 6. The same principle applies if there were multiple terminating gateways at Site 6. All of their IP addresses can be mapped to the WAN edge router—which might or might not be a terminating gateway in its own right.

Figure 4-11 *PSTN Fallback scalability.*

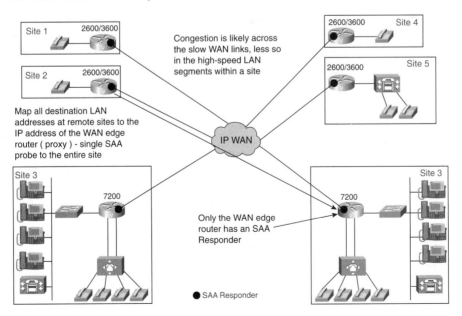

The probe traffic can therefore be reduced significantly by sending probes to IP destinations that represent the portion of the network most likely to be congested (the WAN backbone and WAN edge), and by not sending probe traffic across a high-speed campus or LAN backbone that is much less likely to be congested. This same scalability mechanism also provides a mechanism to support IP destinations that do not support SAA Responder functionality.

PSTN Fallback Summary

PSTN Fallback is a widely deployable, topology-independent CAC mechanism that can be used over any backbone, regardless of whether or not the customer owns the backbone equipment or the technology used in the backbone, or which vendor equipment is used in the backbone.

The following attributes of PSTN Fallback must be considered when designing a network:

- Because it is based on IP probes, PSTN Fallback applies to VoIP networks only.

- PSTN Fallback doesn't reroute calls in progress when network conditions change.

- A slight increase in post-dial delay will apply to only the first call to a destination not yet in the cache.

- There is no interaction between the SAA probe timer and the H.225 timer setting: The SAA probe occurs before the H.323 call-setup is sent to the destination, while the H.225 timer occurs after H.323 call-setup is sent.

- PSTN Fallback is measurement-based, and therefore not absolute. It will perform well in steady traffic that has a gradual ramp-up/ramp-down, but poorly in quickly fluctuating traffic with a bursty ramp-up/ramp-down.

- An erroneous CAC decision could be reached based on non-current information due to the periodic nature of the probes.

- *Proxy* destinations for the probes can be used by mapping destination IP addresses to a smaller number of IP addresses of the nodes located between the outgoing gateway and the terminating gateways.

- No bandwidth measurements are taken by the probes, only delay and loss measurements.

- MD5 key-chain authentication can be configured for security to ensure that probes are initiated only by trusted sources. This circumvents denial-of-service type attacks by untrusted sources initiating large volumes of probes.

Table 4-14 evaluates the PSTN Fallback mechanism against the CAC evaluation criteria described earlier in this chapter.

Table 4-14   *Summary of PSTN Fallback*

	Evaluation Criteria	Value
1	VoX supported	VoIP only
2	Trunking/IP telephony	Trunking
		Calls originating from PBX and terminating to IP telephony destinations
3	Platform/Release	Cisco 2600/3600, MC3810: Cisco IOS Release 12.1(3)T
		AS5300: Cisco IOS Release 12.2(2)T
		7200/7500 support SAA responder
4	PBX trunk types supported	All PBX/PSTN trunk signaling types (analog, Digital CAS and CCS) for analog and digital CAS—alternate IP destination, hairpin for digital CCS—reject the call to PBX/PSTN for rerouting
5	End-to-end/Local/IP cloud	IP cloud
6	Per call/ interface/endpoint	Per active/cached IP destination
7	Topology awareness	None
8	Guarantees QoS for duration of call	None
9	Post-dial delay	Only for first call that initiates probe
10	Messaging network overhead	Periodic SAA probes

Resource-Based CAC Mechanisms

This section discusses the following three resource-based CAC techniques:

- H.323 Resource Availability Indication (RAI)
- Gatekeeper Zone Bandwidth Limitations
- Resource Reservation Protocol (RSVP)

Like the measurement-based CAC techniques, these techniques add visibility into the network itself in addition to the local information on the outgoing gateway that can be used for CAC, as discussed in the preceding sections.

Resource Calculation Versus Resource Reservation

Two types of resource-based CAC mechanisms exist:

- Those that monitor the use of certain resources and calculate a value that will affect the CAC decision
- Those that reserve resources for the call

The reservation mechanisms are the only ones that can guarantee QoS for the duration of the call. All other CAC mechanisms (local, measurement-based and resource calculation-based) simply make a one-time decision prior to call setup based on knowledge of network conditions at that time.

The following resources are of interest to voice calls:

- DS-0 timeslot on the originating and terminating TDM trunks
- DSP resources on the originating and terminating gateways
- CPU use of the nodes—typically the gateways
- Memory use of the nodes—typically the gateways
- Bandwidth availability on one or more links in the path the call will take

In current Cisco IOS Software (Release 12.2), the resource calculation CAC methods take the terminal gateway DS-0 and DSP availability into account (RAI), as well as bandwidth at a high level (gatekeeper zone bandwidth management). The only current resource reservation mechanism (RSVP) takes only bandwidth availability into account.

Resource Availability Indicator

Resource Availability Indication (RAI) is an H.323v2 feature that describes a RAS message that is sent from the terminating gateway to the gatekeeper to deliver information about the current ability of the gateway to take more calls. The gatekeeper doesn't have knowledge of the individual resources or the type of resources that the gateway takes into account. It's a simple yes/no toggle indication sent by the terminating gateway to control whether or not subsequent voice calls are routed to it.

As a CAC mechanism, RAI is unique in its ability to provide information on the terminating POTS connection. Other mechanisms we have discussed in this chapter enable CAC decisions based on local information at the outgoing gateway, and on the condition of the IP cloud between the outgoing gateway and terminating gateways. No other CAC mechanism is able to look at the availability of resources to terminate the POTS call at the terminating gateway—this is the value RAI brings to the table.

Because it is a gateway/gatekeeper indication, RAI CAC applies only to H.323 voice networks that utilize a gatekeeper design. RAI is also unique in that the CAC decision is controlled by the terminating gateway. In all the other methods, the CAC decision is controlled by the outgoing gateway or by the gatekeeper.

Gateway Calculation of Resources

The calculation to reach the yes/no decision is performed on the gateway. Different gateway platforms can use different algorithms. The H.323 standard doesn't prescribe the calculation or the resources to include in the calculation. It merely specifies the RAI message format and the fact that the gatekeeper must stop routing calls to a gateway that has indicated an inability to receive further calls until such time as the gateway informs the gatekeeper that it can take calls again.

To gauge resource availability for a call for the Cisco 2600 and 3600 series routers, the calculation algorithm considers each call as a unit according to the following formula:

- Each free DS-0 is a unit.

- Each hi-complexity DSP is two units.

- Each medium-complexity DSP is four units.

- RAI is calculated per platform, not per T1/E1 interface or per card (per network module, or specifically per NMM-HDV in the case of the Cisco 2600/3600). Only DS-0s reachable through a VoIP dial peer are included in the calculation.

Where and How RAI Is Used in Service Provider Networks

RAI is an indispensable feature in service provider networks that provide VoIP calling services such as debit/credit card calling and VoIP long-distance phone service. The general structure of these networks is shown in Figure 4-12.

Figure 4-12 *Service provider VoIP network topology.*

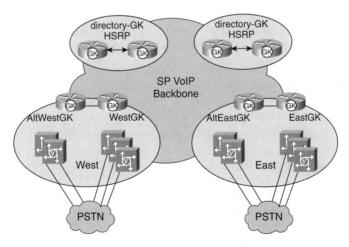

Around the world, there are points of presence (POPs) where racks of gateways (typically Cisco AS5300s) connect to the PSTN with T1/E1 trunks—frequently PRI trunks. Call routing is managed through several levels of gatekeepers. Call volume is high and these gateways handle voice traffic only—no data traffic other than minimal IP routing and network management traffic.

When a customer on the West Coast dials into the network and calls a number on the East Coast, the East Coast gatekeeper must select an East Coast gateway that has an available PSTN trunk to terminate the call; otherwise, the customer call will fail. If the call fails, either the outgoing gateway must retry the call or the customer must redial the call. In either case, there's no guarantee the same out-of-capacity terminating gateway will not be selected again.

Both scenarios are inefficient and provide poor customer service. It's important, therefore, that calls are not routed by the gatekeeper to a terminating gatekeeper that cannot terminate the call—not because of IP capacity in this case, but because of PSTN trunk capacity.

In general, calls will be load-balanced by the gatekeeper across the terminating gateways in its zone. But the gateways could have different levels of T1/E1 capacity, and by sheer load-balancing, one gateway could become shorter on resources than another. In this situation, RAI is imperative—so the overloaded terminating gateway can initiate an indication to the gatekeeper that it is too busy to take more calls.

Where and How RAI Is Used in Enterprise Networks

RAI is generally less applicable in enterprise networks than in service provider networks. This is because there is often only one gateway at each site, as shown in Figure 4-13. This is almost always true for the large number of small sites that connect to a much smaller number of large sites in the typical enterprise network. Even at the large sites, there might be multiple T1/E1 trunks to the attached PBX, but there are seldom multiple gateways.

If there is only one gateway that can terminate a call to a *called user* (where *called user* is a specific PBX and a specific gateway in the network), then RAI does not provide much network intelligence that is not already available. With no alternate gateway to handle excess calls, a call will fail whenever the single terminating gateway is too busy. Also, in enterprise networks, the probability of congestion is typically higher in the IP cloud than in the number of terminating POTS trunks. This is often the other way around for the service provider networks previously discussed.

In spite of these limitations, RAI can still be used for enterprise networks, provided the gateway-PBX connections at the remote sites are T1/E1 trunks. If a terminating gateway is too busy, it triggers a PSTN reroute instead of selecting an alternate gateway, as in the service provider network situation.

Figure 4-13 *Enterprise VoIP network topology.*

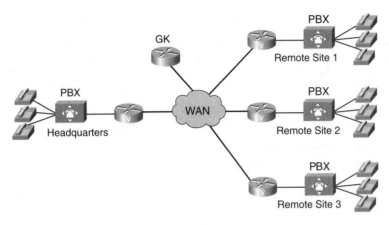

RAI Operation

From the preceding discussion of where and how RAI is used in service provider and enterprise networks, it is clear that RAI is most useful in situations where there are multiple terminating gateways that can reach the same destination [called] phone number. However, RAI has value in any situation where the desire is to prevent a call from being routed to a gateway that does not have the POTS capacity to terminate the call.

When a gatekeeper receives an RAI unavailable indication from a gateway, it removes that gateway from its gateway selection algorithm for the phone numbers that gateway would normally terminate. An RAI available indication received later will return the gateway to the selection algorithm of the gatekeeper.

RAI is an optional H.323 feature. When implementing a network, therefore, it is prudent to verify that both the gateways and gatekeepers under consideration support this feature. Cisco gatekeepers support RAI; Cisco gateway support for RAI is detailed in a later section.

RAI Configuration

RAI on the gateway is configured with high-water and low-water mark thresholds, as shown in Figure 4-14. When resource use, according to the calculation algorithm given earlier, goes above the high-water mark (configured as a percent), an RAI unavailable is sent to the gatekeeper. When resource availability falls below the low-water mark, an RAI available is sent to the gatekeeper. To prevent hysteresis based on the arrival or disconnection of a single call, the high-water and low-water marks should be configured some percentage points apart.

Figure 4-14 *RAI configuration.*

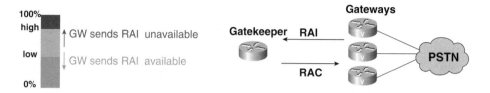

The following is general CLI syntax to configure RAI:

```
resource threshold [all] [high %-value] [low %-value]
```

The following is a sample configuration for RAI:

```
gateway
   resource threshold high 90 low 75
```

RAI Platform Support

The Cisco AS5300 has supported RAI since Cisco IOS Release 12.0(5)T. The Cisco 26x0/
36x0 series routers have supported RAI for T1/E1 connections only, not for analog trunks,
since Cisco IOS Release 12.1(3)T. The other IOS gateways, including the Cisco 1750,
MC3810, 7200, and 7500 do not yet support RAI as of Cisco IOS Release 12.1(5)T or 12.2
mainline). The RAI calculation includes DSPs and DS-0s and might not be the same for all
platforms. In current software, CPU and memory are not yet included in the RAI
availability indication.

Table 4-15 evaluates the RAI mechanism against the CAC evaluation criteria described
earlier in this chapter.

Table 4-15 *Summary of RAI*

	Evaluation Criteria	Value
1	VoX supported	VoIP only
2	Trunking/IP telephony	Trunking
		Potentially IP telephony, but CM does not yet support RAI
3	Platform/Release	AS5300: Cisco IOS Release 12.0(5)T
		2600/3600 T1/E1: Cisco IOS Release 12.1(2)XH / 12.1(3)T
4	PBX trunk types supported	All
5	End-to-end/Local/IP cloud	Local (at the terminating gateway)
		DSP and DS-0 resources; algorithm platform dependent

Table 4-15   *Summary of RAI (Continued)*

	Evaluation Criteria	Value
6	Per call/ interface/endpoint	Per gateway
7	Topology awareness	None
8	Guarantees QoS for duration of call	None
9	Post-dial delay	None
10	Messaging network overhead	Occasional RAI toggle between gateway and gatekeeper

Gatekeeper Zone Bandwidth

Another CAC mechanism that is specific to H.323 gatekeeper networks is the ability of the gatekeeper to impose bandwidth limitations in zones. Different levels of Cisco IOS Software provide different specific capabilities within this feature. In Cisco IOS Release 12.1(5)T and 12.2 mainline, the gatekeeper is able to limit both the bandwidth of calls in its local zone and the bandwidth used between its zone and any other remote zone in the network.

Gatekeeper Zone Bandwidth Operation

Address translation and zone management are two of the primary functions of an H.323 gatekeeper. The zone bandwidth feature enables the gatekeeper to essentially control the number of simultaneous calls that can be active. For the purpose of understanding how the feature operates, let's assume a voice call is equal to 64 kbps of bandwidth. How the number of calls limit of the gatekeeper translates to the actual bandwidth used by those calls will be addressed in a later section.

Single Zone Topology

Figure 4-15 shows a single-zone gatekeeper network with two gateways. This illustrates gatekeeper CAC in its simplest form. If the WAN bandwidth of the link between the two gateways can carry no more than two calls, the gatekeeper has to be configured so it denies the third call. Assuming every call is 64 kbps, the gatekeeper is configured with a zone bandwidth limitation of 128 kbps to achieve CAC in this simple topology.

Figure 4-15 *Simple single-zone topology.*

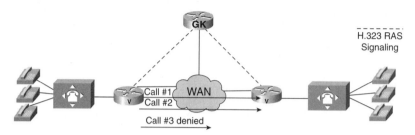

The amount of bandwidth actually used by a voice call is not necessarily the same as the amount of bandwidth requested or tracked by the gatekeeper. Features such as codec, cRTP, Layer 2 and 3 header overheads, and VAD are often transparent to the gatekeeper. Depending on what the voice gateway requests of the gatekeeper, and in some cases, this is a blanket 64 or 128 kbps per call, the zone bandwidth configuration on the gatekeeper should be treated as a "count of calls" more than as an absolute indication of bandwidth really occupied by the calls.

Most networks, however, are not as simple as the preceding one. Figure 4-16 shows a more complex topology, but it's still configured as a single-zone network. In this topology, the legs in the WAN cloud each have separate bandwidth provisioning and therefore separate capabilities of how many voice calls can be carried across that leg. The numbers on the WAN legs in Figure 4-16 show the maximum number of calls that can be carried across that leg.

Figure 4-16 *Complex single-zone topology.*

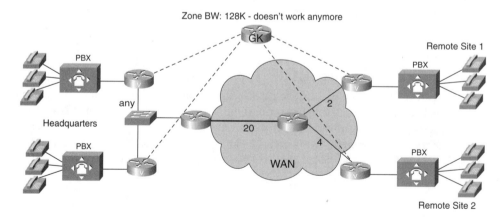

Consider now that the gatekeeper zone bandwidth is still set to a maximum of 128 K, thus allowing no more than two simultaneous calls. This is the desired behavior of the network if both calls involve Site 1—the gatekeeper will protect the bandwidth of the WAN link from Site 1 to the WAN aggregation point by not allowing more than two calls across that link. But if both calls are within the Headquarters site, there is no reason to allow only two calls because there is plenty of bandwidth in the campus backbone.

Multi-Zone Topology

To solve the single-zone problem of reducing the network to the capabilities of the lowest-capacity WAN link anywhere, you can design the network with multiple gatekeeper zones. A good starting point is to create one zone per site, as shown in Figure 4-17.

Figure 4-17 *Simple enterprise multi-zone topology.*

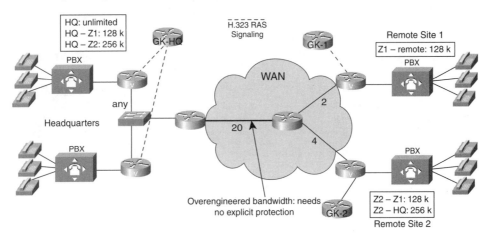

The Site 1 gatekeeper limits the number of calls active in Site 1 (regardless of where those calls originate or terminate) to 2 (128 K). Because only one gateway is at Site 1, there's no need to configure a limit for the intra-zone call traffic. All inter-zone traffic is limited to two calls to protect the WAN link connecting Site 1.

At Site 2, there is also a single gateway and, therefore, no need to limit the intra-zone call traffic. Separate inter-zone limits exist for the following:

- Calls between Site 2 and the Headquarters site (here the limiting factor is the maximum of four calls on the WAN link connecting Site 2)

- Calls between Site 2 and Site 1 (here the limiting factor is the maximum of two calls on the WAN link connecting Site 1)

The Headquarters site has a similar configuration except that calls are unlimited within the Site, not because there is a single gateway, but because ample bandwidth exists between the gateways at that site.

In the preceding network topology, gatekeeper CAC provides sufficient granularity to protect voice traffic across the low-speed WAN access links. But consider another network topology in which there are multiple gateways per zone, with each gateway (the remote sites) having a separate WAN link to the aggregation point (see Figure 4-18).

Figure 4-18 *Complex enterprise multi-zone topology.*

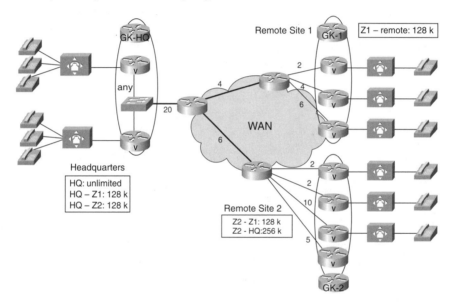

Of the three gateways in remote Site 1, the lowest WAN access link can carry a maximum of two simultaneous calls. As the bandwidth limitation is configured per zone and not per gateway, there is no facility within gatekeeper CAC to limit the calls to specific gateways within the zone. Your best choice is to configure the network for the lowest common denominator link: for both remote Sites 1 and 2, this is 128 kbps of bandwidth, or two calls.

This configuration will ensure proper voice quality at all times, but it's also wasteful of the gateways that could terminate more calls without oversubscribing their WAN bandwidth. In this network configuration, CAC will be activated too soon and will deflect certain calls over to the PSTN when in fact they could have been carried by the WAN. So in this type of topology, gatekeeper CAC isn't sufficient to protect voice quality over the WAN link and also optimize the bandwidth use of all WAN links.

The last configuration to consider is a service provider network where the gateways in the POPs are connected via Fast Ethernet to the WAN edge router. This is shown in Figure 4-19.

Figure 4-19 *Service provider topology with multiple gateways per zone.*

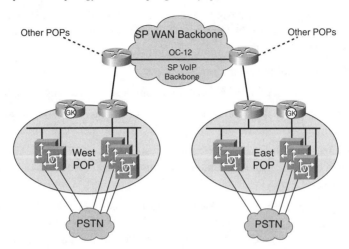

In this network, gatekeeper CAC is again sufficient, although there are multiple gateways per zone. That's because the connections to specific gateways within the zone are not the links that need protection. The bandwidth that needs protection is the WAN access link going into the backbone that aggregates the call traffic from all gateways. A gatekeeper bandwidth limitation for the zone will limit the number of calls over that link. It is assumed that the OC-12 backbone link is over-engineered and requires no protection.

In summary, a multi-zone gatekeeper network offers the following CAC attributes:

- The WAN bandwidth at each connecting site can be protected, provided each site is also a zone. For small remote sites in an enterprise network, this often translates into a zone per gateway, which may or may not be a practical design.

- The bandwidth within a site can be protected if necessary, but this is frequently of little value because there is only one gateway in the site (small remote offices, or a CPE entrypoint to a service provider Managed Network Service) or because there is a high-speed LAN between the gateways (large sites and service provider POPs).

- Gatekeeper CAC is a method well suited to limit calls between sites.

- Gatekeeper CAC cannot protect the bandwidth on WAN segments not directly associated with the zones. For example, the backbone link marked with 20 calls in the simple enterprise topology in Figure 4-17 cannot be protected by gatekeeper CAC unless we follow the lowest common denominator approach. That's why we over-provisioned the bandwidth on this link for the maximum number of calls possible.

Zone-per-Gateway Design

As the zone-per-gateway design offers the finest granularity of gatekeeper CAC, it is worth exploring a little further. In enterprise networks, this often makes sense from the following points of view:

- Geographical considerations.
- CAC to protect the WAN access link into a site containing a single gateway.
- Dialing plans often coincide with sites, so a zone prefix easily translates to the gateway serving that site if the gateway is equivalent to a zone.

A gatekeeper is a logical concept, not a physical concept. Each gatekeeper doesn't mean a separate box in the network; it merely means a separate "local zone" statement in the configuration.

Where combined gateway/gatekeeper software images are available (as in Cisco IOS Release 12.1(5)T and 12.2 mainline), each gateway—at small remote sites in particular—can also be its own gatekeeper, provided the CPU of that platform is sufficient for all these functions. (It likely also serves as the WAN edge router.)

With all this said, a zone-per-gateway design nevertheless thwarts the scalability aspect that gatekeepers bring to H.323 networks, and largely negates the "centralized dial plan" aspect of gatekeeper networks unless the dial plan is implemented entirely on a separate level using directory gatekeepers. You should carefully consider the pros and cons of such a design.

Gatekeeper In CallManager Networks

Of all the CAC mechanisms discussed in this chapter, gatekeeper zone bandwidth is the only method applicable to multi-site distributed CallManager networks. In this scenario, the CallManager behaves like a VoIP gateway to the H.323 gatekeeper, as shown in Figure 4-20.

Zone Bandwidth Calculation

The gatekeeper doesn't have any knowledge of network topology and doesn't know how much bandwidth is available for calls. Nor does the gatekeeper know how much of the configured bandwidth on the links is currently used by other traffic. What the gatekeeper does is take a fixed amount of bandwidth, statically configured on the gatekeeper as we've seen in the preceding network examples, then subtract a certain amount of bandwidth for each call that is set up. Bandwidth is returned to the pool when a call is disconnected. If a request for a new call causes the remaining bandwidth to become less than zero, the call is denied. The gatekeeper therefore does not do bandwidth reservation of any kind; it merely does a static calculation to decide whether or not a new call should be allowed.

Figure 4-20 *Gatekeeper in a CallManager topology.*

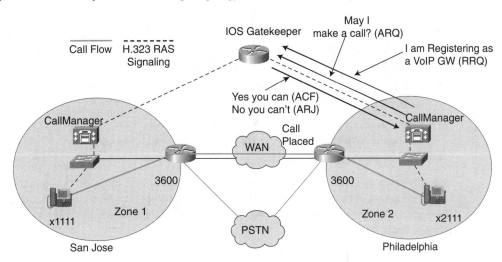

It is up to the gateways to inform the gatekeeper of how much bandwidth is required for a call. Video gateways will therefore potentially request a different bandwidth for every call setup: One video session might require 256 kbps, another 384 kbps. Voice gateways should take codec, Layer 2 encapsulation and compression features such as Compressed Real-Time Protocol (cRTP) into account when requesting bandwidth from the gatekeeper. Sometimes, these features are not known at the time of call setup, in which case a bandwidth change request can be issued to the gatekeeper after call setup to adjust the amount of bandwidth used by the call. At the time this book went to print, this functionality was not yet implemented on Cisco gateways.

In the previous examples, you've assumed a fixed bandwidth of 64 kbps per call. This is how Cisco H.323 gateways are implemented in current software. The codec and other bandwidth-determining features such as cRTP are not currently being taken into account when the bandwidth of a call is considered by the gatekeeper zone bandwidth calculation. This will change in future software releases, but until then, implementing this feature requires a manual mathematical calculation of how many calls should be allowed based on n times 64 kbps per call and the total available WAN bandwidth.

Gatekeeper zone bandwidth nevertheless remains an inexact science because the gateway might not have full knowledge of the bandwidth required by the call. Layer 2 technologies used in the WAN or backbone legs of the network and hop-by-hop features, such as cRTP, might be used deeper into the network than the gateway is aware of. The following are some examples:

- The gateway might be attached to an Ethernet segment in a campus network where cRTP does not apply and where the Layer 2 headers are larger than they would be for Frame Relay or multi-link PPP on the WAN legs.

- A different codec can be used in the campus network from the WAN segments, leveraging codec transcoding functionality at the WAN edge.

- In the backbone of the network, ATM can be used as the transport technology and cell fill should be taken into account for bandwidth calculations.

- cRTP can be used at the WAN edge router.

Both the gateway and the gatekeeper are unaware of the preceding network topology information unless the gateway is also the WAN edge router, in which case it has slightly more visibility. But it probably still won't see an ATM backbone and therefore won't account for it.

Zone Bandwidth Configuration

As of Cisco IOS Releases 12.1(5)T and 12.2 mainline, the following types of zone bandwidth limitations can be configured on the gatekeeper:

- The maximum bandwidth for all H.323 traffic between the local zone and a specified remote zone. (If desired, this configuration can be repeated individually for each remote zone.)

- The maximum bandwidth allowed for a single session in the local zone (typically used for video applications, not for voice).

- The maximum bandwidth for all H.323 traffic allowed collectively to all remote zones.

The following is the syntax for the gatekeeper:

```
[no] bandwidth {interzone | total | session} {default | zone zone-name}
    max-bandwidth
[no] bandwidth remote max-bandwidth
```

Gatekeeper Zone Bandwidth Summary

Gatekeeper CAC works well in network designs where the desire is to limit the number of calls between sites. This might be required due to either bandwidth limitations or business policy. If there are bandwidth limitations on the WAN legs, manual calculations can be done to translate the maximum number of calls to be allowed between sites into a bandwidth figure that will cause the gatekeeper to deny calls exceeding that number.

Gatekeeper zone bandwidth control is a key part of H.323 video network designs. Here bandwidth is more of an issue because video uses much more bandwidth per session than voice. In addition, different video sessions can request different amounts of bandwidth for video transmissions, making the manual calculation method used for voice almost unusable.

One additional thing to keep in mind when designing gatekeeper CAC is that redundant gatekeepers complicate the issues somewhat. For example, if HSRP is used on the gatekeepers for redundancy, there is no shared database between the gatekeepers. If the primary gatekeeper fails, the secondary gatekeeper can take over, but it has no knowledge of how much bandwidth is currently used in the zone or how many calls are currently active. Until its information converges back to reflect reality, the secondary gatekeeper will allow too many calls onto the network. If alternate gatekeepers are used as the redundancy method, this problem is circumvented.

A major advantage of gatekeeper CAC is that it is the only CAC method that can incorporate mixed networks of Cisco IOS gateways and CallManagers with IP phones.

Table 4-16 evaluates the gatekeeper zone bandwidth mechanism against the CAC evaluation criteria described earlier in this chapter.

Table 4-16   *Summary of Gatekeeper Zone Bandwidth*

	Evaluation Criteria	Value
1	VoX supported	VoIP/H.323 only
2	Trunking/IP telephony	Trunking and IP telephony
		Some caveats if both CM and Cisco IOS gateways used in the same zone
3	Platform/Release	Cisco IOS gateways since Cisco IOS Release 11.3
		CM has recent changes in E.164 registration, and bandwidth requested per call
4	PBX trunk types supported	All
5	End-to-end/Local/IP cloud	End to end between outgoing gateway and terminating gateway, although not aware of the network topology (bandwidth availability) in between
6	Per call/ interface/endpoint	Per call
7	Topology awareness	None
8	Guarantees QoS for duration of call	None
9	Post-dial delay	None
10	Messaging network overhead	Part of the gatekeeper RAS messaging

Resource Reservation Protocol

Resource Reservation Protocol (RSVP) is the only CAC mechanism that makes a bandwidth reservation and doesn't make a call admission decision based on a "best guess look-ahead" before the call is set up. This gives RSVP the unique advantage of not only providing CAC for voice, but also guaranteeing the QoS against changing network conditions for the duration of the call.

RSVP Feature Rollout

RSVP is synchronized with the H.323 state machine in Cisco IOS Release 12.1(5)T, and is therefore available in 12.2. mainline code. Various components of this feature appeared in earlier releases of the software, but it was not until Cisco IOS Release 12.1(5)T that all the elements for CAC became available. Following is a short summary of RSVP support:

- RSVP sync with H.323 Standard Connect: Cisco IOS Release 12.1(1)T
- RSVP support for LLQ: Cisco IOS Release 12.1(3)T
- RSVP sync with H.323 FastConnect: Cisco IOS Release 12.1(3)XI / 12.1(5)T
- RSVP support for FR PVCs: Cisco IOS Release 12.1(5)T

RSVP support for ATM PVCs and RSVP support on IP phones are being planned for future software releases.

RSVP Reservation for a Voice Call

Figure 4-21 shows a call flow of the H.323 call setup messages and the RSVP reservation messages.

The H.323 setup is suspended before the destination phone, triggered by the H.225 alerting message, starts ringing. The RSVP reservation is made in both directions because a voice call requires a two-way speech path and therefore bandwidth in both directions.
The terminating gateway ultimately makes the CAC decision based on whether or not both reservations succeed. At that point the H.323 state machine continues either with an H.225 Alerting/Connect (the call is allowed and proceeds), or with an H.225 Reject/Release (call is denied). The RSVP reservation is in place by the time the destination phone starts ringing and the caller hears ringback.

Figure 4-21 *RSVP call setup for H.323 voice call.*

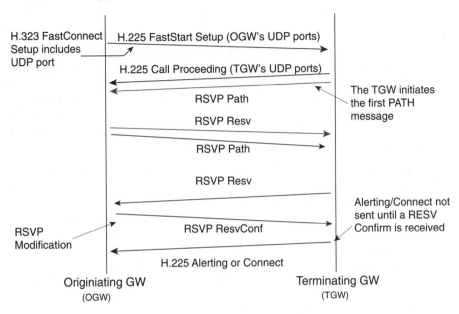

RSVP has the following important differences from other CAC methods discussed in this chapter:

- The ability to maintain QoS for the duration of the call.

- Topology awareness. In concept, the RSVP reservation is installed on every interface the call will traverse through the network (we will look at exceptions to this in later sections), and therefore will ensure bandwidth over every segment without needing to know the actual bandwidth provisioning on an interface, nor the path on which the routing protocols will direct the packets. (RSVP therefore adjusts automatically to network configuration changes, and no manual calculations are necessary to keep different aspects of the configuration synchronized.)

RSVP is an end-to-end reservation per call and only has visibility for that call. It is unaware of how many other calls are active from a site or across an interface, or the source or destination of any other call. Therefore, there is no way to do aggregate levels of CAC with RSVP, such as the site-to-site CAC we can do with gatekeeper zone bandwidth control.

Classification for Voice Packets into Low Latency Queuing

Low latency queuing (LLQ) is one of the key Cisco QoS mechanisms to ensure quality for voice as it prioritizes voice packets over data packets at the router egress interface. For this to work, voice packets must be classified so that they are placed in the priority queue (PQ) portion of LLQ. Traditionally, this is accomplished with access list (ACL) classification, where the TCP (signaling) and UDP (media) ports are matched to funnel voice packets into the appropriate queues.

As a general Cisco IOS feature, RSVP has its own set of reserved queues within weighted fair queuing (WFQ) for traffic with RSVP reservations. These queues, though they have a low weight, are separate from the PQ. Packets in reserved queues do not get priority over packets from other queues other than by virtue of their low weight. It has long been known that this treatment (a low weight queue inside WFQ) is insufficient for voice quality over a congested interface with several different flows of traffic. Therefore, when RSVP is configured for a voice call, it is necessary for the voice packets to be classified into the PQ. RSVP data flow packets should not be classified into the PQ in this case.

RSVP uses a profile to determine whether or not a flow of packets is a voice flow. The profile takes packet sizes and arrival rates and other parameters into account, and, if a packet flow conforms to the parameters, it's considered a voice flow. If not, it's considered a non-voice flow, which includes both data and video. The internal profile is tuned so that all voice traffic originating from a Cisco IOS gateway will fall within the parameters and will therefore be considered a voice flow without needing extra configuration. For third-party applications, such as NetMeeting, the profile might have to be tuned to pick up that kind of traffic. Figure 4-22 shows how this is accomplished.

Figure 4-22 *RSVP packet classification criteria.*

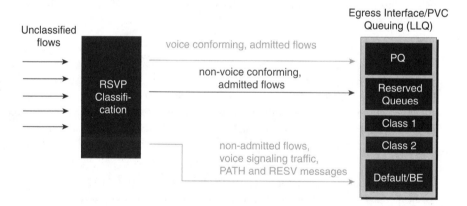

RSVP is the first egress interface classifier to examine an arriving packet. If RSVP considers this a voice flow, the packets will be put into the PQ portion of LLQ. If the flow does not conform to the voice profile, but is nevertheless an RSVP reserved flow, it will be placed into the normal RSVP reserved queues. If the flow is neither a voice flow nor a data RSVP flow, the other egress interface classifiers (such as ACLs and "match" statements within a class map) will attempt to classify the packet for queuing.

It is important to note that RSVP will classify only voice bearer traffic, not signaling traffic. One of the other classification mechanisms such as ACLs or DSCPs must still be used to classify the voice signaling traffic if any treatment better than Best Effort is desired for that traffic. If left up to RSVP alone, signaling traffic will be considered Best Effort traffic as shown in Figure 4-22.

Bandwidth Allocation with RSVP and LLQ

RSVP voice traffic can be mixed with "priority class" traffic (within the policy-map) in the PQ, but the configuration is simpler if a single voice classification mechanism is used. We recommend that you use one or the other for voice, but not both: Either configure RSVP to prioritize voice traffic, or configure policy-maps with priority bandwidth and classify the voice traffic with ACLs into LLQ. Both can be used together, but they don't share bandwidth allocations, which will lead to an inefficient use of bandwidth on the interface.

As bandwidth is defined in the configuration for the egress interfaces, all the bandwidth and priority classes will be allocated bandwidth at configuration time. No bandwidth is allocated to RSVP at configuration time; it requests its bandwidth when the traffic flow starts up—when a voice call starts. RSVP gets allocated bandwidth from the pool that's left after the other features have already allocated their bandwidth.

Bandwidth Per Codec

Both LLQ and RSVP see the Layer 3 IP packet. Layer 2 encapsulations (FR and MLPPP, for example) are added after queuing, so the bandwidth allocated by both LLQ and RSVP for a call is based on the Layer 3 bandwidth of the packets. This number will be slightly different from the actual bandwidth used on the interface once Layer 2 headers and trailers have been incorporated. RSVP bandwidth reserved for a call also excludes both cRTP and VAD. Table 4-17 summarizes the bandwidth RSVP will allocate for calls using different Cisco IOS gateway codecs.

Table 4-17   *RSVP Bandwidth Reservations for Voice Codecs*

Codec	Bandwidth Reserved per Call in LLQ
G.711 (a-law and μ-law)	80 k
G.723.1 and G.723.1A (5.3 k)	22 k
G.723.1 and G.723.1A (6.3 k)	23 k
G.726 (16 k)	32 k
G.726 (24 k)	40 k
G.726 (32 k)	48 k
G.728	32 k
G.729 (all versions)	24 k

RSVP Configuration

The following are three things to configure on a gateway that will originate or terminate voice traffic using RSVP:

- Turn on the synchronization feature between RSVP and H.323. This is a global command and is turned on by default when Cisco IOS Release 12.1(5)T or later is loaded.

- Configure RSVP on both the originating and terminating sides of the VoIP dial-peers. Configure the **guaranteed-delay** keyword on both the **reg-qos** dial-peer configuration command (requested QoS) and the **acc-qos** dial-peer configuration command (acceptable QoS) for RSVP to act as a CAC mechanism. (Other combinations of parameters might lead to a reservation, but no CAC.)

- Enable RSVP and specify the maximum bandwidth on the interfaces that the call will traverse.

The RSVP-related CLI is shown in Example 4-4.

Example 4-4 *RSVP*

```
call rsvp-sync
!
!Global command enabling RSVP as CAC, turned on by default.
controller T1 1/0
 ds0-group 0 timeslots 1-24
 !
 ip rsvp pq-profile voice-like
 !
!RSVP classification profile; default is ok for all IOS gateway voice traffic.
voice-port 1/0:0
 !
dial-peer voice 100 pots
 destination-pattern 2......
 port 1/0:0
 !
dial-peer voice 300 voip
 destination-pattern 3......
 session target ipv4:10.10.2.2
 req-qos guaranteed-delay
!Configure RSVP CAC for voice calls using the dial peer.
 acc-qos guaranteed-delay
 !Configure RSVP CAC for voice calls using the dial peer.
```

The RSVP-related CLI for a PPP interface is shown in Example 4-5.

Example 4-5 *RSVP: PPP Interface Example*

```
interface Serial0/1
 bandwidth 1536
 ip address 10.10.1.1 255.255.255.0
 encapsulation ppp
fair-queue 64 256 36
!Enables WFQ as the basic queuing method. Results in LLQ with RSVP.
ip rsvp bandwidth 1152 24
!Enables RSVP on the interface.
```

The RSVP-related CLI for a Frame Relay interface is shown in Example 4-6.

Example 4-6 *RSVP: Frame Relay Interface Example*

```
interface Serial0/0
 bandwidth 1536
 encapsulation frame-relay
 no fair-queue
 frame-relay traffic-shaping
 !
interface Serial0/0.2 point-to-point
 ip address 10.10.2.2 255.255.255.0
 frame-relay interface-dlci 17
  class VoIPoFR
ip rsvp bandwidth 64 24
 !
!Enables RSVP on the sub-interface.
map-class frame-relay VoIPoFR
 no frame-relay adaptive-shaping
 frame-relay cir 128000
 frame-relay bc 1280
 frame-relay mincir 128000
 frame-relay fair-queue
!Enables WFQ as the basic queuing method. Results in LLQ with RSVP.
 frame-relay fragment 160
```

RSVP Scalability

Concern is often expressed about RSVP scalability in terms of the large number of
individual flow reservations that might be necessary across high-speed backbone links
where many voice calls have aggregated. Indeed, it might not make sense to do individual
flow management over OC-12 backbone network links, for example. For this reason, in
Cisco IOS Release 12.1(5)T code and later, if RSVP is not configured on any interface on
a platform, RSVP messages are passed through transparently. No reservation is made or
managed, but the PATH and RESV packets are not dropped.

This makes it possible to build hybrid topologies where RSVP is used around the edges of the network to protect slower WAN access links from oversubscription, while the high-speed campus and WAN backbone links do not use RSVP. Of course, this topology compromises the true end-to-end reservation and guaranteed QoS promise of RSVP, but it might be a workable compromise. The backbone links can receive a measure of protection from over-engineering or from one of the other CAC mechanisms discussed earlier, while the highest contention links (typically the WAN edge) can make use of RSVP.

Figure 4-23 shows a hypothetical network that is configured for DiffServ in the backbone and campus, but uses RSVP reservations across the WAN edge links.

Figure 4-23 *Hybrid DiffServ/RSVP network topology.*

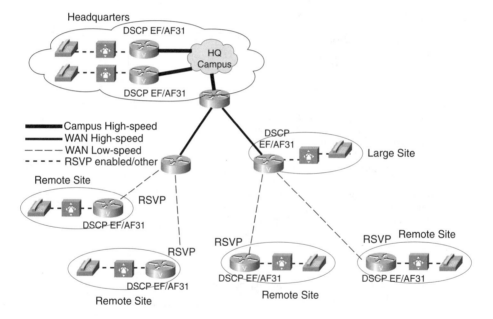

RSVP CAC Summary

Keep these factors in mind regarding the use of RSVP as a CAC mechanism.

In current Cisco IOS Software, H.323 calls are initiated by default using FastConnect when RSVP is configured:

- RSVP packets (PATH and RESV) travel as Best Effort traffic.
- WFQ must be enabled on an interface/PVC as a basis for LLQ.

RSVP is a true end-to-end CAC mechanism only if configured on every interface that a call traverses.

For the unique ability to serve as an end-to-end CAC mechanism, and guarantee the QoS for the entire duration of the call, RSVP does incur some "costs" on the network:

- Signaling (messaging and processing).

- Per flow state (memory).

- Post-dial delays.

- RSVP doesn't provide for call redirection after call setup if a link in the network should fail.

- RSVP is not yet supported on the Cisco IP phones.

Table 4-18 evaluates the RSVP mechanism against the CAC evaluation criteria described earlier in this chapter.

Table 4-18   *Summary of RSVP*

	Evaluation Criteria	Value
1	VoX supported	VoIP/H.323 only
2	Trunking/IP telephony	Currently trunking only
3	Platform/Release	Cisco IOS gateways Cisco IOS Releases 12.1(5)T and 12.2
4	PBX trunk types supported	All
5	End-to-end/Local/IP cloud	End to end between outgoing gateway and terminating gatekeeper (provided all intermediate nodes are RSVP configured)
		Could be used at WAN edge with DiffServ backbone
6	Per call/ interface/endpoint	Per call
7	Topology awareness	Yes
8	Guarantees QoS for duration of call	Yes
9	Post-dial delay	Yes
10	Messaging network overhead	PATH/RESV and periodic keepalives

Feature Combinations, Interactions, and Sequencing

Although some overlap exists between the functionality they provide, several of these solve different aspects of the CAC problem and make sense to use together in a network design. Two questions often arise:

1 Can two CAC methods be used together on the same gateway at the same time for the same calls?

2 If the answer to the preceding question is yes, in what sequence is the CAC decision reached?

Figure 4-24 summarizes the sequencing of CAC features that can be active on an outgoing gateway, based on Cisco IOS Releases 12.1(5)T and 12.2. As features and software releases change, and as bugs are fixed, this information might change without notice. As you can see from the flow diagram in Figure 4-24, the only features that are mutually exclusive are RSVP and PSTN Fallback.

Figure 4-24 *Sequence of CAC feature utilization on an outgoing gateway.*

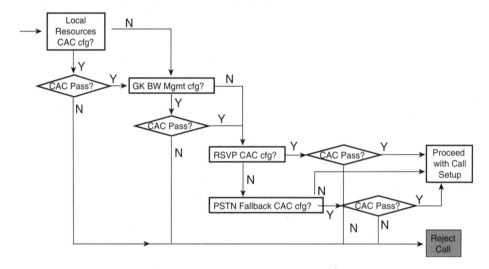

When Should I Use Which CAC Mechanism?

With a plethora of CAC mechanisms available, the immediate design question is, "When should I use which CAC feature?" As has been pointed out during the discussions of the individual features, and through the comparisons and summaries that have been drawn throughout the text, the various features often do different things and solve different aspects of a CAC problem. Some of these aspects can be more important design criteria for your network than others. Thus, there is no single recipe prescribing exactly when to use which mechanism. Like all other software features, you have to make the decision while considering your network design goals.

This section attempts to provide some guidance concerning design criteria that might exist for your network, and if so, which features might fit the solution. Before proceeding, it should be noted that the first feature selection criteria that should be used are the Evaluation Criteria listed at the end of each feature section. For example, if a SIP-based VoIP network is being designed, there is no point in considering an H.323 CAC feature. Provided you have already accomplished that level of screening, use the suggestions in this section to further narrow your choice of features.

CAC in Connection Trunk Networks

Unlike switched networks, where each call is set up individually across the packet network after a user dials, "connection trunk" networks consist of nailed-up connections across the packet network. The PBX might perceive that it makes each call individually, but the packet network has a permanent trunk in place (a point-to-point link—similar in concept to a leased line) that is always present, always ready, and always terminates to a fixed and predetermined destination. These nailed-up packet network configurations are typically used when some signaling is present between the PBXs that must pass transparently and unchanged through the packet network. The gateways cannot interpret the signaling; they merely tunnel it through the packet network.

The following are two major applications for this type of network:

- Networks in which signaling such as flash-hook and Message Waiting Indications (MWI) must be passed through the packet network to a PBX to be activated for OPX (Off Premise Extension) phones—phones that are separated by the packet network from the PBX from which they draw their features.

- Networks in which proprietary signaling is used between PBXs to enable private PBX networking features. (Examples include Lucent DCS, Siemens CorNet, NEC CCIS, and others.)

Cisco IOS gateway connection trunk configurations use the same basic tools (such as dial-peers) as switched networks to set up connections. The difference is that these "calls" are set up only once, when the gateway boots up or when the configuration is inserted, and remain in place indefinitely. If a link in the network should fail and bring the call down, the router will reestablish it at its earliest opportunity. Whether or not there is actually a real call active (with people talking) over this connection is transparent to the gateways. For this reason, the standard CAC mechanisms, in most cases, do not apply. Connection trunk configurations will not come up properly if there is not enough bandwidth for the connection, so once the configuration is in place, it is assumed that there is sufficient bandwidth available for the calls.

The following call-by-call CAC mechanisms apply only to switched networks and should not be used with connection trunk configurations:

- Max connections
- PSTN Fallback
- Gatekeeper bandwidth
- Gatekeeper RAI

Connection trunk configurations can, however, benefit from the PBX busyout CAC features. When something in the network is down and the nailed-up connections fail, or the interfaces they use fail, it would certainly be useful to busyout the trunk to the PBX. These features include:

- LVBO
- AVBO
- Trunk conditioning

In concept, RSVP could be used to guarantee (reserve) bandwidth for the nailed-up calls in order to protect the voice quality from fluctuating network conditions. However, because connection trunk networks are fixed, point-to-point connections, the number of calls active across any network segment (from the router's perspective) is fixed and relatively easily designed by manually engineering the bandwidth and by using standard LLQ configurations to ensure bandwidth. The value-add that RSVP can offer here should be carefully considered.

Areas of the Network to Protect

CAC methods are most useful and most needed in switched networks where it is often impossible to predict exactly how many calls might want to use a particular network leg at a given point in time. Statistical methods for engineering voice networks have existed for decades; nevertheless, there is no mechanism by which to know exactly who will call whom across the network at any given time. Unless the topology of the network is very simple, it is possible that bandwidth, at some point in the network, might be oversubscribed by too many calls. In the PSTN, this condition results in reorder tone or an intercept message indicating "all circuits are busy."

When considering CAC methods to trigger a comparable "all circuits are busy" condition when a packet network is too congested to carry a call, the goals of the network design must be considered. All the aspects of CAC shown in Figure 4-25 exist in every network, but some attributes will almost always be more important to a particular customer than others. The aspects of the network that might need protection with CAC features have been divided into four areas, as shown in Figure 4-25.

Figure 4-25 *Division of areas of the network.*

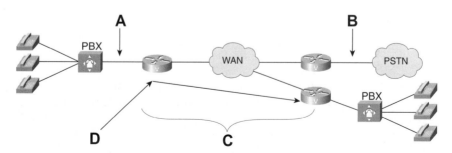

The area labeled A is the originating POTS connection. If it is important to keep the originating PBX from attempting to place a call onto the packet network when the network is incapable of completing the call, then the busyout CAC features should be considered. This might be important if hairpinning is an unacceptable call reject recovery method, or if the PBX/Key System does not have the ability to choose another route for a rejected or hairpinned call.

Area B is the terminating POTS side of the connection. If it is likely because of specific traffic patterns that the terminating POTS side is the part of network most susceptible to oversubscription, then gatekeeper RAI should be used. In enterprise networks, this is seldom of overarching importance, but in service provider networks, this is often an extremely important section of the network to protect.

Area C is the IP backbone part of the network. This is the most typical area of the packet network that enterprise customers (including Service Provider Managed Services networks) wish to protect their calls against, because this infrastructure is not dedicated to voice, but shared by many types of traffic. The CAC features protecting the network "cloud" include:

- PSTN Fallback
- Gatekeeper zone bandwidth
- RSVP

These CAC methods are all IP-based methods, which means that more CAC methods are available for VoIP networks than for VoFR and VoATM networks. VoIP also needs it more, because the Layer 2 technologies like FR and ATM cannot intrinsically protect against VoIP packet loss, as they can with VoFR and VoATM traffic.

Area D is a logical section of the network between sites. Regardless of the actual infrastructure connecting sites together, you might desire not to limit traffic within a site, or to limit it based on very different criteria than the traffic limitations between sites. For example, if the Headquarters location has the capability to handle 24 active calls at once, you might want to make sure that all 24 calls cannot be used by any one other site at any one time, but that there is a certain amount of capacity available to different remote sites so that the low-traffic sites don't get locked out by the high-traffic sites.

The CAC features you would use in this situation include max connections and gatekeeper zone bandwidth.

Network Topology Considerations

At a general level, two network topologies exist:

- Hub-and-spoke
- Multilayer hierarchical network with distribution layers

These two topologies are shown conceptually in Figure 4-26.

Figure 4-26 *Enterprise network topologies.*

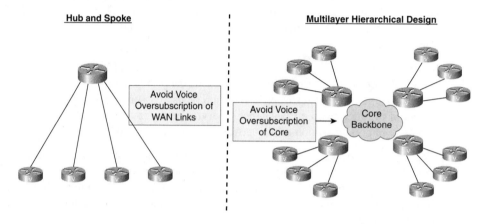

The hub-and-spoke network is the easiest to take care of. In this case, most of the CAC features are useful because only the spokes of the network need protection. There is no invisible backbone, and the spoke links might be the links connected to the gateways at the remote sites. Almost any of the CAC features listed here can be used to good effect in this type of network:

- Physical DS-0 limit
- Max connections
- AVBO
- PSTN Fallback
- Gatekeeper zone bandwidth
- RAI
- RSVP

The multilayer hierarchical network is more representative of larger networks where outlying sites aggregate at one or more layers of intermediate points before a core network that connects the highest-layer aggregation sites. Many of the CAC features will protect the WAN link at the lowest layer of the network, but few of them have visibility into the aggregation and core legs of the network. The ones that have visibility into the network include:

- AVBO
- PSTN Fallback
- RSVP

Summary

Call admission control is a method of deciding whether to accept or reject the establishment of a new voice call. The decision is based on whether or not the required network resources are available to provide suitable QoS for the additional call. In this chapter, we examined 10 different CAC mechanisms in three categories:

- **Local mechanisms** that function on the outgoing gateway and base their decisions on such things as the state of the outgoing LAN/WAN link

- **Measurement-based mechanisms** that look ahead into the packet network and gauge the state of the path to the destination

- **Resource-based mechanisms** that either calculate and compare the available versus the required resources, or compare the required bandwidth to that remaining from a specified bandwidth reservation

While describing the CAC mechanisms in detail, we also explained what resources are needed for a voice call and how they're determined, how the information is gathered to support the CAC decision, and which network component actually makes the CAC decision and when. We evaluated each CAC tool using a standard set of criteria designed to summarize the applicability of the tool and its impact on network operation.

Finally, we showed that, although some overlap exists between the functionality they provide, some CAC mechanisms can be used together in a network design to solve different aspects of the CAC problem.

Network Design Strategies

Designing Static Dial Plans for Large VoIP Networks

A *dial plan* is a numbering plan for a voice-enabled network. It's the way you assign individual or blocks of telephone numbers (E.164 addresses) to physical lines or circuits. The North American telephone network is designed around a 10-digit dial plan consisting of 3-digit area codes and 7-digit telephone numbers. For telephone numbers located within an area code, a 7-digit dial plan is used for the Public Switched Telephone Network (PSTN). Features within a telephone switch (such as Centrex) support a custom 5-digit dial plan for specific customers who subscribe to that service. Private branch exchanges (PBXs) also support variable-length dial plans, containing from 3 to 11 digits.

Dial plans in the H.323 network contain specific dialing patterns so that users can reach a particular telephone number. Access codes, area codes, specialized codes, and combinations of the numbers of digits dialed are all a part of any particular dial plan. Dial plans used with voice-capable routers essentially describe the process of determining which and how many digits to store in each of the configurations. If the dialed digits match the number and patterns, the call is processed for forwarding. Dial plans require knowledge of the network topology, current telephone number dialing patterns, proposed router locations, and traffic routing requirements. Currently, no standard protocol is defined for the dynamic routing of E.164 telephony addresses. Until a standards-based dynamic routing protocol for E.164 telephony addresses is developed, H.323 VoIP dial plans are statically configured and managed on gateway and gatekeeper platforms.

This chapter describes dial plan configuration recommendations on Cisco H.323 gateways and gatekeepers used to support large dial plans. It also illustrates how well-designed network architectures can help reduce the administrative burdens of managing static dial plans.

Components of Large H.323 Networks

The infrastructure of a typical H.323 VoIP network includes both gateways (GWs) and gatekeepers (GKs). In a typical service provider network, a number of gateways are deployed at POPs throughout the service provider's coverage area. A gatekeeper can be used to group these gateways into a logical zone of control and perform all call routing among them.

Larger H.323 VoIP networks might consist of multiple gatekeepers that segment the network into various local zones. In this case, gatekeepers must communicate with each other to route calls between gateways located in different zones. To simplify dial plan administration for these multi-gatekeeper networks, Cisco introduced the concept of a directory gatekeeper (DGK) to handle call routing between local gatekeepers. Figure 5-1 illustrates how these components of an H.323 network relate to one another.

Figure 5-1 *Relationship of gateways, gatekeepers, and directory gatekeepers.*

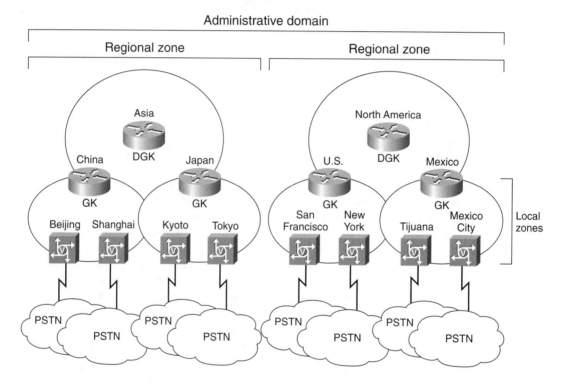

With respect to the VoIP dial plan, each component within the H.323 network has a specific responsibility. Gateways are responsible for edge routing decisions between the PSTN and the H.323 network, while gatekeepers and directory gatekeepers handle the core call routing logic among devices within the H.323 network. This chapter explains the configuration requirements for each of these network components.

For example, when presented with a call, gateways determine whether to send it to the PSTN or into the H.323 VoIP network. If it is sent into the H.323 VoIP network, the gateway then asks the gatekeeper to select the best endpoint to receive the call. Based on its routing table, the gatekeeper might find that this endpoint is a device within its own local zone of control and supply the IP address of the terminating endpoint. Alternatively, it might determine that the endpoint resides under the control of another remote gatekeeper. In this latter case, the gatekeeper would forward the location request (LRQ) to the remote gatekeeper either directly or through a directory gatekeeper. The remote gatekeeper would ultimately respond with the address of the terminating endpoint.

The communication between gateways and gatekeepers is based on standard H.323v2 registration, admission, and status (RAS) messages. Gateways query gatekeepers for routes using RAS admission request (ARQ) and admission confirmation (ACF) messages. Cisco gatekeepers and directory gatekeepers also communicate with each other using RAS location request (LRQ) and location confirmation (LCF) messages. Real-Time Transport Protocol (RTP) provides the end-to-end transport functions. Figure 5-2 shows an example of RAS messages sent between gateways and gatekeepers.

Figure 5-2   *Example of RAS messaging when Phone A calls Phone B.*

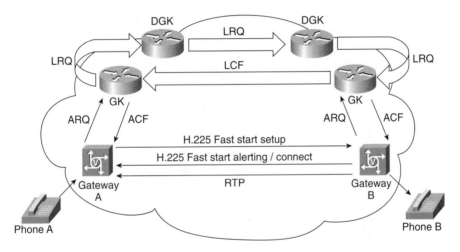

Design Methodology for Large-Scale Dial Plans

It's important to apply some basic design principles when designing a large-scale dial plan. Design options in this chapter will consider the following principles:

- Dial plan distribution
- Hierarchical design
- Simplicity in provisioning
- Reduction in post-dial delay
- Availability, fault tolerance, and redundancy

Dial Plan Distribution

Good dial plan architecture relies on effectively distributing the dial plan logic among the gateway and gatekeeper components. Isolating H.323 devices to a specific portion of the dial plan reduces the complexity of the configuration. Each component can focus on accomplishing specific tasks. Generally, local POP-specific details are handled at the local gateway; higher-level routing decisions are passed along to the gatekeepers and directory gatekeepers. A well-designed network places the majority of the dial plan logic at the gatekeeper and directory gatekeeper devices.

Hierarchical Design

Strive to keep the majority of the dial plan logic (routing decision-making and failover) at the highest component level. The directory gatekeeper is generally considered the highest device. By maintaining a hierarchical design, the addition and deletion of zones becomes more manageable. For example, scaling of the overall network is much easier when configuration changes need to be made to a single directory gatekeeper and a single zone gatekeeper instead of all the zone gatekeepers.

Simplicity in Provisioning

You should keep the dial plan on the gateways and gatekeepers as simple and symmetrical as possible. On the gateways, try to keep consistent dial plans by using translation rules to manipulate the local digit dialing patterns. These number patterns can be normalized into a standard format or pattern before the digits enter the VoIP core. Putting digits into a standard format simplifies gatekeeper zone prefix provisioning and gateway dial-peer management.

This methodology helps reduce dial-peer configurations on the outgoing POTS interface. If the gatekeeper can be provisioned to direct only calls of a certain area code to a particular gateway, then it is unnecessary to provision all of the individual gateways with their respective area codes. Instead, you might be able to generalize the gateway configurations. By normalizing the number, you also reduce the zone prefix search length, reducing the time it takes to search for a zone prefix match. For example, if you have the 0118943xxxx digit pattern, you can send the number as 8943xxxx and have the gatekeeper search on 89 as opposed to 01189.

Reduction in Post-Dial Delay

You should consider the effects of post-dial delay in the network. Gateway and gatekeeper zone design, translation rules, and sequential LRQs all affect post-dial delay. Strive to use these tools most efficiently to reduce post-dial delay.

Availability, Fault Tolerance, and Redundancy

Consider overall network availability and call success rate. Fault tolerance and redundancy within H.323 networks are most important at the gatekeeper level. Use of an alternate gatekeeper, sequential LRQs, and Hot Standby Routing Protocol (HSRP) help provide redundancy and fault tolerance in the H.323 network. As of Cisco IOS Release 12.2, gatekeeper redundancy can be configured for alternate gatekeepers and/or HSRP for gatekeepers.

H.323 Network Components in Large-Scale Dial Plans

This section discusses the basic components of an H.323 network and some of the advanced Cisco IOS commands that can be used when designing large-scale service provider network dial plans. These components are:

- Gateways
- Gatekeepers
- Directory gatekeepers

Gateways in Large-Scale Dial Plans

Gateway dial plan configurations focus on local PSTN access information for the edge of the H.323 network. This includes defining which E.164 prefixes are supported by the PSTN connections of the gateway. In large-scale service provider designs, you might rely on the gateway to perform *digit manipulation*, whereby the gateway takes a calling (or called) number and strips or adds (prefixes) digits before sending the number to its destination. The process of formatting the number to a pre-defined pattern is called *number normalization*.

Figure 5-3 illustrates an example of number normalization from the PSTN to the VoIP core. Digit manipulation can be configured on the incoming POTS port and/or the outgoing VoIP dial-peer to format a 7-, 10-, 11- or x-digit pattern into a fixed 10-digit pattern (USA-centric). The result is a number that has been normalized when it enters the VoIP cloud.

Figure 5-3 *Number normalization from PSTN to VoIP.*

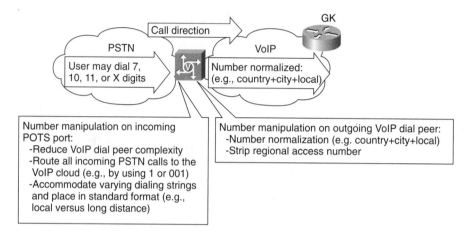

Translation Rules

The gateway uses the Cisco IOS translation rules to accomplish digit manipulation. Translation rules can be configured on the gateway's physical port or on a VoIP dial-peer. For example:

```
translation-rule 1
 Rule 0 ^0111.% 1
 Rule 1 ^0112.% 2
 Rule 2 ^0113.% 3
 Rule 3 ^0114.% 4
 Rule 4 ^0115.% 5
 Rule 5 ^0116.% 6
 Rule 6 ^0117.% 7
 Rule 7 ^0118.% 8
 Rule 8 ^0119.% 9
!
dial-peer voice 1 voip
 destination-pattern 011T
 translate-outgoing called 1
 session target ras
!
```

The preceding translation rule matches digit patterns that begin with 0111 through 0119 and translates this 4-digit pattern into a single digit from 1 to 9, while preserving the remaining digits included in the digit pattern. This effectively strips the 011 (a common international access code) and sends the remaining digits to the VoIP gatekeeper for call routing.

You can use translation rules to manipulate both automatic number identification (ANI) and dialed number identification service (DNIS) numbers. The following commands can be used to match the ANI or DNIS of a call:

- **answer-address**
- **destination-pattern**
- **incoming called-number**
- **numbering-type**

You can test your translation rules by using the **test translation-rule** command.

Likewise, the gateway can perform number manipulation when calls come into the gateway from the VoIP network. Here, the dial peer on the POTS port can either strip or add digits when going out to the PSTN. Figure 5-4 depicts number normalization from the VoIP network to the PSTN.

Figure 5-4   *Number normalization from VoIP back to PSTN.*

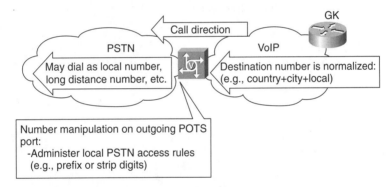

The following example of a POTS dial peer shows how the Cisco IOS **prefix** command can be used to add digits to a calling number:

```
dial-peer voice 20 pots
 destination-pattern 510.......
 prefix 1510
 !
```

The preceding **prefix** command substitutes the 510 with 1510 and effectively adds a 1 to any 10-digit pattern that begins with 510.

Example: Number Normalization for an International Dial Plan

Suppose you are a service provider that provides VoIP transport for calls originating from the San Jose area (408 area code). San Jose subscribers use the following digit patterns when making calls:

- **For local calls within the San Jose area code**—Use a 7-digit number; for example, 555-1000.

- **For long distance calls within the USA**—Use an 11-digit number; for example, 1-212-555-1000.

- **For international calls**—Use a 011 access code, a country code, an area code and the number; for example, 011-33-10-1111-2222.

You'd like long distance calls to go through the VoIP network, but local calls to go back through the PSTN. The gatekeeper should always be queried to make this call routing decision. In this case, ARQs from the gateway to the gatekeeper should be in the standard format:

country code + city (or area) code + local number

This is regardless of whether the user dialed 7 digits (local call), 11 digits (long distance call), or an international call with a 011 access code. You will need to configure the gateway to normalize these patterns. The number normalization logic is shown in Figure 5-5.

Figure 5-5   *Number normalization logic.*

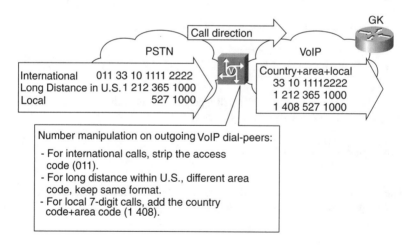

Example Number Normalization Solution

In Example 5-1, translation rules are applied to perform the number normalization.

Example 5-1 *Number Normalization Solution*

```
Hostname SJC-GW
!
translation-rule 2
 Rule 0 ^2...... 14082
 Rule 1 ^3...... 14083
 Rule 2 ^4...... 14084
 Rule 3 ^5...... 14085
 Rule 4 ^6...... 14086
 Rule 5 ^7...... 14087
 Rule 6 ^8...... 14088
 Rule 7 ^9...... 14089
!
translation-rule 1
 Rule 0 ^0111.% 1
 Rule 1 ^0112.% 2
 Rule 2 ^0113.% 3
 Rule 3 ^0114.% 4
 Rule 4 ^0115.% 5
 Rule 5 ^0116.% 6
 Rule 6 ^0117.% 7
 Rule 7 ^0118.% 8
 Rule 8 ^0119.% 9
!
interface Ethernet0/0
 ip address 172.19.49.166 255.255.255.192
 h323-gateway voip interface
 h323-gateway voip id NA-GK ipaddr 172.19.49.168 1719
 h323-gateway voip h323-id US-GW1
!
ip classless
ip route 0.0.0.0 0.0.0.0 172.19.49.129
no ip http server
!
voice-port 1/0/0
!
voice-port 1/0/1
!
dial-peer voice 1408 pots
 destination-pattern 14085551000
 port 1/0/0
!
dial-peer voice 1 voip
 destination-pattern 011T
 translate-outgoing called 1
 session target ras
!
dial-peer voice 2 voip
 destination-pattern 1T
```

continues

Example 5-1 *Number Normalization Solution (Continued)*

```
  session target ras
  !
dial-peer voice 3 voip
  destination-pattern [2-9]T
  translate-outgoing called 2
  session target ras
  !
gateway
  !
```

Example Number Normalization Solution Summary

For international calls, strip the access code. Translation rule 1 strips the 011 access code on numbers that begin with 011. The translation rule is applied to dial peer 1, which matches all numbers beginning with 011 (that is, 011T). The "T" acts as a wild card with interdigit timeout; the digits will be collected when the user doesn't enter a DTMF tone within a certain time. The default value for this timeout is 10 seconds, and is configurable (in seconds) on the voice port. (See the following note.) The user can also enter a termination character (#) after entering the full digit string, to indicate that digits are to be collected.

```
hostname SJC-GW
!
voice-port 0/0/1
  interdigit timeout 3
```

For local 7-digit calls, add the country code + area code (1 408). Translation rule 2 takes any 7-digit number that begins with 2 through 9 and adds a 1408 prefix to that number, where 1 is the country code and 408 is the local area code. This translation rule is applied to dial peer 3, which matches any digit pattern that begins with 2 through 9.

For long distance calls within the USA (different area code), keep the same format. No translation rule is necessary for this case, because the digit pattern is already in the desired format. Dial peer 2 is configured with no translation rule applied.

NOTE   When the "T" timeout indicator is used at the end of the destination pattern in an outbound voice-network dial peer, the router accepts the specified digits and then waits for an unspecified number of additional digits. The router can collect up to 31 additional digits, as long as the interdigit timeout timer has not expired. When the interdigit timeout timer expires, the router places the call.

The default value for the interdigit timeout is 10 seconds. With this setting, all digits will be collected 10 seconds after the last digit is dialed. For example, if you dial 9195556789, but pause for 11 seconds between digits 8 and 9, only 919555678 will be collected by the gateway. You can change the interdigit timeout value using the **timeouts interdigit** command in voice-port configuration mode.

Unless the # character is used as a terminator at the end of the **destination-pattern** command, the T-indicator by default adds 10 seconds to each call setup because the call is not attempted until the timer expires. Therefore, it is recommended that you reduce the interdigit timeout value if you use variable-length dial plans.

The calling party can immediately terminate the interdigit timeout timer by entering the # character while the router is waiting for additional digits. However, if the # character is entered as part of the fixed-length destination pattern that is entered before the router begins waiting for additional digits, it is treated as a dialed digit and is sent across the network when the digits are collected. For example, if the destination pattern is configured as 2222...T, the entire string of 2222#99 is collected. But if the dialed string is 2222#99#99, the #99 at the end of the dialed digits is not collected because the final # character is treated as the **dial-peer terminator** command.

Dial-Peer **preference** Command and Failover Options

You can configure failover options on the gateway by using multiple dial peers with the **preference** command. The **preference** command allows the gateway to select a desired dial peer first, and if the gateway receives an admission reject (ARJ) message from the gatekeeper, the next *preferred* dial peer is used. The default preference value is 0, which is the highest priority. For example, preference 2 is a higher priority than preference 3.

This configuration is commonly referred to as a *rotary dial peer*. This is useful in cases where you want to perform some failover functionality—if the gateway's first dial peer is not able to resolve the termination, then the next preferred dial peer is used. See the section, "Example: Use of Translation Rules, Technology Prefixes, and Dial-Peer Failover" in this chapter for an example of failover functionality.

In Example 5-2, preference commands are configured on two dial peers; dial peer 1 is tried first, then dial peer 2.

Example 5-2 *Commands Configured on Two Dial Peers*

```
dial-peer voice 1 voip
 destination-pattern 1408.......
 session target ras
 preference 1
!
dial-peer voice 2 voip
 destination-pattern 1408.......
 session target osp
 preference 2
```

Gatekeepers in Large-Scale Dial Plans

As more VoIP gateways are added to the network, the adding and changing of dial peers on all remote VoIP gateways can become unmanageable. You can add a gatekeeper to the gateway-to-gateway network to provide centralized dial plan administration. Gatekeepers allow you to logically partition the network into zones and centrally manage the dial plan.

NOTE   A *zone* is a collection of endpoints, gateways, or multipoint control units (MCUs) registered to a single gatekeeper. A single Cisco IOS gatekeeper can control several zones. Think of this as several logical gatekeepers co-existing on a single router. The logical gatekeeper is identified by a gatekeeper name, which is also the name of the zone. When a Cisco IOS gatekeeper is configured, any zone controlled by this router is referred to as a *local zone*. Any zone controlled by a different router is called a *remote zone*.

Without the gatekeeper, explicit IP addresses for each terminating gateway would have to be configured on the originating gateway and matched to a VoIP dial peer. With the gatekeeper in place, the remote VoIP gateways simply reference the dial plan on the gatekeeper when they are trying to establish VoIP calls with other remote VoIP gateways.

When a gatekeeper is added to the network, gateways will register to that gatekeeper in the form of an E.164 address, e-mail alias, or H.323 ID. The gatekeeper will then maintain the call routing information. Gateways can query this information in the RAS ARQ by pointing the session target to the **ras** keyword. This reduces the number of dial peers necessary on the gateway.

For each locally registered gateway, the gatekeeper has information about which prefixes that gateway supports. On the gatekeeper, these prefixes are statically defined using the **zone prefix** command. In the USA, area codes are typically represented by the zone prefix. In European countries, this prefix might be represented as a city or zone code. In addition to containing the local prefixes, the gatekeeper also contains information about the prefixes supported by any remote gatekeepers in the network. The gatekeeper is responsible for ultimately providing the terminating gateway address to the originating gateway. This address can be a local resource, or the gatekeeper can query any one of its remote gatekeepers to supply a terminating gateway address.

The gatekeeper needs to keep track of routing calls that enter the IP cloud. This routing is typically done on E.164 prefixes. The gatekeeper must keep track of which gateways service which prefixes and which prefixes reside on remote gatekeepers, and must maintain resource administration and gateway registrations.

Figure 5-6 illustrates conceptually what a gateway-gatekeeper H.323 network would look like with three gatekeepers. Each gatekeeper manages a zone and is responsible for administering calls to its dedicated zone. Gateways reside within each zone and register to their respective gatekeepers by RAS messages.

Figure 5-6   *Gatekeeper to gatekeeper network, fully meshed.*

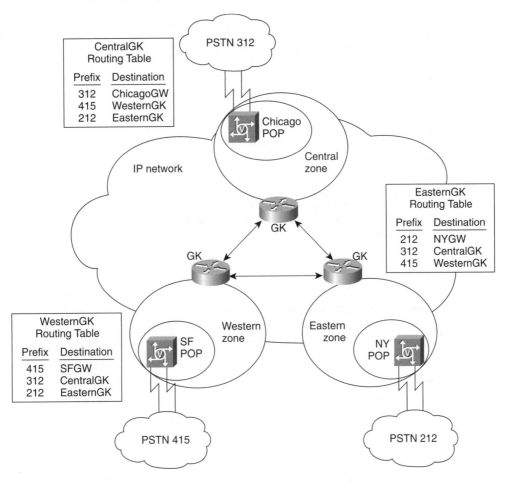

A static zone prefix table has been configured on each of the gatekeepers in Figure 5-6. Each gatekeeper is configured with the zone prefixes in Example 5-3.

Example 5-3   *Zone Prefixes*

```
hostname WesternGK
!
gatekeeper
 zone local WesternGK cisco.com 10.1.1.1
 zone remote CentralGK cisco.com 10.2.1.1 1719
 zone remote EasternGK cisco.com 10.3.1.1 1719
 zone prefix WesternGK 415* gw-priority 10 SFGW
 zone prefix CentralGK 312*
 zone prefix EasternGK 212*
 !
```

continues

Example 5-3 *Zone Prefixes (Continued)*

```
hostname CentralGK
!
gatekeeper
 zone local CentralGK cisco.com 10.2.1.1
 zone remote WesternGK cisco.com 10.1.1.1 1719
 zone remote EasternGK cisco.com 10.3.1.1 1719
 zone prefix CentralGK 312* gw-priority 10 ChicagoGW
 zone prefix WesternGK 415*
 zone prefix EasternGK 212*
!
hostname EasternGK
!
gatekeeper
 zone local EasternGK cisco.com 10.3.1.1
 zone remote CentralGK cisco.com 10.2.1.1 1719
 zone remote WesternGK cisco.com 10.1.1.1 1719
 zone prefix EasternGK 212* gw-priority 10 NYGW
 zone prefix CentralGK 312*
 zone prefix WesternGK 415*
!
```

NOTE   The **zone prefix** command is covered in more detail in the section, "Zone Prefixes."

The following is the call flow for Figure 5-6. For this example, assume that a phone from SFGW (408-555-1000) calls a phone at the NYGW (212-555-3400).

Step 1   SFGW will send an ARQ to the WesternGK, requesting the NYGW address.

Step 2   The WesternGK will look in its zone prefix table to see if it knows where the 212 prefix resides.

Step 3   From the routing table, the WesternGK knows that 212 area codes reside in the EasternGK, so it then sends an LRQ to the EasternGK.

Step 4   The EasternGK checks its routing table and knows that its local zone serves the 212 area code. It also knows that NYGW is the exact terminating gateway for area code 212 phone numbers.

Step 5   The EasternGK sends an LCF message containing the NYGW IP address to the WesternGK.

Step 6   The WesternGK receives this LCF and sends an ACF message, containing the NYGW address, to the SFGW.

Step 7   The SFGW now sends a RAS setup message to the NYGW to begin the peer-to-peer voice communication and RTP stream.

The preceding example shows routers configured for a fully meshed configuration for the routing tables. Each gatekeeper must have a static zone prefix configured for each of the adjacent remote zones.

However, this fully meshed configuration does have limitations. If one of the local gatekeepers were to add another prefix or change a prefix, zone prefix changes would have to be made to every gatekeeper in the fully meshed network. Likewise, if a new zone or gatekeeper were added, all the gatekeepers would need to reflect this change. This would be an administrative burden every time one of these changes occurred.

Gatekeepers with HSRP

Because the gatekeeper maintains the majority of the call routing intelligence (for example, zone prefix tables, technology prefix tables, E.164 registrations), the gatekeeper should be fault tolerant. You can configure gatekeepers to use HSRP so that when one gatekeeper fails, the standby gatekeeper assumes its role, as shown in Figure 5-7.

Figure 5-7   *HSRP on the gatekeeper.*

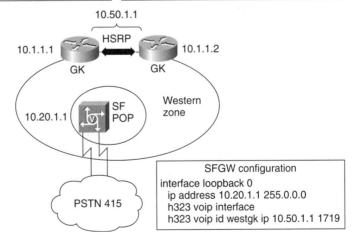

When you configure an active gatekeeper and a standby gatekeeper, they must be on the same subnet. Therefore, the gatekeepers must be located together. HSRP uses a priority scheme to determine which HSRP-configured router is the default active router. To configure a router as the active router, you assign it a priority that is higher than the priority of the other HSRP-configured router. The default priority is 100, so if you configure just one router to have a higher priority, that router will be the default active router.

HSRP works by the exchange of multicast messages that advertise priority among HSRP-configured routers. When the active router fails to send a *hello* message within a configurable period, the standby router with the highest priority becomes the active router after the expiration of a hold timer. The **standby timers** interface configuration command sets the interval (1 to 255 seconds) between hello messages, and sets the time (1 to 255 seconds) that a router waits before it declares the active router to be down. The defaults are 3 seconds and 10 seconds, respectively. If you modify the default values, you must configure each router to use the same hello time and hold time.

NOTE   During the time that the active HSRP gatekeeper transfers to the standby HSRP gatekeeper, the gatekeeper functionality will be lost and will not be able to respond to new LRQs. The secondary directory gatekeeper will address this issue when HSRP is applied to a directory gatekeeper.

In Figure 5-7, notice that a virtual address of 10.50.1.1 has been configured on both the WestGK and the backup GK. The SFGW registers with this virtual address with the **h323 voip id** command.

We recommend the use of HSRP at the directory gatekeeper level because failover from the primary HSRP directory gatekeeper to the secondary HSRP directory gatekeeper will take less time than using an alternate gatekeeper as the main backup. This is because of the time required to send sequential LRQs. Later, we discuss the recommended use of a secondary directory gatekeeper.

Alternate Gatekeepers

In a system where gatekeepers are used, the *alternate gatekeeper* feature provides redundancy. This enhancement allows a gateway to use up to two alternate gatekeepers to provide a backup if the primary gatekeeper fails. More specifically, you can configure a gateway to register with two gatekeepers. If the first gatekeeper fails, the alternate gatekeeper can then be used for call routing, and for maintaining call routing without call failure.

In Example 5-4, the gateway is configured to register with two gatekeepers. The default priority is 127 (the lowest priority); 1 is the highest priority.

Example 5-4 *The Gateway Is Configured to Register with Two Gatekeepers*

```
interface Ethernet 0/1
 ip address 172.18.193.59 255.255.255.0
 h323-gateway voip interface
 h323-gateway voip id GK1 ipaddr 172.18.193.65 1719 priority 120
 h323-gateway voip id GK2 ipaddr 172.18.193.66 1719
 h323-gateway voip h323-id cisco2
```

In Example 5-4, we have configured 172.18.193.65 to be the primary gatekeeper, and 172.18.193.66 as the secondary gatekeeper.

In Figure 5-8, note that the configurations on the WestGK and WestAltGK are very similar with respect to their local and remote zones. Note that there is an entry **zone prefix westaltgk 415*** on the WestGK and **zone prefix westgk 415*** on the WestAltGK. These entries become necessary in the following situation.

Suppose you have two gateways at the SF POP that are both registered to the WestGK (the primary gatekeeper). The WestGK experiences a failure for 30 seconds, then becomes active again. During the 30-second failure, GW1 reregisters to the WestAltGK because its 60-second RRQ timer expires. However, the GW2 RRQ timer does not expire within this time window and it remains registered with the WestGK. We then have a case where the gateways are registered to two different gatekeepers. The extra zone prefix statement ensures that the gatekeeper will check the adjacent gatekeeper for gateways that are not registered with it.

Cisco IOS Release 12.2 introduced a feature that can send LRQs in a sequential fashion instead of in a unicast blast of LRQs. This is a significant advantage over HSRP because backup gatekeepers no longer need to be located in the same geographic area.

Gatekeeper Clusters

Another way to provide gatekeeper redundancy and load sharing is to configure the gatekeepers in a cluster. You can have as many as five gatekeepers in a cluster. Members of a gatekeeper cluster communicate with each other by using Gatekeeper Update Protocol (GUP), a Cisco proprietary protocol based on TCP. Figure 5-9 depicts five gatekeepers in a cluster.

Figure 5-8 *Alternate GK on the zone GKs.*

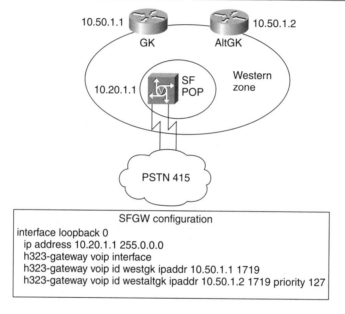

```
                WestGK configuration
gatekeeper
   zone local westgk cisco.com 10.50.1.1 1719
   zone remote westaltgk cisco.com 10.50.1.2 1719
   zone remote dgk cisco.com 10.50.1.100 1719
   zone prefix westgk 415 gw-priority 10 sfgw1
   zone prefix westaltgk 415*
   zone prefix dgk *
   no shutdown
```

```
               WestAltGK configuration
gatekeeper
   zone local westaltgk cisco.com 10.50.1.2 1719
   zone remote westgk cisco.com 10.50.1.1 1719
   zone remote dgk cisco.com 10.50.1.100 1719
   zone prefix westaltgk 415 gw-priority 10 sfgw1
   zone prefix westgk 415*
   zone prefix dgk *
   no shutdown
```

```
               SFGW configuration
interface loopback 0
   ip address 10.20.1.1 255.0.0.0
   h323-gateway voip interface
   h323-gateway voip id westgk ipaddr 10.50.1.1 1719
   h323-gateway voip id westaltgk ipaddr 10.50.1.2 1719 priority 127
```

Figure 5-9 *A gatekeeper cluster.*

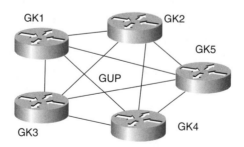

Each gatekeeper in the cluster is configured to know the IP addresses of the member gatekeepers. Upon boot-up, each gatekeeper receives a gatekeeper request (GRQ) message from the other gatekeepers. This GRQ message has the alternate gatekeeper information embedded in the non-standard portion of the message. At this point, a gatekeeper in a cluster opens a TCP connection with all other gatekeepers in the cluster. GUP updates are sent by each gatekeeper at 30-second intervals.

GUP Messages

The following messages are sent by gatekeepers in a cluster:

- **AnnouncementIndication**—Sent periodically, every 30 seconds by default, by each member gatekeeper of the cluster. When a gatekeeper receives this message, it updates the information about call capacity, endpoint capacity, CPU load, memory usage, number of calls, and number of registered endpoints of the alternate gatekeeper (sender).

- **AnnouncementReject**—Sent when there's a configuration mismatch. The receiver will display the error and terminate the GUP connection with the sender.

- **RegistrationIndication**—Sent when the GUP connection is made with a new alternate gatekeeper, or when a new endpoint registers with the gatekeeper.

- **UnregistrationIndication**—Sent when an endpoint is aged out or the gatekeeper is shut down, or when an endpoint unregisters with the gatekeeper.

- **ResourceIndication**—Sent when a gatekeeper receives a Resource Availability Indication (RAI) message from the gateway.

The GUP Protocol

GUP announcements inform other gatekeepers about a gatekeeper's memory and CPU utilization, number of endpoints registered, and the used and available bandwidth. The memory and CPU utilization helps in resource management of the cluster because at any given time, any gatekeeper in the cluster has the load/CPU/memory/call capacity information. If this gatekeeper is overloaded, it can ask the endpoint to use the resources of the alternate gatekeeper with the lowest load.

Each gatekeeper gets the registered endpoint information from all other gatekeepers. Thus the information about any endpoint, registered to any gatekeeper in a cluster, can be obtained from any member gatekeeper. This helps in LRQ processing. Now any gatekeeper in the cluster can resolve LRQ requests sent from an external gatekeeper.

When a new endpoint registers with a gatekeeper in a cluster, that gatekeeper sends a registrationIndication message by GUP. Similarly, an unregistrationIndication is sent when an endpoint unregisters. If a gatekeeper in a cluster does not send six consecutive GUP updates, it is marked as down by all member gatekeepers.

When an endpoint informs a gatekeeper about a new call by an information request response (IRR) message, the gatekeeper increments the total number of active calls it is monitoring, and sends this data by GUP.

If a gatekeeper fails due to a software exception or a power outage, the endpoints are load balanced. Load balancing is achieved during the initial registration confirmation (RCF) message. The initial RCF message contains a list of alternate gatekeepers, listed in order of priority, to which the endpoint can try to register if this (primary) gatekeeper doesn't respond to RAS messages.

When the primary gatekeeper fails to respond to registration request (RRQ) messages, the endpoint will then try to register with other gatekeepers in the cluster, in order of priority, as dictated in the RCF. As soon as the endpoint is registered, an information request (IRQ) message is sent by the gatekeeper to get the information for all calls currently in progress at the endpoint. This ensures that the call information is not lost because of an outage at the gatekeeper.

When a gatekeeper's resources are overloaded (no more call capacity), it can redirect its endpoints to an alternate gatekeeper in the cluster that has sufficient resources. Redirecting endpoints is achieved by sending an ARJ or RRJ reject message in response to an ARQ or RRQ message. The ARJ or RRJ message contains the IP address of the alternate gatekeeper to be used. Upon receipt of this message, the endpoint then tries to register with the new alternate and proceed with new call processing.

Directory Gatekeepers in Large-Scale Dial Plans

Directory gatekeepers simplify the provisioning of large networks. They allow you to confine the configuration requirements to a local area without having to provision the entire network for local changes. Confining configuration requirements to a local area is especially important in networks where local numbers might change more often compared to the general country dial plan. For example, if exchanges are added or rate centers change, these configurations can be isolated to the local area and not propagated through the rest of the network.

Figure 5-10 shows the fully meshed network from Figure 5-6 with a directory gatekeeper added. Notice that each local gatekeeper needs to be configured only with its local information. The rest of the network is "star-routed" out of the directory gatekeeper for resolution. This allows the gatekeepers to be aware of only their own local changes, and isolates the rest of the network from having to cope with these changes. The directory gatekeeper is the only device that needs to know the overall dial plan.

Figure 5-10 *Addition of a directory gatekeeper.*

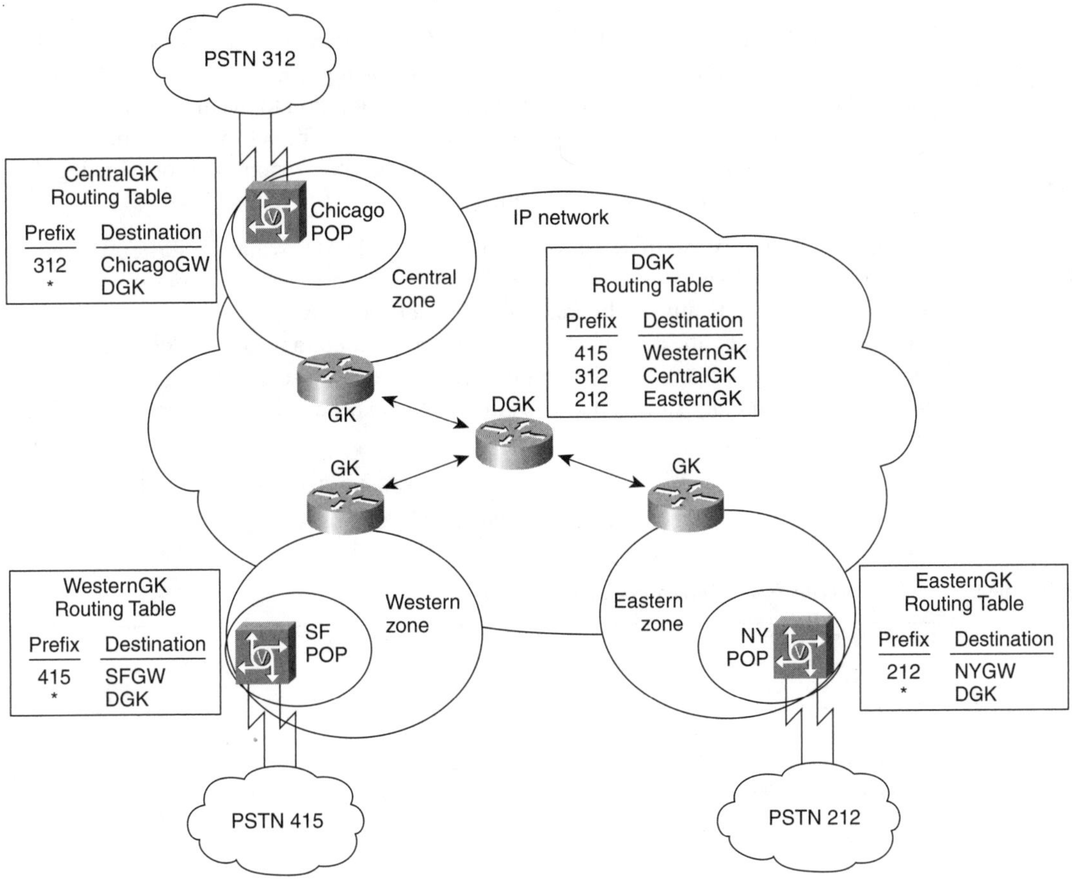

The concept is similar to a Frame Relay WAN. Imagine having to configure a fully meshed network with many dialer maps pointing to each of the adjacent routers in the cloud. The Frame Relay hub-and-spoke configuration simplified much of this by having a hub router, through which all traffic flowed to get to the adjacent routers. You need only configure dialer maps to the hub router.

The same concept can be applied in H.323 networks with the introduction of the directory gatekeeper. The directory gatekeeper will be the hub for the zone prefix routing tables. The remote gatekeepers need to configure only their local zone prefixes and a wildcard (*) default route to the directory gatekeeper.

By adding the directory gatekeeper, we've generated a hierarchical structure with the directory gatekeeper as the highest-level component. We're still able to achieve full connectivity, but with a minimum number of remote zone entries on each of the gatekeepers. The bulk of the remote zone configuration is performed on the directory gatekeeper.

A large service provider network should be divided into various regions to support scaling issues with performance and management. Each regional gatekeeper is responsible for maintaining gateway registrations within its region in addition to making the final routing decisions for the terminating and originating gateways. The directory gatekeepers are responsible for interzone communication across gatekeeper regions and for selecting the proper zone in which to terminate the call.

In Figure 5-10, the WesternGK knows of local area code 415, while the EasternGK is responsible for its own area code of 212 within its local zone. Using zone prefix commands, a routing table is statically configured on each gatekeeper. For area codes local to that particular gatekeeper, the actual gateway can be configured to match the local area code. For area codes that are remote (not within that gatekeeper), use a "star route" or a **zone prefix** * to the directory gatekeeper. The directory gatekeeper will now maintain the master zone prefix table.

The static zone prefix table on each of the gatekeepers has been simplified from Figure 5-6. The zone gatekeepers and directory gatekeeper are now configured as shown in Example 5-5.

Example 5-5 *Zone Gatekeepers and Directory Gatekeeper Configuration*

```
hostname WesternGK
!
gatekeeper
 zone local WesternGK cisco.com 10.1.1.1
 zone remote DGK cisco.com 10.4.1.1 1719
 zone prefix WesternGK 415* gw-priority 10 SFGW
 zone prefix DGK *
!
hostname CentralGK
!
gatekeeper
 zone local CentralGK cisco.com 10.2.1.1
 zone remote DGK cisco.com 10.4.1.1 1719
 zone prefix CentralGK 312* gw-priority 10 ChicagoGW
 zone prefix DGK *
!
hostname EasternGK
!
gatekeeper
 zone local EasternGK cisco.com 10.3.1.1
 zone remote DGK cisco.com 10.4.1.1 1719
 zone prefix EasternGK 212* gw-priority 10 NYGW
 zone prefix DGK *
```

Example 5-5 *Zone Gatekeepers and Directory Gatekeeper Configuration (Continued)*

```
!
hostname DGK
!
gatekeeper
 zone local DGK cisco.com 10.4.1.1
 zone remote WesternGK cisco.com 10.1.1.1 1719
 zone remote CentralGK cisco.com 10.2.1.1 1719
 zone remote EasternGK cisco.com 10.3.1.1 1719
 zone prefix WesternGK 415*
 zone prefix CentralGK 312*
 zone prefix EasternGK 212*
 lrq forward-queries
```

To enable a gatekeeper to forward LRQs that contain E.164 addresses that match zone prefixes controlled by remote gatekeepers, use the **lrq forward-queries** command in the gatekeeper configurations.

Directory Gatekeeper Performance

On average, the directory gatekeeper requires one fourth of the CPU needed by the local zone gatekeepers. Therefore, if the CPU load on the gatekeeper is 40 percent, then you need only 10 percent CPU allocation on the directory gatekeeper. Cisco IOS has a limit of five recursive LRQs; an LRQ is limited to five hops. Local zones and LRQ forwarding zones can be mixed.

Example: Adding a New Zone and a New Rate Center

Suppose you are a service provider that provides VoIP transport for users in San Francisco, Chicago, and New York. The business is growing and you want to design your dial plan to accommodate the following changes:

- Add a new region in the mountain time zone to service area code 406.

- Add a new rate center in the San Francisco area.

San Francisco has added a new set of local numbers in the 415 area code. However, toll charges in the PSTN are applied when callers with 415-626-xxxx numbers call subscribers with 415-961-xxxx numbers. It's less expensive for users to use the VoIP transport than the PSTN when making these calls. Figure 5-11 depicts the addition of the new region and the new rate center.

Figure 5-11 *Adding a rate center and a new mountain zone to a network.*

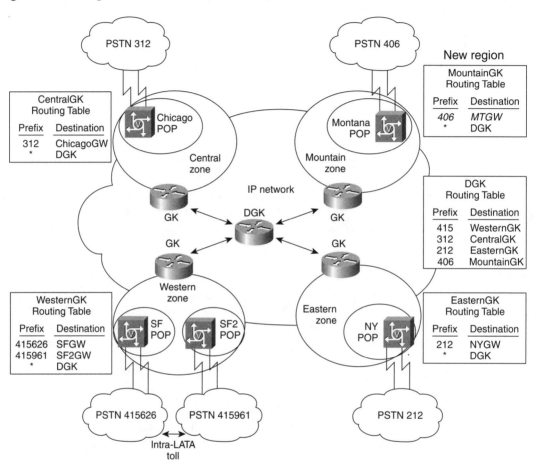

Examples 5-6 through 5-8 show the configuration for this example.

Example 5-6 *WesternGK Configuration*

```
hostname WesternGK
!
interface Ethernet0/0
 ip address 172.19.49.168 255.255.255.192
!
gatekeeper
 zone local WesternGK netman.com 172.19.49.168
 zone remote DGK netman.com 172.19.49.190 1719
 zone prefix WesternGK 1415626* gw-priority 10 SFGW
 zone prefix WesternGK 1415961* gw-priority 10 SF2GW
 zone prefix DGK *
 gw-type-prefix 1#* default-technology
 lrq forward-queries
 no shutdown
```

Example 5-7 *DGK Configuration*

```
gatekeeper
 zone local DGK netman.com 172.19.49.190
 zone remote WesternGK netman.com 172.19.49.168 1719
 zone remote CentralGK netman.com 172.19.49.172 1719
 zone remote EasternGK netman.com 172.19.49.176 1719
 zone remote MountainGK netman.com 172.19.49.200 1719
 zone prefix WesternGK 1415*
 zone prefix CentralGK 1312*
 zone prefix EasternGK 1212*
 zone prefix MountainGK 1406*
 lrq forward-queries
 no shutdown
```

Example 5-8 *MountainGK Configuration*

```
hostname MountainGK
!
!
interface Ethernet0/0
 ip address 172.19.49.200 255.255.255.192
!
!
gatekeeper
 zone local MountainGK netman.com 172.19.49.168
 zone remote DGK netman.com 172.19.49.190 1719
 zone prefix MountainGK 1496* gw-priority 10 MTGW
 zone prefix DGK *
 gw-type-prefix 1#* default-technology
 lrq forward-queries
 no shutdown
```

Secondary Directory Gatekeeper

A *secondary directory gatekeeper* can use the sequential LRQ feature to back up a directory gatekeeper. For example, if a zone gatekeeper sends an LRQ to a primary directory gatekeeper and fails to receive an LCF, another sequential LRQ can be sent from the zone gatekeeper to this alternate gatekeeper. The secondary directory gatekeeper will then provide the normal DGK prefix lookup and call routing in the network until the primary directory gatekeeper is able to function again. We apply this design in the example in Figure 5-12.

Directory Gatekeeper Design Recommendations

We recommend that you use a combination of the alternate gatekeeper, HSRP directory gatekeeper, and secondary directory gatekeeper to provide fault tolerance and redundancy in larger H.323 networks. Several combinations are described here.
(Figure 5-12 illustrates the network topology.)

- **Alternate Gatekeeper at the Zone level**—The gateways are configured to register to a primary gatekeeper and to an alternate gatekeeper in case the primary gatekeeper fails. At any given time, a gateway might be registered to either its primary or its alternate gatekeeper. To accommodate zone fragmentation, you must configure sequential LRQs on the gatekeepers and directory gatekeepers because Cisco gatekeepers do not communicate registration states to each other.

- **HSRP Pair at the Directory Gatekeeper Level**—HSRP is used to provide fault tolerance for the directory gatekeeper. The HSRP failover time can be configured as specified in the section "Gatekeepers with HSRP." A single virtual IP address is shared by the two HSRP directory gatekeepers. Zone gatekeepers need only point to this virtual address.

- **Secondary Directory Gatekeeper at the Directory Gatekeeper Level**—HSRP failover detection might take some time, during which no calls will be processed. To cover this case, you can configure the local gatekeepers to point to an additional secondary directory gatekeeper. Use of sequential LRQs at the gatekeeper level is required. During this time, calls will still be completed, but with additional post-dial delay. The alternate directory gatekeeper is configured the same as the primary HSRP directory gatekeeper pair (See Steps 2a and 2b in Figure 5-12).

The following is the high-level failover flow for the topology shown in Figure 5-12. Assume that a user in the SF POP calls 12125551000 at the NY POP.

1 LRQ is sent from WesternGK to DGK.

1a LRQ is sent from DGK to EasternGK, with no response from EasternGK.

1b LRQ is sent from DGK to EasternAltGK (sequential LRQ).

Either the EasternGK or EasternAltGK will send the LCF back to the WesternGK, depending on whether there is a 1a or a 1b condition.

Suppose one of the directory gatekeepers fails. In this case, assume DGK1 is the primary and it experiences a failure. HSRP will function to activate the secondary, DGK2. Some time will elapse during this failover. During this failover time, no new calls can be processed because neither of the DGKs will respond. To provide redundancy for this interval, we recommend that a secondary directory gatekeeper be used to receive the LRQ during this time.

The following is the call flow from the Western Zone to the Eastern Zone:

1 LRQ is sent from WesternGK to DGK; no response from DGK (HSRP failover interval).

2 Second LRQ is sent from WesternGK to AltDGK (sequential LRQ).

2a LRQ is sent from AltDGK to EasternGK; no response from EasternGK.

2b LRQ is sent from AltDGK to EasternAltGK.

Either the EasternGK or EasternAltGK will send the LCF back to the WesternGK, depending on whether there is a 2a or a 2b condition.

Figure 5-12 *Fault-tolerant design recommendation.*

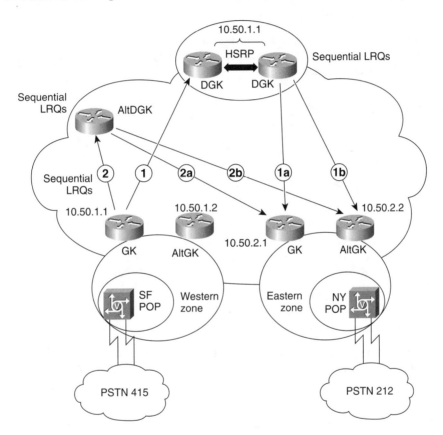

Dial Plan Call RoutingTools and Features

Cisco IOS Software provides the following tools and features to make administration and scaling easier for call routing in large-scale dial plans:

- Zone prefixes
- Technology prefixes
- Hopoff zones

These tools and features are discussed in the following sections.

Zone Prefixes

A *zone prefix* is the part of a called number, usually the NPA (area code) or NPA-NXX (area code and local office) that identifies the zone where a call hops off. There is currently no protocol by which gatekeepers can advertise which zone prefixes can be accessed from their zones, so these zone prefixes must be statically configured.

Zone prefixes are typically used to associate an area code or a set of area codes with a particular configured zone. First, local and remote zones are defined on the gatekeeper by the following commands:

```
gatekeeper
  zone local west-gk cisco.com 10.1.1.1
  zone remote east-gk cisco.com 10.1.1.2 1719
  zone remote central-gk cisco.com 10.1.1.3 1719
```

Then, the zone prefixes are configured on the gateway to identify which gatekeeper manages remote area codes:

```
zone prefix east-gk 312.......
zone prefix west-gk 408.......
zone prefix central-gk 212*
```

This is similar to configuring static routes in an IP environment. Note that currently no method exists for dynamically propagating dial plans to routers in a network. Therefore, you must configure these static zone prefixes to let gatekeepers know where they should forward LRQs to resolve the gateway or endpoint's IP address.

The idea of a zone prefix on the gatekeeper is to associate an E.164 address to a particular trunking gateway. Because the trunking gateways can terminate a range of addresses, the range must be manually defined on the gatekeeper.

Another type of endpoint that can register with the gatekeeper is an *analog gateway* or H.323 endpoint. These devices typically register with the full E.164 address. In this case, the zone prefix is used to partition a specific H.323 zone that will manage this set of addresses.

You can display the statically configured zone prefixes on the gatekeeper by using the **show gatekeeper zone prefix** command:

```
NA-GK# show gatekeeper zone prefix
      ZONE PREFIX TABLE
      =================
GK-NAME                   E164-PREFIX
-------                   -----------
east-gk                   312.......
west-gk                   408.......
Central-gk                212*
```

For a specific zone prefix (range of E.164 addresses), you can configure the gatekeeper to hand a call to a specific gateway, or pool of gateways, each at configured levels of priority. Note that only currently registered gateways from the priority list will be considered. Gateways that are too busy, as indicated by an RAI message, are excluded from the selection.

For use by the gateway selection algorithm, you can specify gateway priorities ranging from 10 (highest priority) to 0 (usage prohibited) for different zone prefixes within a zone. Gateway priorities are implemented with the **gw-pri** command, as shown here:

```
router-sj(config-gk)# zone local west-gk cisco.com 10.1.1.1
router-sj(config-gk)# zone prefix west-gk  408....... gw-pri 10 gw408
router-sj(config-gk)# zone prefix west-gk  415....... gw-pri 10 gw415
router-sj(config-gk)# zone prefix west-gk  650....... gw-pri 10 gw650
router-sj(config-gk)# zone prefix west-gk  510.......
```

All three gateways can now register in the same zone. If a zone prefix has any defined gateway priorities, a separate gateway list is kept for that zone prefix. The list contains all registered gateways, ordered by priority. When a gateway is inserted in such a list, a default priority of 5 is used for unnamed gateways.

Zone prefixes that do not have any priorities defined (for example, the 510 area code) do not have any special lists associated with them. Calls to the 510 area code will be serviced out of the master gateway list for the zone.

With the preceding configuration, when gw408 registers, it is placed in the 408 list at priority 10, and in the 415 and 650 lists at the default priority of 5. When all three gateways are registered, the zones' lists will look like the following:

```
resultant Master list
master list: gw408, gw415, gw650
408 list: pri 10 gw408; pri 5 gw650, gw415
415 list: pri 10 gw415; pri 5 gw650, gw408
650 list: pri 10 gw650; pri 5 gw408, gw415
```

Any call to the 408 area code will be directed to gw408 because it has the highest priority. However, if gw408 is busy (that is, it has sent an RAI message saying that it is almost out of resources) the call will be routed to either gw415 or gw650. If you do not want either of these gateways to be used for 408 calls, then you can specify that they have a zero priority for that area code, as shown here:

```
router-sj(config-gk)# zone prefix west-gk 408....... gw-pri 10 gw408
router-sj(config-gk)# zone prefix west-gk 408....... gw-pri 0 gw415 gw650
```

This configuration ensures that only gw408 will be used for calls to the 408 area code.

You must be aware that gateway priority lists come with some overhead costs; they should be used with discretion. If you can partition your zones to avoid using gateway priorities, you should do so. If you must use this feature, try to keep the number of zone prefixes with priority definitions to fewer than 50 per zone. Whenever a gateway registers in a zone, it will need to be inserted into each prioritized list in that zone, and removed from all lists when it unregisters.

As we've seen, zone prefixes are created to identify particular area codes with zones that have been established. Specific gateways within the zone can be prioritized so that the gatekeeper will hand off the call to those gateways first.

Technology Prefixes

Technology prefixes allow special characters to be included in the called number. These special characters are most commonly designated as 1#, 2#, 3#, and so on, and can be configured to prepend the called number on the outgoing VoIP dial peer. The gatekeeper can then check its gateway technology prefix table for gateways that have registered with that particular technology prefix. Technology prefixes can also be used to identify a type, class, or pool of gateways.

There are two places where technology prefix commands can be entered on both gateways and gatekeepers, depending on how you want to design the technology prefix decision intelligence:

- Gateway VoIP interface
- Gateway dial peer

Technology Prefix on the Gateway VoIP Interface

To realize the advantages of the routing efficiencies that technology prefixes provide, the gateway first needs to identify itself with a technology prefix number, such as 1#, 2#, and so on. This prefix number can be configured on the VoIP interface of the gateway, as shown in Example 5-9. Here the gateways first register their technology prefix with an RRQ message to the gatekeeper. This technology prefix registration determines the gatekeeper's selection of a gateway for an incoming call.

Example 5-9 *GW1*

```
hostname gw1
!
interface Ethernet 0/0
 ip address 10.1.1.1 255.255.255.0
 h323-gateway voip tech-prefix 2#
```

In Example 5-9, GW1 registers to the gatekeeper with **2#** as the technology prefix. This technology prefix registration determines the gatekeeper's selection of a gateway for an incoming call.

You can display this registration on the gatekeeper with the **show gatekeeper gw-type-prefix** command, as indicated here:

```
vn-gk# show gatekeeper gw-type-prefix
GATEWAY TYPE PREFIX TABLE
=========================
Prefix: 2#*
  Zone vn-gk master gateway list:
    10.71.3.101:1720 gw1
```

Technology Prefix on the Gateway Dial Peer

You can also configure a technology prefix on a specific VoIP dial peer:

```
dial-peer voice 1 voip
  destination-pattern  1408.......
  session target ras
  tech-prefix  2#
```

The preceding commands prepend a 2# to the 1408....... called number. A called number of 5554321 then becomes 2#14085554321.

The gatekeeper first looks for a technology prefix match; then it tries to find a zone prefix match. It must find a gateway that's registered with that zone prefix and that also matches the zone prefix table. If these two matches occur, the gatekeeper directs the call to that *egress gateway*.

Example 5-10 shows how to configure the technology prefix and how to display it on the gatekeeper, along with the technology prefixes that have been registered.

Example 5-10 *How to Configure the technology prefix and How to Display It on the Gatekeeper*

```
hostname vn-gw1
!
interface Ethernet0
 ip address 10.71.3.101 255.255.255.0
 h323-gateway voip interface
 h323-gateway voip id vn-gk ipaddr 10.71.3.201 1719
 h323-gateway voip h323-id vn-gw1
 h323-gateway voip tech-prefix 1#
!
hostname vn-gw2
!
interface Ethernet0/0
 ip address 10.71.3.105 255.255.255.0
 h323-gateway voip interface
 h323-gateway voip id vn-gk ipaddr 10.71.3.201 1719
 h323-gateway voip h323-id vn-gw2
 h323-gateway voip tech-prefix 2#
!
hostname vn-gk
!
gatekeeper
 zone local vn-gk cisco.com 10.71.3.201
 zone remote k-gk cisco.com 10.71.3.200 1719
 zone remote hopoff cisco.com 10.71.3.202 1719
 zone prefix vn-gk 1212*
 zone prefix k-gk 1212*
!
 no shutdown
```

continues

Example 5-10 *How to Configure the technology prefix and How to Display It on the Gatekeeper (Continued)*

```
vn-gk#show gatekeeper gw-type-prefix
GATEWAY TYPE PREFIX TABLE
==========================
Prefix: 2#*
  Zone vn-gk master gateway list:
    10.71.3.101:1720 vn-gw1
Prefix: 1#*
  Zone vn-gk master gateway list:
    10.71.3.105:1720 12125557777
```

The gatekeeper now has the vn-gw1 (10.71.3.101) registered with the 1# prefix, and will consider this gateway if incoming calls arrive with a 1# prepended to the DNIS. Vn-gw2 is registered with the 2# prefix.

NOTE   Cisco trunking gateways must be configured to register with a technology prefix of 1# in order to be placed into the gateway selection table on the gatekeeper. Analog gateways register their full E.164 address, so they do not necessarily need to register a technology prefix to the gatekeeper.

Technology Prefix Commands on the Gatekeeper

The following additional technology prefix commands are available on the gatekeeper to allow additional control.

Define a default technology prefix:

```
gatekeeper
 gw-type-prefix 1# default-technology
```

This command tells the gatekeeper to use gateways that are registered with 1# if no technology prefixes are sent with the called number.

Define the gatekeeper to receive a particular technology prefix and forward the LRQ to the hopoff zone:

```
gatekeeper
 gw-type-prefix 7# hopoff spacezone
```

After receiving a called number with 7# preceding, send an LRQ to the spacezone gatekeeper. This takes priority over other gateway selections.

Configure a static technology prefix registration entry into the gatekeeper:

```
gatekeeper
 gw-type-prefix 8# gw ipaddr 1.1.1.1
```

This command creates a static entry into the gw-type-prefix table on the gatekeeper. It's the equivalent of having a gateway (IP address 1.1.1.1) register with an 8#.

Example 5-11 uses these optional commands.

Example 5-11 *Technology Prefix Commands*

```
gatekeeper
 !
 gw-type-prefix 7#* hopoff spacezone
 gw-type-prefix 1#* default-technology
 gw-type-prefix 8#* gw ipaddr 1.1.1.1 1720

vn-gk# show gatekeeper gw-type-prefix
GATEWAY TYPE PREFIX TABLE
==========================
Prefix: 7#*                              (Hopoff zone spacezone)
  Zone vn-gk master gateway list:
    10.71.3.101:1720 vn-gw1
Prefix: 1#*                              (Default gateway-technology)
  Zone vn-gk master gateway list:
   10.71.3.105:1720 12125557777  (Here, 10.71.3.105 GW has registered with a 1#,
                                  so it  belongs to the 1# pool)
Prefix: 8#*
  Statically-configured gateways:  (Not necessarily currently registered)
    1.1.1.1:1720
```

Figure 5-13 shows technology prefix configurations. Figure 5-14 shows the use of technology prefixes in a network.

Figure 5-13 *Technology prefix configurations.*

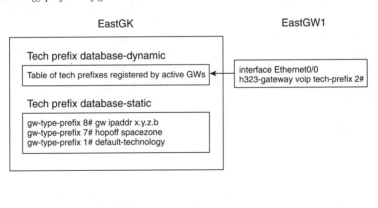

Figure 5-14 *Use of technology prefixes in a network.*

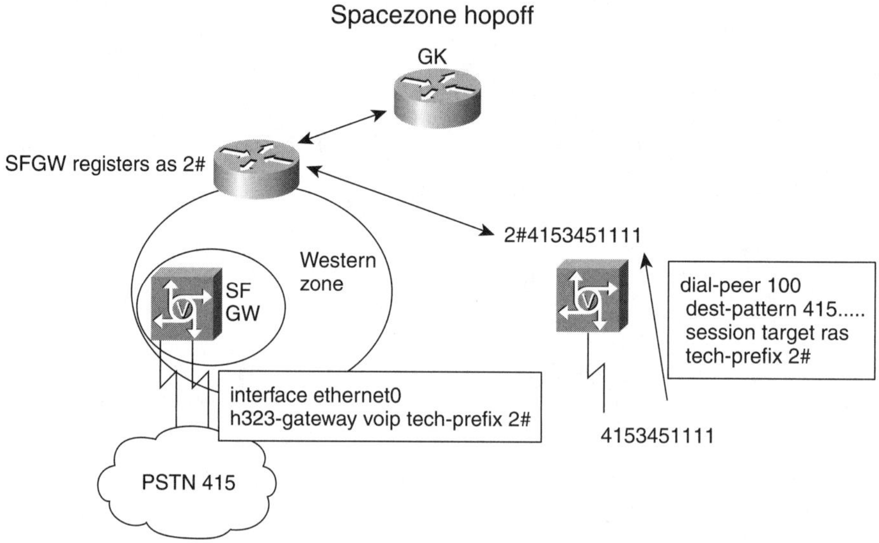

NOTE Normally, when an endpoint or gateway sends an ARQ message to its gatekeeper, the gatekeeper resolves the destination address by first looking for the technology prefix. When that technology prefix is matched, the remaining string is compared against known zone prefixes. If the address resolves to a remote zone, the entire address, including both the technology and zone prefixes, is sent to the remote gatekeeper in an LRQ message. That remote gatekeeper then uses the technology prefix to decide which of its gateways to hop off of. This behavior can be overridden by associating a *forced hop off zone* with a particular technology prefix. This forces the call to the specified zone, regardless of the zone prefix in the address.

Hopoff Zones

The *hopoff zone* refers to the point where a call transitions from H.323 to non-H.323 (PSTN or H.320, for example) via a gateway. You can configure a gatekeeper to administer a zone dedicated for traffic that is not locally serviced. For example, if phone A calls 3155559999, which is outside of the local area codes defined by gatekeeper X, then a hopoff zone can be configured to handle such phone numbers. Think of a hopoff zone as a default gateway in the IP world.

The hopoff zone is used in conjunction with technology prefixes and is configured as an option with the **gw-type-prefix** command, as shown here:

```
gatekeeper
  gw-type-prefix 2# hopoff hopoffgk
```

This configuration is often referred to as *technology prefix forced hopoff*. A sample configuration is depicted in Figure 5-15.

Figure 5-15 *Application of the hopoff zone.*

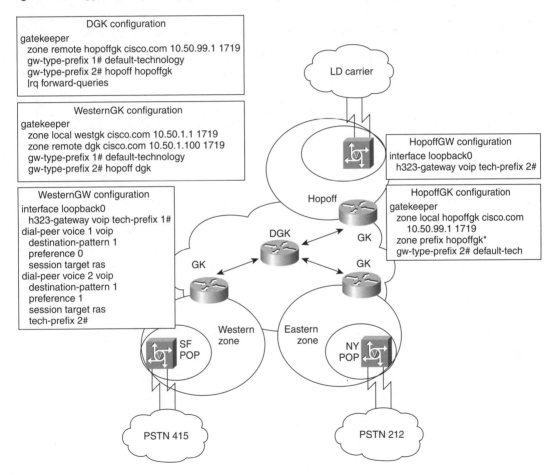

In Figure 5-15 a hopoff zone has been added, consisting of a hopoff gateway and a hopoff gatekeeper. The WesternGK and DGK are configured with a static **gw-type-prefix** command. This command will cause all called numbers with a 2# technology prefix to send an LRQ message to its next hopoff gatekeeper. In this case, the WesternGK will forward these LRQs to the DGK, and the DGK will forward the LRQs to the hopoffGK.

Note that the WesternGK has been configured with 2 dial-peers. The **preference** command assigns the dial-peer order. This command is generally used for failover purposes when you have the same destination pattern assigned to multiple dial peers.

Dial peer 1 first sends an ARQ message to the WesternGK to determine if it knows the called number's terminating gateway address. If the WesternGK does not know this, the WesternGK will send an ARJ message to the gateway. The second dial peer will then append a 2# technology prefix to the called number and again try an ARQ message to the WesternGK. This time, the 2# matches the **gw-type-prefix 2#** command to hop off to the DGK. The DGK also recognizes the 2# and matches its **gw-type-prefix 2#** command to hop off to the hopoffGK. Note that the 2# gets propagated with the called number.

You can enter the **hopoff** keyword and gatekeeper ID multiple times in the same command to define a group of gatekeepers that will service a given technology prefix. Only one of the gatekeepers in the hopoff list can be local.

If the technology prefix does not have any forced zone attribute, the gatekeeper uses *zone prefix matching* to determine the zone. If the matching zone prefix is associated with a remote zone, an LRQ message is sent to the remote gatekeeper. The LRQ message contains the entire called number, including the previously stripped technology prefix. If the matching prefix is for a local zone, that zone is used to satisfy the request.

If no zone prefix match is found, the default behavior is to attempt to use a local zone for hopoff rather than to fail the call. However, this might not be the desired behavior. You might prefer that an ARJ message be returned to the gateway so that it can fall through to an alternate dial peer (for example, one that specifies that the next hop is through a special-rate PSTN). To override the default behavior, use the **arq reject-unknown-prefix** gatekeeper command.

Example: Use of Translation Rules, Technology Prefixes, and Dial-Peer Failover

This example demonstrates the use of Cisco IOS tools and features to provide better call routing control with hierarchical design and to minimize dial-peer configuration.

Figure 5-16 illustrates the topology of the example network.

Figure 5-16 *Example network using failover scenarios.*

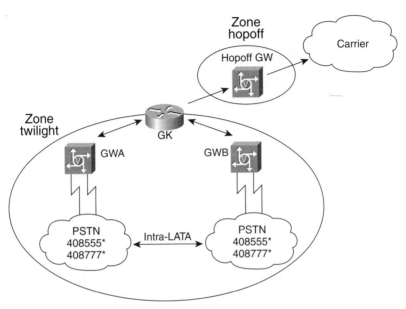

Business Case

In this example, the service provider has two gateways that serve both the 408555* and the 408777* numbering plan area (NPA) NXX zones. The gatekeeper has two local zones twilight and hopoff.

Calls from GWA to GWB should be made through the gatekeeper VoIP network. However, if GWB is unavailable because of failure or a resource allocation issue (RAI), you should make the following provisions:

- Calls to 408555* should be hairpinned back through the PSTN (GWA POTS) and completed to the destination. These calls through the PSTN do not incur any intra-LATA toll charges.

- Calls to 408777* should be sent through to the hopoff zone, not to the PSTN. An intra-LATA toll charge is associated with these calls, so the customer wants to redirect these calls to the hopoff zone, which has a better rate.

Applying Cisco IOS Tools

The following tools are used in this example:

- Translation rules
- **preference** command
- Technology prefixes
- Hopoff zone

Translation Rules

Use translation rules to strip or add a 1 to the calling number. This will be used to allow additional call-routing control in the gateway selection order.

preference Command

Use the **preference** command on dial peers to allow a dial peer selection order. For instance, the gateway will match first on dial peer 1. If the gateway receives a location reject (LRJ) message from the gatekeeper, the next preferred dial peer will be used. This will allow for failover scenarios and greater call control.

Technology Prefixes

Use technology prefixes to allow certain dial peers to use a hopoff zone technology prefix (that is, 27#). When dial-peer failover occurs, the 27# technology prefix will force the call to go to the hopoff zone.

Hopoff Zone

Create a hopoff zone and a hopoff gateway within the network. This zone has a special negotiated rate for VoIP calls, so the calls cost less than those going through the PSTN.

Example Solution and Configurations

Examples 5-12 through 5-15 show the configurations for the use of translation rules, technology prefixes, and dial-peer failover.

Example 5-12 *GWA Configuration*

```
hostname GWA
!
translation-rule 1
  Rule 0 ^2.% 12
  Rule 1 ^3.% 13
  Rule 2 ^4.% 14
  Rule 3 ^5.% 15
  Rule 4 ^6.% 16
  Rule 5 ^7.% 17
  Rule 6 ^8.% 18
  Rule 7 ^9.% 19
 !
 translation-rule 2
  Rule 0 ^12.% 2
  Rule 1 ^13.% 3
  Rule 2 ^14.% 4
  Rule 3 ^15.% 5
  Rule 4 ^16.% 6
  Rule 5 ^17.% 7
  Rule 6 ^18.% 8
  Rule 7 ^19.% 9
 !
interface loopback0
  h323-gateway voip interface
  h323-gateway voip id GK ipaddr 172.20.10.9 1719
  h323-gateway voip h323-id GWA
  h323-gateway voip tech-prefix 1#
 !
voice-port 0:D
 translate called 1
 no modem passthrough
 !
dial-peer voice 2 voip
 preference 5
 destination-pattern 1408.......
 session target ras
 tech-prefix 27#
 !
dial-peer voice 100 pots
 destination-pattern .......
 direct-inward-dial
 port 0:D
 prefix 1408
 !
dial-peer voice 1 voip
 preference 1
 destination-pattern 1408.......
 translate-outgoing called 2
 session target ras
```

Example 5-13 *GWB Configuration*

```
hostname GWB
!
interface loopback0
 h323-gateway voip interface
 h323-gateway voip id GK ipaddr 172.20.10.9 1719
 h323-gateway voip h323-id GWB
 h323-gateway voip tech-prefix 1#
```

Example 5-14 *Hopoff GW Configuration*

```
hostname hopoff-gw
!
interface loopback0
 h323-gateway voip interface
 h323-gateway voip id GK ipaddr 172.20.10.9 1719
 h323-gateway voip h323-id hopoff-gw
```

Example 5-15 *GK Configuration*

```
hostname GK
!
gatekeeper
 zone local twilight-zone cisco.com 172.20.10.10
 zone local hopoff-zone cisco.com
 zone prefix twilight-zone 408555* gw-priority 10 GWB
 zone prefix twilight-zone 408555* gw-priority 5 GWA
 zone prefix twilight-zone 408777* gw-priority 10 GWB
 zone prefix twilight-zone 408777* gw-priority 0 GWA
 zone prefix hopoff-zone 1408777* gw-priority 10 hopoff-gw
 gw-type-prefix 1#* default-technology
 gw-type-prefix 27#* hopoff hopoff-zone
 no shutdown

GK# show gatekeeper gw-type-prefix
GATEWAY TYPE PREFIX TABLE
==========================
Prefix: 1#*                               (Default gateway-technology)
  Zone twilight-zone master gateway list:
    172.20.10.3:1720 GWA
    172.20.10.5:1720 GWB
  Zone twilight-zone prefix 408777* priority gateway list(s):
   Priority 10:
    172.20.10.5:1720 GWB
  Zone twilight-zone prefix 408555* priority gateway list(s):
   Priority 10:
    172.20.10.5:1720 GWB
   Priority 5:
    172.20.10.3:1720 GWA
Prefix: 27#*                              (Hopoff zone hopoff-zone)
  Zone hopoff-zone master gateway list:
    172.20.10.4:1720 hopoff-gw
```

Example 5-15 *GK Configuration (Continued)*

```
Zone hopoff-zone prefix 1408777* priority gateway list(s):
 Priority 10:
  172.20.10.4:1720 hopoff-gw
```

Configuration Review and Dial Plan Logic

This section shows the following flows:

- GWA calls 1408555* on GWB—Success
- GWA calls 1408555* on GWB—Failover through zone prefixes
- GWA calls 1408777* on GWB—Success
- GWA calls 1408777* on GWB—Failover using dial-peer failover (**preference** command)

Flow #1: Success

GWA calls 1408555* on GWB:

1 Voice-port translation rule 1 adds 1 to the NPA.

2 Match dial-peer 1 translation rule 2, which strips the digit 1. Send an ARQ message to the GK.

3 Match zone prefix twilight-zone 408555* gw-priority 10 GWB.

4 The call is successful through VoIP.

Flow #2: Failover through Zone Prefixes

GWA calls 1408555* on GWB:

1 Voice-port translation rule 1 adds 1 to the NPA.

2 Match dial-peer 1 translation rule 2, which strips the digit 1. Send an ARQ message to the GK.

3 Match zone prefix twilight-zone 408555* gw-priority 10 GWB.

4 GWB is down (or RAI unavailable), so GWB is removed from the GK selection table. Look for the next match.

5 Match zone prefix twilight-zone 408555* gw-priority 5 GWA.

6 Select GWA (itself).

7 Match on pots dial-peer, and destination pattern ....

8 Hairpin the call back through the PSTN.

9 The call is successful through the PSTN.

Flow #3: Success

GWA calls 1408777* on GWB:

1 Voice-port translation rule 1 adds 1 to the NPA.

2 Match dial-peer 1 translation rule 2, which strips the digit 1. Send an ARQ message to the GK.

3 Match zone prefix twilight-zone 408777* gw-priority 10 GWB.

4 The call is successful through VoIP.

Flow #4: Failover Using Dial-Peer Failover (**preference** Command)

GWA calls 1408777* on GWB:

1 Voice-port translation rule 1 adds 1 to the NPA.

2 Match dial-peer 1 translation rule 2, which strips the digit 1. Send an ARQ message to the GK.

3 Match zone prefix twilight-zone 408777* gw-priority 10 GWB.

4 GWB is down (or RAI unavailable), so GWB is removed from the GK selection table. Look for the next match.

5 Match, but zone prefix twilight-zone 408777* gw-priority 0 GWA.

6 The GK sends an ARJ message to GWA.

7 Roll over to next preferred dial-peer, dial-peer 2.

8 Dial-peer 2 does not strip the 1 (no translation rule) but does add a technology prefix of 27#.

9 27#14087771000.

10 GWA sends an ARQ message to the GK.

11 Match the gw-type-prefix 27#* hopoff hopoff-zone.

12 Match the zone prefix hopoff-zone 1408777* gw-priority 10 hopoff-gw.

13 In an ACF message, the GK sends the hopoff-gw address to GWA.

14 The call is successful to the hopoff gw.

Example: Implementing an International Dial Plan

This implementation provides an example of an international dialing plan using several of the methods covered to reduce dial-peer configuration at the gateway, simplify prefix searches at the gatekeeper, and provide fault tolerance at the gatekeeper and the directory gatekeeper level. Figure 5-17 depicts the topology of the example network.

Figure 5-17 *Topology of an international service provider network.*

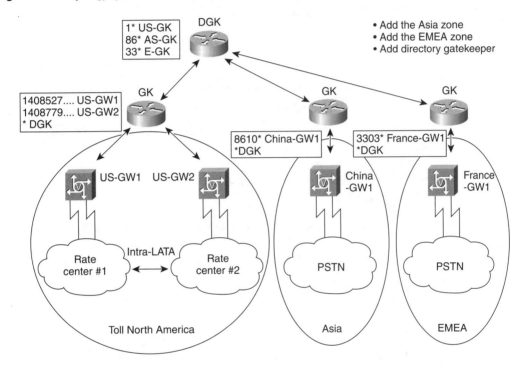

The service provider wants to provide wholesale voice services with a presence in North America, Asia, and EMEA. You need to design and configure a gateway, gatekeeper, and directory gatekeeper H.323 network that will provide for the following POP locations:

- **North America**—The gateway is in the United States.
- **Asia**—The gateway is in China.
- **EMEA**—The gateway is in France.

The design goals of the network are as follows:

- Successful inter-carrier calls between countries
- Hierarchical GW/GK/DGK design
- Number normalization into the VoIP from the PSTN
- Fault tolerance at the GK and DGK level

Figure 5-18 shows an example topology with these design goals implemented.

Figure 5-18 *Network topology with country-specific calling information.*

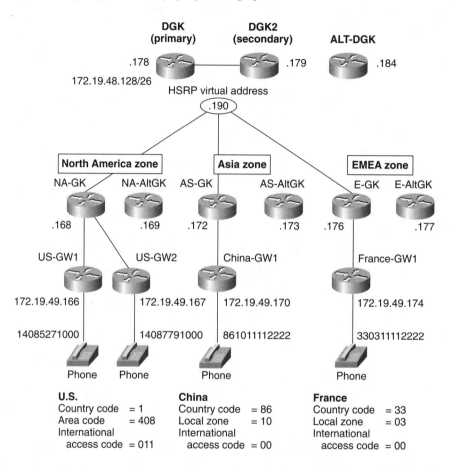

To accomplish the design goals of the network, the following design strategies are implemented:

- Number normalization to reduce the number of dial peers on the gateway
- Directory gatekeeper and local zone prefix search
- Alternate gatekeepers and HSRP pairs used for fault tolerance

Number Normalization to Reduce the Number of Dial-Peers on the Gateway

To reduce the number of gateway dial peers, create translation rules on each of the gateways to accommodate the local country dialing habits.

U.S. Gateways

The setup includes the following elements:

- Two gateways are located in the US POP.
- US-GW1 has phone 1-408-527-1000.
- US-GW2 has phone 1-408-779-1000.

The local dialing habits in the US are:

- For local numbers in the 408 area code, use 7-digit dialing.
- For long-distance numbers within the US, use 1 + area code + local number.
- For international numbers (outside of North America), use 011 (access code) + country code + local city code + local number.

Normalize these numbers into the following formula:

Country code + city code + local number.

China Gateway

The setup is as follows:

- One gateway is located in the China POP.
- The country code = 86, and the local city code = 010.
- CHINA-GW1 has phone 861011112222.

The local dialing habits in China are:

- For local numbers in the 010 city code, use 8-digit dialing, beginning with 1–9.
- For long-distance numbers within China, use the area code (dialed with 0x or 0xx) + local number.
- For international numbers (outside of China), use 00 (access code) + country code + local city code + local number.

Normalize these numbers into the following formula:

Country code + city code + local number.

France Gateway

The setup for France is as follows:

- One gateway is located in the France POP.
- The country code = 33, and the local city code = 03.
- FRANCE-GW1 has phone 330311112222.

The local dialing habits in France are:

- For local numbers in the 03 area code, use the area code (0x) + 8-digit dialing.
- For long-distance numbers within France, use the area code (dialed with 0x) + 8-digit local number.
- For international numbers (outside of France), use 00 (access code) + country code + local city code + local number.

Normalize these numbers into the following formula:

Country code + city code + local number.

The translation rules should be configured to match the local dialing habits within the country in which the gateway resides. Match the translation rule with the appropriate outgoing VoIP dial-peer.

Directory Gatekeeper and Local Zone Prefix Search

Gatekeepers are configured to administer their local country zones and city/area codes (for example, 8610*) to their specific gateways. A directory gatekeeper is used to handle call routing on just the country code number. The GK applies translation rules to present this country code first, before it enters the VoIP gatekeeper core. In addition, zone prefix tables on the zone gatekeepers are greatly simplified because the directory gatekeeper has been designed in.

Alternate Gatekeepers and HSRP Pairs for Fault Tolerance

Alternate gatekeepers are configured at the zone gatekeeper level to back up the primary gatekeepers. A primary and secondary HSRP pair is used at the directory gatekeeper level to back up each other. A secondary directory gatekeeper is used to back up the directory gatekeeper pair.

NOTE The configurations for the alternate gatekeeper in the US POP are shown. The configurations for the alternate gatekeeper in the Asia and France POPs are not shown.

Configuration Listings

Examples 5-16 through 5-26 show configuration listings for implementing the international dial plan.

Example 5-16 *US-GWI Configuration*

```
!
! No configuration change since last restart
!
version 12.1
service timestamps debug uptime
service timestamps log uptime
no service password-encryption
!
hostname US-GW1
!
enable password xxx
!
username cisco password 0 xxx
!
clock timezone PDT -7
ip subnet-zero
no ip domain-lookup
!
translation-rule 2
 Rule 0 ^2...... 14082
 Rule 1 ^3...... 14083
 Rule 2 ^4...... 14084
 Rule 3 ^5...... 14085
 Rule 4 ^6...... 14086
 Rule 5 ^7...... 14087
 Rule 6 ^8...... 14088
 Rule 7 ^9...... 14089
!
translation-rule 1
 Rule 0 ^0111.% 1
 Rule 1 ^0112.% 2
 Rule 2 ^0113.% 3
 Rule 3 ^0114.% 4
 Rule 4 ^0115.% 5
 Rule 5 ^0116.% 6
 Rule 6 ^0117.% 7
 Rule 7 ^0118.% 8
 Rule 8 ^0119.% 9
!
interface Ethernet0/0
 ip address 172.19.49.166 255.255.255.192
 h323-gateway voip interface
 h323-gateway voip id NA-GK ipaddr 172.19.49.168 1719 priority 1
 h323-gateway voip id NA-ALTGK ipaddr 172.19.49.169 1719 priority 2
 h323-gateway voip h323-id US-GW1
 h323-gateway voip tech-prefix 1#
 !
```

continues

Example 5-16 *US-GWI Configuration (Continued)*

```
ip classless
ip route 0.0.0.0 0.0.0.0 172.19.49.129
no ip http server
!
voice-port 1/0/0
 timeouts interdigit 3
 !
voice-port 1/0/1
 !
dial-peer cor custom
 !
dial-peer voice 1408 pots
 destination-pattern 14085271000
 port 1/0/0
 !
dial-peer voice 1 voip
 destination-pattern 011T
 translate-outgoing called 1
 session target ras
 !
dial-peer voice 4 voip
 destination-pattern [2-9]......
 translate-outgoing called 2
 session target ras
 !
dial-peer voice 99 voip
 destination-pattern 2601
 session target ipv4:172.19.49.4
 !
dial-peer voice 2 voip
 destination-pattern 1T
 session target ras
 !
gateway
 !
line con 0
 transport input none
line aux 0
line vty 0 4
 exec-timeout 0 0
 password xxx
 !
end
```

Example 5-17 *US-GW2 Configuration*

```
 !
version 12.1
service timestamps debug uptime
service timestamps log uptime
no service password-encryption
```

Example 5-17 *US-GW2 Configuration (Continued)*

```
!
hostname US-GW2
!
enable password xxx
!
username cisco password 0 xxx
!
ip subnet-zero
no ip domain-lookup
!
call rsvp-sync
!
translation-rule 1
 Rule 0 ^0111.% 1
 Rule 1 ^0112.% 2
 Rule 2 ^0113.% 3
 Rule 3 ^0114.% 4
 Rule 4 ^0115.% 5
 Rule 5 ^0116.% 6
 Rule 6 ^0117.% 7
 Rule 7 ^0118.% 8
 Rule 8 ^0119.% 9
!
translation-rule 4
 Rule 0 ^2...... 14082
 Rule 1 ^3...... 14083
 Rule 2 ^4...... 14084
 Rule 3 ^5...... 14085
 Rule 4 ^6...... 14086
 Rule 5 ^7...... 14087
 Rule 6 ^8...... 14088
 Rule 7 ^9...... 14089
!
interface Ethernet0/0
 ip address 172.19.49.167 255.255.255.192
 h323-gateway voip interface
 h323-gateway voip id NA-GK ipaddr 172.19.49.168 1719 priority 1
 h323-gateway voip id NA-ALTGK ipaddr 172.19.49.169 1719 priority 2
 h323-gateway voip h323-id US-GW2
!
ip classless
ip route 0.0.0.0 0.0.0.0 172.19.49.129
no ip http server
!
voice-port 1/0/0
!
voice-port 1/0/1
!
dial-peer cor custom
!
dial-peer voice 1 voip
 destination-pattern 011T
```

continues

Example 5-17 *US-GW2 Configuration (Continued)*

```
  translate-outgoing called 1
  session target ras
 !
dial-peer voice 2 voip
  destination-pattern 1T
  session target ras
 !
dial-peer voice 1408 pots
  destination-pattern 14087791000
  port 1/0/0
 !
dial-peer voice 4 voip
  destination-pattern [2-9]......
  translate-outgoing called 4
  session target ras
 !
gateway
 !
line con 0
  transport input none
line aux 0
line vty 0 4
  exec-timeout 0 0
  password xxx
 !
end
```

Example 5-18 *CHINA-GW1 Configuration*

```
 !
version 12.1
service timestamps debug uptime
service timestamps log uptime
no service password-encryption
 !
hostname CHINA-GW1
 !
username cisco password 0 xxx
 !
ip subnet-zero
no ip domain-lookup
 !
translation-rule 2
 Rule 0 ^01.% 8601
 Rule 1 ^02.% 8602
 Rule 2 ^03.% 8603
 Rule 3 ^04.% 8604
 Rule 4 ^05.% 8605
 Rule 5 ^06.% 8606
 Rule 6 ^07.% 8607
 Rule 7 ^08.% 8608
```

Example 5-18 *CHINA-GW1 Configuration (Continued)*

```
 Rule 8 ^09.% 8609
!
translation-rule 1
 Rule 0 ^001.% 1
 Rule 1 ^002.% 2
 Rule 2 ^003.% 3
 Rule 3 ^004.% 4
 Rule 4 ^005.% 5
 Rule 5 ^006.% 6
 Rule 6 ^007.% 7
 Rule 7 ^008.% 8
 Rule 8 ^009.% 9
!
interface Ethernet0/0
 ip address 172.19.49.170 255.255.255.192
 h323-gateway voip interface
 h323-gateway voip id AS-GK ipaddr 172.19.49.172 1719
 h323-gateway voip h323-id CHINA-GW1
 h323-gateway voip tech-prefix 1#
!
interface Ethernet0/1
 no ip address
 shutdown
!
ip classless
ip route 0.0.0.0 0.0.0.0 172.19.49.129
no ip http server
!
voice-port 1/0/0
 timeouts interdigit 3
!
voice-port 1/0/1
!
dial-peer cor custom
!
dial-peer voice 1 voip
 destination-pattern 00T
 translate-outgoing called 1
 session target ras
!
dial-peer voice 2 voip
 destination-pattern 86T
 session target ras
!
dial-peer voice 3 voip
 destination-pattern 0[1-9]T
 translate-outgoing called 2
 session target ras
!
dial-peer voice 8610 pots
 destination-pattern 861011112222
 port 1/0/0
```

continues

Example 5-18 *CHINA-GW1 Configuration (Continued)*

```
!
gateway
!
line con 0
 transport input none
line aux 0
line vty 0 4
 exec-timeout 0 0
 password xxx
!
end
```

Example 5-19 *FRANCE-GW1 Configuration*

```
!
version 12.1
service timestamps debug uptime
service timestamps log uptime
no service password-encryption
!
hostname FRANCE-GW1
!
no logging console
enable password xxx
!
username cisco password 0 xxx
!
ip subnet-zero
no ip domain-lookup
!
call rsvp-sync
!
dial-control-mib retain-timer 60
dial-control-mib max-size 1200
!
translation-rule 2
 Rule 0 ^01.% 3301
 Rule 1 ^02.% 3302
 Rule 2 ^03.% 3303
 Rule 3 ^04.% 3304
 Rule 4 ^05.% 3305
 Rule 5 ^06.% 3306
!
translation-rule 1
 Rule 0 ^0011.% 1
 Rule 1 ^0012.% 2
 Rule 2 ^0013.% 3
 Rule 3 ^0014.% 4
 Rule 4 ^0015.% 5
 Rule 5 ^0016.% 6
 Rule 6 ^0017.% 7
```

Example 5-19 *FRANCE-GW1 Configuration (Continued)*

```
 Rule 7 ^0018.% 8
 Rule 8 ^0019.% 9
 !
translation-rule 3
 Rule 0 ^001.% 1
 Rule 1 ^002.% 2
 Rule 2 ^003.% 3
 Rule 3 ^004.% 4
 Rule 4 ^005.% 5
 Rule 5 ^006.% 6
 Rule 6 ^007.% 7
 Rule 7 ^008.% 8
 Rule 8 ^009.% 9
 !
interface Ethernet0/0
 ip address 172.19.49.174 255.255.255.192
 h323-gateway voip interface
 h323-gateway voip id E-GK ipaddr 172.19.49.176 1719
 h323-gateway voip h323-id FRANCE-GW1
 h323-gateway voip tech-prefix 1#
 !
interface Ethernet0/1
 no ip address
 shutdown
 !
ip classless
ip route 0.0.0.0 0.0.0.0 172.19.49.129
no ip http server
 !
voice-port 1/0/0
 timeouts interdigit 3
 !
voice-port 1/0/1
 !
voice-port 1/1/0
 !
voice-port 1/1/1
 !
dial-peer cor custom
 !
dial-peer voice 3301 pots
 destination-pattern 330311112222
 port 1/0/0
 !
dial-peer voice 1 voip
 destination-pattern 00T
 translate-outgoing called 3
 session target ras
 !
dial-peer voice 2 voip
 destination-pattern 0[1-6]........
 translate-outgoing called 2
```

continues

Example 5-19 *FRANCE-GW1 Configuration (Continued)*

```
  session target ras
 !
 gateway
 !
 line con 0
  transport input none
 line aux 0
 line vty 0 4
  exec-timeout 0 0
  password xxx
  login local
 !
 no scheduler allocate
 end
```

Example 5-20 *NA-GK (North America Gatekeeper) Configuration*

```
 !
 version 12.1
 service timestamps debug uptime
 service timestamps log uptime
 no service password-encryption
 !
 hostname NA-GK
 !
 no logging console
 enable password xxx
 !
 username cisco password 0 xxx
 !
 ip subnet-zero
 no ip domain-lookup
 !
 dial-control-mib retain-timer 60
 dial-control-mib max-size 1200
 !
 interface Ethernet0/0
  ip address 172.19.49.168 255.255.255.192
  !
 interface Ethernet0/1
  no ip address
  shutdown
 !
 ip classless
 ip route 0.0.0.0 0.0.0.0 172.19.49.129
 no ip http server
 !
 snmp-server engineID local 00000009020000001969C63E0
 snmp-server community public RW
 snmp-server packetsize 4096
 !
```

Example 5-20 *NA-GK (North America Gatekeeper) Configuration (Continued)*

```
dial-peer cor custom
!
gatekeeper
 zone local NA-GK netman.com 172.19.49.168
 zone remote NA-ALTGK netman.com 172.19.49.169 1719
 zone remote DGK netman.com 172.19.49.190 1719
 zone remote ALTDGK netman.com 172.19.49.180 1719
 zone prefix NA-GK 1408527* gw-priority 10 US-GW1
 zone prefix NA-GK 1408779* gw-priority 10 US-GW2
 zone prefix NA-GK 1408*
 zone prefix NA-ALTGK 1408*
 zone prefix DGK *
 zone prefix ALTDGK *
 gw-type-prefix 1#* default-technology
 lrq forward-queries
 no shutdown
!
line con 0
 transport input none
line aux 0
line vty 0 4
 exec-timeout 0 0
 password xxx
 login local
!
no scheduler allocate
end
```

Example 5-21 *NA-ALTGK (North America Alternate Gatekeeper) Configuration*

```
!
version 12.1
service timestamps debug uptime
service timestamps log uptime
no service password-encryption
!
hostname NA-ALTGK
!
enable password xxx
!
ip subnet-zero
!
interface Ethernet0/0
 ip address 172.19.49.169 255.255.255.0
!
interface Ethernet0/1
 no ip address
 shutdown
!
ip classless
no ip http server
```

continues

Example 5-21 *NA-ALTGK (North America Alternate Gatekeeper) Configuration (Continued)*

```
!
dial-peer cor custom
!
gatekeeper
 zone local NA-ALTGK netman.com 172.19.49.169
 zone remote NA-GK netman.com 172.19.49.168 1719
 zone remote DGK netman.com 172.19.49.190 1719
 zone remote ALTDGK netman 172.19.49.180 1719
 zone prefix NA-ALTGK 1408527* gw-priority 10 US-GW1
 zone prefix NA-ALTGK 1408779* gw-priority 10 US-GW2
 zone prefix NA-GK 1408*
 zone prefix DGK *
 zone prefix ALTDGK *
 gw-type-prefix 1#* default-technology
 lrq forward-queries
 no shutdown
!
line con 0
 transport input none
line aux 0
line vty 0 4
 password xxx
 login
!
end
```

Example 5-22 *AS-GK (Asia Gatekeeper) Configuration*

```
!
version 12.1
service timestamps debug uptime
service timestamps log uptime
no service password-encryption
!
hostname AS-GK
!
no logging console
enable password xxx
!
username cisco password 0 xxx
!
ip subnet-zero
no ip domain-lookup
!
interface Ethernet0/0
 ip address 172.19.49.172 255.255.255.192
!
interface Ethernet0/1
 no ip address
 shutdown
!
```

Example 5-22 *AS-GK (Asia Gatekeeper) Configuration (Continued)*

```
ip classless
ip route 0.0.0.0 0.0.0.0 172.19.49.129
no ip http server
!
snmp-server engineID local 00000000902000001969C63A0
snmp-server community public RW
!
dial-peer cor custom
!
gatekeeper
 zone local AS-GK netman.com 172.19.49.172
 zone remote DGK netman.com 172.19.49.190 1719
 zone remote ALTDGK netman.com 172.19.49.184 1719
 zone prefix AS-GK 8610* gw-priority 10 CHINA-GW1
 zone prefix DGK *
 zone prefix ALTDGK *
 no shutdown
!
line con 0
 transport input none
line aux 0
line vty 0 4
 exec-timeout 0 0
 password xxx
 login local
!
no scheduler allocate
end
```

Example 5-23 *E-GK (EMEA Gatekeeper) Configuration*

```
!
version 12.1
service timestamps debug uptime
service timestamps log uptime
no service password-encryption
!
hostname E-GK
!
no logging console
enable password xxx
!
username cisco password 0 xxx
!
clock timezone PDT -7
ip subnet-zero
no ip domain-lookup
!
interface Ethernet0/0
 ip address 172.19.49.176 255.255.255.192
 !
```

continues

Example 5-23 *E-GK (EMEA Gatekeeper) Configuration (Continued)*

```
interface Ethernet0/1
 no ip address
 shutdown
 !
ip classless
ip route 0.0.0.0 0.0.0.0 172.19.49.129
no ip http server
 !
snmp-server engineID local 00000009020000024B8FEF60
snmp-server community public RW
 !
dial-peer cor custom
 !
gatekeeper
 zone local E-GK netman.com 172.19.49.176
 zone remote DGK netman.com 172.19.49.190 1719
 zone remote ALTDGK netman.com 172.19.49.180 1719
 zone prefix E-GK 3303* gw-priority 10 FRANCE-GW1
 zone prefix DGK *
 zone prefix ALTDGK *
 no shutdown
 !
line con 0
 transport input none
line aux 0
line vty 0 4
 exec-timeout 0 0
 password xxx
 login local
 !
ntp clock-period 17207746
ntp server 172.19.49.166
no scheduler allocate
end
```

Example 5-24 *DGK (Directory Gatekeeper—Primary HSRP) Configuration*

```
 !
version 12.1
service timestamps debug uptime
service timestamps log uptime
no service password-encryption
 !
hostname DGK
 !
enable password xxx
 !
ip subnet-zero
```

Example 5-24 *DGK (Directory Gatekeeper—Primary HSRP) Configuration (Continued)*

```
!
interface FastEthernet0/0
 ip address 172.19.49.178 255.255.255.192
 duplex auto
 speed auto
 standby 1 priority 110
 standby 1 ip 172.19.49.190
!
interface FastEthernet0/1
 no ip address
 duplex auto
 speed auto
!
no ip classless
ip route 0.0.0.0 0.0.0.0 172.19.49.129
no ip http server
!
dial-peer cor custom
!
gatekeeper
 zone local DGK netman.com 172.19.49.190
 zone remote NA-GK netman.com 172.19.49.168 1719
 zone remote AS-GK netman.com 172.19.49.172 1719
 zone remote E-GK netman.com 172.19.49.176 1719
 zone remote NA-AGK netman.com 172.19.49.169 1719
 zone prefix NA-GK 1*
 zone prefix E-GK 33*
 zone prefix AS-GK 86*
 lrq forward-queries
 no shutdown
!
line con 0
 transport input none
line aux 0
line vty 0 4
 password xxx
 login
```

Example 5-25 *DGK2 (Directory Gatekeeper—Secondary HSRP) Configuration*

```
!
version 12.1
service timestamps debug uptime
service timestamps log uptime
no service password-encryption
!
hostname DGK2
!
boot system flash c3640-ix-mz.121-2.T.bin
enable password xxx
!
```

continues

Example 5-25 *DGK2 (Directory Gatekeeper—Secondary HSRP) Configuration (Continued)*

```
ip subnet-zero
!
interface FastEthernet0/0
 ip address 172.19.49.179 255.255.255.192
 no ip redirects
 duplex auto
 speed auto
 standby 1 ip 172.19.49.190
!
interface FastEthernet0/1
 no ip address
 shutdown
 duplex auto
 speed auto
!
no ip classless
no ip http server
!
gatekeeper
 zone local DGK netman.com 172.19.49.190
 zone remote NA-GK netman.com 172.19.49.168 1719
 zone remote AS-GK netman.com 172.19.49.172 1719
 zone remote E-GK netman.com 172.19.49.176 1719
 zone remote NA-AGK netman.com 172.19.49.169 1719
 zone prefix NA-GK 1*
 zone prefix E-GK 33*
 zone prefix AS-GK 86*
 lrq forward-queries
 no shutdown
!
line con 0
 transport input none
line aux 0
line vty 0 4
 password xxx
 login
!
end
```

Example 5-26 *ALT-DGK (Secondary Directory Gatekeeper) Configuration*

```
!
version 12.1
service timestamps debug uptime
service timestamps log uptime
no service password-encryption
!
hostname ALT-DGK
!
boot system flash c3640-ix-mz.121-2.T.bin
enable password xxx
```

Example 5-26 *ALT-DGK (Secondary Directory Gatekeeper) Configuration (Continued)*

```
!
ip subnet-zero
no ip domain-lookup
!
interface FastEthernet0/0
 ip address 172.19.49.184 255.255.255.192
 duplex auto
 speed auto
!
interface FastEthernet0/1
 no ip address
 shutdown
 duplex auto
 speed auto
!
no ip classless
no ip http server
!
gatekeeper
 zone local DGK netman.com 172.19.49.190
 zone remote NA-GK netman.com 172.19.49.168 1719
 zone remote AS-GK netman.com 172.19.49.172 1719
 zone remote E-GK netman.com 172.19.49.176 1719
 zone remote NA-AGK netman.com 172.19.49.169 1719
 zone prefix NA-GK 1*
 zone prefix E-GK 33*
 zone prefix AS-GK 86*
 lrq forward-queries
 no shutdown
!
line con 0
 transport input none
line aux 0
line vty 0 4
 password xxx
 login
!
end
```

Summary

This chapter discussed how to configure and manage static H.323 dial plans on gateway and gatekeeper platforms for large VoIP networks. We described the relationships between gateways, gatekeepers, and directory gatekeepers, and explained the responsibilities of each of these network components in implementing a large-scale dial plan.

We talked about using translation rules to accomplish digit manipulation, and we talked about using the **preference** command, HSRP, and other tools to configure failover options. We also discussed how to use zone prefixes, technology prefixes, and hopoff zones to simplify administration and scaling for call routing in large-scale dial plans.

## CHAPTER 6

Designing a Long-Distance VoIP Network

The long-distance VoIP network solution is a set of network design and configuration strategies that provides trunk-level transport of global switched telephone traffic distributed over VoIP. Calls originate in the PSTN and are routed through interexchange carriers (IXCs) before being handed off to a wholesale VoIP carrier for transport. To the subscriber, the service seems like any other inexpensive long-distance service. To the originating long-distance carrier, the wholesale carrier is only one of a number of termination options.

The long-distance VoIP network solution offers service providers the required architecture design, network components, software features, functional groups, and provisioning methodologies needed to run a VoIP wholesale service. The solution enables you to build a wholesale network and sell unbranded voice services to retailers, such as Internet telephony service providers (ITSPs), application service providers (ASPs), IXCs, and Post Telephone and Telegraph administrations (PTTs).

This chapter describes the fundamentals of designing a long-distance VoIP network solution.

Long-Distance VoIP Network Features and Benefits

The long-distance VoIP network solution includes multiple components in various combinations from both Cisco and third-party vendors. Voice points of presence (POPs) that are interconnected to other service providers are a central component in the delivery of wholesale voice services. The types of interconnections or call topologies you support will determine the specific components and design methods we recommend. You use the call topologies to build a set of deployment scenarios that enables wholesale applications. Figure 6-1 shows some of the interconnection possibilities.

Figure 6-1 *Long-distance VoIP interconnection possibilities.*

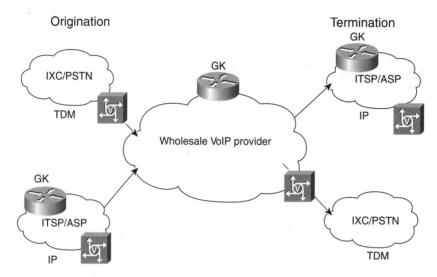

The long-distance VoIP network solution provides the following benefits:

- Voice quality that is indistinguishable from that of the PSTN
- A cost-effective, reliable VoIP network infrastructure
- Support for least-cost routing and other enhanced call-routing methods
- Intercarrier call authorization and accounting (peer-to-peer)
- Support for intercarrier clearing and settlement services
- Support for local, national, and international dial plans
- Connectivity with the PSTN over carrier interfaces
- Connectivity with other VoIP service providers and VoIP equipment from other vendors
- A worldwide network of other VoIP service providers interested in interconnecting

Long-Distance VoIP Design Methodology

To design your own personalized long-distance VoIP solution, we recommend that you systematically perform the following steps:

Step 1 Identify the service or services you plan to sell.

Step 2 Determine the type of carriers or providers you plan to interconnect with.

Step 3 Determine the interconnection types you plan to use.

Step 4   Determine the call topologies you plan to use.

Step 5   Identify the appropriate deployment scenario.

Step 6   Identify the functional areas you require.

Step 7   Identify the required hardware and software components.

Step 8   Identify design and scalability issues.

Step 9   Configure and provision components.

Step 1: Identify Services

A key feature of the Cisco long-distance VoIP solution is its ability to support various mixes of services to suit the needs of a single service provider or multiple partnering service providers. Supported services include:

- Minutes aggregation and termination (including ASP termination)
- Calling card services
- Clearinghouse services
- Service options

Figure 6-2 depicts all of the components that might be needed to provide these services. These components include gatekeepers (GKs), gateways (GWs), signaling link termination equipment (SLTs), signaling controllers (SCs), and intermachine trunks (IMTs).

Minutes Aggregation and Termination (Including ASP Termination)

The Cisco long-distance VoIP solution supports the originating carrier that hands calls over to a VoIP wholesaler at a profit. Termination settlement rates are generally lower than PSTN termination rates—the key reason why long-distance carriers will choose a VoIP carrier for termination. Furthermore, termination bandwidth is often available over VoIP to countries where PSTN termination is unavailable because of congested international gateway facilities or other reasons. The average call success rate is as good as or better than that provided by PSTN carriers, and voice quality, including echo cancellation, is uncompromised.

Key features of this service include the following:

- H.323 VoIP interconnect using standards-based H.323 implementation
- Gatekeeper LRQ forwarding for call routing and accurate call accounting
- Support for voice, modem, and fax calls
- Support for SS7, T1/E1 E&M, E1 R2, and E1 PRI interfaces

Figure 6-2 *High-level view of end-to-end service possibilities.*

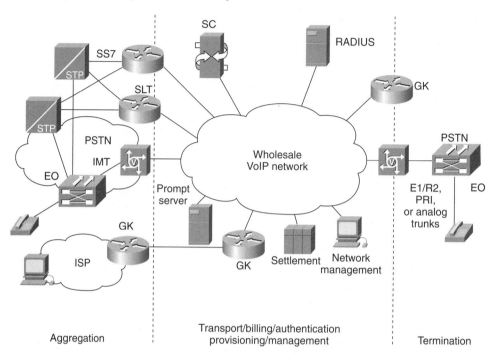

As part of this service, ASP carrier-to-carrier termination services are supported. The ASP originates the call, often over an Internet-enabled PC-telephony application, or through a PSTN portal for cellular phone callers. The ASP provides pre-call services, such as content delivery (prerecorded messages, voice mail, private number dialing) or supervision-related services, such as "find me/follow me." The ASP then hands off any long-distance calls to a wholesale carrier for termination by the PSTN. This requires accurate call accounting.

Calling Card Services

The Cisco long-distance VoIP solution supports the following calling card services:

- **Prepaid**—A wholesale VoIP carrier can host prepaid services for multiple service providers on its infrastructure. In addition, most prepaid service providers use VoIP wholesalers to terminate long-distance calls that are placed by prepaid subscribers. Using the integrated voice response (IVR) feature in Cisco wholesale VoIP gateways (for example, Cisco 2600 and 3600 series, Cisco AS5300 and AS5400 series, and Cisco 7200 series), and the real-time authorization and call accounting systems provided by Cisco Ecosystem Partners, you can offer this service over a VoIP network and lower the cost and deployment time of calling-card services.

- **Postpaid**—Like the prepaid service, this service can be hosted by a wholesale VoIP carrier. An example is basic calling that's accessed by the 800 prefix, a calling card number, or a PIN. Postpaid is similar to prepaid service, except that with postpaid the authorization is not tied to call rating. Consequently, call rating does not have to happen in real time, and there might be more partner billing-system options that perform adequately at scale. After calls are made, a billing system contracted by the company charges the carrier.

Figure 6-3 illustrates a variety of calling card services, including those provided by third parties.

Figure 6-3 *Calling card services.*

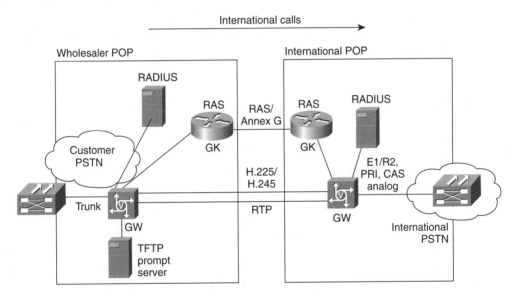

Clearinghouse Services

When multiple partners join to provide long-distance VoIP services, the services previously described might require the assistance of clearinghouse services for billing and settlement. The Cisco long-distance voice solution supports call termination agreements through Open Settlement Protocol (OSP) in Cisco devices.

OSP relies upon Cisco's Open Packet Telephony (OPT) framework at the call control layer. Service providers that use OSP (the only standard IP interface for VoIP clearinghouse functions) have to do business with only one settlements provider. As a result, there is no need to negotiate separate agreements with carriers in multiple countries, meet varied technical requirements for interconnection, make repeated arrangements for call accounting, or establish multiple credit accounts. The OSP clearinghouse solution virtually eliminates the risk of doing business with new service providers that have a limited credit history, or with carriers in countries subject to currency fluctuations. In addition, it gives virtually every VoIP provider the worldwide calling reach that it requires.

OSP uses a standard protocol approved by the Internet Protocol Harmonization over Networks organization of the European Telecommunications Standards Institute (ETSI TIPHON). By allowing gateways to transfer accounting and routing information securely, this protocol provides common ground among VoIP service providers. Consequently, third-party clearinghouses with an OSP server can offer call authorization, call accounting, and settlement—including all the complex rating and routing tables necessary for efficient and cost-effective interconnections.

In most cases, a wholesale provider will subcontract with a clearinghouse partner to provide wholesale voice services with proper settlement. However, a clearinghouse solutions vendor can also independently take advantage of the Cisco long-distance VoIP solution to achieve market objectives.

Service Options

In addition to the services previously listed, two additional service options are available:

- Limited egress carrier-sensitive routing
- Interconnect to Clarent-based clearinghouses

Limited Egress Carrier-Sensitive Routing

As an enhancement to simple carrier-interconnect applications, the Cisco long-distance VoIP solution makes it possible to route a call to different destination carriers. You have the same considerations as with simple carrier-interconnect models, but with slightly increased call-routing responsibilities. The directory gatekeeper can make limited egress carrier-sensitive routing (CSR) decisions by using the sequential location request (LRQ) feature, which is available to the applications using directory gatekeeper routing. Generally speaking, this means any TDM partners and directory gatekeeper peering partners, but also includes any OSP partners in which an OSP interconnection zone is used, as opposed to a direct implementation on your gateways.

In this CSR application, the sequential LRQ feature is used to route a call to different carriers, each of which supports a different destination. For example, you can provision your gatekeepers to route certain destination patterns to carrier A first. If carrier A (an ITSP) is unavailable as a result of a location reject (LRJ) or LRQ timeout, you might decide to route the call to carrier B (an IXC), then to carrier C, and so on. Figure 6-4 illustrates this application.

Figure 6-4   *Limited egress carrier-sensitive routing.*

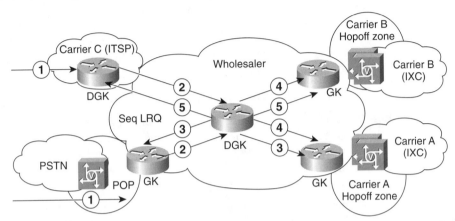

The three restrictions to keep in mind with limited egress CSR are explained here:

- **Independence of ingress and egress carriers**—The egress carrier is selected independently of the source carrier. The gatekeeper routes calls on the basis of DNIS (Dialed Number Identification Service). The list of possible egress carriers that you statically configure are tried in order, although routing decisions are not based on which carrier sourced the call. For example, the fact that carrier A sourced the call doesn't influence the choice of carrier on which the call will be terminated.

- **Independence of destination carriers**—Each destination carrier must be contained in its own zone. For ITSP carriers, this is fairly simple. Interconnected ITSPs are seen as single remote zones to which your directory gatekeeper sends LRQ messages. For interconnected TDM carriers, this implies (1) that the gateways that are capable of sending calls to the carrier are grouped into their own hopoff zone that's managed by a gatekeeper, and (2) that multiple carriers are never supported by a single gateway.

- **Static versus dynamic routing**—Dynamic routing decisions are not supported; you configure the order of sequential LRQs statically. Consequently, there's no provision for percentage-based routing, maximum-minute cutoffs, and so forth. Egress carriers are always chosen from a statically configured list of routes. If the directory gatekeeper determines that an OSP interconnection zone handles a route, it's possible that the OSP server will return a terminating gateway on the basis of advanced routing logic (if so provisioned). For example, the OSP server might dynamically select a least-cost terminating carrier on the basis of time of day or best voice quality.

Interconnect to Clarent-Based Clearinghouses

You can interconnect with a Clarent-based service provider (see www.clarent.com) provided that the gateways register to a Clarent gatekeeper; however, this means dedicating specific gateways as part of the Clarent zone. Back-to-back gateways can be used to provide a "transit" zone between the Cisco- and the Clarent-based network. One of the back-to-back gateways registers to a Clarent gatekeeper in the Clarent-based service provider's network; the other registers to a Cisco gatekeeper in your network. This is similar to using back-to-back gateways to interconnect OSP partners, except that here the relationship is H.323 gateway to gatekeeper instead of OSP.

The following are two limitations to using Clarent-based interconnect:

- **IP-to-IP interconnect**—The use of back-to-back gateways enables Clarent-based interconnect partners to exchange traffic not only with wholesaler TDM-based interconnects, but also with other IP-based interconnect partners. Those partners can be either directory gatekeeper or OSP-based. It might be necessary to modify the dial plan architecture to support directory gatekeeper-based IP carrier interconnects.

- **Interoperability considerations**—To interconnect with Clarent-based networks, H.323 interoperability must be sustained between Cisco gateways and Clarent gatekeepers. Currently, only voice-bearer interoperability is supported for G.711, G.723.1, and G.729 codec types. Because of tandem compression, back-to-back gateways impair voice quality.

Step 2: Determine Carriers or Providers

As a long-distance VoIP service provider, you need to interconnect with other service providers (ITSPs and ASPs) and carriers (IXCs and PSTNs) to offer the services you selected in Step 1. This interconnection method is referred to as a *call topology*. Because each call topology is specific to the carrier or service provider with which you plan to connect, you need to first identify the targeted carriers and service providers.

Step 3: Determine Interconnection Types

Basically, you can use two application interconnection types to interconnect with other service providers: IP and TDM. The application interconnect type you use determines your call topology, and the line of demarcation between you and the other service providers determines whether the interconnection type is IP or TDM.

Step 4: Determine Call Topologies

The call topology influences the ultimate configuration requirements of the functional areas within the network to support a given application. For example, if you enable simple carrier interconnect between an ASP and an IXC, then you'd use an IP-to-TDM call topology. You'd then have to address the configuration requirements for that application (such as call routing and shared support services needed for billing, settlement, and security options) as influenced by that topology type.

The four call topologies or interconnection methods are listed here:

- Originating TDM/Terminating TDM

- Originating TDM/Terminating IP

- Originating IP/Terminating TDM

- Originating IP/Terminating IP (transit VoIP network)

Figure 6-5 summarizes each of these topologies.

Figure 6-5   *Summary of call topologies.*

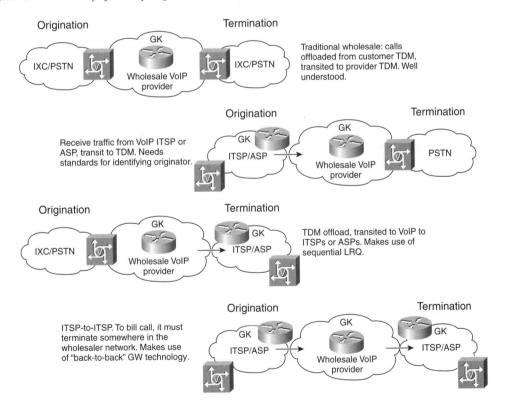

Originating TDM/Terminating TDM Call Topology

The originating TDM/terminating TDM call topology is a single administrative domain and the most fundamental call topology. With this topology, you receive and terminate traffic from other service providers via TDM interfaces. Figure 6-6 illustrates this topology.

Figure 6-6   *Topology 1: originating TDM/terminating TDM.*

Because interconnect is confined to the TDM interfaces on gateways that you administer, deployment considerations in the areas of routing, security, billing, and settlement are fairly straightforward. Limited-egress CSR applications demand additional call routing provisioning tasks. Your concerns are primarily confined to supporting the proper TDM signaling and the transparency of bearer traffic, such as voice, fax, or modem pass-through.

The originating TDM/terminating TDM call topology is appropriate for the following applications:

- Card services
- IXC-to-IXC interconnect
- IXC offload
- LEC-to-LEC interconnect (simple toll bypass)
- LEC-to-IXC interconnect

Originating TDM/Terminating IP Call Topology

If you want to increase call volume or coverage area by adding interconnections with other IP-based service providers, use the originating TDM/terminating IP call topology. With this topology, you receive traffic from IXC or PSTN providers over TDM interfaces. If the provider can't terminate the call within its own network POPs, it can send traffic to other service providers such as ITSPs or ASPs over IP. Figure 6-7 illustrates this topology.

In addition to the TDM-related issues described in the originating TDM/terminating TDM call topology, you have with this topology the added considerations of IP interconnect. You must consider issues pertaining to call routing, interoperable bearer transport, billing, settlement, and security.

Figure 6-7   *Topology 2: originating TDM/terminating IP.*

The originating TDM/terminating IP call topology is appropriate for the following applications:

- Card services
- LEC-to-ASP interconnect
- LEC-to-ITSP interconnect (simple toll bypass)
- IXC-to-ASP interconnect
- IXC-to-ITSP interconnect

Originating IP/Terminating TDM Call Topology

This call topology is essentially the same as the originating TDM/terminating IP call topology, but the call direction is reversed. With this topology, you receive traffic from other service providers via IP and terminate traffic at your POPs to IXC or LEC providers through TDM interfaces. Figure 6-8 illustrates this topology.

Figure 6-8   *Topology 3: originating IP/terminating TDM.*

Because you're now receiving traffic from other providers through IP interconnect, you must be concerned with call routing, originating carrier identification for billing and settlement, interoperable bearer transport, and security.

The originating IP/terminating TDM call topology is appropriate for the following applications:

- ITSP-to-LEC interconnect (toll bypass)
- ASP-to-LEC interconnect (toll bypass)
- ITSP-to-IXC interconnect
- ASP-to-IXC interconnect

Originating IP/Terminating IP (Transit VoIP Network) Call Topology

If you want to provide transit between different IP-based interconnect partners, use the originating IP/terminating IP call topology. With this topology, you exchange traffic between other service providers using only IP connections. Figure 6-9 illustrates this topology.

Figure 6-9   *Topology 4: originating IP/terminating IP.*

Typically, you receive traffic from an ITSP or ASP, and if you can't terminate the call at one of your own POPs, you send the call to another service provider.

When sending and receiving traffic between two IP interconnects, you have increased challenges in the areas of call routing, carrier identification, billing, settlement, security, and masking originating carrier information from the terminating carrier.

The originating IP/terminating IP call topology is appropriate for the following applications:

- ASP-to-ITSP interconnect
- ASP-to-ASP interconnect
- ITSP-to-ITSP interconnect
- ITSP-to-ASP interconnect

IP Interconnection Variations

In addition to using the call topologies previously described, you can interconnect with other IP-based service providers (ITSPs and ASPs) using one of the following methods:

- Directory gatekeeper-based interconnection method
- OSP-based interconnection method

Each method has its own provisioning requirements.

Directory Gatekeeper-Based Interconnection Method

With this interconnection method, you provision call routing between your IP interconnect partners by peering directory gatekeepers to which you send LRQ RAS messages. You can direct certain destination patterns to specific interconnect partners. These destination patterns potentially could have been modified upon ingress into your network to provide limited ingress carrier-sensitive routing applications. Additionally, you can use sequential LRQ features to provide limited egress carrier-sensitive routing applications.

With directory gatekeeper-based interconnect, you benefit by centralizing route provisioning in the directory gatekeeper rather than pushing it to the edge gateways as with OSP. However, billing/settlement functions and security options are processes external to call routing that require some configuration in the gateways, gatekeepers, and related shared-services components.

If you are a large service provider with many POP gateways, provisioning complexities can determine that this is the best option for interconnect. Figure 6-10 illustrates a directory gatekeeper-based interconnect with other ITSP/ASP partners.

OSP-Based Interconnection Method

With this interconnection method, an OSP server performs call routing, billing/settlement, and security functions; however, additional provisioning is required. All edge gateways must be registered with the OSP server, and rotary dial-peer failover must be provisioned to route calls through the OSP interconnect.

OSP might be an attractive interconnect option if you want to combine call routing, security, and billing/settlement into one architecture. However, in current Cisco implementations, limitations with OSP deployments require extensive provisioning in the gateways so that they can interact with the required shared services, support the dial plan architecture, and cover termination caveats.

Figure 6-11 illustrates an OSP-based interconnect with other ITSP/ASP service partners.

Figure 6-10 *Directory gatekeeper-based interconnect with other service providers.*

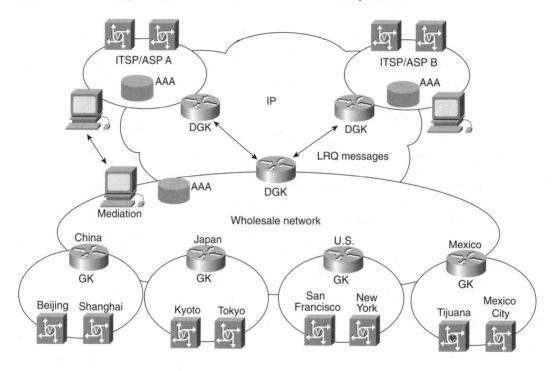

Figure 6-11 *OSP-based interconnect with other service partners.*

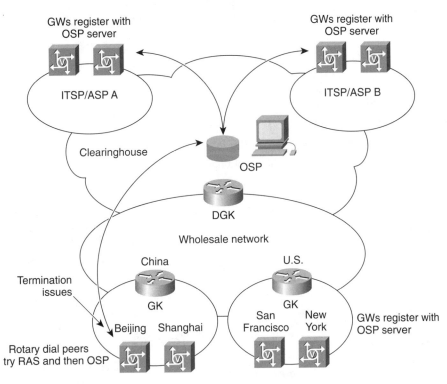

Step 5: Identify Deployment Scenario

Select the appropriate deployment scenario based on *functional areas* (described later in this chapter) and call topologies.

The Cisco long-distance VoIP solution supports the following deployment scenarios:

- TDM to TDM
- TDM to IP
- TDM to IP with OSP
- IP to IP with directory gatekeeper
- IP to IP with OSP

Step 6: Identify Functional Areas

The Cisco long-distance VoIP solution encompasses the following primary functional areas:

- Gatekeeper core
- Shared services
- Non-SS7-based POP
- SS7-based POP
- Back-to-back gateway system

Figure 6-12 shows each of the functional areas.

Figure 6-12 *Functional areas of the Cisco long-distance VoIP solution.*

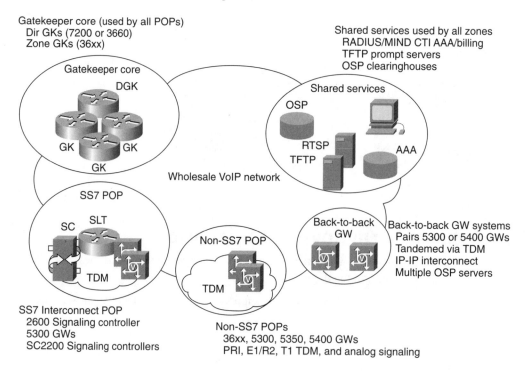

Gatekeeper core (used by all POPs)
  Dir GKs (7200 or 3660)
  Zone GKs (36xx)

Shared services used by all zones
  RADIUS/MIND CTI AAA/billing
  TFTP prompt servers
  OSP clearinghouses

Gatekeeper core
  DGK
  GK   GK
    GK

Shared services
  OSP
  RTSP
  TFTP   AAA

Wholesale VoIP network

SS7 POP
  SC   SLT
  TDM

Non-SS7 POP
  TDM

Back-to-back
  GW

Back-to-back GW systems
  Pairs 5300 or 5400 GWs
  Tandemed via TDM
  IP-IP interconnect
  Multiple OSP servers

SS7 Interconnect POP
  2600 Signaling controller
  5300 GWs
  SC2200 Signaling controllers

Non-SS7 POPs
  36xx, 5300, 5350, 5400 GWs
  PRI, E1/R2, T1 TDM, and analog signaling

NOTE   The platforms shown in Figure 6-12 are suggestions and are not intended to be a comprehensive list of available and/or applicable platforms.

Your wholesale VoIP cloud can include some or all of the areas depicted previously, depending on the issues specific to your interconnection methods, billing services, call control, settlement, IVR options, and network management.

Gatekeeper Core

The gatekeeper core functional area, illustrated in Figure 6-13, is used by all POPs and is the foundation of a large-scale H.323 network design. It consists of Cisco GKs, Cisco directory gatekeepers (DGKs), and optionally, Ecosystem Partner gatekeeper platforms.

Figure 6-13 *Role of gatekeepers and directory gatekeepers in the gatekeeper core.*

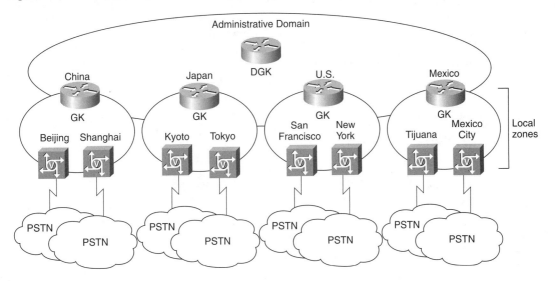

Gatekeepers enable a network to scale in growth, performance, and dial plan administration. Gatekeepers and directory gatekeepers provide for resource management, call routing, security, fault tolerance, external Gatekeeper Transaction Message Protocol (GKTMP) applications, and call detail record (CDR) generation. Gatekeepers support interactions with shared services and provide gatekeeper-based interconnect with other providers if the application demands it.

Inbound directory gatekeepers are Cisco 7200 series routers or Cisco 3660 routers. Zone gatekeepers are Cisco 3600 series routers. Cisco 3640s, 3660s, AS5300s, AS5350s, and AS5400s are examples of gateway platforms.

Shared Services

Shared support services are central resources that enable network applications in the areas of card services, call routing, billing, settlement, security, and network management. The primary elements that enable these applications are OSP servers, TFTP servers, AAA servers, billing systems, NMS platforms, and EMS platforms.

Non-SS7-Based POP

Wholesale service provider networks consist of POPs that house gateways to transport voice traffic between TDM and IP networks. POPs are active components in the originating TDM/terminating TDM, originating TDM/terminating IP, and originating IP/terminating TDM call topologies. Non-SS7-based POPs receive signaling from the TDM network on the same physical interface that supports bearer traffic. There can be a logical separation of signaling and bearer traffic within the interface, such as with ISDN. Actual gateway platforms used at these POPs will depend on the signaling type offered by the TDM interconnect. Figure 6-14 shows non-SS7-based POP signaling. The following interfaces are supported through in-band signaling:

- FXO/FXS
- E&M
- BRI/PRI
- DS1/DS3
- E1/R2
- T1 CAS

Figure 6-14 *Non-SS7-based POP signaling.*

Gateway components include the Cisco 3600 series routers and the Cisco AS5300 universal access servers.

In addition to the physical interface and signaling variations, a number of platform-independent software features and functions must be enabled on the POP gateways to support an application. These include POP size, dial plan, fault-tolerance, security, billing, network management, and bearer transport responsibilities.

SS7-Based POP

SS7-based POPs generally have the same deployment considerations with billing, security, network management, transparent bearer transport, and TFTP servers as the non-SS7 based POPs. However, these POPs have additional considerations related to SS7 interconnect signaling, which is required to conform to the PSTN TDM network. Additional considerations appear in POP size, dial-plan responsibilities, and fault tolerance.

Gateway components include Cisco 2600 Signaling Link Terminals (SLTs) and Cisco AS5300 universal access servers. Support is provided for Q.767 and TR-113 signaling.

Back-to-Back Gateway System

The back-to-back gateway system is a special component used to provide a variety of functions for numerous applications. Gateways are deployed as a pair in a back-to-back TDM trunk, single-stage-dialing configuration.

Depending on the application, back-to-back gateways can function as unidirectional or bidirectional call devices. For example, in an IVR application, the back-to-back gateway has a dedicated half that receives all calls, while the other half is dedicated to originating calls. In contrast, for an OSP interconnect zone application, the back-to-back gateway can process calls in both directions, although each gateway is responsible for separate protocols. For added clarity when discussing back-to-back gateway pairs, we refer to the individual gateways in a pair as an inbound VoIP gateway and an outbound VoIP gateway with respect to the call direction for unidirectional applications. For bidirectional applications, we refer to the gateway by the protocol it supports, where possible.

Figure 6-15 shows the relationship of the back-to-back gateway to an ingress and egress carrier and to your wholesale VoIP cloud.

Figure 6-15 *Relationship of back-to-back gateways to wholesaler and carriers.*

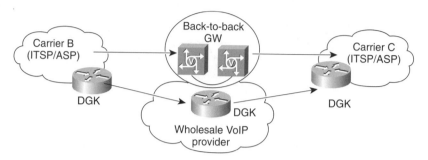

In many ways, the back-to-back gateway system functions just like a normal non-SS7-based POP. The gateway pair helps with applications that use different bearer transport options (such as codec type or security options) on the two interconnecting networks for which you are providing transit. It allows you to have a presence in the call-signaling path in IP-to-IP interconnect call topologies so that you can generate usage records through AAA, interconnect with Clarent-based and OSP-based environments, and front-end PC-to-phone applications for IP-based interconnect partners. It also provides a way to obscure information about interconnect partners.

The platforms that can be used as back-to-back gateways are the Cisco 3600 series routers, the Cisco AS5300 universal access server, and the Cisco AS5400 universal gateway.

Step 7: Identify Required Hardware and Software Components

This section describes the actual hardware and software components, both Cisco's and those of third-party vendors, that can be used to implement a wholesale voice solution.

Major Components

The following major components are used to implement a wholesale voice solution:

- Cisco voice GWs
- Cisco H.323 GKs and DGKs
- Cisco signaling controllers
- Cisco SS7 signaling link termination systems

Cisco Voice Gateways

Wholesale solutions require a range of small- to large-scale PSTN interconnects with the wholesaler's TDM-based customers (typically IXCs, PTTs, or other wholesalers), depending on anticipated call volumes. Similar interconnects might be required to offload traffic. Gateways can handle their own signaling, or they can provide intermachine trunks (IMTs) and receive external SS7 signaling through a Cisco SC2200 running Cisco SS7 Interconnect for Voice Gateways Solution software with Q.931 signaling backhaul.

Gateway platform examples include Cisco 3640, 3660, AS5300, AS5350, and AS5400, along with various supporting network modules.

NOTE   The Cisco long-distance VoIP solution does not support gateway platforms that use MGCP call signaling. Cisco AS5800 gateways cannot be used in SS7 POPs that are using the Cisco SS7 Interconnect for Voice Gateways Solution software.

Cisco H.323 Gatekeepers and Directory Gatekeepers

Gatekeepers and directory gatekeepers are mandatory network elements used to scale a wholesale network to large sizes. They consist of specialized Cisco IOS software images running on a dedicated Cisco 3660 or 7200 series router.

DGKs further supplement network scalability and are mandatory if GK-based carrier interconnect is desired. Cisco GKs perform the following tasks:

- **Resource management**—Cisco GKs determine the health of H.323 gateways by monitoring registration and unregistration (RRQ/URQ) request messages and resource availability indicator (RAI) messages.

- **Call routing**—Cisco GKs provide call routing based on destination E.164 addresses. They can use their knowledge of local gateway health levels to make routing decisions to increase the availability of the gateways on the network. Cisco gatekeepers can also route calls between remote GKs within the same administrative domain, using inter-gatekeeper LRQ RAS messages. Similarly, Cisco DGKs can also route calls to other carrier administrative domains using LRQ RAS messages.

- **Security**—In conjunction with an external server (such as RADIUS), Cisco GKs can be used for secure call admission of intradomain call scenarios (calls within the same service provider). Cisco GKs also have limited application in implementing interdomain security functions for calls sent between carriers through IP interconnect.

- **External Gatekeeper Transaction Message Protocol (GKTMP) applications**— Cisco GKs can act as a control point from which an application server can provide call routing, number translation, call admission/blocking, and so on. These application servers interface with a Cisco GK or DGK using GKTMP.

- Call Detail Record (CDR) generation—Cisco GKs have limited abilities to generate CDRs for calls. This is an option if you don't own the gateways at a POP, or if you want to reduce the amount of messaging overhead associated with AAA in your smaller POPs. Billing in this manner has limitations.

Cisco Signaling Controllers

These are optional components, but are required in SS7 interconnect solutions. The supported platform is the Cisco SC2200.

Cisco Signaling Link Termination Systems

These are optional Cisco 2600 series routers (Cisco 2611 and Cisco 2651) capable of terminating Message Transfer Part (MTP) Levels 1 and 2 SS7 layers and backhauling Level 3 and higher SS7 layers to the Cisco SC2200 in an SS7 interconnect solution.

Additional Components for Shared Services

The following additional components, provided by third parties, support shared services:

- RADIUS/OSS servers
- Ecosystem partner H.323 gatekeepers
- GK application servers
- OSP servers
- Prompt servers
- TFTP servers
- Network management systems
- Element management systems

RADIUS/OSS Servers

Ecosystem partner OSS servers interface with Cisco gateway and gatekeeper components through AAA RADIUS vendor-specific attributes (VSAs) and are mandatory elements of the wholesale network. Current examples include Cisco Secure and Cisco ecosystem partners, such as MIND/CTI and Belle Systems billing platforms. Cisco has defined a set of VSAs in the document *RADIUS Vendor-Specific Attributes Voice Implementation Guide*. VSAs can be used to achieve the following functions:

- **CDR collection and billing system front-ending**—Cisco gateways send call start/stop records to a RADIUS server using AAA. The billing application can extract these records to generate CDRs. CDRs can then be shared between carriers as a method of settlement through billing system mediation applications.

- **User authentication and authorization**—For card services, an AAA RADIUS server can validate end users based on ANI or username and password combinations. AAA interaction occurs directly on the Cisco gateway.

- **Application hosting**—A Cisco gateway can run a call script that interacts with an application mounted on the RADIUS server. The server is capable of manipulating call information through VSAs in AAA. An example would be a debit card application. The AAA server interacts with a debit card billing application to determine account balances, call rates, and time remaining for an individual user. This information is sent to the gateway script in AAA VSAs.

NOTE	Cisco Secure doesn't support applications that depend on VSAs, such as debit cards.

- **Security**—GKs can administer security options to perform secure endpoint registrations and to verify that incoming calls are from authorized users or endpoints. Access-control lists are the recommended solution for security. H.235-based intradomain security (access tokens) is not supported.

- **Settlement**—Some billing system vendors support interdomain settlement based on CDRs collected from each local domain. This offers a viable alternative to OSP in some cases. Mediation vendors such as XACCT also provide servers dedicated to settling CDRs between different vendors' billing systems. These are known as mediation servers and are optional components in a wholesale network.

Ecosystem Partner H.323 Gatekeepers

These optional gatekeepers can be used on the network fringe to complement the Cisco GK/DGK infrastructure and to host a variety of applications. Individual applications will vary among ecosystem partners.

NOTE	The Cisco long-distance VoIP solution doesn't require or specify the use of these GKs, but the architecture doesn't exclude them from being inserted into your network.

Gatekeeper Application Servers

Enhanced call-routing applications might optionally reside on an external server and interface with a Cisco wholesale VoIP network through the Cisco GKs or DGKs using the GKTMP interface specification.

NOTE   The Cisco long-distance VoIP solution doesn't require or specify the use of specific GKTMP applications, but the architecture doesn't prohibit you from adding them to your network.

OSP Servers

To support carrier interconnect, you might choose to use OSP servers. Using OSP for secure settlement transactions requires a clearinghouse entity, or at least a dominant carrier in the interconnect relationship that administers the OSP server. GRIC and TransNexus currently provide OSP-based clearinghouse services. OSP servers perform the following functions:

- **Authentication of gateways or carriers**—An OSP server can verify whether an originating or terminating carrier's gateway is a valid participant in the OSP interconnect by using a secure exchange of certificates.

- **Call authorization**—An OSP server generates an access token for each call sent from an originating gateway into the OSP-based interconnect. The originating gateway includes this token in the SETUP message to the terminating gateway. Upon receiving SETUP, the terminating gateway can either send the token back to the OSP server for validation or perform the validation locally.

- **Call routing**—The OSP server provides the originating gateway with a terminating gateway selected from registered OSP endpoints.

- **CDR collection**—OSP usage indications are sent to the OSP server from both the originating and terminating endpoints after a call has ended. The OSP server uses this information to generate a CDR.

- **CDR correlation and settlement**—Once CDRs are collected, the OSP server can interface with a billing application to generate settlement billing between the two interconnecting carriers.

Prompt Servers

A prompt server is an optional component that maintains a prompt database for gateways running IVR functionality for applications such as card services. Prompt databases can be stored locally on the gateway in flash memory if they're not too large. Larger prompt databases, such as those needed when there are many branded retailers or when many languages must be supported, can be dynamically downloaded as needed from a prompt server using TFTP. TFTP servers are generic third-party devices that can be hosted on a wide variety of platforms.

TFTP Servers

TFTP servers are used to store audio (IVR) files, IOS files, configuration files, dial plans, and other files that don't need to reside on a local machine. These files can be downloaded as needed.

Network Management Systems

Network Management Systems (NMS) are optional components used for network monitoring, fault management, trap correlation, and reporting. Any NMS can extract this information from wholesale components using SNMP. The Cisco wholesale voice solution recognizes CiscoWorks Internet Protocol Manager (IPM) to monitor network QoS and Cisco Info Center (CIC) for fault management and trap correlation. For reporting, it's possible for third-party vendors, such as Trinagy, to provide reports by interfacing with Cisco Voice Manager (CVM).

Element Management Systems

Element Management Systems (EMSs) are optional components that are used for managing or provisioning other components in the solution. CVM provides limited provisioning support and is the only EMS currently supported in the Cisco long-distance VoIP solution.

Detailed Component Inventory

The following component hardware and software products and subordinate solutions are relevant to the Cisco wholesale voice solution:

- VoIP gateways
- H.323 gatekeepers
- SS7 elements
- Shared services components

VoIP Gateways

The following Cisco devices are candidates for VoIP gateways:

- Cisco 3620
- Cisco 3640
- Cisco 3660
- Cisco AS5300 series
- Cisco AS5350
- Cisco AS5400 series
- Cisco 7200 series

These platforms support a variety of analog and digital interfaces. For more information about supported interfaces for a specific platform, refer to the documentation for that specific platform at the Cisco Web site (www.cisco.com).

H.323 Gatekeepers

Candidate gatekeepers are as follows:

- Cisco 3660
- Cisco 7200 series

SS7 Elements

Candidate SS7 elements are as follows:

- Cisco SC2200
- Cisco 2600 SLT

Shared-Services Components

Candidate shared-services components are as follows:

- Cisco Voice Manager (CVM)
- Trinagy Trend Reporting Application
- Cisco Info Center (CIC)
- Internet Performance Module (IPM)
- AAA RADIUS Security Server (various vendors)
- MIND/CTI Billing System
- OSP server (various vendors)
- Generic TFTP server

Step 8: Identify Design and Scalability Issues

Some of the design issues associated with the Cisco long-distance VoIP solution have been mentioned in previous steps. The following paragraphs look at these issues in detail and organize them into the following groups:

- General design issues
- Functional areas design issues
- Services design issues

General Design Issues

Because of the many ways in which multi-functional groups interact, there are general design issues associated with the following topics:

- Call routing
- Billing and settlement
- Basic dial plans
- Fault tolerance in dial plans
- Security considerations associated with dial plans

Call Routing

Call routing between IP service providers can be either DGK-based or OSP-based. The billing and call routing functions that you desire will determine whether your network will be DGK-based or OSP-based.

DGK-based call routing uses LRQ RAS messages to resolve call routing for desired prefixes. An LRQ message is sent from the originating service provider's DGK to the terminating service provider's DGK to request the terminating gateway IP address. The DGK method of call routing can be used when the originating and terminating service providers are trusted peers.

OSP-based call routing uses a separate OSP clearinghouse entity that maintains OSP servers. The OSP servers contain the prefix call-routing tables of all service providers that subscribe to the OSP clearinghouse. The originating gateway sends an OSP authorization request to the OSP server; the OSP server responds with an authorization response containing a list of possible IP addresses of the terminating gateway plus a security token. This token is included in the setup message to provide security validation at the terminating gateway. The OSP method of call routing is used when carriers want a third party to provide the billing and settlement.

Billing and Settlement

To properly bill for service, you must accurately identify the originating carrier and terminating carrier for calls. The degree of difficulty of this depends on the call topology used. Furthermore, the usage indication must be extracted from a reliable source. This implies that the devices supplying call usage indications are somewhere within the H.225 call-signaling path. Therefore, if billing is desired, you must own at least one gateway in any given conversation.

Billing and settlement functionality can be AAA/RADIUS-based or OSP-based. These methods can be used either individually or in conjunction with each other and will directly depend on the method of interconnect. Though differing in protocol, each method addresses the same basic needs for call accounting.

AAA billing must be used for any intradomain calls because OSP is designed to bill for interdomain calls only. AAA can also be used for interdomain calls if interconnect is handled by a peering DGK relationship rather than by an OSP server. In this scenario, the billing application correlates the usage records to generate CDRs. The CDRs are then distributed to customers in the form of a periodic bill. Customers can verify this bill against their own records before exchanging money or settling the call. Various mediation vendors exist that help automate the verification and settlement stages.

For interconnect using OSP, you can either own an OSP server or depend on a third-party clearinghouse OSP server to provide accounting services. The OSP server receives accounting information from your gateway in much the same manner as with AAA. Because usage indications are received from both gateways across administrative domains, the OSP server gets accurate terminating and originating carrier information. The usage records are then correlated to generate CDRs, which might be distributed as periodic bills to customers. Customers can verify this bill against their own records before exchanging money or settling the call. To provide personal accounting records for verification, parallel AAA accounting records can be used.

A third party could manage an interconnecting TDM POP. If so, you can't depend on gateways to send them CDR information. You can, therefore, choose to do billing from the terminating gateways only (if you own them) or from the gatekeeper.

Billing from the gatekeeper has limitations. Cisco gatekeepers can send call start/stop records to a AAA RADIUS server based on receipt of ARQ and DRQ RAS messages from gateways. However, RAS messages are sent over UDP and aren't guaranteed to arrive at the gatekeeper. Furthermore, this method of billing lacks answer supervision. Also, if there are firewalls between gatekeepers and AAA servers, there can be problems because certain ports need to be open for these messages to be received. Therefore, billing is most reliable and accurate if performed at the gateway.

Basic Dial Plans

Dial plan responsibilities are distributed among gateways, gatekeepers, and directory gatekeepers. Because SS7 deployments leverage NI-2 type Q.931 backhaul signaling, the basic H.323 dial plan architecture is the same regardless of whether the POPs in the network are SS7 based, non-SS7 based, or a mixture of both. Figure 6-16 depicts a typical large-scale H.323 network design.

Figure 6-16 *Typical large-scale H.323 network design.*

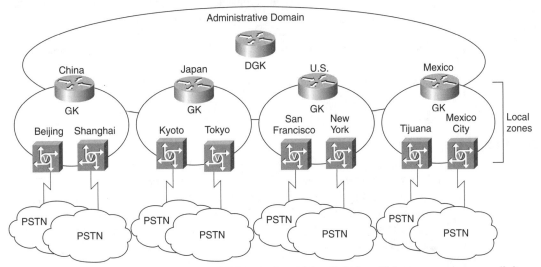

Gateways deal with the local POP portion of the dial plan. This encompasses any digit manipulation needed to normalize numbers or to implement local PSTN access rules. It also includes notifying a gatekeeper when RAI thresholds are crossed, to increase call-completion rates. Furthermore, the gateway can implement rotary dial-peers to handle call failover routing options (such as trying OSP) if normal gatekeeper RAS call routing offers no possible termination.

For example, you might want the gateway to notify the gatekeeper when its resource limits are nearly exhausted, thereby prompting the gatekeeper to select a different gateway. Additionally, to simplify route provisioning in the gatekeepers and directory gatekeepers, you might want to normalize numbers into a standard format (for example, country code + area code + local number) before sending calls into the VoIP network. Or, you might need to prepend or strip digits such as area codes or access codes, as PSTN access rules require, before sending calls via the TDM interfaces.

Local gatekeepers monitor gateway health levels and maintain detailed routing tables, mapping destination patterns to specific terminating gateways within one or more local zones. The local gatekeepers can use features such as lightweight registration, RAI, and static gateway-priority assignments to influence gateway selection. For all other non-locally supported destination patterns, the local gatekeeper configures a wild-card route to the directory gatekeeper.

The DGK maintains an overall routing table of destination patterns and the corresponding local gatekeepers that support them. It simply forwards LRQ messages to the local gatekeeper that handles that destination pattern.

This use of gatekeepers and directory gatekeepers allows the addition of new gatekeeper zones, POPs, and certain types of IP interconnect partners with minimal impact to dial plan provisioning. Changes are isolated to the local gatekeeper and the directory gatekeeper. The rest of the elements in the network are untouched. Often, the level of dial plan resolution at the directory gatekeeper level can be simplified. For example, a DGK might know to route all calls beginning with a country code of 1 to the local U.S. gatekeeper. The local U.S. gatekeeper can then expand selection to more digits to route the call to the proper terminating gateway.

Fault Tolerance in Dial Plans

For intradomain calls and directory gatekeeper-based IP interconnects, you have the option of overlaying fault tolerance onto the basic H.323 VoIP network dial plan design. This is accomplished by using a combination of Cisco IOS software features such as alternate gatekeepers on the gateway, Hot Standby Router Protocol (HSRP) on the directory gatekeeper, and sequential LRQs on the gatekeepers and directory gatekeepers. Figure 6-17 illustrates a fault-tolerant architecture using alternate gatekeepers.

Gateways can be configured to register to a primary gatekeeper and an alternate gatekeeper if the primary gatekeeper fails. This implies that, at any given time, gateways can be registered to either a primary or alternate gatekeeper. Because Cisco gatekeepers don't communicate registration states to each other, sequential LRQs must be configured on the gatekeepers and directory gatekeepers to accommodate zone fragmentation.

For example, a gatekeeper in the Western Zone supports gateways in San Jose (408) and San Francisco (415). Under normal circumstances, when San Jose calls San Francisco, the route is resolved in the local primary gatekeeper. However, say that San Jose fails over to the alternate gatekeeper while San Francisco remains on the primary gatekeeper. To continue to support regional call completion within the Western Zone, the primary and alternate gatekeepers must be provisioned to send local prefixes to each other if no local resource exists—that is, if the terminating gateway has failed over to the other gatekeeper. In this case, for San Francisco to complete calls to San Jose, the primary gatekeeper must know to send LRQ messages for the San Jose prefix to the alternate gatekeeper. Similar provisioning is required on both primary and alternate gatekeepers to support calls in both directions.

Figure 6-17 *Fault-tolerant architecture using alternate gatekeepers.*

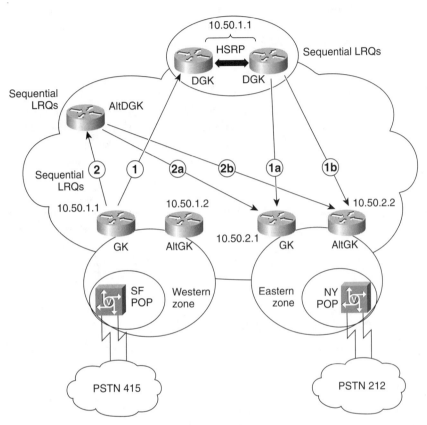

Provisioning is also required on the directory gatekeeper to prevent zone fragmentation when calls are originated from other zones. For example, if San Francisco sends a call to New York, the directory gatekeeper doesn't know with which gatekeeper (primary or alternate) the NY gateway is registered. The directory gatekeeper must be provisioned to send sequential LRQs to both primary and alternate terminating local gatekeepers for all Eastern Zone-supported prefixes (messages 1a and 1b in Figure 6-17). Similar provisioning is required for the Western Zone prefixes to support calls in the other direction.

HSRP is used to provide fault tolerance for the directory gatekeeper. However, HSRP failover detection can take some time, during which no calls will be processed. To cover this possibility, local gatekeepers can be configured to point to more than one directory gatekeeper (that is, an alternate directory gatekeeper, or AltDGK) for their wild-card routes using sequential LRQs.

For example, the gatekeeper can point to an HSRP directory gatekeeper pair as its primary option (message 1). If no response is received because HSRP failover has not yet been detected, the gatekeeper might initiate another LRQ (message 2) to an AltDGK after a configurable timeout of 100 to 1000 ms. During this time, calls will still be completed, but with additional post-dial delay. The AltDGK is configured exactly the same as the primary directory gatekeeper HSRP pair (messages 2a and 2b).

Security Considerations Associated with Dial Plans

You can implement various security mechanisms throughout your H.323 VoIP network. The security mechanism you select might have different provisioning needs within multiple functional areas. For intradomain calls, you can use complex access-lists. For interdomain calls, you can use either complex access-lists or, where OSP is used, OSP access tokens.

NOTE   The Cisco long-distance VoIP solution doesn't support Cisco H.235 access tokens.

You can provision your gateways with complex access-lists to accept calls only from known entities; however, this is neither scalable nor friendly to network changes or to elements that use DHCP.

Functional Areas Design Issues

You must consider design issues for each of the following functional areas:

- Gatekeeper core
- Shared services
- SS7-based POPs
- Non-SS7-based POPs
- Back-to-back gateways

Gatekeeper Core

Consider the following issues when designing the gatekeeper core:

- **Network size scaling**—Large H.323 VoIP networks are segmented into different regional zones, each managed by a gatekeeper. Segmentation is based on several factors, such as desired call throughput, the dial plan, and the number of active endpoints. As network coverage and capacity grow, you can expand by adding new gateways or POPs to gatekeepers until performance limitations for the gatekeeper platform are reached. At that point, you can expand by adding new gatekeepers. Traffic is routed between gatekeeper zones using LRQ/LCF RAS messages.

- **Dial plan scaling**—As more gatekeepers are added to the network, inter-gatekeeper routing configurations increase dramatically. The smallest change to the dial plan requires configuration changes to all gatekeepers in the network. When the number of zones is relatively small, these changes can be managed by having a single dial plan that's downloaded through TFTP to all the gatekeepers within your administrative domain. As the scale increases, the number of zones and the rate of dial plan updating increases. At this point, rather than burdening every gatekeeper with routing information for the entire network, a directory gatekeeper should be used to isolate and alleviate dial plan provisioning. For information on dial plan provisioning, refer to Chapter 5, "Designing Static Dial Plans for Large VoIP Networks."

- **Fault tolerance**—Cisco gatekeepers and directory gatekeepers can be designed to enable redundancy in the dial plan. At the edge, gateways at each POP are configured to support registration with an alternate gatekeeper in case the primary gatekeeper fails. In the core, gatekeepers are configured to support sequential LRQ messages to provide redundant paths to alternate directory gatekeepers and to accommodate local zone fragmentation conditions. To accommodate zone fragmentation at the directory gatekeeper level, both sequential LRQs and HSRP are configured to provide redundancy at the highest layer.

- **Directory gatekeeper-based IP interconnect**—If you choose to interconnect routes with other service providers by using a directory gatekeeper, configure the DGKs to exchange LRQ RAS messages between their administrative domains to resolve call routing for the desired prefixes. Sequential LRQs can be implemented on the directory gatekeeper to support limited egress CSR applications. Back-to-back gateways can be used to support IP-to-IP call topologies.

- **Security**—To validate whether a call originated from a valid endpoint, Cisco gateways and gatekeepers can implement access lists to provide secure gateway registration and admission. To support this, gatekeepers must be configured to interact with a AAA server.

- **Network management**—Gatekeepers must be enabled to support SNMP community strings so that external management platforms, such as CVM and CIC, can provision, access reporting information, and receive traps using SNMP.

- **TFTP server access**—If you desire, the gatekeeper can be configured to support the remote downloading of software images and configurations through a TFTP server.

Shared Services

Consider the following issues when designing shared services:

- **Call routing**—For OSP-based interconnect scenarios, an OSP server handles call routing functions along with some complimentary provisioning on the OSP gateway dial-peers. The impact on the dial plan is discussed in more detail in Chapter 5.

"Designing Static Dial Plans for Large VoIP Networks." Additionally, it's possible for an external server to provide enhanced call routing functions by interfacing with Cisco gatekeepers and directory gatekeepers via GKTMP.

- **Billing**—A AAA server collects usage records directly from the gateways. Alternatively, an OSP server might collect usage records for interdomain calls. Details on billing implementations vary, depending on the application enabled.

- **Security**—You can provision complex access lists on the gateways to implement security functions. Where IOS configurations exceed the router's NVRAM capacity, a TFTP server can be employed to centrally store, administer, and upload gateway configurations. Cisco H.235 access tokens are not currently supported. An OSP server supplies security functions for OSP interconnect methods.

- **Network management**—Standard SNMP NMS platforms can be deployed to provide generic SNMP management functions. CVM provides SNMP-based statistics collection along with a very limited dial plan and component-provisioning tool. Reports can be generated by using ecosystem partner reporting engines that integrate with CVM. Cisco recognizes Trinagy as one of these vendors. CIC can be used if fault management is desired. Additionally, Cisco IPM can be used to provide monitoring of network QoS.

- **Remote download**—A TFTP server can be used to remotely store IVR prompts, TCL scripts, software images, and configurations for download.

SS7 POP

Consider the following issues when designing SS7 POPs:

- **Signaling**—SS7 POPs are large and consist of DS1 and DS3 IMTs to the gateways. PSTN-side call control is provided using Q.931 backhaul from the Cisco SC2200 to Cisco AS5300 and AS5400 gateways. POPs might optionally support Cisco 2600 SLT gateways to terminate SS7 layers MTP1 and MTP2 on behalf of the SC2200 signaling controller.

  Figure 6-18 shows the signaling used in an SS7 POP, and the relationship among Cisco SC2200 nodes and hosts, Cisco AS5x00 gateways, and Cisco SC26xx SLTs.

- **Dial plan**—For SS7-based POPs, you can perform number modification in either the gateway, the Cisco SC2200 signaling controller, or both. The Cisco SC2200 allows digits in the called-party number or calling-party number fields to be added, deleted, or modified. It's also possible to modify the nature of address (NOA), perform black-listing and white-listing, and AIN triggering. The gateway must be provisioned with an RLM group to interface with the Cisco SC2200 in addition to normal H.323 configurations. After the Cisco SC2200 and gateway are provisioned to interface with each other, the rest of the H.323 dial plan remains the same.

Figure 6-18 *SS7 POP signaling.*

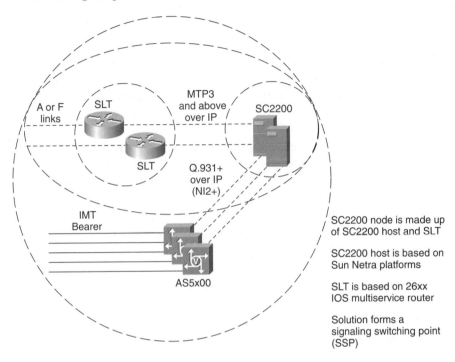

- **Fault tolerance**—Gateways can support a backup Cisco SC2200 if the primary SC2200 fails. It might take up to three seconds for the gateway to detect and failover to the new SC2200. During this time, any new calls will not be processed. Furthermore, any calls that were in the process of being set up will be lost. Active calls at the point of failover, however, remain in progress.

Non-SS7 POP

Consider the following issues when designing Non-SS7 POPs:

- **Signaling types**—Signaling types can vary greatly and include analog FXO, analog E&M, BRI, DS1 interfaces (E1/R2 variations, T1 CAS variations, PRI), and perhaps DS3 interfaces on the upper boundary.

  Low-density analog interfaces generally discourage carrier interconnects, so calls that ingress the POP will almost always be for card services, and calls that egress the POP are reoriginated into the PSTN, usually to bypass PTT interconnect tariffs. DS1 and DS3 interfaces generally provide either card services or interconnect wholesale systems to their customers.

- **Size**—Additional considerations surface at small-scale POPs. The hardware footprint of the equipment must be minimized in addition to the amount of non-bearer traffic, because the IP network bandwidth coming into the POP is likely to be sub-E1 bandwidth.

- **Dial plan**—Dial plan responsibilities are distributed among gateways, gatekeepers, and directory gatekeepers. The gateways have to deal with the local POP portion of the dial plan. This includes provisioning needed dial-peers, translation rules, and RAI thresholds. Dial plans encompass more than one functional area and are discussed in greater detail in Chapter 5.

- **Billing**—For performance and accuracy reasons, it's recommended that billing be done from the gateway whenever possible. You must configure the Cisco gateways to interact with shared AAA services to support billing and optional debit card applications.

- **Fault tolerance**—If you desire, you can configure a gateway to support an alternate gatekeeper with which it will register should the primary gatekeeper fail. This requires a related configuration in the gatekeeper functional area.

- **Security**—To support security, gateways can be configured with complex access lists. For OSP-based interconnect scenarios, the gateways must be provisioned to interact with the OSP server to support OSP security options.

- **Network management**—Gateways must be configured to support SNMP community strings so that external management platforms, such as CVM and CIC, can provision, access reporting information, and receive traps using SNMP.

- **Transparent bearer transport**—Unless you've previously agreed to limit the types of calls exchanged between other carriers, you might receive traffic of any bearer type. Your gateways must be able to transparently pass voice, real-time fax, and modem traffic across the VoIP network.

- **TFTP server**—If you desire, you can configure a gateway to support remote downloading of prompts, software images, and configurations through a TFTP server.

Back-to-Back Gateways

Consider the following issues when designing back-to-back gateways:

- **Signaling**—Back-to-back gateways need to be configured with similar TDM signaling types.

- **Voice quality and bearer issues**—Voice quality suffers, especially in the case of tandem compression. The addition of back-to-back gateways introduces additional post-dial delay and added latency for all calls. There is even greater impact if more than one back-to-back zone is traversed. Fax relay can also suffer. Modem passthrough is highly unreliable, and is not supported in scenarios that employ back-to-back gateways.

- **Dial plan**—The back-to-back gateway is responsible for manipulating digits and tech prefixes to fit into the general gatekeeper and directory gatekeeper dial plan. This also includes separating ingress and egress gateways in the gatekeeper call-routing table. The extent of these considerations depends on the application and the DGK/GK dial plan design. Dial plan responsibilities are discussed in greater detail in Chapter 5.

- **Billing**—One of the main benefits of the back-to-back gateway is establishing a point in the call-signaling path from which to bill for IP-to-IP call topologies. The back-to-back gateway largely functions as a normal POP gateway. Billing options vary by application type.

- **Fault tolerance**—If you desire, a back-to-back gateway system can be configured just like a normal TDM POP gateway to support an alternate gatekeeper with which it will register should the primary gatekeeper fail.

- **Security**—Back-to-back gateways have the same security options and implications as normal POP gateways.

- **Network Management**—Back-to-back gateways have the same network responsibilities as in a normal TDM POP.

Service Design Issues

This section describes the issues you should consider for service design. We consider solutions for the following two kinds of services and discuss the issues associated with each, depending on the call topology used:

- Minutes aggregation and termination (including ASP termination)
- Card services (prepaid and postpaid)

Minutes Aggregation and Termination

This solution enables you to collect traffic from multiple originating providers, then aggregate and deliver it to the termination providers you select. This can include target greenfields, resellers, dial-around callback operators, and international ISPs.

TDM-to-TDM Call Topology

If you select the TDM-to-TDM call topology for this service, consider the following issues:

- **Dial plan—gatekeeper core.** This application uses the basic large-scale H.323 dial plan concept as previously discussed in this chapter.

- **Shared services—billing and settlement.** Dedicate separate gateways for each TDM interconnect partner. Provision the billing system to identify carriers by using originating and terminating gateway IP addresses. This allows you to generate appropriate CDRs to settle with customers.

- **Security.** Calls in this template type are all intradomain calls.

TDM-to-IP Call Topology Using Directory Gatekeeper-Based IP Interconnect

If you select the TDM-to-IP call topology using directory gatekeeper-based IP interconnect for this service, consider the following issues:

- **Dial plan**—The basic large-scale H.323 dial plan concept is still used. To interconnect your POPs with your IP interconnect partners, you must add additional LRQ route statements to the peering directory gatekeepers to direct certain destination patterns between you and your interconnect partners. Because these routes are added and modified in the directory gatekeepers, the rest of the network remains untouched.

- **Billing and settlement**—In this scenario, you own only one of the gateways in the conversation, either the originating or terminating gateway, depending on the call direction. Your billing application must be able to extract enough information from one side of the call to generate a CDR.

  This requires correlating either source or destination IP addresses with a particular IP interconnecting carrier, depending on the call direction. Your billing system must maintain a database of this information to bill the interconnecting customer accurately. For calls sourced from ASPs, the list of possible originating IP addresses is typically limited to a few call-signaling proxy servers. However, for ITSPs with many gateways or PC clients, this list can be quite extensive. The list might be reduced if the ITSP forgoes performance and uses gatekeeper RCS. Once carrier identification issues are solved, AAA billing and settlement is done on the gateways.

  Alternatively, the originating ITSP or ASP can include a mutually recognized carrier ID (for example, prepend ANI) in the H.323 SETUP message. The terminating gateway will then include this information in the AAA record. You can provision the billing application to recognize this carrier ID and associate it with an originating carrier. Bear in mind that this implies a trusting relationship between service providers.

- **Security**—Security can be accomplished by using Cisco H.235 access tokens. However, this means you must share a database of all gateway user IDs and passwords with all IP-based interconnecting partners.

TDM-to-IP-Based Interconnect with OSP Call Topology

If you select the TDM-to-IP-based interconnect with OSP call topology for this service, consider the following issues:

- **Dial plan**—An OSP-based interconnect partner can connect to your network by implementing OSP directly on the gateway, or through a back-to-back OSP interconnection zone.

  From a call-routing perspective, OSP is most readily accepted into the network if an OSP interconnection zone consisting of back-to-back gateways is used. One gateway handles the RAS side of the call; the other handles the OSP side of the call. From the perspective of the directory gatekeeper, this looks like another TDM zone managed by a local gatekeeper. The directory gatekeeper simply adds LRQ routes to the OSP interconnect zone gatekeeper for specific destination patterns serviced by the OSP interconnect partner.

  Provisioning requirements for the gateways within this OSP interconnection zone are only slightly different from the requirements for a normal wholesaler TDM POP. The OSP-side gateway is configured to interface with the OSP server. The RAS-side gateway is configured like a normal POP RAS gateway. The back-to-back gateways are then configured to send all calls received through IP out the TDM interfaces to the opposite gateway, using single-stage dialing. This method of OSP interconnect isolates provisioning tasks to the back-to-back gateway pair, the local hopoff gatekeeper configuration, and an added LRQ route in the directory gatekeeper. The rest of the network is unaffected.

  If OSP is implemented without using the interconnect zone, dial-peer provisioning increases dramatically to support OSP directly on the gateways. Separate dial-peers are needed on all POP gateways to send calls to the OSP server for route resolution instead of through RAS. You might provision dial-peers on the gateways to send calls to OSP for specific destination patterns.

  For example, if an interconnect partner knows that all calls to Australia need to be terminated by OSP, you can insert a dial-peer into your gateways that sends all calls beginning with a "61" country code to an OSP session target. However, any changes to the OSP dial plan require modification to the dial-peers on all gateways in the network.

  You might choose to configure the gateway with rotary dial-peers to handle OSP-based interconnects instead of explicit patterns. Although this might reduce the dial plan's sensitivity to changes, it still requires additional dial-peer provisioning to support failover. In this case, gateways are configured to try to terminate the call within their own administrative domain, first through RAS. If RAS offers no termination possibilities, either by explicit ARJ or RAS timeout, the gateways might fall back to a secondary dial-peer to reoriginate the VoIP call through OSP.

Consider a gateway provisioned with two dial-peers having identical generic destination patterns. One dial-peer points to session target RAS; the other points to session target settlement. The RAS dial-peer is given a higher priority than the settlement dial-peer, so it's always attempted first. If the RAS dial-peer fails, then the gateway attempts to send the call to an OSP server through the secondary dial-peer.

This reduces the amount of maintenance of OSP dial-peers to accommodate dial plan changes, but adds post-dial delay to all OSP-based interconnect calls.

- **Billing and settlement**—In any OSP implementation, the OSP server collects usage information and generates CDRs. This usage information is extracted directly from the gateways registered to the OSP server, regardless of whether they are functioning as back-to-back gateways or as normal POP gateways.

  You can also send duplicate records to a AAA server for internal accounting. These CDRs can be used to cross-check any settlement issues with the OSP provider. You might optionally employ a mediation application to automate this process.

- **Security**—If OSP is performed directly on the terminating gateway, intradomain security continues to (optionally) use Cisco access lists. Interdomain security uses OSP H.235 tokens, with the noted caveats to the dial plan. If a back-to-back gateway zone is used, the OSP token management is offloaded from your POP gateways and is instead handled by the OSP gateway in the back-to-back zone. The OSP gateway in the back-to-back pair supports the H.235 OSP tokens, whereas the RAS gateway optionally implements Cisco access lists. This use of the back-to-back OSP transit zone allows security caveats previously mentioned in the direct method to be sidestepped.

IP-to-IP-Based Interconnect (Transit Network) with DGK Call Topology

If you select the IP-to-IP-based interconnect (transit network) with directory gatekeeper call topology for this service, consider the following issues:

- **Dial plan**—Interconnections between IP-based service providers are sent to a back-to-back gateway transit zone. Each IP interconnecting partner has a dedicated transit zone. If both interconnecting partners are made through a directory gatekeeper peering relationship, this adds complexity to the large-scale H.323 dial plan architecture. The dial plan must be altered to provide dedicated ingress and egress directory gatekeepers to route calls properly through your network. IP interconnect from one carrier (using directory gatekeeper peering) and an OSP-based interconnection partner (using a back-to-back OSP interconnection zone) is accomplished in essentially the same way as discussed for the TDM-to-IP call topology using directory gatekeeper-based IP interconnect.

- **Billing and settlement**—The back-to-back gateway provides a point in the call-signaling path from which you can gather accounting information. Billing can be done from the back-to-back gateway in the same manner as described in the simple interconnect method of the TDM-to-TDM solution.

- **Security**—The back-to-back gateway zone also allows you to obscure originating ITSP carrier information from the terminating ITSP carrier, if desired. Calls sent into the terminating ITSP B look as if you sourced them. The terminating ITSP B has no idea that ITSP A originated the call.

  You still must share gateway IDs and passwords with your interconnecting partners. However, the back-to-back gateway allows you to isolate interdomain security information between service providers. That is, ITSP A doesn't need to know ITSP B's security information, and vice versa, for the two to complete calls between each other.

IP-to-IP-Based Interconnect (Transit Network) with OSP Call Topology

If you select the IP-to-IP-based interconnect (transit network) with OSP call topology for this service, consider the following issues:

- **Dial plan**—This extends the method described in the TDM-to-IP-based interconnect with OSP solution to include sending calls to another OSP provider through another back-to-back gateway zone or another directory gatekeeper-based service provider, depending on LRQ routing entries in the directory gatekeeper.

- **Billing and settlement**—Billing between OSP providers is done just as discussed in the TDM-to-IP-based interconnect with OSP solution, but for two OSP back-to-back gateway zones. The originating zone provides settlement CDRs for the originating carrier; the terminating zone provides settlement CDRs for the terminating carrier. If the call is instead sent to a directory gatekeeper interconnect, AAA RADIUS records are used on that side. The AAA can be reconciled with the OSP usage records by means of a mediation application.

- **Security**—Security is accomplished as described in the TDM-to-IP-based interconnect with OSP solution.

Card Services (Prepaid and Postpaid)

You can host prepaid services for multiple service providers on their infrastructure. In addition, most prepaid service providers use VoIP wholesalers to terminate long-distance calls that are placed by prepaid subscribers. Using the integrated voice response (IVR) feature in the Cisco VoIP gateways, and real-time authorization and call accounting systems provided by Cisco ecosystem partners, service providers can offer this service over a VoIP network and lower the cost and deployment time of calling-card services.

Like prepaid services, you can also host postpaid services. An example is basic calling that's accessed by the 800 prefix, a calling card number, or a PIN. With postpaid service, the authorization is not tied to call rating. Consequently, call rating doesn't have to happen in real time, and there might be more partner billing-system options that perform adequately at scale. After calls are made, a billing system contracted by the company charges the carrier.

TDM-to-TDM Call Topology

If you select the TDM-to-TDM call topology for this service, consider the following issues:

- **Dial plan**—Card services typically affect dialing habits by employing two-stage dialing. Aside from this, dial plans remain basic. Once inside your network, the call can either be terminated at one of your POPs or sent to another service provider through a TDM hopoff, using the basic large-scale H.323 dial plan architecture.

- **Billing and settlement**—Your originating gateway supports card services for TDM-based interconnecting partners. AAA-based billing is done on the gateways and settled as discussed in the TDM-to-TDM solution. However, the billing server must interact in real time with the AAA server to offer prepaid services.

- **Fault tolerance**—Basic H.323 fault tolerance is used.

- **Security**—An IVR script running on the originating gateway performs user authentication. This IVR script interacts with a AAA RADIUS security server. On top of this, either user-level or gateway-level security can be implemented for registration and call admission.

- **Prompting**—To support branding requirements, you must be able to identify the necessary IVR script for the carrier. Different call scripts might be invoked, depending on the supplied DNIS. Prompts can be stored remotely on a TFTP server, if desired.

TDM-to-IP Call Topology Using Directory Gatekeeper-Based IP Interconnect

If you select the TDM-to-IP call topology using directory gatekeeper-based IP interconnect for this service, consider the following issues:

- **Dial plan**—For card services provided to TDM interconnect partners, the same considerations exist as outlined in the TDM-to-TDM template. However, you might want to provide card services for IP interconnecting partners. In this case, you might route incoming VoIP calls directly to the terminating gateway as normal and then implement the IVR.

Alternatively, you can configure the gatekeepers and directory gatekeepers to first route the call to a back-to-back gateway for IVR services, based on the end user dialing a specific access number. The directory gatekeeper knows to send calls destined to this access number to a particular IVR zone consisting of back-to-back gateways. The local gatekeeper is configured to send calls destined to this access number to a designated ingress-only gateway of the back-to-back pair. The egress gateway is explicitly given a gateway priority of 0 to avoid sending calls through the back-to-back gateway in the reverse direction.

The ingress back-to-back gateway is configured to pass this call through TDM to the egress gateway. The egress gateway then applies the required IVR script, based on the DNIS received. The egress gateway collects the desired destination pattern and reoriginates the call into the H.323 network as if it were a normal TDM POP.

- **Billing and settlement**—AAA-based billing is done on the gateways. However, the billing server must interact in real time with the AAA server to offer prepaid services. For back-to-back gateway scenarios, billing is done on one of the gateways as if it were a normal TDM POP.

- **Fault tolerance**—Basic H.323 fault tolerance is used.

- **Security**—Security is accomplished as described previously in the simple interconnect application. Added security is provided by the IVR script in authenticating IP-based users either before the call enters your network (as with the back-to-back implementation), or before the call is completed through your network (as with the terminating gateway implementation).

- **Prompting**—Prompting for TDM interconnects is the same as in the TDM-to-TDM solution. To support the proper welcome announcements and local languages required for branding in IP interconnections, you must be able to identify the source carrier before authenticating the user.

Where IVR is implemented directly on the terminating gateway, the called number is supplied by the end user and is routed to the destination. It's unreliable to identify the originating carrier based on DNIS. Modifications can be made to ANI, but this is also unreliably enforced on originating PC endpoints. Therefore, multiple branding is not supported in this implementation for IP interconnect partners.

For IP interconnects front-ended with a back-to-back gateway, you can support branding services to individual carriers by providing separate access numbers that PC users dial to reach various back-to-back gateway zones. For example, carrier A is given a special destination number to dial into a back-to-back gateway IVR pool.

TDM-to-IP-Based Interconnect with OSP Call Topology

If you select the TDM-to-IP-based interconnect with OSP call topology for this service, consider the following issues:

- **Dial plan**—Dial plans can be administered in a similar manner as discussed in the card services application in the TDM-to-TDM solution. However, in this case, front-ending IVR calls don't require routing to separate back-to-back gateway IVR zones. IVR services can be performed directly on the interconnecting OSP back-to-back gateway pair.

- **Billing and settlement**—Billing is done as discussed in the card services application in the TDM-to-TDM solution.

- **Fault tolerance**—Basic H.323 fault tolerance is used.

- **Security**—Security is implemented as discussed previously in the simple carrier-interconnect application. Added security is provided by the IVR script in authenticating IP-based users either before the call enters your network (as with the back-to-back gateway implementation), or before the call is completed through your network (as with the terminating gateway implementation).

- **Prompting**—Prompting is implemented in the same manner as discussed in the card services application in the TDM-to-TDM solution. For OSP interconnects using a back-to-back gateway zone, the IVR services can be implemented on the RAS-side gateway as if it were a normal POP gateway.

IP-to-IP-Based Interconnect (Transit Network) with Directory Gatekeeper Call Topology

If you select the IP-to-IP-based interconnect (transit network) with directory gatekeeper call topology for this service, consider the following issues:

- **Dial plan**—You might want to provide card services for IP interconnecting partners by using a back-to-back gateway IVR zone as the front-ending application. This is done the same way as the TDM-to-IP call topologies using directory gatekeeper-based IP interconnect solution.

- **Billing and settlement**—Billing is done on one of the gateways as if it were a normal TDM POP. AAA-based billing is done on the gateways as previously discussed.

- **Security**—Security is accomplished as in the IP-to-IP-based interconnect (transit network) with OSP solution. The IVR script provides additional security by authenticating IP-based users before the call traverses the network in the back-to-back gateway.

- **Prompting**—Prompting is done as in the TDM-to-IP call topologies using a directory gatekeeper-based IP interconnect solution. The back-to-back gateway essentially operates as the front-end application.

IP-to-IP-Based Interconnect (Transit Network) with OSP Call Topology

If you select the IP-to-IP-based interconnect (transit network) with OSP call topology for this service, consider the following issues:

- **Dial plan**—You might want to provide card services for OSP-based IP interconnecting partners by using a back-to-back gateway zone, as discussed in the TDM-to-IP call topologies using the directory gatekeeper-based IP interconnect solution.

- **Billing and settlement**—Billing is done on one of the gateways as if it were a normal TDM POP, as in the TDM-to-IP call topologies using directory gatekeeper-based IP interconnect solution.

- **Security**—Security is accomplished as in the IP-to-IP-based interconnect (transit network) with OSP solution. The IVR script provides additional security by authenticating IP-based users before the call traverses the network in the back-to-back gateway.

- **Prompting**—Prompting is done as in the TDM-to-IP call topologies using directory gatekeeper-based IP interconnect solution. The back-to-back gateway essentially operates as the front-end application.

Step 9: Configure and Provision Components

Describing how to configure and provision the components associated with your long-distance VoIP solution is beyond the scope of this book. For more information about configuring specific devices, refer to the configuration material that shipped with your network devices, or, for Cisco products, refer to the Cisco Web site (www.cisco.com).

Summary

In this chapter, we outlined and described the step-by-step methodology used to design a personalized long-distance VoIP solution. We summarized the features and benefits of the Cisco long-distance VoIP solution, we described the services that can be provided at wholesale, and we identified the hardware and software components that are available from Cisco and from third-party vendors to implement wholesale voice services.

PART III

Network Services

## CHAPTER 7

Managed Multiservice Networks and Packet Voice VPNs

This chapter discusses two classes of hosted voice networks: Managed Multiservice (MMS) networks and packet voice Virtual Private Networks (VPNs). Hosted voice networks are enterprise networks that are owned and operated by service providers (SPs). The SPs then contract with enterprise customers who require voice service but who do not want to maintain their own WAN and customer premises equipment (CPE). Instead, the enterprise customers use the SP's WAN as a virtual WAN. Hosted voice networks enable SPs to offer inexpensive voice service to their enterprise customers, who can then focus on their core business responsibilities.

MMS networks are relatively simple VoIP networks that are intended for enterprise customers who want dependable, inexpensive voice service between two or more sites. Although MMS networks do not support more advanced VoIP features, they are relatively simple and inexpensive for SPs to implement on top of their existing networks. A VPN is an MMS with more advanced features and functionality. We will discuss the differences between the two in this chapter.

Packet voice VPNs should not be confused with data VPNs. While both types of VPNs enable enterprise customers to outsource their IT responsibilities to SPs, data VPNs use technologies such as Multiprotocol Label Switching (MPLS), Layer 2 Tunneling (L2F, L2TP, and PPTP), and encryption (IPSec and MPPE) to enable geographically dispersed sites to communicate securely over a shared backbone. Packet voice VPNs are MMS networks that include devices such as gatekeepers and route servers. These devices provide more network intelligence and support advanced voice features such as overlapping dial plans, digit manipulation, priority routing, load balancing, and multiple-stage dialing.

In this chapter, we explain how H.323 MMS solutions can be designed, the features and elements of the solution, and what network design options exist with software available today and with capabilities coming in the near future. This chapter focuses only on the voice functionality of an H.323 MMS network service offering. ATM AAL5-based and AAL2-based MMS solutions will not be covered here. In addition, data managed services and data VPNs are mature technologies that are necessary precursors to an MMS network and, therefore, are not explicitly discussed here.

Managed Multiservice Networks

An MMS network is essentially an enterprise network that is hosted by an SP on its shared backbone. The CPE equipment and features are the same as the enterprise would use to create its own network, but instead they are managed and sometimes owned by the SP. Instead of maintaining its own WAN, the enterprise uses the SP backbone, which is shared by many different enterprises, as a virtual WAN. The enterprise's network thus becomes a *VPN*.

An MMS network has the same configuration, features, and performance issues as any enterprise network. Additionally, security, billing, network management, compliance with service-level agreements (SLAs) including traffic policing and shaping, and voice quality issues must be considered.

An MMS network has the following characteristics:

- **Combined services**—In addition to managing data traffic between multiple sites for the enterprise customer, voice services are included in an overall solution managed and deployed by the SP.

- **Tandem/class 4 replacement**—SPs offer business connect services that replace those that would ordinarily connect an enterprise's telephony equipment to the IXC's Class 4 switch.

- **Not a local services solution**—MMS solutions don't support the features required to address the residential market (Class 5).

Evolution of Managed Voice Networks

Managed voice networks began with the advent of circuit-switched telephone solutions. The following is a timeline of the significant developments that have occurred:

- **Mid-1980s**—Sprint USA invented a time-division multiplexed (TDM) voice VPN to compete against AT&T's Private Line PBX networks.

- **Early 1990s**—U.S. long-distance companies such as AT&T and several international companies such as SITA-Equant started providing Managed Router Services over Frame Relay.

- **Late 1990s**—Fifty international carriers ratified Circuit-Switched Voice VPN as an international standard.

Today, SPs such as AT&T and MCI offer feature-rich, worldwide voice VPN services to enterprises.

The following pressures are driving the industry toward packet-based solutions:

- Competition to duplicate existing services on packet networks.

- Desire to provide advanced, revenue-generating services that can be deployed only over packet-based networks.

- New entrants want to complement existing packet-based voice services with voice VPNs.

- Mobile carriers want to interconnect mobile and PBX networks with voice VPNs.

Now that data managed services have matured and become commodities, enterprises can switch relatively easily among different SP offerings, which are often competitively priced. By adding voice and other value-added services to their existing data managed service offerings, SPs can maintain a competitive edge, increase revenues, and encourage customer loyalty.

MMS Solution Market Drivers

The following factors were the original market drivers for MMS networks:

- To leverage the convergence of data and voice over packet networks, the traditional data providers had to upgrade their offerings to be multiservice.

- To increase revenues, SPs wanted to attract more traffic onto their packet backbone.

However, simply transporting voice traffic is no longer a cutting-edge service. The industry is moving toward value-added services and applications leveraging a combined infrastructure, particularly packet voice VPNs. The factors driving this market include the following:

- As competitive pressures force enterprise customers to focus on their own business plans, they are increasingly turning to SPs for network outsourcing.

- Enterprise customers are comfortable with VPNs, because both voice VPN (circuit-switched) and data VPN services are mature technologies.

- VPNs offer cost-effective communication with remote offices and business partners.

- For large, multisite enterprises, internal voice traffic typically is greater than external traffic.

The following enterprise customers are ideally suited for MMS network solutions:

- Larger enterprise customers who want to interconnect multiple sites (a more important goal than Internet access or e-business connectivity, although these are often secondary goals).

- Customers who need to integrate existing dial plans, PBXs, and key systems.

- Customers who would prefer to outsource the management of their WAN.
- Customers who need to improve the efficiency and reduce the overall cost of their networks. Specifically, retail and financial enterprises have benefitted from MMS networks.

Peer-to-Peer Managed Multiservice Networks

A peer-to-peer MMS network is a network that has the same architecture as the older, data-only networks, as shown in Figure 7-1. Each customer has data and voice traffic coming in from edge CPE devices resident at their various customer sites.

Figure 7-1 *Peer-to-peer MMS network architecture.*

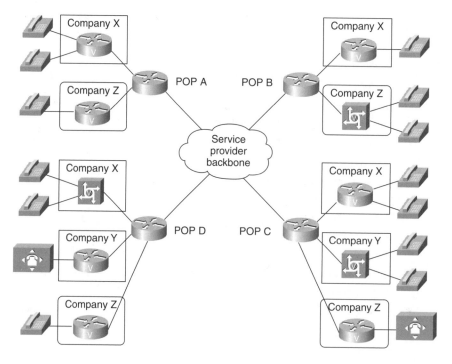

This architecture is designed primarily for customers that are outsourcing their enterprise WANs. Note that the traffic on the network is from one Company X location to another Company X location. A peer-to-peer MMS network is not well suited for SP value-added services offered on common or shared equipment accessed by multiple end customers such as voice VPNs or Unified Messaging services. In contrast, there is additional secure traffic on a voice VPN between different customers and traffic from customers to shared servers that provide services such as Unified Messaging or web applications.

Peer-to-Peer MMS Network Elements

A peer-to-peer MMS network has a relatively simple architecture consisting of the following:

- **CPE router(s)**—This is typically a Cisco 2600 series, 3600 series, or MC3810 concentrator. Customer data traffic enters the SP network through this router, which is typically connected by an Ethernet or Token Ring LAN on the customer side, and a Frame Relay, ATM, or IP connection on the SP side.

  The customer PBX, phone sets, and/or key system are also connected to this router and are responsible for originating and terminating the voice traffic. Earlier incarnations of MMS networks frequently used Voice over Frame Relay (VoFR) and Voice over ATM (VoATM) technologies. Many of the carriers that currently offer VoFR or VoATM solutions are planning or considering VoIP-based services, to either replace or augment their existing services.

  A variation on CPE voice traffic that is also under consideration is IP telephony. In this architecture, the CPE router doesn't originate or terminate the voice. IP phones, softphones, and/or other H.323, SIP, or VoIP endpoints originate and terminate voice traffic, and the CPE router aggregates and routes the traffic destined for the SP backbone. More challenges (billing, security, call admission control, and so on) exist with this design than with traditional telephony equipment connecting via the CPE router (which also acts as the voice gateway).

- **SP Points of Presence (POP)**—These are geographically dispersed aggregation points of CPE traffic that typically use Frame Relay or ATM connectivity.

- **SP backbone**—The backbone carries traffic between the POP, usually using an ATM-based, high-speed network (Frame Relay is more often used as a CPE access technology).

- **Network management**—The premise of an MMS network is that it can be managed. SPs run elaborate Network Operations Centers (NOCs) where the status of the network is monitored and alarms are raised when outages occur. SPs can use Cisco management platforms such as CiscoWorks, or they can write their own applications and use various products as elements in their network management scheme.

  There is also a network management overlay network, typically using a separate PVC to the CPE equipment and separate IP addressing, to carry SNMP and remote-access traffic to allow the SP to gather the information necessary to manage the network.

- **Billing**—This function is key to the SP's ability to charge accurately for services rendered. Peer-to-peer MMS networks tend to use a relatively simple, flat-rate basis for billing, such as CPE access bandwidth or committed information rate (CIR).

Peer-to-Peer MMS Network Features and Characteristics

Peer-to-peer MMS networks are relatively simple and straightforward. They don't include call agents, gatekeepers, or any other type of server-based call control or call assistance. Because of this lack of high-level network intelligence, these networks typically have the following voice characteristics:

- On-net to on-net calls only between sites belonging to the same customer.

- No on-net to on-net calls between different customers (note that regulatory rules in different geographic regions might not allow this type of service).

- On-net to off-net traffic possible (although not typical, because of IP security risks).

- No off-net to on-net traffic (DID/DDI functionality).

- Relatively small number of customer sites (about 10–20 maximum) because the flat dial-peer architecture doesn't scale without becoming unmanageable and complex.

- One customer per gateway. Peer-to-peer MMS networks can't support multitenant gateways shared among multiple customers—for example, a Cisco 3660 gateway in a building with different customers on different floors of the building.

Peer-to-peer MMS networks have been in operation for several years and were the first networks to be deployed with combined data and voice services. However, advanced call features, such as those discussed in more detail later in this chapter, typically are not yet offered. The primary purpose of these networks is to make and receive on-net calls across a shared packet backbone between sites belonging to the same customer. Advanced call features such as contact centers, on-net and off-net routing of calls, digit manipulation, VPN services, and time-of-day routing require more intelligence in the network than peer-to-peer dial plans allow.

Peer-to-Peer MMS Network Customer Dialing Plans

The voice dial plan for a peer-to-peer MMS network is created as a flat direct dial-peer architecture, where every Company X site has a dial-peer pointing to every other Company X site. Calls between Company X and Company Y are not possible because there are no dial peers entered for such calls.

In VoATM and H.323 VoIP-based peer-to-peer MMS networks, the dial peers for each customer are fully meshed between the customer's sites, precluding scalability to a large number of sites. In VoFR-based networks, the VoFR tandeming function provides a certain measure of centralization of some of the dial plan in the POPs or aggregation points in the network, simplifying the CPE configuration and easing the deployment of slightly larger networks.

Customer dial plans can overlap—Company X has an extension 2211, as does Company Y—but typically do not. Overlapping dial plans can be supported because there is no visibility or connectivity between Company X and Company Y voice networks. An exception to this, shown in Figure 7-2, is the VoFR tandem switching functionality in the SP network, which either precludes overlapping dial plans or forces the tandeming to be performed by a device dedicated to a particular customer. For example, all Company X branch office CPE equipment could tandem their VoFR calls through a Cisco 7200 CPE device at Company X headquarters or a large site location. SPs who have deployed VoFR tandeming have typically opted not to support overlapping dial plans.

Figure 7-2   *VoFR tandem switching.*

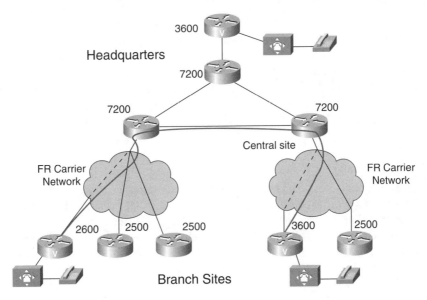

In summary, peer-to-peer dial plans tend to have the following characteristics:

- Fully meshed between sites belonging to a particular customer.
- On-net to on-net calling only within the same customer.
- Non-overlapping—each site, regardless of customer, has a unique phone number or range.
- Prescribed by the SP rather than fitting in with the custom dialing plan that the company might already have on its PBXs.

Peer-to-Peer MMS Network Call Routing Characteristics

In peer-to-peer MMS networks, call routing is determined exclusively through the flat dial plan configured on the CPE gateways and through the IP routes they use. There are no database lookups, address translation, call servers, or any other intelligence in the network to aid with call setup, routing, admission decisions, or billing information.

On-Net to On-Net Calls

Calls between sites belonging to the same customer are fully supported. Calls between sites belonging to different customers are typically not supported. Because of the flat dial plan, this functionality requires that the IP addressing of Company X be visible from Company Y network, which is insecure.

It is technically possible to implement inter-customer calling by making all voice calls from all customers share the same IP addressing plane—separate from the per-customer data IP addressing space. Yet there is still risk because there is no control point, such as a gatekeeper, to authenticate calls between different customers. If the H.323 voice traffic originates on the CPE voice gateway, the security concern is negligible. But if the traffic originates on the LAN segment behind the CPE router, which is the case when using a gatekeeper, the IP addresses are visible to end users, which is very insecure.

On-Net to Off-Net Calls

It's technically possible to support calls from customer locations to PSTN destinations by using common, SP-owned PSTN gateways, but typically this functionality isn't offered. In this situation, each customer gateway has a dial peer that points PSTN destination patterns to the shared, SP-owned, PSTN-entry gateway, which is called a *hopoff*. Because this gateway destination IP address is visible to all end customers' networks, this is also insecure.

Off-Net to On-Net Calls

Off-net to on-net DID calls—calls from the PSTN to a customer location—are typically not supported. These calls usually terminate through existing PSTN connections to the customer PBX. Although such calls can be supported, they cause complexities in routing and dial plans. If you need to support off-net to on-net calls, you should use a gatekeeper to perform functions such as digit translation and manipulation.

Peer-to-Peer MMS Network Billing Features

First generation peer-to-peer MMS networks are typically billed at a flat rate. For data service, the customer pays for a given amount of bandwidth on the SP network access link. For voice connectivity, the customer usually pays for a certain maximum number of allowed simultaneous calls. The actual use of network bandwidth for voice calls is monitored by the SP, but not charged for.

As peer-to-peer MMS networks evolve toward value-added services such as Unified Messaging and voice VPNs, where off-net calling should be charged only for actual calls made, usage-based billing models become much more important. For voice traffic, this means call detail record (CDR) information collected from the network with details and accurate information on the parameters of the call.

Packet Voice Virtual Private Networks

Packet voice VPNs (PV-VPNs) are voice networks with a packet-based backbone that offer end-user features similar to traditional circuit-switched voice VPNs. These voice features can be offered by a SP entirely independent of data VPN offerings such as MPLS, IPSec, and other tunneling and security technologies.

Figure 7-3 illustrates the difference between a peer-to-peer MMS voice network and a PV-VPN, where each customer has a separate voice network customized to the individual needs of the company.

Figure 7-3 *Peer-to-peer voice MMS versus PV-VPN.*

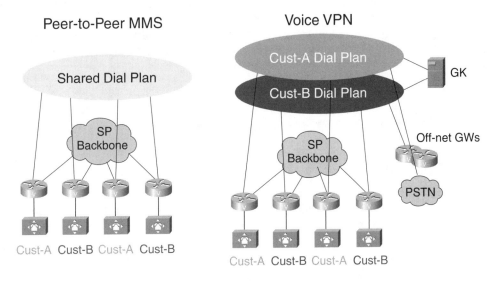

The key differences between the two voice architectures are shown in Table 7-1.

Table 7-1 *Comparison Between Peer-to-Peer MMS and PV-VPN*

Peer-to-Peer MMS Voice	PV-VPNs
Shared dial plan	Custom dial plan per customer
Typically no gatekeepers	Gatekeepers, call routing servers, and/or call agents
Point-to-point pipes between customer sites	Switched calls between any endpoints
Primarily on-net calling	On-net and off-net calling, and any combination of these
Basic calling	Feature rich

PV-VPN Architecture

A PV-VPN consists of the same elements as a peer-to-peer MMS network, with the addition of gatekeepers and/or route servers to add intelligence to the network for the purpose of controlling call routing. Optionally, PV-VPNs can also include several other application servers to offer various additional features and applications. This equipment can be either physically centralized or dispersed. The servers provide services to the network and they can be connected at any point where it makes logistical and geographical sense. Figure 7-4 gives a high-level view of a PV-VPN.

The architecture is designed to offer advanced voice features in addition to simple outsourcing of an enterprise WAN. It is scalable and extendable and provides the basis for value-added applications such as Unified Messaging and call center outsourcing.

PV-VPN Elements

A PV-VPN has all the elements of a peer-to-peer MMS network to provide for the core infrastructure of the network. In addition, it includes advanced call servers and services. There are many pieces of equipment in this category, and how many of these you deploy in your solution will depend on the features and applications offered in the VPN. Any or all of these servers can potentially accomplish digit manipulation functions. The different types of servers include the following:

- **Gatekeepers**—These are used both in the infrastructure of the network to improve dial plan scalability, and in applications that implement call routing to specific destinations, such as a shared database or applications built on an API into the gatekeeper.

Figure 7-4   *PV-VPN architecture.*

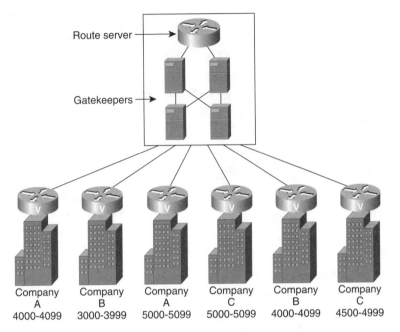

Route server

Gatekeepers

| Company A | Company B | Company A | Company C | Company B | Company C |
| 4000-4099 | 3000-3999 | 5000-5099 | 5000-5099 | 4000-4099 | 4500-4999 |

- **Call Agents**—These appear in MGCP-based networks and implement the core call control logic, which is centralized in an MGCP architecture rather than distributed, as in an H.323 architecture.

- **Call Route Servers**—These work in conjunction with a gatekeeper to control call routing decisions such as least-cost routing and time-of-day routing. You can implement this application as a database accessed by the gatekeeper or as a peer application communicating with the gatekeeper.

- **Proxies**—These are often deployed for reasons such as security (to hide IP addresses), scalability (to hide the complexity of the rest of the network), and feature invocation (to invoke QoS features on behalf of an end-station that isn't capable of QoS).

- **Specialized application servers**—These include Unified Messaging, Call Center applications, customized announcement servers, IVR applications, speech recognition servers, Follow-Me applications, and the like.

- **OSP connectivity (optional)**—An off-net call termination capability includes at least interconnectivity with the traditional PSTN. To offer lower-cost alternatives to off-net destinations not served directly by the service provider's POP, the SP can use an OSP clearinghouse to hand off calls to other low-cost, packet-based carriers to lessen the traditional long-distance PSTN charges for off-net calls.

- **Enhanced billing services**—Billing systems for VPNs are more complex than those for peer-to-peer MMS network offerings, because per-usage-based billing is an important value-added VPN feature. Consolidated billing for off-net and business-to-business on-net calls is also necessary.

PV-VPN Characteristics and Features

Simple PV-VPNs can be implemented today using Cisco and NetSpeak gatekeepers and NetSpeak route servers. Cisco and its partner vendors are still developing more advanced features.

Currently, SP PV-VPN networks include one or more of the following features:

- **Intra-business on-net calling (on-net to on-net calls, same customer)**—This functionality includes the following features to connect different sites belonging to the same customer:

  — Private Dialing Plan—Private or custom number plan for intra-company voice and fax. Dialing plans can overlap; therefore, customers can keep the dialing plan already implemented on their PBX private line network, and can have the same numbers as other customers.

  — On-net Calling—Inter-PBX extension calls using the Private Dialing Plan.

  — Virtual On-Net—Expands VPN coverage of the dial plan to sites not connected to the VPN network. An on-net number is assigned to the offsite location, and when this number is dialed, the network connects the call to the PSTN number. To the end user it looks like an on-net location.

  — Private Network Interface—The physical connection (such as E1 PRI or T1 CAS) between the PBX and the VPN CPE.

  — Forced On-Net—If an offsite PSTN number is dialed to an on-net location, the servers in the network convert this to an on-net call.

- **Inter-business on-net calling (on-net to on-net calls, different customers)**—This functionality includes various value-added features to connect different customers who each contract their PV-VPN service from the same SP. These calls would otherwise traverse the PSTN, but because both enterprises are connected to the same physical SP network, the SP can provide better rates and services to these customers for business-to-business calling.

- **PSTN Access (on-net to off-net)**—This functionality includes the following features to route calls that originate on the VPN but terminate on the PSTN:

  — **Off-net Calling**—Calls routed from the VPN to worldwide PSTN destinations. Calls are carried on-net as long as possible and use the closest or least-cost remote POP to connect to the destination local PSTN or other carriers.

  — **Dedicated Termination Overflow**—If trunks on the VPN to the distant PBX are blocked or fail, calls are allowed to overflow to the PSTN.

- **Off-net Access to VPN (off-net to on-net)**—This functionality includes the following features to route calls that originate on the PSTN but terminate on the VPN:

  — **Calling Card Access**—Employees at remote locations have access to the VPN by way of a toll-free or local PSTN number and a PIN.

  — **Toll-free VPN Access**—Allows for end users to have a toll-free access number for customers and other services.

  — **Off-net Access**—Allows small branch offices, telecommuters, and home locations to have PSTN access to the enterprise VPN with automatic number identification (ANI) authorization.

  — **Customer Care**—Allows for Customer Care toll-free services to terminate on the SP's network and the calls to be routed over the on-net network to the appropriate end-customer Call Center location.

All the preceding features are capable of performing sophisticated digit manipulation at various points in the network.

PV-VPN Customer Dial Plans

One of the key features that differentiates a VPN from a peer-to-peer MMS network is the support for customized dial plans. Custom dial plans imply overlapping, or non-unique, dial plans within the SP network. This means, for example, that both Company X and Company Y can have an extension 2211. Theoretically, peer-to-peer MMS networks can support custom overlapping dial plans, but they are difficult to manage. PV-VPNs support overlapping dial plans with the following, more advanced, features:

- Access rights for Company X extension 2211 that might be different from those for Company Y extension 2211.

- On-net calling access between Company X extension 2211 and Company Y extension 2211.

- Off-net to on-net (PSTN to on-net) calling for each of these extensions.

The interpretation of the dial plan is implemented by the gatekeepers and/or route servers in the network. The dialed string is not interpreted in isolation, but in conjunction with some indication of which enterprise customer (closed user group) the caller belongs to. One method of accomplishing this identification is to assign each gateway to a specific customer. The combination of the originating gateway and the dial string then provides a unique identification of the VPN to which the call belongs. Another method is to use digit manipulation features on the gateway such as number expansion, translation rules, and technology prefixes, to assign a unique "site ID" to the dialed number before attempting the call setup with the gatekeeper and then delete it before the call exits the network to a PBX or the PSTN.

Custom dial plans provide the following two major benefits to enterprise customers:

- **End-user transparency**—Customers can maintain their pre-existing private PBX dial plans.

- **Closed user groups**—The establishment of user groups that have custom calling patterns between members of the group, with appropriate security and access rights restrictions (such as international dialing access) imposed by the network.

Custom dial plans also provide the following benefits to service providers:

- The network is more manageable and economical.

- The SP can offer better service to ensure the loyalty of existing customers and to attract new customers.

Gateway Partitioning

In all currently deployable VPN offerings, the implementation of the overlapping dial plan still relies on the fact that gateways are not shared among customers. Often the non-unique dial plan is resolved by associating the originating or terminating gateway with a particular customer in the gatekeeper and/or route server configurations. This association is typically transparent to the gateway: The gateway is aware only of its unique dial plan, while the gatekeeper and/or route server handle the overlapping portions of the dial plan. This means that if there are two or more extension 2211s in the network, each resides on a separate gateway.

Gateway partitioning is a concept that allows a single gateway to be partitioned between different customers. This enables an SP to offer VPN service to small offices sharing a common building—such as a tall downtown building or shops in a mall—by putting a single gateway in the building and providing different T1/E1 trunks or analog connections to each customer. In this scenario, instead of gatekeepers associating customers with the originating gateway, the gateway associates customers with the originating voice interface and then forwards this information to the gatekeeper to decide on the proper routing.

Multiple-Stage Dialing

Multiple-stage dialing capability enables a caller to hear one or two additional dial tones and dial one or two additional numbers to access a VPN. The possible dialing scenarios are as follows:

- **Single-stage dialing**—The caller hears a dial tone, dials a string of digits, and the call gets connected to the terminating point. If the call is an on-net call, it might be connected based on the exact digits dialed. For calls involving the PSTN, digit manipulation is usually required. For example, an American user calls a friend in the UK by dialing 9.011.44.1582.845544. Because the hopoff gateway is in the UK, but not local to the 1582 area code, the number delivered to the UK PSTN is 01582.845544. This digit manipulation is transparent to the caller.

- **Two-stage dialing**—The caller hears a dial tone, dials a number, hears another dial tone, and then dials the terminating phone number. This can be used for several features—for example, the off-net access feature. A small or home office has a PSTN number to gain access to the VPN. The caller dials the PSTN number, hears a second dial tone supplied by a VPN gateway (authentication can be accomplished using ANI/CLID), and then dials the VPN destination.

- **Three-stage dialing**—The caller hears a dial tone (or some other tone) twice and dials three distinct numbers before the call is connected. An example of this application is calling card access to the VPN for traveling employees. The first number is a local or toll-free PSTN number terminating on the SP network. Next, the caller dials an authorization number and/or PIN and, finally, the VPN destination of the call. The sequence of the last two stages can be reversed depending on how the application is implemented.

Digit Manipulation

Digit manipulation is a key feature when implementing PV-VPN dialing plans, and every element of the network (PBXs, gateways, POPs, gatekeepers, application servers, and the billing system) potentially can manipulate the calling and called digits of every call. This is common practice in the TDM voice world.

PV-VPN Call Routing Characteristics

The design, implementation, and interpretation of dial plans are key elements in performing successful call routing in a PV-VPN. Digit manipulation by various network elements is also important because it directs the decisions of the next element in the network to which a call is routed. In addition, the following features are necessary to perform advanced call routing:

- Priority routing
- Load balancing and fault tolerance
- Gatekeeper call-signaling models

Priority Routing

If multiple paths exist to connect a call to its destination, some paths might be preferred over others due to cost, distance, quality, delay, partner hand-offs, traffic load, and various other considerations. The following priority routing features keep an updated list of possible routes and the preferences among these routes:

- **Least-cost routing**—This is most useful for on-net to off-net and off-net to on-net calls. When there are multiple PSTN entry-points or OSP partners available to deliver a call or when a PSTN gateway has trunks to different PSTN carriers at different cost levels, least-cost routing will determine the cheapest route for the call.

- **Time-of-day routing**—This provides customized routing based on the time of day and day of the week. Situations where time-of-day routing is useful include:

  — Travel and roaming features

  — Call Center call diversion during or after business hours

  — Technical support centers with 24/7 service offered by different locations and time zones

  — Call diversion for holidays or off-site meetings

  — Call diversion or announcements during outages

Load Balancing and Fault Tolerance

For traffic to destinations with multiple gateways (such as PSTN hopoff gateways or gateways into a large customer site), load balancing is often required. The H.323 Resource Availability Indication (RAI) feature is often part of this functionality. H.323 RAI instructs gatekeepers to route calls to gateways only when they have adequate capacity available. For more information, see Chapter 4, "Understanding Call Admission Control."

Gatekeeper Call Signaling Models

The call signaling model you choose for your network influences what type of network topology and which call routing features you will be able to implement. The following two call signaling models are available:

- **Directed call signaling**—In this model, both the H.225 and H.245 call signaling and the RTP media stream flow directly between the gateways. The only signaling passed to the gatekeeper (and therefore visible to the gatekeeper-based applications) is the H.225 RAS messaging.

  For many features, this is sufficient. This call model scales well because the gatekeeper is not a bottleneck or a single point-of-failure for all call signaling in the network (HSRP and other gatekeeper redundancy features can mitigate the single point-of-failure risks). A possible downside is that CDR information from the gatekeeper might not be accurate enough for billing purposes; therefore, CDRs have to be drawn from the gateways in the network. Because there are many more gateways than gatekeepers in a network, there will be more CDR traffic on the network.

- **Gatekeeper-routed signaling**—In this model, only the RTP media stream passes directly between the gateways, while the call signaling passes only through the gatekeepers. In some implementations, the RTP stream also passes through the gatekeepers and not through the gateways.

  This call model doesn't scale as well as directed call signaling, particularly when the RTP stream doesn't pass through the gateways. It also introduces an additional point of failure in the network However, gatekeeper-routed signaling offers the most flexibility to gatekeeper-based applications. Billing information from the gatekeeper is also accurate and often obviates the need to gather CDR information from the gateways.

Some third-party gatekeepers can operate in either mode; the mode you choose will depend on the features and services required in your network.

PV-VPN Billing Features

PV-VPN billing can be quite sophisticated and can include the following:

- Single or multisite billing
- Consolidated PSTN (off-net) billing
- Volume discounts
- Inter-business (Company X to Company Y) on-net call billing at different rates than either intra-business (Company X Site 1 to Site 2) on-net calling or off-net calling
- Account code billing

Cisco doesn't offer billing solutions. Third-party billing systems such as Mind-CTI, Belle, or Portal are generally used with Cisco networks. Some of the exact billing system features required for new PV-VPN features might not be available yet, and you will need to evaluate billing criteria on a case-by-case basis. VSA extensions to RADIUS might be required to support the information required by the billing system.

Summary

This chapter compared and contrasted the features and characteristics of peer-to-peer Managed Multiservice (MMS) networks and packet voice Virtual Private Networks (PV-VPNs). Peer-to-peer MMS voice networks enable SPs to offer basic VoIP service to enterprise customers. MMS networks are intended for enterprises that want dependable, inexpensive voice service between two or more sites, but also want the responsibility of maintaining their own WAN.

We explained that the primary purpose of MMS networks is to make and receive on-net calls between sites belonging to the same customer across a shared packet backbone. Because MMS networks are relatively simple to deploy and maintain, SPs often introduce MMS networks as their first VoIP offerings while they plan more advanced VoIP services.

PV-VPNs are MMS networks that include devices such as gatekeepers and route servers that enable the support of advanced features such as overlapping dial plans, digit manipulation, priority routing, load balancing, and multiple-stage dialing.

Peer-to-peer MMS networks are being widely deployed today. PV-VPNs with entry-level features are also being deployed, but the process of integrating various components and ensuring their interoperability is not yet fully defined. Cisco customers have implemented solutions by using Cisco gateways and gatekeepers and, in some cases, by using gatekeepers and call-routing servers from vendors such as NetSpeak and Clarent.

## CHAPTER 8

Fax Services

Traditional Fax over Circuit-Switched Networks

Fax has a long tradition as a telephony application for sending documents between terminal devices. We use the phrase *traditional facsimile* or *G3 Fax* to denote implementations of International Telecommunications Union (ITU) recommendations T.30 and T.4. The T.30 protocol describes the formatting of non-page data, such as messages that are used for capabilities negotiation. The T.4 protocol describes the formatting of page data.

The transmission of fax data end to end is accompanied by two actions:

- Negotiation—to ensure that the scanned data can be rendered at the recipient's end
- Confirmation of delivery—to give the sender assurance that the final data has been received and processed

All fax machines use the V.21 protocol (300 baud) for the negotiation stage (LS fax) of fax transmission. The page transfer stage (HS) is negotiated at higher speeds (V.17, V.27, and so on).

Figure 8-1 illustrates a typical fax call flow.

The information conveyed in the transmission consists of both *protocol* and *document content*. Protocol comprises identification, control information, and capabilities. Document content consists primarily of the *document image* plus additional metadata accompanying the image. The *image data representation* is the means by which an image of a document is encoded within the fax content.

When the fax has been successfully transmitted, the sender receives a *confirmation:* an indication that the fax content was delivered. This confirmation is an internal signal and is not normally visible to the sender. Some error messages are visible, however, to allow a page to be retransmitted.

The traditional fax is transmitted over the PSTN using a point-to-point switched circuit for each call. At startup, the T.30 engines synchronize, negotiate connection/transmission parameters, transmit page data, signal success or failure, and then disconnect.

Figure 8-1 *PSTN fax call flow.*

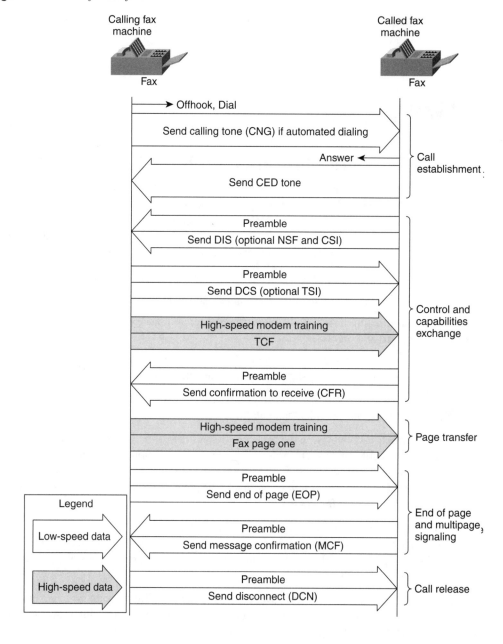

Reducing Fax Costs

The cost of using the PSTN for traditional fax transmissions can be very expensive, especially if the fax communication is international. Heavily used corporate fax machines can generate thousands of dollars of calling charges per month. When these long-distance calls are instead sent over the Internet, the savings can be dramatic. Standards are currently being defined for two types of Internet (IP packet-based) fax: store and forward fax and real-time fax.

Store and Forward Fax and the T.37 Standard

Store and forward fax gateways can take calls from G3 fax machines, convert them into e-mail messages, and transmit them over the Internet. Another store and forward fax gateway at the terminating end of the call receives the e-mail message, converts it back into a fax message, and delivers it to a G3 fax machine.

Store and forward fax is generally sent as an e-mail attachment. An extension to the Simple Mail Transport Protocol (SMTP) called Multipurpose Internet Mail Extensions (MIME) is available for this fax service from the Internet Engineering Task Force (IETF). These standards are covered by Request for Comments (RFC) 2301 through 2306. Fax images are attached to e-mail headers and are encoded in Tag Image File Format (TIFF). TIFF-F describes the data format for compressed fax images.

The ITU developed the T.30 protocol and other fax standards and has adopted the SMTP/MIME protocol for fax as part of a new ITU standard called T.37. This standard defines store and forward fax by e-mail and has approved *simple mode* (RFC 2305). Extended, or *full mode*, is still under study. Simple mode restricts TIFF-F encoding to the *s-profile*, which is based on the minimum set of TIFF for facsimile, limiting fax transmission to only the most popular fax machine formats. These formats are Modified Huffman (MH) image compression with standard or fine resolution. In T.37 terminology, fax gateways can send faxes to a conventional PSTN-connected fax machine or to another fax gateway over an IP network. The originating (transmitting) gateway is referred to as an *on-ramp gateway*; the terminating (receiving) gateway is an *off-ramp gateway*.

Cisco fax gateways support ITU-T standard T.37 as independent on-ramp gateways, independent off-ramp gateways, or on-ramp/off-ramp combinations. Because the mail server first stores the fax message (page by page) and then forwards it, the confirmation that the sender receives is delayed. Although the lack of an immediate confirmation message is a disadvantage, store and forward fax has several advantages, including delivery at off-peak hours, sophisticated retry-on-busy algorithms, and the ability to broadcast a single fax to multiple receiving fax machines. Figure 8-2 illustrates the store and forward fax service model.

Figure 8-2 *Store and forward fax service model.*

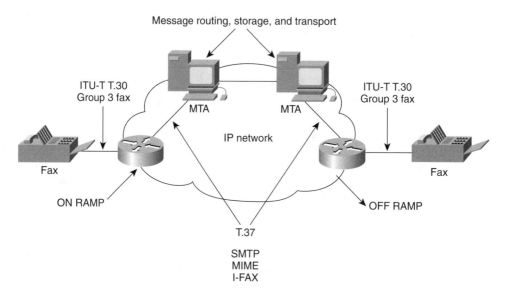

Real-Time Fax and the T.38 Standard

Real-time fax gateways can deliver a fax to a remote fax machine while the sending fax machine is still processing additional fax pages. Delivery confirmation is the processing of the last page without an error message. In the real-time fax model, delivery confirmation is immediate.

The T.38 standard defines the IP network protocol used by Internet-aware T.38 fax devices and T.38 IP fax gateways. T.38 fax gateways provide the following functions:

* Demodulate incoming T.30 fax signals at the transmitting gateway
* Translate T.30 fax signals into T.38 Internet Fax Protocol (IFP) packets
* Exchange IFP packets between the transmitting and receiving T.38 gateways
* Translate T.38 IFP packets back into T.30 signals at the receiving gateway

You can deploy the ITU T.38 recommendation using two implementations:

* Fax relay
* Real-time fax with spoofing

These implementations differ in their ability to deal with IP network delay.

Fax Relay

With fax relay, the gateway receives an analog fax signal and demodulates it into its digital form using a fax modem. The digital, demodulated fax is then packetized and transmitted over the IP network. At the receiving end, the fax gateway remodulates the digital fax packets into T.30 analog fax signals to be transmitted to the destination fax machine through a gateway modem. There is no requirement that the gateway provide T.30 signals of its own, just fax modems and the T.38 IP data protocol.

Network delay becomes a factor when deploying real-time fax. In controlled private data networks and networks that have been tuned for VoIP traffic, delay has been reduced to less than 500 ms end to end and fax relay can be used effectively. If delays become too large, such as with gateways employed over the Internet, where delay is out of the direct control of the administrator, real-time fax with spoofing can be used.

Real-Time Fax with Spoofing

Spoofing techniques are employed to extend the delay tolerance of fax machines. These techniques add to the T.30 protocol used by fax machines to communicate, keeping them on line beyond their normal T.30 timeout intervals. Extra line padding techniques, T.30 protocol spoofing, and sending of redundant data are used to provide image packet jitter tolerance. Spoofing and jitter compensation allow the fax machines to tolerate network delay without losing communication. This is sufficient for faxing over the Internet.

The T.38 standard defines different protocols depending on the real-time fax transport mechanism used.

UDP/IP Transport

User Datagram Protocol (UDP) is a fast but unreliable transport protocol. The speed of UDP allows it to be employed for real-time fax without the need for spoofing. In addition, the T.38 protocol provides two methods to improve the reliability of the UDP transport mechanism. One method uses redundancy of the image data; the other uses a simple forward-error-correction (FEC) scheme.

TCP/IP Transport

Although Transport Control Protocol (TCP) adds reliability through the use of error-checking mechanisms at each router it transits, it also adds delay. T.38 specifies a simple protocol for transport by TCP that includes no error checking.

The T.38 real-time fax-over-IP service model is illustrated in Figure 8-3.

Figure 8-3   *Real-time fax service model.*

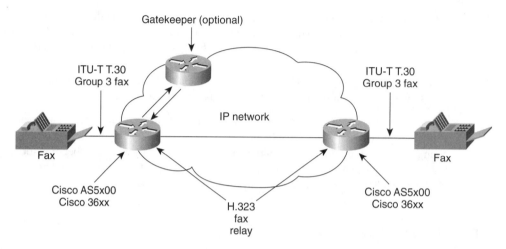

The Cisco AS5300 access server and Cisco 3600 router families of voice gateways support both ITU recommendations: T.37 for store and forward fax, and T.38 for real-time fax as of Cisco IOS Release 12.1(3)XI. The Cisco MC3810 Multiservice Concentrator and Cisco 2600 router families support ITU recommendation T.38 as of Cisco IOS Release 12.1(3)T. The Cisco AS5300 also requires the recommended VCWare Version 7.16. The proper VCWare is bundled within Cisco IOS software for the Cisco 3600 series. Real-time fax works like a VoIP call and requires no extra configuration. Store and forward fax configuration and testing are the focus of this chapter.

This chapter also documents the *never-busy* fax solution. This solution uses a Tool Command Language (TCL) Interactive Voice Response (IVR) script to *roll over* a T.38 fax that receives a busy signal into a T.37 fax. This feature is documented in the last section of the chapter.

Cisco Store and Forward Fax

Store and forward fax enables Cisco AS5300 voice gateways to transmit and receive faxes across packet-based networks without the timeout restrictions imposed by real-time fax transport methods. Store and forward fax is an implementation of the RFC 2305 and RFC 2532 proposed standards from the IETF. RFC 2305 proposes a standard aligned with the T.37 recommendation from the ITU.

With this feature, your access server becomes a multiservice platform, providing both data and fax communication. Store and forward fax enables you to do the following:

- Send and receive faxes to and from Group 3 fax devices.
- Receive faxes that will be delivered as e-mail attachments.
- Create and send a standard e-mail message that will be delivered as a fax to a standard Group 3 fax device.

Store and forward fax functionality is facilitated through SMTP. Additional functionality described in RFC 2532, *Extended Facsimile Using Internet Mail*, confirms delivery using existing SMTP mechanisms. Examples of such mechanisms are delivery status notifications (DSNs) in RFC 1891 and message disposition notifications (MDNs) in RFC 2298.

When store and forward fax is configured, the on-ramp gateway receives faxes from traditional Global Switched Telephone Network (GSTN)-based Group 3 fax devices and converts them into TIFF file attachments. It then creates a standard MIME e-mail message and attaches the TIFF file(s) to it. The on-ramp gateway then forwards this fax mail to the messaging infrastructure of a designated SMTP server, where the fax-mail message is stored. The messaging infrastructure performs message routing, message storage, and transport, and can be either custom store-and-forward SMTP software or a standard Internet mail transport agent (MTA) such as UNIX sendmail or Netscape MailServer.

After the fax mail is stored on the SMTP server, it can be delivered in two ways: as an e-mail message with an attachment, or as a fax to a standard GSTN-based Group 3 fax device. In the latter case, the SMTP server mail delivery infrastructure delivers the fax mail to the Cisco off-ramp gateway. The off-ramp gateway router converts the attached TIFF file back into standard fax format and transmits the information to a standard GSTN-based Group 3 fax device. The off-ramp gateway is also responsible for generating DSNs and MDNs, as appropriate. This simple topology is illustrated in Figure 8-4.

Store and forward fax is used in conjunction with the VoIP software feature for Cisco voice gateways. The supporting digital signal processor (DSP) technology can be either c542 or c549. To understand the voice feature card (VFC) and VoIP technology and architecture, search for these topics on the Cisco web site, www.cisco.com. To learn about VCWare and DSP technology in particular, see the following web site:

> http://www.cisco.com/univercd/cc/td/doc/product/access/acs_serv/5300/53modgd/53mvopv2.htm

Compatibility issues are addressed at the following link:

> http://www.cisco.com/univercd/cc/td/doc/product/access/acs_serv/5300/iosrn/vcwrn/vcwrmtrx.htm

Figure 8-4 *Topology of store and forward fax functionality.*

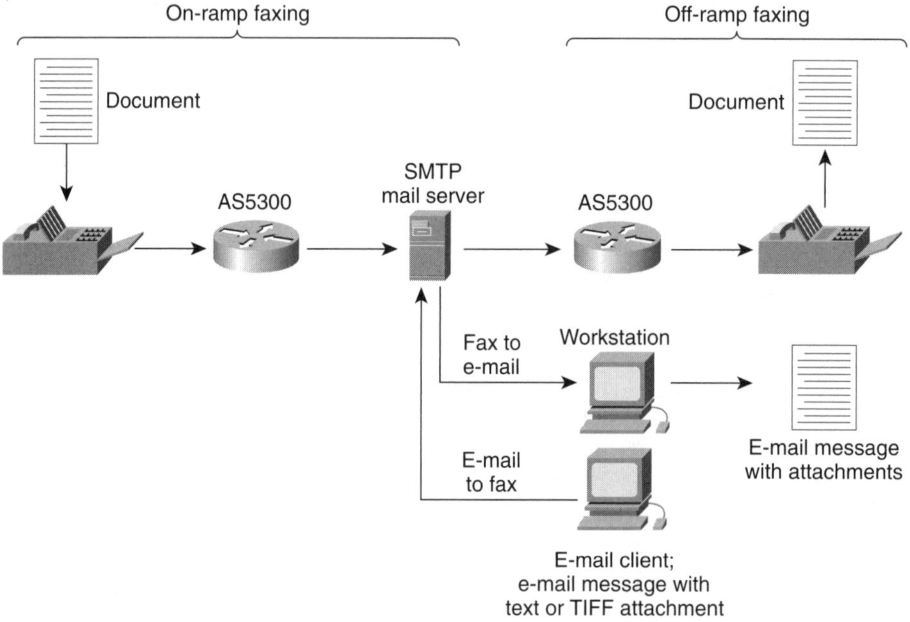

Handling of Enclosures

Store and forward fax can process e-mail with the following MIME media content types:

- Text/plain
- Text/enriched
- Image/TIFF (Group 3 Profile S [RFC 2301 Section 3] ImageWidth = 1728

Cisco's implementation uses an enriched "Profile S" media content type that allows modified read (MR) and modified modified read (MMR) image encoding. The important property of the TIFF images supported by Cisco gateways is that the TIFF image file descriptor (IFD) header precedes the actual TIFF data. This header location allows TIFF-to-fax conversion in streaming mode without storing the TIFF image on the gateway. (Note that Cisco store-and-forward gateways support only the specific TIFF format described previously.)

Store and forward fax supports the following MIME content-transfer encodings:

- Seven-bit
- Eight-bit
- Base 64
- Quotable printable

These content transfer encodings can be wrapped in any multipart content type. Nesting of multiparts (multipart-in-multipart) is not supported.

When a Cisco off-ramp gateway receives a message with the content type of multipart/ alternative, it processes the first part of the multipart/alternative message and records a count of what was and was not successfully transmitted to the GSTN-based Group 3 fax device. The off-ramp gateway then discards the other parts of the message. For example, if a multipart/alternative message has two parts, a text/plain part and a text/HTML part (and the text/plain part is first), the off-ramp gateway transmits only the first part (the text/plain part) to the GSTN-based Group 3 fax device.

NOTE	An e-mail client can determine the content type described previously. In the Eudora e-mail client, for example, this is configurable in the /Tools/Options/Styled text section. If you select the option *send both plain and styled text*, that is the same as enabling multipart/ alternative, and the behavior described in the preceding paragraph will be observed. Choosing *send styled text only* enables multipart/*. If you want to send both text and TIFF attachments to an off-ramp fax gateway, you must choose *send styled text only* in the Eudora client. Other e-mail clients have similar configuration options.

NOTE	The TIFF file format must conform to RFC 2301 (file format for Internet fax). The Cisco off-ramp gateway doesn't support UUencoded files, JPEG, JBIG, Word, PDF, or multiraster content.

WARNING	The Cisco off-ramp gateway recognizes only the listed file attachment types for store and forward fax activities. If the Cisco gateway receives a file format different from one of the defined acceptable formats, it discards the data.

T.37 Fax Connection Protocol

The 300-baud V.21 protocol is used by all fax machines for the negotiation stage (LS) of fax transmission. The page transfer stage (HS) is negotiated at higher speeds.

Image Encoding and Image Resolution

Depending on your specific needs, you might want to increase or decrease the resolution of the received fax image. As a default, image resolution in store and forward fax is set to *passthrough*, which means that the image is forwarded exactly as it is received. If you want to specify a different resolution for the fax TIFF image, whether greater or lesser, use the **image resolution** dial-peer configuration command as an attribute of the on-ramp multimedia mail over IP (MMoIP) dial peer.

Depending on the capacity of the fax machines in your network, you might want to use a different image encoding (compression) scheme for the fax TIFF image that store and forward fax creates. As a default, image encoding in store and forward fax is set to *passthrough*, which means that the image is forwarded exactly as it is received. If you want to specify a specific encoding (compression) scheme for the fax TIFF image, use the **image encoding** dial-peer configuration command as an attribute of the on-ramp MMoIP dial-peer.

NOTE   This is an on-ramp-only command. Even though the CLI will allow configuration of passthrough mode on the off-ramp dial peers, it is unacceptable to do so. Configuring encoding and resolution values on off-ramp dial peers can cause problems and should be avoided.

Quality of Service and Cisco T.37 Fax

Quality of service (QoS) is an important issue in voice packet networks and is discussed in detail elsewhere in this book. The following QoS mechanisms are employed in Cisco gateway-based T.37 fax to improve fax quality:

- Received fax data is checked for quality when it is totally decoded and re-encoded in TIFF format.
- The IOS code has magic values for the allowed number of bad lines versus good lines on a page.
- Bad lines are recovered by replicating good lines.
- T.37 has some level of protocol deviation correction.
- Normal training and retraining in the initial message exchange.
- Middle fax retraining, but no retransmissions.

Benefits of Cisco T.37 Store and Forward Fax

The following are the benefits of Cisco T.37 store and forward fax:

- Cost savings
- Universal inbox for fax and e-mail
- E-mail can be sent as a fax transmission
- Toll bypass
- Broadcast to multiple recipients

Cost Savings

The worldwide IP fax service market is projected to reach about $2 billion by 2002. Analysts estimate that corporate customers can shave 30 to 50 percent off their annual fax bills by using converged IP voice/data/fax networks.

In addition, corporate users can continue to use their existing applications. For example, existing e-mail programs such as Eudora, Netscape, or Outlook can be used to send a fax by inserting a fax number in the *To:* field: fax=+5551212@off-ramp.cisco.com and clicking the Send button. You can also send and receive both fax and e-mail messages from your private e-mail inboxes, and you can use existing standalone fax machines with no user retraining.

Universal Inbox for Fax and E-Mail

The Cisco AS5300 allows configuration of direct-inward-dial (DID) numbers to deliver faxes to a specific electronic mailbox. This feature greatly simplifies the receiving of faxes while traveling. Receiving e-mail on the road is commonplace, whereas receiving faxes on the road can be problematic.

E-Mail Can Be Sent as a Fax Transmission

The Cisco AS5300 can receive an e-mail message with both TIFF image files and text files attached, and send that message to a GSTN-based Group 3 fax device. This feature allows you to easily combine e-mail and fax recipients from their existing user agent (Eudora, Netscape, Outlook) and send faxes to multiple recipients by using group e-mail aliases.

Toll Bypass

In an enterprise environment in which offices in different cities are connected by a WAN, you can bypass toll charges by transmitting faxes over the WAN to the same city as the GSTN-based Group 3 fax recipient and use the off-ramp gateway to deliver the faxes in that city. Because the fax message is stored on the mail server until SMTP forwards messages to the recipient, you can configure SMTP to forward fax e-mail attachments to the Cisco off-ramp gateway during off-peak hours (for example, during evenings and weekends), thereby reducing peak-time bandwidth demands. As another example, some estimates show that as much as 60 percent of all long-distance traffic to Japan is faxes. Routing this fax traffic over e-mail data links represents a considerable savings potential.

Broadcast to Multiple Recipients

Because store and forward fax uses e-mail messages as the transporting vehicle for the fax, you can send e-mail fax attachments to multiple recipients by addressing the fax mail to an e-mail list alias. The e-mail server will generate multiple e-mails, one for each recipient from the list, and forward them to the off-ramp gateway for faxing.

Restrictions for Cisco T.37 Store and Forward Fax

Store and forward fax on-ramp faxing has been designed to work in one of two ways: using the DID feature, or using a redialer. A redialer is an interface hardware device that interconnects between a fax device and the PSTN. If you choose not to enable DID, you must configure and enable a redialer on the originating fax machine for store and forward fax to be operational. And, you must add a TCL IVR script on the incoming dial peer to inform the processing engine to look for the second dialed number.

A third alternative is available that requires user training. This method entails setting up a two-stage dial scenario in which the caller dials the access number of the on-ramp gateway, waits for a secondary dial tone, and then dials the actual destination fax machine number.

When implementing authentication, authorization, and accounting (AAA) for T.37 fax, it might be necessary to use the H.323 *AAA method list* to perform authentication for both on-ramp and off-ramp faxes. The aaa method list is configured as shown here:

```
gateway1 (config)# aaa new-model
gateway1 (config)# aaa authentication login fax group radius
gateway1 (config)# aaa authentication login h323 group radius
```

The method list is in boldface in the preceding configuration lines. It doesn't hurt to include the fax method list, but if you want authentication to succeed, you must configure the H.323 method list.

The second item concerns accounting records. Accounting is configured also, as shown here:

```
gateway1 (config)# aaa accounting connection fax stop-only group radius
```

This configuration item is successful with the fax method list. Unfortunately, some TCL IVR scripts available on the Cisco Web site do not have the configuration line that supports accounting. When accounting is enabled using one of the faulty scripts, the debug output message received is:

```
moip_aaa_offramp: NULL acct list
```

This message is an indication that accounting is not enabled in the TCL IVR script. The solution is to obtain a script in which accounting is enabled. The Cisco Technical Assistance Center (TAC) should be able to provide links to the proper scripts.

Configuration Guidelines for On-Ramp Store and Forward Fax

On-ramp store and forward fax functionality includes accepting a fax from a GSTN-based Group 3 fax machine, converting the fax to a TIFF file attachment, and delivering that fax mail to a mail transfer agent (MTA). In this scenario, the fax mail will be delivered to the recipient e-mail account with the fax portion of the message contained in a TIFF attachment. If the fax portion is more than one page, the recipient is required to use a graphics program that can create a multipage TIFF file.

The on-ramp gateway can also be configured to forward the fax mail to an off-ramp gateway. For now, we will concentrate on the delivery to an MTA and subsequently to a recipient's e-mail inbox. Figure 8-5 shows a model of an on-ramp gateway.

Figure 8-5   *On-ramp fax service model.*

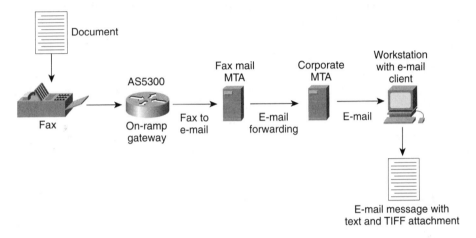

The configuration of the on-ramp gateway consists of the following tasks:

Step 1   Configuring on-ramp dial peers

Step 2   Configuring TCL IVR and call application parameters

Step 3   Configuring on-ramp fax and MTA parameters

Step 4   Configuring other on-ramp variables

Configuring On-Ramp Dial Peers

Cisco fax over IP technology uses the concept of dial peers to identify the properties of a call. A dial peer can be incoming (answer) or outgoing (originate), and either from/to the PSTN (telephony) or from/to the IP network (VoIP). A call entering or leaving a voice gateway is identified with a dial peer configured in the gateway. This dial peer contains information about the call, including encoding technique, call properties, and how the call should be handled.

POTS Dial Peers

Plain old telephone service (POTS) dial peers can be thought of as the answering/destination number of the gateway. If a call is coming from the telephony side, the POTS dial peer is an *answer* telephony dial peer. If the POTS dial peer is sending a call to the GSTN, then it's an *originate* telephony dial peer. The line coming into the fax gateway is assigned a certain number or numbers by the service provider. These are the dialed numbers that the fax gateway answers. If the gateway dial-in port answers only one dialed number, then it can have only one POTS dial peer of significance. If the gateway is configured with more than one access number, these numbers can be differentiated by the configuration parameters in the POTS dial peers.

MMoIP Dial Peers

MMoIP dial peers can be thought of as mapping between a dialed number and a data network location. In the case of on-ramp fax mail, that location is an e-mail address. VoIP dial peers are equivalent to MMoIP dial peers. They both serve the same function for different call types. MMoIP dial peers are used for T.37 fax; VoIP dial peers are used for voice and T.38 fax.

On-Ramp Dial Peer Call Routing

When the fax on-ramp gateway receives a call, it decides how to route the call based on the configuration of the gateway. The call-processing engine determines the call type according to the dialed number identification service (DNIS) that was received in the call setup messages. The DNIS is also referred to as the *called party number.*

After receiving the DNIS, the gateway examines its POTS dial peers and searches for a match between the DNIS (called number) and the *incoming called number* in a POTS dial peer. For example, consider a DNIS of 9991144 and the following POTS dial peer:

```
dial-peer voice 999 pots
  application on-ramp
  incoming called-number 99911..
  direct-inward-dial
```

The DNIS is matched as the called number in this POTS dial peer because the trailing dots are wild cards (the "." represents one and only one legal digit). Because of the wild cards, all of the numbers from 9991100 through 9991199 are matches. Finding a match, the on-ramp gateway next sees that the **application on-ramp** dial-peer configuration command and **direct-inward-dial** dial-peer configuration command are configured on this dial-peer.

The **application on-ramp** dial-peer configuration command tells the processing engine to look for a TCL IVR call application script reference in the call application parameters (to be discussed shortly). The **direct-inward-dial** dial-peer configuration command tells the gateway to look for an outbound MMoIP dial peer that matches the dialed number,

9991144. In this case, it finds **mmoip dial-peer 990**. The **destination-pattern** dial-peer
configuration command in the MMoIP dial peer matches the dialed number.

```
dial-peer voice 990 mmoip
  application fax_on_vfc_onramp_app out-bound
  destination-pattern 9991144
  information-type fax
  session target mailto:owner@domain.cisco.com
  dsn success
```

Assuming that there is an exact match, the on-ramp gateway now knows what to do with
the call to 9991144: Run the C-based application called "fax_on_vfc_onramp_app" with
the keyword **out-bound**. This application is compiled into Cisco IOS for the purpose of
setting up the fax call after all the authentication and other activities are successfully
completed. If they do not successfully complete, the call is handed to the application with
the failure flag and the call is torn down.

After the preliminary steps are successfully completed, the application sets up the call with
the destination specified in the **session target** dial-peer configuration command. In this
example, it sends an e-mail with the fax content as a TIFF attachment to
owner@domain.cisco.com. The session target is hardcoded to represent a static address
assignment; the hardcoded SMTP address requires an exact match to the dialed number in
the dial peer.

Dynamic matching can be achieved with the following session target statement:

```
  session target mailto:$d$@domain.cisco.com
```

This target statement could be matched to a range of dialed numbers. The d substitution
inserts the string *fax=<dialed number>* into the mailto: statement. After substitution, the
session target (IP destination) becomes *fax=<dialed number>@domain.cisco.com*. An
alias must be configured in the MTA that will accept *fax=<dialed number>@
domain.cisco.com* and translate that address to a viable target e-mail address, which might
be another off-ramp fax gateway or a normal user mailbox. The MTA alias procedure is
covered in the section on mailers, but be aware that there are many MTAs on the market,
and most of them are configured differently.

Dedicating a mailer to your fax-mail function is an excellent idea. If you do this, you are
better positioned to experiment with the properties of your mailer without risking the
company's e-mail system. Be sure to obtain permission from the postmaster if the e-mail
system is the company's live e-mail system!

Figure 8-5 shows how you can deploy a specialized fax-mail MTA to receive fax mail from
the on-ramp gateway. This allows for configuring aliases and other fax-specific variables on
the fax-mail MTA that might conflict with the settings on the corporate mailer. The fax-mail
MTA thus can be devoted to fax mail and can simply forward the fax mail-turned-e-mail to
the corporate MTA for delivery to the recipient in the regular way.

Direct Inward Dial Versus Redialers

When on-ramp functionality is implemented, a telephone number translation is required at the on-ramp gateway so the sender of the fax needs to dial only one telephone number. The sender dials the telephone number of the destination fax machine, but the fax gateway on-ramp access number is the number actually reached. The on-ramp gateway maps the number dialed by the sender to the desired destination. This mapping is accomplished by the **direct-inward-dial** dial-peer configuration command in the POTS dial-peer.

An alternative to DID in the on-ramp configuration is to use a redialer, or prompt the sender for the destination number after the access number has been dialed. A redialer is a device that sits between the fax machine and the POTS RJ-11 connector and is programmed to capture the digits of the destination number that the sender dials into the fax machine. It then dials the access number of the fax on-ramp gateway (this number is programmed into the redialer) and transmits the captured digits to the fax on-ramp gateway when the fax on-ramp gateway requests them. The on-ramp gateway then matches the captured digits to an MMoIP dial peer and performs the same steps as described previously for the DID method. Many redialers are available; exploring their use and functionality is not covered in this book.

If neither the redialer access method nor direct inward dial are configured, the default access method is to prompt the sender. This can also be configured explicitly in the call application options. When *prompt user* is the access method, after the access gateway is dialed, the on-ramp TCL IVR script plays the prompt, "Please enter the phone number you want to reach." The sender then dials the destination fax number and sends the fax.

Configuring On-Ramp TCL IVR and Call Application Parameters

When voice feature cards (VFCs) are used, Cisco store and forward fax makes use of TCL IVR scripts for call control. T.37 store and forward fax on VFCs requires TCL IVR Version 2.0 and Cisco voice extensions that are available in Cisco IOS Release 12.1(3)XI or later.

TCL IVR scripts are loaded dynamically by the voice/fax gateway either at the time they are configured or upon reboot. Configuring a call application script requires a tag and a URL for the script and is accomplished in the following way:

```
mmoip-b(config)# call application voice on-ramp tftp://sleepy/sffax_onramp
   9.2.0.0.tcl
Loading sffax_onramp9.2.0.0.tcl from 172.19.49.14 (via FastEthernet0): !!!
[OK - 11013/21504 bytes]
Read script succeeded. size=11013, url=tftp://sffax_onramp9.2.0.0.tcl
```

The keyword in the preceding configuration line is **on-ramp** and is the name that will be referred to by the dial peer to have that script activated. The URL is the machine **sleepy**, the base directory is **/tftpboot** (understood by the Trivial File Transfer Protocol [TFTP] server), and the actual filename is "sffax_onramp9.2.0.0.tcl." The command is entered in global configuration mode. As soon as the command is entered, the gateway attempts to access the TFTP server and download the particular TCL IVR file named in the configuration line.

After the script is successfully loaded, you can enter other parameters to control the behavior of the script. For basic on-ramp faxing, two other call application parameters are required: one to tell the script which language to use, the other to tell the gateway where to find the audio files required for the prompts, even if the prompts are not going to be used. The required command lines are as follows:

```
call application voice on-ramp language 1 en
call application voice on-ramp set-location en 0 tftp://sleepy/prompts/en/
```

In the first line, English is chosen as the language. Languages are referred to with their International Organization for Standardization (ISO) two-character code. The second line gives the path for the gateway to find the audio file prompts to use. It's important to remember to enter the final slash (/) at the end of the path to the audio prompts. The TCL IVR script prepends the path to the prompt name, and if the slash is not at the end of the path, the language code will be concatenated onto the audio filename and the script will not be able to load the file. The result will be silence and a failed call.

You can download TCL IVR scripts and associated audio file prompts from the Cisco Web site at http://www.cisco.com/cgi-bin/tablebuild.pl/tclware.

NOTE It is important when entering a TCL IVR filename into the Cisco CLI that you spell it exactly as it appears on Cisco.com. You can display a list of possible TCL IVR filenames by entering the **show call application voice summary** privileged EXEC command, but some of the filenames might not display in their entirety due to the limitations of the CLI parser.

To display the TCL IVR script in its entirety, enter the **show call application voice on-ramp** Privileged EXEC command. (Note that the **on-ramp** argument is the keyword name that we've assigned to the filename **sffax_onramp9.2.0.0.tcl**.) At the beginning of the output is an explanation of the call flow decisions made by the script.

Configuring On-Ramp Fax Receive and MTA Send Parameters

Fax receive, MTA send, and MMoIP AAA parameters are configured using a series of global configuration commands. The AAA parameters are considered in a separate section. Table 8-1 lists the necessary and optional on-ramp parameters.

Table 8-1 *On-Ramp Fax and MTA Parameters*

Global Command	Description
fax receive called-subscriber d	Substitutes the string **fax=<*dialed fax number*>** for d in the session target parameter in the MMoIP dial peer. The session target can also be hardcoded, as in the MMoIP dial peer previously, in which case this variable will not be used.

continues

Table 8-1 *On-Ramp Fax and MTA Parameters (Continued)*

Global Command	Description
fax interface-type vfc	Tells the gateway that fax calls are processed in DSPs rather than modems.
mta send server *server@domain.com*	Specifies the destination mail server. It can be an IP address or a fully qualified domain name.
mta send subject *fax subject line*	The variable configured here will be listed in the subject line of the e-mail message that is generated.
mta send postmaster *name@mailserver.domain.com*	Defines the address of a person to whom undeliverable mail is sent.
mta send mail-from username *username* **mta send mail-from hostname** *mailserver.domain.com*	Together these two commands comprise the *From* header of the fax-mail message, for example, username@mailserv.domain.com.
mta send return-receipt-to hostname *mail.domain.com* **mta send return-receipt-to username** *username*	These two commands configure the e-mail address of the person to whom MDNs are sent, for example, postmaster@mailserv.domain.com

Fax and MTA Variables

The fax and MTA variables configured in the gateway control the behavior of the faxes and fax mail leaving the gateway. A minimal configuration for on-ramp faxing requires the following fax and MTA variables:

```
1. fax receive called-subscriber $d$
2. fax interface-type vfc
3. mta send server 171.69.167.33
4. mta send server earlgrey.cisco.com
5. mta send subject VoIP TME Faxmail
6. mta send postmaster mailman@172.19.49.30
7. mta send mail-from hostname earlgrey.cisco.com
8. mta send mail-from username $s$
9. mta send return-receipt-to hostname cisco.com
10. mta send return-receipt-to username thuff
```

Line 1 substitutes the DNIS for d, which is used in the MMoIP dial peer as the username part of the session target.

Line 2 is necessary to define the interface type being used for fax. Although VFCs are used exclusively in the latest Cisco IOS software, the first implementation of T.37 fax in Cisco gateways used modems.

Lines 3 and 4 configure the MTAs to which the fax mail is sent from the on-ramp gateway. Use the **mta send server** global configuration command to provide a backup destination server in case the first configured mail server is unavailable. (This command is not intended to be used for load distribution.)

You can configure up to ten different destination mail servers using the **mta send server** global configuration command. If you configure more than one destination mail server, the Cisco gateway attempts to contact the first mail server configured. If that mail server is unavailable, it contacts the next configured destination mail server, and so on.

Line 5 configures the message that is inserted into the subject line of the fax mail sent.

Line 6 configures the e-mail address of the postmaster to whom the DSN messages are sent.

Lines 7 and 8 configure the ID of the fax mail sender. The **s** substitution for the username inserts the automatic number identification (ANI) of the caller. This should not be confused with the phone number configured in the fax machine. The number configured in the fax machine by the person who maintains the fax machine doesn't always coincide with the ANI. In our case, the following appears in the *From:* line of a received fax mail in a Eudora 4.3.2 e-mail client:

> From: "4085151827" FAX=408@earlgrey.Cisco.com

The number in quotes is the number configured in the fax machine itself, while the 408 in FAX=408@... represents the ANI that is delivered from the Cisco Centrex system. Thus, the **s** variable referenced in Line 8 is the ANI from the PSTN. To further confuse things, it is the number in quotes that appears in the subject line of a Eudora mail client, not the PSTN ANI. When you actually open the fax mail, then you can see both numbers, as in the preceding paragraph.

Lines 9 and 10 configure the recipient of return receipts if message disposition notification (MDN) is configured in the MMoIP dial peer. It takes the form of *username@hostname*.

Configuring Other On-Ramp Variables

The variables that don't fit into any of the preceding categories are discussed in this section.

If you are resolving machine names with the Domain Name System (DNS), you will need to enter the following commands on the gateway:

```
ip domain-lookup         (this command is ON by default)
ip domain-name domain.com (domain name is the domain name of your network)
ip name-server 10.10.10.10  (the IP address of your DNS server)
```

These commands attach the gateway to a domain and point it to a DNS server. Six different DNS servers can be configured; the gateway tries them in turn.

To perform accurate accounting, both the gateways and the RADIUS server need to agree on the time of day. The typical way to do this with IP-based devices is through the use of Network Time Protocol (NTP). The first command sets the gateway in a particular time zone with a certain offset in hours from Greenwich Mean Time (GMT). The default is to use GMT (also referred to as Coordinated Universal Time, or UTC).

```
clock timezone PST -8     (Pacific Standard Time, minus 8 hours from GMT)
```

If you do not enter a time zone, the gateway assumes that it's GMT. The next command tells the gateway where to go to get the correct time.

```
ntp server 172.19.49.11.Cisco Systems
```

A list of freely accessible NTP servers in every time zone can be found at www.eecis.udel.edu/~mills/ntp/clock2.htm.

Configuration Example for On-Ramp Store and Forward Fax

If we start with a configuration that has IP connectivity and then configure all the items in the preceding sections, the gateway configuration should resemble Example 8-1.

Example 8-1 *Configuration Example for On-Ramp Store and Forward Fax*

```
mmoip-b# write terminal
Building configuration...
Current configuration:
!
version 12.2
service timestamps debug uptime
service timestamps log uptime
no service password-encryption
service internal
service udp-small-servers
service tcp-small-servers
!
hostname mmoip-b
!
enable secret 5 $1$CF2w$GbYL.9.Y5ccJKSdEBh13f0
!
resource-pool disable
!
clock timezone PST -8
ip subnet-zero
ip host sleepy 172.19.49.14
!This maps sleepy to its IP address.
ip domain-name cisco.com
ip name-server 172.18.10.70
ip name-server 172.18.10.140
!
isdn switch-type primary-5ess
isdn voice-call-failure 0
call application voice on-ramp tftp://sleepy/ifax/sffax_onramp9.2.0.0.tcl
call application voice on-ramp language 1 en
call application voice on-ramp set-location en 0 tftp://sleepy/prompts/en/
!
fax receive called-subscriber $d$
fax interface-type vfc
mta send server earlgrey.cisco.com
mta send server 172.29.187.33
mta send subject VoIP TME Faxmail
mta send origin-prefix "Cisco Powered Fax Mail"
```

Example 8-1 *Configuration Example for On-Ramp Store and Forward Fax (Continued)*

```
mta send postmaster mailman@172.31.149.30
mta send mail-from hostname voip-tme.cisco.com
mta send mail-from username $s$
mta send return-receipt-to hostname cisco.com
mta send return-receipt-to username thuff
!
controller T1 0
!Only one controller port is active on this router.
 framing esf
 clock source line primary
 linecode b8zs
 pri-group timeslots 1-24
!
controller T1 1
 clock source line secondary 1
!
controller T1 2
 clock source line secondary 2
!
controller T1 3
 clock source line secondary 3
!
!interface Ethernet0
!Any interface in "shutdown" mode is not in service,
!nor is it needed for this operation.
 no ip address
 shutdown
!
interface Serial0
 no ip address
 no ip mroute-cache
 shutdown
 no fair-queue
 clockrate 2015232
!
interface Serial1
 no ip address
 shutdown
 no fair-queue
 clockrate 2015232
!
interface Serial2
 no ip address
 shutdown
 no fair-queue
 clockrate 2015232
!
interface Serial3
 no ip address
 shutdown
 no fair-queue
```

continues

Example 8-1 *Configuration Example for On-Ramp Store and Forward Fax (Continued)*

```
 clockrate 2015232
!
interface Serial0:23
!This interface relates to the signaling channel of Port 0;
!these are the numbers serviced.
description 3590576 and 5551460-1479
no ip address
 ip mroute-cache
 isdn switch-type primary-5ess
 isdn incoming-voice modem
!This provides voice bearer capability.
 isdn disconnect-cause 1
!
interface FastEthernet0
 ip address 172.19.49.20 255.255.255.128
 duplex auto
 speed auto
!
ip classless
ip route 0.0.0.0 0.0.0.0 172.19.49.1
no ip http server
!
!
!
voice-port 0:D
!
dial-peer voice 1 pots
!This POTS port answers incoming calls that begin with 361 and have seven digits.
!It runs the application "on-ramp" referenced previously. DID directs it to look for
!an MMoIP dial peer with that destination pattern.
 application on-ramp
 incoming called-number 361....
 direct-inward-dial


port 0:D
!
dial-peer voice 60 mmoip
!This MMoIP dial peer will be found if the dialed number is 5551460. It will run
!the application fax_on_vfc_onramp and will direct the fax mail to
!owner@cisco.com. The target can be any valid e-mail address;
!the postmaster will be informed of successful message delivery.
 application fax_on_vfc_onramp_app out-bound
 destination-pattern 5551460
 information-type fax
 session target mailto:owner@cisco.com
 mdn
 dsn success
dial-peer voice 73 mmoip
!This dial peer answers to 5551473 and is the same as the preceding dial peer 60
!except that it directs the fax mail to FAX=5551473@earlgrey.cisco.com.
 application fax_on_vfc_onramp_app out
```

Example 8-1   *Configuration Example for On-Ramp Store and Forward Fax (Continued)*

```
 destination-pattern 5551473
 information-type fax
 session target mailto:$d$@earlgrey.cisco.com
!There is an MTA at this address that has an alias configured to translate
!FAX=5551473 into a valid username and send the fax mail on.
 mdn
 dsn success
 !
 !
line con 0
 exec-timeout 0 0
 transport input none
line aux 0
line vty 0 4
 no login
 !
ntp clock-period 17180024
ntp server 172.19.49.11
end
```

Verifying On-Ramp Fax Operation

With the configuration in Example 8-1, on-ramp faxing should now be in service. To ensure that the TCL IVR script is working properly, enter the debug commands as in Example 8-2.

Example 8-2   *Verifying On-Ramp Fax Operation*

```
mmoip-b# debug voip ivr
mmoip-b# show debug
ivr:
  ivr errors debugging is on
  ivr state transitions debugging is on
  ivr settlement activities debugging is on
  ivr script debugging is on
  ivr script debugging is on
  ivr app library debugging is on
  ivr tcl commands debugging is on
  ivr digit collect debugging is on
  ivr call setup debugging is on
```

To examine the different call states of a successful on-ramp call, enter the following debug command:

```
mmoip-b# debug foip on-ramp
FOIP On ramp faxmail debugging is on
```

If there's a problem with the configuration or with the on-ramp fax operation, the debug output will indicate where the problem is occurring. The actual debug output is too lengthy to include in this book. For more information about problem-solving on-ramp fax operations, go to this Cisco Web site:

http://www.cisco.com/cpropart/salestools/cc/so/cuso/sp/faxov_in.htm.

As an example of a fax mail application, the Primary Rate Interface (PRI) line that is terminated in a Cisco Technical Marketing Group on-ramp gateway has 21 numbers mapped to it. (The service provider that manages the phone lines provides this functionality.) Each person in the group has an MMoIP dial peer that corresponds to an individual phone number. The POTS dial peer with that same number maps its DID to the corresponding MMoIP dial peer. That MMoIP dial peer is mapped to the e-mail address of the person having that phone number. Now every person with their own fax-mail number can receive faxes through e-mail wherever they are. Receiving e-mail on the road is commonplace; receiving a fax on the road is problematic at best. That problem is solved with store and forward fax mail.

Fine-Tuning the Fax Mail Transport Agent

The configurations in this chapter utilize two different MTAs. For both on-ramp and off-ramp functionality, both MTAs are used. The on-ramp gateway receives the fax mail, converts the pages into a TIFF file, and sends the message to its primary MTA, which is a Netscape Messaging Server V3.6. The Netscape MTA finds an alias for fax=number and sends the mail on to the recipient that was configured in its alias file. This second mailer is the Cisco corporate mailer, which is a Solaris UNIX machine running sendmail. Extreme caution should be used when dealing with the corporate mail system. E-mail systems are maximized for delivering e-mail, and the demands and behavior of fax mail might cause problems if configured improperly.

The off-ramp gateway accepts an e-mail and turns any TIFF or text attachments into T.4 fax format. It then attempts to deliver the T.4 fax format to a GSTN-based Group 3 fax device. The chance of creating problems is more severe with the off-ramp gateway than with the on-ramp gateway.

Many MTAs are on the market that will work without modification with both the on-ramp and off-ramp features of store and forward fax. Cisco recommends that you dedicate a mail server to fax mail and avoid the conflicting configuration requirements of traditional e-mail and fax-mail servers. Optimize each mail server for its individual functions—for example, fax messages should usually retry transmissions every 5 minutes versus normal e-mail, which retries every 30 minutes; fax messages should give up after 3 to 4 hours versus normal e-mail, which tries for 4 to 5 days.

To avoid any complications arising from the difference between the SMTP e-mail and fax delivery requirements, modify the following parameters:

- Delivery to one recipient
- Message priority
- Connection cache size
- Minimum queue age

NOTE	In some countries it's illegal to try to send a fax more than three times in a row if the transmission fails.

WARNING	It is extremely important to modify SMTP delivery requirement parameters. Failure to do so can result in a monopoly of network bandwidth and off-ramp fax resources.

NOTE	Sendmail is a freeware mailer included with many UNIX implementations; it's also available from sendmail.org and from sendmail.com. It's not the only MTA available; there are many others, including qmail, Netscape Messaging Server, Post.Office, Microsoft Exchange, PMDF, and vmailer, to name a few.

Configuring the SMTP Server to Support Store and Forward Fax

If you choose to configure your SMTP server, edit the SMTP server alias file to include an alias for fax transmissions. For example, suppose you create the following alias: fax=5551212: user@hostname.com.

In this example, if a fax is sent to the telephone number 5551212, the on-ramp gateway will automatically forward it to the mailbox for user@hostname.com. If you create aliases to forward faxes to particular e-mail addresses, you need to configure the on-ramp MMoIP **session target** dial-peer configuration command as follows:

```
router(config-dial-peer)# session target mailto:$d$@hostname.com
```

The **d** keyword specifies that the destination fax machine telephone number is inserted into the *Envelope to:* field of the fax mail that is sent to the SMTP server.

The Cisco AS5300 off-ramp gateway accepts only one e-mail recipient per SMTP transaction because:

- The SMTP server in the Cisco AS5300 off-ramp gateway doesn't queue messages because of their size and the lack of non-volatile storage in the Cisco AS5300.

- SMTP doesn't provide a mechanism to allow the receiving MTA to indicate the success or failure of each recipient. Instead, the receiving MTA must indicate the success or failure of the entire transaction.

The Cisco AS5300 prevents multiple recipients in one SMTP transaction by responding to the second and subsequent RCPT commands with a 450 reply code. Because of the typical mailer configuration, there will be a cumulative 30-minute delay for each recipient (immediate delivery for the first recipient, 30-minute delay for the second recipient, 60-minute delay for the third recipient, and so on).

Forcing All Mail Through One Mailer

To simplify system administration, it's often desirable to have all mail to the Cisco AS5300 go through one mailer. One way to accomplish this is to set up a Domain Name Service (DNS) MX record for the Cisco AS5300 pointing to the one mailer, and set up that mailer to skip MX record-processing when delivering mail to the Cisco AS5300.

For example, the following two records would be added to the DNS:

```
sj-offramp in mx 10 sj-mailer
sj-offramp in a 1.2.3.4
```

To help prevent unauthorized use of the fax off-ramp gateway, and to force all mail to go through sj-mailer, we recommend that you configure the Cisco AS5300 with access control lists (ACLs) to block incoming connections to its mail port (TCP Port 25) from any other IP address. For more information about ACLs, refer to the *Cisco IOS Security Configuration Guide* and the "Security Considerations" section of this chapter.

Tuning the Sending Mailer for a Single Recipient

It's possible to tune the sending mailer to work faster with store and forward fax off-ramp gateways and to reduce delays caused by attempting to send to multiple recipients. You can do this by configuring the mailer to send to each recipient serially, but without delays between each transmission. Configuring the mailer to send messages in parallel would require sending each message back through the mailer again (perhaps on a different port) and also running multiple client processes on the system. Such configuration changes are beyond the intended scope of this chapter.

WARNING Modifying the sending mailer configuration can break all e-mail into and out of the fax gateway for your entire enterprise. Perform sendmail configuration modifications only after you have notified the postmaster at your site.

Configuration Guidelines for Off-Ramp Store and Forward Fax

Off-ramp faxing requires the off-ramp gateway to communicate with a GSTN-based Group 3 fax device using standard fax protocols. The off-ramp gateway is capable of transmitting a message containing a TIFF image, a text message, or a message containing both.

The off-ramp gateway performs the following functions:

- It converts a TIFF file or text file into a standard fax format and transmits it to a GSTN-based Group 3 fax device. Store and forward fax doesn't alter the TIFF or text file in any way from its original format when converting it to the standard fax format. The off-ramp gateway uses the dial peers to dial the correct telephone number for the GSTN-based Group 3 fax device.

- It delivers an e-mail message as a standard fax transmission, which is received and processed by a Group 3 fax device. The source of this transmission is an e-mail message. The Cisco off-ramp gateway generates information to be appended to the top of each text-to-fax page and creates a fax cover sheet. The off-ramp gateway uses the receiving MTA, dial peers, and commands specific to formatting the appended information and generating a fax cover sheet to deliver e-mail messages as fax transmissions.

Configuration guidelines for the off-ramp gateway are described in the following sections. Off-ramp configuration consists of the same four tasks as on-ramp configuration. Figure 8-6 shows a suggested off-ramp gateway model. Call flow is similar and is handled by the same service modules.

Figure 8-6   *Off-ramp fax service model.*

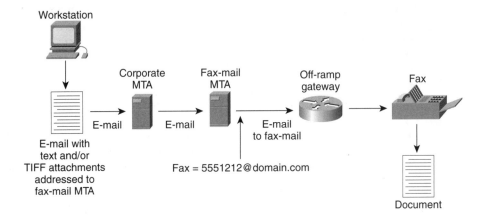

The configuration of the off-ramp gateway consists of the following tasks:

Step 1   Configuring off-ramp dial peers

Step 2   Configuring TCL IVR and call application parameters

Step 3   Configuring off-ramp fax send and MTA receive parameters

Step 4   Configuring other off-ramp variables

Configuring Off-Ramp Dial Peers

Off-ramp faxing is the second half of the store and forward fax topology illustrated in Figure 8-4. With off-ramp faxing, the package delivered to the voice/fax gateway is an SMTP message. The content of the message is encoded by the gateway into a TIFF attachment file and the message headers are transferred to a cover page for the fax.

Because an off-ramp fax is delivered to a terminating gateway, it's delivered using IP, and the dial peer that it finds in the gateway is an MMoIP dial peer. This MMoIP dial peer runs the off-ramp fax TCL IVR script, which hands the call to a matching POTS dial peer. The POTS dial peer sets up a call to a fax machine on the telephony side of the gateway, remodulates the IP packets into a G3 fax, and delivers the fax to a G3 fax machine.

Following is an example of a pair of dial peers configured for off-ramp faxing:

```
dial-peer voice 100 mmoip
 application off
 incoming called-number 8......
 information-type fax
!
dial-peer voice 101 pots
 destination-pattern 8......
 port 0:D
 prefix 8
```

The DNIS of the destination fax machine is a seven-digit number beginning with *8*. This is received by MMoIP dial peer 100 in the off-ramp fax gateway. SMTP directs the call to the IP address of the gateway, while the number configured in the username portion of the SMTP message (*fax=8531827@*) links the message to a particular dial peer in the gateway.

This dial peer is configured with the TCL IVR application named *off*. After the off-ramp parameters are collected, the script hands off the call to POTS dial peer 101 for delivery to the destination fax machine.

POTS Dial Peers

To configure the POTS dial peers on the off-ramp gateway, simply enter the various phone numbers for the fax machines that will be receiving fax mail. An example follows:

```
dial-peer voice 1 pots
 destination-pattern .......
 port 0:D
```

The preceding dial peer will initiate a connection to any fax machine within the present area code because the seven dots represent wild cards. This dial peer requires seven digits because there are seven dots. If you want to enable long-distance fax machines, configure the POTS dial peers as shown here:

```
dial-peer voice 1 pots
  destination-pattern 1408.......
  port 0:D
  prefix 1408
```

The preceding dial peer will match an incoming number of 1408 plus seven more digits represented by the seven dots. Because POTS dial peers strip all numbers that aren't wild cards, the dial peer will strip the 1408. The **prefix** dial-peer configuration command will prepend the 1408 back onto the dial peer, thus allowing any fax machine number in the 408 area code to be reachable. You can enable or restrict dial peers for any or all area codes in this manner.

MMOIP Dial Peers

The primary function of the MMoIP dial peer is to run the TCL IVR application for the off-ramp fax. The incoming IP call setup matches the *incoming called-number* configured in the MMoIP dial peer to the actual DNIS of the call being established. If that dial peer is configured with an application, then that application is launched.

Configuring Off-Ramp TCL IVR and Call Application Parameters

The TCL IVR script for an off-ramp gateway is very similar to the on-ramp script discussed earlier in this chapter. The primary function of the off-ramp script is to gather authentication, accounting, and calling parameters and, if so configured, communicate these to a RADIUS server. After the parameter gathering is completed, the call is handed off to the internal off-ramp application with the related call-control information. You can view the TCL IVR script name and a short description by entering the **show call application voice summary** privileged EXEC command in privileged EXEC mode.

For a complete discussion of TCL IVR script-loading, configuring, and call flow control, see the section "Configuring On-Ramp TCL IVR and Call Application Parameters" earlier in this chapter.

Configuring Off-Ramp Fax Send and MTA Receive Parameters

With on-ramp faxing, the fax and MTA parameters are **fax receive** and **mta send**; for off-ramp faxing, the parameters are **fax send** and **mta receive**. Table 8-2 and Table 8-3 list the necessary and optional off-ramp parameters.

Table 8-2   *Off-Ramp MTA Receive Parameters*

Global Command	Description
mta receive aliases *string*	Defines a host name to be used as an alias for the off-ramp gateway. You can define up to ten different aliases.
	Note: The SMTP server of the off-ramp device will accept incoming mail only if the destination host name of the incoming mail matches one of the aliases as configured by the **mta receive aliases** global configuration command.
	Note: This command doesn't automatically include reception for a domain IP address: It must be explicitly added. If you add an IP address, you must enclose the address in brackets as follows: [xxx.xxx.xxx.xxx]. Note that RFC1123 requires that mail servers accept mail for all of their IP interfaces; however, in practice, this is usually not a requirement in most mail environments.
mta receive generate-mdn	(Optional) Configures the off-ramp gateway to generate an MDN message when requested to do so. Some sites might want to enable or disable this feature, depending on corporate policy or the types of mail user agents in use.
mta receive maximum-recipients number	Defines the number of simultaneous SMTP recipients handled by this device. This is intended to limit the number of resources (modems) allocated for fax transmissions.
	Note: Only one recipient will be accepted per SMTP transaction, and it is not controllable by this setting.

Table 8-3   *Off-Ramp Fax Send Parameters*

Global Command	Description
fax send transmitting-subscriber {**d** | *string*}	Defines the number that appears in the LCD of the receiving fax device. This parameter defines the transmitting subscriber identifier (TSI).
fax send left-header {**a** | **d** | **p** | **s** | **t** | *string*}	Specifies the header information to be displayed in the left header position. The wild cards used in this command insert the following information: **a**—Date **d**—Destination address **s**—Sender's address **p**—Page count **t**—Transmission time The variables can be preceded by words; for example, Page:p. Use the string variable in this command to insert a personalized text string.
fax send center-header {**a** | **d** | **p** | **s** | **t** | *string*}	Specifies the header information to be displayed in the center header position. The wild cards used in this command insert the same information as in the **fax send left-header** global configuration command.
fax send right-header {**a** | **d** | **p** | **s** | **t** | *string*}	Specifies the header information to be displayed in the right header position. The wild cards used in this command insert the same information as in the **fax send left-header** global configuration command.
fax send coverpage enable	Enables the off-ramp gateway to send a cover sheet with faxes that originate from e-mail messages.
fax send coverpage show-detail	(Optional) Prints all of the e-mail header information as part of the fax cover sheet text.
fax send coverpage comment *string*	(Optional) Adds personalized text in the title field of the fax cover sheet.

Configuring Other Off-Ramp Variables

For off-ramp faxing, only one additional variable exists that doesn't fit into the MTA receive and fax send categories:

```
fax interface-type vfc
```

This global command tells Cisco IOS software to use the voice feature card DSPs for fax processing rather than modems.

Configuration Example for Off-Ramp Store and Forward Fax

After the preceding commands have been entered, the off-ramp gateway configuration should look similar to Example 8-3 (IP routing commands and command lines not associated with store and forward fax have been removed from Example 8-3 in an effort to save space).

Example 8-3 *Configuration Example for Off-Ramp Store and Forward Fax*

```
mmoip-b# write terminal
!
hostname mmoip-b
!
call rsvp-sync
call application voice off tftp://snoopy/sffax_offramp5.2.0.0.tcl
clock timezone PST -8
!
isdn switch-type primary-5ess
isdn voice-call-failure 0
!
!
fax send left-header $s$
fax send center-header $t$
fax send right-header Page: $p$
fax send coverpage enable
fax send coverpage email-controllable
fax send coverpage comment VoIP TME Generated Fax
fax interface-type vfc
mta receive aliases offramp.cisco.com
mta receive aliases cisco.com
mta receive aliases [xxx.xxx.xxx.xxx]
mta receive maximum-recipients 255
mta receive generate-mdn
!
!

controller T1 0
 framing esf
 clock source line primary
 linecode b8zs
 pri-group timeslots 1-24
!
controller T1 1
 clock source line secondary 1
!
controller T1 2
 clock source line secondary 2
!
controller T1 3
 clock source line secondary 3
!
interface Serial0:23
 no ip address
 ip mroute-cache
```

Example 8-3 *Configuration Example for Off-Ramp Store and Forward Fax (Continued)*

```
 isdn switch-type primary-5ess
 isdn incoming-voice modem
 isdn disconnect-cause 1
 !
interface FastEthernet0
 ip address 172.31.149.20 255.255.255.128
 duplex auto
 speed auto
 !
ip classless
ip route 0.0.0.0 0.0.0.0 172.31.149.1
 !
voice-port 0:D
 !
dial-peer voice 100 mmoip
 application off
 incoming called-number 8......
 information-type fax
 !
dial-peer voice 101 pots
 destination-pattern 8......
 port 0:D
 prefix 8
 !
dial-peer voice 1000 pots
 destination-pattern 1831.......
 port 0:D
 prefix 1831
 !
dial-peer voice 1001 mmoip
 application off
 incoming called-number 1831.......
 information-type fax
ntp clock-period 17179630
ntp server xx.xx.xxx.xxx
 !
```

Complete On-Ramp/Off-Ramp Gateway Configuration

Example 8-4 shows a sample of a Cisco gateway configured for both on-ramp and off-ramp store and forward fax. (IP routing commands and command lines not associated with store and forward fax have been removed from Example 8-4 in an effort to save space.)

Example 8-4 *Complete On-Ramp/Off-Ramp Gateway Configuration*

```
mmoip-b# write terminal
 !
hostname mmoip-b
 !
enable secret 5 $1$CF2w$GbYL.9.Y5ccJKSdEBh13f0
 !
```

continues

Example 8-4 *Complete On-Ramp/Off-Ramp Gateway Configuration (Continued)*

```
resource-pool disable
!
clock timezone PST -8
!
isdn switch-type primary-5ess
isdn voice-call-failure 0
call application voice roll tftp://snoopy/fax_rollover_on_busy.tcl
call application voice off tftp://snoopy/t37_offramp.0.0.6.tcl
call application voice off accounting enable
call application voice off accounting-list fax
call application voice off language 1 en
call application voice off set-location en 0 tftp://snoopy/prompts/en/
!
call application voice onramp tftp://snoopy/t37_onramp13.tcl
call application voice onramp password 1234
call application voice onramp authen-method dnis
call application voice onramp authen-list fax
call application voice onramp authentication enable
call application voice onramp accounting enable
call application voice onramp accounting-list fax
call application voice onramp language 1 en
call application voice onramp set-location en 0 tftp://sleepy/prompts/en/
voice hunt user-busy
!
voice service voip
!
fax receive called-subscriber $d$
fax send max-speed 9600
fax send left-header $s$
fax send center-header $t$
fax send right-header Page: $p$
fax send coverpage enable
fax send coverpage email-controllable
fax send coverpage comment VoIP TME Generated Fax
fax interface-type vfc
mta send server earlthepearl.cisco.com
mta send server mail.cisco.com
mta send subject VoIP TME Faxmail
mta send origin-prefix "Cisco Powered Fax Mail"
mta send postmaster mailman@xxx.xxx.xxx.xxx
mta send mail-from hostname voip-tme.cisco.com
mta send mail-from username $s$
mta send return-receipt-to hostname cisco.com
mta send return-receipt-to username thuff
mta receive aliases mmoip-b.cisco.com
mta receive aliases cisco.com
mta receive aliases [xxx.xxx.xxx.xxx]
mta receive aliases [xxx.xxx.xxx.xxx]
mta receive maximum-recipients 255
mta receive generate-mdn
!
!
```

Example 8-4 *Complete On-Ramp/Off-Ramp Gateway Configuration (Continued)*

```
controller T1 0
 framing esf
 clock source line primary
 linecode b8zs
 pri-group timeslots 1-24
!
controller T1 1
 clock source line secondary 1
!
controller T1 2
 clock source line secondary 2
!
controller T1 3
 clock source line secondary 3
!
gw-accounting h323
gw-accounting h323 vsa
gw-accounting voip
!
interface Serial0:23
 no ip address
 ip mroute-cache
 isdn switch-type primary-5ess
 isdn incoming-voice modem
 isdn disconnect-cause 1
!
interface FastEthernet0
 ip address xxx.xxx.xxx.xxx 255.255.255.128
 duplex auto
 speed auto
!
voice-port 0:D
!
dial-peer voice 1 pots
 application sandf
 incoming called-number XXX....
 direct-inward-dial
!
dial-peer voice 2 pots
 application sandf
 incoming called-number XXX....
 direct-inward-dial
!
dial-peer voice 3 pots
 application sandf
 incoming called-number XXXX.......
 direct-inward-dial
!
dial-peer voice 68 mmoip
 application fax_on_vfc_onramp_app out-bound
 destination-pattern xxxxxxx
 information-type fax
```

continues

Example 8-4 *Complete On-Ramp/Off-Ramp Gateway Configuration (Continued)*

```
  session target mailto:user1@cisco.com
  mdn
  dsn delayed
  dsn success
  dsn failure
 !
 dial-peer voice 69 mmoip
  application fax_on_vfc_onramp_app out-bound
  destination-pattern xxxxxxx
  information-type fax
  session target mailto:user2@cisco.com
  mdn
  dsn delayed
  dsn success
  dsn failure
 !
 dial-peer voice 1477 pots
  application roll
  incoming called-number xxxxxxx
  direct-inward-dial
 !
 dial-peer voice 77 voip
  preference 1
  application roll
  destination-pattern xxxxxxx
  session target ipv4:xxx.xx.xxx.xx
  fax rate 14400
 !
 dial-peer voice 771 mmoip
  preference 2
  application fax_on_vfc_onramp_app out-bound
  destination-pattern xxxxxxx
  information-type fax
  session target mailto:user3@cisco.com
 !
 dial-peer voice 79 mmoip
  application fax_on_vfc_onramp_app out-bound
  destination-pattern xxxxxxx
  information-type fax
  session target mailto:jamesbond@earlgrey.cisco.com
  mdn
  dsn success
 !
 dial-peer voice 853 mmoip
  application off
  incoming called-number 8......
  information-type fax
 !
 dial-peer voice 1853 pots
  destination-pattern 8......
  port 0:D
  prefix 8
```

Example 8-4   *Complete On-Ramp/Off-Ramp Gateway Configuration (Continued)*

```
 !
 dial-peer voice 831 mmoip
  application off
  incoming called-number 1831.......
  information-type fax
 !
 dial-peer voice 1831 pots
  destination-pattern 1831.......
  port 0:D
  prefix 1831
 !
 line con 0
  exec-timeout 0 0
  transport input none
 line aux 0
 line vty 0 4
 !
 ntp clock-period 17179630
 ntp server xxx.xx.xx.xxx
 end
 !
```

Sending an Off-Ramp Fax

A debug function is built into Cisco IOS software so you can determine whether or not off-ramp faxing is working. The application sends an off-ramp fax from the off-ramp gateway to the number that's entered on the command line. The following is an example:

```
mmoip-b# debug mmoip send fax 8531827
  mmoip_send_test_fax: phone num=8531827
 Test succeed!
```

The test command sends a one-page fax with the following short message to the number specified: "This is a test fax sent by Cisco Powered Libretto Faxmail." If the test fax doesn't succeed, use the **debug foip offramp** privileged EXEC command to try to determine the cause of the problem.

We mentioned earlier that an off-ramp fax can be sent by using an e-mail client such as Netscape or Eudora. Because the off-ramp gateway contains a compliant SMTP engine, off-ramp faxes can also be sent by a direct Telnet connection to the SMTP port (Port 25) of the off-ramp gateway. This method is employed by many bulk fax service providers.

A typical off-ramp fax session using Telnet consists of the following steps:

Step 1   Telnet to Port 25 of the off-ramp gateway.

Step 2   Signal the connection.

Step 3   Send the sender's address.

Step 4   Send the recipient's address.

Step 5   Enable Xacct (optional).

Step 6   Send cover-page data and attachments (optional).

Step 7   Send test data.

Step 8   Disconnect.

From a machine enabled with a Telnet client, start a Telnet session to Port 25 of the off-ramp gateway. Commands entered at the Telnet client are in boldface type; responses from the off-ramp gateway are in regular type.

```
orange% telnet 172.19.49.20 25
Trying 172.19.49.20...
Connected to 172.19.49.20.
Escape character is '^]'.
220 mmoip-b.cisco.com Cisco NetWorks ESMTP server
ehlo world
250-mmoip-b.cisco.com, hello world [172.19.49.14] (really )
250-ENHANCEDSTATUSCODES
250-8BITMIME
250-PIPELINING
250-HELP
250-DSN
250 XACCOUNTING
mail from:sender@cisco.com
250 2.5.0 Sender <sender@cisco.com> ok
rcpt to:fax=8531827@mmoip-b.cisco.com
250 2.1.5 Recipient <fax=8531827@mmoip-b.cisco.com> ok, maps to '8531827' (cp=yes)
data
354 Enter mail, end with a single "."
subject: Store and Forward fax mail
date: Dec 12, 2000
(empty line sent here)
Now is the time for all good men to come to the aid of their party.
.
250 2.5.0 Message delivered to remote fax machine
```

The fax process begins when you enter the **data** command, but text data isn't received until you enter a blank line. The data entered before the blank line is extra cover-page material such as the date and subject of the fax mail. This is also where you add attachments. After entering cover-page data and attachments, you must enter a blank line.

After entering the blank line, you can enter fax-page text data. Different third-party applications have different ways of generating text and attaching TIFF files. You can create a UNIX script, for example, that will automatically generate an off-ramp fax with an attachment through a Telnet connection.

After all of the text and attachments have been entered, signal the end of the transmission by entering a dot (.) on a line by itself. If the fax transmission is successful, the remote fax machine will send a successful transfer message to the off-ramp gateway, and the last line in the preceding example will be displayed on your Telnet client.

T.38 Real-Time Fax and Never-Busy Fax Service

The configuration of T.38 real-time fax on Cisco voice gateways is similar to the configuration of VoIP calls. Telephony dial peers are POTS dial peers; network dial peers are VoIP dial peers. In the following T.38 dial-peer configuration example, dial peers 1 and 2 are on the originating gateway; dial peer 3 is on the terminating gateway:

```
dial-peer 1 pots
 incoming called-number 555. . .
 direct-inward-dial
 dial-peer voice 2 voip
 destination-pattern 5551212
 session target ipv4:172.19.26.49

dial-peer voice 3 pots
 destination-pattern.
 port 0:D
```

This configuration assumes that the fax machine is plugged directly into the gateway or that a redialer is being used. Refer to "Configuration Guidelines for On-Ramp Store and Forward Fax" earlier in this chapter for more details. This section examines the *never-busy* functionality of T.38 fax.

In the preceding scenario described, if the far-end fax machine is busy or unreachable, the near-end fax machine tries to redial for a configurable number of times and then quits without success if the far-end gateway is down. With the addition of some dial peers and call application parameters, a T.38 fax can be configured to roll over to a T.37 fax session when the far end is busy or unreachable.

First, add the TCL IVR rollover application to the on-ramp gateway. Refer to "Configuring On-Ramp TCL IVR and Call Application Parameters" for details on TCL IVR scripts. The script in the 2.0 TCL IVR bundle is named *fax_rollover_on_busy.2.0.0.tcl*, and is added to the originating gateway with the following command:

```
mmoip-b(config)# $call application voice roll
    tftp://sleepy/ifax/fax_rollover_on_busy.tcl
Loading ifax/fax_rollover_on_busy.tcl from 172.19.49.14 (via FastEthernet0): !
[OK - 4803/9216 bytes]
Read script succeeded. size=4803,
url=tftp://sleepy/ifax/fax_rollover_on_busy.tcl
```

Notice that the rollover application is given the name *roll* in the previous **call application voice** global configuration command. After installing the script in the originating gateway, add the application to the POTS dial peer that will answer T.38 calls and run the rollover application.

```
dial-peer voice 1 pots
 application roll
 incoming called-number 325....
 direct-inward-dial
```

The preceding POTS dial peer will answer all calls to seven-digit numbers starting with 325. The rollover application will be launched, and because the **direct-inward-dial** dial-peer configuration command is configured, it will pass the call to a VoIP dial peer that matches the DNIS. The TCL IVR application has a procedure for setting up the call, waiting for success, and, upon receiving a busy or gateway-down message, setting up the same call again with new destination parameters. When the call is returned to the originating gateway, the gateway searches for a new VoIP dial peer with the same destination number and a preference equal to or greater than the first dial peer that it found. If it finds one, it sets up the call again. The VoIP dial peers in question follow. The first is the T.38 dial peer and the second is the T.37 dial peer:

```
dial-peer voice 78 voip
 preference 1
 destination-pattern 5551478
 session target ipv4:172.19.49.12
 fax rate 14400
 fax protocol t38 ls-redundancy 0 hs-redundancy 0
!
dial-peer voice 781 mmoip
 preference 2
 application fax_on_vfc_onramp_app out-bound
 destination-pattern 5551478
 information-type fax
 session target mailto:$d$@cisco.com
```

Because the dial peers are configured with the same destination pattern and different preferences, the gateway will try the destination with the lowest preference number (meaning the highest preference) first, and then, if required, try the next preferential choice, and so on. Should several dial peers be configured with the same preference, the gateway will choose the first one present in the configuration.

If a T.38 call is initiated to the number 5551478, the first choice will be to send the fax according to the details in dial-peer 78. If the destination number is busy or the gateway at 172.19.49.12 is down, the call will be retried with the details contained in dial peer 781, namely a T.37 fax to d@cisco.com. This model results in the fax being delivered, regardless of the fact that the far-end fax machine is busy.

NOTE   If the destination fax machine is an extension on a PBX, this feature might not function correctly. Typically, the PBX answers the call request and then makes the connection to the end device. The proper behavior of the PBX would be to connect to the far end before sending a connection signal back to the near end. If, for various configuration reasons, the PBX sends a connect acknowledgment to the near-end fax machine before actually connecting to the far-end fax machine, the rollover function will never take place, even if the far end is busy. Because the originating fax machine receives a connect acknowledgment followed by a setup failure, it just tries to redial the same number again. It will retry for the configured number of times, and then ultimately fail.

Assuming no PBX, or a properly configured PBX, the preceding scenario will provide a *never-busy* model for faxing.

Security Considerations

Security for connections is supported in Cisco gateways through the use of the AAA protocol. Security on the off-ramp gateway can be further enhanced by using Cisco IOS access lists.

AAA On-Ramp Authentication

AAA is utilized on the on-ramp gateway to perform authentication and accounting. Authentication is employed to restrict access, and is performed in conjunction with a RADIUS or TACACS+ server. Access can be restricted through authentication of one of the following attributes:

- Gateway ID
- DNIS
- ANI
- Redialer ID
- Redialer DNIS
- Prompt of the user

An authentication method is chosen with the following command:

```
call application voice tag authen-method method
```

To authenticate an on-ramp fax using one of the preceding methods, there must be an authentication server configured with the chosen authentication parameters.

AAA authentication for on-ramp gateways uses the **fax** method list. This method list authenticates the incoming call according to the authentication method configured in the call application parameters. All AAA configuration begins with the **aaa new-model** global configuration command. The AAA command lines for authentication are shown here:

```
aaa new-model
aaa authentication login fax group radius local
aaa authorization exec fax group radius
```

The RADIUS protocol does authentication (who) and authorization (what) together. Without the authorization command, authentication will fail. After entering the **AAA** global configuration commands, you can enter the **radius-server** global configuration commands. Trying to enter **radius-server** global configuration commands before enabling AAA with the **aaa new-model** global configuration command will result in the "Unrecognized Command" error message.

The following RADIUS commands are required for authentication:

```
radius-server host {hostname | ip-address} auth-port 1645 acct-port 1646
radius-server key test
```

The **auth-port 1645** and **acct-port 1646** values shown in the preceding **radius-server host** global configuration command are the default port assignments from the fax gateway. Other ports can be configured if the RADIUS server in the network requires it. If no port assignments are specified, the default ports will be assigned automatically.

The **radius-server key** global configuration command denotes the password that is exchanged with the RADIUS server through the use of the Challenge Handshake Authentication Protocol (CHAP).

Other RADIUS commands can be entered at this point, but they aren't necessary to successful authentication. Other RADIUS commands control the behavior of the RADIUS client in the gateway by controlling parameters such as timeout, retry count, and retry interval. Consult the Cisco security documentation for a complete list.

In addition to enabling authentication and specifying the authentication method and the authentication list, you must also configure **call application voice** global configuration commands for the authentication portion of AAA. The nature of the TCL IVR script also requires at least one language selection, and its corresponding URL must point to the location of the audio files. Following is an example showing the commands you must use:

```
call application voice onramp authentication enable
call application voice onramp authen-list fax
call application voice onramp authen-method dnis
call application voice onramp password foip
call application voice onramp language 1 en
call application voice onramp set location en 0 tftp://sleepy/prompts/en/
```

The preceding configured variables are retrieved by the TCL IVR on-ramp application. To observe the actions of the TCL IVR script, use the **debug voip ivr** privileged EXEC command.

Problems with authentication can occur in many different forms. For example, you might need to use the *h323* method-list instead of the *fax* method-list for authentication to work properly. This *h323* method list is configured with the following command:

```
aaa authentication login h323 group radius
```

Other problems with on-ramp authentication can be uncovered with the following debug commands:

```
debug mmoip aaa
debug aaa authentication
debug aaa authorization
```

In summary, on-ramp authentication is accomplished by creating a username/password in the RADIUS server that conforms to the method chosen for authentication. This method doesn't make sense for off-ramp faxing because the connection is coming from an MTA rather than from dual-tone multifrequency (DTMF) or redialer information from the PSTN side.

AAA Off-Ramp Authentication

Off-ramp authentication is the process of allowing or denying other MTAs to connect to the gateway MTA. This can be easily accomplished with access control lists (ACLs). An ACL is configured on the off-ramp gateway that allows only specified MTAs (identified by their IP addresses) to connect to the gateway and deliver an SMTP message to be sent out as a T.37 fax.

A simple ACL configuration follows. For more detailed information about ACLs, refer to the *Cisco IOS Security Configuration Guide*.

First, configure the list and specify the allowed hosts as shown here:

```
access-list 1 permit <ip address of allowed host> 0.0.0.0
```

There is an implicit *deny all* at the end of every access list. The result of the preceding list would be to allow only one host to connect to the gateway. The following command would permit any host in the range of 172.19.49.1 to 172.19.49.126:

```
access-list 2 permit 172.19.49.0 0.0.0.127
```

To activate an access list, you must apply it to an interface as shown here:

```
gateway (config)# interface FastEthernet 0
gateway (config-if)# ip access-group 1 in
```

You can apply the access list to incoming or outgoing connections. The connection from the MTA is incoming, and therefore is applied with the keyword **in**.

NOTE Activating AAA in gateways outlined in this chapter and conforming to T.37 fax on VFCs is a different model from previous configurations of T.37 on Cisco gateways. AAA is now under the control of the TCL IVR scripts. Commands such as:

```
mmoip aaa receive-id primary
mmoip aaa global-password
mmoip aaa send-accounting enable
```

are no longer used or recognized by the T.37 gateway.

NOTE Be aware that when you configure access lists, you can inadvertently restrict all connectivity to your gateway, or break connectivity that you want to keep. Advanced access lists can be very specific to accomplish the level of security that you seek.

Billing and Accounting

Fax over IP (I-fax) accounting records can be obtained through the use of RADIUS, TACACS+, SNMP, and SMTP. The supported SNMP Management Information Bases (MIBs) involved in store and forward fax are as follows:

- MMoIP DIAL-CONTROL-MIB
- MODEM-MANAGEMENT-MIB
- CISCO-ANALOG-VOICE-IF-MIB
- CISCO-VOICE-DIAL-CONTROL-MIB
- CISCO-VOICE-IF-MIB

This section covers RADIUS and SMTP accounting. SNMP accounting is not covered. Implementation of TACACS+ is similar to RADIUS and is also not covered.

RADIUS Accounting and Billing

RADIUS records sent to the RADIUS server include both standard RADIUS attributes and Cisco vendor-specific attributes (VSAs). The RADIUS server must be able to understand VSAs as described in RFC 2138 (Attribute 26). For a description of standard RADIUS attributes, refer to the following documents:

- RFC 2138, *Remote Authentication Dial-in User Service (RADIUS)*
- RFC 2139, *RADIUS Accounting*
- *Configuration Guide for AAA Billing Features in Cisco Voice-Enabled Routers and Access Servers* at http://www.cisco.com/warp/public/cc/so/cuso/sp/sms/acct/caaaf_cg.htm
- *VSA Implementation Guide* at http://www.cisco.com/univercd/cc/td/doc/product/access/acs_serv/vapp_dev/vsaig3.htm

VSA call detail record (CDR) variables used in store and forward fax billing and accounting are listed in Table 8-4.

Table 8-4   *Cisco VSAs*

VSA Attribute Number	VSA Name	Description
VSA 3	cisco_fax_account_id_origin	Indicates the account ID origin as defined by the system administrator for the **mmoip aaa receive-id** or **mmoip aaa send-id** global configuration commands.
VSA 4	cisco_fax_msg_id	Indicates a unique fax message identification number assigned by store and forward fax.

Table 8-4   *Cisco VSAs (Continued)*

VSA Attribute Number	VSA Name	Description
VSA 5	cisco_fax_pages	Indicates the number of pages transmitted or received during this fax session; this page count includes cover pages.
VSA 6	cisco_fax_cover_page	Boolean (true or false) describing whether or not the fax includes a cover page (off-ramp gateway-specific).
VSA 7	cisco_fax_modem_time	Delivers two values in seconds; the first describes the modem transmission time, the second describes the total fax session time.
VSA 8	cisco_fax_connect_speed	Modem transmission speed in bps; possible values are 1200, 4800, 9600, and 14,400.
VSA 9	cisco_fax_recipient_count	Indicates the number of recipients for this fax transmission; until e-mail servers support session mode, the number should be 1.
VSA 10	cisco_fax_process_about_flag	Indicates that the fax session was either aborted or successful; true means that the session was aborted; false means that the session was successful.
VSA 11	cisco_fax_dsn_address	Indicates the address to which DSNs will be sent.
VSA 12	cisco_fax_dsn_flag	Indicates whether DSN has been enabled; true indicates that DSN has been enabled; false means that DSN has not been enabled.
VSA 13	cisco_fax_mdn_address	Indicates the address to which MDNs will be sent.
VSA 14	cisco_fax_mdn_flag	Indicates whether MDN has been enabled; true indicates that MDN was enabled; false means that MDN was not enabled.
VSA 15	cisco_fax_auth_status	Indicates whether authentication for this fax session was successful; possible values for this field are success, failed, bypassed, or unknown.
VSA 16	cisco_email_server_address	Indicates the IP address of the e-mail server handling the on-ramp fax-mail message.
VSA 17	cisco_email_server_ack_flag	Indicates that the on-ramp gateway has received a positive acknowledgment from the e-mail server accepting the fax-mail message.

continues

Table 8-4   *Cisco VSAs (Continued)*

VSA Attribute Number	VSA Name	Description
VSA 18	cisco_gateway_id	Indicates the name of the gateway that processed the fax session; the name appears in the following format: hostname.domain name.
VSA 19	cisco_call_type	Describes the type of fax activity: fax receive or fax send.
VSA 20	cisco_port_used	Indicates the slot/port number of the Cisco AS5300 used to either transmit or receive this fax mail.
VSA 21	cisco_abort_cause	If the fax session aborts, indicates the system component that signaled the abort. Examples of system components that could trigger an abort are FAP (fax application process), TIFF (the TIFF reader or the TIFF writer), fax-mail client, fax-mail server, Extended Simple Mail Transfer Protocol (ESMTP) client, or ESMTP server.

Mmoip Accounting

Store and forward fax was designed to use the fax accounting method-list. This adds the ability to receive accounting records through the *mmoip-aaa* facility. These CDRs can be viewed in the off-ramp or on-ramp gateway through the use of the **debug mmoip aaa** privileged EXEC command. Example 8-5 shows a configuration snippet from the offramp gateway and an accounting session from an off-ramp fax, with this debug turned on.

Example 8-5   *The Off-Ramp Gateway and an Accounting Session from an Off-Ramp Fax*

```
aaa new-model
aaa authentication login default local
aaa authentication login fax group radius
aaa authentication login h323 group radius
aaa authorization exec fax group radius
aaa accounting connection fax stop-only group radius
enable secret 5 $1$4L6w$W0SoUHw2YgkK4IPJ7VtHc1
fl---------configuration items deleted ---------------‡
call application voice off tftp://sleepy/ifax/t37_offramp6.2.0.0.tcl
call application voice off accounting enable
call application voice off accounting-list fax
call application voice off authentication enable
call application voice off password foip
call application voice off authen-list fax_call application voice off authen-method
   gateway
call application voice off language 1 en
```

Example 8-5 *The Off-Ramp Gateway and an Accounting Session from an Off-Ramp Fax (Continued)*

```
call application voice off set-location en 0 tftp://sleepy/prompts/en/

1w0d: %ISDN-6-DISCONNECT: Interface Serial0:22 disconnected from 5551827 , call
  lasted 121 seconds
1w0d: mmoip_aaa_offramp: Called-Station-Id = fax=5551827@[172.19.49.20]
1w0d: mmoip_aaa_offramp: authenID = sleepytime.cisco.com
1w0d: mmoip_aaa_offramp: fax_account_id_origin = GATEWAY_ID
1w0d: mmoip_aaa_offramp: fax_msg_id =
1w0d: mmoip_aaa_offramp: fax_pages = 5
1w0d: mmoip_aaa_offramp: fax_modem_time = 121/123
1w0d: mmoip_aaa_offramp: fax_connect_speed = 9600
1w0d: mmoip_aaa_offramp: fax_auth_status = USER AUTHENTICATED
1w0d: mmoip_aaa_offramp: email_server_ack_flag = TRUE
1w0d: mmoip_aaa_offramp: gateway_id = sleepytime.cisco.com
1w0d: mmoip_aaa_offramp: call_type = Fax Send
1w0d: mmoip_aaa_offramp: port_used = 0:D (60)
1w0d: mmoip_aaa_offramp: abort_cause = 10
1w0d: mmoip_aaa_offramp: Called-Station-Id = fax=5551827@[172.19.49.20]
1w0d: mmoip_aaa_offramp: authenID = sleepytime.cisco.com
1w0d: mmoip_aaa_offramp: fax_account_id_origin = GATEWAY_ID
1w0d: mmoip_aaa_offramp: fax_msg_id =
1w0d: mmoip_aaa_offramp: fax_connect_speed = 9600
1w0d: mmoip_aaa_offramp: fax_auth_status = USER AUTHENTICATED
1w0d: mmoip_aaa_offramp: email_server_ack_flag = TRUE
1w0d: mmoip_aaa_offramp: gateway_id = sleepytime.cisco.com
1w0d: mmoip_aaa_offramp: call_type = Fax Send
1w0d: mmoip_aaa_offramp: abort_cause = 10
```

The debug call details come only at the call's termination because *stop-only* accounting is enabled. They cover some of the same variables as the radius debugs but are more fax-centric. The variable *fax_modem_time* records the time spent sending fax information and the total time of the connection. In this example, the connection was up for 123 seconds and fax page information was sent for 121 seconds.

SMTP Accounting

The Cisco AS5300 off-ramp gateway can send account records by SMTP. This functionality is activated by using an intelligent fax client. To send a fax transmission, the fax client initiates a Telnet session to the SMTP port (Port 25) of the off-ramp gateway and executes a series of commands. In a typical operation, the client executes the following commands:

```
telnet 10.14.120.2 25
ehlo anyserver.com
mail from: <>
rcpt to: <FAX=555-0839@cisco.com>
xact        (<<< this command verb enables the output of esmtp accounting data)
data
header info     (info supplied after the data command comprises header details)
```

```
Testing 1 2 3    (after a carriage return/line feed the text body of the
Testing 1 2 3     transmission is entered)
Testing 1 2 3
Testing 1 2 3
Testing 1 2 3
Testing 1 2 3
Testing 1 2 3
     .                 (<<< a period on a line by itself signals the end of transmission)
```

Example 8-6 shows an actual session in which the accounting application was activated manually. The commands required to activate the application are in boldface; the output from the off-ramp gateway is in italics.

NOTE   If you have an access list configured that filters connections to the SMTP port, you will have to Telnet to the SMTP port of the off-ramp gateway from a machine that is permitted in the access list.

Example 8-6   *Session in which the Accounting Application Was Activated Manually*

```
earlgrey.cisco.com% telnet monarda 25
Trying 172.19.42.57...
Connected to monarda.cisco.com.
Escape character is '^]'.
220 earlgrey.cisco.com Cisco NetWorks ESMTP server
ehlo monarda
250-earlgrey.cisco.com, hello monarda [172.19.42.60] (really )
250-ENHANCEDSTATUSCODES
250-8BITMIME
250-PIPELINING
250-HELP
250-DSN
250-XSESSION
250 XACCOUNTING
mail from:<thuff@cisco.com>
250 2.5.0 Sender <thuff@cisco.com> ok
rcpt to:<fax=5551111@earlgrey.cisco.com>
250 2.1.5 Recipient <fax=5551111@earlgrey.cisco.com> ok, maps to '5551111' (cp=yes)
xact
250 2.5.0 XACCOUNTING enabled
data
354 Enter mail, end with a single "."
Subject:Faxmail accounting enabled  (Message details will go here, and then a
Date:March 2, 2001      carriage return/line feed before the text of the message)
This is the time for all good men to come to the aid of their party.
     .                  (A period on a line by itself signals the end of a message.)
250-2.5.0 Message delivered to remote fax machine
250-2.5.0 fax_modem_time = 51/60    (These numbers are actual fax transmission
                                             time/total connection time.)
250-2.5.0 fax_pages = 2
250-2.5.0 gateway_id = monarda.cisco.com
250-2.5.0 fax_connect_speed = 14400bps
250-2.5.0 transmit_bytes = 22585
```

Example 8-6 *Session in which the Accounting Application Was Activated Manually (Continued)*

```
250-2.5.0 port_used = slot:1 port:5
250-2.5.0 call_type = Fax Send
250-2.5.0 abort_cause = 0
250-2.5.0 T30_error_code = 0
250-2.5.0 ISDN_disconnect_code = 16
250 2.5.0 CSID =5551111
quit
221 2.3.0 Goodbye from earlgrey.cisco.com; closing connection
Connection closed by foreign host.
earlgrey.cisco.com%
```

Figure 8-7 depicts the fax that was received from the preceding transmission.

Figure 8-7 *Received fax.*

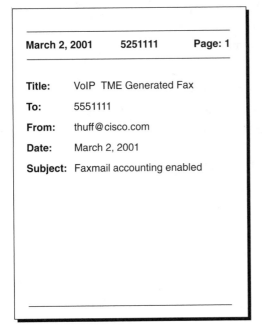

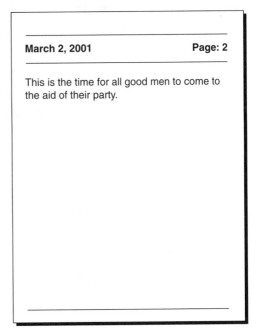

Note that all the accounting fields are preceded by a number string. In the preceding example, the string is *250-2.5.0.*

The SMTP server replies to the terminating period (.) following standard SMTP rules, which require that each line of the reply string start with a three-digit number, and that continuation lines have a hyphen (-) in the fourth position. Because the Cisco AS5300 SMTP server also implements enhanced SMTP error codes (RFC2034), each line will also contain a one-to-three-digit number, a period, a one-to-three-digit number, a period, a one-to-three-digit number, and a space. The following accounting information is sent after the

SMTP response code and the SMTP enhanced error code. Accounting information is always sent one per line.

Some typical responses sent by the SMTP server application after the terminating period (.) follow. Note that *250* represents success, *450* is a transient error, (meaning that the e-mail client should/will retry); *554* means permanent error.

```
250-2.5.0 Message delivered to remote fax machine
450 4.3.2 Could not reserve a modem
450-4.4.2 A fax protocol delivery error occurred.
554-5.1.1 Destination is not a receive FAX
```

Following are definitions of the accounting fields:

- **fax_modem_time**—Indicates the amount of time in seconds the modem sent fax data (x) and the amount of time in seconds of the total fax session (y), including both fax mail and PSTN time, in the form x/y. In the previous example, 51/60 means that the transfer time took 51 seconds and the total fax session took 60 seconds.

- **fax_pages**—number of pages, including cover.

- **gateway_id**—hostname.domain, name of the gateway.

- **fax_connect_speed**—connection speed in bps.

- **transmit_bytes**—amount of data transmitted, in bytes.

- **port_used**—slot refers to carrier card shelf; port refers to modem on the card.

- **call_type**—can be fax send or fax receive. For an off-ramp gateway, it's always fax send.

- **abort_cause**—defines the internal gateway component that signaled an abort condition, if any.

The following are valid abort codes:

```
NO_ABORT 0
FAP_ABORT, (Fax application process) 1
ESMTP_ABORT 2
TIFF_ABORT 3
T2F_ABORT, (Text to Fax process) 4
AUTHENTICATION_ABORT 5
```

The following are valid T30_error_code—standard Rockwell error codes:

```
/* Rockwell Class2 Hangup Status Codes */
/* Call Placement */
NORMAL_CONNECTION 0
RING_DETECT_NOCONNECT 1
USER_ABORT 2
NO_LOOP_CURRENT 3
/* Start proprietary codes */
AT_TIMEOUT 4
AT_ERROR 5
AT_NO_DIALTONE 6
AT_BUSY 7
AT_NO_CARRIER 8
/* End proprietary codes */
/* Transmit Phase A & Miscellaneous Errors */
```

```
PHASE_A_ERROR 10
NO_ANSWER_T30_TIMEOUT 11
/* Transmit Phase B Hangup Codes */
TRANSMIT_PHASE_B_ERROR 20
REMOTE_CANNOT_RECEIVE_SEND 21
COMREC_ERR_TRANSMIT_PHASE_B 22
COMREC_INVALID_COMMAND 23
RSPEC_ERROR_B 24
DCS_NO_RESPONSE 25
DIS_DTC_RECEIVED_3_TIMES 26
FTT_2400 27
RSPREC_INVALID_RESPONSE_B 28
/* Transmit Phase C Hangup Codes */
TRANSMIT_PHASE_C_ERROR 40
DTE_DCE_UNDERFLOW 43
/* Transmit Phase D Hangup Codes */
TRANSMIT_PHASE_D_ERROR 50
RSPREC_ERROR_D 51
NO_RESPONSE_MPS 52
INVALID_RESPONSE_MPS 53
NO_RESPONSE_EOP 54
INVALID_RESPONSE_EOP 55
NO_RESPONSE_EOM 56
INVALID_RESPONSE_EOM 57
UNABLE_CONTINUE 58
/* Receive Phase B Hangup Codes */
RECEIVE_PHASE_B_ERROR 70
RXSPREC_ERROR 71
COMREC_ERROR_RXB 72
T30_T2_TIMEOUT_PAGE 73
T30_T1_TIMEOUT_EOM 74
/* Receive Phase C Hangup Codes */
RECEIVE_PHASE_C_ERROR 90
MISSING_EOL 91
UNUSED_CODE 92
DCE_TO_DTE_OVERFLOW 93
/* Receive Phase D Hangup Codes */
RECEIVE_PHASE_D_ERROR 100
RSPREC_INVALID_RESPONSE_RECEIVED_D 101
COMREC_INVALID_RESPONSE_RECEIVED_102
UNABLE_TO_CONTINUE_AFTER_PIN_PIP 103
```

The following are valid ISDN_disconnect_code values:

```
CC_CAUSE_UNINITIALIZED = 0, /* un-initialized (0) */
CC_CAUSE_UANUM = 1, /* unassigned num */
CC_CAUSE_NO_ROUTE_TO_TRANSIT_NETWORK = 2,
CC_CAUSE_NO_ROUTE = 3, /* no rt to dest */
CC_CAUSE_SEND_INFO_TONE = 4,
CC_CAUSE_MISDIALLED_TRUNK_PREFIX = 5,
CC_CAUSE_CHANNEL_UNACCEPTABLE = 6,
CC_CAUSE_CALL_AWARDED = 7,
CC_CAUSE_PREEMPTION = 8,
CC_CAUSE_PREEMPTION_RESERVED = 9,
CC_CAUSE_NORM = 16,
CC_CAUSE_BUS = 17, /* user busy */
CC_CAUSE_NORS = 18, /* no user response*/
CC_CAUSE_NOAN = 19, /* no user answer. */
CC_CAUSE_SUBSCRIBER_ABSENT = 20,
CC_CAUSE_REJECT = 21, /* call rejected. */
CC_CAUSE_NUMBER_CHANGED = 22,
CC_CAUSE_NON_SELECTED_USER_CLEARING = 26,
CC_CAUSE_DESTINATION_OUT_OF_ORDER = 27,
CC_CAUSE_INVALID_NUMBER = 28,
```

```
CC_CAUSE_FACILITY_REJECTED = 29,
CC_CAUSE_RESPONSE_TO_STATUS_ENQUIRY = 30,
CC_CAUSE_UNSP = 31, /* unspecified. */
CC_CAUSE_NO_CIRCUIT = 34, /* no circuit. */
CC_CAUSE_REQUESTED_VPCI_VCI_NOT_AVAILABLE = 35
CC_CAUSE_VPCI_VCI_ASSIGNMENT_FAILURE = 36,
CC_CAUSE_CELL_RATE_NOT_AVAILABLE = 37,
CC_CAUSE_NETWORK_OUT_OF_ORDER = 38,
CC_CAUSE_PERM_FRAME_MODE_OUT_OF_SERVICE = 39,
CC_CAUSE_PERM_FRAME_MODE_OPERATIONAL = 40,
CC_CAUSE_TEMPORARY_FAILURE = 41,
CC_CAUSE_SWITCH_CONGESTION = 42,
CC_CAUSE_ACCESS_INFO_DISCARDED = 43,
CC_CAUSE_NO_REQ_CIRCUIT = 44,
CC_CAUSE_NO_VPCI_VCI_AVAILABLE = 45,
CC_CAUSE_PRECEDENCE_CALL_BLOCKED = 46,
CC_CAUSE_NO_RESOURCE = 47, /* no resource. */
CC_CAUSE_QOS_UNAVAILABLE = 49,
CC_CAUSE_FACILITY_NOT_SUBCRIBED = 50,
CC_CAUSE_CUG_OUTGOING_CALLS_BARRED = 53,
CC_CAUSE_CUG_INCOMING_CALLS_BARRED = 55,
CC_CAUSE_BEARER_CAPABILITY_NOT_AUTHORIZED = 57,
CC_CAUSE_BEARER_CAPABILITY_NOT_AVAILABLE = 58,
CC_CAUSE_INCONSISTENCY_IN_INFO_AND_CLASS = 62,
CC_CAUSE_NOSV = 63,
/* service or option * not available, * unspecified. */
CC_CAUSE_BEARER_CAPABILITY_NOT_IMPLEMENTED = 65,
CC_CAUSE_CHAN_TYPE_NOT_IMPLEMENTED = 66,
CC_CAUSE_FACILITY_NOT_IMPLEMENTED = 69,
CC_CAUSE_RESTRICTED_DIGITAL_INFO_BC_ONLY = 70,
CC_CAUSE_SERVICE_NOT_IMPLEMENTED = 79,
CC_CAUSE_INVALID_CALL_REF_VALUE = 81,
CC_CAUSE_CHANNEL_DOES_NOT_EXIST = 82,
CC_CAUSE_CALL_EXISTS_CALL_ID_IN_USE = 83,
CC_CAUSE_CALL_ID_IN_USE = 84,
CC_CAUSE_NO_CALL_SUSPENDED = 85,
CC_CAUSE_CALL_CLEARED = 86,
CC_CAUSE_USER_NOT_IN_CUG = 87,
CC_CAUSE_INCOMPATIBLE_DESTINATION = 88,
CC_CAUSE_NON_EXISTENT_CUG = 90,
CC_CAUSE_INVALID_TRANSIT_NETWORK = 91,
CC_CAUSE_AAL_PARMS_NOT_SUPPORTED = 93,
CC_CAUSE_INVALID_MESSAGE = 95,
CC_CAUSE_MANDATORY_IE_MISSING = 96,
CC_CAUSE_MESSAGE_TYPE_NOT_IMPLEMENTED = 97,
CC_CAUSE_MESSAGE_TYPE_NOT_COMPATIBLE = 98,
CC_CAUSE_IE_NOT_IMPLEMENTED = 99,
CC_CAUSE_INVALID_IE_CONTENTS = 100,
CC_CAUSE_MESSAGE_IN_INCOMP_CALL_STATE = 101,
CC_CAUSE_RECOVERY_ON_TIMER_EXPIRY = 102,
CC_CAUSE_NON_IMPLEMENTED_PARAM_PASSED_ON = 103,
CC_CAUSE_UNRECOGNIZED_PARAM_MSG_DISCARDED = 110,
CC_CAUSE_PROTOCOL_ERROR = 111,
CC_CAUSE_INTERWORKING = 127,
CC_CAUSE_NEXT_NODE_UNREACHABLE = 128,
CC_CAUSE_DTL_TRANSIT_NOT_MY_NODE_ID = 160,
CSID—called subscriber ID (the number or ID of the called fax machine)
```

Using SMTP accounting, vendors implementing proprietary intelligent fax applications can collect accounting and CDR information on fax transmissions without the deployment of a RADIUS server.

Summary

This chapter discussed traditional fax over circuit-switched networks and described how store and forward fax gateways can take calls from G3 fax machines, convert them into e-mail messages, and transport them over the Internet as e-mail attachments. At the terminating end of the call, another store and forward fax gateway receives the e-mail message, converts it back into a fax message, and delivers it to a G3 fax machine. We explained how the ITU developed the T.30 protocol and adopted the SMTP for fax called MIME as part of the T.37 standard for store and forward fax.

We also described the ITU T.38 recommendation for fax relay and real-time fax with spoofing. Using this standard, real-time fax gateway can deliver faxes to remote fax machines while the sending fax machines are still processing fax pages. With fax relay, the gateway receives an analog fax signal and demodulates it into its digital form using a fax modem. The digital, demodulated fax is then packetized and transmitted over the IP network. At the receiving end, the fax gateway remodulates the digital fax packets into T.30 analog fax signals to be transmitted to the destination fax machine through a gateway modem.

We described in detail how Cisco implements T.37 store and forward fax, and we gave configuration guidelines and examples for both on-ramp and off-ramp fax gateways. Finally, we described how Cisco implements T.38 real-time fax and fax rollover, or *never-busy* fax, and we gave configuration guidelines for those applications.

## CHAPTER 9

Unified Messaging

From audio e-mail for car or train commuters to mobile retrieval of faxes and e-mails from a wireless device, Unified Communications integrates the two separate worlds of phone and Internet over a single unified network. Unified Open Network Exchange (uOne) is an enhanced, IP-based software solution that gives subscribers the ability to receive voice mail, e-mail, and fax messages using a single mailbox that can be accessed by the phone or from a desktop browser or e-mail client.

Unlike TDM-based proprietary messaging solutions, the Cisco Unified Communications (UC) platform is built on Open Packet Telephony (OPT), Cisco's standards-based, open-protocol voice/data architecture. The standards-based services platform is designed to carrier-class specifications, providing scalability to support millions of subscribers. It combines synchronous and asynchronous message types, including Voice over IP, Internet fax, store and forward voice mail, and e-mail under a common message store and directory. This eliminates the need to synchronize disparate message stores and directories, such as different voice mail and e-mail systems, and dramatically reduces operational and maintenance costs. Competitive products that use old-world PSTN networks can't offer this level of integration or scalability.

This chapter discusses various unified messaging concepts and features that apply to Cisco's uOne unified messaging (UM) solution. This chapter also provides high-level examples showing how to deploy UM in different service provider and enterprise environments.

Market Scope

Cisco's UM solution delivers new revenue opportunities to a service provider company by consolidating voice, e-mail, and fax communications within an IP infrastructure, independent of location, time, or device. Standards-based OPT enables a service provider to offer new revenue-generating services over its existing communications framework, reducing implementation time and cost.

You can deploy services like fax, e-mail, and voice mail over IP using the Cisco AS5x00 dial infrastructure and best-of-breed applications from a variety of partner companies. Here are some of the cost-effective services you can offer to build brand identity and increase customer loyalty:

- Unified voice mail, fax, and e-mail
- Voice, fax, and e-mail retrieval by phone
- Integration of electronic documents with faxes
- Personal message agents
- Never-busy fax lines
- Broadcast fax
- Single number reach

Moving to a unified communications platform also enables you to combine traditional telephony products with Internet applications. Cisco's new architecture lets you move call-handling services from application platforms into your existing Cisco edge devices. This makes it easier to deploy new services and new territories more cost effectively.

You can begin deployment of UM solutions based on the core services you currently offer, and add new, revenue-producing services incrementally, without replacing your existing infrastructure down the line.

Unified Messaging Features

This section describes the features associated with Unified Messaging. They include:

- Voice over IP
- E-mail messaging over IP
- Fax messaging over IP
- Single number reach

Voice Messaging over IP

Voice messaging over IP allows service provider subscribers to check and access messages from any phone and perform the following tasks:

- Create multiple personalized greetings programmed to play at different times, including times when the line is busy, when there is no answer, and when calls are received after the close of business.

- Place a new call or respond to a message without leaving the messaging system (known as the "Return Call" feature). This allows subscribers to respond to the message, forward it to someone else, or place a new call and return to the messaging system to continue processing additional messages. All messages and calls can be handled with a single call.

- Leave messages for multiple recipients with a single call.

- Designate or prioritize messages so that they can retrieve messages based on priorities.

- Locate a subscriber mailbox by name or telephone number.

- Forward voice messages as e-mail attachments to any e-mail user, enabling users of different voice-mail systems to share voice mail messages.

- Receive message-waiting indication by pager, stutter dial tone, or indicator light on telephone.

E-Mail Messaging over IP

E-mail messaging over IP allows subscribers to access e-mail messages from a phone and do the following:

- Identify voice, e-mail, and fax messages in an e-mail inbox and save time by using one access device for all messages. Voice messages can be played as streaming audio or .wav files.

- Listen to e-mail messages from a telephone using the text-to-speech (TTS) feature.

- Respond to an e-mail message over the phone with an audio attachment.

- Receive paging notification on arrival of new e-mail messages.

E-mail messaging over IP supports both Point of Presence (POP) and Internet Messaging Access Protocol (IMAP) clients.

Fax Messaging over IP

Fax messaging over IP allows subscribers to receive faxes anywhere by redirecting fax messages from their UM mailbox to a nearby fax machine. Fax messaging over IP also enables subscribers to:

- Determine, by using their telephone, the number of pages, what faxes have arrived, the arrival time, and the sender's identification.

- View faxes as .tiff files from an e-mail client and save them in separate folders.

- Forward fax messages to other people as e-mail attachments.

- Receive immediate paging notification when new fax messages arrive.
- Have greater privacy by printing faxes from their mailboxes when they are ready to view them.

Single Number Reach

Single Number Reach improves accessibility by providing a single phone number that callers use to locate a subscriber in multiple locations. With Single Number Reach, callers can do the following:

- Use a single number to dial a subscriber work phone, home phone, or wireless phone.
- Choose to either try to locate the subscriber or leave a message. Callers are not trapped in the system waiting for the subscriber to be located.

With Single Number Reach, subscribers can do the following:

- Decide whether or not to accept an incoming call or transfer it to voice mail. Callers are prompted to speak their name if they attempt to locate the subscriber. Subscribers can then choose to accept the call or transfer it to voice mail, depending on who is calling.
- Define different reach numbers for different time periods, such as business hours, non-business hours, and holidays.
- Choose to be paged for incoming calls so that they know they've been called.

Components of a Unified Messaging System

uOne is built on a *distributed agent platform* (DAP)—an open systems distributed computing environment that permits easy integration of new, non-proprietary voice- and information-processing technologies. DAP is based on a client/server model and consists of several components that are networked to provide all the functions of a unified messaging system.

The architecture is a distributed, object-based framework providing native support for all major industry standards such as LDAP, IMAP4, SMTP/MIME, VPIM, HTTP/HTML, and support for centralized SNMP management and Web-based administration. Cisco's uOne applications reside on a gateserver that interfaces with the circuit-switched network through a Registration, Admission, and Status (RAS) gateway to any telephone, cellular phone, or fax machine. Gateserver applications then communicate over the IP network to directory services, media services, and management services. This allows uOne and other enhanced services applications to communicate with anyone, anywhere, using the IP network.

Figure 9-1 shows a complete unified messaging solution based on a three-tiered model, which includes access services, application services, and backend services.

Figure 9-1   *The unified messaging three-tier model.*

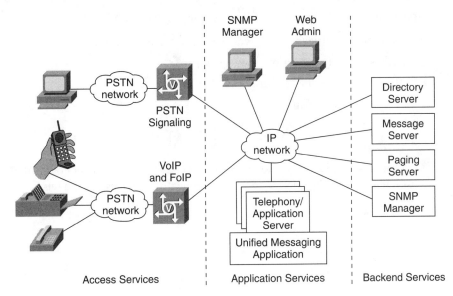

Access Services

Access services provide access to application services and the front-end user interface of the unified messaging system. Subscribers can access messaging services with traditional telephony equipment, like phones and fax machines, or via workstations connected to an IP network. Access services provide call recognition and routing, media translation, and telco signaling.

Access services include the following components:

- PSTN and its components
- H.323 components like gateways (Cisco AS5X00) and gatekeepers

A gateway is an H.323 component that facilitates translation among various transmission formats and communication procedures (signaling). It is responsible for call setup and teardown on both the network and PSTN sides.

A gatekeeper provides call control services to the H.323 endpoints. The main functions of a gatekeeper in an H.323 network are to:

- Provide address translation between phone numbers and transport addresses.
- Authorize network access (admission control) using H.225 messages.
- Provide bandwidth control and zone management.

Application Services

Application services provide all the messaging logic required for:

- Storing and retrieving messages (voice mail, e-mail, and fax)
- Translating among various message types
- User authentication
- Changing user profiles
- Message waiting indication
- SNMP services

Application services are the endpoints for all H.323 calls into and out of the unified messaging system. Figure 9-2 shows how application services are laid out.

Figure 9-2   *Application services.*

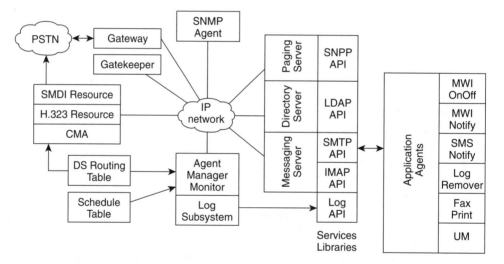

Application services consist of three major components:

- Agent Communication Broker (ACB)
- Call Control/Media Control Agent (CMA)
- SNMP agent

Agent Communications Broker

The ACB is a set of distributed software modules that provides communication services to other DAP agents. The ACB includes:

- **Agent manager and monitor (AMM)**—The AMM provides scheduling, routing, launching, monitoring, and terminating services for all other DAP agent instances.

- **Schedule tables**—The AMM uses the information in the schedule tables to decide how and when applications should be launched. Some applications are started as soon as the AMM starts; others are dynamically launched as needed, depending on a token that is passed to the AMM. Dynamic launches of agents and applications are usually triggered by external events such as an incoming call or a notification request.

- **Domain services routing table**—The AMM uses the information in the domain services routing table to bind agents together to access specific services. The domain services routing table is used when messages need to be routed to other objects or application instances. Internal object routines use a token and the information in the domain services routing table to determine where to route the message. The AMM also monitors and manages agent instances for abnormal termination and state transition changes.

- **A set of services libraries**—Services libraries provide APIs (application programming interface) for various software services supported by unified messaging. These APIs are used to develop application agents, such as the UM and fax print agents.

- **Local agent communications services (LACS)**—The LACS handle communications among all agents on a gateserver.

- **Logging subsystems**—A logging subsystem is also part of the ACB and provides centralized log-management services to DAP agents.

Call Control/Media Control Agent

The CMA supports call control, media control, and media resources. It uses H.323 call control signaling to accept, drop, and manage calls from an H.323 gateway or gatekeeper. It uses RAS to register with an H.323 gatekeeper, and it provides DTMF detection services. The CMA also provides media services such as playing, recording, and deleting messages.

The CMA and the ACB must reside on the same gateserver. The CMA uses dialed number identification service (DNIS) or redirected number (RDN) as the token to search the domain services routing table and determine which application will handle the request.

LDAP Directory Services

Lightweight directory access protocol (LDAP) is a directory service protocol that runs over TCP/IP. A directory is like a database but it usually contains more descriptive, attribute-based information. Directory information is generally read much more often than it is written. Consequently, directories don't usually use the same complicated transaction or roll-back schemes that regular databases do for high-volume, complex updates. Instead, directories are tuned to give quick response to high-volume lookup or search operations. They have the ability to replicate information widely and to increase availability and reliability while reducing response time. The basic function of a directory service is to allow you to store and retrieve information about your enterprise or subscribers. You can retrieve the information by either directly searching for that information, or by searching for related, more easily remembered information, such as a name.

The LDAP directory service model is based on entries. An *entry* is a collection of attributes that has a name, called a distinguished name (DN), which is a unique reference for the entry. In LDAP, directory entries are arranged in a hierarchical tree-like structure that reflects, for example, political, geographic, and/or organizational boundaries. LDAP defines operations for interrogating and updating entries in the directory—for adding and deleting entries from the directory, changing existing entries, and changing the names of entries. LDAP query requests permit a portion of the directory to be searched for entries that match certain criteria specified by a search filter. Information can be requested from each entry that matches the criteria.

LDAP is based on the client/server model and uses TCP as its transport protocol. One of the objectives of LDAP is to minimize the complexity of clients, to facilitate large-scale deployment and hence scalability. Each Directory Server instance is capable of supporting millions of entries and thousands of queries per second. By using replication and referrals, the Directory Server can be scaled to support even the largest of enterprises and subscriber bases, including multinational corporations and very large ISPs. Figure 9-3 shows a typical LDAP session call flow.

Figure 9-3 *LDAP session call flow.*

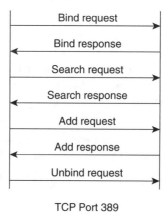

TCP Port 389

Unified messaging uses the directory server primarily to store and retrieve user profile information. You perform administrative tasks on the directory server by using vendor-supplied tools, like the Netscape console and admin server. UM subscribers interact with the directory server using Cisco's web-based tools such as Personal Mailbox Administration (PMA), which permits subscribers to administer their personal preferences. Unified Messaging System Administration (UMSA) is Cisco's web-based tool that you can use to create new classes of service, add subscribers, manage broadcast lists, and manage user mailboxes.

You can use communities of interest (COI) as a mechanism to split a large directory into smaller, more manageable directories, each of which has its own access control and well-defined search base that restricts the view of the directory. COI usually defines a subscriber group that subscribes to a customized set of services under a single administrative authority. Service providers can use the same set of shared resources to create multiple communities of interest. The COI is based on the directory tree structure on the directory server and is defined by a specific node in the tree. Users within a COI have restricted visibility to everything below their node in the hierarchical directory tree structure.

Referrals in LDAP are a redirection mechanism that is used by a directory service to scale the service beyond the millions of users that can be supported with a single server. When an LDAP client queries a directory service and the query does not match any of the directory suffixes it supports, the server can return a referral to the client, requesting it to direct the query to a different LDAP server. Upon receipt of the referral, the client reformats the original LDAP request to fit the boundaries set by the referral, and reissues the request to the new server. Referrals are not returned if the directory names do not match, or if the client attempts to modify an entry that does not exist.

LDAP version 3 supports smart referrals, which allow you to map your directory entries to specific LDAP URLs. Smart referrals permit a directory server to refer the query to another server that services the same name space, or to refer it to a different name space within the same server. With smart referrals, if a client attempts to modify a directory entry and is referred elsewhere, the client will reformat the modification request to fit the boundaries set by the referral, and reissue the request to the new server. If the client has sufficient privileges, the operation is performed without the user ever knowing that the activity occurred on a remote server.

Cisco's unified messaging server uses LDAP version 2 APIs. The server does not process any LDAP referrals because there is no easy way to permit directory entry modification across multiple directory servers with referrals in LDAP version 2. The current version of UM will not support a model with multiple LDAP servers, even though it is possible to handle directory changes by processing smart referrals. However, the UM application is fully compatible with both versions of LDAP in the single directory service model.

Messaging Server

Messaging server is a messaging service that provides open, standards-based, flexible, cross-platform e-mail and messaging solutions, scalable to many thousands of simultaneous users. Messaging server provides the UM application with a common message store and allows access to its message store by standard Internet protocols such as IMAP4, POP3, and HTTP. Messaging server is an LDAP client, and uses the directory server as the centralized store for mail-user account storage, authentication, and mail routing control. The messaging server also provides a facility for specialized HTTP service for Web-based e-mail. HTTP clients send mail to the specialized HTTP service, which then transfers the requests to a mail transfer agent.

Cisco's unified messaging application uses Simple Mail Transfer Protocol (SMTP) to store e-mail, voice mail, and fax mail messages on the common message store provided by the messaging server. The messages are stored in Multipurpose Internet Mail Extensions (MIME) format. UM subscribers use IMAP4, POP3, or HTTP to retrieve these messages from the message store.

Messaging servers use SMTP to accept and route messages. The following steps summarize how the messaging server accepts and routes a message:

Step 1   The messaging server queries the directory server (LDAP) to determine whether the recipient is local or remote.

Step 2   If the recipient is local, the messaging server delivers the message, typically placing it in the message store.

Step 3   If the recipient is remote, the messaging server:

   3.1   Queries the Domain Name System (DNS) to find the mail exchange (MX) servers for the remote domain.

   3.2   Queries DNS to find the IP address of the remote messaging server (resolves the server name [from Step 3.1] to an IP address).

   3.3   Establishes a TCP/IP connection to TCP port 25 of the remote messaging server.

   3.4   Optionally establishes a Secure Sockets Layer (SSL) connection to the remote messaging server.

   3.5   Sends the message to the remote messaging server (SMTP-Deliver).

To retrieve a message, the client must know the IP address of the messaging server, establish a connection to the server, then retrieve the message using one of the retrieval protocols: POP3, IMAP4, or HTTP. The following steps summarize how the client retrieves a message:

Step 1   Queries DNS to find the IP address of the server.

Step 2   Establishes a TCP/IP connection to the server.

Step 3   Optionally establishes an SSL connection to the server.

Step 4   Establishes a POP3, IMAP4, or HTTP connection to the server to retrieve the message.

uOne uses IMAP4 for storage and retrieval of messages from the messaging server. A typical IMAP session is summarized in Figure 9-4.

Figure 9-4   *IMAP session.*

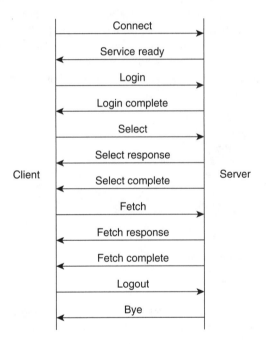

Typical uOne Call Flows

This section discusses the following typical uOne call flows:

- Subscriber does not answer call.
- Caller leaves a message for a subscriber.
- Subscriber is notified to retrieve messages.

- Subscriber calls the UM server to retrieve messages.
- Inbound fax message to a subscriber.
- Printing a fax message from a subscriber's mailbox to an alternate fax number.
- Overall uOne protocol flow sequence.

Subscriber Does Not Answer Call

When someone calls a subscriber and there is no answer, the call is forwarded to the gateserver. When the local exchange carrier (LEC) switch detects an incoming call that is destined for a busy or non-answering party, the switch formulates a Q.931 setup message with the redirected number (RDN) field set to the original destination number, and sends it to the gateway. The called-party number of the setup message is set to one of the DNIS access numbers of the gateway. The original called number is then the RDN, and the number that was called to access the server is the DNIS. Whenever the RDN field is populated, the UM application uses it to retrieve (using LDAP) the subscriber's profile from a directory server. If there is a matching subscriber, UM retrieves and plays the subscriber's personal greeting. Figure 9-5 shows an example of how this process works.

Figure 9-5 *Retrieve subscriber's personal greeting.*

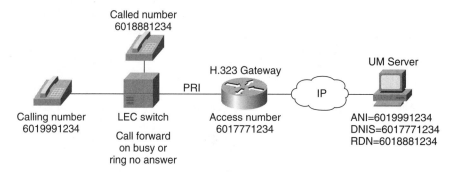

In this example, the presence of RDN indicates a call to the subscriber. The UM searches for the subscriber profile using 6018881234, retrieves it, and plays the personal greeting.

When a subscriber calls the UM server to access messages, automatic number identification (ANI) is set to the calling number, DNIS is set to the called number, and RDN is not populated. In this case, UM plays the general welcome message and requests the caller's phone number and PIN. A subscriber calling from his or her own phone can simply press the # key, in which case UM uses the ANI to retrieve the subscriber's profile, as shown in Figure 9-6.

Figure 9-6 *ANI profile retrieval.*

In this example, an unpopulated RDN field indicates a call from the subscriber to retrieve messages. The UM requests that the subscriber enter his or her phone number or simply press #. If the subscriber enters a phone number, it is used in a directory search (LDAP). If the subscriber enters #, 6016661234 is used to search the directory for his or her profile.

Caller Leaves a Message for a Subscriber

When someone calls a subscriber's phone number and does not get an answer, the subscriber's switch forwards the call to the Cisco AS5300 gateway. Figure 9-7 shows how the messaging server accepts and routes a message to the subscriber.

Figure 9-7 *User calls and leaves a message.*

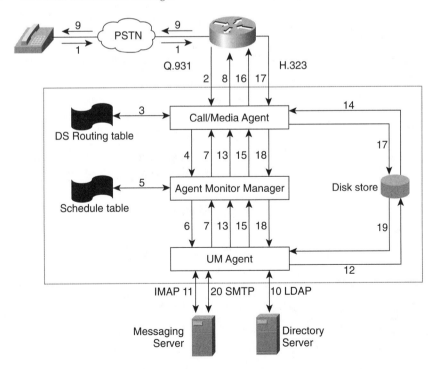

The following describes each step in the call flow diagram shown in Figure 9-7:

Step 1   A caller makes a call to the subscriber's phone number and does not get an answer. The call is forwarded across the PSTN to the gateway (Cisco AS5300). DNIS is the number that was called to reach the gateway, and RDNIS is set to the original called number.

Step 2   The gateway, based on its configuration (matching dial-peers), selects the session target IP address as the call recipient. It sends an H.225 setup message to the target IP address.

Step 3   The target IP address is that of the gateserver (CMA), which looks in its DS routing table to figure out which AMM to contact.

Step 4   The CMA then sends a **start app** command to the appropriate AMM.

Step 5   The targeted AMM looks in the "schedule table" to determine which application agent to activate. In this case, the application agent is UM.

Step 6   The AMM forks and executes a new UM process to handle this call. (An instance of the UM agent is executed for each incoming call.)

Step 7   The new UM agent sends a message to the CMA via the AMM to accept the call.

Step 8   The CMA sends an H.225 connect message to the gateway, requesting it to connect the call.

Step 9   The gateway sends a Q.931 connect message to the PSTN and connects the call to the gateserver (CMA).

Step 10 Using RDN, the UM agent gets the subscriber's profile from the directory server and determines which greetings are active and what their locations are—on which messaging server they reside.

Step 11 Subscriber greetings are stored as an audio file in an e-mail attachment in the greeting administrator's e-mail account. The UM retrieves the greeting from the messaging server using IMAP.

Step 12 The UM application detaches the greeting audio file and stores it on the file system.

Step 13 The UM application provides a pointer to the greeting's location on the file system and issues a command to the CMA (via the AMM) to play the greeting.

Step 14 The CMA loads the audio file from the file system and plays the greeting.

Step 15 The UM application sends a message to the CMA to record a message from the caller.

Step 16 The CMA plays the "beep" to start recording the caller's message.

Step 17 The caller leaves a message for the subscriber, which is stored by the CMA as an audio file on the file system.

Step 18 The CMA uses the AMM to send a "record complete" notification to the UM application.

Step 19 The UM application retrieves the message from the file system and, using the subscriber's e-mail address, composes an e-mail message and attaches the audio file to it. While composing the e-mail message, the UM application sets the content-type attribute to voice mail, as specified in the Voice Profile for Internet Mail version 2 (VPIM v2) specification.

Step 20 Using SMTP, the UM agent sends this e-mail to the subscriber's messaging server. The messaging server deposits the message in the subscriber's mailbox.

Subscriber Is Notified to Retrieve Messages

For a message-waiting indicator or stutter dial tone, the gateserver must have an RS-232 connection to a switch that has access to the telephone handset. For paging services, a Hylafax Simple Network Paging Protocol (SNPP) server must be installed and accessible to the gateserver. The flow diagram in Figure 9-8 shows the subscriber notification process.

The following describes each step in the subscriber notification process flow diagram, as shown in Figure 9-8:

Step 21 When the messaging server accepts a new message, it calls a configured message waiting indicator (MWI) plug-in. This plug-in must be installed as an additional messaging server component during installation.

Step 22 The MWI plug-in inserts a notification message in a local queue (FIFO).

Step 23 MWI_PassOff monitors the queue and receives the notification request.

Step 24 Using a TCP connection, MWI_PassOff forwards the notification request to the MWI_Notify process, which is resident on a notification access server. Typically, this is the UM server where the CMA and AMM components are running.

Step 25 MWI_Notify receives the request and uses AMM to forward it to the MWI_OnOff process.

Step 26 Using LDAP, MWI_OnOff retrieves the subscriber's profile from the directory server and determines the type of notification to use for that subscriber.

Step 27 If the subscriber's notification requires an MWI light or dial tone stutter, the MWI_OnOff process issues a command to the CMA, using the AMM for Simplified Message Desk Interface (SMDI) signaling.

Step 28 Using SMDI signaling, the CMA sends the appropriate notification message to the switch.

Step 29 The switch turns on the stutter tone (by sending an SMDI message to the central office switch) or MWI light on the handset as appropriate.

Step 30 If the subscriber has requested to be notified by a page, MWI_OnOff issues a command to the paging server using Simple Network Paging Protocol (SNPP). SNPP is an Internet standard (RFC 1861) for sending one-way or two-way wireless messages to pagers.

Step 31 The paging server notifies the paging provider to send a page using TAP/IXO.

Figure 9-8 *The subscriber notification process.*

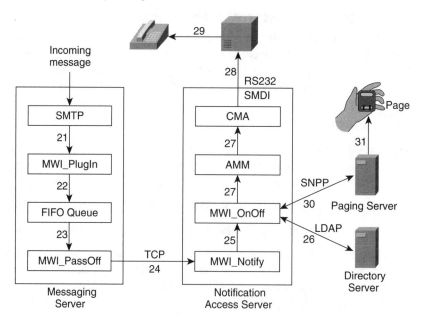

Subscriber Calls the UM Server to Retrieve Messages

After being notified by an MWI or a page, the subscriber can retrieve messages. Figure 9-9 shows how the subscriber retrieves messages.

Figure 9-9 *Subscriber calls to retrieve messages.*

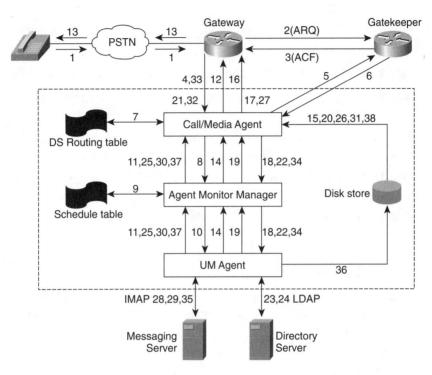

The following describes each step in the message retrieval flow diagram shown in Figure 9-9:

Step 1   The subscriber makes a call to access the UM server. DNIS is set to the called number, and ANI is set to the calling number (the number that the subscriber is calling from).

Step 2   The gateway has a matching dial peer for the called number with the session target set to RAS. It sends an admission request (ARQ) to the gatekeeper.

Step 3   The gatekeeper looks at all of its registered gateways and, in an admission confirm message (ACF), returns the IP address of the gateway to which this call has to be forwarded.

Step 4   The target IP address is that of the gateserver (CMA) that is registered with the gatekeeper. The gateway sends an H.225 setup message to the gateserver.

Step 5   The CMA sends an ARQ to the gatekeeper for permission to accept the call.

Step 6 The CMA receives an ACF from the gatekeeper, permitting it to accept the call.

Step 7 The CMA looks in its DS routing table to determine which AMM to contact.

Step 8 The CMA then sends a **start app** command to the appropriate AMM.

Step 9 The targeted AMM looks in the schedule table to determine which application agent to activate. In this case, the application agent is UM.

Step 10 The AMM forks and executes a new UM process to handle this call. An instance of the UM agent is executed for each incoming call.

Step 11 The new UM agent sends a message to the CMA via the AMM to accept the call.

Step 12 The CMA sends an H.225 connect message to the gateway, requesting it to connect the call.

Step 13 The gateway sends a Q.931 connect message to the PSTN, and connects the call to the UM server (CMA).

Step 14 Because RDNIS is unpopulated, the UM agent sends a message to CMA to play the message that asks for the caller's phone number, and collects the DTMF.

Step 15 The CMA retrieves the message from the file system.

Step 16 The CMA plays the message. The subscriber hears "Good morning, please enter your …".

Step 17 The subscriber enters a phone number followed by a #, or presses the # key if calling from his or her own phone, or does nothing (times out). DTMF is transported across the H.323 network to the CMA using Cisco's Real-time Transport Protocol (RTP) encapsulation.

Step 18 The CMA uses the AMM to pass DTMF information to the UM application.

Step 19 The UM application sends a message to the CMA to play the message, prompts the user for a password, and collects the DTMF.

Step 20 The CMA retrieves and plays the message.

Step 21 The subscriber password is keyed in. The DTMF is transported to CMA using RTP encapsulation.

Step 22 The CMA uses the AMM to pass the DTMF information to the UM application.

Step 23 The UM application requests user profile information from the directory server. The subscriber's profile is retrieved using the keyed-in phone number or the ANI (calling number) if the caller simply pressed #.

Step 24 The directory server returns the entire profile and authentication to the UM application. The UM application verifies the caller as a valid subscriber.

Step 25 The UM application sends a "Play prompt" message to the CMA via the AMM.

Step 26 The CMA retrieves the welcome-message.wav file from disk storage.

Step 27 The CMA plays the prompt to the caller and the caller hears the welcome message.

Step 28 The UM agent determines the messaging server for the subscriber (based on the messaging server host name specified in the subscriber's profile) and sets up an IMAP4 connection to it using information from the subscriber's profile.

Step 29 The UM application retrieves the message headers and inventories the subscriber's mailbox.

Step 30 If the subscriber has urgent messages, the UM application passes them as a .wav file to the CMA via AMM. If there are no urgent messages, the UM application sends the **inventory prompt** command to the CMA.

Step 31 The CMA retrieves the prompt from the file system.

Step 32 The CMA plays the prompt. The caller hears something like "You have one voice message and three e-mail messages. . . "

Step 33 The subscriber enters a "1" to retrieve the messages.

Step 34 The digit is collected by the gateway and sent to the CMA, which uses the AMM to pass it on to the UM application.

Step 35 Using IMAP, the UM application retrieves any urgent messages for the subscriber from the subscriber's messaging server.

Step 36 Depending on whether headers are on or off in the subscriber's profile, the UM application retrieves and stores just the message body .wav file or both the message body and header .wav files

Step 37 The UM application sends a command to the CMA to play the audio files.

Step 38 The CMA retrieves the .wav files from the file system and plays them.

Inbound Fax Message to a Subscriber

The gateserver does not participate in handling incoming fax messages. When a fax account is created on the UM server, it creates an alias file on the messaging server, where it maps the subscriber's fax number to his or her e-mail address. This alias is used in Step 4 of the fax delivery process described later in this section.

With store and forward fax, the AS5300 acts as an on-ramp gateway, which receives faxes from end users and converts them into Tag Image File Format-Fax (TIFF-F) files. It attaches this TIFF-F file to a MIME e-mail message and forwards it to a designated SMTP server where the e-mail is stored. Figure 9-10 shows how the fax delivery process works.

Figure 9-10   *The fax delivery process.*

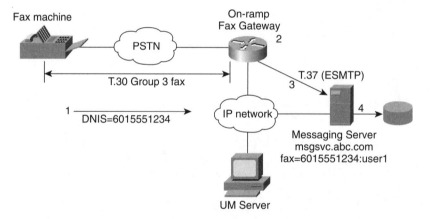

The following describes each step in the fax delivery process flow diagram shown in Figure 9-10:

Step 1   A fax is sent to the subscriber telephone number (6015551234). The fax machine connects to a fax gateway (Cisco AS5300 access server).

Step 2   The fax gateway receives the call. The incoming call is determined to be a fax call because the DNIS matches a fax inbound dial-peer (dial-peer voice 1 mmoip). The gateway converts the T.30 Group 3 fax to a .tiff file. Because the dial-peer that it matches identifies the call as a fax or a voice call, two separate numbers need to be used for fax and voice mail for each subscriber.

Step 3   The gateway creates a mail message, attaches the .tiff file, and delivers it to the messaging server using Extended SMTP (ESMTP). The session target statement under the fax dial peer determines the delivery e-mail address. The statement *session target mailto:d@mailserver.com* sets the destination e-mail address to *<DNIS>@mailserver.com*. In this case,

the destination e-mail address is set to fax=6015551234@
msgsvc.abc.com. The **mta send server msgsvc.abc.com** global
configuration command specifies the messaging server that this e-mail
with the .tiff attachment is sent to.

Step 4 The messaging server contains a list of aliases that map phone numbers
to valid e-mail addresses on the server. For example, *fax=6015551234* is
mapped to *faxuser@msgsvc.abc.com*. The server accepts the e-mail from
the gateway, looks up the alias file, and deposits the fax in the
subscriber's mailbox. The receipt to e-mail address is the DNIS-based e-
mail alias (*fax=6015551234@msgsvc.abc.com*). This enables the UM
server to determine that this is a fax message when retrieving messages
from the message store.

A working configuration of an on-ramp fax gateway is presented in Chapter 8, "Fax
Services."

Printing a Fax Message from a Subscriber's Mailbox to an Alternate Fax Number

After successfully logging in using a telephone, the subscriber can choose to retrieve faxes
or e-mail messages containing faxes and redirect these messages to another fax number to
be printed. Figure 9-11 shows how the subscriber retrieves fax messages by printing them
to an alternate fax number.

Figure 9-11 *Printing to an alternate fax number.*

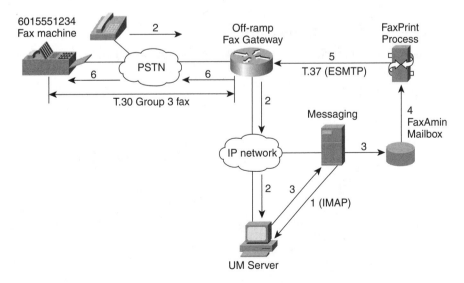

The following describes each step in the redirect fax printing process flow diagram shown in Figure 9-11:

Step 1   The UM application uses the subscriber information from the directory server to log in to the subscriber's mailbox, and uses IMAP to retrieve the fax or e-mail message from the messaging server.

Step 2   The subscriber chooses the option to print the message (redirect it to a fax machine close by). The subscriber keys in the phone number of the fax machine where the message is to be sent—for example, 6015551234.

Step 3   Every subscriber mailbox is associated with a faxadmin account. The UM application adds the destination fax information to the message and uses SMTP to forward it to the subscriber's faxadmin e-mail account.

Step 4   The FaxPrint application, which runs on the messaging server, constantly monitors the faxadmin's mailbox for new messages. It uses IMAP to retrieve the message sent in the previous step.

Step 5   The FaxPrint application addresses the message to the destination fax machine and sends the message to the off-ramp fax gateway using ESMTP (T.37). The faxprint.ini and dialmap.ini files define the gateway to use. The destination e-mail address would be fax=6015551234@gateway.abc.com.

Step 6   The fax gateway extracts the destination phone number from this e-mail address, converts any text to .tiff format, and sends the fax to the destination as a T.30 Group 3 fax.

Overall uOne Protocol Flow Sequence

Figure 9-12 summarizes the overall uOne protocol flow sequence.

Figure 9-12 *Overall protocol flow sequence.*

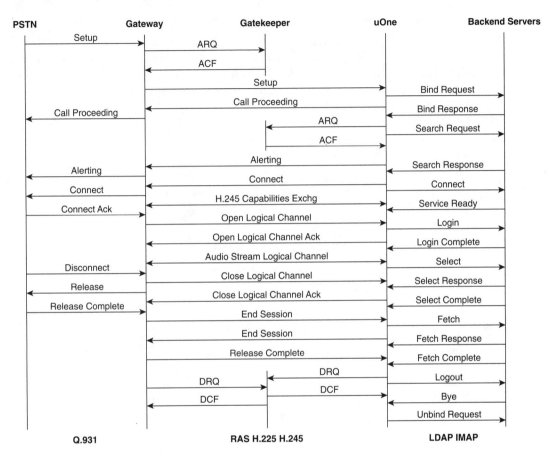

Deploying Unified Messaging Services in a Service Provider Environment

Service providers typically have a large set of users with varying requirements. They also provide Internet service to a number of small corporations. UM services can be deployed across the entire service provider network and sold at different levels to individual users as well as corporations. A typical deployment in a service provider environment would be decentralized (as shown in Figure 9-13) to provide for local-number access to services.

Ideally, there are one or more gateservers per POP, with their own messaging servers connected locally. However, they all share a common centralized directory service. From a unified messaging point of view, a totally self-contained POP has a gateserver, a messaging server (for local message store), an H.323 gateway (for local access to the gateserver), and an access gateway that allows users to dial in to the service provider network.

In this scenario, LDAP and RAS are the only UM-related protocols that use the WAN. E-mail messages to the user are relayed (using SMTP) to messaging servers located at each POP. Depending on the subscriber base at each POP, multiple gateservers can share the same central messaging server or one that is located at one of the POP sites.

Figure 9-13 *Service provider deployment scenario.*

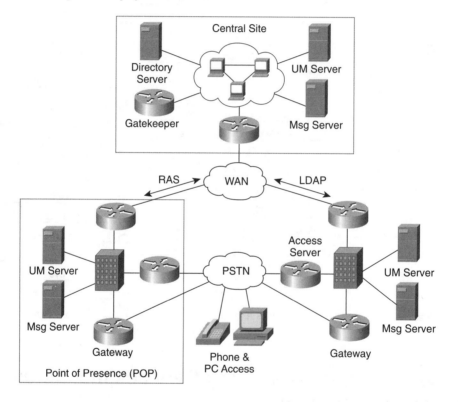

Initially, you can provide service to your subscribers at the central site, then add messaging servers and gateservers at POP installations as the subscriber base grows. If subscribers travel from one POP to another, they can still access their services with a local call. The local gateserver will be able to service all requests, but because the subscribers' messaging server is not local, they might notice a small degradation in service, depending on network bandwidth availability.

For subscribers who travel out of your service area, you have the option of providing 800-number access to a gateway at the central site for an additional fee. In the preceding scenario, the distributed architecture allows any gateserver to service any subscriber because they all have access to a common directory server. This provides for complete redundancy and also helps with maintenance of the gateservers.

After the services are deployed, they can be used to support many different COIs, enabling you to sell different levels and classes of service to individual subscribers, corporations, and resellers.

To deploy UM services in a service provider environment, you need to do the following:

Step 1   Determine where to place the uOne components for an optimal solution.

Step 2   Create multiple COIs.

Step 3   Define various classes of service (CoS).

Step 4   Add greeting and fax administrators.

Step 5   Add Unified Messaging System Administrators (UMSAs) and subscribers.

Step 6   Deploy fax services.

Step 7   Plan for redundancy and load balancing.

Determine Optimal Design

A typical service provider services both individual subscribers (with dial Internet access) and corporations, with their own dedicated Internet access solutions. The decision where to place various components of a uOne solution depends on the subscriber base, the available bandwidth, and the quality of the UM services offered. The various network components associated with a uOne solution affect service quality in different ways. The following is a list of the major components, a brief description of their main functions, and how they affect service quality.

Gateserver

In the unified communication solution, the gateserver is the termination point for an H.323 connection. Depending on its proximity to the H.323 gateway, and the available bandwidth between the gateserver and H.323 gateway, the gateserver affects call setup times as well as voice quality. Other factors that influence the performance of the gateserver are the number of simultaneous calls that can be handled and available resources, such as memory and CPU.

Directory Server

Directory services are used to authenticate, store, and retrieve subscriber profile information. Directory services directly influence authentication and message response times. Authentication time is the time a user has to wait for the system to respond after a user ID and PIN have been entered. Directory services are also used to store subscribers' mailbox and login information so that uOne can retrieve subscribers' messages from their mailboxes. Login information must be retrieved from the directory server to be able to log in to the messaging server and retrieve the message. Message response time is the time a subscriber has to wait to hear the message after the message has been selected. We recommend that directory services be centralized and deployed at the core because all uOne servers in an ISP share the same directory.

Messaging Server

The messaging server is used to store and retrieve personal greetings, and voice, e-mail, and fax messages. It directly affects message response time as well as greeting response time. Greeting response time is the time it takes the system to retrieve and play a personal greeting after it has determined which greeting to play. Other factors that can influence the performance of a messaging server are the size of the subscriber base that is served by the server, and available resources, such as CPU and memory.

H.323 Gateway

The H.323 gateway serves as the protocol translator between the PSTN and the H.323 networks. Depending on its proximity to the subscriber base, subscribers might not have local number access to the unified messaging system. The gateway directly affects call setup times and voice quality.

H.323 Gatekeeper

Primarily, the gatekeeper determines which gateserver will handle an incoming call. It has a direct influence on call setup times.

Create Multiple COIs

The concept of COI involves taking a large set of users and logically grouping them into smaller communities under a single administrative authority. This allows the same UM service infrastructure to be used by multiple communities at the same time, and permits delegation of administrative tasks to the UM administrators for that community. Every administrator can customize their own greetings, provide different classes of service, and perform other administrative tasks within their own COI. A COI translates to a point in the directory tree on a directory server. Figure 9-14 illustrates a sample directory tree for a typical service provider.

Data in a directory is hierarchical, and is represented as attribute-data pairs. The attributes used in this directory example are as follows:

- **o**—Organization name.
- **ou**—Organizational unit. This attribute is typically used to represent smaller divisions within your enterprise.
- **cn**—Group. "CN" stands for common name.
- **uid**—User ID.

Figure 9-14 *Sample directory tree.*

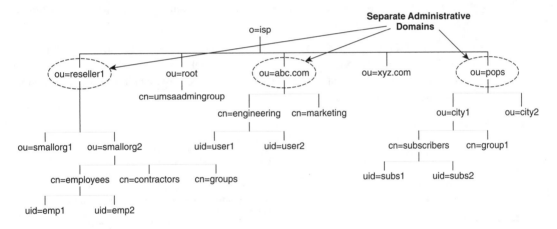

The top level "o=isp" and the admin account are created at installation time. The top-level administrator (admin) has the capability to create more organizations and organizational units, groups, and users. uOne requires an organizational unit called "root" and a group under "root" for UMSA administrators. The administrator accesses the LDAP directory server using a web interface at http:\\directoryServer:2500.

Once logged in as the admin, you can create more organizational units and groups, as shown in Figure 9-14. You should refer to the directory server user guide for details on how to create additional organizational units, groups, and users. Creating organizational units, groups, and a few sample users will create database entries with directory branch points.

If you export the directory, the resulting LDAP Data Interchange Format (LDIF) file will have the format of individual entries in the directory database. You can then use this LDIF file as a template for creating a large number of entries in the directory. For example, you can use an existing subscriber database as a source to create a large number of directory entries by using a scripting language to automate the creation of the LDIF file, which can then be imported into the directory.

You can also use the bulk add tool that comes with the UM server to add a large number of entries to your directory. Once again, you should refer to the directory user and deployment guides that came with the directory server for details about directory design.

Define Classes of Service

A class of service (CoS) defines a common set of unified communication services for a group of subscribers that is administered by a central authority. Subscriber groups use CoSs to bundle various feature sets into distinct packages that facilitate administration of common features. A CoS is unique within a COI and is identified by a number (for example, CoS=1). CoSs are defined by identifying sets of features that you can market as different levels of services to subscribers and resellers.

In the example in Figure 9-15, "DL" stands for directory listing. "DL Entries" specifies how many listings are permitted per list, and "Number of DLs" specifies the maximum number of lists that the user can create. Since a CoS is unique per organizational unit, it is possible to have the same CoS number under different organizational units.

Figure 9-15 *Classes of service (CoS).*

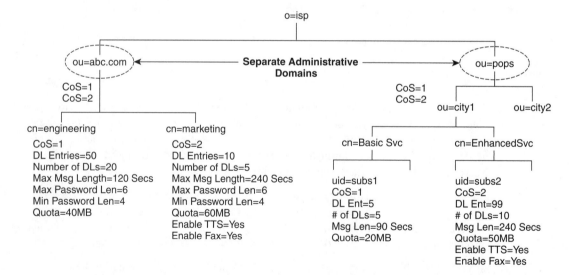

Two CoSs are defined for subscribers at POP sites. Basic services include voice mail and e-mail, with each voice message restricted to a maximum length of 90 seconds. Enhanced services include basic services and permit fax as well as text-to-speech (TTS) services, and increase the maximum length of voice messages to 240 seconds. Also, enhanced services subscribers can create more and larger distribution lists.

Every organizational unit needs one CoS defined for each feature set being offered to users. You can define CoSs by using the Web-based administration tool, UMSA, under "CoS Administration." The entry in the "DN" field in "add a new CoS" associates the CoS with an organizational unit. In the Figure 9-15 example, the Distinguished Name (DN) entry for abc.com would be "ou=abc.com,o=isp." The complete entry is:

> Entry DN: ou=abc.com, o=isp
> Class of Service ID: 1
> Class of Service Name: EngSvc
> Search Base: ou=abc.com,o=isp
> Personal Access UM Ini File Name: UM.ini

Refer to the UM administrator guide for more details.

Add Greeting and Fax Administrators

The greeting administrator account is a special mailbox used to store personal greetings and distribution list names for subscribers. The greeting administrator is identified by msgadmin@<organizational unit name>. Each organizational unit requires its own greeting and faxadmin accounts and can have more than one of each.

Every subscriber account has a greeting and a faxadmin associated with it. When a subscriber is added to the system, a set of folders is added to the greeting admin account to store the subscriber personal greetings and distribution list information. These folders are separate from the subscriber message mailbox, which stores their voice, fax, and e-mail messages. When a subscriber first logs in to the system and records a personal greeting, the greeting is stored in a folder under the subscriber's greeting administrator. Figure 9-16 shows how the centralized greeting admin works.

When a call comes in for a subscriber, a personal greeting needs to be played to the caller. Using IMAP, the greeting is retrieved from the greeting admin account where it is stored. However, the voice mail message left by the caller will be stored in the subscriber's mailbox, which can be accessed by an e-mail client. Centralized greeting admins and local subscriber message stores will result in personal greetings being retrieved across the WAN, with voice messages being stored and retrieved locally for subscribers at POPs. In Figure 9-16, the only traffic local to the POP is the storage of voice messages in the subscriber's mailbox. If you created the greeting and faxadmin accounts on the local message store to service all local subscribers, all IMAP traffic will be local to the POP. The greeting and faxadmin accounts can be added using UMSA under "Global Administration." We recommend that you create a greeting and faxadmin account on a messaging server to service all subscribers who have a message stored on that server.

Figure 9-16 *Protocol flows for centralized greeting admin.*

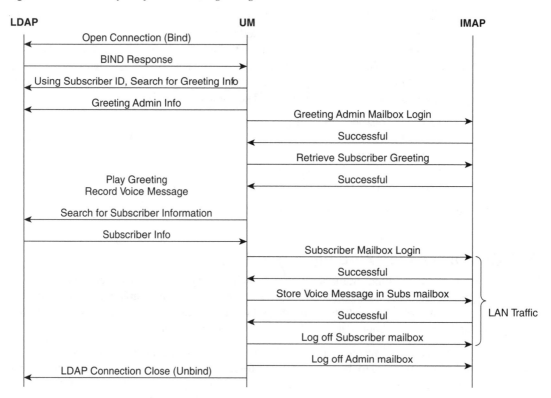

Add Organizational Unit UMSA Administrators and Subscribers

Each organizational unit requires a UMSA administrator who will manage its COI. UMSA administrators have add, change, and delete privileges over subscribers and CoSs within their COI. These unique admin accounts have privileges within their own COI and are added as subscribers. Any subscriber can be made a UMSA administrator by adding them to the UMSA administrator group created under ou=root.

UMSA administrators can add subscribers within their own COI using the web-based UMSA tool. While adding subscribers, administrators can select the messaging server and greeting and fax admins that service the subscriber. All messaging servers known to the LDAP directory service, and the defined greeting and fax admins, are listed in the drop-down menu on the web interface. Selecting the appropriate message store and greeting admin is an important consideration when adding new subscribers because they define the message store for personal greetings and faxes as well as the message store for incoming e-mail, voice mail, and fax.

Deploy Fax Services

When you enable fax services for subscribers, they are assigned a fax number, where incoming faxes will be accepted and stored in their mailbox. Subscribers also have the ability to redirect e-mail and fax messages from their mailboxes to any fax machine. Depending on the volume of subscribers wanting fax services, fax gateways can be local to the POP or centralized.

Fax services are described in detail in Chapter 8, "Fax Services."

Deploying Unified Messaging for Dial Internet Access

In this section, we describe the following four scenarios for deploying unified messaging for dial Internet access, along with associated call flows:

- Completely Centralized
- Partially Centralized
- More Distributed
- Completely Distributed

Completely Centralized

The completely centralized configuration is a good starting point for deployment of uOne services where, except for an H.323 gateway to provide local-number access, all other uOne components are centrally located at your core network. This is an acceptable model when the subscriber base is small and services are just being introduced. Figure 9-17 shows an example of a completely centralized unified messaging deployment; Figure 9-18 shows the flow sequence for this deployment.

Partially Centralized

As the subscriber base at a POP site grows, we recommend that a uOne server be dedicated to servicing the site while still maintaining backend services at the core. This improves call setup times and voice quality and is easy to deploy. The server at the POP will now service existing subscribers from the POP using the core uOne server because the gatekeeper can be configured to forward calls to the POP to a local server. No other changes to the configuration or user profile information will be necessary. Figure 9-19 shows an example of a partially centralized unified messaging deployment; Figure 9-20 shows the flow sequence for this deployment.

Figure 9-17 *Completely centralized deployment.*

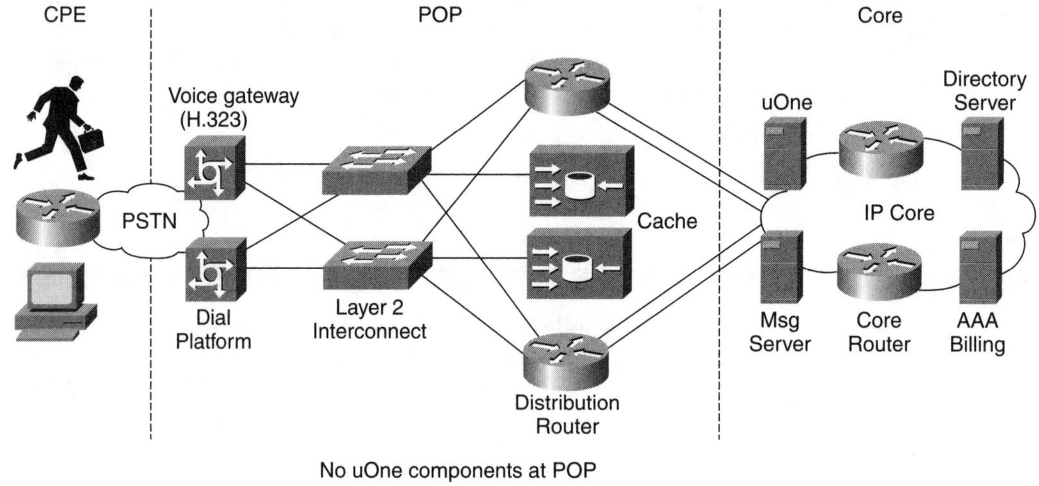

No uOne components at POP

More Distributed

As the subscriber base at a POP site continues to grow, we recommend that you dedicate a messaging server to service the site. Dedicating a messaging server greatly improves message response times as well as voice quality because all messages are stored and retrieved locally across the LAN. However, your subscribers could notice a slight increase in message response times if they attempt to access their messages from another POP site because the messages have to be retrieved across the WAN from the messaging server at its home site. Figure 9-21 shows an example of this unified messaging deployment; Figure 9-22 shows the flow sequence for this deployment.

Figure 9-18 *Completely centralized flow sequence.*

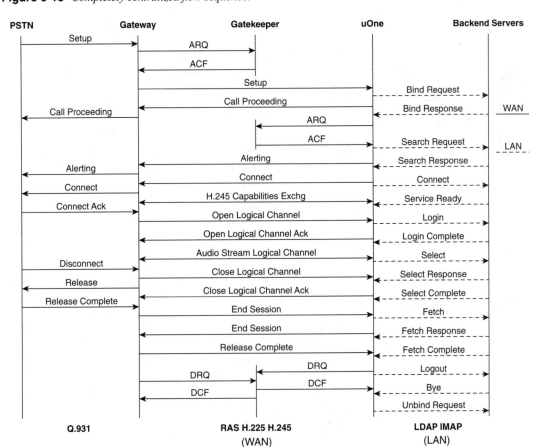

Figure 9-19 *Partially centralized deployment.*

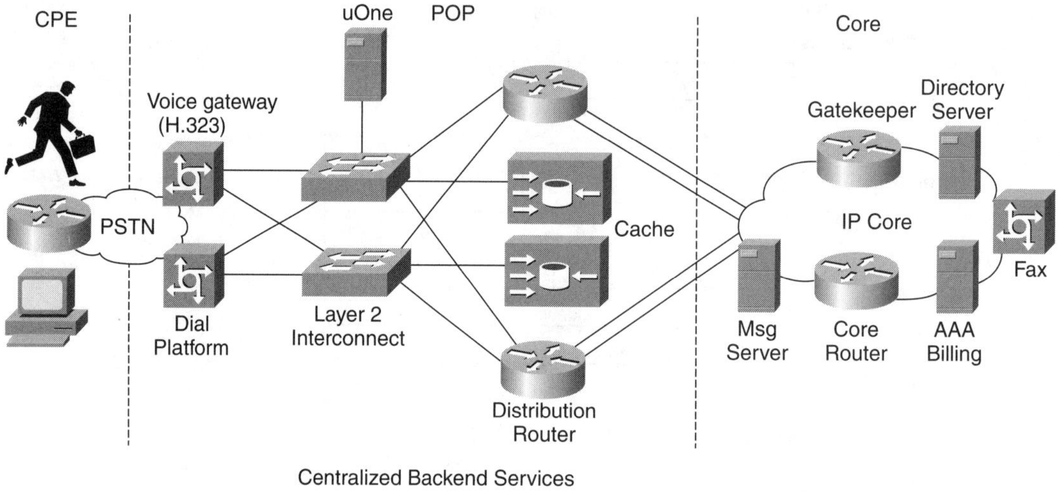

Completely Distributed

In a completely distributed deployment, everything but directory services is moved to the local POP. Except for authentication and retrieving of user profile information, all the other services are local to the POP. Because the gatekeeper is local as well, call setup times are very good and service quality is at its best. Each POP will have its own zone and can be designed for fault tolerance by using redundant gateservers and redundant gatekeepers running HSRP. In normal operation, both gateservers have equal priority and share the call load on a per-call basis. (Call balancing and redundancy are discussed in the "Redundancy and Load Balancing" section later in this chapter.) Figure 9-23 shows an example of a completely distributed unified messaging deployment; Figure 9-24 shows the flow sequence for this deployment.

Figure 9-20 *Partially centralized flow sequence.*

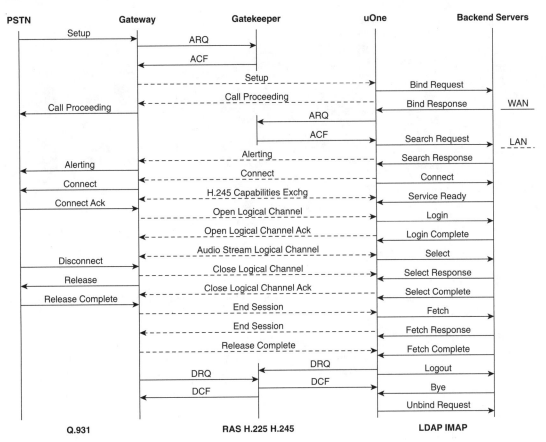

Figure 9-21 *More distributed deployment.*

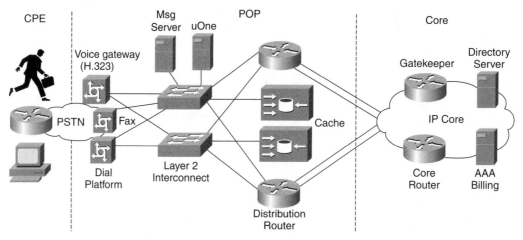

uOne and Messaging server at each POP

Table 9-1 summarizes the qualities of each of the described dial Internet access deployment scenarios.

Table 9-1 *Deployment Summary*

Quality Feature	Fully Centralized	Partially Centralized	Fully Distributed	Partially Distributed
Call Setup Time[1]	Long	Good	Best	Good
Voice Quality[2]	Average	Good	Good	Good
Authentication[3]	Good	Good	Good	Good
Message Response[4]	Acceptable	Acceptable	Good	Good

1. Call Setup Time: The time taken to set up the call and hear ringing at the far end.

2. Voice Quality: The quality of the messages being played back from uOne.

3. Authentication: The time that the subscriber has to wait for the system after entering a user ID and PIN.

4. Message Response: The time that the subscriber has to wait to hear a message after selecting that message.

Figure 9-22 *More distributed flow sequence.*

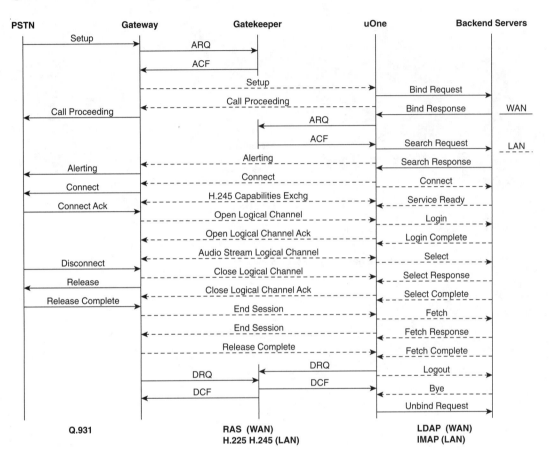

Figure 9-23 *Completely distributed deployment.*

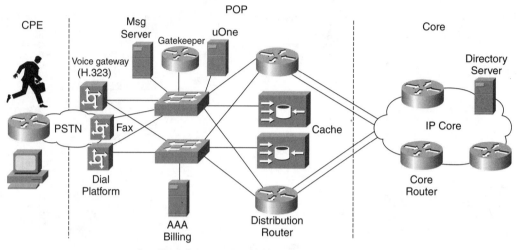

Local gatekeeper zone for each POP

Figure 9-24 *Completely distributed flow sequence.*

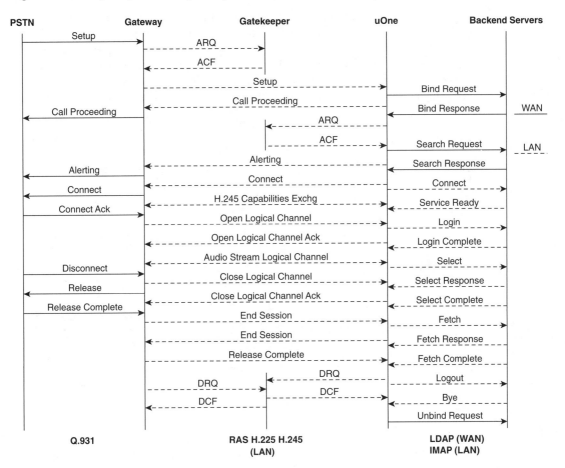

Deploying Unified Messaging for Dedicated Internet Access

In this section, we describe the following three scenarios for deploying UM for dedicated Internet access:

- Sharing uOne Resources at the POP
- Local Gateway
- Dedicated uOne Resources

Sharing uOne Resources at the POP

Small and large corporations use dedicated lines to the service provider for Internet access. A separate COI is set up for each corporation, and administrative authority for this COI is delegated to a system administrator within the organization. The corporation can then set up accounts for its employees on a trial basis and share uOne resources at the POP to which they connect. Employees with unified messaging accounts can access their messages by calling the POP site. Figure 9-25 shows an example of sharing uOne resources at the POP to deploy unified messaging.

Figure 9-25 *Shared POP gateway.*

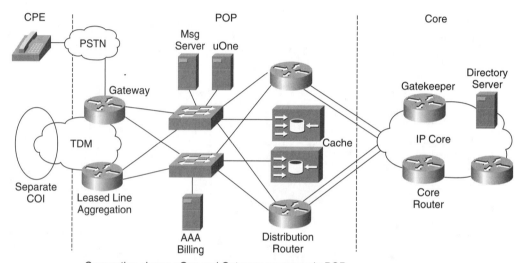

Corporation shares uOne and Gateway resources in POP

Local Gateway

As more users within the organization use unified messaging services, it is more economical for the corporation to have its own local gateway, especially if users have to pay toll charges to access the services at a POP site. Figure 9-26 shows an example where the corporation has its own local gateway.

Dedicated uOne Resources

When the subscriber base within the organization grows even more, it justifies dedicated uOne resources to handle all unified communication services. In this case, the uOne server is at the customer site, and messaging servers need to be integrated into existing mail servers. However, directory services are centralized at the core, and billing records can be collected at the POP site or at the core. Figure 9-27 shows an example of using dedicated uOne resources to deploy unified messaging.

Figure 9-26 *Local gateway.*

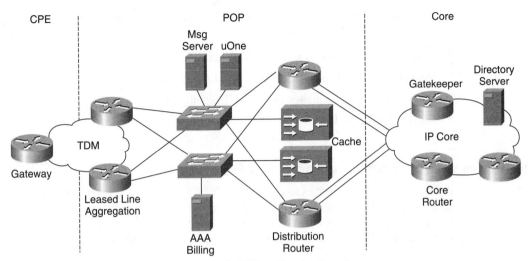

Corporation shares uOne resources in POP and has local number access

Figure 9-27 *Dedicated uOne resources.*

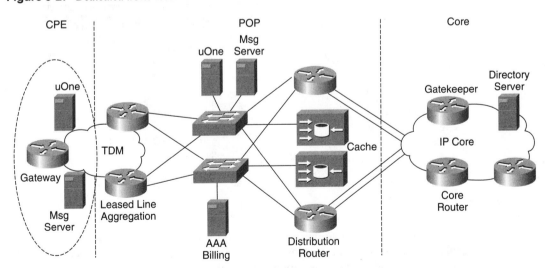

Corporation has dedicated uOne resources

Redundancy and Load Balancing

This section describes how to provide redundancy and load balancing for unified messaging services, and includes the following:

- uOne Server Redundancy and Load Balancing
- Fax Gateway (off-ramp) Redundancy and Load Balancing
- H.323 Gateway Redundancy and Load Balancing
- Gatekeeper Redundancy

uOne Server Redundancy and Load Balancing

Gateservers register themselves as gateways with an H.323 gatekeeper. If multiple gateservers register with the same gatekeeper, and they can all handle any service call, the gatekeeper automatically rotates the calls among all the registered gateways of equal priority. Figure 9-28 shows an example of load balancing between two UM servers, Server1 and Server2.

Figure 9-28 *uOne server redundancy and load balancing.*

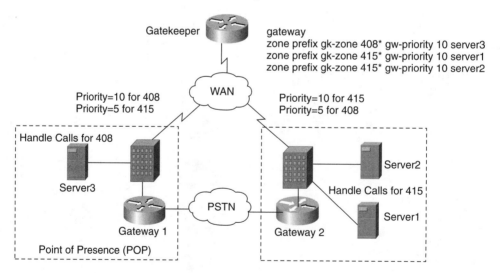

In Figure 9-28, calls are load-balanced between Server1 and Server2 because they have equal priority to handle calls starting with "415." However, because all calls are not of the same duration, load balancing is only on a per-call basis. If one of the UM servers is down, it loses its registration with the gatekeeper and the other server handles all incoming calls.

Based on the geographic location of a UM server, you can configure the gatekeeper with different levels of priority for each gateserver, as illustrated in Figure 9-29.

Figure 9-29 *uOne server redundancy across POPs.*

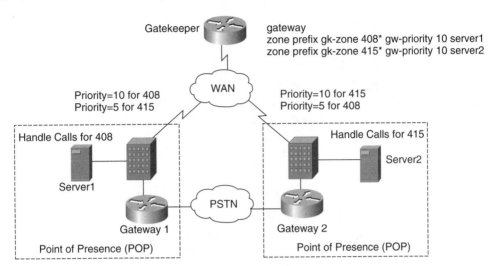

Server1 has been assigned a priority of 10 for handling calls to area code 408. Server2 has priority 10 for area code 415. The default priority for a gateway is 5. If one of the servers fails, the server with a lower priority will take over.

Even though a server in one geographic location can service a call in another geographic location, the server still needs to access the message store for the subscriber, which might be local to the POP. Access to this message store is across the WAN, so the subscriber might notice a slight degradation in service depending on existing traffic loads and bandwidth across the WAN.

Note that there is no redundancy for active calls being currently serviced by a uOne server. If the server becomes unavailable, another uOne server will handle new incoming calls but existing calls will be disrupted and will have to be reestablished by the caller.

Fax Gateway (Off-Ramp) Redundancy and Load Balancing

By using Cisco IOS Server Load Balancing (IOS SLB), you can configure multiple fax gateways at a POP site to balance the outbound fax load and provide redundancy and load balancing as shown in Figure 9-30. IOS SLB is an IOS-based feature that provides load balancing among multiple servers.

A virtual server is a group of real fax gateways that can handle outbound fax calls. The virtual server is assigned an IP address, which is also configured as a secondary address on each of the constituent fax gateways. The uOne faxprint process is configured to connect to this virtual IP address in the faxprint.ini and dialmap.ini files.

Figure 9-30 *Redundancy and load balancing with IOS SLB.*

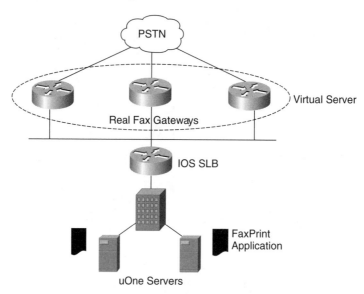

When the faxprint process initiates a connection to the virtual IP address, the IOS SLB software chooses a real fax gateway to service this connection based on the configured load-balancing algorithm. IOS SLB software tracks each connection attempt to a fax gateway. If several consecutive TCP "SYN" open connections are not acknowledged, the session is assigned to a new fax gateway.

The number of connection attempts before the session is reassigned is configurable. Every failed connection attempt increments a failure counter. If the failure counter exceeds a configurable threshold, the gateway is considered out of service and is removed from the list of active gateways. The failed gateway is not assigned any new connections for a specified configurable time interval called "retry timer." After the timer expires, IOS SLB will assign the next qualified connection to the failed gateway. If it succeeds, the gateway is placed back on the list of active real gateways. If it fails again, no new connections are attempted until the retry timer expires again.

IOS SLB supports two load-balancing algorithms: weighted round robin and weighted least connections. In weighted round robin, each gateway is assigned a weight that represents its capacity to handle connections. The gateway is assigned the number of connections equal to its weight before another real gateway is chosen. In weighted least connections, the gateway chosen to service a connection request is the one with the fewest active connections. Here, also, you can assign weights to gateways. They represent the relative capacity of the gateway to service connection requests compared to the total service capacity of all the gateways that share the same virtual IP address.

H.323 Gateway Redundancy and Load Balancing

Gateways report resource availability to their gatekeepers using RAS Resource Availability Indication (RAI) messages. DSP channels can be monitored, and based on a configured threshold, gateways send an RAI message to notify the gatekeeper that it is almost out of resources. When resources become available and are more than another configurable threshold, they send another RAI message to the gatekeeper, notifying it that resources are now available.

When there are multiple gateways registered with the gatekeeper, and all other factors are equal, a gatekeeper will choose a gateway with available resources over a gateway with depleted resources. Because the gateway monitors DSP resources, it will send an RAI message to the gatekeeper when it loses its connection to the PSTN. When there are multiple resources with equal priority registered with the gatekeeper, the gatekeeper rotates the calls with equal priority among all the registered gateways that are qualified to handle the calls, as shown in Figure 9-31.

Figure 9-31 *Gateway load balancing and redundancy.*

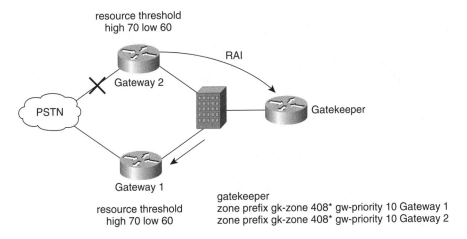

In Figure 9-31, both gateways are configured to send RAI messages to the gatekeeper and both have equal priority to handle calls destined for area code 408. In normal mode, calls are load balanced by turns between the two gateways. When Gateway 2 loses its connection to the PSTN, its DSP resource drops below the configured threshold and it sends an RAI message to the gatekeeper, which then forwards all outbound area code 408 calls to Gateway 1.

Gatekeeper Redundancy

Cisco gatekeepers can be configured to use Hot Standby Routing Protocol (HSRP) so a standby gatekeeper assumes the role if an active gatekeeper fails. A virtual HSRP IP address is configured on all gatekeepers in the HSRP group and is the common IP address that the active gatekeeper responds to. HSRP uses a priority scheme to identify one gatekeeper as active within a group. All remaining gatekeepers in the group are on standby. When the active gatekeeper fails to send a "hello" within a configurable interval of time, the next gatekeeper in the group with the highest priority becomes the active gatekeeper and starts responding to the virtual HSRP IP address.

There is no load balancing among the multiple gatekeepers. Two or more gatekeepers can be grouped as an HSRP group, with the one having the highest priority being the active gatekeeper at any given time. The RAS address for all gatekeepers in the group will be the HSRP virtual address. Endpoints and gateways use this HSRP virtual address as their gatekeeper address. This works even if the gateways attempt to discover the gatekeeper by using multicasting, because only the active gatekeeper responds. All other gatekeepers are in standby mode and do not respond to a multicast or unicast request.

When a standby gatekeeper takes over because of the failure of an active gatekeeper, it does not have the state or the registrations of the failed gatekeeper. When a gateway or an endpoint attempts to initiate a new call by sending an Admission Request (ARQ), it will get an Admission Reject (ARJ), indicating that the endpoint is not recognized. The gateways and uOne servers will have to reregister with the new gatekeeper before being able to make any calls.

Figure 9-32 shows an example of gatekeepers grouped in an HSRP group to provide redundancy.

In Figure 9-32, GK1 has higher priority than GK2, and will become active and respond to the virtual HSRP IP address 10.1.1.3. The gateway and uOne server are configured to use 10.1.1.3 as the IP address of the gatekeeper. If GK1 fails, GK2 starts responding to the virtual IP address but does not yet have the gateway or the uOne server registered as H.323 gateways. When the gateway and the uOne server make the next attempt to register with the gatekeeper by sending a Registration Request (RRQ) message, they will get a Registration Confirmation (RCF) response from GK2.

Figure 9-32 *Redundant gatekeepers using HSRP.*

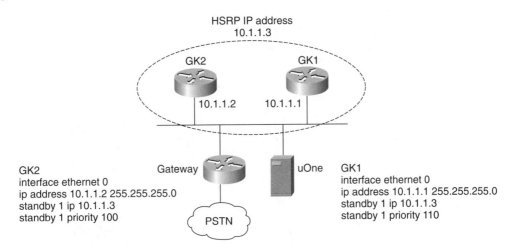

A Fully Redundant Configuration

A fully redundant POP site has multiple gateways, gatekeepers, fax gateways, and uOne servers. By implementing replication, the LDAP directory server can be made redundant at the core. A fully redundant configuration is shown in Figure 9-33.

GW1 and GW2 are redundant gateways configured to send RAI messages to the gatekeeper based on their available resources and the state of their connection to the PSTN. When a gateway loses its connection to the PSTN, it will send an RAI message to the gatekeeper and force all outgoing calls to the other gateway.

GK1 and GK2 are two redundant gatekeepers configured for HSRP. They constantly monitor each other for availability, and take over each other's functions when the other gatekeeper is not available. The two uOne servers register with the gatekeeper with equal priority (the default is 5) and, in normal operation, handle incoming calls on a round robin basis. However, if one of the servers becomes unavailable, it loses its active registration with the gatekeeper, forcing all new calls to be handled by the remaining uOne server. The IOS SLB feature can be used for load balancing and redundancy on outbound faxes (off-ramp fax gateways).

Figure 9-33 *Fully redundant configuration.*

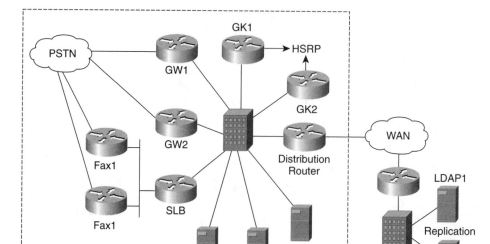

Unified Messaging Configuration Examples

This section provides the following UM configuration examples:

- Interoperability with Cisco and NetSpeak gatekeepers
- Cisco gateway and gatekeeper configuration for two-stage dialing

Interoperability with Cisco and NetSpeak Gatekeepers

In this configuration example, the Cisco AS5300 gateway and uOne gateserver 4.1S are configured to use a NetSpeak gatekeeper to route calls. Direct inward dial can be used at the Cisco AS5300 gateway to accommodate single-stage dialing. Figure 9-34 illustrates the details of the network topology.

Figure 9-34 *Interoperability with NetSpeak gatekeeper.*

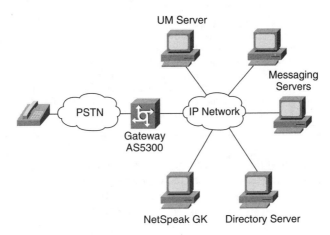

NetSpeak Gatekeeper Configuration Example

Example 9-1 shows how to configure the NetSpeak gatekeeper in Figure 9-34.

Example 9-1 *NetSpeak Gatekeeper Configuration Example*

```
From the NetSpeak control center
Select the route server (RS)
Route configuration
Gatekeeper Zones (You will see your NetSpeak Gatekeeper defined here and Online)
Associated gateways
        Add Gateway
        Primary alias (This is the H323-ID field defined in the AS5300)
        Alias type (H323)
        Vendor (Other)
        Country Code (1)
        Area Code (XXX)
        National Prefix (1)
        International Prefix (011)
        Time To Live - TTL (60)
        Number of ports (20)
Associated Hunt Groups (From the Gateways Menu after you have added a gateway)
        Group Name (Name of a hunt group you want associated with your gateway)
        Beginning port number (0)
        Ending port number (19)
        Associated Codec Compatibility
                Standard G.723.1 Audio
                Standard GSM audio
                Standard PCMCA audio
                Standard PCMU audio
        Associated Route Sets
                Route Set management
```

continues

Example 9-1 *NetSpeak Gatekeeper Configuration Example (Continued)*

```
                        Add a route set
                Associated routes
                        Add E.164
                                Country Code (1)
                                Area Code (XXX)
                                Beginning subscriber number (9933301)
                                Ending Subscriber number (9933347)
                                Number to dial (SN) - Subscriber Number
        Add the newly created route set with associated routes to the
        newly created hunt group.
```

You need to repeat this configuration process on the NetSpeak gatekeeper for the other gateway. When you go to "Associated Gateways," you should see both gateways on line: This is an indication that they have registered with the gatekeeper. If you do not associate codecs with a gateway, it will fail registration with the NetSpeak gatekeeper.

Cisco AS5300 Gateway Configuration Example

Example 9-2 shows how to configure the Cisco AS5300 gateway in Figure 9-34.

Example 9-2 *Cisco AS5300 Gateway Configuration Example*

```
router# show running-config
!
version 12.0
service timestamps debug uptime
service timestamps log uptime
no service password-encryption
!
hostname tokyo-5300
!
enable password xxxx
!
resource-pool disable
!
ip subnet-zero
no ip domain-lookup
isdn switch-type primary-dms100
cns event-service server
mta receive maximum-recipients 1024
!
controller T1 0
 framing esf
 clock source line primary
 linecode b8zs
 pri-group timeslots 1-24
!
controller T1 1
 framing esf
 clock source line secondary 1
```

Example 9-2 *Cisco AS5300 Gateway Configuration Example (Continued)*

```
 linecode b8zs
 pri-group timeslots 1-24
!
controller T1 2
 framing esf
 linecode b8zs
 pri-group timeslots 1-24
!
controller T1 3
 framing esf
 linecode b8zs
 pri-group timeslots 1-24
!
voice-port 0:D
voice-port 1:D
voice-port 2:D
voice-port 3:D
!
dial-peer voice 1 voip
 destination-pattern 9933...
 dtmf-relay cisco-rtp
 codec g711ulaw
 session target ras
!
dial-peer voice 2 pots
 incoming called-number 9933...
 direct-inward-dial
!
process-max-time 200
gateway
 !
interface Ethernet0
 ip address 172.26.106.4 255.255.255.0
 no ip directed-broadcast
 h323-gateway voip interface
 h323-gateway voip id GK@hope.cisco.com ipaddr 172.26.106.10 1719
 h323-gateway voip h323-id tokyo-5300
 h323-gateway voip tech-prefix 8
!
interface Serial0:23
 no ip address
 no ip directed-broadcast
 isdn switch-type primary-dms100
 isdn tei-negotiation first-call
 isdn incoming-voice modem
 fair-queue 64 256 50
 no cdp enable
!
interface Serial1:23
 no ip address
 no ip directed-broadcast
 isdn switch-type primary-dms100
```

continues

Example 9-2 *Cisco AS5300 Gateway Configuration Example (Continued)*

```
 isdn tei-negotiation first-call
 isdn incoming-voice modem
 fair-queue 64 256 0
 no cdp enable
!
interface Serial2:23
 no ip address
 no ip directed-broadcast
 isdn switch-type primary-dms100
 isdn tei-negotiation first-call
 fair-queue 64 256 0
 no cdp enable
!
interface Serial3:23
 no ip address
 no ip directed-broadcast
 isdn switch-type primary-5ess
 fair-queue 64 256 0
 no cdp enable
!
interface FastEthernet0
 no ip address
 no ip directed-broadcast
 shutdown
 duplex auto
 speed auto
!
ip classless
ip route 0.0.0.0 0.0.0.0 172.26.106.1
no ip http server
!
line con 0
 transport input none
line aux 0
line vty 0 4
 password xxxx
 login
!
end
```

Cisco Gateway and Gatekeeper Configuration for Two-Stage Dialing

In the following configuration examples, the UM server registers with the gatekeeper with a technology prefix of 4#, which also happens to be the default technology prefix defined in the gatekeeper. The gateway also has to be registered with the gatekeeper, as all calls to the UM server must be routed via the gatekeeper. This particular example illustrates a two-stage dialing model, where subscribers dial a phone number to access the gateway and then use a token (265) to access the UM services.

Example 9-3 shows how to configure the gateway described in the preceding scenario.

Example 9-3   *Gateway Configuration to Support Two-Stage Dialing*

```
Gateway# show running-config
!
version 12.0
service timestamps debug uptime
service timestamps log uptime
no service password-encryption
!
hostname Gateway
!
enable password xxxx
!
resource-pool disable
!
ip subnet-zero
no ip domain-lookup
ip host hope.cisco.com 172.26.106.6
ip host faith.cisco.com 172.26.106.3
ip host charity.cisco.com 172.26.106.2
!
isdn switch-type primary-dms100
cns event-service server
mta receive maximum-recipients 1024
!
controller T1 0
 framing esf
 clock source line primary
 linecode b8zs
 pri-group timeslots 1-24
!
controller T1 1
 framing esf
 clock source line secondary 1
 linecode b8zs
 pri-group timeslots 1-24
!
controller T1 2
 framing esf
 linecode b8zs
 pri-group timeslots 1-24
!
controller T1 3
 framing esf
 linecode b8zs
 pri-group timeslots 1-24
!
voice-port 0:D
voice-port 1:D
voice-port 2:D
voice-port 3:D
!
```

continues

Example 9-3   *Gateway Configuration to Support Two-Stage Dialing (Continued)*

```
dial-peer voice 1 voip
 destination-pattern 265
 dtmf-relay cisco-rtp
 codec g711ulaw
 session target ras
 !
process-max-time 200
gateway
 !
interface Ethernet0
 ip address 172.26.106.4 255.255.255.0
 no ip directed-broadcast
 h323-gateway voip interface
 h323-gateway voip id gk-splob ipaddr 172.26.106.8 1719
 h323-gateway voip h323-id tokyo-5300
 h323-gateway voip tech-prefix 8
 !
interface Serial0:23
 no ip address
 no ip directed-broadcast
 isdn switch-type primary-dms100
 isdn tei-negotiation first-call
 isdn incoming-voice modem
 fair-queue 64 256 50
 no cdp enable
 !
interface Serial1:23
 no ip address
 no ip directed-broadcast
 isdn switch-type primary-dms100
 isdn tei-negotiation first-call
 isdn incoming-voice modem
 fair-queue 64 256 0
 no cdp enable
 !
interface Serial2:23
 no ip address
 no ip directed-broadcast
 isdn switch-type primary-dms100
 isdn tei-negotiation first-call
 fair-queue 64 256 0
 no cdp enable
 !
interface Serial3:23
 no ip address
 no ip directed-broadcast
 isdn switch-type primary-5ess
 fair-queue 64 256 0
 no cdp enable
 !
```

Example 9-3 *Gateway Configuration to Support Two-Stage Dialing (Continued)*

```
interface FastEthernet0
 no ip address
 no ip directed-broadcast
 shutdown
 duplex auto
 speed auto
!
ip classless
ip route 0.0.0.0 0.0.0.0 172.26.106.1
no ip http server
!
line con 0
 transport input none
line aux 0
line vty 0 4
 password xxxx
 login
!
end
```

The **show** command output in Example 9-4 displays the current status of this gateway.

Example 9-4 *Status of the Gateway Supporting Two-Stage Dialing*

```
Gateway# show gateway
 Gateway  tokyo-5300  is registered to Gatekeeper gk-splob

Alias list (CLI configured)
 H323-ID tokyo-5300
Alias list (last RCF)
 H323-ID tokyo-5300

 H323 resource thresholding is Disabled
```

Example 9-5 shows how to configure the gatekeeper described in the preceding scenario.

Example 9-5 *Gatekeeper Configuration to Support Two-Stage Dialing*

```
Gatekeeper# show running-config
!
version 12.0
service timestamps debug uptime
service timestamps log uptime
no service password-encryption
!
hostname Gatekeeper
!
boot system flash c2600-ix-mz.120-5.T1
boot system flash c2600-js-mz.120-5.XK1
enable password xxxx
!
ip subnet-zero
no ip domain-lookup
```

continues

Example 9-5 *Gatekeeper Configuration to Support Two-Stage Dialing (Continued)*

```
!
ip dvmrp route-limit 20000
!
process-max-time 200
!
interface Ethernet0/0
 ip address 172.26.106.8 255.255.255.0
 no ip directed-broadcast
!
interface Ethernet0/1
 no ip address
 no ip directed-broadcast
 shutdown
!
ip classless
ip route 0.0.0.0 0.0.0.0 172.26.106.1
no ip http server
!
gatekeeper
 zone local gk-splob cisco.com
 gw-type-prefix 4#* default-technology
 no use-proxy gk-splob default inbound-to terminal
 no shutdown
!
line con 0
 transport input none
line aux 0
line vty 0 4
 password xxxx
 login
```

The **show** command output in Example 9-6 displays the gateway technology prefix table for this gatekeeper.

Example 9-6 *Example of Gateway Technology Prefix Table for Gatekeeper*

```
Gatekeeper# show gateway gw-type-prefix
GATEWAY TYPE PREFIX TABLE
==========================
Prefix: 4#*    (Default gateway-technology)
  Zone gk-splob master gateway list:
    172.26.106.2:1720 Charity-UM

Prefix: 8*
  Zone gk-splob master gateway list:
    172.26.106.4:1720 tokyo-5300
```

The **show** command output in Example 9-7 displays the status of all registered endpoints for this gatekeeper.

Example 9-7   *Example of Registered Endpoints for Gatekeeper*

```
Gatekeeper# show gatekeeper endpoints
Total number of active registrations = 2
      GATEKEEPER ENDPOINT REGISTRATION
      ================================
CallSignalAddr  Port  RASSignalAddr   Port  Zone Name     Type      F
--------------- ----- --------------- ----- ---------     ----     --
172.26.106.2    1720  172.26.106.2    32795 gk-splob      VOIP-GW
   H323-ID: Charity-UM
172.26.106.4    1720  172.26.106.4    1803  gk-splob      VOIP-GW
   H323-ID: tokyo-5300
```

Summary

Cisco's unified messaging provides the seamless unification of Internet and voice applications by combining e-mail, voice mail, and fax services in an integrated, robust, scalable solution. This chapter described the components of a unified messaging system and the call flows for the various messaging features of the system. We saw several design and deployment scenarios and considerations for expanding subscriber services, and learned how the COI feature allows service providers to leverage their equipment investment. The chapter also provided gateway and gatekeeper configuration information, and details of operation with a NetSpeak gatekeeper in a unified messaging environment.

## CHAPTER 10

Prepaid Services

Prepaid services enable Internet telephony service providers (ITSPs) to offer calling card services that customers can pay for in advance. Basically, prepaid services can be managed in two ways: through your own internal network infrastructure or through an Open Settlement Protocol (OSP) clearinghouse. In your own internal network infrastructure, prepaid services are implemented through a debit card application that works in conjunction with the following:

- Interactive Voice Response (IVR)
- Authentication, Authorization, and Accounting (AAA) security services
- Remote Authentication Dial-In User Service (RADIUS) security system
- An integrated third-party billing system

This combination of services enables you (as a carrier) to authorize voice calls and debit individual user accounts in real time at the edges of a VoIP network without requiring external service nodes. If you rely on an OSP clearinghouse to manage prepaid services, configure your voice gateway to register with an OSP server. OSP is designed to offer billing and accounting record consolidation for voice calls that traverse ITSP boundaries. Third-party clearinghouses with an OSP server can offer services such as route selection, call authorization, call accounting, and inter-carrier settlements, including all the complex rating and routing tables necessary for efficient and cost-effective interconnections.

This chapter discusses how to design and implement a prepaid services solution that's managed either through your internal network infrastructure or through an OSP clearinghouse.

Debit Card Application Overview

The key to managing prepaid services within your own network is the Cisco Systems debit card application. The debit card application integrates the functionality of IVR, AAA, RADIUS, and a third-party billing system. The IVR software infrastructure uses Tool Command Language (TCL) IVR scripts, dynamically combining prerecorded audio files to play the time, date, and dollar amount of remaining credit. AAA security services, in combination with a RADIUS server, provide the infrastructure for both authentication and accounting. The integrated third-party billing system maintains per-user credit balance information. RADIUS vendor-specific attributes (VSAs) are used with AAA to communicate with the third-party billing system.

With Cisco IOS Release 12.1 and later, the debit card application offers the following functionality to support internally managed prepaid services:

- Rates a call according to the caller ID, PIN, and destination number.
- Plays the credit (dollar amount) remaining on a card in $$$$$$.$$ format.
- Announces the time-remaining credit on the card in hours and minutes (HH:MM).
- Plays a "time-running-out" message based on the configurable timeout value.
- Plays a warning "time-has-run-out" message when the credit runs out.
- Makes more than one successive call to different destinations during a single call session by using the "long pound key" feature. This feature also allows the caller to make additional calls if the called party hangs up.
- Reauthorizes each new call.
- Allows type-ahead keypad entries to be made before the prompt has been completed.
- Allows the caller to skip past announcements by pressing a touch-tone key.
- Allows retry when entering data (user-ID/PIN/destination number) by using a special key.
- Terminates a field by size rather than by using a terminating character (#).
- Supports multiple languages.
- Sends an off-net tone to the caller.
- Provides voice-quality information to the RADIUS server on a call-by-call basis.
- Creates dynamic prompts by using prerecorded audio files.
- Supports local announcements with customized audio files.
- Determines how many languages are configured and plays the language selection menu only if needed.
- Supports extended TCL IVR scripting.

IVR and TCL IVR Scripts

The debit card application uses IVR as the mechanism at the voice gateway to present a customized interface to prepaid services customers. The IVR application provides simple voice prompting and digit collection to gather caller information for authenticating users and identifying destination telephone numbers.

IVR uses TCL scripts and audio files to provide voice prompting and digit collection. TCL scripts contain both executable files and audio files that interact with the system software. When a TCL IVR script is activated by an incoming call, the C code is activated in run-time mode and performs the work of these commands. Examples of the commands used by TCL IVR scripts include:

- **Play**—Plays an audio file prompt for the caller.
- **Collect**—Collects dual tone multi-frequency (DTMF) digits, such as a PIN.
- **Send**—Sends information collected to a RADIUS server and expects results.

As of Cisco IOS Release 12.1 and later, TCL IVR scripts and audio files are stored on an external TFTP server for dynamic access by the voice gateways. The scripts are loaded into RAM and remain resident as long as the gateway remains active.

New TCL IVR scripts are being developed on a continuous basis. Table 10-1 lists the TCL IVR scripts available as of Cisco IOS Release 12.1.

Table 10-1   *TCL IVR Scripts*

TCL IVR Script Name	Description
clid_col_dnis_3.tcl	Authenticates the caller ID three times, first with DNIS; if unsuccessful, attempts to authenticate with the caller PIN up to three times.
clid_col_npw_3.tcl	Authenticates with NULL; if unsuccessful, attempts to authenticate using the caller PIN up to three times.
clid_4digits_npw_3.tcl	Authenticates with NULL; if unsuccessful, attempts to authenticate with the caller PIN up to three times using the 14-digit account number and password entered together.
clid_4digits_npw_3_cli.tcl	Authenticates the account number and PIN, respectively, using ANI and NULL. The length of digits allowed for the account number and password are configurable through the CLI. If authentication fails, allows the caller to retry. The retry number is also configured through the CLI.
clid_authen_col_npw_cli.tcl	Authenticates the account number and PIN, respectively, using ANI and NULL. If authentication fails, allows the caller to retry. The retry number is configured through the CLI. The account number and PIN are collected separately.
clid_authen_collect_cli.tcl	Authenticates the account number and PIN using ANI and DNIS. If authentication fails, allows the caller to retry. The retry number is configured through the CLI. The account number and PIN are collected separately.
clid_col_npw_3_cli.tcl	Authenticates using ANI and NULL for account and PIN, respectively. If authentication fails, allows the caller to retry. The retry number is configured through the CLI.

continues

Table 10-1   *TCL IVR Scripts (Continued)*

TCL IVR Script Name	Description
clid_col_npw_npw_cli.tcl	Authenticates using ANI and NULL for account and PIN, respectively. If authentication fails, allows the caller to retry. The retry number is configured through the CLI. The account number and PIN are collected together.
debitcard.tcl	Collects account ID and PIN with a single prompt.
debitcard_acct_pin.tcl	Requests the account and PIN with two separate prompts.

Cisco provides a set of professionally recorded audio prompts (IVR audio files) in several languages. New audio prompts are being developed on a continuous basis. Table 10-2 and Table 10-3 list some of the IVR audio files available as of Cisco IOS Release 12.1.

Table 10-2   *Number Audio File Set*

Audio File Name	Recorded Prompt	Audio File Name	Recorded Prompt
en_zero.au	Zero	en_fifteen.au	Fifteen
en_one.au	One	en_sixteen.au	Sixteen
en_two.au	Two	en_seventeen.au	Seventeen
en_three.au	Three	en_eighteen.au	Eighteen
en_four.au	Four	en_nineteen.au	Nineteen
en_five.au	Five	en_twenty.au	Twenty
en_six.au	Six	en_thirty.au	Thirty
en_seven.au	Seven	en_forty.au	Forty
en_eight.au	Eight	en_fifty.au	Fifty
en_nine.au	Nine	en_sixty.au	Sixty
en_ten.au	Ten	en_seventy.au	Seventy
en_eleven.au	Eleven	en_eighty.au	Eighty
en_twelve.au	Twelve	en_ninety.au	Ninety
en_thirteen.au	Thirteen	en_hundred.au	Hundred
en_fourteen.au	Fourteen	en_thousand.au	Thousand

Table 10-3 *Additional Miscellaneous Prompts*

Audio File Name	Recorded Prompt
en_second.au	Second
en_seconds.au	Seconds
en_minute.au	Minute
en_minutes.au	Minutes
en_hour.au	Hour
en_hours.au	Hours
en_cent.au	Cent
en_cents.au	Cents
en_dollar.au	Dollar
en_dollars.au	Dollars
en_welcome.au	"Welcome to Cisco Debit Card Demo."
en_lang_select.au	"Please press 1 for English, 2 for Mandarin."
en_wrong_lang_sel.au	"You have made an invalid selection. Please press 1 for English or press 2 for Mandarin."
en_no_lang_sel.au	"You did not select any language. Press 1 for English or press 2 for Mandarin."
en_final.au	"We are having difficulties connecting your call. Please try again later."
en_generic_final.au	"Please hang up and try again."
en_enter_card_num.au	"Please enter card number followed by pound."
en_invalid_digits.au	"You have entered an invalid number of digits. Please reenter your card number followed by pound."
en_auth_fail.au	"You have entered an invalid card number. Please reenter your card number followed by pound."
en_no_card_entered.au	"You did not enter any digits. Please enter card number followed by pound."
en_technical_problem.au	"We are having technical difficulties. Please call back later."
en_zero_bal.au	"You have zero balance. Please call the operator or hang up."
en_enter_dest.au	"Please enter destination number."
en_disconnect.au	"Your call will be disconnected."
en_disconnected.au	"You have been disconnected."

continues

Table 10-3 *Additional Miscellaneous Prompts (Continued)*

Audio File Name	Recorded Prompt
en_dest_collect_fail.au	"Sorry, the number you have dialed is blocked. If you feel you have reached a number in error, please call the customer service number."
en_invalid_amt.au	"You have more than one million."
en_dest_busy.au	"The party you called is busy. Please enter a new number or hang up and try again later."
en_enter_acct.au	"Please enter your account number followed by the pound key."
en_no_acct_entered.au	"We did not get any input. Please enter your account number followed by the pound key."
en_invalid_digits_acct.au	"You have entered an invalid number of digits. Please enter your account number followed by the pound key."
en_invalid_account.au	"You have entered an invalid account number. Please enter your account number followed by the pound key."
en_enter_pin.au	"Please enter your PIN number followed by the pound key."
en_no_pin_entered.au	"We did not get any input. Please enter your PIN number followed by the pound key."
en_invalid_digits_pin.au	"You have entered an invalid number of digits. Please enter your PIN number followed by the pound key."
en_invalid_pin.au	"You have entered an invalid PIN. Please enter your pin number followed by the pound key."
en_card_expired.au	"We're sorry, your card has expired."
en_account_blocked.au	"This account is currently in use."
en_no_dest_entered.au	"We did not get any input. Please enter the destination number you are calling."
en_no_dialpeer_match.au	"You have entered an invalid destination. Please reenter the destination number you are calling."
en_connect_cust_ser.au	"You will be connected to Customer Service."
en_dial_cust_ser.au	"Please hang up and dial the calling card customer service number."
en_no_service.au	"We're sorry, this service is not available."
en_dest_unreachable.au	"We're sorry, the destination you have called is unreachable."
en_toll_free.au	"You can only make toll-free calls."

You can find TCLWare (TCL scripts) and audio files at the following URL:

http://www.cisco.com/cgi-bin/tablebuild.pl/tclware

AAA and RADIUS

The debit card application uses AAA security services as the infrastructure with which to provide authentication and accounting services. AAA is an architectural framework for configuring a set of three independent functions: authentication, authorization, and accounting. Authentication is the way a user is identified prior to being allowed access to services. Authorization provides a method for remote access control. Accounting provides a method for collecting and sending security server information used for billing, auditing, and reporting data such as user identities and start and stop times.

Typically, AAA works in tandem with a remote security server such as RADIUS. RADIUS uses IETF-standard, vendor-specific, and vendor-proprietary attributes to define specific AAA elements in a user profile that's stored on the RADIUS database. RADIUS and AAA authenticate, authorize, and perform accounting functions by associating attribute/value (AV) pairs with the appropriate user. For internally managed prepaid services, AAA works in tandem with IVR to enable voice gateways to interact with a RADIUS security server to authenticate users (typically incoming calls) and to perform accounting services.

Authentication

The gateway normally uses AAA in conjunction with IVR to check the legitimacy of a prospective gateway user based on an account number collected by IVR, or based on automatic number identification (ANI). When the gateway uses AAA with IVR, the IVR application collects the user account and PIN information and then passes it to the AAA interface. The AAA interface makes a RADIUS authentication request with the given information, and, based on the information received from the RADIUS server, forwards either a pass or a fail message to the IVR application.

Accounting

The RADIUS server collects basic start-stop connection accounting data during the accounting process for each call leg created on the gateway. The RADIUS server can be configured to collect accounting data using one of the following two methods:

- **Start-stop**—The RADIUS server collects a call-start record and a call-stop record for each call leg, producing a total of eight records for each call.

- **Stop-only**—The RADIUS server collects a call-stop record for each call leg, producing a total of four call records for each call.

The various call leg start and stop records generated by the gateway can be organized by their *Connection ID*, which is the same for all call legs of a connection. The Connection ID is a 128-bit field displayed in hexadecimal format that can vary in appearance. In the examples cited in this chapter, the Connection ID is of the form 3C5AEAB9 95C80008 0 587F34 (one 4-octet string, a space, one 4-octet string, a space, a zero, a space, and one 3-octet string). The billing application uses the Connection ID to generate all of the information needed for accurate and timely billing.

Start records by definition can't contain the time connection details required for billing by time; these details are contained in the stop records. (All RADIUS billing information pertaining to the call is contained in the stop records.) However, some deployments choose to use start-stop records so that they will know when a call was terminated abnormally and thus has no stop record. Start records, in conjunction with update records, provide a more accurate and deterministic real-time measurement technique for identifying when a call started, or in case packets get lost. Stop-only accounting records are configured if RADIUS network traffic or storage needs are an issue.

Update records can be obtained from Cisco routers by using the **aaa accounting update** global configuration command.

Call Detail Records

For debit card networks, the voice gateways can send accounting data in the form of call detail records (CDRs) to the RADIUS server in one of two ways:

- Using the overloaded Acct-Session-ID RADIUS attribute
- Using vendor-specific RADIUS attributes

After sending a CDR, if the gateway doesn't receive a response from the RADIUS server within a certain period of time, it will produce duplicate CDRs and deliver them to the RADIUS server. This can happen when the gateway doesn't receive a timely response from the RADIUS server acknowledging receipt of the original record. The only difference in these duplicate CDRs is in the AV pair Acct-Delay-Time (attribute 41). The first value for Acct-Delay-Time is 0; when duplicate records are created, the Acct-Delay-Time value is incremented in each subsequent record. All other fields in the duplicate CDRs remain the same. The particular billing application is responsible for discarding these duplicate records.

Overloaded Acct-Session-ID

To take advantage of standard RADIUS implementations that don't support VSAs, the unsupported information is embedded in the IETF-standard RADIUS attribute 44, the Acct-Session-ID. The Acct-Session-ID field has a maximum length of 256 characters and is defined to contain ten fields, separated by slashes. One of these fields is the Connection

ID. The overloaded *Acct-Session-ID* field also contains connect and disconnect times, remote IP address, and disconnect cause. The following string format is used for the *Acct-Session-ID* field to support the additional fields:

```
<session id>/<call leg setup time>/<gateway id>/<connection id>/<call origin>/
<call type>/<connect time>/<disconnect time>/<disconnect cause>/
<remote ip address>
```

Table 10-4 describes the fields in the *Acct-Session-ID* attribute.

Table 10-4   *Overloaded* Acct-Session-ID *Field Descriptions*

Field	Description
Session ID	The standard (RFC 2139) RADIUS *account-session-id*.
Call leg setup time	The Q.931 setup time for this connection in NTP format.
Gateway ID	The name of the underlying gateway; the name string is in the form of gateway.domain_name.
Connection ID	A unique global identifier used to correlate call legs that belong to the same end-to-end call. The field consists of four long words (128 bits). Each long word is displayed in hexadecimal and separated by a space character.
Call origin	Indicates the origin of the call relative to the gateway; possible values are originate and answer.
Call type	Indicates call leg type; possible values are Telephony and VoIP.
Connect time	The Q.931 connect time for this call leg in NTP format (stop packets only).
Disconnect time	The Q.931 disconnect time for this call leg in NTP format (stop packets only).
Disconnect cause	Documented in Q.931 specification; valid range is from 1 to 160 (stop packets only).
Remote IP address	IP address of the remote gateway used in this connection (stop packets only).

NOTE   The last four attributes (connect time, disconnect time, disconnect cause, and remote IP address) packed in the overloaded *Acct-Session-ID* listed previously are available only in stop packets. In start packets and update packets, these fields are blank.

Vendor-Specific Attributes (VSAs)

VSAs are defined as Attribute 26 of the IETF standard group of attribute/value (AV) pairs. For the RADIUS server to receive accounting information from the gateway using attribute 26, configure the gateway to recognize RADIUS VSAs. After you configure the gateway to recognize VSAs, the RADIUS server will no longer overload the *Acct-Session-ID* attribute. Instead, the information elements in the overloaded *Acct-Session-ID* attribute will be captured in separate VSAs.

The following example shows the value string for a typical VSA:

```
Attribute 26 23 0000000967146833
```

In this example:

- Attribute 26 indicates a VSA.

- The value 23 represents the length in bytes.

- The next value is broken into three parts:

  — For the first four octets, **00000009**, the high-order octet is 0. The three low-order octets are the assigned vendor network management private enterprise code as defined in RFC 1700 (Cisco Systems' assigned vendor code is 9).

  — The next octet, **67**, represents the VSA attribute number in hex (hex 67 = attribute 103 or return code).

  — The last three octets, **146833**, are vendor configurable.

Table 10-5 and Table 10-6 list the information the voice gateway sends to the RADIUS server and the information the RADIUS server sends to the voice gateway. Table 10-7 lists the RADIUS codes that identify what kind of packet RADIUS is sending. Table 10-8 lists RADIUS return codes, which you can define by using TCL IVR scripts as long as the RADIUS server is configured to understand what response or return message is required.

Table 10-5   *VSAs Sent from the Voice Gateway to the RADIUS Server*

VSA Name	VSA No.	Sample	Purpose	RADIUS Codes
Gateway ID	22	bowie.cisco.com	Name of the gateway emitting the message	1 and 4
Remote Gateway ID	23	172.16.17.128	Address of remote gateway	4—stop record
Connection ID	24	3C5AEB9 95C80008 0 58F7F34	Unique call identifier, four long words (128 bits), space separated; used to associate CDRs from all call legs	4—start and stop record
Setup Time	25	18:27:28.032 UTC Wed Dec 9 1998	Q.931 setup time in NTP format	4—stop record
Connect Time	26	18:27:30.094 UTC Wed Dec 9 1998	Q.931 connect time in NTP format	4—stop record

Table 10-5   *VSAs Sent from the Voice Gateway to the RADIUS Server (Continued)*

VSA Name	VSA No.	Sample	Purpose	RADIUS Codes
Disconnect Time	27	18:27:49.095 UTC Wed Dec 9 1998	Q.931 disconnect time in NTP format	4—stop record
Disconnect Cause	28	27 in dec.1B in hex	Q.931 disconnect cause	4—stop record
Call Origin	29	answer	Indicates origin of call relative to gateway (answer or originate)	4—start and stop record
Call Type	30	VoIP	Call leg type (VoIP or POTS)	4—start and stop record
Voice Quality	31	25	Value representing ICPIF (expectation factor, IT G.113) calculation of voice quality	4—stop record
IVR out AVpair	32	color=stardust	User-definable AV pairs to be sent from voice gateway to RADIUS server.	1 and 4

Table 10-6   *VSAs Sent to the Voice Gateway from the RADIUS Server*

VSA Name	VSA No.	Sample	Purpose	RADIUS Codes
IVRin Avpair	100	Bowie=from_mars	User-definable AV pairs to be sent from RADIUS server to voice gateway	2, 3, 5
Amount Balance	101	123.45	Currency or unit balance remaining in user's account (based on UID and OIN)	2

continues

Table 10-6   *VSAs Sent to the Voice Gateway from the RADIUS Server (Continued)*

VSA Name	VSA No.	Sample	Purpose	RADIUS Codes
Time Balance	102	16345	Seconds remaining based on called number (DNIS) and user balance; translates to hold time for the call	2
Return Code	103	51	Conveys action to take (re-prompt for UID, etc.) as listed in Table 10-7	2, 3, 5
Prompt ID	104	10	An index into an array of prompts known to the IVR script; can be used with Return code (103) to indicate how/when to play out	2, 3, 5
Time of Day	105	22:10:31	Time of day at called number	2
Redirect Number	106	4085551212	Provide phone number for caller redirect; can be used with return code, in failure conditions, etc.	2, 3
Preferred Language	107	en	ISO language indication to inform caller's language of preference	2, 3
Redirect IP Address	108	172.16.243.15	IP address of terminating gateway (can be used with Return code)	2, 3

Table 10-7 *RADIUS Codes*

Code	Meaning
1	Access-Request
2	Access-Accept
3	Access-Reject
4	Accounting-Request
5	Accounting-Response
11	Access-Challenge
12	Status-Server (experimental)
13	Status-Client (experimental)
255	Reserved

Table 10-8 *RADIUS Return Codes*

Code	Meaning
0	Success, proceed
1	Failed—Invalid Account number
2	Failed—Invalid Password
3	Failed—Account in use
4	Failed—Zero balance
5	Failed—Card expired
6	Failed—Credit limit
7	Failed—User denied
8	Failed—Service not available
9	Failed—Called number blocked
10	Failed—Number of retries exceeded
11	Failed—Invalid argument
12	Failed—Insufficient funds
13	Toll-Free call
14	Failed—Invalid card number
50	Redirect—Call will be hairpinned back to PSTN network
51	Redirect to Called party (use redirect number)
52	Redirect to Customer Service (use redirect number)
53	Connect IP leg to Redirect IP Address (108)

Debit Card Application Functional Call Flow

The following step list describes a high-level call flow sequence for a debit card application. The actual call flow varies, depending on the parameters passed to the application and on the features that are available on the RADIUS billing system that's being used. Figures 10-1a through 10-1e provide a detailed flow diagram of this process.

Step 1　A customer calls the access number of the ITSP or other company offering the service. The application begins with a welcome message (Figure 10-1a).

Step 2　If you've configured the application for multiple languages, the customer is prompted to select a preferred language (Figure 10-1a).

Step 3　After selecting the preferred language, the customer is prompted for his or her account number (Figure 10-1b). The account number is the combination of the user identification number (UID) and PIN. This entry must have the same number of digits as configured in the gateway call application parameters. If the account number is the proper length and is a valid account number, the customer is authorized.

Step 4　After successful completion of this first authorization phase, the prompt returns the amount of credit available in the customer's account (Figure 10-1d).

Step 5　The next prompt asks for a destination number. A second authorization phase then occurs, authorizing a call to the number entered (Figure 10-1d).

Step 6　If authorized, the prompt returns the amount of time left in the customer's account for a call to that destination (Figure 10-1e).

Step 7　The call is completed when a caller hangs up. If instead, the caller presses and holds the pound (#) button on the telephone keypad for more than one second, the authorization process begins again at the second authorization phase.

Step 8　The prompt returns a new credit amount to the caller and the call to the new destination begins. If customers do not disconnect, they can make repeated calls without having to repeat first-phase authentication.

Step 9　If, at any time during a call, the credit amount left in the customer's account reaches the preconfigured warning amount (typically, one minute of service left), a warning prompt is played (Figure 10-1e).

Step 10　If a caller continues to talk until all the time is consumed, a disconnect message is played (Figure 10-1e).

Figure 10-1a   *Debit card application call flow.*

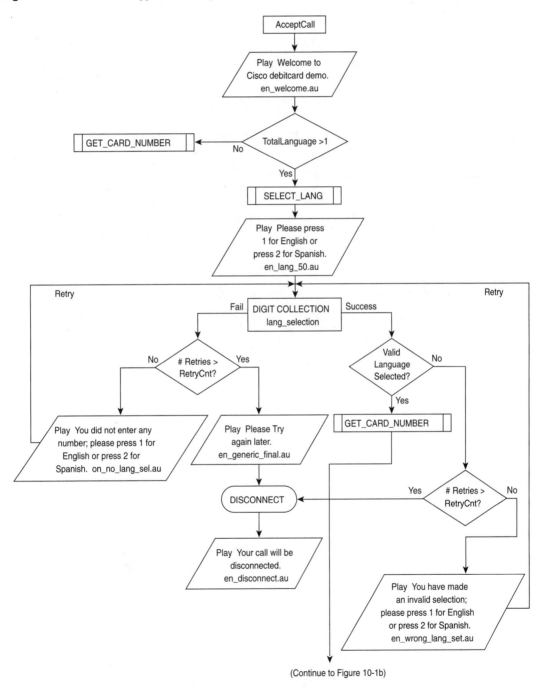

(Continue to Figure 10-1b)

Figure 10-1b   *Debit card application call flow.*

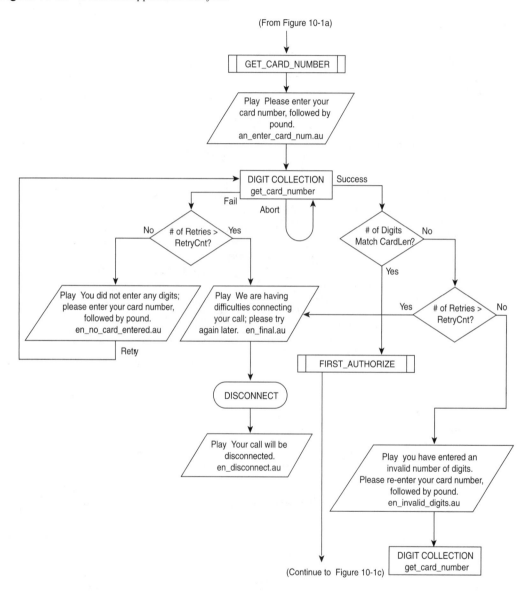

Figure 10-1c   *Debit card application call flow.*

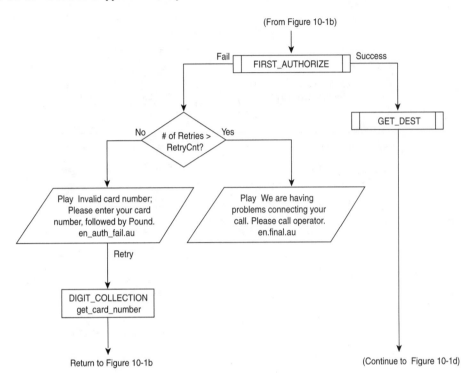

Figure 10-1d *Debit card application call flow.*

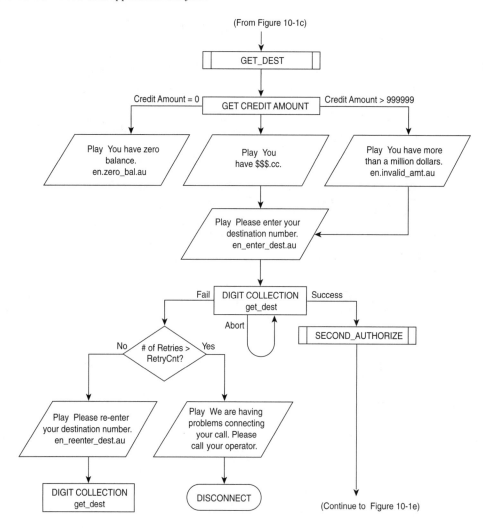

Figure 10-1e   *Debit card application call flow.*

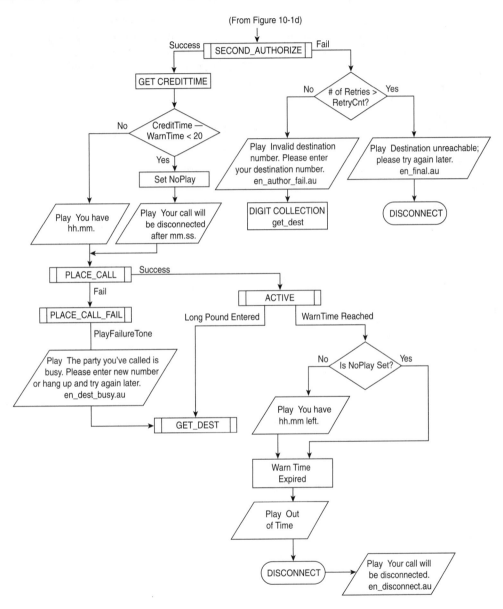

Architecture for Internally Managed Prepaid Services

The architecture for a network designed to manage prepaid services from within its own infrastructure can vary depending on the relative locations of the voice gateways. Figure 10-2 illustrates an architectural model in which the FTP/TFTP servers are local to the gateways and the RADIUS server is centralized. Both FTP/TFTP and RADIUS servers can be centralized or geographically dispersed, depending on the nature of the packet telephony network involved.

Figure 10-2   *Internally managed prepaid services network topology.*

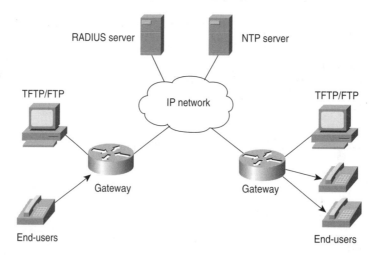

The billing and accounting components of prepaid services consist of VoIP gateways, TCL IVR scripts, audio files, a TFTP server, and an integrated third-party, RADIUS-based billing system.

Hardware and Software Requirements

This section covers the following:

- Network devices
- System platform requirements
- Cisco IOS software and VCWare requirements
- Memory

Network Devices

Given the network topology shown in Figure 10-2, you need the following devices to support internally managed prepaid services:

- **Gateways**—The debit card application operates on Cisco VoIP H.323 gateways, including the Cisco AS5300 universal access servers and the Cisco 2600 series, 3620, and 3640 routers.

- **RADIUS server**—A standard RADIUS server performs the back-end billing process. This server must be enabled to parse and understand VSAs and must be able to respond with the required VSAs, RADIUS codes, and RADIUS return codes. For smaller-scale deployments, the RADIUS and TFTP servers can be on the same device.

- **TFTP/FTP server**—This server stores the audio files and TCL script files necessary to operate the debit card application. The TCL IVR scripts and audio files prompt the user for information such as account number or destination number, and return values such as time or money remaining on the card. Approximately 175 audio files exist.

- **NTP server**—This server has a stratum-1 or stratum-2 clock. All of the devices in the network must synchronize their clocks to the NTP server to ensure accurate and consistent accounting records.

System Platform Requirements

The IVR and debit card applications are supported on the following Cisco platforms:

- Cisco AS5300 universal access servers
- Cisco 3620, 3640, 3660 routers
- Cisco 2600 series routers

Cisco IOS Software and VCWare Requirements

To support prepaid services, the Cisco devices in your network must have the following versions of Cisco IOS software and VCWare installed:

- Cisco IOS Release 12.1 or higher
- VCWare Version 4.10

NOTE   Various versions of VCWare and DSPWare are required to complement different versions of Cisco IOS software. For complete information, please consult the compatibility matrix at http://www.cisco.com/univercd/cc/td/doc/product/access/acs_serv/5300/iosrn/ioscm/vcwrmtrx.htm.

Memory

To support prepaid services, the Cisco devices in your network must have the following minimum memory installed:

- 16 MB Flash memory
- 64 MB DRAM memory

Loading TCL IVR Scripts and Storing Sound Files

With a Cisco.com password, you can download the most recent TCL IVR scripts and audio files from the following URL:

http://www.cisco.com/cgi-bin/tablebuild.pl/tclware

After you've downloaded the scripts and audio files, you need to load them onto the TFTP server so that they'll be available for the voice gateway. When you unzip the TCLWare bundle into the /tftpboot directory of the TFTP server, the various TCL and audio files will be positioned in the recommended subdirectory hierarchy. Table 10-9 gives the recommended directory structure.

Table 10-9 *TCL Script and Audio File Directory Structure*

Directory	Contents
/tftpboot/tcl	TCL IIVR scripts
/tftpboot/au/en	English language prompts and audio files
/tftpboot/au/ch	Chinese language prompts and audio files

After you've downloaded the TCL IVR scripts and audio files into the appropriate subdirectories on the TFTP server, you are ready to configure your voice gateway to support prepaid services.

Prepaid Services Configuration Guidelines

This section offers general guidelines on how to configure a typical voice gateway to support prepaid services. The following tasks must be completed:

- Load Call Application Script
- Configure Call Application Parameters
- Configure Dial Peers
- Configure AAA
- Configure RADIUS and VSA Parameters
- Configure Network Time Protocol

Load Call Application Script

Example 10-1 shows how the TCL script is loaded into DRAM on the voice gateway.

Example 10-1 *Loading the TCL Script*

```
pmeas1(config)# call application voice debit tftp://george/tcl/debitcard.tcl
Loading tcl/debitcard.tcl from 10.19.21.101 (via Ethernet0): !!!!
[OK--16098/31744 bytes]
```

The command in Example 10-1 instructs the gateway to load the TCL call application script **debitcard.tcl** from the */tftpboot/ tcl* subdirectory on the machine *george* and refer to it with the tag **debit**. The debit card application will then be available for association with an incoming dial peer and its corresponding destination number. When a user calls the number configured on that dial peer in the originating gateway, the debit card application is activated. After the application is loaded, it's available in the gateway and remains available until you enter the **no** form of the command or reboot the gateway. If the gateway is rebooted, the debitcard.tcl file will be loaded automatically.

You must receive successful feedback when loading the TCL script. If the application fails to load properly, it won't function and the entire debit card procedure will fail. Failure to load the debit card script is indicated by negative feedback that resembles the following:

```
pmeas1(config)# call application voice debit tftp://george/tcl/debitcard.tcl
%Error opening tftp://george/tcl/derbitcard.tcl (Timed out)
Sep 30 09:41:00.565 UTC: %IVR-3-NOSCRIPT: Could not open IVR script
tftp://george/tcl/derbitcard.tcl
errno=66568=
```

If you receive an error message similar to the previous one while trying to load the application, you must remedy that situation before you continue.

Example 10-2 shows how to fix a failed call application load.

Example 10-2 *Fixing a Failed TCL Script Load*

```
pmeas1(config)# show running-config
-----------output suppressed----------------
clock timezone PST -7
ip subnet-zero
no ip domain-lookup
ip domain-name cisco.com
ip name-server 192.168.8.69
ip name-server 192.168.0.21
!
cns event-service server
call application voice debit tftp://george/tcl/derbitcard.tcl
-----------output suppressed----------------
pmeas01(config)#
pmeas01(config)#call app voice debit tftp://george/tcl/debitcard.tcl
                                    ^
% Invalid input detected at '^' marker.
pmeas01(config)#
```

continues

Example 10-2 *Fixing a Failed TCL Script Load (Continued)*

```
pmeas01(config)# no call application voice debit
Deleting TCL IVR App: debit with url
tftp://george/tcl/debitcard.tcl
pmeas01(config)#
pmeas01(config)# call app voice debit tftp://george/tcl/debitcard.tcl
Loading tcl/debitcard.tcl from 10.19.21.101 (via FastEthernet0): !!!!
[OK-16098/31744 bytes]
```

To fix a failed call application load, you must first remove the failed script. In Example 10-2, the script that failed to load properly is still displayed in the **show running-config** command output. If you try to reload the application script with the same tag (debit) before removing the failed script, you'll be unsuccessful. In this example, the first attempt to reload the script is unsuccessful because the failed script wasn't removed. The output indicates that the keyword **debit** is still in use.

Scripts can fail to load for various reasons, but the most common reason is that there's a problem reaching the application file. Make sure you can manually reach the directory path (by Telneting from the voice gateway) in which the application is located.

Configure Call Application Parameters

At this point, a call to 555-1200 would return the built-in IVR response, "No prompts available." The TCL call application script begins the IVR process, but because no configuration parameters detail the location of the audio files, it defaults to the embedded audio file *noPromptPrompt*, as illustrated in the following output from the **debug voip ivr all** EXEC command:

```
4w1d: $ $ta_PromptCmd() url=Tcl_GetVar2() [flash:enter_account.au]
4w1d: $ $ta_PromptCmd() Get prompt url=[flash:enter_account.au] name=[enter_acco
unt.au]
4w1d: $ $ta_PromptCmd() >>mc_createFromFileUrl
4w1d: $ $mc_createFromFileUrl (url:[flash:enter_account.au], name:[enter_account
.au]):::
4w1d: mc_load can not open flash:enter_account.au. errno=2=No such file or direc
tory
4w1d: mc_load can not open flash:enter_account.au. errno=2=No such file or direc
tory
4w1d: $ $mc_createFromFileUrl(name[enter_account.au]) load failed.
4w1d: $ $mc_createFromFileUrl(url[flash:enter_account.au]) load failed.
4w1d: $ $mc_delete()::
4w1d: $ $ta_PromptCmd() pArgs->content = 61D15750 noPromptPrompt;
4w1d: $ $ta_PromptCmd() >> ccGetApp(pcapp)
```

The call application parameters are contained in the configuration commands that govern the authentication parameters and location of the audio files. Example 10-3 configures the user ID (UID) and PIN lengths of the account number, and the location of the sets of language sound files used in the IVR scripts. This configuration is necessary only on originating gateways.

Example 10-3 *Configuring Call Application Parameters*

```
pmeas01(config)# call application voice debit uid-len 10
pmeas01(config)# call application voice debit pin-len 4
pmeas01(config)# call application voice debit language 1 en
Please make sure to use the corresponding set-location command
pmeas01(config)# call application voice debit set-location en 0 tftp:
    //george/au/en/
pmeas01(config)# call application voice debit language 2 ch
Please make sure to use the corresponding set-location command
pmeas01(config)# call application voice debit set-location ch 0 tftp:
    //george/au/ch/
```

The first two commands in Example 10-3 configure the length of the UID and the PIN. The lengths for the PIN and UID appear in the configuration output only if they are different from the default values.

The last four commands deal with labeling and storing the audio files. The **language 1 en** and **set-location en** lines go together in a pair in addition to the **language 2 ch** and **set-location ch** lines, as mentioned in the feedback from the session output.

In Example 10-3, **language 1 en** references the choice of language (in this case, English) and **set-location en** defines the machine or path where the files can be found. The number tag corresponds to the number that the IVR prompt will request ("Please press 1 for English.").

When a call is placed to the gateway, IVR looks in the audio file directory that was configured for the beginning IVR messages (en_welcome.au, en_lang_sel1.au, and ch_lang_sel2.au). These three messages play the welcome message in English and the "select language" message in English and then Mandarin. Because these files have to play to initiate the IVR process, they must be located in both language directories. In this case, because the **set-location** command for the Mandarin audio files was entered last, (the **call application voice debit set-location ch 0 tftp://george/au/ch/** command), the TCL application looks in the Chinese audio file subdirectory for the welcome message and the select language option messages. Placing a call to the gateway with the **debug voip ivr all** EXEC command enabled produces the output in Example 10-4, confirming the expected behavior. Important items are in boldface for emphasis.

Example 10-4 *Output Produced with the **debug voip ivr all** Command Enabled*

```
4d11h: App debit: Handling callID 58
4d11h: callingNumber=408, calledNumber=5710961, redirectNumber=
4d11h: accountNumber=, finalDestFlag=0,
guid=86db.7ca8.8c6c.0096.0000.0000.1729.90ac
4d11h: peer_tag=1
4d11h: settlement_validate_token: cid(58), target=, tokenp=0x0
4d11h: :/acceptCall/
```

continues

Example 10-4 *Output Produced with the **debug voip ivr all** Command Enabled (Continued)*

```
4d11h: Accepting CallID=58
4d11h: :/getVariable/
4d11h: :/setVariable/
4d11h: ta_SetVariableCmd. language type set to 1
4d11h: :/getVariable/
4d11h: :/setVariable/
4d11h: ta_SetVariableCmd. language type set to 2
4d11h: :/getVariable/
4d11h: :/setVariable/
4d11h: ta_SetVariableCmd. long pound enabled
4d11h: :[callID]
4d11h: :/puts/
4d11h: cid( 58) app running state select_language
4d11h: ta_PlayPromptCmd() 4d11h
4d11h: ta_PlayPromptCmd. CallID=58
4d11h: $ $pc_mc_makeDynamicS() calloc mcDynamicS_t
4d11h: $ $mc_createFromFileUrl (url:[tftp://george/au/ch/en_welcome.au], name:
[en_welcome.au])::
4d11h: $ $mc_getFromUrlName() en_welcome.au on ram mc_waitq_delete: mc=619219A4
mc_waitq_unlink: elm=61D88ECC
mc_waitq_unlink: prompt_free=2D2F4 prompt_active=0
mc_waitq_delete: prompt_free=2D2F4 prompt_active=6584
4d11h: $ $du_get_vpPromptName() OK###
4d11h: $ $du_mcDynamicS_silence() ms_int 1000 postSilence 1000
4d11h: $ $mc_createFromFileUrl (url:[tftp://george/au/ch/en_lang_sel1.au], nam
e:[en_lang_sel1.au])::
4d11h: $ $mc_getFromUrlName() en_lang_sel1.au on ram mc_waitq_delete: mc=61D8EFA 8
mc_waitq_unlink: elm=61DA3090
mc_waitq_unlink: prompt_free=291A8 prompt_active=6584
mc_waitq_delete: prompt_free=291A8 prompt_active=A6D0
4d11h: $ $du_get_vpPromptName() OK###
4d11h: $ $du_mcDynamicS_silence() ms_int 1000 postSilence 1000
4d11h: $ $mc_createFromFileUrl (url:[tftp://george/au/ch/ch_lang_sel2.au],
name: [ch_lang_sel2.au])::
4d11h: $ $mc_getFromUrlName() ch_lang_sel2.au on ram mc_waitq_delete: mc=61D8F07
0
mc_waitq_unlink: elm=61CD1EA0
mc_waitq_unlink: prompt_free=2537C prompt_active=A6D0
mc_waitq_delete: prompt_free=2537C prompt_active=E4FC
```

The debug output in Example 10-4 indicates that the IVR application is looking in the
Chinese language subdirectory of the TFTP server for the English language audio files.
This scenario is the proper behavior and the preceding output is derived from a successful
call.

After the IVR variables are correctly configured, the next step is to associate the debit card
application with an incoming POTS dial peer.

Configure Dial Peers

The debit card TCL application is initiated dynamically by reference to a POTS dial peer in the originating voice gateway. By matching a certain dialed number to a POTS dial peer, the debit card application begins a TCL application referenced in the dial peer. Example 10-5 shows a POTS dial peer configured for the originating gateway.

Example 10-5 *Configuring a POTS Dial Peer on the Originating Gateway*

```
dial-peer voice 555 pots
  destination-pattern 5551200
  application debit
  port 0:D
```

In Example 10-5, if a user called the number 555-1200, it would match the configured POTS dial peer and activate the TCL application with the tag **debit**, provided that the application exists and is reachable according to the application access commands configured in the gateway. The name **debit** is a tag given to the actual TCL script (debitcard.tcl) stored on the TFTP server.

The debitcard.tcl script is listed in its entirety in Appendix C, "TCL IVR Scripts." You can display all the TCL scripts available in a gateway with the following **show** command:

```
pmeas11# show call application voice summary
name                description
session             Basic app to do DID, or supply dialtone.
fax_hop_on          Script to talk to a fax redialer
clid_authen         Authenticate with (ani, dnis)
clid_authen_        collect Authenticate with (ani, dnis), collect if that fails
clid_authen_npw     Authenticate with (ani, NULL)
clid_authen_col_npw Authenticate with (ani, NULL), collect if that fails
clid_col_npw_3      Authenticate with (ani, NULL), and 3 tries collecting
clid_col_npw_npw    Authenticate with (ani, NULL) and 3 tries without pw
SESSION             Default system session application
debit               tftp://george/tcl/debitcard.tcl
```

To display an application in its entirety, replace the **summary** keyword with the appropriate name of the application. For example, the **show call application voice debit** privileged EXEC command would display the debitcard.tcl script.

Example 10-6 shows a VoIP dial peer configured for the terminating gateway.

Example 10-6 *Configuring a Dial Peer on the Terminating Gateway*

```
dial-peer voice 514 voip
  destination-pattern 1514.......
  session target ipv4:10.10.12.23
dial-peer voice 213 voip
  destination-pattern 1213.......
  session target ipv4:10.20.120.14
```

VoIP dial peers associate a number dialed to a network destination—in this case, an IP address. The terminating gateway VoIP dial peer doesn't need to be associated with an application.

Configure AAA

In order for the debit card application to work with the RADIUS server to collect the appropriate connection accounting information, you must configure AAA on your voice gateways to support H.323 gateway-specific accounting. Example 10-7 configures AAA to use RADIUS on the gateways. The same configuration is used on both the originating and terminating gateways.

Example 10-7 *Configuring AAA*

```
aaa new-model
aaa authentication login h323 group radius
aaa authentication login NONE none
aaa authorization exec h323 group radius
aaa accounting connection h323 start-stop group radius
line con 0
 login authentication NONE
gw-accounting h323 vsa
```

In Example 10-7, AAA is enabled and a named list called **h323** defines that RADIUS should be used to provide authentication, authorization, and accounting. The named list **NONE** enables network administrators to log in to the console port and bypass authentication. CDRs will be delivered to the RADIUS server using the VSA method.

Configure RADIUS and VSA Parameters

In Example 10-8, both the originating and terminating gateways are configured to support RADIUS. The same configuration is used on both gateways. (Note that you must enable AAA before you can configure any RADIUS parameters.)

Example 10-8 *Configuring RADIUS*

```
radius-server host 172.22.42.49 auth-port 1645 acct-port 1646
radius-server key testing123
radius-server vsa send accounting
radius-server vsa send authentication
```

In Example 10-8, the first command configures the IP address of the RADIUS server and the ports on which the gateway expects the RADIUS server to be listening. The authentication and accounting ports are the default ports for Cisco gateways. The second command configures the password used for authenticating the RADIUS server. The last two commands enable the use of VSAs for H.323 authentication and accounting.

Configure Network Time Protocol

You must configure Network Time Protocol (NTP) in order to pass time stamps that are synchronized between the gateways and servers. To instruct the gateway to synchronize its time-of-day clock with an NTP server, use the **ntp server** *ip-address* global configuration command. For test purposes, one of the gateways can act as the authoritative NTP server by issuing the **ntp master** global configuration command. Then other gateways can synchronize with the master by pointing to the master in their configurations with the **ntp server** *ip-address* global configuration command.

The clocks on Cisco routers, however, are typically stratum 8 clocks as opposed to stratum 1 and stratum 2 NTP servers. Stratum 8 clocks are not considered accurate enough to keep time for a production network.

Internally Managed Prepaid Services Call Example

The following sample debug output is from a successful prepaid services call. In this example, a pair of gateways is used to make a debit card call with a MindCTI RADIUS back-end billing system performing the AAA. This example shows the behavior and characteristics of the debit card application. Basic voice connectivity has been established, so this example doesn't verify the call control system. However, we've set some billing debug commands so that you can see how IVR and AAA operate. The following debug session is the output received for a successful call, then long pound, then another successful call.

Originating Gateway Debug Output

The following debug commands were activated on the originating gateway:

```
debug voip ivr all
debug radius
debug aaa authentication
debug aaa authorization
debug aaa accounting
```

In the following output, a call was placed through a PBX. The number that the PBX sends out is configurable—the PBX in this example was configured to send the area code for San Jose (408).

NOTE   In this debug output, pertinent information is in boldface. Added comments are in regular type, and unnecessary parts are deleted. Look for successful voice prompt loads, RADIUS authentication and authorization transactions, VSA output, and RADIUS return codes.

```
pmeas11#
1w6d: AAA: parse name=<no string> idb type=-1 tty=-1
1w6d: AAA/MEMORY: create_user (0x61BEFB38) user='408' ruser='5550961' port='' re
m_addr='408/5710961' authen_type=NONE service=H323_VSA priv=0
1w6d: AAA/ACCT/CONN: Found list "h323"
1w6d: AAA/ACCT/CONN/START User 408, Port , Location "unknown"
1w6d: AAA/ACCT/CONN/START User 408, Port ,refers to the AAA accounting list
in the gateway

task_id=81 start_time=939938654 timezone=PST service=connection protocol=h323
1w6d: AAA/ACCT: user 408, acct type 1 (397058159): Method=radius (radius)
1w6d: RADIUS: ustruct sharecount=2
1w6d: RADIUS: added cisco VSA 33 len 23 "h323-gw-id=sj7_pmeas11."
1w6d: RADIUS: added cisco VSA 24 len 41 "h323-conf-id=86DB7CA8 8C6C016E 0 466555
A0"
1w6d: RADIUS: added cisco VSA 26 len 23 "h323-call-origin=answer"
1w6d: RADIUS: added cisco VSA 27 len 24 "h323-call-type=Telephony"
1w6d: RADIUS: added cisco VSA 25 len 48 "h323-setup-time=14:03:46.180 PST Thu Oc
t 14 1999"
1w6d: App debit: Handling callID 142
1w6d: callingNumber=408,
```

In the following output, all the call setup variables are listed, both standard IETF RADIUS attributes and VSAs. The start record is for the answer telephony call leg (call leg 1). IVR is shown beginning next.

```
calledNumber=5710961, redirectNumber=
1w6d: accountNumber=, finalDestFlag=0,
guid=86db.7ca8.8c6c.016e.0000.0000.4665.55a0
1w6d: peer_tag=1
1w6d: RADIUS: Initial Transmit id 19 172.22.42.52:1646, Accounting-Request, len
278
1w6d: Attribute 4 6 AC162758
1w6d: Attribute 61 6 00000000
1w6d: Attribute 1 5 3430381E
1w6d: Attribute 30 9 35373130
1w6d: Attribute 31 5 34303828
1w6d: Attribute 40 6 00000001 start record
1w6d: Attribute 6 6 00000001
1w6d: Attribute 26 31 0000000921196833 h323-gw-id
1w6d: Attribute 26 49 00000009182B6833 h323-conf-id
1w6d: Attribute 26 31 000000091A196833 answer
1w6d: Attribute 26 32 000000091B1A6833 telephony
1w6d: Attribute 26 56 0000000919326833 setup time
1w6d: Attribute 44 10 30303030
1w6d: Attribute 41 6 00000000
```

In this output, we see that English is set as language number 1 and Chinese is set as language number 2.

```
1w6d: settlement_validate_token: cid(142), target=, tokenp=0x0
1w6d: :/acceptCall/
1w6d: Accepting CallID=142
1w6d: :/getVariable/
1w6d: :/setVariable/
1w6d: ta_SetVariableCmd. language type set to 1 English is set as language
number 1
1w6d: :/getVariable/
1w6d: :/setVariable/
1w6d: ta_SetVariableCmd. language type set to 2
```

The long-pound feature is enabled, which means that the user can press the pound key to make another call without having to be reauthenticated.

```
1w6d: :/getVariable/
1w6d: :/setVariable/
1w6d: ta_SetVariableCmd. long pound enabled
```

The welcome message is loaded from the */tftpboot/au/ch* subdirectory of the TFTP server and copied into RAM and played.

```
1w6d: :[callID]
1w6d: :/puts/
1w6d: cid( 142) app running state select_language
1w6d: ta_PlayPromptCmd() 1w6d
1w6d: ta_PlayPromptCmd. CallID=142
1w6d: $ $pc_mc_makeDynamicS() calloc mcDynamicS_t
1w6d: $ $mc_createFromFileUrl (url:[tftp://george/au/ch/en_welcome.au], name:[
en_welcome.au])::
```

The prompt, "Select 1 for English," is loaded and played.

```
1w6d: $ $mc_getFromUrlName() en_welcome.au on ram mc_waitq_delete: mc=619219A4
mc_waitq_unlink: elm=61CD27B0
mc_waitq_unlink: prompt_free=A433B prompt_active=0
mc_waitq_delete: prompt_free=A433B prompt_active=6584
1w6d: $ $du_get_vpPromptName() OK###
1w6d: $ $du_mcDynamicS_silence() ms_int 1000 postSilence 1000
1w6d: $ $mc_createFromFileUrl (url:[tftp://george/au/ch/en_lang_sel1.au], name
:[en_lang_sel1.au])::
```

The Chinese prompt, "Select 2 for Chinese," is loaded and played.

```
1w6d: $ $mc_getFromUrlName() en_lang_sel1.au on ram mc_waitq_delete: mc=61D8EFA8
mc_waitq_unlink: elm=61D82198
mc_waitq_unlink: prompt_free=A01EF prompt_active=6584
mc_waitq_delete: prompt_free=A01EF prompt_active=A6D0
1w6d: $ $du_get_vpPromptName() OK###
1w6d: $ $du_mcDynamicS_silence() ms_int 1000 postSilence 1000
1w6d: $ $mc_createFromFileUrl (url:[tftp://george/au/ch/ch_lang_sel2.au], name
:[ch_lang_sel2.au])::
```

After the language is chosen, IVR begins the authentication process by loading and playing the "Enter card number" prompt. Now that the IVR application knows that the chosen language is English, it goes to the */au/en* subdirectory for the files, as shown here:

```
1w6d: $ $mc_getFromUrlName() ch_lang_sel2.au on ram mc_waitq_delete: mc=61D8F070
-----------output suppressed----------------
1w6d: $ $pc_mc_makeDynamicS() calloc mcDynamicS_t
1w6d: $ $mc_createFromFileUrl (url:[tftp://george/au/en/en_enter_card_num.au],
name:[en_enter_card_num.au])::
1w6d: $ $mc_getFromUrlName() en_enter_card_num.au on ram mc_waitq_delete: mc=619
21618
```

The script returns a success upon matching the card number against the database, as shown here:

```
-----------output suppressed----------------
1w6d: pcapp CallID 142 returning PCAPP_MATCHED. string=0000701234
1w6d: $ $pcapp_finished() >>pcapp_return()
1w6d: $ $pcapp_finished() >>ms_delete()
```

The following RADIUS records concern the authentication phase of the call:

```
------------output suppressed---------------
1w6d: cid(142) ta_get_event returning collect success
1w6d: :[called]
1w6d: :/puts/
1w6d: cid( 142) app running state second_authorize
1w6d: :/ani/
1w6d: :[authorize]
1w6d: authorization
1w6d: account=000070 the account number is broken out into uid
1w6d: password=1234 and pin numbers
1w6d: destination= destination is blank because it has not yet been entered
1w6d: password=1234
1w6d: AAA: parse name=<no string> idb type=-1 tty=-1
1w6d: AAA/MEMORY: create_user (0x61C27260) user='000070' ruser='' port='' rem_ad
dr='408/5255233' authen_type=ASCII service=LOGIN priv=0
1w6d: unknown AAA/AUTHOR/EXEC (1758884971): Port='' list='h323' service=EXEC
1w6d: AAA/AUTHOR/EXEC: unknown (1758884971) user='000070'
1w6d: unknown AAA/AUTHOR/EXEC (1758884971): found list "h323"
1w6d: unknown AAA/AUTHOR/EXEC (1758884971): Method=radius (radius)
```

The call is assigned a conference ID. This number will be consistent through all legs of this call. It's used to identify records concerning the same call.

```
1w6d: RADIUS: authenticating to get author data
1w6d: RADIUS: ustruct sharecount=2
1w6d: RADIUS: added cisco VSA 24 len 41 "h323-conf-id=86DB7CA8 8C6C016E 0 466555
A0"
1w6d: RADIUS: Initial Transmit id 21 172.22.42.52:1645, Access-Request, len 121
1w6d: Attribute 4 6 AC162758
1w6d: Attribute 61 6 00000000
1w6d: Attribute 1 8 30303030
1w6d: Attribute 26 49 00000009182B6833
1w6d: Attribute 30 9 35323535
1w6d: Attribute 31 5 34303802
1w6d: Attribute 2 18 7B8D2364
1w6d: RADIUS: Received from id 21 172.22.42.52:1646, Access-Accept, len 76
```

The following RADIUS VSAs are received from the RADIUS server in response to the authentication request. The user's credit amount is kept in the RADIUS database and is accessed in real time at the time of the call. The **h323-credit-amount** will be played to the caller via the TCL IVR scripts. The script will build the amount $32.91 from (thirty) and (two) and (dollars) and (ninety) and (one) and (cents). The credit amount shows up as a minus so that credit spent on a call will be subtracted from the total until the credit amount reaches 0. Note that not all attributes returned are supported.

```
1w6d: Attribute 26 26 0000000967146833 h323-return-code
1w6d: Attribute 26 30 000000096B186833 h323-preferred-lang
1w6d: Attribute 26 33 00000009651B6833 h323-credit-amount
1w6d: Attribute 26 23 000000096D116269 unsupported VSA
1w6d: Attribute 26 25 000000096E136375 unsupported VSA
1w6d: RADIUS: saved authorization data for user 61C4C2D0 at 61C4C3E4
1w6d: RADIUS: cisco AVPair ":h323-return-code=0"
1w6d: RADIUS: cisco AVPair ":h323-preferred-lang=en"
1w6d: RADIUS: cisco AVPair ":h323-credit-amount=-32.91"
1w6d: RADIUS: unrecognized cisco VS option 109
1w6d: RADIUS: Bad attribute (unsupported attribute): type 26 len 23 data 0x9
1w6d: RADIUS: unrecognized cisco VS option 110
1w6d: RADIUS: Bad attribute (unsupported attribute): type 26 len 25 data 0x9
```

After passing authentication, the system prompts for the destination number, as shown here:

```
1w6d: AAA/AUTHOR (3803615862): Post authorization status = PASS_ADD
------------output suppressed----------------
1w6d: cid( 142) app running state get_dest
1w6d: :/getVariable/
1w6d: ta_PlayPromptCmd() 1w6d
1w6d: ta_PlayPromptCmd. CallID=142
1w6d: $ $du_get_vpPromptName() OK###
1w6d: $ $du_mcDynamicS_silence() ms_int 1000 postSilence 1000
1w6d: $ $mc_createFromFileUrl (url:[tftp://george/au/en/en_enter_dest.au], nam
e:[en_enter_dest.au])::
```

The "Enter destination" prompt is loaded and played and the user enters the destination number. The destination string entered is 555-5233.

```
1w6d: $ $mc_getFromUrlName() en_enter_dest.au on ram mc_waitq_delete: mc=61D9F56
0
------------much output suppressed----------------
1w6d: pcapp CallID 142 returning PCAPP_MATCHED. string=5555233
------------output suppressed----------------
1w6d: cid(142) ta_get_event returning collect success
1w6d: :[callID]
1w6d: :/puts/
1w6d: cid( 142) app running state second_authorize
1w6d: :/ani/
1w6d: :[authorize]
1w6d: authorization
```

Authorization is performed for the particular destination.

```
1w6d: account=000070
same UID and PIN as deserved in CDR for the first call.
1w6d: password=1234
1w6d: destination=5555233
```

Now the destination is added.

```
1w6d: AAA: parse name=<no string> idb type=-1 tty=-1
1w6d: AAA/MEMORY: create_user (0x61C27260) user='000070' ruser='' port='' rem_ad
dr='408/5555233' authen_type=ASCII service=LOGIN priv=0
1w6d: unknown AAA/AUTHOR/EXEC (1758884971): Port='' list='h323' service=EXEC
1w6d: AAA/AUTHOR/EXEC: unknown (1758884971) user='000070'
1w6d: unknown AAA/AUTHOR/EXEC (1758884971): found list "h323"
```

The AAA authorization list configured in the router is found. The user is authorized for a call to 555-5233 and returns time left for this destination to be 20,900 seconds (5 hours, 48 minutes, and 20 seconds).

```
1w6d: unknown AAA/AUTHOR/EXEC (1758884971): Method=radius (radius)
1w6d: RADIUS: authenticating to get author data
1w6d: RADIUS: ustruct sharecount=2
1w6d: RADIUS: added cisco VSA 24 len 41 "h323-conf-id=86DB7CA8 8C6C016E 0 466555
A0"
1w6d: RADIUS: Initial Transmit id 21 172.22.42.52:1645, Access-Request, len 121
1w6d: Attribute 4 6 AC162758
1w6d: Attribute 61 6 00000000
1w6d: Attribute 1 8 30303030
1w6d: Attribute 26 49 00000009182B6833
1w6d: Attribute 30 9 35323535
1w6d: Attribute 31 5 34303802
```

```
1w6d: Attribute 2 18 7B8D2364
1w6d: RADIUS: Received from id 21 172.22.42.52:1646, Access-Accept, len 76
1w6d: Attribute 26 26 0000000967146833
1w6d: Attribute 26 30 0000000966186833
1w6d: RADIUS: saved authorization data for user 61C27260 at 61C4C4E4
1w6d: RADIUS: cisco AVPair ":h323-return-code=0"
1w6d: RADIUS: cisco AVPair ":h323-credit-time=20900"
1w6d: AAA/AUTHOR (1758884971): Post authorization status = PASS_ADD
```

In the following output, the authorized user is prompted with the remaining time available
(5 hours and 48 minutes) for a call to the specified destination.

```
1w6d: ta_PlayPromptCmd. CallID=142
1w6d: $ $pc_mc_makeDynamicS() calloc mcDynamicS_t
1w6d: $ $mc_createFromFileUrl (url:[tftp://george/au/en/en_you_have.au], name:
[en_you_have.au])::
-----------output suppressed----------------
1w6d: $ $mc_createFromFileUrl (url:[tftp://george/au/en/en_five.au], name:[en_
five.au])::
-----------output suppressed----------------
1w6d: $ $mc_createFromFileUrl (url:[tftp://george/au/en/en_hours.au], name:[en
_hours.au])::
-----------output suppressed----------------
1w6d: $ $mc_createFromFileUrl (url:[tftp://george/au/en/en_and.au], name:[en_a
nd.au])::
-----------output suppressed----------------
1w6d: $ $mc_createFromFileUrl (url:[tftp://george/au/en/en_forty.au], name:[en
_forty.au])::
-----------output suppressed----------------
1w6d: $ $mc_createFromFileUrl (url:[tftp://george/au/en/en_eight.au], name:[en
_eight.au])::
-----------output suppressed----------------
1w6d: $ $mc_createFromFileUrl (url:[tftp://george/au/en/en_minutes.au], name:
[en_minutes.au])::
```

The following RADIUS output is the start packet, call leg 2, for the active call. The VSAs,
spelled out at the top of this section, deliver call details to the RADIUS server.

```
-----------output suppressed----------------
1w6d: Placing call for callID 142 to destination=5555233
1w6d: placecall CallID 142 got event CC_EV_CALL_HANDOFF
1w6d: Matched peers(1)
1w6d: placecall pc_setupPeer cid(142), destPat(5555233), matched(1), prefix(), p
eer(61C2BD34)
1w6d: placecall cid(142) state change PC_CS_INIT to PC_CS_CALL_SETTING
-----------output suppressed----------------
1w6d: RADIUS: ustruct sharecount=2
1w6d: RADIUS: added cisco VSA 33 len 23 "h323-gw-id=sj7_pmeas11."
1w6d: RADIUS: added cisco VSA 24 len 41 "h323-conf-id=86DB7CA8 8C6C016E 0 466555
A0"
1w6d: RADIUS: added cisco VSA 26 len 26 "h323-call-origin=originate"
1w6d: RADIUS: added cisco VSA 27 len 19 "h323-call-type=VoIP"
1w6d: RADIUS: added cisco VSA 25 len 48 "h323-setup-time=14:04:54.450 PST Thu Oc
t 14 1999"
1w6d: RADIUS: Initial Transmit id 22 172.22.42.52:1646, Accounting-Request, len
279
1w6d: Attribute 4 6 AC162758
1w6d: Attribute 61 6 00000000
1w6d: Attribute 1 8 30303030
1w6d: Attribute 30 9 35323535
1w6d: Attribute 31 5 34303828
1w6d: Attribute 40 6 00000001
1w6d: Attribute 6 6 00000001
```

```
1w6d: Attribute 26 31 0000000921196833
1w6d: Attribute 26 49 00000009182B6833
1w6d: Attribute 26 34 000000091A1C6833
1w6d: Attribute 26 27 000000091B156833
1w6d: Attribute 26 56 0000000919326833
1w6d: Attribute 44 10 30303030
1w6d: Attribute 41 6 00000000
1w6d: RADIUS: Received from id 22 172.22.42.52:1646, Accounting-response, len 46
1w6d: Attribute 26 26 0000000967146833
```

In the following output, the user presses the pound key 543 seconds (9 minutes and 3 seconds) into the call.

```
-----------output suppressed----------------
1w6d: cid(142) ta_get_event returning active
1w6d: :[callID]
1w6d: :/puts/
1w6d: cid( 142) app running state active
1w6d: :/startTimer/
1w6d: Wait for 21380 seconds Now the timer starts for the call
1w6d: cid(142) ta_get_event returning digit
1w6d: ta_StartTimerCmd(): ta_get_event [digit]
1w6d: :/startTimer/
1w6d: Wait for 20837 seconds the long pound is pressed 543 seconds into the call
1w6d: cid(142) ta_get_event returning longpound
1w6d: ta_StartTimerCmd(): ta_get_event [longpound]
```

The following is the stop record for the first call. Notice the conf-id for comparison. We know it's a stop record because it has connect-time, disconnect-time, and disconnect-cause (present only in stop records) and it is type "originate VoIP" (call leg 2).

```
-----------output suppressed----------------
1w6d: RADIUS: ustruct sharecount=1
1w6d: RADIUS: added cisco VSA 33 len 23 "h323-gw-id=sj7_pmeas11."
1w6d: RADIUS: added cisco VSA 24 len 41 "h323-conf-id=86DB7CA8 8C6C016E 0 466555A0"
1w6d: RADIUS: added cisco VSA 26 len 26 "h323-call-origin=originate"
1w6d: RADIUS: added cisco VSA 27 len 19 "h323-call-type=VoIP"
1w6d: RADIUS: added cisco VSA 25 len 48 "h323-setup-time=14:04:54.450 PST Thu Oc
t 14 1999"
1w6d: RADIUS: added cisco VSA 28 len 50 "h323-connect-time=14:05:02.260 PST Thu
Oct 14 1999"
1w6d: RADIUS: added cisco VSA 29 len 53 "h323-disconnect-time=14:05:34.740 PST T
hu Oct 14 1999"
1w6d: RADIUS: added cisco VSA 30 len 24 "h323-disconnect-cause=10"
1w6d: RADIUS: added cisco VSA 31 len 20 "h323-voice-quality=0"
1w6d: RADIUS: added cisco VSA 23 len 30 "h323-remote-address=10.10.1.15"
1w6d: :[callID]
1w6d: :/puts/
1w6d: cid( 142) app running state first_authorize
1w6d: :/ani/
1w6d: :[authorize]
1w6d: authorization
1w6d: account=000070
1w6d: password=1234
1w6d: destination=
```

In the following output, the next call is authorized. Notice that the conf-id is the same as with the first call. It is, in effect, the same session. A new credit amount is given and a new destination is prompted for. This call proceeds in the same manner as the previous one.

```
-----------output suppressed----------------
1w6d: AAA: parse name=<no string> idb type=-1 tty=-1
1w6d: AAA/MEMORY: create_user (0x61C67F20) user='000070' ruser='' port='' rem_ad
dr='408' authen_type=ASCII service=LOGIN priv=0
1w6d: unknown AAA/AUTHOR/EXEC (3696672751): Port='' list='h323' service=EXEC
1w6d: AAA/AUTHOR/EXEC: unknown (3696672751) user='000070'
1w6d: unknown AAA/AUTHOR/EXEC (3696672751): found list "h323"
1w6d: unknown AAA/AUTHOR/EXEC (3696672751): Method=radius (radius)
1w6d: RADIUS: authenticating to get author data
1w6d: RADIUS: ustruct sharecount=2
1w6d: RADIUS: added cisco VSA 24 len 41
"h323-conf-id=86DB7CA8 8C6C016E 0 466555A0"
-----------output suppressed----------------
1w6d: RADIUS: saved authorization data for user 61C67F20 at 620157E0
1w6d: RADIUS: cisco AVPair ":h323-return-code=0"
1w6d: RADIUS: cisco AVPair ":h323-preferred-lang=en"
1w6d: RADIUS: cisco AVPair ":h323-credit-amount=-33.75"
-----------output suppressed----------------

1w6d: $ $mc_createFromFileUrl (url:[tftp://george/au/en/en_enter_dest.au], nam
e:[en_enter_dest.au]):::
1w6d: $ $mc_getFromUrlName() en_enter_dest.au on ram mc_waitq_delete: mc=61D9F560
-----------output suppressed----------------
1w6d: prompt and collect app got callID 142
-----------output suppressed----------------
1w6d: $ $mc_make_packets_DQ()::
1w6d: $ $mc_make_packets_DQ() post pak silence = 1000
1w6d: $ $mc_make_packets_DQ() mc:61D9F560 name:en_enter_dest.au
1w6d: $ $mc_make_packets_DQ() count: 36 ##
-----------output suppressed----------------
1w6d: pcapp CallID 142 returning PCAPP_MATCHED. string=5554094
-----------output suppressed----------------
1w6d: cid(142) ta_get_event returning collect success
-----------output suppressed----------------
1w6d: RADIUS: added cisco VSA 33 len 23 "h323-gw-id=sj7_pmeas11."
1w6d: RADIUS: added cisco VSA 24 len 41 "h323-conf-id=86DB7CA8 8C6C016E 0 466555
A0"
1w6d: RADIUS: added cisco VSA 26 len 26 "h323-call-origin=originate"
1w6d: RADIUS: added cisco VSA 27 len 19 "h323-call-type=VoIP"
1w6d: RADIUS: added cisco VSA 25 len 48 "h323-setup-time=14:05:58.760 PST Thu Oc
t 14 1999"
-----------output suppressed----------------
1w6d: ta_StartTimerCmd(): ta_get_event [digit]
1w6d: :/startTimer/
1w6d: Wait for 20794 seconds
-----------output suppresse----------------
```

The following is another stop record created at the termination of the second call. Connect and disconnect times are sent to the RADIUS server.

```
1w6d: AAA/ACCT: user 408, acct type 1 (953168740): Method=radius (radius)
1w6d: RADIUS: ustruct sharecount=1
1w6d: RADIUS: added cisco VSA 33 len 23 "h323-gw-id=sj7_pmeas11."
1w6d: RADIUS: added cisco VSA 24 len 41 "h323-conf-id=86DB7CA8 8C6C016E 0 466555
A0"
1w6d: RADIUS: added cisco VSA 26 len 23 "h323-call-origin=answer"
1w6d: RADIUS: added cisco VSA 27 len 24 "h323-call-type=Telephony"
1w6d: RADIUS: added cisco VSA 25 len 48 "h323-setup-time=14:03:46.180 PST Thu Oc
t 14 1999"
1w6d: RADIUS: added cisco VSA 28 len 50 "h323-connect-time=14:03:46.200 PST ThuOct
14 1999"
1w6d: RADIUS: added cisco VSA 29 len 53 "h323-disconnect-time=14:07:36.320 PST T
hu Oct 14 1999"
1w6d: RADIUS: added cisco VSA 30 len 24 "h323-disconnect-cause=10"
```

```
1w6d: RADIUS: added cisco VSA 31 len 20 "h323-voice-quality=0"
1w6d: cid(142) incoming disconnected
1w6d: cid(0) ta_get_event returning incoming disconnected
1w6d: TCL script eval for callID 142 completed. code=OK
1w6d: incoming disconnected
1w6d: RADIUS: Initial Transmit id 29 172.22.42.52:1646, Accounting-Request, len
------------output suppressed----------------
1w6d: AAA/MEMORY: free_user (0x61BEFB38) user='408' ruser='5550961' port='' rem_
addr='408/5554094' authen_type=NONE service=H323_VSA priv=0
sj7_pmeas11#
```

Terminating Gateway Debug Output

The following debug commands were activated on the terminating gateway:

```
debug radius
deb aaa authentication
debug aaa authorization
debug aaa accounting
```

The following debug output shows the activity on the terminating gateway for the activities and calls described in the previous debug output. Because IVR is not running on the terminating gateway, we've restricted debug data to AAA and RADIUS.

The important items in this output are those that compare the times and billing amounts to the originating gateway records. From this output you can see that the records collected from either gateway are sufficient to generate accurate billing records.

Notice in the following output that the conf-ID values match. There's a two-second difference, however, in the setup times. This delay reflects the time it took to make the call setup.

```
sj7_pmeas01#
Oct 14 14:05:22.600 PST: AAA: parse name=<no string> idb type=-1 tty=-1
Oct 14 14:05:22.600 PST: AAA/MEMORY: create_user (0x61C024B0) user='408' ruser='
5255233' port='' rem_addr='408/5555233' authen_type=NONE service=H323_VSA priv=0
Oct 14 14:05:22.600 PST: AAA/ACCT/CONN: Found list "h323"
Oct 14 14:05:22.600 PST: AAA/ACCT/CONN/START User 408, Port , Location "unknown"
Oct 14 14:05:22.600 PST: AAA/ACCT/CONN/START User 408, Port ,
task_id=56 start_time=939938722 timezone=PST service=connection protoco
l=h323
Oct 14 14:05:22.600 PST: AAA/ACCT: user 408, acct type 1 (2416182195): Method=ra
dius (radius)
Oct 14 14:05:22.600 PST: RADIUS: ustruct sharecount=2
Oct 14 14:05:22.600 PST: RADIUS: added cisco VSA 33 len 23 "h323-gw-id=sj7_pmeas
01."
Oct 14 14:05:22.604 PST: RADIUS: added cisco VSA 24 len 41
"h323-conf-id=86DB7CA8 8C6C016E 0 466555A0"
Oct 14 14:05:22.604 PST: RADIUS: added cisco VSA 26 len 23
"h323-call-origin=answer"
Oct 14 14:05:22.604 PST: RADIUS: added cisco VSA 27 len 19
"h323-call-type=VoIP"
Oct 14 14:05:22.604 PST: RADIUS: added cisco VSA 25 len 48
"h323-setup-time=14:04:56.620 PST Thu Oct 14 1999"
```

The following information is the start record for call leg 4 (originate Telephony):

```
------------output suppressed----------------
Oct 14 14:05:22.756 PST: RADIUS: added cisco VSA 33 len 23 "h323-gw-id=sj7_pmeas
01."
Oct 14 14:05:22.756 PST: RADIUS: added cisco VSA 24 len 41 "h323-conf-id=86DB7CA
8 8C6C016E 0 466555A0"
Oct 14 14:05:22.756 PST: RADIUS: added cisco VSA 26 len 26 "h323-call-
  origin=originate"
Oct 14 14:05:22.756 PST: RADIUS: added cisco VSA 27 len 24 "h323-call-type=Telephony"
Oct 14 14:05:22.756 PST: RADIUS: added cisco VSA 25 len 48 "h323-setup-time=14:0
4:56.770 PST Thu Oct 14 1999"
Oct 14 14:05:22.756 PST: RADIUS: Initial Transmit id 155 172.22.42.52:1646,
Accounting-Request, len 281
Oct 14 14:05:22.756 PST: Attribute 4 6 AC16275A
Oct 14 14:05:22.756 PST: Attribute 61 6 00000000
Oct 14 14:05:22.756 PST: Attribute 1 5 3430381E
Oct 14 14:05:22.756 PST: Attribute 30 9 35323535
Oct 14 14:05:22.756 PST: Attribute 31 5 34303828
Oct 14 14:05:22.756 PST: Attribute 40 6 00000001
Oct 14 14:05:22.756 PST: Attribute 6 6 00000001
Oct 14 14:05:22.756 PST: Attribute 26 31 0000000921196833
Oct 14 14:05:22.756 PST: Attribute 26 49 00000009182B6833
Oct 14 14:05:22.756 PST: Attribute 26 34 000000091A1C6833
Oct 14 14:05:22.756 PST: Attribute 26 32 000000091B1A6833
Oct 14 14:05:22.756 PST: Attribute 26 56 0000000919326833
Oct 14 14:05:22.760 PST: Attribute 44 10 30303030
Oct 14 14:05:22.760 PST: Attribute 41 6 00000000
Oct 14 14:05:22.772 PST: RADIUS: Received from id 155 172.22.42.52:1646,
Accounting-response, len 46
Oct 14 14:05:22.772 PST: Attribute 26 26 0000000967146833
```

The connect time is approximately one second after call leg 2.

```
------------output suppressed----------------
Oct 14 14:06:02.885 PST: RADIUS: added cisco VSA 33 len 23 "h323-gw-id=sj7_pmeas
01."
Oct 14 14:06:02.885 PST: RADIUS: added cisco VSA 24 len 41 "h323-conf-id=86DB7CA
8 8C6C016E 0 466555A0"
Oct 14 14:06:02.885 PST: RADIUS: added cisco VSA 26 len 23 "h323-call-origin=answer"
Oct 14 14:06:02.885 PST: RADIUS: added cisco VSA 27 len 19 "h323-call-type=VoIP"
Oct 14 14:06:02.885 PST: RADIUS: added cisco VSA 25 len 48 "h323-setup-time=14:0
4:56.620 PST Thu Oct 14 1999"
Oct 14 14:06:02.885 PST: RADIUS: added cisco VSA 28 len 50 "h323-connect-time=14
:05:03.780 PST Thu Oct 14 1999"
```

The disconnect time is about two seconds after call leg 2. The time of the call (disconnect-time minus connect-time) is 32.48 seconds for call leg 2 and 33.12 seconds for call leg 3 (a 0.640-second difference between call leg 2 and call leg 3).

```
Oct 14 14:06:02.885 PST: RADIUS: added cisco VSA 29 len 53 "h323-disconnect-time
=14:05:36.900 PST Thu Oct 14 1999"
```

Using OSP for Clearinghouse Services

Packet telephony service providers interested in expanding their geographic coverage are faced with limited options. To help alleviate this problem, Cisco has implemented the Open Settlement Protocol (OSP), a client-server protocol defined by the ETSI TIPHON standards organization. OSP is designed to offer billing and accounting record consolidation for voice calls that traverse ITSP boundaries; it also allows service providers to exchange traffic with each other without establishing multiple bilateral peering agreements.

Because of OSP, you can employ a reliable third-party clearinghouse to handle VoIP call termination while leveraging the bandwidth efficiencies and tariff arbitrage advantages inherent in IP. You can use a clearinghouse as both a technical and business bridge; by signing on with such an organization and using OSP, you can extend service beyond the boundaries of your network and immediately access the entire clearinghouse network of affiliated service providers.

OSP Background

In the TDM circuit-switched world, interconnecting carriers calculated settlements based on minutes used in circuits exchanged between their switches, often exchanging Signaling System 7 (SS7) information and voice paths. Call authorization was based simply on the physical demarcation point; if a call arrived, it was deemed "authorized." This scenario required a stable business relationship except in the case of international traffic, where third-party wholesale carriers often provided such services.

VoIP service providers have had to adapt to such arrangements by terminating calls on the PSTN and reoriginating the call on a circuit switch. However, such an approach limits the cost-effectiveness of today's packet telephony. Even interconnection between VoIP networks was problematic—solutions were usually tightly integrated with individual vendors' proprietary and nonstandard implementations of H.323 protocols.

OSP avoids this problem. By allowing gateways to transfer accounting and routing information securely, this protocol provides common ground among VoIP service providers.

Third-party clearinghouses with an OSP server can offer route selection, call authorization, call accounting, and inter-carrier settlements, including all the complex rating and routing tables necessary for efficient and cost-effective interconnections. Cisco has worked with a variety of leading OSP clearinghouses to ensure interoperability with their OSP server applications. OSP-based clearinghouses provide the least cost and the best route-selection algorithms based on a variety of parameters their subscriber carriers provide, including cost, quality, and specific carrier preferences. Prepaid calling services, click-to-dial, and clearinghouse settlements can be offered over the same packet infrastructure.

Benefits of Using OSP Clearinghouses

The OSP clearinghouse solution gives virtually all VoIP providers the worldwide calling reach they require. This service can be used separately or in conjunction with internally-managed prepaid calling services.

The benefits of using an OSP clearinghouse include the following:

- End-to-end VoIP support
- Cost-effective worldwide calling coverage
- Guaranteed settlement of authorized calls
- Incremental revenue increase by terminating calls from other service providers
- Simplified business and credit relationships
- Outsourced complex rating and routing tables
- Flexibility in selecting appropriate termination points
- Secure transmission using widely accepted encryption for sensitive data
- Single authentication for the actual gateway or platform at initialization time
- Secure interface between the settlement client and the settlement server

OSP Clearinghouse Operation and Call Flow

The following step list describes a high-level call flow sequence for an OSP clearinghouse application:

Step 1 A customer places a call via the PSTN to a VoIP gateway, which authenticates the customer by communicating with a RADIUS server.

Step 2 The originating VoIP gateway attempts to locate a termination point within its own network by communicating with a gatekeeper using H.323 RAS. If there's no appropriate route, the gatekeeper tells the gateway to search for a termination point elsewhere.

Step 3 The gateway contacts an OSP server at the third-party clearinghouse. The gateway then establishes a Secure Socket Layer (SSL) connection to the OSP server and sends an authorization request to the clearinghouse. The authorization request contains pertinent information about the call, including the destination number, the device ID, and the customer ID of the gateway.

Step 4 The OSP server processes the information and, assuming the gateway is authorized, returns routing details for the possible terminating gateways that can satisfy the request of the originating gateway.

NOTE Although it depends on OSP server implementation, most OSP servers can supply the least-cost and best-route selection algorithms according to your requirements for cost, quality, and other parameters, selecting up to three routes.

Step 5   The clearinghouse creates an authorization token, signs it with a clearinghouse certificate and private key, and then replies to the originating gateway with a token and up to three selected routes. If any or all of the three routes have identical cost and quality parameters, the settlement server randomizes the qualifying routes. The originating gateway uses the IP addresses supplied by the clearinghouse to set up the call.

Step 6   The originating gateway sends the token it received from the settlement server in the setup message to the terminating gateway.

Step 7   The terminating gateway accepts the call after validating the token and completes the call setup.

At the end of the call, both the originating and terminating gateways send usage indicator reports (call detail records) to the OSP server. The usage indicator reports contain the call detail information that the OSP server uses to provide settlement service between the originating and terminating service providers.

Figure 10-3 illustrates call flow for a typical call settled by a clearinghouse server.

Architecture for OSP

Figure 10-4 shows an OSP architecture model where all inter-ISP calls are routed and settled by an OSP server. Intra-ISP calls are routed and billed in the typical postpaid or prepaid model.

OSP Hardware and Software Requirements

This section covers the following:

- System Platform Requirements
- Memory and Software Requirements
- Hardware Components

System Platform Requirements

OSP is supported on the following Cisco platforms:

- Cisco AS5300 and AS5800 universal access servers; Cisco AS5400 universal gateway
- Cisco 2600 series routers
- Cisco 3620, 3640, and 3660 routers

Figure 10-3 *Typical call flow for an OSP clearinghouse application.*

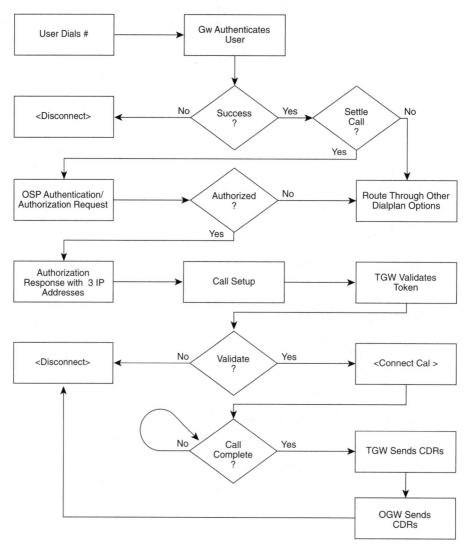

Figure 10-4 *OSP architecture model.*

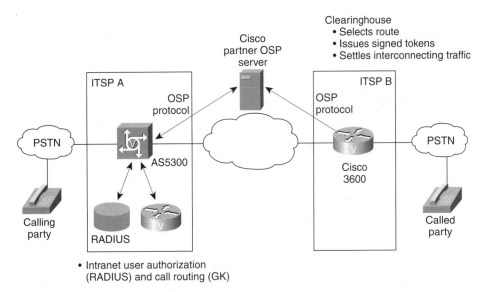

Memory and Software Requirements

The following are the memory and software requirements:

- 16 MB Flash

- 128 MB DRAM

- TCL IVR script for settlements (session application embedded in IOS software)

- Cisco IOS Release 12.2(1) or later with -ik8s- or -jk8s- cryptographic images

- VCWare, DSPWare versions as listed in the following compatibility matrix:

  http://www.cisco.com/univercd/cc/td/doc/product/access/acs_serv/5300/iosrn/
  vcwrn/vcwrmtrx.htm

Hardware Components

The following are the hardware components:

- VoIP gateway that supports 56-bit encryption, SSL, and OSP
- Certificate Authority (CA)
- OSP server

The following are OSP server vendors:

- Concert: www.concert.com
- GRIC: www.gric.com
- NeTrue: www.netrue.com
- OpenOSP: www.openosp.org
- TransNexus: www.transnexus.com

NOTE   The settlement feature cannot be enabled on dial peers that use Registration, Admission, and Status (RAS) as the session target. The settlement software is offered only in cryptographic images; therefore, the images are under export controls.

OSP Clearinghouse Solution Configuration Guidelines

Configuring a Cisco router or access server to register with an online TransNexus Phase 1 OSP server consists of the following steps:

- Define gateway identity parameters.
- Use Network Time Protocol.
- Configure the Public Key Infrastructure (PKI).
- Enroll with the OSP server.
- Configure settlement parameters.
- Configure incoming and outgoing dial peers.

The specific configuration parameters might be different from those shown here, depending on the OSP server with which you are registering.

Define Gateway Identity Parameters

OSP servers typically locate gateways and clients using DNS. For this reason, you need to make sure that the voice gateway can locate the OSP server and other IP resources using DNS. Example 10-9 shows how to configure the domain name in which the gateway resides and identify a DNS server in that domain.

Example 10-9 *Defining Gateway Identity Parameters*

```
Router(config)# ip domain-name cisco.com
Router(config)# ip name-server 172.22.30.32
```

In Example 10-9, both the domain name and DNS are identified. Typically, the **ip domain-lookup** global configuration command is enabled by default in Cisco routers and gateways.

When you've configured the **ip domain-name** and the **ip name-server** global configuration commands and confirmed that the **ip domain-lookup** global configuration command is enabled, the gateway can refer to the OSP server by its domain name.

NOTE   You should check to make sure that the **ip domain-lookup** global configuration command hasn't been overridden in the gateway. If the command is NOT listed in the **show running-config** privileged EXEC command output, the command is active.

Use Network Time Protocol

The OSP server requires accurate time stamps from gateways in order to rate calls adequately. Unless the gateway time-of-day clock (not to be confused with the system controller clock) is within a certain tolerance range (minutes) of the OSP server clock, token validation will fail. Gateways, servers, and other IP devices can synchronize their time-of-day clocks with each other through the Network Time Protocol (NTP). Similar to DNS, a hierarchy of NTP servers is available on the Internet. Any gateway with access to the Internet can point to an available NTP server for accurate time-of-day synchronization. A list of Stratum 2 NTP servers can be found at the following URL:

http://www.eecis.udel.edu/~mills/ntp/clock2.htm

The following global configuration command configures a Cisco gateway to synchronize its time to an authoritative NTP source:

```
Router(config)# ntp server ip-address
```

Although not required for simple time synchronization, the **ntp** global configuration command can be used to configure a variety of other NTP parameters, as shown in Table 10-10.

Table 10-10 *NTP Global Configuration Command Parameters*

Command	Description
ntp access-group	Controls NTP access
ntp authenticate	Authenticates time sources
ntp authentication-key	Configures the authentication key for trusted time sources
ntp broadcastdelay	Displays the estimated round-trip delay
ntp clock-period	Length of hardware clock tick
ntp master	Acts as NTP master clock
ntp max-associations	Sets the maximum number of associations
ntp peer	Configures NTP peer
ntp server	Configures NTP server
ntp source	Configures interface for source address
ntp trusted-key	Configures key numbers for trusted time sources
ntp update-calendar	Periodically updates calendar with NTP time

NTP time formats are displayed in the following format, which is described in Table 10-11:

```
%H:%M:%S.%k %Z %tw %tn %td %Y
```

Table 10-11 *NTP Record Field Descriptions*

Value	Description and Range
%H	Hour (00 to 23)
%M	Minutes (00 to 59)
%S	Seconds (00 to 59)
%k	Milliseconds (000 to 999)
%Z	Time zone string
%tw	Day of the week (Saturday to Sunday)
%tn	Month (January to December)
%td	Day of the month (01 to 31)
%Y	Year, including century (for example, 1998)

Enabling the **debug ntp adjust** EXEC command is a quick way to see if your gateway is communicating with the configured NTP server. Example 10-10 shows this debug command output.

Example 10-10 *debug ntp adjust Command*

```
Router# debug ntp adjust
NTP clock adjustments debugging is on
Router#
00:27:12: NTP: adj(-0.000000317), rem. offset = 0.000000000, adj = -0.000000317
00:27:13: NTP: adj(-0.000000838), rem. offset = 0.000000000, adj = -0.000000838
00:27:14: NTP: adj(-0.000000842), rem. offset = 0.000000000, adj = -0.000000842
00:27:15: NTP: adj(-0.000000933), rem. offset = 0.000000000, adj = -0.000000933
00:27:16: NTP: adj(-0.000001029), rem. offset = 0.000000000, adj = -0.000001029
00:27:17: NTP: adj(-0.000000290), rem. offset = 0.000000000, adj = -0.000000290
```

You can use the **show clock** privileged EXEC command to confirm the correct time.

Configure the Public Key Infrastructure (PKI)

To configure the PKI for secured communication between the gateway and the OSP server, perform the following steps:

- Generate a Rivest-Shamir-Adleman (RSA) key pair.
- Configure the enrollment parameters.
- Obtain the certification authority (CA) certificate.

Generate an RSA Key Pair

Example 10-11 shows you how to generate an RSA key pair.

Example 10-11 *Generating an RSA Key Pair*

```
Router(config)# crypto key generate rsa
```

When you enter this command, you will receive the following feedback from the gateway:

```
The name for the keys will be: Group10_B.cisco.com
```

Choose the size of the key modulus in the range of 360 to 2048 for your general-purpose keys. Choosing a key modulus greater than 512 might take a few minutes.

```
How many bits in the modulus [512]:
```

When you press **Enter**, you generate a 512-bit key. The system confirms that the RSA keys have been generated by displaying the following output:

```
Generating RSA keys ...
[OK]
```

Configure the Enrollment Parameters

Example 10-12 shows how to configure the enrollment parameters.

Example 10-12 *Configuring the Enrollment Parameters*

```
Router(config)# crypto ca identity transnexus
Router(ca-identity)# enrollment url http://enroll.transnexus.com:2378
Router(ca-identity)# enrollment retry count 3
Router(ca-identity)# enrollment retry period 1
Router(ca-identity)# no enrollment mode ra
Router(ca-identity)# exit
```

In Example 10-12, the **crypto ca identity** global configuration command opens identity configuration mode and matches the OSP parameters to the identity tag **transnexus**. The next three commands configure the enrollment URL of the OSP server and the retry parameters. The fourth command makes sure you are not in resource authority mode. Finally, the **exit** command exits the identity configuration mode.

Obtain the CA Certificate

Example 10-13 shows you how to obtain a CA certificate.

Example 10-13 *Obtaining a CA Certificate*

```
Router(config)# crypto ca authenticate transnexus
```

When you enter this command, you will receive the following feedback from the gateway:

```
Certificate has the following attributes:
Fingerprint: 96D254B4 0AEF4F23 7A545BF9 70DC4D17
% Do you accept this certificate? [yes/no]: Y
<To accept this certificate, you type "Y" here.>
```

The tag-name must be the same as the one used when declaring the CA with the **crypto ca identity** global configuration command (in this example, **transnexus**).

Enroll with the OSP Server

Example 10-14 shows you how to enroll your voice gateway with the OSP server.

Example 10-14 *Enrolling with the OSP Server*

```
Router(config)# crypto ca enroll transnexus
```

When you enter this command, the system will prompt you for a series of responses. All of the responses that you should enter are in boldface type:

```
%
% Start certificate enrollment ..
% Create a challenge password. You will need to verbally provide this
password to the CA Administrator in order to revoke your certificate.
For security reasons your password will not be saved in the configuration.
Please make a note of it.
Password: xxxx <You enter your password here.>
Re-enter password: xxxx <You re-enter your password here.>
% The subject name in the certificate will be: Group10_B.cisco.com
% Include the router serial number in the subject name? [yes/no]: Y
% The serial number in the certificate will be: 006CE956
% Include an IP address in the subject name? [yes/no]: Y
Interface: Ethernet 0
Request certificate from CA? [yes/no]: y
% Certificate request sent to Certificate Authority
% The certificate request fingerprint will be displayed.
% The 'show crypto ca certificate' command will also show the fingerprint
Wait here for the feedback below:
(config)# Fingerprint: 24D05F87 1DE1D0C9 4DF974D1 7AE064C6
11:15:12: %CRYPTO-6-CERTRET: from Certificate Authority
```

If you don't get the CERTRET feedback, your enrollment most likely has failed. If you continue without a proper certificate, you won't be able to register. After you receive a certificate, you need to display your gateway configuration to confirm the presence of certificates (see Example 10-15).

Example 10-15   *show running-config output*

```
Router# show running-config
Current configuration:
!
version 12.0
service timestamps debug uptime
service timestamps log uptime
no service password-encryption
!
hostname ogw
!
enable secret level 14 5 $1$gB9t$cNIAO.XGbV/2ebLeiYXPc.
enable secret 5 $1$W1Wx$KtFgICn0Q7X8BbxwFnR991
!
clock timezone GMT 0
ip subnet-zero
ip domain-name cisco.com
!
crypto ca identity transnexus
enrollment url http://10.100.1.3
crypto ca certificate chain transnexus
certificate AFADA65D4DF416847B6B284AB197146E
30820231 3082019A A0030201 02021100 AFADA65D 4DF41684 7B6B284A B197146E
300D0609 2A864886 F70D0101 04050030 6E310B30 09060355 04061302 55533110
300E0603 55040813 0747656F 72676961 31183016 06035504 0A130F54 72616E73
4E657875 732C204C 4C433114 30120603 55040B13 0B446576 656C6F70 6D656E74
311D301B 06035504 03131454 52414E53 4E455855 53204245 54412043 41203130
1E170D39 39303332 39323235 3235395A 170D3030 30333239 32323532 35395A30
72317030 0D060355 04051306 36434232 31413017 06092A86 4886F70D 01090813
0A31302E 3130302E 312E3130 1A06092A 864886F7 0D010902 160D6F67 772E6369
```

continues

Example 10-15 *show running-config output (Continued)*

```
73636F2E 636F6D30 2A060355 04031423 5B747261 6E736E65 7875732E 636F6D20
47574944 3D313030 20435349 443D3430 30305D30 5C300D06 092A8648 86F70D01.
01010500 034B0030 48024100 C871D5F7 8529C9AE 9E7BC554 C5510B75 A66C9E78
405FECDB 60896552 80106C8F 7F7F9B3B 89A50D55 0578881D 3672CCFE 9BB5E515
47D03E95 CE4CC0F1 3DC20593 02030100 01A30F30 0D300B06 03551D0F 04040302
05A0300D 06092A86 4886F70D 01010405 00038181 00256D3C 087E8005 74D05759
0B9924B2 842675D5 C37A913C A2E16AC1 B146161C DFF7F96A 0053DCFC F5E1E22D
E51D4C82 9A97D2E8 B38E5CE0 902CEFE1 13181486 5929DF21 B882775E 830563A2
D15C61DE 0EFDC39D 334ECD0D E826E953 1C37ED56 2DA5D765 5B9949E6 1D33E3CE
FB3E2818 78355CDF 4A9A6118 52B6FF48 D07A6DEB 33
quit
certificate ca 0171
3082024C 308201B5 02020171 300D0609 2A864886 F70D0101 04050030 6E310B30
09060355 04061302 55533110 300E0603 55040813 0747656F 72676961 31183016
06035504 0A130F54 72616E73 4E657875 732C204C 4C433114 30120603 55040B13
0B446576 656C6F70 6D656E74 311D301B 06035504 03131454 52414E53 4E455855
53204245 54412043 41203130 1E170D39 39303332 32313334 3630395A 170D3030
30333231 31333436 30395A30 6E310B30 09060355 04061302 55533110 300E0603
55040813 0747656F 72676961 31183016 06035504 0A130F54 72616E73 4E657875
732C204C 4C433114 30120603 55040B13 0B446576 656C6F70 6D656E74 311D301B
06035504 03131454 52414E53 4E455855 53204245 54412043 41203130 819F300D
06092A86 4886F70D 01010105 0003818D 00308189 02818100 B1B8ACFC D78F0C95
0258D164 5B6BD8A4 6F5668BD 50E7524B 2339B670 DC306537 3E1E9381 DE2619B4
4698CD82 739CB251 91AF90A5 52736137 658DF200 FAFEFE6B 7FC7161D 89617E5E
4584D67F F018EDAB 2858DDF9 5272F108 AB791A70 580F994B 4CA54F08 38C32DF5
B44077E8 79830F95 96F1DA69 4CAE16F2 2879E07B 164F5F6D 02030100 01300D06
092A8648 86F70D01 01040500 03818100 2FDCB580 C29E557C 52201151 A8DB5F47
C06962D5 8FDA524E A69DE3EE C3FE166A D05C8B93 2844CD66 824A8859 974F22E0
46F69F7E 8027064F C19D28BC CA750E4E FF2DD68E 1AA9CA41 8BB89C68 7A61E9BF
49CBE41E E3A42B16 AAEDAEC7 D3B4F676 4F1A817B A5B89ED8 F03A15B0 39A6EBB9
0AFA6968 17A9D381 FD62BBB7 A7D379E5
quit
---------- output suppressed --------
ntp clock-period 17182503
ntp server 10.100.1.3
end
```

You should find two large blocks of hex strings similar to the previous ones. One block is a representation of the OSP server certificate, and the other represents the key from the certificate authority. The presence of both keys is an indication (although not a guarantee) that the registration has occurred correctly.

Configure Settlement Parameters

Example 10-16 shows you how to configure settlement parameters on your gateway.

Example 10-16 *Configuring Settlement*

```
Router(config)# settlement 0
Router(config-settlement)# type osp
Router(config-settlement)# url https://192.168.152.17:8444/
Router(config-settlement)# response-timeout 20
Router(config-settlement)# device-id 1039928734
Router(config-settlement)# customer-id 805311438
Router(config-settlement)# no shutdown
Router(config-settlement)# exit
```

The first command in Example 10-16 opens settlement configuration mode. The next five commands configure the settlement parameters, including the settlement URL. Notice that settlement is using the SSL protocol (denoted by https://) as the transport mechanism. The device ID and customer ID are both TransNexus-specific. Finally, the **exit** command exits settlement configuration mode.

Configure Incoming and Outgoing Dial Peers

The incoming POTS dial peer on the originating gateway is associated with the session application that initiates the OSP activities. Example 10-17 shows how to configure the incoming POTS dial peer on the originating gateway.

Example 10-17 *Configuring the Incoming POTS Dial Peer on the Originating Gateway*

```
Router(config)# dial-peer voice 1 pots
Router(config-dial-peer)# application session
Router(config-dial-peer)# incoming called-number 1415.......
Router(config-dial-peer)# port 1/0/0
```

The first command in Example 10-17 opens the dial-peer configuration mode and defines the tag number of the dial peer you are configuring. The **application** dial-peer configuration command associates the session application with the call. The last two commands configure general POTS dial-peer parameters.

The outbound VoIP dial peer on the originating gateway has a session target of **settlement**, which directs the call to the OSP server. Example 10-18 shows how to configure the outbound VoIP dial peer on the originating gateway.

Example 10-18 *Configuring the Outbound VoIP Dial-Peer on the Originating Gateway*

```
Router(config)# dial-peer voice 10 voip
Router(config-dial-peer)# destination-pattern 1219.......
Router(config-dial-peer)# session target settlement
```

The first command in Example 10-18 opens dial-peer configuration mode and defines the tag number of the dial peer you are configuring. The **session target settlement** dial-peer configuration command sends the call to the OSP server. The other commands configure general VoIP dial peer parameters.

The VoIP dial peer on the terminating gateway matches the outgoing VoIP dial peer on the originating gateway and must also point to the **settlement** session target. Example 10-19 shows how to configure the inbound VoIP and outbound POTS dial peers on the terminating gateway.

Example 10-19 *Configuring the Inbound VoIP Dial Peer and the Outbound POTS Dial Peer on the Terminating Gateway*

```
Router(config)# dial-peer voice 10 voip
Router(config-dial-peer)# application session
Router(config-dial-peer)# incoming called-number 1415.......
Router(config-dial-peer)# session target settlement:0
Router(config-dial-peer)# exit
Router(config)# dial-peer voice 1 pots
Router(config-dial-peer)# incoming called-number 1219.......
Router(config-dial-peer)# port 1/0/0
```

The first command in Example 10-19 opens the dial-peer configuration mode and defines the tag number of the inbound VoIP dial-peer you are configuring. The **application** dial-peer configuration command associates the session application with the call. The **session target settlement** dial-peer configuration command identifies the settlement server.

The next command defines the outbound POTS dial peer and defines its tag number. The last two commands configure general POTS dial-peer parameters.

Troubleshooting OSP

In general, the following commands are useful in debugging an OSP installation:

- **debug voip ivr settlement**—displays IVR settlement information
- **debug voip settlement network**—shows the messages exchanged between a router and a settlement provider
- **debug voip settlement errors**—displays all settlement errors
- **debug voip settlement transaction**—displays the attributes of the transactions on the settlement gateway
- **debug voip settlement misc**—shows the details on the code flow of each settlement transaction

Common Problems with Settlement Configuration

The following are the problems covered in this section:

- Settlement database not set up properly
- TCL IVR script not called
- No destination pattern set
- No session target settlement set on originating gateway
- No VoIP inbound dial peer on terminating gateway
- No application attribute on terminating gateway
- Terminating gateway not synchronized with settlement server
- Settlement provider not running
- Router and server not using SSL to communicate
- Multiple dial peers have random order
- H.323 setup connection timeout

Settlement Database Not Set Up Properly

Problem: Calls are routed through a settlement server, but the originating gateway gets no response, or negative response.

Solution: Check with the settlement provider to make sure the router is properly registered with that provider. Router registration with the settlement provider is normally done outside of OSP.

TCL IVR Script Not Called

Problem: TCL IVR script is not used on the originating gateway or terminating gateway.

Solution: You can do the following:

- Configure a TCL IVR script for the dial peer using the **application** dial-peer configuration command.
- Use the **show call application voice summary** EXEC command to list all the available scripts on the router, as shown here:

```
router# show call application voice summary
name                  description
session               Basic app to do DID, or supply dialtone.
fax_hop_on            Script to talk to a fax redialer
clid_authen           Authenticate with (ani, dnis)
clid_authen_collect   Authenticate with (ani, dnis), collect if that fails
clid_authen_npw       Authenticate with (ani, NULL)
clid_authen_col_npw   Authenticate with (ani, NULL), collect if that fails
clid_col_npw_3        Authenticate with (ani, NULL), and 3 tries collecting
clid_col_npw_npw      Authenticate with (ani, NULL) and 3 tries without pw
SESSION               Default system session application
```

No Destination Pattern Set

Problem: The inbound POTS dial peer on the originating gateway has no destination pattern set.

Solution: Because some PBX devices don't pass along the calling number in the setup message, the router uses the destination pattern number or answer-address as an alternative, and calling number is a required field for settlement.

No Session Target Settlement Set on Originating Gateway

Problem: The originating gateway outbound VoIP dial peer doesn't have the session target configured for settlement.

NOTE   The router can make successful calls, but not through a settlement server. The session target attribute dictates how the router resolves the terminating gateway address for a particular called number.

Solution: Configure the **session target settlement** *provider-number* dial-peer configuration command.

No VoIP Inbound Dial-Peer on Terminating Gateway

Problem: The terminating gateway has no VoIP inbound dial-peer. Because the settlement token in the incoming setup message from the originating gateway can't be validated, the terminating gateway rejects the call.

Solution: Create an inbound dial-peer with the **session target settlement** *provider-number* dial-peer configuration command.

No Application Attribute on Terminating Gateway

Problem: The terminating gateway has an inbound dial-peer configured, but with no application attribute. The default session application (SESSION) processes the call, but it doesn't support settlement.

Solution: Configure the **application** dial-peer configuration command in the inbound dial peer.

Terminating Gateway Not Synchronized with Settlement Server

Problem: The terminating gateway clock is not synchronized with the settlement server. The terminating gateway rejects the call because it's too soon or too late to use the settlement token in the incoming setup message.

Solution: Use the **ntp** or **clock set** EXEC command to synchronize the clocks between the terminating gateway and the settlement server.

Settlement Provider Not Running

Problem: The settlement provider on the originating or terminating gateway isn't running. No settlement transaction processing is allowed unless the provider is running.

Solution: Enable settlement using the **no shutdown** command in settlement configuration mode. Use the **show settlement** privileged EXEC command to verify the provider status.

Router and Server Not Using SSL to Communicate

Problem: The router can't use SSL to communicate with the server because the server URL should be "https," not "http."

Solution: Configure a secured URL using "https."

Problem: The router can't use SSL to communicate with the server because the certificates of the server or router weren't properly obtained.

Solution: Check the certificate enrollment process for both the server and the router.

Multiple Dial Peers Have Random Order

Problem: The originating gateway has multiple dial peers for the same called number and settlement is never used. The order for rotary dial peers is random unless a dial peer preference is specified. The dial peer with lower preference is chosen first.

Solution: Define dial-peer preference using the **preference** dial-peer configuration command.

H.323 Setup Connection Timeout

Problem: The originating gateway can't successfully set up a call with the first terminating gateway that's returned from the OSP server. The problem occurs when a gateway attempts to set up the call with the terminating gateways in the order that they are received. If for some reason the H.323 call setup is not successful, there's a 15-second default timeout before the next terminating gateway on the list is contacted.

Solution: The H.323 call setup timeout can be tuned using the **h225 timeout tcp establish** voice class configuration command:

```
voice class h323 1
 h225 timeout tcp establish <value 0 to 30 seconds>

dial-peer voice 919 voip
 application session
 destination-pattern 919555....
 voice-class codec 1
 voice-class h323 1
 session target settlement
```

OSP Problem Isolation

If you are having trouble isolating the problems that are occurring with settlement, try the following:

- Check the originating and terminating gateway configurations for dial peers, settlement providers, and certificates.

- Check the network between the originating gateway, terminating gateway, and the server. Ping each device to make sure that the machines are running.

- Verify that IP calls can be made successfully. If so, the problem is specific to settlement.

- Use the **debug voip ivr settlement** EXEC command on the originating gateway to see if the TCL IVR script initiates a settlement request to the server.

- Use the **debug voip settlement network** EXEC command on the originating gateway to capture the HTTP requests sent to the server and the response from the server. If the originating gateway gets no response from the server, contact the settlement provider.

- Use the **debug voip settlement misc** EXEC command to see the list of TGWs returned from the server. If this list is incorrect, contact the settlement provider.

- If the terminating gateway rejects the settlement token because it's too soon or too late to use it, synchronize the terminating gateway clock with the server.

OSP Clearinghouse Configuration Examples

This section shows two examples:

- Configuring OSP on the originating gateway
- Configuring OSP on the terminating gateway

Configuring OSP on the Originating Gateway

Example 10-20 shows an originating gateway configured to register with an OSP server.

NOTE   The first tuplet in each IP address in this example has been replaced with a unique variable.

Example 10-20 *Configuring OSP on the Originating Gateway*

```
version 12.1
service timestamps debug uptime
service timestamps log uptime
no service password-encryption
!
hostname Group2_A
!
boot system flash c3640-js56i-mz_120-4_XH.bin
enable password pme123
!
clock timezone PST -7
ip subnet-zero
ip domain-name cisco.com
ip name-server xxx.156.128.1
ip name-server xxx.156.128.10
!
cns event-service server
!
crypto ca identity transnexus
! Certificate authority identity parameters
 enrollment retry count 3
 enrollment url http://enroll.transnexus.com:2378
! Clearinghouse server address
crypto ca certificate chain transnexus
! The following 2 blocks of characters are a hexidecimal representation of the
! certificates present on the gateway.
certificate 73A39A2746B2BFFC373AF35B70F427CC
 30820246 308201AF A0030201 02021073 A39A2746 B2BFFC37 3AF35B70 F427CC30
 0D06092A 864886F7 0D010104 0500306E 310B3009 06035504 06130255 53311030
 0E060355 04081307 47656F72 67696131 18301606 0355040A 130F5472 616E734E
 65787573 2C204C4C 43311430 12060355 040B130B 44657665 6C6F706D 656E7431
 1D301B06 03550403 13145452 414E534E 45585553 20424554 41204341 2031301E
 170D3939 31303132 31353430 33345A17 0D303031 30313231 35343033 345A3081
 87318184 300D0603 55040513 06413137 30443030 1A06092A 864886F7 0D010908
 130D3230 392E3234 2E313431 2E333430 1F06092A 864886F7 0D010902 16124772
 6F757032 5F412E63 6973636F 2E636F6D 30360603 55040314 2F5B7472 616E736E
 65787573 2E636F6D 20475749 443D3130 37333734 36393333 20435349 443D3830
 35333131 3433385D 305C300D 06092A86 4886F70D 01010105 00034B00 30480241
 00E288FF 7C275A55 5C375387 99FB9682 7BFC554C F2DFA453 BFFD88AB 657C0FD5
 7FC510BA 13DDEB99 DF7E5FAA 5BE5952E B974F8DB 1B333F2C D4C5689D 61812121
 DB020301 0001A30F 300D300B 0603551D 0F040403 0205A030 0D06092A 864886F7
 0D010104 05000381 81007D83 08924EFD F2139D01 504FAC21 35108FCF 083D9DA7
 495649F6 6D1E28A6 1A687F1C CAF5BDBD 37E8E8A1 54401F4A 73BBFB05 786E01BC
```

continues

Example 10-20 *Configuring OSP on the Originating Gateway (Continued)*

```
 AF966529 AC92648B 2A4B9FEC 3BFFEBF8 81A116B5 4D3DAA93 7E4C24FB E3624EB3
 D630C232 D016149D 427557A1 F58F313E F92F9E9D ADBA3873 92EBF7F0 861E0413
 F81CD5C0 E4E18A03 2FA2
quit
certificate ca 0171
 3082024C 308201B5 02020171 300D0609 2A864886 F70D0101 04050030 6E310B30
 09060355 04061302 55533110 300E0603 55040813 0747656F 72676961 31183016
 06035504 0A130F54 72616E73 4E657875 732C204C 4C433114 30120603 55040B13
 0B446576 656C6F70 6D656E74 311D301B 06035504 03131454 52414E53 4E455855
 53204245 54412043 41203130 1E170D39 39303332 32313334 3630395A 170D3030
 30333231 31333436 30395A30 6E310B30 09060355 04061302 55533110 300E0603
 55040813 0747656F 72676961 31183016 06035504 0A130F54 72616E73 4E657875
 732C204C 4C433114 30120603 55040B13 0B446576 656C6F70 6D656E74 311D301B
 06035504 03131454 52414E53 4E455855 53204245 54412043 41203130 819F300D
 06092A86 4886F70D 01010105 0003818D 00308189 02818100 B1B8ACFC D78F0C95
 0258D164 5B6BD8A4 6F5668BD 50E7524B 2339B670 DC306537 3E1E9381 DE2619B4
 4698CD82 739CB251 91AF90A5 52736137 658DF200 FAFEFE6B 7FC7161D 89617E5E
 4584D67F F018EDAB 2858DDF9 5272F108 AB791A70 580F994B 4CA54F08 38C32DF5
 B44077E8 79830F95 96F1DA69 4CAE16F2 2879E07B 164F5F6D 02030100 01300D06
 092A8648 86F70D01 01040500 03818100 2FDCB580 C29E557C 52201151 A8DB5F47
 C06962D5 8FDA524E A69DE3EE C3FE166A D05C8B93 2844CD66 824A8859 974F22E0
 46F69F7E 8027064F C19D28BC CA750E4E FF2DD68E 1AA9CA41 8BB89C68 7A61E9BF
 49CBE41E E3A42B16 AAEDAEC7 D3B4F676 4F1A817B A5B89ED8 F03A15B0 39A6EBB9
 0AFA6968 17A9D381 FD62BBB7 A7D379E5
quit
!
voice-port 1/0/0
!
voice-port 1/0/1
!
voice-port 1/1/0
!
voice-port 1/1/1
!
dial-peer voice 1 pots
! The incoming pots dial peer on the originating gateway is associated
! with the session application that initiates the OSP activities.
 application session
 destination-pattern 9549204
 port 1/0/0
!
dial-peer voice 10 voip
 destination-pattern 7671234
 session target ipv4:xxy.24.141.35
!
dial-peer voice 101 voip
! The outgoing VoIP dial peer has a session target of settlement,
! which directs the call to the OSP server.
 application session
 destination-pattern 1T
 session target settlement
!
```

Example 10-20 *Configuring OSP on the Originating Gateway (Continued)*

```
process-max-time 200
settlement 0
 type osp
! The settlement parameters include the URL to the settlement server;
! in this case, using SSL
 url https://xxy.144.152.17:8444/
 device-id 1073746933
 customer-id 805311438
 no shutdown
!
interface Ethernet0/0
 no ip address
 no ip directed-broadcast
 shutdown
!
interface Ethernet0/1
 description flat management network
 ip address xxy.24.141.34 255.255.255.240
 no ip directed-broadcast
!
ip classless
ip route 0.0.0.0 0.0.0.0 xxy.24.141.33
no ip http server
!
line con 0
 exec-timeout 0 0
 transport input none
line aux 0
 speed 115200
line vty 0 4
 exec-timeout 0 0
 password pme123
 no login
!
ntp clock-period 17180168
ntp source Ethernet0/1
! NTP parameters are pointing to a Stratum 2 NTP server
ntp server 209.24.141.33
end
```

Configuring OSP on the Terminating Gateway

Example 10-21 shows a terminating gateway configured to support OSP.

NOTE The first tuplet in each IP address in this example has been replaced with a unique variable.

Example 10-21 *Configuring OSP on the Terminating Gateway*

```
version 12.1
service timestamps debug uptime
service timestamps log uptime
no service password-encryption
!
hostname Group2_B
!
enable password pme123
!
clock timezone PST -7
ip subnet-zero
ip domain-name cisco.com
ip name-server xxx.156.128.1
ip name-server xxx.156.128.10
!
cns event-service server
!
crypto ca identity transnexus
! Certificate authority identity parameters
 enrollment retry count 3
 enrollment url http://enroll.transnexus.com:2378
crypto ca certificate chain transnexus
certificate 0172
 30820264 308201CD 02020172 300D0609 2A864886 F70D0101 04050030 6E310B30
 09060355 04061302 55533110 300E0603 55040813 0747656F 72676961 31183016
 06035504 0A130F54 72616E73 4E657875 732C204C 4C433114 30120603 55040B13
 0B446576 656C6F70 6D656E74 311D301B 06035504 03131454 52414E53 4E455855
 53204245 54412043 41203130 1E170D39 39303332 32313334 3631345A 170D3030
 30333231 31333436 31345A30 8185310B 30090603 55040613 02555331 10300E06
 03550408 13074765 6F726769 61311830 16060355 040A130F 5472616E 734E6578
 75732C20 4C4C4331 31302F06 0355040B 13285472 616E736E 65787573 20536574
 746C656D 656E7420 53657276 65722044 6576656C 6F706D65 6E743117 30150603
 55040313 0E747261 6E736E65 7875732E 636F6D30 819F300D 06092A86 4886F70D
 01010105 0003818D 00308189 02818100 AF4E4E7A 7AE56E12 8526027B 4FAA7E16
 07710217 72EF63B9 8C0CAD75 C40724FE 71779746 937C8499 0EE9B19E FE7E76D0
 12A9FD09 DA7FE092 979FA5C6 066F6FAB 3614229A A352708E 87BE67A0 B7D1B8F1
 2238DCD7 E1D5D538 E632974E 2B15A124 E72BEBCA 054A7000 43090FF6 A62E05DD
 86452268 12EA8BF9 D7E63996 116426D5 02030100 01300D06 092A8648 86F70D01
 01040500 03818100 7DDBBA3F 2EF28952 6458090A E005C659 F26D690C 3CEB89A3
 B4C4BF49 8CA7B624 EF75AA02 3C723BCD 028C04FF 191EE516 49AE9092 CADED3F9
 D652EE75 E0BCF22E EBA6908F BD7D8248 F19F3BCE D06B0A26 5FADFA19 1C5E9721
 6BCD8EFA 249DD629 5024EA19 5B2B0732 CE5DF1DD 7758EB41 B3F3FE1C D0E34AAA
 5E3CA3D2 9FEA6CA2
quit
certificate ca 0171
 3082024C 308201B5 02020171 300D0609 2A864886 F70D0101 04050030 6E310B30
 09060355 04061302 55533110 300E0603 55040813 0747656F 72676961 31183016
 06035504 0A130F54 72616E73 4E657875 732C204C 4C433114 30120603 55040B13
```

Example 10-21 *Configuring OSP on the Terminating Gateway (Continued)*

```
0B446576 656C6F70 6D656E74 311D301B 06035504 03131454 52414E53 4E455855
53204245 54412043 41203130 1E170D39 39303332 32313334 3630395A 170D3030
30333231 31333436 30395A30 6E310B30 09060355 04061302 55533110 300E0603
55040813 0747656F 72676961 31183016 06035504 0A130F54 72616E73 4E657875
732C204C 4C433114 30120603 55040B13 0B446576 656C6F70 6D656E74 311D301B
06035504 03131454 52414E53 4E455855 53204245 54412043 41203130 819F300D
06092A86 4886F70D 01010105 0003818D 00308189 02818100 B1B8ACFC D78F0C95
0258D164 5B6BD8A4 6F5668BD 50E7524B 2339B670 DC306537 3E1E9381 DE2619B4
4698CD82 739CB251 91AF90A5 52736137 658DF200 FAFEFE6B 7FC7161D 89617E5E
4584D67F F018EDAB 2858DDF9 5272F108 AB791A70 580F994B 4CA54F08 38C32DF5
B44077E8 79830F95 96F1DA69 4CAE16F2 2879E07B 164F5F6D 02030100 01300D06
092A8648 86F70D01 01040500 03818100 2FDCB580 C29E557C 52201151 A8DB5F47
C06962D5 8FDA524E A69DE3EE C3FE166A D05C8B93 2844CD66 824A8859 974F22E0
46F69F7E 8027064F C19D28BC CA750E4E FF2DD68E 1AA9CA41 8BB89C68 7A61E9BF
49CBE41E E3A42B16 AAEDAEC7 D3B4F676 4F1A817B A5B89ED8 F03A15B0 39A6EBB9
0AFA6968 17A9D381 FD62BBB7 A7D379E5
quit
!
voice-port 1/0/0
 description Pac Bell 954 9173
!
voice-port 3/0/0
 input gain 14
!
voice-port 3/0/1
!
voice-port 3/1/0
!
voice-port 3/1/1
!
!
dial-peer voice 1 pots
 application clid_authen_collect
 incoming called-number 9549172
 port 3/0/0
!
dial-peer voice 767 pots
 destination-pattern 7......
 port 3/0/0
 prefix 7
!
dial-peer voice 513 pots
 ! The outgoing pots dial peer is associated with the default application and
 ! does not need an OSP application association.
 destination-pattern 1513.......
 port 3/0/0
!
dial-peer voice 1513 voip
 ! The incoming VoIP dial peer, which matches the outgoing VoIP dial peer on
 ! the originating gateway, must also point to a session target of settlement.
 application session
 incoming called-number 1513.......
```

continues

Example 10-21 *Configuring OSP on the Terminating Gateway (Continued)*

```
 session target settlement
!
dial-peer terminator #
process-max-time 200
settlement 0
 type osp
 url https://xxy.144.152.17:8444/
 device-id 1140855798
 customer-id 805311438
 no shutdown
!
interface Ethernet0/0
 no ip address
 no ip directed-broadcast
 shutdown
!
interface Serial0/0
 no ip address
 ni ip directed-broadcast
 no ip mroute-cache
 shutdown
!
interface Ethernet0/1
 description Transnexus enrollment
 ip address xxy.24.141.35 255.255.255.240
 no ip directed-broadcast
!
ip classless
ip route 0.0.0.0 0.0.0.0 xxy.24.141.33
ni ip http server
!
line con 0
 exec-timeout 0 0
 transport input none
line aux 0
line vty 0 4
 no login
!
ntp clock-period 17180148
ntp source Ethernet0/1
ntp server xxy.24.141.33
end
```

Summary

Prepaid services can be managed either internally within the infrastructure of your own network, or through the services of an OSP clearinghouse. Depending on the needs of your particular network, you can use one or both of these solutions to provide and manage prepaid services.

The key to providing internally managed prepaid services is Cisco Systems' debit card application, which coordinates the functionality of four separate applications: IVR, AAA, RADIUS, and a third-party billing system. IVR provides the customer interface; AAA and RADIUS form the infrastructure to provide authentication and billing; and IVR, AAA, and RADIUS communicate with the third-party billing system through VSAs. In this chapter, we discussed the architecture of an internally managed prepaid solution and the required hardware and software elements. We also provided configuration guidelines, and led you through the steps of a typical prepaid services call.

OSP is used for inter-carrier interconnect authorization and accounting, enabling carriers to admit and bill for each VoIP call accepted from another service provider. This capability is critical to toll-bypass applications, specifically international wholesale voice, because the terminating carrier must deliver the call to the PSTN, incurring a fee that must be funded out of the settlement payment from the originating carrier. Because of OSP, you can employ reliable third-party clearinghouses to handle VoIP call termination while leveraging the bandwidth efficiencies and tariff arbitrage advantages that are inherent in IP. This chapter discussed the architecture of an OSP clearinghouse solution and the required hardware and software elements. We provided configuration guidelines and troubleshooting tips and the complete configuration files for typical originating and terminating gateways configured to register with an OSP server.

PART IV

Appendixes

Erlang B Traffic Model

Traffic models are mathematical formulas used in traffic engineering to determine the number of telephone trunks needed to support a given amount of traffic. Traffic models simulate voice traffic patterns. In general, the Erlang B traffic model assumes that calls that cannot get through simply disappear. In the Erlang B model, if a caller receives some sort of denial (such as a busy signal), the caller will either be rerouted to a more expensive circuit or the caller will give up trying to place the call. Use Erlang B when traffic is random and no queuing mechanism is in place. For more information about the Erlang B traffic model, refer to Chapter 1, "Understanding Traffic Analysis."

If you determine that the Erlang B traffic model is appropriate, you can use the Erlang B distribution table to determine the number of circuits needed for a given grade of service (see Table A-1). The grade of service is used to determine the percentage of calls that will experience a busy tone on the first attempt during the busy hour. For example, a grade of service of P.05 means that 5 out of 100 callers will encounter a busy tone when calling during the busy hour.

To use the Erlang B distribution table, you must first determine the amount of traffic your network experiences during its busy hour and express that value in Erlangs. Use the following formula to determine the busy hour traffic in Erlangs:

Erlangs = N 3 A / 3600

N = the number of calls handled during the busy hour and A = the average length of a call, in seconds.

To determine the number of circuits you need, you must first select the grade of service that you want to offer. Trace down the appropriate grade of service column until you find the busy hour traffic of your network (in Erlangs). The number of circuits needed is listed to the far left; the busy hour traffic value is the intersection point between the grade of service and the number of circuits needed.

Table A-1 *Erlang B*

Circuits	\multicolumn{14}{c}{Grade of Service}													
	0.001	0.002	0.003	0.004	0.005	0.01	0.02	0.03	0.04	0.05	0.1	0.2	0.3	0.4
1	0.0000	0.0000	0.0000	0.0000	0.0000	0.0101	0.0204	0.0309	0.0416	0.0526	0.1111	0.2500	0.4282	0.6660
2	0.0457	0.0653	0.0806	0.0937	0.1053	0.1526	0.2234	0.2815	0.3333	0.3811	0.5952	1.0000	1.4482	2.0000
3	0.1938	0.2487	0.2885	0.3210	0.3490	0.4554	0.6021	0.7148	0.8119	0.8990	1.2708	1.9292	2.6323	3.4775
4	0.4392	0.5349	0.6021	0.6555	0.7012	0.8694	1.0920	1.2588	1.3994	1.5244	2.0449	2.9443	3.8887	5.0195
5	0.7620	0.8997	0.9943	1.0690	1.1319	1.3605	1.6571	1.8750	2.0569	2.2180	2.8809	4.0088	5.1855	6.5918
6	1.1459	1.3250	1.4465	1.5417	1.6216	1.9087	2.2756	2.5430	2.7642	2.9597	3.7573	5.1064	6.5098	8.1855
7	1.5785	1.7983	1.9461	2.0610	2.1572	2.5007	2.9352	3.2496	3.5085	3.7375	4.6655	6.2275	7.8545	9.7959
8	2.0513	2.3105	2.4834	2.6177	2.7295	3.1270	3.6270	3.9863	4.2822	4.5420	5.5957	7.3672	9.2109	11.4141
9	2.5573	2.8548	3.0526	3.2053	3.3322	3.7820	4.3440	4.7472	5.0790	5.3701	6.5457	8.5210	10.5732	13.0430
10	3.0920	3.4265	3.6478	3.8190	3.9606	4.4604	5.0830	5.5286	5.8948	6.2146	7.5098	9.6826	11.9482	14.6680
11	3.6510	4.0213	4.2660	4.4540	4.6097	5.1596	5.8411	6.3271	6.7260	7.0751	8.4863	10.8550	13.3311	16.3066
12	4.2312	4.6362	4.9036	5.1086	5.2786	5.8755	6.6138	7.1396	7.5718	7.9497	9.4717	12.0352	14.7188	17.9531
13	4.8302	5.2693	5.5582	5.7803	5.9636	6.6063	7.4014	7.9663	8.4297	8.8344	10.4673	13.2190	16.1040	19.5889
14	5.4461	5.9186	6.2284	6.4668	6.6625	7.3512	8.1997	8.8030	9.2969	9.7275	11.4707	14.4102	17.5000	21.2324
15	6.0768	6.5817	6.9122	7.1658	7.3755	8.1079	9.0088	9.6497	10.1733	10.6311	12.4823	15.6042	18.8965	22.8809
16	6.7212	7.2578	7.6084	7.8779	8.0986	8.8750	9.8281	10.5039	11.0586	11.5430	13.5000	16.8047	20.2969	24.5313
17	7.3778	7.9449	8.3163	8.5996	8.8331	9.6507	10.6551	11.3679	11.9510	12.4595	14.5181	18.0044	21.6982	26.1807
18	8.0453	8.6429	9.0330	9.3318	9.5779	10.4359	11.4895	12.2366	12.8496	13.3835	15.5479	19.2129	23.0977	27.8438
19	8.7236	9.3510	9.7598	10.0729	10.3303	11.2291	12.3319	13.1135	13.7537	14.3126	16.5786	20.4194	24.5015	29.4834
20	9.4110	10.0671	10.4956	10.8221	11.0913	12.0300	13.1812	13.9966	14.6631	15.2490	17.6123	21.6309	25.9082	31.1328
21	10.1071	10.7922	11.2383	11.5792	11.8586	12.8366	14.0350	14.8835	15.5782	16.1858	18.6493	22.8457	27.3164	32.7920
22	10.8120	11.5250	11.9883	12.3428	12.6342	13.6506	14.8940	15.7776	16.5000	17.1311	19.6904	24.0625	28.7246	34.4609
23	11.5239	12.2644	12.7459	13.1130	13.4162	14.4691	15.7592	16.6744	17.4241	18.0782	20.7343	25.2798	30.1426	36.1172
24	12.2432	13.0107	13.5088	13.8896	14.2031	15.2944	16.6289	17.5752	18.3516	19.0283	21.7793	26.4961	31.5469	37.7578
25	12.9684	13.7627	14.2792	14.6729	14.9963	16.1240	17.5034	18.4814	19.2841	19.9829	22.8302	27.7100	32.9590	39.4287
26	13.6998	14.5211	15.0535	15.4597	15.7946	16.9578	18.3812	19.3921	20.2173	20.9409	23.8799	28.9326	34.3789	41.0820

Table A-1   *Erlang B (Continued)*

| Circuits | Grade of Service | | | | | | | | | | | | | |
	0.001	0.002	0.003	0.004	0.005	0.01	0.02	0.03	0.04	0.05	0.1	0.2	0.3	0.4
27	14.4377	15.2847	15.8335	16.2537	16.5965	17.7962	19.2645	20.3027	21.1564	21.9012	24.9368	30.1641	35.7935	42.7412
28	15.1809	16.0533	16.6199	17.0505	17.4043	18.6399	20.1489	21.2188	22.0972	22.8662	25.9902	31.3838	37.2012	44.4063
29	15.9302	16.8276	17.4090	17.8524	18.2170	19.4861	21.0385	22.1394	23.0421	23.8315	27.0494	32.6108	38.6289	46.0488
30	16.6827	17.6056	18.2025	18.6584	19.0338	20.3357	21.9305	23.0603	23.9868	24.7998	28.1104	33.8379	40.0342	47.7246
31	17.4413	18.3873	19.0023	19.4696	19.8537	21.1895	22.8262	23.9841	24.9377	25.7703	29.1685	35.0566	41.4443	49.3760
32	18.2041	19.1748	19.8037	20.2832	20.6768	22.0469	23.7227	24.9141	25.8887	26.7422	30.2344	36.2891	42.8750	51.0313
33	18.9714	19.9654	20.6099	21.1003	21.5032	22.9070	24.6251	25.8417	26.8407	27.7189	31.3000	37.5198	44.2293	52.6904
34	19.7413	20.7603	21.4202	21.9224	22.3353	23.7714	25.5291	26.7742	27.7993	28.6958	32.3647	38.7480	45.7041	54.3535
35	20.5164	21.5588	22.2328	22.7466	23.1685	24.6371	26.4337	27.7090	28.7579	29.6765	33.4277	39.9731	47.1338	56.0205
36	21.2959	22.3594	23.0493	23.5745	24.0051	25.5059	27.3428	28.6436	29.7158	30.6563	34.4971	41.2031	48.5508	57.6914
37	22.0771	23.1645	23.8680	24.4055	24.8458	26.3770	28.2513	29.5837	30.6768	31.6388	35.5682	42.4380	49.9717	59.3301
38	22.8629	23.9727	24.6917	25.2390	25.6878	27.2522	29.1633	30.5225	31.6404	32.6191	36.6362	43.6777	51.3965	61.0078
39	23.6514	24.7844	25.5176	26.0746	26.5328	28.1265	30.0784	31.4661	32.6063	33.6061	37.7146	44.9033	52.8062	62.6895
40	24.4434	25.5981	26.3452	26.9141	27.3804	29.0063	30.9961	32.4097	33.5742	34.5947	38.7842	46.1328	54.2188	64.3359
41	25.2384	26.4145	27.1765	27.7546	28.2300	29.8867	31.9136	33.3550	34.5387	35.5797	39.8589	47.3662	55.6543	65.9844
42	26.0359	27.2344	28.0085	28.5994	29.0826	30.7694	32.8330	34.3044	35.5093	36.5706	40.9336	48.6035	57.0527	67.6758
43	26.8369	28.0560	28.8447	29.4457	29.9378	31.6542	33.7565	35.2524	36.4807	37.5620	42.0079	49.8447	58.4951	69.3291
44	27.6396	28.8804	29.6833	30.2943	30.7952	32.5408	34.6812	36.2012	37.4526	38.5537	43.0869	51.0791	59.8984	70.9844
45	28.4464	29.7070	30.5228	31.1449	31.6544	33.4314	35.6067	37.1530	38.4274	39.5453	44.1595	52.3169	61.3257	72.6416
46	29.2540	30.5370	31.3667	31.9984	32.5164	34.3203	36.5327	38.1050	39.4021	40.5420	45.2363	53.5469	62.7559	74.3008
47	30.0649	31.3687	32.2121	32.8518	33.3796	35.2127	37.4589	39.0596	40.3792	41.5381	46.3173	54.7798	64.1660	75.9619
48	30.8774	32.2017	33.0586	33.7090	34.2451	36.1084	38.3906	40.0137	41.3555	42.5332	47.3965	56.0156	65.6016	77.6250
49	31.6927	33.0385	33.9058	34.5698	35.1111	37.0012	39.3220	40.9729	42.3337	43.5330	48.4736	57.2544	67.0161	79.2900
50	32.5104	33.8745	34.7580	35.4294	35.9802	37.8998	40.2527	41.9312	43.3136	44.5313	49.5605	58.4961	68.4570	80.9570
51	33.3302	34.7154	35.6104	36.2921	36.8508	38.7979	41.1885	42.8881	44.2950	45.5277	50.6389	59.7407	69.8760	82.6260
52	34.1520	35.5564	36.4641	37.1560	37.7241	39.6982	42.1230	43.8496	45.2747	46.5283	51.7207	60.9756	71.2969	84.2969

continues

Table A-1 *Erlang B (Continued)*

Circuits	\	\	\	\	\	Grade of Service	\	\	\	\	\	\	\	\
	0.001	0.002	0.003	0.004	0.005	0.01	0.02	0.03	0.04	0.05	0.1	0.2	0.3	0.4
53	34.9753	36.4003	37.3206	38.0226	38.5968	40.6008	43.0560	44.8093	46.2585	47.5331	52.8059	62.2129	72.7197	85.9697
54	35.8017	37.2453	38.1797	38.8883	39.4717	41.5020	43.9937	45.7734	47.2401	48.5354	53.8879	63.4526	74.1445	87.6445
55	36.6292	38.0928	39.0378	39.7595	40.3503	42.4081	44.9326	46.7352	48.2257	49.5349	54.9731	64.6948	75.5713	89.2676
56	37.4592	38.9409	39.8997	40.6294	41.2275	43.3125	45.8726	47.7012	49.2119	50.5381	56.0547	65.9258	77.0000	90.9453
57	38.2899	39.7911	40.7617	41.5010	42.1064	44.2216	46.8135	48.6643	50.1951	51.5449	57.1392	67.1726	78.4028	92.6250
58	39.1227	40.6432	41.6273	42.3743	42.9885	45.1284	47.7551	49.6313	51.1819	52.5483	58.2266	68.4077	79.8350	94.2500
59	39.9575	41.4970	42.4927	43.2489	43.8719	46.0361	48.6973	50.5987	52.1724	53.5552	59.3097	69.6592	81.2402	95.9326
60	40.7941	42.3523	43.3594	44.1248	44.7546	46.9482	49.6436	51.5662	53.1592	54.5654	60.3955	70.8984	82.6758	97.6172
72	50.9436	52.7168	53.8638	54.7383	55.4546	57.9551	61.0313	63.2417	65.0742	66.6914	73.4590	85.7813	99.7734	117.5625
90	66.4810	68.5547	69.8950	70.9140	71.7517	74.6823	78.3051	80.9143	83.0786	85.0122	93.1421	108.1714	125.4199	147.5684
96	71.7275	73.8926	75.2930	76.3623	77.2383	80.3027	84.0996	86.8359	89.1152	91.1367	99.7148	115.6406	133.9688	157.5000
120	92.9626	95.4822	97.1118	98.3569	99.3787	102.9602	107.4170	110.6470	113.3496	115.7666	126.0645	145.5469	168.2227	197.4609
144	114.5127	117.3560	119.2017	120.6079	121.7637	125.8286	130.9043	134.6045	137.7158	140.5020	152.5078	175.4648	202.5000	237.5156
150	119.9387	122.8638	124.7543	126.2009	127.3911	131.5704	136.7981	140.6158	143.8202	146.7041	159.1187	182.9590	211.0840	247.4121
168	136.2949	139.4480	141.4885	143.0522	144.3340	148.8560	154.5161	158.6689	162.1758	165.3135	178.9717	205.4063	236.7422	277.4297
180	147.2607	150.5566	152.6935	154.3304	155.6763	160.4114	166.3660	170.7385	174.4299	177.7478	192.2168	220.3857	253.8281	297.4219
192	158.2646	161.7012	163.9336	165.6387	167.0449	171.9961	178.2305	182.8125	186.7031	190.1953	205.4766	235.3594	271.0313	317.4375
210	174.8419	178.4821	180.8533	182.6605	184.1537	189.4153	196.0675	200.9637	205.1294	208.8849	225.3552	257.8345	296.7480	347.4023
216	180.3812	184.0924	186.5017	188.3474	189.8701	195.2358	202.0188	207.0220	211.2803	215.1167	231.9785	265.3594	305.2266	357.3281
240	202.6208	206.5942	209.1797	211.1572	212.7905	218.5547	225.8643	231.2842	235.8984	240.0879	258.5449	295.3125	339.6094	397.5000
264	224.9656	229.1873	231.9386	234.0454	235.7856	241.9409	249.7720	255.5889	260.5518	265.0635	285.1084	325.2305	373.8281	437.2500
270	230.5646	234.8492	237.6425	239.7766	241.5482	247.7939	255.7452	261.6696	266.7371	271.3184	291.7529	332.7539	382.3242	447.4512
288	247.3989	251.8682	254.7773	257.0098	258.8467	265.3770	273.7090	279.9316	285.2402	290.0918	311.6602	355.2188	408.0938	477.2813
300	258.6456	263.2324	266.2170	268.5059	270.4010	277.1210	285.6995	292.1082	297.6013	302.6001	324.9756	370.2393	425.2441	497.4609
312	269.9103	274.6139	277.6750	280.0269	281.9692	288.8723	297.6987	304.2876	309.9624	315.1230	338.2412	385.2012	442.4063	517.3594
330	286.8416	291.7108	294.8932	297.3303	299.3445	306.5149	315.6995	322.5879	328.5095	333.9075	358.1982	407.6660	468.0908	547.2070

Table A-1 *Erlang B (Continued)*

Circuits	Grade of Service													
	0.001	0.002	0.003	0.004	0.005	0.01	0.02	0.03	0.04	0.05	0.1	0.2	0.3	0.4
336	292.4927	297.4248	300.6343	303.1055	305.1460	312.4058	321.7061	328.6992	334.6875	340.1836	364.8340	415.2422	476.6016	557.1563
360	315.1318	320.2844	323.6462	326.2280	328.3704	335.9729	345.7507	353.1006	359.4507	365.2515	391.4648	445.1660	510.8203	597.3047
384	337.8281	343.1953	346.6992	349.3945	351.6270	359.5781	369.8203	377.5547	384.2109	390.3281	418.0313	475.1250	545.2500	637.5000
390	343.5114	348.9326	352.4734	355.1930	357.4484	365.4822	375.8368	383.6682	390.4285	396.6174	424.7058	482.6440	553.7695	647.4609
408	360.5797	366.1516	369.7998	372.6013	374.9235	383.2097	393.9053	401.9985	408.9961	415.4458	444.6563	505.1191	579.5273	677.3438
420	371.9669	377.6514	381.3620	384.2139	386.5851	395.0317	405.9650	414.2322	421.4099	427.9980	457.9395	520.0781	596.5723	697.2656
432	383.3657	389.1533	392.9304	395.8374	398.2500	406.8721	418.0254	426.4629	433.7930	440.5430	471.2871	535.1484	613.8281	717.1875
450	400.4929	406.4255	410.3050	413.2919	415.7707	424.6216	436.1160	444.8364	452.4170	459.3933	491.2537	557.6660	639.4043	747.0703
456	406.2015	412.1854	416.1028	419.1086	421.6135	430.5476	442.1536	450.9624	458.6162	465.6577	497.8594	565.1016	647.9297	757.0313
480	429.0674	435.2490	439.2993	442.4121	445.0049	454.2627	466.2891	475.4590	483.4277	490.7813	524.5313	595.0781	682.2656	797.3438
504	451.9742	458.3496	462.5255	465.7478	468.4087	477.9910	490.4648	499.9702	508.2759	515.9355	551.1270	625.0781	716.6250	837.2109
510	457.7051	464.1252	468.3353	471.5804	474.2729	483.9148	496.4905	506.1090	514.4824	522.2021	557.8125	632.5195	725.1563	847.1777
528	474.9148	481.4729	485.7832	489.0945	491.8499	501.7354	514.6260	524.4873	533.0918	541.0840	577.7578	655.1016	750.7500	877.0781
540	486.3922	493.0499	497.4170	500.7788	503.5803	513.6163	526.7175	536.7700	545.5371	553.6450	591.0864	670.1221	767.8125	897.0117
552	497.8832	504.6299	509.0603	512.4716	515.3101	525.5017	538.8267	549.0352	557.9634	566.2178	604.4238	685.1484	785.1445	917.4844
570	515.1187	522.0071	526.5298	530.0175	532.9138	543.3334	556.9711	567.4255	576.5753	585.0989	624.3420	707.4902	810.7471	947.4023
576	520.8750	527.8096	532.3535	535.8691	538.7871	549.2813	563.0273	573.5742	582.8203	591.3633	630.9844	715.0781	819.5625	957.3750
600	543.8965	551.0101	555.6793	559.2865	562.2803	573.0652	587.2192	598.1323	607.6538	616.5161	657.6416	745.0195	853.7109	997.2656
624	566.9377	574.2312	579.0205	582.7148	585.7998	596.8828	611.4507	622.6670	632.5313	641.6719	684.3281	775.1250	887.8594	1037.1563
630	572.7063	580.0410	584.8572	588.5870	591.6824	602.8336	617.5031	628.8080	638.7671	647.9956	690.9851	782.5781	896.3965	1047.1289
648	590.0087	597.4739	602.3782	606.1750	609.3292	620.6902	635.6799	647.2485	657.4131	666.8657	710.9648	804.9375	922.3342	1077.0469
660	601.5491	609.1022	614.0671	617.9041	621.1066	632.6074	647.7942	659.5166	669.8291	679.4568	724.2920	820.0049	939.4043	1096.9922
672	613.1016	620.7305	625.7549	629.6411	632.8711	644.5400	659.9209	671.7949	682.2949	692.0156	737.5430	835.0781	956.4844	1116.9375
690	630.4294	638.1889	643.3058	647.2540	650.5389	662.4152	678.1027	690.2527	700.9497	710.9308	757.5513	857.4463	982.1045	1146.8555
696	636.2087	644.0145	649.1547	653.1266	656.4294	668.3771	684.1692	696.3823	707.1724	717.1978	764.2236	865.0723	990.9844	1156.8281
720	659.3335	667.3096	672.5610	676.6260	680.0098	692.2266	708.4204	720.9668	732.0410	742.4121	790.8398	895.0781	1025.1563	1196.7188

continues

Table A-1 *Erlang B (Continued)*

Circuits	Grade of Service													
---	0.001	0.002	0.003	0.004	0.005	0.01	0.02	0.03	0.04	0.05	0.1	0.2	0.3	0.4
744	682.4806	690.6204	695.9901	700.1338	703.5963	716.0955	732.6929	745.5439	756.9419	767.5679	817.4736	924.9141	1059.3281	1237.3359
750	688.2706	696.4531	701.8433	706.0204	709.4994	722.0764	738.7390	751.6937	763.1836	773.8495	824.1577	932.5562	1067.8711	1247.3145
768	705.6445	713.9531	719.4258	723.6680	727.1953	739.9688	756.9375	770.1563	781.8281	792.7500	844.1250	954.9375	1093.5000	1277.2500
780	717.2415	725.6204	731.1548	735.4395	739.0100	751.9116	769.0979	782.4518	794.2822	805.3271	857.5049	970.0488	1110.5859	1297.2070
792	728.8319	737.2914	742.8746	747.2010	750.8145	763.8662	781.2202	794.7554	806.7437	817.9585	870.7939	984.9727	1127.6719	1317.1641
810	746.2244	754.8143	760.4750	764.8627	768.5211	781.7706	799.4202	813.2135	825.4248	836.8451	890.7825	1007.3584	1153.6963	1347.0996
816	752.0259	760.6545	766.3447	770.7524	774.4380	787.7607	805.4912	819.3618	831.6387	843.1436	897.4805	1015.0195	1162.2422	1357.0781
840	775.2338	784.0265	789.8199	794.3188	798.0615	811.6479	829.7974	843.9478	856.5601	868.3521	924.0820	1045.0781	1196.4258	1396.9922
864	798.4644	807.4028	813.3091	817.8838	821.7070	835.5762	854.0859	868.5879	881.4551	893.5313	950.6953	1074.9375	1230.6094	1436.9063
870	804.2747	813.2487	819.1827	823.7759	827.6257	841.5381	860.1498	874.7260	887.6825	899.8425	957.4036	1082.4023	1239.1553	1446.8848
888	821.7008	830.7927	836.8088	841.4700	845.3588	859.4912	878.3796	893.2031	906.3735	918.7310	977.3203	1105.0137	1265.2266	1476.8203
900	833.3267	842.5003	848.5565	853.2669	857.1945	871.4493	890.5243	905.4932	918.8416	931.3110	990.7471	1119.9463	1282.3242	1496.7773
912	844.9526	854.2068	860.3159	865.0613	869.0273	883.4165	902.6763	917.8169	931.2598	943.9512	1004.0684	1135.1016	1299.4219	1516.7344
930	862.4027	871.7615	877.9628	882.7592	886.7752	901.3632	920.9180	936.3007	949.9805	962.8088	1023.9990	1157.5049	1325.0684	1546.6699
936	868.2166	877.6285	883.8413	888.6687	892.6963	907.3499	927.0022	942.4556	956.2236	969.1348	1030.7197	1164.9727	1333.6172	1556.6484
960	891.5039	901.0547	907.3682	912.2754	916.3770	931.2891	951.2988	967.0605	981.1230	994.3359	1057.2656	1194.8438	1367.8125	1597.5000
984	914.7825	924.4819	930.9082	935.8931	940.0671	955.2319	975.6218	991.6875	1006.0415	1019.5547	1083.9375	1224.9551	1402.0078	1637.4375
990	920.6097	930.3456	936.7960	941.7961	945.9805	961.2076	981.6916	997.8552	1012.2968	1025.8319	1090.6677	1232.4243	1410.5566	1647.4219
1008	938.0863	947.9377	954.4592	959.5195	963.7493	979.1763	999.9404	1016.3057	1030.9482	1044.7910	1110.6211	1255.0781	1436.2031	1677.3750
1020	949.7443	959.6585	966.2265	971.3315	975.6116	991.1444	1012.0935	1028.6536	1043.4082	1057.3535	1123.9673	1270.0195	1453.3008	1697.3438
1032	961.3980	971.3895	978.0033	983.1526	987.4515	1003.1199	1024.2524	1040.9443	1055.8726	1069.9819	1137.3164	1284.9609	1470.3984	1717.3125
1050	978.8876	988.9893	995.6863	1000.8774	1005.2353	1021.0968	1042.5018	1059.4208	1074.6094	1088.9008	1157.2815	1307.3730	1496.5576	1747.2656
1056	984.7148	994.8501	1001.5693	1006.7900	1011.1729	1027.0928	1048.5879	1065.6035	1080.8145	1095.1875	1163.8945	1314.8438	1505.1094	1757.2500
1080	1008.0505	1018.3337	1025.1398	1030.4462	1034.8792	1051.0620	1072.9468	1090.2502	1105.7739	1120.4077	1190.6104	1344.9902	1539.3164	1797.1875
1104	1031.3950	1041.8225	1048.7292	1054.1030	1058.6008	1075.0254	1097.2617	1114.8823	1130.6836	1145.6426	1217.2031	1374.8789	1573.5234	1837.1250
1110	1037.2206	1047.6878	1054.6152	1060.0182	1064.5404	1081.0373	1103.3606	1121.0431	1136.8964	1151.9366	1223.9539	1382.3511	1582.0752	1847.1094

Table A-1 *Erlang B (Continued)*

Circuits	Grade of Service													
	0.001	0.002	0.003	0.004	0.005	0.01	0.02	0.03	0.04	0.05	0.1	0.2	0.3	0.4
1128	1054.7375	1065.3056	1072.3195	1077.7756	1082.3368	1099.0151	1121.5972	1139.5320	1155.6079	1170.8232	1243.9395	1405.0430	1607.7305	1877.0625
1140	1066.4191	1077.0474	1084.1098	1089.6066	1094.1989	1111.0025	1133.7726	1151.8634	1168.1104	1183.4180	1257.1729	1419.9902	1624.8340	1897.0313
1152	1078.1016	1088.8066	1095.9082	1101.4453	1106.0684	1122.9961	1145.9531	1164.1641	1180.5469	1196.0156	1270.5469	1434.9375	1641.9375	1917.0000
1170	1095.6253	1106.4262	1113.6031	1119.1910	1123.8684	1140.9714	1164.2157	1182.6755	1199.2786	1214.9890	1290.5420	1457.3584	1667.5928	1946.9531
1176	1101.4592	1112.3156	1119.5112	1125.1099	1129.8113	1146.9661	1170.2937	1188.8481	1205.5005	1221.2915	1297.1602	1464.8320	1676.1445	1956.9375
1200	1124.8352	1135.8215	1143.1091	1148.8037	1153.5645	1170.9595	1194.6533	1213.4766	1230.4688	1246.5088	1323.9258	1494.7266	1710.9375	1996.8750
1224	1148.2284	1159.3411	1166.7371	1172.4895	1177.3081	1194.9763	1218.9946	1238.1196	1255.3770	1271.7378	1350.5537	1524.9199	1745.1563	2036.8125
1230	1154.0634	1165.2306	1172.6440	1178.4059	1183.2481	1200.9654	1225.0827	1244.3015	1261.6058	1278.0469	1357.1741	1532.3950	1753.7109	2046.7969
1248	1171.6187	1182.8730	1190.3569	1196.1841	1201.0591	1218.9595	1243.3535	1262.7773	1280.2969	1296.9023	1377.1875	1554.8203	1779.3750	2076.7500
1260	1183.3072	1194.6313	1202.1680	1208.0319	1212.9538	1230.9686	1255.5396	1275.1117	1292.7612	1309.5264	1390.4297	1569.7705	1796.4844	2096.7188
1272	1195.0135	1206.4067	1213.9860	1219.8864	1224.8357	1242.9639	1267.6912	1287.4497	1305.2673	1322.1533	1403.8271	1585.0313	1813.5938	2116.6875
1290	1212.5638	1224.0591	1231.6965	1237.6033	1242.6604	1260.9663	1285.9845	1305.9439	1323.9743	1341.0992	1423.8501	1607.4609	1839.2578	2146.6406
1296	1218.4211	1229.9502	1237.6033	1243.5952	1248.5984	1266.9697	1292.0449	1312.1367	1330.2114	1347.4160	1430.4727	1614.9375	1847.8125	2156.6250
1320	1241.8304	1253.4924	1261.2469	1267.2894	1272.3651	1290.9961	1316.4148	1336.7578	1355.1270	1372.6099	1457.1240	1644.8438	1882.0313	2196.5625
1344	1265.2500	1277.0420	1284.8965	1291.0078	1296.1553	1315.0020	1340.8008	1361.4316	1380.0938	1397.8125	1483.7813	1674.7500	1916.2500	2236.5000
1350	1271.1044	1282.9285	1290.7974	1296.9360	1302.0859	1320.9961	1346.8689	1367.5919	1386.3373	1404.1351	1490.4053	1682.2266	1924.8047	2246.4844
1368	1288.6787	1300.5978	1308.5508	1314.7295	1319.9271	1339.0269	1365.1611	1386.1187	1405.0723	1423.1074	1510.4443	1704.6563	1950.4688	2276.4375
1380	1300.4041	1312.3856	1320.3662	1326.5991	1331.8213	1351.0254	1377.3468	1398.4460	1417.5238	1435.6750	1523.8623	1719.9463	1967.5781	2296.4063
1392	1312.1155	1324.1693	1332.1875	1338.4534	1343.7209	1363.0283	1389.5361	1410.7764	1429.9775	1448.3291	1537.1133	1734.9023	1984.6875	2316.3750
1410	1329.6957	1341.8408	1349.9304	1356.2558	1361.5485	1381.0410	1407.8055	1429.2773	1448.7268	1467.2296	1557.1619	1757.3364	2010.3516	2346.3281
1416	1335.5592	1347.7452	1355.8477	1362.2000	1367.5151	1387.0474	1413.8826	1435.4458	1454.9780	1473.5596	1563.7881	1764.8145	2018.9063	2356.3125
1440	1359.0088	1371.3135	1379.5093	1385.9253	1391.3086	1411.0840	1438.2422	1460.1270	1479.9023	1498.7109	1590.4688	1794.7266	2053.1250	2396.2500
1464	1382.4520	1394.9059	1403.1936	1409.6719	1415.1002	1435.1158	1462.6150	1484.7751	1504.8354	1523.9575	1617.1553	1824.9961	2087.3438	2436.1875
1470	1388.3196	1400.7909	1409.1014	1415.6062	1421.0568	1441.1096	1468.7439	1490.9500	1511.0925	1530.2930	1623.7830	1832.4756	2095.8984	2446.1719
1488	1405.9098	1418.4771	1426.8552	1433.4170	1438.9116	1459.1646	1487.0010	1509.4336	1529.7773	1549.2129	1643.6660	1854.9141	2121.5625	2476.1250
1500	1417.6483	1430.2826	1438.7054	1445.2744	1450.8133	1471.1609	1499.1760	1521.7896	1542.2974	1561.7981	1657.1045	1869.8730	2138.6719	2496.0938

continues

Table A-1   *Erlang B (Continued)*

Circuits														
							Grade of Service							
	0.001	0.002	0.003	0.004	0.005	0.01	0.02	0.03	0.04	0.05	0.1	0.2	0.3	0.4
1512	1429.3817	1442.0709	1450.5381	1457.1595	1462.7197	1483.1840	1511.4001	1534.1484	1554.7280	1574.4771	1670.3613	1884.8320	2155.7813	2516.0625
1530	1446.9818	1459.7754	1468.2967	1474.9736	1480.5766	1501.2144	1529.6732	1552.5989	1573.5168	1593.4076	1690.4333	1907.2705	2182.1924	2546.0156
1536	1452.8438	1465.6641	1474.2188	1480.8984	1486.5234	1507.2188	1535.7656	1558.7813	1579.6875	1599.6563	1697.0625	1914.7500	2190.7500	2556.0000
1560	1476.3181	1489.2673	1497.8961	1504.6564	1510.3455	1531.2689	1560.1428	1583.4705	1604.6558	1624.9365	1723.7695	1944.6680	2224.9805	2595.9375
1584	1499.7920	1512.8679	1521.5933	1528.4092	1534.1616	1555.3103	1584.5317	1608.1699	1629.6328	1650.1289	1750.2891	1974.5859	2259.2109	2635.8750
1590	1505.6671	1518.7683	1527.5267	1534.3684	1540.1184	1561.3229	1590.6308	1614.3100	1635.9027	1656.4764	1757.1130	1982.0654	2267.7686	2645.8594
1608	1523.2890	1536.4772	1545.2856	1552.1803	1557.9708	1579.3663	1608.9324	1632.8306	1654.6187	1675.4253	1777.0049	2004.8965	2293.4414	2675.8125
1620	1535.0276	1548.2895	1557.1390	1564.0604	1569.8941	1591.3751	1621.0876	1645.1642	1667.0654	1688.0273	1790.4639	2019.8584	2310.5566	2695.7813
1632	1546.7842	1560.1069	1568.9971	1575.9448	1581.7969	1603.4121	1633.2949	1657.5000	1679.5137	1700.6309	1803.7266	2034.8203	2327.6719	2715.7500
1650	1564.3982	1577.8175	1586.7680	1593.7798	1599.6712	1621.4493	1651.6113	1676.0330	1698.2391	1719.5892	1823.6206	2057.2632	2353.3447	2745.7031
1656	1570.2638	1583.7067	1592.7023	1599.7269	1605.6398	1627.4465	1657.6677	1682.1782	1704.5156	1725.8423	1830.2520	2064.7441	2361.9023	2755.6875
1680	1593.7646	1607.3383	1616.4001	1623.5010	1629.4482	1651.5198	1682.1021	1706.8652	1729.4751	1751.0596	1856.9824	2094.6680	2396.1328	2797.2656
1704	1617.2867	1630.9633	1640.1156	1647.2659	1653.2981	1675.5809	1706.4961	1731.5610	1754.4419	1776.2827	1883.7188	2125.0078	2430.3633	2837.2266
1710	1623.1510	1636.8626	1646.0472	1653.2227	1659.2500	1681.5852	1712.5571	1737.7103	1760.6717	1782.6416	1890.3516	2132.4902	2438.9209	2847.2168
1728	1640.7905	1654.5938	1663.8223	1671.0469	1677.1377	1699.6289	1730.8477	1756.2656	1779.3633	1801.5117	1910.2500	2154.9375	2464.5938	2877.1875
1740	1652.5433	1666.4026	1675.6819	1682.9434	1689.0500	1711.6708	1743.0798	1768.5681	1791.8793	1814.1284	1923.7280	2169.9023	2481.7090	2897.1680
1752	1664.3011	1678.2292	1687.5458	1694.8440	1700.9659	1723.6893	1755.2615	1780.9255	1804.3975	1826.8535	1936.9951	2184.8672	2498.8242	2917.1484
1770	1681.9402	1695.9574	1705.3427	1712.6619	1718.8467	1741.7496	1773.5651	1799.4388	1823.0438	1845.7306	1956.8958	2207.3145	2524.4971	2947.1191
1776	1687.8179	1701.8690	1711.2590	1718.6301	1724.8088	1747.7622	1779.6313	1805.5928	1829.3320	1851.9873	1963.7461	2214.7969	2533.0547	2957.1094
1800	1711.3403	1725.5127	1734.9884	1742.4042	1748.6664	1771.8201	1804.0649	1830.3223	1854.2725	1877.2339	1990.2832	2244.7266	2567.2852	2997.0703
1824	1734.8679	1749.1597	1758.7061	1766.1929	1772.5107	1795.8896	1828.4531	1854.9492	1879.2188	1902.4863	2017.0430	2274.6563	2601.5156	3037.0313
1830	1740.7562	1755.0671	1764.6449	1772.1423	1778.4810	1801.9089	1834.5236	1861.1627	1885.5121	1908.8562	2023.6780	2282.1387	2610.0732	3047.0215
1848	1758.4001	1772.7953	1782.4391	1789.9962	1796.3690	1819.9709	1852.8501	1879.6948	1904.2273	1927.7446	2043.5830	2304.5859	2636.6484	3076.9922
1860	1770.1730	1784.6191	1794.2972	1801.9034	1808.2892	1832.0160	1865.0519	1892.0142	1916.7059	1940.3760	2057.0801	2319.5508	2653.7695	3096.9727
1872	1781.9363	1796.4470	1806.1875	1813.7856	1820.2126	1844.0354	1877.2559	1904.3350	1929.1860	1953.0088	2070.3516	2334.5156	2670.8906	3116.9531
1890	1799.5894	1814.1964	1823.9873	1831.6585	1838.1184	1862.0837	1895.5371	1922.8766	1947.9089	1971.9031	2090.2588	2356.9629	2696.5723	3146.9238

Table A-1 *Erlang B (Continued)*

Circuits	Grade of Service													
	0.001	0.002	0.003	0.004	0.005	0.01	0.02	0.03	0.04	0.05	0.1	0.2	0.3	0.4
1896	1805.4760	1820.1149	1829.9224	1837.5890	1844.0695	1868.1108	1901.6704	1929.0388	1954.1506	1978.2788	2096.8945	2364.9082	2705.1328	3156.9141
1920	1829.0186	1843.7695	1853.6426	1861.4063	1867.9395	1892.1680	1926.0352	1953.7500	1979.1211	2003.4375	2123.6719	2394.8438	2739.3750	3196.8750
1944	1852.5635	1867.4396	1877.4064	1885.2078	1891.7930	1916.2650	1950.4666	1978.4092	2004.0974	2028.7178	2150.2178	2424.7793	2773.6172	3236.8359
1950	1858.4599	1873.3521	1883.3199	1891.1751	1897.7509	1922.2687	1956.5460	1984.6344	2010.3424	2034.9792	2156.8542	2432.2632	2782.1777	3246.8262
1968	1876.1104	1891.0950	1901.1398	1909.0225	1915.6589	1940.3430	1974.8467	2003.1343	2029.0195	2054.0039	2177.0039	2454.7148	2807.8594	3276.7969
1980	1887.8975	1902.9282	1913.0191	1920.9348	1927.6117	1952.3859	1987.0697	2015.4694	2041.5125	2066.5283	2190.2783	2469.6826	2824.9805	3296.7773
1992	1899.6736	1914.7650	1924.8867	1932.8199	1939.5374	1964.4009	1999.2949	2027.8059	2054.0068	2079.1743	2203.5527	2484.6504	2842.1016	3316.7578
2010	1917.3454	1932.5272	1942.7097	1950.6839	1957.4313	1982.4889	2017.6062	2046.3135	2072.7512	2098.0847	2223.4644	2507.1021	2867.7832	3346.7285
2016	1923.2227	1938.4497	1948.6318	1956.6606	1963.3975	1988.4990	2023.6904	2052.5449	2079.0000	2104.4707	2230.3477	2514.5859	2876.3438	3356.7188
2040	1946.8030	1962.1179	1972.3901	1980.4523	1987.2693	2012.6074	2048.0933	2077.2290	2103.9990	2129.6484	2256.8994	2545.0195	2910.5859	3396.6797
2064	1970.3679	1985.8000	1996.1616	2004.2871	2011.1528	2036.6631	2072.5034	2101.9189	2128.9409	2154.9551	2283.7031	2574.9609	2944.8281	3436.6406
2070	1976.2537	1991.7149	2002.0908	2010.2399	2017.1255	2042.7100	2078.5913	2108.0923	2135.1929	2161.2195	2290.3418	2582.4463	2953.3887	3446.6309
2088	1993.9164	2009.4802	2019.9144	2028.1025	2035.0162	2060.7594	2096.9209	2126.6147	2153.8872	2180.1401	2310.2578	2604.9023	2979.0703	3476.6016
2100	2005.7121	2021.3173	2031.7795	2040.0146	2046.9681	2072.8271	2109.1003	2138.9648	2166.3940	2192.7979	2323.5352	2619.8730	2996.1914	3496.5820
2112	2017.4956	2033.1738	2043.6797	2051.9297	2058.8906	2084.8652	2121.3457	2151.3164	2178.9023	2205.4570	2336.8125	2634.8438	3013.3125	3516.5625
2130	2035.1777	2050.9245	2061.4874	2069.8077	2076.8280	2102.9265	2139.6204	2169.7815	2197.6025	2224.3835	2356.9885	2657.2998	3038.9941	3546.5332
2136	2041.0735	2056.8484	2067.4248	2075.7686	2082.7760	2108.9480	2145.7126	2176.0239	2203.8582	2230.6494	2363.6279	2664.7852	3047.5547	3556.5234
2160	2064.6497	2080.5359	2091.2146	2099.5862	2106.6724	2133.0396	2170.1514	2200.6714	2228.8184	2255.8447	2390.1855	2694.7266	3081.7969	3596.4844
2184	2088.2234	2104.2195	2114.9835	2123.4148	2130.5464	2157.1399	2194.5308	2225.3899	2253.7830	2281.1763	2417.0098	2724.6680	3116.0391	3636.4453
2190	2094.1273	2110.1507	2120.9276	2129.3820	2136.5332	2163.1329	2200.6934	2231.5704	2260.0415	2287.4432	2423.6499	2732.1533	3124.5996	3646.4355
2208	2111.8110	2127.9155	2138.7473	2147.2544	2154.4307	2181.2153	2218.9834	2250.0469	2278.7520	2306.3789	2443.5703	2754.6094	3150.2813	3676.4063
2220	2123.6101	2139.7852	2150.6250	2159.1614	2166.3766	2193.2730	2231.1786	2262.4109	2291.2720	2319.0491	2456.8506	2769.5801	3167.4023	3696.3867
2232	2135.4126	2151.6240	2162.5225	2171.0880	2178.3252	2205.3329	2243.3752	2274.7764	2303.7935	2331.5845	2470.1309	2784.5508	3184.5234	3716.3672
2250	2153.0972	2169.3878	2180.3398	2188.9572	2196.2357	2223.3925	2261.6730	2293.3273	2322.5098	2350.5249	2490.3259	2807.0068	3210.2051	3746.3379
2256	2158.9937	2175.3278	2186.2917	2194.9321	2202.2300	2229.4248	2267.8418	2299.5117	2328.7031	2356.9307	2496.9668	2814.4922	3218.7656	3756.3281
2280	2182.5879	2199.0262	2210.0720	2218.7695	2226.1102	2253.5248	2292.2461	2324.1833	2353.6853	2382.1436	2523.5303	2844.4336	3253.0078	3796.2891

continues

Table A-1 *Erlang B (Continued)*

Circuits	Grade of Service													
	0.001	0.002	0.003	0.004	0.005	0.01	0.02	0.03	0.04	0.05	0.1	0.2	0.3	0.4
2304	2206.1953	2222.7363	2233.8633	2242.6172	2250.0000	2277.6328	2316.6563	2348.8594	2378.6719	2407.3594	2550.0938	2874.3750	3287.2500	3836.2500
2310	2212.0816	2228.6481	2239.7864	2248.5631	2255.9651	2283.6346	2322.7597	2355.0467	2384.8663	2413.6285	2556.7346	2881.8604	3295.8105	3846.2402
2328	2229.7804	2246.4404	2257.6300	2266.4396	2273.8993	2301.7134	2341.0723	2373.6108	2403.5918	2432.5781	2576.9414	2904.3164	3321.4922	3876.2109
2340	2241.5955	2258.3057	2269.5172	2278.3722	2285.8347	2313.7921	2353.2825	2385.9888	2416.1243	2445.2600	2590.2246	2919.8584	3338.6133	3896.1914
2352	2253.3779	2270.1379	2281.4249	2290.3074	2297.8081	2325.8372	2365.4941	2398.2964	2428.6582	2457.9434	2603.5078	2934.8320	3355.7344	3916.1719
2370	2271.0933	2287.9454	2299.2645	2308.1969	2315.7188	2343.8901	2383.8144	2416.8677	2447.3895	2476.7542	2623.4326	2957.2925	3381.4160	3946.1426
2376	2276.9879	2293.8646	2305.2123	2314.1492	2321.6902	2349.9327	2389.9219	2422.9863	2453.5854	2483.1694	2630.0742	2964.7793	3389.9766	3956.1328
2400	2300.6104	2317.5659	2328.9917	2338.0005	2345.6177	2374.0356	2414.3555	2447.6807	2478.5156	2508.3984	2656.9336	2994.7266	3424.2188	3996.0938
2424	2324.2083	2341.2964	2352.7994	2361.8613	2369.5177	2398.1459	2438.7209	2472.3794	2503.5967	2533.6304	2683.5029	3024.6738	3458.4609	4036.0547
2430	2330.1096	2347.2215	2358.7344	2367.8188	2375.4941	2404.1931	2444.8315	2478.5733	2509.7937	2539.9017	2690.1453	3032.1606	3467.0215	4046.0449
2448	2347.8179	2365.0005	2376.5801	2385.6943	2393.4265	2422.2634	2463.1655	2497.1572	2528.5342	2558.8652	2710.0723	3054.6211	3492.7031	4076.0156
2460	2359.6271	2376.8752	2388.4927	2397.6141	2405.3467	2434.3250	2475.3900	2509.4733	2541.0040	2571.5588	2723.6572	3069.5947	3509.8242	4095.9961
2472	2371.4392	2388.7337	2400.3702	2409.5550	2417.3064	2446.3506	2487.6160	2521.7900	2553.4746	2584.1030	2736.9434	3084.5684	3526.9453	4115.9766
2490	2389.1629	2406.5263	2418.2286	2427.4612	2435.2501	2464.4678	2505.9576	2540.3046	2572.2198	2603.0713	2756.8726	3107.0288	3552.6270	4145.9473
2496	2395.0532	2412.4585	2424.1699	2433.4248	2441.2324	2470.4824	2511.9961	2546.5020	2578.4180	2609.3438	2763.5156	3114.5156	3561.1875	4155.9375
2520	2418.6786	2436.1743	2447.9791	2457.2845	2465.1288	2494.5831	2536.4575	2571.2183	2603.4412	2634.5874	2790.0879	3144.4629	3595.4297	4195.8984
2544	2442.2959	2459.9194	2471.7784	2481.1337	2489.0332	2518.6904	2560.8472	2595.9390	2628.4688	2659.8340	2816.6602	3175.0313	3629.6719	4235.8594
2550	2448.2117	2465.8379	2477.7443	2487.0827	2495.0203	2524.7086	2566.9647	2602.1393	2634.6680	2666.1072	2823.6145	3182.5195	3638.2324	4245.8496
2568	2465.9242	2483.6356	2495.5869	2504.9912	2512.9457	2542.8435	2585.3196	2620.6641	2653.4224	2685.0835	2843.5459	3204.9844	3663.9141	4275.8203
2580	2477.7425	2495.5170	2507.4847	2516.9330	2524.9246	2554.8834	2597.5580	2632.9889	2665.9003	2697.7881	2856.8335	3219.9609	3681.0352	4295.8008
2592	2489.5635	2507.3811	2519.3848	2528.8572	2536.8662	2566.9248	2609.7188	2645.3145	2678.3789	2710.3359	2870.1211	3234.9375	3698.1563	4315.7813
2610	2507.2703	2525.1718	2537.2389	2546.7572	2554.8019	2585.0294	2628.0807	2663.8440	2697.1381	2729.3170	2890.0525	3257.4023	3723.8379	4345.7520
2616	2513.1738	2531.0966	2543.1914	2552.7316	2560.7948	2591.0519	2634.1622	2670.0476	2703.3384	2735.5913	2896.6963	3264.8906	3732.3984	4355.7422
2640	2536.8146	2554.8413	2567.0068	2576.5942	2584.6912	2615.1855	2658.6108	2694.7852	2728.3008	2760.8496	2923.5938	3294.8438	3766.6406	4395.7031
2664	2560.4456	2578.5956	2590.8107	2600.4650	2608.6355	2639.2852	2683.0239	2719.4458	2753.2661	2786.1108	2950.1719	3324.7969	3800.8828	4435.6641
2670	2566.3550	2584.5255	2596.7681	2606.4441	2614.5923	2645.3110	2689.1483	2725.6522	2759.5486	2792.3859	2956.8164	3332.2852	3809.4434	4445.6543

Table A-1 *Erlang B (Continued)*

Circuits	Grade of Service													
	0.001	0.002	0.003	0.004	0.005	0.01	0.02	0.03	0.04	0.05	0.1	0.2	0.3	0.4
2688	2584.0869	2602.3184	2614.6230	2624.3438	2632.5469	2663.3906	2707.4414	2744.1914	2778.2344	2811.3750	2976.7500	3354.7500	3835.1250	4475.6250
2700	2595.9114	2614.1830	2626.5427	2636.2656	2644.5053	2675.4456	2719.6930	2756.5247	2790.8020	2823.9258	2990.0391	3369.7266	3852.2461	4495.6055
2712	2607.7178	2626.0706	2638.4231	2648.1892	2656.4656	2687.5433	2731.8633	2768.9414	2803.2883	2836.6421	3003.3281	3384.7031	3869.3672	4515.5859
2730	2625.4630	2643.8752	2656.3097	2666.0989	2674.4302	2705.6310	2750.2451	2787.4026	2821.9775	2855.4694	3023.5950	3407.1680	3895.0488	4545.5566
2736	2631.3794	2649.8112	2662.2521	2672.0837	2680.3916	2711.6609	2756.2896	2793.6123	2828.2632	2861.9121	3030.2402	3414.6563	3903.6094	4555.5469
2760	2655.0092	2673.5605	2686.0684	2695.9442	2704.3250	2735.7843	2780.7202	2818.2861	2853.2410	2887.0166	3056.8213	3444.6094	3937.8516	4595.5078
2784	2678.6697	2697.2974	2709.8928	2719.8120	2728.2656	2759.9136	2805.1553	2843.0479	2878.2217	2912.2910	3083.4023	3474.5625	3973.4531	4635.4688
2790	2684.5704	2703.2382	2715.8395	2725.8014	2734.2307	2765.9042	2811.2860	2849.1751	2884.5099	2918.7378	3090.0476	3482.0508	3982.0166	4645.4590
2808	2702.2972	2721.0641	2733.7039	2743.6871	2752.1708	2784.0059	2829.5947	2867.7283	2903.2053	2937.5684	3109.9834	3504.5156	4007.7070	4675.4297
2820	2714.1252	2732.9292	2745.6230	2755.6274	2764.1473	2796.0754	2841.8591	2880.0696	2915.6982	2950.2942	3123.6182	3519.4922	4024.8340	4695.4102
2832	2725.9556	2744.7964	2757.5442	2767.5696	2776.1041	2808.1465	2854.0386	2892.4116	2928.1919	2962.8486	3136.9102	3534.4688	4041.9609	4715.3906
2850	2743.6947	2762.6118	2775.3971	2785.5080	2794.0315	2826.2558	2872.3526	2910.9695	2946.8903	2981.8542	3156.8481	3556.9336	4067.6514	4745.3613
2856	2749.6234	2768.5585	2781.3490	2791.4594	2800.0444	2832.2930	2878.4868	2917.1851	2953.0942	2988.1318	3163.4941	3564.4219	4076.2148	4755.3516
2880	2773.2568	2792.3071	2805.1831	2815.3564	2823.9697	2856.4014	2902.9395	2941.8750	2978.0859	3013.4180	3190.0781	3594.3750	4110.4688	4795.3125
2904	2796.9212	2816.0638	2829.0027	2839.2166	2847.9016	2880.5149	2927.3522	2966.5679	3003.0806	3038.5298	3216.6621	3624.3281	4144.7227	4835.2734
2910	2802.8332	2821.9931	2834.9588	2845.2159	2853.8745	2886.5552	2933.4448	2972.6971	3009.3741	3044.9854	3223.3081	3631.8164	4153.2861	4845.2637
2928	2820.5724	2839.8285	2852.8297	2863.1279	2871.8401	2904.6782	2951.7686	2991.2637	3028.0781	3063.8203	3243.2461	3654.2813	4178.9766	4875.2344
2940	2832.4013	2851.7139	2864.7459	2875.0415	2883.7894	2916.7172	2964.0454	3003.6127	3040.5780	3076.5564	3256.8970	3669.2578	4196.1035	4895.2148
2952	2844.2324	2863.5787	2876.6640	2887.0016	2895.7852	2928.8024	2976.2336	3015.9624	3053.0786	3089.1138	3270.1904	3684.2344	4213.2305	4915.1953
2970	2861.9831	2881.4021	2894.5445	2904.9225	2913.7143	2946.8875	2994.5627	3034.5337	3071.8762	3108.1311	3290.1306	3706.6992	4238.9209	4945.1660
2976	2867.9011	2887.3594	2900.4829	2910.8818	2919.6914	2952.9316	3000.6577	3040.6641	3078.0820	3114.4102	3296.7773	3714.1875	4247.4844	4955.1563
3000	2891.5558	2911.1023	2924.3317	2934.7687	2943.6493	2977.0660	3025.0854	3065.3687	3103.0884	3139.5264	3323.3643	3744.1406	4281.7383	4995.1172
3024	2915.2419	2934.8756	2948.1647	2958.6621	2967.5676	3001.2056	3049.5630	3090.1685	3128.0977	3164.8271	3349.9512	3774.0938	4315.9922	5035.0781
3030	2921.1417	2940.8144	2954.1298	2964.6249	2973.5481	3007.2066	3055.6137	3096.2997	3134.3042	3171.1066	3356.5979	3781.5820	4324.5557	5045.0684
3048	2938.8904	2958.6334	2972.0046	2982.5621	2991.5383	3025.3037	3073.9519	3114.8796	3153.0168	3190.1309	3376.9102	3804.7910	4350.2461	5075.0391
3060	2950.7410	2970.5383	2983.9156	2994.4913	3003.5028	3037.4011	3086.1942	3127.2363	3165.5237	3202.6904	3390.2051	3819.7705	4367.3730	5095.0195

continues

Table A-1 *Erlang B (Continued)*

Circuits	\multicolumn													
	Grade of Service													
	0.001	0.002	0.003	0.004	0.005	0.01	0.02	0.03	0.04	0.05	0.1	0.2	0.3	0.4
3072	2962.5703	2982.4219	2995.8281	3006.4453	3015.4688	3049.4531	3098.4375	3139.5938	3177.9375	3215.4375	3403.5000	3834.7500	4384.5000	5115.0000
3090	2980.3299	3000.2271	3013.7119	3024.3677	3033.4204	3067.5568	3116.7810	3158.0841	3196.7468	3234.2780	3423.4424	3857.2192	4410.1904	5144.9707
3096	2986.2350	3006.1708	3019.6582	3030.3347	3039.4050	3073.6077	3122.8330	3164.3108	3202.9541	3240.5581	3430.0898	3864.7090	4418.7539	5154.9609
3120	3009.9078	3029.9506	3043.4949	3054.2542	3063.3472	3097.7197	3147.3267	3189.0308	3227.9736	3265.8691	3456.6797	3894.6680	4453.0078	5194.9219
3144	3033.5887	3053.7136	3067.3381	3078.1322	3087.2952	3121.8362	3171.7288	3213.6577	3252.9961	3291.1831	3483.2695	3924.6270	4487.2617	5234.8828
3150	3039.4981	3059.6615	3073.3120	3084.1026	3093.2831	3127.8900	3177.8778	3219.8868	3259.2041	3297.4640	3489.9170	3932.1167	4495.8252	5244.8730
3168	3057.2534	3077.5078	3091.1880	3102.0161	3111.2490	3146.0054	3196.1338	3238.3828	3277.9248	3316.3066	3509.8594	3954.5859	4521.5156	5274.8438
3180	3069.1008	3089.3834	3103.1154	3113.9845	3123.2281	3158.0676	3208.4344	3250.8435	3290.4382	3329.0625	3523.5425	3969.5654	4538.6426	5294.8242
3192	3080.9502	3101.2606	3115.0444	3125.9302	3135.1844	3170.1310	3220.6392	3263.1108	3302.8550	3341.6250	3536.8389	3984.5449	4555.7695	5314.8047
3210	3098.6913	3119.0918	3132.9044	3143.8515	3153.1334	3188.2526	3238.9476	3281.7078	3321.6760	3360.4688	3556.7834	4007.0142	4581.4600	5344.7754
3216	3104.6305	3125.0446	3138.8829	3149.8260	3159.1252	3194.2610	3245.0508	3287.8418	3327.8848	3366.9463	3563.4316	4014.5039	4590.0234	5354.7656
3240	3128.2938	3148.8354	3162.7277	3173.7277	3183.0963	3218.4448	3269.4653	3312.5757	3352.9175	3392.0728	3590.0244	4044.4629	4624.2773	5394.7266
3264	3151.9893	3172.6084	3186.5537	3197.6353	3207.0234	3242.5840	3293.9824	3337.3125	3377.8535	3417.3984	3616.6172	4074.4219	4658.5313	5434.6875
3270	3157.9081	3178.5402	3192.5361	3203.5881	3213.0185	3248.5945	3300.0375	3343.4473	3384.1626	3423.6804	3623.2654	4081.9116	4667.0947	5444.6777
3288	3175.6674	3196.3879	3210.4358	3221.5236	3230.9808	3266.7275	3318.4036	3362.0522	3402.7910	3442.7271	3643.2100	4104.3809	4692.7852	5474.6484
3300	3187.5092	3208.2802	3222.3541	3233.4824	3242.9489	3278.7506	3330.6152	3374.3225	3415.4114	3455.2917	3656.9092	4119.3604	4709.9121	5494.6289
3312	3199.3528	3220.1741	3234.2739	3245.4426	3254.9436	3290.8250	3342.8276	3386.6938	3427.8311	3467.8564	3670.2070	4134.3398	4727.0391	5514.6094
3330	3217.1217	3238.0053	3252.1564	3263.3858	3272.8876	3308.9639	3361.1984	3405.2014	3446.5622	3486.9067	3690.1538	4156.8091	4752.7295	5544.5801
3336	3223.0455	3243.9413	3258.1179	3269.3421	3278.8865	3314.9769	3367.2546	3411.4387	3452.8740	3493.1895	3696.8027	4164.2988	4761.2930	5554.5703
3360	3246.7456	3267.7405	3281.9678	3293.2471	3302.8345	3339.1333	3391.6846	3436.1865	3477.8174	3518.3203	3723.3984	4194.2578	4795.5469	5594.5313
3384	3270.4272	3291.5204	3305.8235	3317.1575	3326.7876	3363.2424	3416.1174	3460.8340	3502.7622	3543.6577	3749.9941	4224.2168	4829.8008	5634.4922
3390	3276.3551	3297.4599	3311.7883	3323.1166	3332.7896	3369.3091	3422.2778	3467.0737	3508.9728	3549.9408	3756.6431	4231.7065	4838.3643	5644.4824
3408	3294.1157	3315.3065	3329.6851	3341.0735	3350.7458	3387.4072	3440.5532	3485.5869	3527.8125	3568.9980	3776.5898	4255.0078	4864.0547	5674.4531
3420	3305.9756	3327.2150	3341.6180	3353.0205	3362.7269	3399.4913	3452.8244	3497.9645	3540.2344	3581.5649	3789.8877	4269.9902	4881.1816	5694.4336
3432	3317.8112	3339.0989	3353.5263	3364.9688	3374.7092	3411.5764	3465.0443	3510.3428	3552.7610	3594.1318	3803.1855	4284.9727	4898.3086	5714.4141
3450	3335.5808	3356.9275	3371.4306	3382.9067	3392.6720	3429.6799	3483.3755	3528.8589	3571.4996	3613.1927	3823.5535	4307.4463	4923.9990	5744.3848

Table A-1   *Erlang B (Continued)*

Circuits	Grade of Service													
	0.001	0.002	0.003	0.004	0.005	0.01	0.02	0.03	0.04	0.05	0.1	0.2	0.3	0.4
3456	3341.5137	3362.8711	3377.3730	3388.8691	3398.6777	3435.6973	3489.4863	3534.9961	3577.7109	3619.4766	3830.2031	4314.9375	4932.5625	5754.3750
3480	3365.1965	3386.6757	3401.2518	3412.8012	3422.6248	3459.8749	3513.9844	3559.7571	3602.7686	3644.6118	3856.8018	4344.9023	4966.8164	5794.3359
3504	3388.9127	3410.4598	3425.1097	3436.7120	3446.5767	3484.0034	3538.3792	3584.4141	3627.7222	3669.9609	3883.4004	4374.8672	5001.0703	5834.2969
3510	3394.8228	3416.4068	3431.0550	3442.6772	3452.5854	3490.0227	3544.4916	3590.6589	3634.0411	3676.2451	3890.0500	4382.3584	5009.6338	5844.2871
3528	3412.6089	3434.2767	3448.9731	3460.6280	3470.5602	3508.1356	3562.8300	3609.1802	3652.6772	3695.0977	3909.9990	4404.8320	5035.3242	5874.2578
3540	3424.4595	3446.1740	3460.8934	3472.5879	3482.5269	3520.2301	3575.0565	3621.5643	3665.2094	3707.8821	3923.2983	4419.8145	5052.4512	5894.2383
3552	3436.3118	3458.0728	3472.8149	3484.5220	3494.4946	3532.2715	3587.2295	3633.9492	3677.7422	3720.4512	3936.5977	4434.7969	5069.5781	5914.2188
3570	3454.0796	3475.8964	3490.7133	3502.4796	3512.4756	3550.3894	3605.6259	3652.4734	3696.3794	3739.3048	3956.5466	4457.2705	5095.2686	5944.1895
3576	3459.9939	3481.8474	3496.6891	3508.4480	3518.4880	3556.4656	3611.6858	3658.6121	3702.5918	3745.5894	3963.1963	4464.7617	5103.8320	5954.1797
3600	3483.7097	3505.6549	3520.5414	3532.3792	3542.4316	3580.6091	3636.1450	3683.2764	3727.6611	3770.9473	3989.7949	4494.7266	5138.0859	5994.1406
3624	3507.4321	3529.4407	3544.4264	3556.2878	3566.3796	3604.7563	3660.6072	3708.0527	3752.7334	3796.0869	4016.8359	4524.6914	5172.3398	6034.1016
3630	3513.3499	3535.3949	3550.3777	3562.2588	3572.3950	3610.7799	3666.7786	3714.1919	3758.9465	3802.5934	4023.4863	4532.1826	5180.9033	6044.0918
3648	3531.1333	3553.2598	3568.2891	3580.2012	3590.3599	3628.9072	3685.0723	3732.8320	3777.5859	3821.4492	4043.4375	4554.6563	5206.5938	6074.0625
3660	3542.9723	3565.1436	3580.1944	3592.1457	3602.3378	3640.9561	3697.3059	3745.1111	3790.1239	3834.0198	4056.7383	4569.6387	5223.7207	6094.0430
3672	3554.8407	3577.0567	3592.1569	3604.1193	3614.3448	3653.0618	3709.5403	3757.5022	3802.6626	3846.5903	4070.0391	4584.6211	5240.8477	6114.0234
3690	3572.6042	3594.9010	3610.0470	3622.0681	3632.2874	3671.1942	3727.8369	3776.0339	3821.3031	3865.6714	4089.9902	4607.0947	5266.5381	6143.9941
3696	3578.5543	3600.8591	3616.0298	3628.0422	3638.3064	3677.2200	3734.0112	3782.1738	3827.6294	3871.9570	4096.6406	4614.5859	5275.1016	6153.9844
3720	3602.2458	3624.6387	3639.8795	3651.9699	3662.2723	3701.3818	3758.3716	3806.9604	3852.5977	3897.0996	4123.2422	4644.5508	5309.3555	6193.9453
3744	3625.9717	3648.4519	3663.7339	3675.9023	3686.2427	3725.4902	3782.8477	3831.6357	3877.5674	3922.4707	4149.8438	4674.5156	5343.6094	6233.9063
3750	3631.8970	3654.4132	3669.7197	3681.8504	3692.2073	3731.5750	3789.0244	3837.8906	3883.8959	3928.7567	4156.4941	4682.0068	5352.1729	6243.8965
3768	3649.6750	3672.2706	3687.6218	3699.8108	3710.1887	3749.6591	3807.3267	3856.4275	3902.5386	3947.6147	4176.4453	4704.4805	5377.8633	6273.8672
3780	3661.5289	3684.1676	3699.5389	3711.7667	3722.1776	3761.7160	3819.5673	3868.7091	3915.0824	3960.4175	4189.7461	4719.4629	5394.9902	6293.8477
3792	3673.3843	3696.0659	3711.4860	3723.7236	3734.1387	3773.8315	3831.8086	3881.1064	3927.6270	3972.9902	4203.5098	4734.4453	5412.1172	6313.8281
3810	3691.1700	3713.9303	3729.3945	3741.6902	3752.1547	3791.9197	3850.1138	3899.6457	3946.2708	3991.8494	4223.4631	4756.9189	5437.8076	6343.7988
3816	3697.0994	3719.8663	3735.3549	3747.6409	3758.1218	3797.9495	3856.1770	3905.7869	3952.4854	3998.1357	4230.1143	4764.4102	5446.3711	6353.7891
3840	3720.8203	3743.6719	3759.2285	3771.5625	3782.1094	3822.1289	3880.6641	3930.5859	3977.5781	4023.5156	4256.7188	4794.3750	5480.6250	6397.5000

continues

Table A-1 *Erlang B (Continued)*

| Circuits | Grade of Service | | | | | | | | | | | | | |
	0.001	0.002	0.003	0.004	0.005	0.01	0.02	0.03	0.04	0.05	0.1	0.2	0.3	0.4
3864	3744.5471	3767.4825	3783.1069	3795.4885	3806.0718	3846.3120	3905.1541	3955.2700	4002.4380	4048.6626	4283.3232	4824.3398	5514.8789	6437.4844
3870	3750.4797	3773.4508	3789.0699	3801.5002	3812.0705	3852.3436	3911.2180	3961.4117	4008.7711	4054.9493	4289.9744	4831.8311	5523.4424	6447.4805
3888	3768.2798	3791.2983	3806.9604	3819.4189	3830.0383	3870.4395	3929.5283	3979.9556	4027.5352	4074.0469	4309.9277	4854.3047	5549.1328	6477.4688
3900	3780.1186	3803.2082	3818.9186	3831.3858	3842.0380	3882.5043	3941.7755	3992.3584	4039.9658	4086.6211	4323.2300	4869.2871	5566.2598	6497.4609
3912	3791.9885	3815.1193	3830.8482	3843.3538	3854.0387	3894.5698	3954.0234	4004.6426	4052.5159	4099.1953	4336.5322	4884.2695	5583.3867	6517.4531
3930	3809.7661	3832.9733	3848.7447	3861.3078	3872.0119	3912.7295	3972.3367	4023.3087	4071.2823	4118.2965	4356.4856	4906.7432	5609.0771	6547.4414
3936	3815.7026	3838.9453	3854.7407	3867.2930	3877.9834	3918.7632	3978.5215	4029.4512	4077.4980	4124.5840	4363.1367	4914.2344	5617.6406	6557.4375
3960	3839.4223	3862.7463	3878.6078	3891.2366	3901.9922	3942.8998	4002.9016	4054.1418	4102.4817	4149.7339	4389.7412	4944.1992	5651.8945	6597.4219
3984	3863.1475	3886.5520	3902.4792	3915.1542	3925.9446	3967.1001	4027.4048	4078.8340	4127.4668	4175.1270	4416.8320	4974.1641	5688.0938	6637.4063
3990	3869.0872	3892.5270	3908.4782	3921.1418	3931.9180	3973.0746	4033.4702	4085.0986	4133.6829	4181.4148	4423.4839	4981.6553	5696.6602	6647.4023
4008	3886.8781	3910.3625	3926.3551	3939.0758	3949.9006	3991.2429	4051.7886	4103.6499	4152.4534	4200.2783	4443.4395	5004.1289	5722.3594	6677.3906
4020	3898.7608	3922.2849	3938.2947	3951.0535	3961.9107	4003.3154	4064.0424	4115.9363	4165.0085	4212.8540	4456.7432	5019.1113	5739.4922	6697.3828
4032	3910.6143	3934.1777	3950.2354	3963.0322	3973.9219	4015.3887	4076.2969	4128.3457	4177.4414	4225.4297	4470.0469	5034.0938	5756.6250	6717.3750
4050	3928.4122	3952.0500	3968.1484	3980.9715	3991.8789	4033.4999	4094.6182	4146.8994	4196.0907	4244.5404	4490.0024	5056.5674	5782.3242	6747.3633
4056	3934.3559	3957.9977	3974.1200	3986.9312	3997.8856	4039.5374	4100.6843	4153.0430	4202.4309	4250.8286	4496.6543	5064.0586	5790.8906	6757.3594
4080	3958.0719	3981.8225	3998.0090	4010.8960	4021.8530	4063.6890	4125.1978	4177.7417	4227.4219	4275.9814	4523.2617	5094.0234	5825.1563	6797.3438
4104	3981.7930	4005.6520	4021.9025	4034.8026	4045.8241	4087.8435	4149.5889	4202.4419	4252.4143	4301.3848	4549.8691	5123.9883	5859.4219	6837.3281
4110	3987.7398	4011.6023	4027.8452	4040.7955	4051.8331	4093.9453	4155.7809	4208.7112	4258.6313	4307.6733	4556.5210	5131.4795	5867.9883	6847.3242
4128	4005.5193	4029.4548	4045.7688	4058.7444	4069.7988	4112.0010	4174.1074	4227.2695	4277.4082	4326.5391	4576.4766	5153.9531	5893.6875	6877.3125
4140	4017.4159	4041.3895	4057.7193	4070.7010	4081.8192	4124.0808	4186.3678	4239.5581	4289.8425	4339.1162	4589.7803	5168.9355	5910.8203	6897.3047
4152	4029.2823	4053.2937	4069.6392	4082.6902	4093.7772	4136.1614	4198.5022	4251.9734	4302.4036	4351.6934	4603.0840	5183.9180	5927.9531	6917.2969
4170	4047.0685	4071.1521	4087.5684	4100.6442	4111.7793	4154.3472	4216.8311	4270.5341	4321.1829	4370.8136	4623.0396	5206.3916	5953.6523	6947.2852
4176	4052.9872	4077.1055	4093.5454	4106.6082	4117.7593	4160.3247	4223.0259	4276.6787	4327.4004	4377.1025	4629.6914	5213.8828	5962.2188	6957.2813
4200	4076.7288	4100.9216	4117.4240	4130.5618	4141.7450	4184.4910	4247.4243	4301.3855	4352.2705	4402.2583	4656.8115	5243.8477	5996.4844	6997.2656
4224	4100.4756	4124.7422	4141.3066	4154.5195	4165.7344	4208.6602	4271.9531	4326.0938	4377.3984	4427.6719	4683.4219	5273.8125	6030.7500	7037.2500
4230	4106.3969	4130.7303	4147.2860	4160.4854	4171.7162	4214.7029	4278.0212	4332.2388	4383.6163	4433.9612	4690.0745	5281.3037	6039.3164	7047.2461

Table A-1   *Erlang B (Continued)*

Circuits	Grade of Service													
	0.001	0.002	0.003	0.004	0.005	0.01	0.02	0.03	0.04	0.05	0.1	0.2	0.3	0.4
4248	4124.1951	4148.5671	4165.2257	4178.4489	4189.7274	4232.8323	4296.3552	4350.8035	4402.2700	4452.8291	4710.0322	5303.7773	6065.0156	7077.2344
4260	4136.0728	4160.4813	4177.1544	4190.3824	4201.6928	4244.9194	4308.6218	4363.2239	4414.8358	4465.4077	4723.3374	5318.7598	6082.1484	7097.2266
4272	4147.9519	4172.3965	4189.0840	4202.3818	4213.7241	4257.0073	4320.8240	4375.5146	4427.4023	4477.9863	4736.6426	5333.7422	6099.2813	7117.2188
4290	4165.7565	4190.2714	4206.9965	4220.3503	4231.6750	4275.1405	4339.1606	4394.0817	4446.0571	4497.1161	4756.6003	5356.2158	6124.9805	7147.2070
4296	4171.6811	4196.2302	4212.9787	4226.3185	4237.6917	4281.1853	4345.2949	4400.3584	4452.2754	4503.4058	4763.2529	5363.7070	6133.5469	7157.2031
4320	4195.4150	4220.0684	4236.8774	4250.2588	4261.6626	4305.3662	4369.7021	4424.9414	4477.2803	4528.5645	4789.8633	5393.6719	6167.8125	7197.1875
4344	4219.1869	4243.9109	4260.7471	4274.2028	4285.6699	4329.4838	4394.2434	4449.7896	4502.2866	4553.8557	4816.4736	5424.6973	6202.0781	7237.1680
4350	4225.1141	4249.8390	4266.7316	4280.1727	4291.5301	4335.5301	4400.3128	4455.9357	4508.5052	4560.2783	4823.1262	5432.1899	6210.6445	7247.1680
4368	4242.8972	4267.7245	4284.6537	4298.1504	4309.6476	4353.6702	4418.6543	4474.5073	4527.2944	4579.1484	4843.0840	5454.6680	6236.3438	7277.1563
4380	4254.7874	4279.6495	4296.5918	4310.0922	4321.6544	4365.7645	4430.9271	4486.7999	4539.8657	4591.7285	4856.3892	5469.6533	6253.4766	7297.1484
4392	4266.6454	4291.5421	4308.5643	4322.1017	4333.6285	4377.8595	4443.0667	4499.2266	4552.3037	4604.3086	4869.6943	5484.6387	6270.6094	7317.1406
4410	4284.4682	4309.4332	4326.4579	4340.0171	4351.6248	4395.9361	4461.4105	4517.6660	4570.9607	4623.3133	4889.6521	5507.1167	6296.3086	7347.1289
4416	4290.3984	4315.3975	4332.4453	4346.0229	4357.6465	4401.9844	4467.6152	4523.9473	4577.1797	4629.7383	4896.8438	5514.6094	6304.8750	7357.1250
4440	4314.1562	4339.2233	4356.3300	4369.9475	4381.6003	4426.1792	4492.0313	4548.6694	4602.3267	4654.8999	4923.4570	5544.5801	6339.1406	7397.1094
4464	4337.8846	4363.0532	4380.2183	4393.9094	4405.6252	4450.3088	4516.4487	4573.3931	4627.2041	4680.0615	4950.0703	5574.5508	6373.4063	7437.0938
4470	4343.8174	4369.0199	4386.2080	4399.8834	4411.6150	4456.3586	4522.5874	4579.5401	4633.4235	4686.3519	4956.7236	5582.0435	6381.9727	7447.0898
4488	4361.6517	4386.8871	4404.1102	4417.8750	4429.5853	4474.5092	4540.9362	4598.1182	4652.2185	4705.4971	4976.6836	5604.5215	6407.6719	7477.0781
4500	4373.5199	4398.7885	4416.0576	4429.8248	4441.5665	4486.6104	4553.1464	4610.4126	4664.7949	4718.0786	4989.9902	5619.5068	6424.8047	7497.0703
4512	4385.3892	4410.7251	4428.0059	4441.8098	4453.5828	4498.6436	4565.4258	4622.8447	4677.2344	4730.6602	5003.2969	5634.4922	6441.9375	7517.0625
4530	4403.1951	4428.5976	4445.9473	4459.7717	4471.5916	4516.7976	4583.7772	4641.4252	4695.8936	4749.5325	5023.2568	5656.9702	6467.6367	7547.0508
4536	4409.1310	4434.5325	4451.9052	4465.7479	4477.5835	4522.8494	4589.8484	4647.5728	4702.1133	4755.8232	5029.9102	5664.2031	6476.2031	7557.0469
4560	4432.8772	4458.3783	4475.8081	4489.6893	4501.5527	4546.9885	4614.2725	4672.3022	4727.2705	4781.2646	5056.5234	5694.4336	6510.4688	7597.0313
4584	4456.6278	4482.2281	4499.7147	4513.6340	4525.5599	4571.1998	4638.7679	4697.0332	4752.1509	4806.4292	5083.1367	5724.4043	6544.7344	7637.0156
4590	4462.5661	4488.1650	4505.6744	4519.6120	4531.5534	4577.2531	4644.9097	4703.1812	4758.3710	4812.7203	5089.7900	5731.8970	6553.3008	7647.0117
4608	4480.3828	4506.0469	4523.6250	4537.6172	4549.5703	4595.3438	4663.2656	4721.7656	4777.1719	4831.5938	5109.7500	5754.3750	6579.0000	7677.0000
4620	4492.2620	4517.9929	4535.5463	4549.5749	4561.5591	4607.4518	4675.4095	4734.0619	4789.7534	4844.1760	5123.0566	5769.3604	6596.1328	7696.9922

continues

Table A-1 *Erlang B (Continued)*

Circuits	Grade of Service													
	0.001	0.002	0.003	0.004	0.005	0.01	0.02	0.03	0.04	0.05	0.1	0.2	0.3	0.4
4632	4504.1422	4529.9046	4547.5036	4561.5333	4573.5487	4619.4899	4687.6948	4746.4995	4802.1943	4857.0410	5136.3633	5784.3457	6613.2656	7716.9844
4650	4521.9646	4547.7917	4565.4236	4579.5078	4591.5344	4637.6541	4706.0532	4764.9445	4820.8557	4875.9155	5156.3232	5806.8237	6638.9648	7746.9727
4656	4527.9060	4553.7308	4571.3855	4585.4879	4597.5300	4643.7092	4712.1255	4771.0928	4827.0762	4882.2070	5162.9766	5814.3164	6647.5313	7756.9688
4680	4551.6563	4577.5964	4595.3064	4609.4458	4621.5143	4667.8601	4736.5576	4795.9717	4852.2437	4907.3730	5190.1611	5844.2871	6681.7969	7796.9531
4704	4575.4109	4601.4302	4619.1951	4633.3711	4645.5015	4692.0132	4761.0630	4820.5664	4877.1270	4932.8262	5216.7773	5874.2578	6716.0625	7836.9375
4710	4581.3547	4607.3712	4625.1947	4639.3888	4651.4987	4698.0698	4767.2076	4826.7151	4883.3478	4939.1180	5223.4314	5881.7505	6724.6289	7846.9336
4728	4599.1696	4625.2676	4643.0870	4657.3354	4669.4916	4716.1685	4785.5706	4845.3054	4902.1545	4957.9937	5243.3936	5904.2285	6750.3281	7876.9219
4740	4611.0416	4637.1877	4655.0523	4669.3369	4681.4877	4728.2831	4797.7167	4857.7478	4914.7412	4970.5774	5256.7017	5919.2139	6767.4609	7896.9141
4752	4622.9326	4649.1086	4667.0186	4681.3030	4693.4846	4740.3984	4810.0078	4870.0459	4927.1836	4983.1611	5270.0098	5934.1992	6784.5938	7916.9063
4770	4640.7349	4666.9736	4684.9514	4699.2535	4711.4813	4758.5001	4828.3731	4888.6386	4945.8472	5002.0367	5289.9719	5956.6772	6810.2930	7946.8945
4776	4646.6816	4672.9534	4690.9173	4705.2374	4717.4806	4764.5585	4834.4465	4894.7878	4952.0684	5008.6201	5296.6260	5964.1699	6818.8594	7956.8906
4800	4670.4346	4696.8018	4714.8193	4729.2114	4741.4795	4788.7207	4858.8867	4919.5313	4977.0996	5033.7891	5323.2422	5994.1406	6853.1250	7996.8750
4824	4694.1916	4720.6538	4738.7247	4753.1519	4765.4813	4812.8851	4883.3284	4944.2761	5002.1323	5058.9580	5349.8584	6024.1113	6887.3906	8036.8594
4830	4700.1407	4726.5990	4744.6923	4759.1375	4771.4822	4818.9450	4889.4759	4950.4257	5008.3539	5065.2502	5356.5125	6031.6040	6895.9570	8046.8555
4848	4717.9526	4744.4725	4762.6333	4777.1323	4789.4861	4837.0518	4907.7715	4969.0225	5027.0186	5084.1270	5376.4746	6054.0820	6921.6563	8076.8438
4860	4729.8532	4756.4017	4774.5703	4789.1052	4801.4896	4849.1730	4920.0677	4981.3220	5039.6100	5097.0081	5389.7827	6069.0674	6938.7891	8096.8359
4872	4741.7177	4768.3317	4786.5452	4801.0789	4813.4938	4861.2206	4932.2161	4993.6216	5052.2021	5109.5933	5403.0908	6084.0527	6955.9219	8116.8281
4890	4759.5348	4786.2099	4804.4534	4819.0407	4831.5015	4879.4046	4950.5878	5012.2202	5070.8679	5128.4711	5423.0530	6106.5308	6981.6211	8146.8164
4896	4765.4868	4792.1572	4810.4604	4825.0283	4837.5044	4885.3916	4956.7368	5018.5195	5077.0898	5134.7637	5429.7070	6114.0234	6990.1875	8156.8125
4920	4789.2599	4816.0236	4834.3414	4848.9807	4861.5179	4909.5648	4981.2598	5043.1201	5101.9775	5159.9341	5456.3232	6143.9941	7024.4531	8196.7969
4944	4813.0371	4839.8558	4858.2631	4872.9360	4885.4967	4933.7402	5005.7095	5067.8716	5127.1670	5185.4063	5482.9395	6173.9648	7058.7188	8236.7813
4950	4818.9537	4845.8427	4864.2345	4878.9253	4891.5012	4939.8033	5011.7844	5074.0219	5133.3893	5191.6992	5489.5935	6181.4575	7067.2852	8246.7773
4968	4836.7804	4863.7293	4882.1880	4896.8943	4909.4780	4957.9178	5030.1606	5092.6245	5152.0562	5210.5781	5510.1621	6203.9355	7092.9844	8276.7656
4980	4848.6534	4875.6294	4894.1327	4908.8745	4921.4886	4970.0455	5042.3108	5104.9255	5164.5007	5223.1641	5523.4717	6218.9209	7110.1172	8296.7578
4992	4860.5654	4887.5684	4906.0781	4920.8555	4933.5000	4982.0977	5054.6133	5117.3789	5176.9453	5235.7500	5536.7813	6233.9063	7127.2500	8316.7500
5010	4878.3782	4905.4594	4923.9977	4938.8283	4951.5184	5000.2148	5072.9919	5135.8310	5195.7651	5254.6289	5556.7456	6256.3843	7152.9492	8346.7383

Table A-1   *Erlang B (Continued)*

Circuits	Grade of Service													
	0.001	0.002	0.003	0.004	0.005	0.01	0.02	0.03	0.04	0.05	0.1	0.2	0.3	0.4
5016	4884.3162	4911.4107	4929.9712	4944.8196	4957.5249	5006.2797	5079.0674	5142.1348	5202.1406	5260.9219	5563.4004	6263.8770	7161.5156	8356.7344
5040	4908.0899	4935.2563	4953.9056	4968.7866	4981.4758	5030.4639	5103.5229	5166.7383	5227.0313	5286.4014	5590.0195	6293.8477	7195.7813	8396.7188
5064	4931.8674	4959.1439	4977.8047	4992.7180	5005.5062	5054.6503	5127.9800	5191.4963	5251.9219	5311.5747	5616.6387	6323.8184	7230.0469	8436.7031
5070	4937.7882	4965.0970	4983.7800	4998.7109	5011.5143	5060.7166	5134.0558	5197.8021	5258.2993	5317.8680	5623.2935	6331.3110	7238.6133	8446.6992
5088	4955.6294	4982.9575	5001.7068	5016.6907	5029.5007	5078.8389	5152.4385	5216.2559	5277.1230	5336.7480	5643.2578	6353.7891	7264.3125	8476.6875
5100	4967.5117	4994.9043	5013.6589	5028.6392	5041.4795	5090.8951	5164.6683	5228.5583	5289.5691	5349.3347	5656.5674	6368.7744	7281.4453	8496.6797
5112	4979.3950	5006.8130	5025.6508	5040.6273	5053.4978	5103.0297	5176.8984	5241.0168	5302.0151	5362.2334	5669.8770	6385.0078	7298.5781	8516.6719
5130	4997.2412	5024.7166	5043.5815	5058.6108	5071.5266	5121.1546	5195.2835	5259.4711	5320.6842	5381.1145	5689.8413	6407.4902	7324.2773	8546.6602
5136	5003.1643	5030.6719	5049.5588	5064.6057	5077.5366	5127.1443	5201.3599	5265.7793	5326.9072	5387.4082	5696.4961	6414.9844	7332.8438	8556.6563
5160	5026.9373	5054.5340	5073.4698	5088.5870	5101.4996	5151.3391	5225.8228	5290.3857	5351.9568	5412.5830	5723.1152	6444.9609	7367.1094	8596.6406
5184	5050.7139	5078.3994	5097.3838	5112.5317	5125.5439	5175.5361	5250.2871	5315.1504	5377.0078	5437.7578	5749.7344	6474.9375	7401.3750	8636.6250
5190	5056.6586	5084.3564	5103.3627	5118.5282	5131.5159	5181.6055	5256.3638	5321.3022	5383.2312	5444.0515	5756.3892	6482.4316	7409.9414	8646.6211
5208	5074.4941	5102.2284	5121.3007	5136.4790	5149.5117	5199.7354	5274.7529	5339.9165	5401.9014	5463.2505	5776.3535	6504.9141	7435.6406	8676.6094
5220	5086.3857	5114.1838	5133.2602	5148.4735	5161.5363	5211.7960	5286.9067	5352.2205	5414.3481	5475.8386	5789.6631	6519.9023	7452.7734	8696.6016
5232	5098.2781	5126.1002	5145.1805	5160.4688	5173.5216	5223.8569	5299.2202	5364.6841	5426.9546	5488.4268	5802.9727	6534.8906	7469.9063	8716.5938
5250	5116.0984	5144.0163	5163.1222	5178.4229	5191.5207	5241.9891	5317.6117	5383.1406	5445.7855	5507.3090	5822.9370	6557.3730	7495.6055	8746.5820
5256	5122.0256	5149.9753	5169.1031	5184.4213	5197.5341	5248.0602	5323.6890	5389.2927	5452.0093	5513.6030	5829.5918	6564.8672	7504.1719	8756.5781
5280	5145.8167	5173.8135	5193.0286	5208.3765	5221.5491	5272.2656	5348.1592	5414.0625	5476.9043	5538.7793	5856.2109	6594.8438	7538.4375	8796.5625
5304	5169.5912	5197.6545	5216.9165	5232.3746	5245.5667	5296.3923	5372.6309	5438.8337	5501.9612	5564.2793	5882.8301	6624.8203	7572.7031	8836.5469
5310	5175.5404	5203.6558	5222.8990	5238.3341	5251.5411	5302.4648	5378.7085	5444.9863	5508.1851	5570.5737	5890.1331	6632.3145	7581.2695	8846.5430
5328	5193.3691	5221.5392	5240.8477	5256.2944	5269.5461	5320.6018	5397.1040	5463.6064	5527.0195	5589.4570	5910.0996	6654.7969	7606.9688	8876.5313
5340	5205.2696	5233.4624	5252.8143	5268.2959	5281.5775	5332.6666	5409.2596	5475.9119	5539.4678	5602.0459	5923.4106	6669.7852	7624.1016	8896.5234
5352	5217.1302	5245.3863	5264.7817	5280.2981	5293.5687	5344.8135	5421.5786	5488.2173	5551.9160	5614.6348	5936.7217	6684.7734	7641.2344	8916.5156
5370	5234.9634	5263.2735	5282.7342	5298.2618	5311.5770	5362.9532	5439.8126	5506.8393	5570.5884	5633.5181	5956.6882	6707.2559	7666.9336	8946.5039
5376	5240.9355	5269.2363	5288.7188	5304.2227	5317.5938	5368.9453	5446.0547	5512.9922	5576.8125	5639.8125	5963.3438	6714.7500	7675.5000	8956.5000
5400	5264.7034	5293.1305	5312.6175	5328.2318	5341.5802	5393.1610	5470.4498	5537.7686	5602.0386	5665.3198	5989.9658	6744.7266	7709.7656	8996.4844

continues

Table A-1 *Erlang B (Continued)*

Circuits	Grade of Service													
	0.001	0.002	0.003	0.004	0.005	0.01	0.02	0.03	0.04	0.05	0.1	0.2	0.3	0.4
5424	5288.4745	5316.9866	5336.5188	5352.1611	5365.5688	5417.2961	5494.8457	5562.3809	5626.9365	5690.4990	6016.5879	6774.7031	7744.0313	9036.4688
5430	5294.4489	5322.9510	5342.5049	5358.1645	5371.5871	5423.3716	5501.0898	5568.6996	5633.1610	5696.7938	6023.2434	6782.1973	7752.5977	9046.4648
5448	5312.2489	5340.8456	5360.4642	5376.1342	5389.6013	5441.5159	5519.3254	5587.1594	5651.8345	5715.6782	6043.2100	6804.6797	7778.2969	9076.4531
5460	5324.1582	5352.7762	5372.3964	5388.1009	5401.5976	5453.5849	5531.6492	5599.6326	5664.2834	5728.2678	6056.5210	6819.6680	7795.4297	9096.4453
5472	5336.0475	5364.7075	5384.3708	5400.1099	5413.6362	5465.6543	5543.8066	5611.9395	5676.8994	5740.8574	6069.8320	6834.6563	7812.5625	9116.4375
5490	5353.8725	5382.6059	5402.2920	5418.0828	5431.6118	5483.8010	5562.2104	5630.3998	5695.7410	5759.9094	6089.7986	6857.1387	7838.2617	9146.4258
5496	5359.8286	5388.5724	5408.2800	5424.0881	5437.6318	5489.8781	5568.2893	5636.5532	5701.9658	5766.3721	6096.4541	6864.6328	7846.8281	9156.4219
5520	5383.6130	5412.4402	5432.2339	5448.0688	5461.6296	5514.0198	5592.7734	5661.3354	5726.8652	5791.5527	6123.0762	6894.6094	7881.0938	9196.4063
5544	5407.3795	5436.3109	5456.1484	5472.0099	5485.6296	5538.2476	5617.2590	5686.1191	5751.7646	5816.7334	6149.6982	6924.5859	7915.3594	9236.3906
5550	5413.3587	5442.2791	5462.0956	5478.0167	5491.6512	5544.2413	5623.3383	5692.2729	5757.9895	5823.0286	6156.3538	6932.0801	7923.9258	9246.3867
5568	5431.1704	5460.1421	5480.0654	5495.9956	5509.6318	5562.3926	5641.7461	5710.9043	5776.8340	5841.9141	6176.3203	6954.5625	7949.6250	9276.3750
5580	5443.0884	5472.0799	5492.0036	5507.9681	5521.6763	5574.5508	5653.9050	5723.2123	5789.4543	5854.5044	6189.6313	6969.5508	7966.7578	9296.3672
5592	5454.9646	5484.0185	5503.9850	5519.9839	5533.6362	5586.6244	5666.2346	5735.5203	5801.9048	5867.0947	6202.9424	6984.5391	7983.8906	9316.3594
5610	5472.8231	5501.9277	5521.9157	5537.9233	5551.6624	5604.6927	5684.4736	5754.1534	5820.5804	5886.3226	6222.9089	7007.0215	8009.5898	9346.3477
5616	5478.7621	5507.8978	5527.9072	5543.9319	5557.6857	5610.7727	5690.6389	5760.3076	5826.8057	5892.6182	6229.5645	7014.5156	8018.1563	9356.3438
5640	5502.5414	5531.7371	5551.8320	5567.8821	5581.6946	5635.0085	5715.0439	5785.0964	5851.8787	5917.8003	6256.1865	7044.4922	8052.4219	9396.3281
5664	5526.3237	5555.6221	5575.7593	5591.8777	5605.7058	5659.1602	5739.5361	5809.7139	5876.9531	5942.9824	6282.8086	7074.4688	8086.6875	9436.3125
5670	5532.2644	5561.5938	5581.7523	5597.8445	5611.6873	5665.1550	5745.6161	5816.0413	5883.1787	5949.2780	6289.4641	7081.9629	8095.2539	9446.3086
5688	5550.1309	5579.5100	5599.6891	5615.8325	5629.7192	5683.3132	5764.0298	5834.5049	5901.8555	5968.1646	6310.1250	7104.4453	8120.9531	9476.2969
5700	5562.0140	5591.4116	5611.6333	5627.8107	5641.7267	5695.3903	5776.1902	5846.8140	5914.3066	5980.7556	6323.4375	7119.4336	8138.0859	9496.2891
5712	5573.8978	5603.3573	5623.6216	5639.8330	5653.7347	5707.5549	5788.5249	5859.1230	5926.7578	5993.6953	6336.7500	7134.4219	8155.2188	9516.2813
5730	5591.7468	5621.2335	5641.5179	5657.7805	5671.7697	5725.6284	5806.8535	5877.7615	5945.4346	6012.5830	6356.7188	7156.9043	8180.9180	9546.2695
5736	5597.7114	5627.2072	5647.5128	5663.7924	5677.7525	5731.7113	5813.0215	5883.9163	5951.8352	6018.8789	6363.3750	7164.3984	8189.4844	9556.2656
5760	5621.4844	5651.1035	5671.4502	5687.7539	5701.7285	5755.8691	5837.4316	5908.7109	5976.9141	6044.0625	6390.0000	7194.3750	8223.7500	9596.2500

Extended Erlang B Traffic Model

Traffic models are mathematical formulas used in traffic engineering to determine the number of telephone trunks needed to support a given amount of traffic. Traffic models simulate voice traffic patterns. In general, the Erlang B traffic model assumes that calls that cannot get through simply disappear. In the Extended Erlang B model, if a caller receives some sort of denial (such as a busy signal), it is assumed that the caller will try immediately to call again. The Extended Erlang B model is designed to take into account calls retried at a certain rate. This model assumes a random call arrival pattern; blocked callers make multiple attempts to complete their calls and no overflow is allowed. The Extended Erlang B model is commonly used for standalone trunk groups with a retry probability (such as a modem pool). For more information about the Extended Erlang B traffic model, refer to Chapter 1, "Understanding Traffic Analysis."

If you determine that the Extended Erlang B traffic model is appropriate, you can use the Extended Erlang B distribution tables (Tables B-1 through B-3) to determine the number of circuits needed for a given grade of service. The grade of service is used to determine the percentage of calls that will experience a busy tone on the first attempt during the busy hour. For example, a grade of service of P.05 means that 5 out of 100 callers will encounter a busy tone when calling during the busy hour. With Extended Erlang B, you must also take into account the percentage of calls that will be retried. In this appendix, we offer three different retry percentage rates: 40 percent, 50 percent, and 60 percent. Use Table B-1 if your model assumes a 40 percent possible retry rate. Use Table B-2 if your model assumes a 50 percent possible retry rate. Use Table B-3 if your model assumes a 60 percent possible retry rate.

To use any of the Extended Erlang B distribution tables, you must first determine the amount of traffic your network experiences during its busy hour and express that value in Erlangs. Use the following formula to determine the busy hour traffic in Erlangs:

Erlangs = N 3 A / 3600

where N = the number of calls handled during the busy hour and A = the average length of a call, in seconds.

To determine the number of circuits you need, first select the appropriate table based on the assumed retry percentage. Then select the grade of service you want to offer. Trace down the appropriate grade of service column until you find the busy hour traffic of your network (in Erlangs). The number of circuits needed is listed to the far left; the busy hour traffic value is the intersection point between the grade of service and the number of circuits needed.

Table B-1　*Extended Erlang B with 40 Percent Retry Possibility*

Circuits

	0.001	0.002	0.003	0.004	0.005	0.01	0.02	0.03	0.04	0.05	0.1	0.2	0.3	0.4
1	0.0000	0.0000	0.0000	0.0000	0.0000	0.0101	0.0202	0.0305	0.0410	0.0516	0.1066	0.2300	0.3770	0.5596
2	0.0457	0.0653	0.0805	0.0936	0.1052	0.1520	0.2217	0.2781	0.3279	0.3735	0.5713	0.9199	1.2744	1.6797
3	0.1937	0.2485	0.2881	0.3204	0.3483	0.4536	0.5973	0.7064	0.7987	0.8811	1.2195	1.7754	2.3159	2.9209
4	0.4391	0.5345	0.6013	0.6545	0.6997	0.8657	1.0835	1.2437	1.3770	1.4937	1.9629	2.7090	3.4219	4.2148
5	0.7617	0.8990	0.9930	1.0672	1.1298	1.3550	1.6437	1.8524	2.0239	2.1741	2.7649	3.6890	4.5654	5.5371
6	1.1453	1.3240	1.4451	1.5396	1.6183	1.9014	2.2573	2.5122	2.7202	2.9004	3.6079	4.6992	5.7305	6.8789
7	1.5778	1.7970	1.9438	2.0580	2.1529	2.4908	2.9113	3.2103	3.4530	3.6624	4.4792	5.7302	6.9111	8.2305
8	2.0503	2.3086	2.4805	2.6138	2.7241	3.1147	3.5977	3.9385	4.2139	4.4512	5.3730	6.7773	8.1055	9.5859
9	2.5562	2.8526	3.0487	3.2003	3.3256	3.7672	4.3099	4.6901	4.9977	5.2625	6.2842	7.8398	9.3076	10.9512
10	3.0905	3.4235	3.6432	3.8129	3.9526	4.4427	5.0427	5.4626	5.8008	6.0913	7.2095	8.9087	10.5176	12.3242
11	3.6493	4.0182	4.2606	4.4473	4.6010	5.1388	5.7941	6.2520	6.6185	6.9341	8.1466	9.9875	11.7305	13.6963
12	4.2294	4.6326	4.8977	5.1006	5.2676	5.8521	6.5610	7.0547	7.4502	7.7900	9.0938	11.0713	12.9492	15.0762
13	4.8282	5.2654	5.5518	5.7708	5.9517	6.5801	7.3419	7.8711	8.2948	8.6582	10.0499	12.1621	14.1743	16.4531
14	5.4440	5.9139	6.2216	6.4565	6.6497	7.3213	8.1339	8.6970	9.1482	9.5344	11.0127	13.2583	15.4014	17.8418
15	6.0745	6.5762	6.9040	7.1548	7.3599	8.0750	8.9374	9.5334	10.0104	10.4187	11.9824	14.3555	16.6260	19.2188
16	6.7188	7.2520	7.5996	7.8652	8.0830	8.8389	9.7490	10.3789	10.8809	11.3125	12.9590	15.4609	17.8594	20.6094
17	7.3747	7.9387	8.3060	8.5861	8.8154	9.6123	10.5700	11.2310	11.7601	12.2104	13.9391	16.5684	19.0918	21.9971
18	8.0420	8.6364	9.0225	9.3164	9.5581	10.3942	11.3983	12.0916	12.6431	13.1155	14.9238	17.6748	20.3291	23.3789
19	8.7201	9.3434	9.7482	10.0566	10.3094	11.1850	12.2333	12.9558	13.5333	14.0273	15.9153	18.7866	21.5605	24.7705
20	9.4073	10.0598	10.4822	10.8044	11.0693	11.9824	13.0750	13.8281	14.4287	14.9438	16.9067	19.9023	22.8027	26.1621
21	10.1033	10.7839	11.2248	11.5600	11.8356	12.7853	13.9222	14.7067	15.3296	15.8628	17.9033	21.0205	24.0454	27.5522
22	10.8073	11.5156	11.9749	12.3233	12.6086	13.5956	14.7759	15.5869	16.2355	16.7874	18.9036	22.1343	25.2817	28.9395
23	11.5190	12.2545	12.7311	13.0926	13.3895	14.4115	15.6342	16.4751	17.1447	17.7161	19.9060	23.2527	26.5264	30.3335
24	12.2373	13.0005	13.4927	13.8677	14.1753	15.2329	16.4971	17.3643	18.0586	18.6475	20.9121	24.3750	27.7617	31.7227
25	12.9631	13.7520	14.2616	14.6484	14.9658	16.0599	17.3645	18.2602	18.9743	19.5831	21.9177	25.5005	29.0039	33.1177
26	13.6951	14.5092	15.0360	15.4359	15.7628	16.8895	18.2336	19.1572	19.8936	20.5220	22.9277	26.6221	30.2529	34.5059

Table B-1 *Extended Erlang B with 40 Percent Retry Possibility (Continued)*

Circuits	0.001	0.002	0.003	0.004	0.005	0.01	0.02	0.03	0.04	0.05	0.1	0.2	0.3	0.4
27	14.4327	15.2724	15.8154	16.2274	16.5635	17.7253	19.1096	20.0605	20.8169	21.4629	23.9414	27.7449	31.4956	35.9121
28	15.1758	16.0405	16.5994	17.0232	17.3701	18.5647	19.9883	20.9658	21.7451	22.4082	24.9512	28.8750	32.7441	37.2969
29	15.9231	16.8134	17.3887	17.8241	18.1799	19.4083	20.8703	21.8739	22.6740	23.3536	25.9697	29.9983	33.9844	38.6855
30	16.6763	17.5909	18.1815	18.6292	18.9954	20.2551	21.7548	22.7838	23.6041	24.3054	26.9861	31.1279	35.2295	40.0781
31	17.4347	18.3741	18.9786	19.4374	19.8140	21.1063	22.6426	23.6965	24.5385	25.2556	28.0029	32.2563	36.4795	41.4746
32	18.1973	19.1602	19.7803	20.2510	20.6348	21.9590	23.5352	24.6133	25.4746	26.2109	29.0234	33.3906	37.7344	42.8750
33	18.9633	19.9503	20.5847	21.0681	21.4609	22.8164	24.4277	25.5315	26.4137	27.1650	30.0472	34.5146	38.9780	44.2793
34	19.7341	20.7437	21.3932	21.8871	22.2897	23.6759	25.3236	26.4546	27.3552	28.1230	31.0698	35.6519	40.2256	45.6709
35	20.5089	21.5417	22.2061	22.7103	23.1226	24.5389	26.2222	27.3779	28.2965	29.0826	32.0947	36.7773	41.4771	47.0654
36	21.2871	22.3418	23.0208	23.5371	23.9568	25.4048	27.1230	28.3008	29.2412	30.0410	33.1216	37.9160	42.7236	48.4453
37	22.0681	23.1465	23.8409	24.3659	24.7961	26.2731	28.0255	29.2292	30.1867	31.0065	34.1455	39.0505	43.9736	49.8633
38	22.8536	23.9541	24.6615	25.1984	25.6356	27.1432	28.9314	30.1583	31.1348	31.9697	35.1750	40.1802	45.2178	51.2480
39	23.6418	24.7642	25.4866	26.0341	26.4792	28.0146	29.8380	31.0876	32.0850	32.9348	36.2007	41.3137	46.4648	52.6348
40	24.4336	25.5774	26.3135	26.8701	27.3267	28.8916	30.7471	32.0215	33.0371	33.9014	37.2314	42.4512	47.7148	54.0430
41	25.2284	26.3932	27.1440	27.7120	28.1750	29.7665	31.6584	32.9547	33.9882	34.8690	38.2623	43.5825	48.9678	55.4341
42	26.0257	27.2126	27.9752	28.5546	29.0262	30.6464	32.5715	33.8917	34.9427	35.8400	39.2930	44.7173	50.2236	56.8477
43	26.8264	28.0337	28.8106	29.3985	29.8788	31.5283	33.4861	34.8273	35.8981	36.8114	40.3282	45.8555	51.4824	58.2432
44	27.6289	28.8575	29.6484	30.2460	30.7334	32.4119	34.4019	35.7661	36.8564	37.7856	41.3628	46.9971	52.7227	59.6406
45	28.4340	29.6837	30.4871	31.0954	31.5912	33.2968	35.3210	36.7081	37.8149	38.7570	42.3962	48.1311	53.9758	61.0400
46	29.2427	30.5132	31.3288	31.9479	32.4504	34.1827	36.2407	37.6501	38.7732	39.7334	43.4282	49.2681	55.2314	62.4189
47	30.0534	31.3429	32.1719	32.8002	33.3137	35.0721	37.1605	38.5920	39.7308	40.7062	44.4641	50.4080	56.4780	63.8218
48	30.8657	32.1768	33.0176	33.6563	34.1763	35.9619	38.0830	39.5361	40.6934	41.6836	45.5039	51.5391	57.7266	65.2031
49	31.6807	33.0116	33.8669	34.5129	35.0423	36.8547	39.0050	40.4824	41.6578	42.6597	46.5416	52.6846	58.9771	66.6094
50	32.4982	33.8486	34.7168	35.3729	35.9085	37.7472	39.9323	41.4276	42.6208	43.6401	47.5769	53.8208	60.2295	68.0176
51	33.3178	34.6874	35.5668	36.2329	36.7776	38.6422	40.8585	42.3745	43.5853	44.6188	48.6156	54.9595	61.4839	69.4277
52	34.1393	35.5278	36.4213	37.0957	37.6479	39.5396	41.7866	43.3228	44.5510	45.6016	49.6514	56.1006	62.7402	70.8145

continues

Table B-1 *Extended Erlang B with 40 Percent Retry Possibility (Continued)*

Circuits	0.001	0.002	0.003	0.004	0.005	0.01	0.02	0.03	0.04	0.05	0.1	0.2	0.3	0.4
53	34.9624	36.3712	37.2753	37.9611	38.5208	40.4390	42.7131	44.2723	45.5178	46.5820	50.6903	57.2441	63.9985	72.2021
54	35.7869	37.2156	38.1335	38.8273	39.3926	41.3372	43.6443	45.2263	46.4854	47.5631	51.7324	58.3770	65.2456	73.6172
55	36.6141	38.0626	38.9908	39.6957	40.2698	42.2369	44.5734	46.1780	47.4536	48.5480	52.7710	59.5251	66.4941	75.0073
56	37.4438	38.9102	39.8518	40.5645	41.1455	43.1416	45.5068	47.1270	48.4224	49.5298	53.8125	60.6621	67.7578	76.3984
57	38.2743	39.7598	40.7130	41.4349	42.0229	44.0442	46.4412	48.0833	49.3949	50.5151	54.8569	61.8010	68.9956	77.7905
58	39.1068	40.6113	41.5760	42.3070	42.9017	44.9479	47.3728	49.0366	50.3641	51.5005	55.8972	62.9419	70.2627	79.1836
59	39.9413	41.4628	42.4423	43.1805	43.7837	45.8525	48.3084	49.9937	51.3369	52.4857	56.9402	64.0847	71.5029	80.6064
60	40.7776	42.3175	43.3081	44.0552	44.6667	46.7615	49.2444	50.9473	52.3096	53.4741	57.9785	65.2295	72.7734	81.9727
72	50.9238	52.6750	53.7979	54.6504	55.3425	57.7222	60.5435	62.4814	64.0283	65.3555	70.5234	78.9258	87.8203	98.7891
90	66.4563	68.4998	69.8099	70.8014	71.6089	74.3829	77.6788	79.9420	81.7548	83.3093	89.4177	99.5361	110.3906	123.9258
96	71.6982	73.8340	75.2051	76.2393	77.0859	79.9805	83.4258	85.7930	87.6914	89.3203	95.7305	106.4063	117.9375	132.3281
120	92.9260	95.4053	96.9946	98.1995	99.1809	102.5500	106.5564	109.3213	111.5405	113.4521	121.0327	133.9160	148.0664	165.9375
144	114.4666	117.2637	119.0566	120.4146	121.5220	125.3276	129.8584	132.9961	135.5098	137.6895	146.4082	161.4375	178.2070	199.5469
150	119.8929	122.7631	124.6078	125.9995	127.1393	131.0486	135.7086	138.9313	141.5222	143.7653	152.7466	168.3105	185.7422	207.8613
168	136.2437	139.3352	141.3193	142.8215	144.0469	148.2612	153.2856	156.7720	159.5815	162.0117	171.8145	189.0000	208.3594	233.1328
180	147.2003	150.4358	152.5122	154.0833	155.3632	159.7742	165.0366	168.6841	171.6394	174.1992	184.5264	202.7637	223.4180	249.8730
192	158.2031	161.5723	163.7344	165.3750	166.7109	171.3105	176.8066	180.6211	183.7148	186.3984	197.2500	216.5625	238.5000	266.6250
210	174.7714	178.3411	180.6354	182.3721	183.7885	188.6591	194.4974	198.5541	201.8481	204.7064	216.3574	237.2241	261.1157	291.8262
216	180.3120	183.9441	186.2776	188.0475	189.4878	194.4580	200.4038	204.5435	207.9053	210.8188	222.7236	244.1074	268.6289	300.2695
240	202.5439	206.4294	208.9270	210.8203	212.3657	217.6831	224.0625	228.5156	232.1338	235.2832	248.2031	271.6992	298.8281	333.8672
264	224.8770	229.0060	231.6606	233.6748	235.3143	240.9741	247.7739	252.5273	256.3945	259.7783	273.7002	299.2559	328.9688	367.3828
270	230.4739	234.6638	237.3541	239.3976	241.0620	246.8051	253.7018	258.5303	262.4689	265.8966	280.0854	306.1560	336.5112	375.8643
288	247.3022	251.6660	254.4697	256.5967	258.3369	264.3223	271.5293	276.5742	280.6875	284.2910	299.2148	326.8125	359.1563	401.0625
300	258.5449	263.0219	265.8966	268.0847	269.8608	276.0132	283.4106	288.6108	292.8406	296.5576	311.9751	340.6494	374.2676	417.7734
312	269.8055	274.3901	277.3418	279.5793	281.4075	287.7202	295.3184	300.6504	305.0112	308.8198	324.7207	354.4277	389.3145	434.6367
330	286.7258	291.4792	294.5407	296.8570	298.7503	305.2963	313.1818	318.7207	323.2526	327.2406	343.8776	375.1172	411.9360	459.8730

Table B-1 *Extended Erlang B with 40 Percent Retry Possibility (Continued)*

Circuits	0.001	0.002	0.003	0.004	0.005	0.01	0.02	0.03	0.04	0.05	0.1	0.2	0.3	0.4
336	292.3799	297.1838	300.2754	302.6235	304.5410	311.1548	319.1426	324.7515	329.3452	333.3750	350.2734	382.0195	419.5078	468.2344
360	315.0110	320.0317	323.2617	325.7117	327.7112	334.6326	342.9932	348.8818	353.6938	357.9565	375.7983	409.5703	449.6484	501.8555
384	337.6992	342.9258	346.2891	348.8379	350.9297	358.1367	366.8672	373.0195	378.0703	382.5469	401.3438	437.1563	479.8125	535.5000
390	343.3804	348.6530	352.0509	354.6277	356.7343	364.0182	372.8375	379.0622	384.1681	388.6908	407.7100	444.0820	487.3096	543.8672
408	360.4365	365.8590	369.3516	372.0037	374.1764	381.6782	390.7676	397.1799	402.4717	407.1284	426.8760	464.7773	510.0000	568.9688
420	371.8195	377.3438	380.9070	383.6050	385.8160	393.4552	402.7222	409.2719	414.6680	419.4360	439.6619	478.5498	525.0000	585.7031
432	383.2207	388.8369	392.4624	395.2112	397.4590	405.2373	414.6768	421.3608	426.8716	431.7363	452.4346	492.3281	540.1055	602.4375
450	400.3349	406.0959	409.8175	412.6328	414.9399	422.9324	432.6279	439.5081	445.1797	450.1923	471.5881	513.0615	562.7197	627.7588
456	406.0415	411.8584	415.6018	418.4476	420.7716	428.8359	438.6189	445.5630	451.2825	456.3618	477.9873	519.9023	570.2227	636.1289
480	428.9063	434.9048	438.7720	441.7090	444.1113	452.4463	462.5684	469.7607	475.7080	480.9814	503.5547	547.5000	600.4688	669.8438
504	451.7974	457.9805	461.9718	465.0018	467.4781	476.0760	486.5427	493.9717	500.1394	505.6150	529.1016	575.1211	630.6152	703.3359
510	457.5261	463.7595	467.7750	470.8255	473.3235	481.9849	492.5372	500.0391	506.2491	511.7743	535.4938	581.9678	638.2471	711.7090
528	474.7295	481.0942	485.1951	488.3130	490.8669	499.7212	510.5171	518.2031	524.5840	530.2559	554.6836	602.7012	660.7734	736.8281
540	486.2027	492.6544	496.8237	499.9878	502.5751	511.5564	522.5153	530.3265	536.8030	542.5708	567.4548	616.4648	675.7910	753.5742
552	497.6810	504.2256	508.4454	511.6545	514.2825	523.3960	534.5142	542.4485	549.0352	554.8975	580.2334	630.2988	690.9434	770.5898
570	514.9187	521.5897	525.9036	529.1739	531.8527	541.1591	552.5180	560.6241	567.3734	573.3746	599.3976	650.9912	713.6133	795.7178
576	520.6729	527.3877	531.7207	535.0166	537.7148	547.0840	558.5273	566.6836	573.4863	579.5508	605.8125	657.8438	721.1250	804.0938
600	543.6859	550.5707	555.0110	558.3984	561.1633	570.7764	582.5317	590.9546	597.9492	604.2114	631.3477	685.4736	751.1719	837.8906
624	566.7188	573.7742	578.3254	581.7913	584.6287	594.4929	606.5566	615.2021	622.4194	628.8750	656.9443	713.1211	781.5234	871.4063
630	572.4852	579.5796	584.1650	587.6450	590.5000	600.4303	612.5620	621.2714	628.5388	635.0372	663.3380	719.9780	789.0381	879.7852
648	589.7813	596.9993	601.6663	605.2061	608.1130	618.2183	630.5977	639.4768	646.8926	653.5371	682.4883	740.7070	811.5820	904.9219
660	601.3174	608.6188	613.3319	616.9171	619.8578	630.0897	642.6178	651.6211	659.1339	665.8813	695.2881	754.4238	826.6113	921.6797
672	612.8555	620.2383	625.0063	628.6465	631.6099	641.9561	654.6504	663.7559	671.3848	678.1934	708.0938	768.3047	841.8047	938.4375
690	630.1767	637.6836	642.5372	646.2222	649.2439	659.7725	672.6910	681.9772	689.7473	696.6962	727.2711	788.9685	864.5215	963.5742
696	635.9539	643.5048	648.3794	652.0858	655.1232	665.7114	678.6892	688.0349	695.8726	702.8818	733.6377	795.9141	872.0391	971.9531
720	659.0808	666.7822	671.7590	675.5493	678.6475	689.4800	702.7515	712.3315	720.3516	727.5586	759.2432	823.4473	902.1094	1005.4688

continues

Table B-1 *Extended Erlang B with 40 Percent Retry Possibility (Continued)*

Circuits	0.001	0.002	0.003	0.004	0.005	0.01	0.02	0.03	0.04	0.05	0.1	0.2	0.3	0.4
744	682.2195	690.0754	695.1614	699.0212	702.2000	713.2460	726.8236	736.6208	744.8401	752.2192	784.8237	850.9863	932.1797	1039.3477
750	688.0074	695.9038	701.0078	704.8988	708.0803	719.1925	732.8339	742.6987	750.9613	758.4000	791.1987	857.9407	939.6973	1047.7295
768	705.3750	713.3789	718.5703	722.5078	725.7422	737.0156	750.8906	760.9219	769.3359	776.9063	810.3750	878.6250	962.4375	1072.8750
780	716.9559	725.0372	730.2740	734.2612	737.5223	748.9124	762.9327	773.0731	781.5948	789.2596	823.1799	892.4487	977.6660	1089.6387
792	728.5419	736.7113	741.9924	746.0167	749.3159	760.8087	774.9844	785.2324	793.8369	801.6196	835.9893	906.2754	992.7070	1106.4023
810	745.9277	754.2087	759.5728	763.6514	766.9885	778.6560	793.0426	803.3494	812.2247	820.1349	855.1868	926.8726	1015.2686	1131.5479
816	751.7271	760.0444	765.4233	769.5322	772.8816	784.5981	799.0664	809.5254	818.3408	826.2847	861.5713	933.8379	1022.7891	1139.9297
840	774.9261	783.3984	788.8715	793.0499	796.4722	808.4180	823.1580	833.8477	842.8711	850.9717	887.1680	961.4063	1052.8711	1173.8672
864	798.1479	806.7568	812.3335	816.5918	820.0723	832.2275	847.2568	858.1729	867.3750	875.6807	912.7266	989.0859	1082.9531	1207.4063
870	803.9561	812.5983	818.2004	822.4750	825.9663	838.1927	853.2733	864.2386	873.5046	881.8414	919.1180	995.9546	1090.6860	1215.7910
888	821.3756	830.1423	835.8062	840.1285	843.6650	856.0496	871.3608	882.4717	891.8752	900.3574	938.2969	1016.5605	1113.2520	1240.9453
900	832.9971	841.8274	847.5540	851.9073	855.4779	867.9611	883.4106	894.6442	904.1473	912.7167	951.0864	1030.4077	1128.5156	1257.7148
912	844.6187	853.5249	859.2861	863.6836	867.2878	879.8818	895.4678	906.8232	916.3975	925.0811	963.8789	1044.2578	1143.5625	1274.4844
930	862.0551	871.0661	876.9127	881.3544	885.0014	897.7588	913.5672	925.0616	934.7964	943.5947	983.0731	1064.8682	1166.1328	1299.6387
936	867.8738	876.9287	882.7844	887.2548	890.9110	903.7222	919.5754	931.1440	940.9131	949.7681	989.4727	1071.7383	1173.6563	1308.0234
960	891.1377	900.3369	906.2842	910.8252	914.5459	927.5684	943.7109	955.4590	965.4492	974.4727	1015.0781	1099.4531	1203.7500	1341.5625
984	914.4221	923.7462	929.7971	934.3916	938.1753	951.4182	967.8142	979.7959	989.9758	999.1948	1040.6353	1126.9395	1233.8438	1375.1016
990	920.2396	929.6054	935.6781	940.3006	944.0923	957.3706	973.8666	985.8911	996.1029	1005.3479	1047.0410	1133.8110	1241.3672	1383.4863
1008	937.7095	947.1841	953.3210	957.9814	961.8267	975.2695	991.9424	1004.1548	1014.4907	1023.8730	1066.2012	1154.6719	1263.9375	1408.6406
1020	949.3552	958.8959	965.0748	969.7906	973.6505	987.1912	1004.0158	1016.3269	1026.7548	1036.2488	1079.0186	1168.4180	1279.2334	1425.4102
1032	961.0122	970.6179	976.8380	981.5779	985.4832	999.1201	1016.0955	1028.4727	1039.0232	1048.5974	1091.8389	1182.1641	1294.2832	1442.1797
1050	978.4950	988.2042	994.5007	999.2912	1003.2326	1017.0273	1034.1705	1046.7316	1057.4341	1067.1112	1111.0107	1202.9114	1316.8579	1467.3340
1056	984.3281	994.0605	1000.3770	1005.1948	1009.1426	1023.0000	1040.2090	1052.8096	1063.5410	1073.3057	1117.4238	1209.7852	1324.6406	1475.7188
1080	1007.6468	1017.5262	1023.9203	1028.7982	1032.8192	1046.8597	1064.3445	1077.1655	1088.0750	1097.9956	1143.0176	1237.4121	1354.7461	1509.2578
1104	1030.9739	1040.9802	1047.4827	1052.4185	1056.4951	1070.7466	1088.5020	1101.5068	1112.6250	1122.7324	1168.5527	1264.9102	1384.8516	1542.7969
1110	1036.8141	1046.8579	1053.3618	1058.3244	1062.4063	1076.7014	1094.5193	1107.5949	1118.7396	1128.9020	1174.9713	1271.7847	1392.3779	1551.1816

Table B-1   *Extended Erlang B with 40 Percent Retry Possibility (Continued)*

Circuits	0.001	0.002	0.003	0.004	0.005	0.01	0.02	0.03	0.04	0.05	0.1	0.2	0.3	0.4
1128	1054.3158	1064.4536	1071.0286	1076.0544	1080.1681	1094.6089	1112.6470	1125.8657	1137.1567	1147.4150	1194.1626	1292.5459	1414.9570	1576.8867
1140	1065.9842	1076.1951	1082.8226	1087.8671	1092.0071	1106.5668	1124.7272	1138.0518	1149.4281	1159.7955	1206.9360	1306.4355	1430.0098	1593.6621
1152	1077.6621	1087.9365	1094.6074	1099.6699	1103.8535	1118.4961	1136.7773	1150.2070	1161.7031	1172.1445	1219.7813	1320.1875	1445.0625	1610.4375
1170	1095.1790	1105.5515	1112.2820	1117.4057	1121.6368	1136.4189	1154.8965	1168.5004	1180.0690	1190.7092	1238.9832	1340.8154	1467.6416	1635.6006
1176	1101.0286	1111.4183	1118.1654	1123.3154	1127.5503	1142.3903	1160.9268	1174.5645	1186.2283	1196.8872	1245.3369	1347.6914	1475.1680	1643.9883
1200	1124.3958	1134.9243	1141.7542	1146.9543	1151.2573	1166.2903	1185.0952	1198.9380	1210.7666	1221.6064	1270.8984	1375.3418	1505.2734	1677.5391
1224	1147.7615	1158.4259	1165.3363	1170.6218	1174.9548	1190.1951	1209.2454	1223.2903	1235.3181	1246.3000	1296.5405	1402.9980	1535.6777	1711.0898
1230	1153.6130	1164.2921	1171.2364	1176.5291	1180.8833	1196.1607	1215.2856	1229.3994	1241.4487	1252.4844	1302.8961	1409.8755	1543.2056	1719.4775
1248	1171.1426	1181.9304	1188.9287	1194.2607	1198.6597	1214.1035	1233.4131	1247.6572	1259.8447	1271.0039	1322.1152	1430.5078	1565.7891	1744.6406
1260	1182.8458	1193.6893	1200.7260	1206.1093	1210.5313	1226.0468	1245.4843	1259.8462	1272.1124	1283.3789	1334.9048	1444.2627	1580.8447	1761.4160
1272	1194.5380	1205.4459	1212.5303	1217.9260	1222.3901	1237.9951	1257.5596	1272.0000	1284.3831	1295.7568	1347.6958	1458.1729	1595.9004	1778.1914
1290	1212.0815	1223.0848	1230.2399	1235.6726	1240.1802	1255.9273	1275.6898	1290.2756	1302.7945	1314.2505	1366.8457	1478.9648	1618.7988	1803.3545
1296	1217.9268	1228.9614	1236.1399	1241.5979	1246.1067	1261.9072	1281.7222	1296.3955	1308.9331	1320.4424	1373.2822	1485.8438	1626.3281	1811.7422
1320	1241.3370	1252.4954	1259.7363	1265.2753	1269.8273	1285.8197	1305.9009	1320.7654	1333.4949	1345.1770	1398.8745	1513.3594	1656.4453	1845.2930
1344	1264.7476	1276.0371	1283.3584	1288.9570	1293.5508	1309.7520	1330.0547	1345.1074	1358.0273	1369.9219	1424.4727	1540.8750	1686.5625	1879.5000
1350	1270.5997	1281.9191	1289.2731	1294.8761	1299.4904	1315.7227	1336.1160	1351.1948	1364.1724	1376.0788	1430.9143	1547.7539	1694.0918	1887.8906
1368	1288.1673	1299.5750	1306.9852	1312.6421	1317.2970	1333.6622	1354.2231	1369.5029	1382.6118	1394.6353	1450.0767	1568.5576	1716.6797	1913.0625
1380	1299.8776	1311.3327	1318.7869	1324.4724	1329.1681	1345.6348	1366.3129	1381.6846	1394.8663	1406.9952	1462.8809	1582.3169	1731.7383	1929.8438
1392	1311.5845	1323.2179	1330.6051	1336.3293	1341.0234	1357.5908	1378.4063	1393.8691	1407.1230	1419.3574	1475.6865	1596.2461	1746.7969	1946.6250
1410	1329.1685	1340.7758	1348.3383	1354.0828	1358.8376	1375.5331	1396.5317	1412.1515	1425.5768	1437.8833	1494.8547	1616.8872	1769.3848	1971.7969
1416	1335.0190	1346.6649	1354.2380	1360.0177	1364.7711	1381.5161	1402.6040	1418.2471	1431.6863	1444.0884	1501.2158	1623.7676	1776.9141	1980.1875
1440	1358.4595	1370.2148	1377.8723	1383.7061	1388.5181	1405.4590	1426.7725	1442.5928	1456.2598	1468.8281	1526.8359	1651.2891	1807.0313	2013.7500
1464	1381.9047	1393.7889	1401.5182	1407.4156	1412.2855	1429.3748	1450.9541	1466.9934	1480.7988	1493.5320	1552.4619	1678.8105	1837.1484	2047.3125
1470	1387.7701	1399.6806	1407.4191	1413.3408	1418.2082	1435.3674	1456.9904	1473.0505	1486.9574	1499.6979	1558.8245	1685.6909	1844.6777	2055.7031
1488	1405.3535	1417.3531	1425.1523	1431.1238	1436.0281	1453.3293	1475.1262	1491.3604	1505.3467	1518.2432	1578.0029	1706.5137	1867.2656	2080.8750
1500	1417.0761	1429.1382	1436.9888	1442.9626	1447.9065	1465.3015	1487.2284	1503.5248	1517.6239	1530.6244	1590.8203	1720.4590	1882.3242	2097.6563

continues

Table B-1 *Extended Erlang B with 40 Percent Retry Possibility (Continued)*

Circuits	0.001	0.002	0.003	0.004	0.005	0.01	0.02	0.03	0.04	0.05	0.1	0.2	0.3	0.4
1512	1428.8049	1440.9174	1448.8077	1454.8293	1459.7897	1477.2546	1499.3108	1515.7375	1529.9033	1543.0078	1603.6392	1734.2227	1897.3828	2114.4375
1530	1446.3982	1458.6081	1466.5457	1472.6157	1477.6117	1495.2145	1517.4399	1534.0155	1548.3032	1561.5170	1622.8235	1754.8682	1919.9707	2139.6094
1536	1452.2578	1464.4922	1472.4609	1478.5313	1483.5469	1501.2188	1523.4844	1540.1250	1554.4688	1567.6875	1629.1875	1761.7500	1927.8750	2148.0000
1560	1475.7349	1488.0890	1496.1108	1502.2522	1507.3224	1525.1514	1547.6697	1564.4751	1579.0430	1592.4683	1654.8340	1789.2773	1957.9980	2181.5625
1584	1499.1998	1511.6594	1519.7805	1525.9680	1531.0920	1549.0986	1571.8667	1588.8823	1603.5776	1617.1611	1680.3896	1816.8047	1988.1211	2215.1250
1590	1505.0727	1517.5674	1525.7071	1531.9180	1537.0372	1555.0877	1577.9178	1594.9493	1609.7003	1623.3838	1686.8518	1823.6865	1995.6519	2223.5156
1608	1522.6756	1535.2504	1543.4454	1549.7021	1554.8547	1573.0605	1596.0754	1613.2507	1628.1196	1641.9089	1705.9482	1844.5283	2018.2441	2248.6875
1620	1534.4220	1547.0535	1555.2850	1561.5637	1566.7548	1585.0223	1608.1595	1625.4382	1640.4181	1654.2609	1718.7781	1858.2935	2033.3057	2265.4688
1632	1546.1616	1558.8618	1567.1294	1573.4297	1578.6343	1597.0122	1620.2461	1637.6279	1652.7188	1666.6641	1731.6094	1872.2578	2048.3672	2282.2500
1650	1563.7688	1576.5587	1584.8671	1591.2369	1596.4737	1614.9788	1638.3934	1655.9418	1671.1487	1685.1974	1750.8087	1892.9077	2071.3623	2307.4219
1656	1569.6447	1582.4559	1590.7945	1597.1748	1602.4307	1620.9525	1644.4270	1662.0139	1677.2761	1691.3760	1757.1753	1899.7910	2078.8945	2315.8125
1680	1593.1366	1606.0565	1614.4775	1620.8990	1626.2183	1644.9316	1668.6438	1686.4087	1701.8408	1716.0938	1782.7441	1927.3242	2109.0234	2349.3750
1704	1616.6367	1629.6632	1638.1655	1644.6398	1649.9960	1668.8727	1692.8196	1710.8123	1726.3608	1740.8174	1808.4199	1954.8574	2139.1523	2382.9375
1710	1622.5117	1635.5580	1644.0772	1650.5743	1655.9363	1674.8795	1698.8846	1716.8884	1732.5439	1746.9992	1814.7876	1961.7407	2146.6846	2391.3281
1728	1640.1313	1653.2754	1661.8447	1668.3838	1673.7891	1692.8525	1717.0313	1735.1719	1750.9395	1765.5469	1833.9961	1982.3906	2169.2813	2416.5000
1740	1651.8796	1665.0751	1673.6774	1680.2618	1685.6781	1704.8209	1729.1409	1747.3810	1763.2581	1777.9138	1846.7322	1996.1572	2184.3457	2433.2813
1752	1663.6461	1676.8925	1685.5274	1692.1172	1697.5708	1716.8188	1741.2532	1759.5923	1775.5254	1790.2822	1859.5752	2010.1377	2199.4102	2450.0625
1770	1681.2650	1694.6070	1703.2901	1709.9341	1715.4167	1734.7815	1759.3858	1777.8864	1793.9291	1808.8376	1878.7885	2030.7898	2222.0068	2475.2344
1776	1687.1404	1700.5140	1709.2266	1715.8660	1721.3672	1740.7705	1765.4312	1783.9673	1800.0645	1815.0234	1885.1572	2037.6738	2229.5391	2483.6250
1800	1710.6537	1724.1394	1732.9285	1739.6301	1745.1782	1764.7339	1789.6179	1808.3496	1824.6643	1839.7705	1910.7422	2065.4297	2259.6680	2517.1875
1824	1734.1860	1747.7681	1756.6187	1763.3818	1768.9761	1788.7090	1813.8413	1832.7393	1849.2158	1864.5234	1936.3301	2092.9688	2289.7969	2550.7500
1830	1740.0581	1753.6709	1762.5366	1769.3221	1774.9347	1794.7046	1819.8917	1838.8239	1855.3546	1870.6567	1942.8113	2099.8535	2297.3291	2559.1406
1848	1757.7092	1771.3854	1780.3242	1787.1482	1792.7878	1812.6958	1838.0460	1857.1362	1873.7732	1889.2258	1961.9209	2120.5078	2319.9258	2584.3125
1860	1769.4635	1783.2001	1792.1686	1799.0085	1804.6848	1824.6936	1850.1517	1869.3375	1886.0541	1901.6071	1974.7742	2134.2773	2334.9902	2601.0938
1872	1781.2222	1795.0188	1804.0166	1810.9006	1816.5850	1836.6658	1862.2595	1881.5405	1898.3364	1913.9897	1987.5146	2148.0469	2350.0547	2617.8750
1890	1798.8684	1812.7544	1821.7955	1828.7169	1834.4559	1854.6432	1880.4254	1899.8053	1916.7627	1932.5089	2006.7407	2168.7012	2372.6514	2643.0469

Table B-1 *Extended Erlang B with 40 Percent Retry Possibility (Continued)*

Circuits

	0.001	0.002	0.003	0.004	0.005	0.01	0.02	0.03	0.04	0.05	0.1	0.2	0.3	0.4
1896	1804.7527	1818.6683	1827.7236	1834.6670	1840.3953	1860.6467	1886.4529	1905.9521	1922.9055	1938.7017	2013.1113	2175.5859	2380.1836	2651.4375
1920	1828.2861	1842.3047	1851.4453	1858.4180	1864.2188	1884.6387	1910.6836	1930.3125	1947.4805	1963.4766	2038.7109	2203.1250	2410.3125	2685.0000
1944	1851.8368	1865.9564	1875.1520	1882.2118	1888.0258	1908.6119	1934.8638	1954.7380	1972.0613	1988.1980	2064.3135	2230.9014	2440.4414	2718.5625
1950	1857.7160	1871.8643	1881.0883	1888.1401	1893.9720	1914.5920	1940.9248	1960.8307	1978.2074	1994.3939	2070.6848	2237.7869	2447.9736	2726.9531
1968	1875.3746	1889.5935	1898.8726	1905.9595	1911.8452	1932.5955	1959.0813	1979.1108	1996.5879	2012.9238	2089.9189	2258.4434	2470.5703	2752.1250
1980	1887.1422	1901.4175	1910.7381	1917.8531	1923.7445	1944.5911	1971.1780	1991.2994	2008.8831	2025.3186	2102.7832	2272.4561	2485.6348	2768.9063
1992	1898.9138	1913.2452	1922.6071	1929.7500	1935.6467	1956.5892	1983.3069	2003.4895	2021.1797	2037.6541	2115.5273	2286.2285	2500.6992	2785.6875
2010	1916.5787	1930.9937	1940.3787	1947.5862	1953.5362	1974.5760	2001.4737	2021.8387	2039.6274	2056.2506	2134.6436	2306.8872	2523.2959	2810.8594
2016	1922.4536	1936.8962	1946.3247	1953.5229	1959.4907	1980.5625	2007.5098	2027.9355	2045.7773	2062.3887	2141.1387	2313.7734	2530.8281	2819.2500
2040	1946.0248	1960.5615	1970.0555	1977.3083	1983.3160	2004.5453	2031.7200	2052.3267	2070.3186	2087.1277	2166.7529	2341.3184	2560.9570	2852.8125
2064	1969.5806	1984.2253	1993.7681	2001.0747	2007.1216	2028.5376	2055.9375	2076.7236	2094.9272	2111.8711	2192.2441	2368.8633	2591.0859	2886.3750
2070	1975.4640	1990.1198	1999.7060	2007.0181	2013.0826	2034.5293	2061.9772	2082.8238	2101.0172	2118.0734	2198.6169	2375.7495	2599.1235	2894.7656
2088	1993.1358	2007.8712	2017.5090	2024.8687	2030.9700	2052.5394	2080.1624	2101.1265	2119.4780	2136.6189	2217.8628	2396.4082	2621.7246	2919.9375
2100	2004.9110	2019.6991	2029.3762	2036.7622	2042.8665	2064.5279	2092.2455	2113.3301	2131.7871	2148.9624	2230.7373	2410.1807	2636.7920	2936.7188
2112	2016.6899	2031.5464	2041.2305	2048.6426	2054.7979	2076.5186	2104.3945	2125.5352	2144.0332	2161.3711	2243.4844	2423.9531	2651.8594	2953.5000
2130	2034.3652	2049.2995	2059.0498	2066.4926	2072.6678	2094.5087	2122.5247	2143.8130	2162.5012	2179.9219	2262.6050	2444.6118	2674.4604	2978.6719
2136	2040.2587	2055.2025	2064.9803	2072.4441	2078.6367	2100.5391	2128.6014	2149.8845	2168.5928	2186.0625	2269.1089	2451.4980	2681.9941	2987.0625
2160	2063.8257	2078.8879	2088.7097	2096.2244	2102.4536	2124.5032	2152.8149	2174.3042	2193.2227	2210.8228	2294.7363	2479.3066	2712.1289	3020.6250
2184	2087.3903	2102.5532	2112.4508	2120.0156	2126.2974	2148.5087	2177.0350	2198.7297	2217.7917	2235.5874	2320.2334	2506.8545	2742.2637	3054.1875
2190	2093.2919	2108.4631	2118.3879	2125.9735	2132.2559	2154.5114	2183.0827	2204.8370	2223.8846	2241.7291	2326.6077	2513.7415	2749.7974	3062.5781
2208	2110.9688	2126.2310	2136.2036	2143.8179	2150.1519	2172.5229	2201.2617	2223.0938	2242.3652	2260.2891	2345.8652	2534.4023	2772.3984	3087.7500
2220	2122.7632	2138.0745	2148.0844	2155.7231	2162.0576	2184.4995	2213.3606	2235.3113	2254.6198	2272.7087	2358.7500	2548.4473	2787.4658	3104.5313
2232	2134.5612	2149.9211	2159.9341	2167.6311	2173.9658	2196.5120	2225.4609	2247.5303	2266.8750	2285.0618	2371.5000	2562.2227	2802.5332	3121.3125
2250	2152.2388	2167.6712	2177.7649	2185.4725	2191.8755	2214.5004	2243.6485	2265.8272	2285.3622	2303.6270	2390.6250	2582.8857	2825.1343	3146.4844
2256	2158.1331	2173.5894	2183.6927	2191.4209	2197.8237	2220.5090	2249.7004	2271.9038	2291.4565	2309.8389	2397.0000	2589.7734	2832.6680	3154.8750
2280	2181.7181	2197.2693	2207.4454	2215.2209	2221.6571	2244.5142	2273.9117	2296.3513	2316.0425	2334.5508	2422.6392	2617.3242	2863.3594	3188.4375

continues

Table B-1 *Extended Erlang B with 40 Percent Retry Possibility (Continued)*

Circuits	0.001	0.002	0.003	0.004	0.005	0.01	0.02	0.03	0.04	0.05	0.1	0.2	0.3	0.4
2304	2205.3164	2220.9609	2231.1914	2239.0313	2245.5176	2268.5273	2298.1641	2320.7344	2340.6328	2359.2656	2448.2813	2644.8750	2893.5000	3222.0000
2310	2211.2004	2226.8857	2237.1428	2244.9678	2251.4886	2274.5407	2304.2194	2326.8484	2346.7987	2365.4800	2454.6570	2651.7627	2901.0352	3230.3906
2328	2228.8923	2244.6465	2254.9481	2262.8340	2269.3524	2292.5486	2322.3875	2345.1218	2365.2275	2383.9834	2473.7842	2672.4258	2923.6406	3256.6992
2340	2240.7028	2256.4847	2266.8393	2274.7302	2281.3000	2304.5444	2334.5013	2357.3529	2377.4908	2396.4148	2486.6785	2686.2012	2938.7109	3273.4863
2352	2252.4807	2268.3435	2278.7153	2286.6467	2293.2144	2316.5420	2346.6167	2369.5496	2389.7549	2408.7759	2499.4307	2699.9766	2953.7813	3290.2734
2370	2270.1892	2286.1011	2296.5161	2304.5082	2311.0899	2334.5599	2364.7563	2387.8647	2408.1885	2427.2827	2518.7036	2720.6396	2976.3867	3315.4541
2376	2276.0815	2292.0337	2302.4751	2310.4512	2317.0677	2340.5427	2370.8156	2393.9824	2414.3577	2433.5002	2525.0801	2727.5273	2983.9219	3323.8477
2400	2299.6765	2315.7349	2326.2268	2334.2651	2340.9302	2364.5508	2395.0562	2418.3838	2438.9648	2458.2275	2550.5859	2755.0781	3014.0625	3357.4219
2424	2323.2836	2339.4285	2349.9884	2358.0886	2364.7833	2388.5662	2419.2656	2442.7896	2463.5024	2483.0317	2576.2397	2782.6289	3044.2031	3390.9961
2430	2329.1826	2345.3490	2355.9350	2364.0367	2370.7480	2394.5897	2425.3281	2448.8731	2469.6744	2489.1779	2582.6166	2789.5166	3051.7383	3399.3896
2448	2346.8840	2363.1328	2373.7599	2381.8843	2388.6453	2412.5889	2443.5176	2467.1997	2488.1177	2507.7656	2601.8965	2810.4785	3074.3438	3424.5703
2460	2358.6887	2374.9796	2385.6400	2393.7854	2400.5795	2424.6030	2455.6458	2479.3689	2500.3894	2520.0586	2614.6509	2824.2554	3089.4141	3441.3574
2472	2370.4962	2386.8289	2397.5224	2405.7076	2412.4971	2436.5812	2467.7377	2491.6143	2512.6619	2532.5024	2627.4053	2838.0322	3104.4844	3458.1445
2490	2388.1940	2404.6076	2415.3410	2423.5858	2430.3868	2454.6272	2485.8966	2509.9091	2531.1099	2551.0190	2646.5369	2858.6975	3127.0898	3483.3252
2496	2394.1011	2410.5352	2421.2944	2429.5400	2436.3574	2460.6182	2491.9629	2516.0332	2537.2852	2557.2422	2653.0664	2865.5859	3134.6250	3491.7188
2520	2417.7173	2434.2517	2445.0568	2453.3432	2460.2069	2484.6240	2516.1932	2540.3796	2561.8359	2581.9849	2678.5767	2893.4473	3164.7656	3525.2930
2544	2441.3254	2457.9591	2468.8477	2477.1548	2484.0839	2508.6365	2540.4287	2564.8066	2586.3896	2606.7305	2704.2422	2921.0039	3194.9063	3558.8672
2550	2447.2389	2463.8924	2474.7871	2483.1139	2490.0398	2514.6698	2546.4981	2570.9335	2592.5674	2612.8784	2710.6201	2927.8931	3202.4414	3567.2607
2568	2464.9446	2481.6764	2492.6089	2500.9944	2507.9496	2532.6555	2564.6693	2589.2380	2610.9463	2631.4790	2729.7539	2948.5605	3225.0469	3592.4414
2580	2476.7583	2493.5289	2504.4928	2512.9175	2519.8856	2544.6872	2576.7719	2601.4160	2623.3044	2643.8544	2742.6672	2962.3389	3240.1172	3609.2285
2592	2488.5549	2505.3838	2516.3789	2524.8230	2531.8037	2556.6812	2588.9150	2613.6738	2635.5850	2656.2305	2755.4238	2976.1172	3255.1875	3626.0156
2610	2506.2746	2523.1606	2534.2122	2542.6950	2549.7043	2574.7147	2607.0529	2631.9836	2653.9673	2674.7562	2774.5587	2996.7847	3277.7930	3651.1963
2616	2512.1759	2529.1007	2540.1577	2548.6600	2555.6854	2580.7134	2613.1260	2638.0342	2660.1482	2680.9050	2781.0967	3003.6738	3285.3281	3659.5898
2640	2535.8075	2552.8070	2563.9252	2572.4854	2579.5551	2604.7119	2637.3413	2662.4780	2684.7144	2705.6616	2806.6113	3031.2305	3315.4688	3693.1641
2664	2559.4294	2576.5225	2587.7010	2596.3187	2603.4324	2628.7570	2661.6017	2686.8450	2709.2834	2730.4211	2832.1260	3058.7871	3345.6094	3726.7383
2670	2565.3365	2582.4680	2593.6514	2602.2681	2609.3774	2634.7591	2667.6370	2692.9779	2715.4669	2736.6522	2838.5046	3065.6763	3353.1445	3735.1318

Table B-1   *Extended Erlang B with 40 Percent Retry Possibility (Continued)*

Circuits	0.001	0.002	0.003	0.004	0.005	0.01	0.02	0.03	0.04	0.05	0.1	0.2	0.3	0.4
2688	2583.0615	2600.2471	2611.4854	2620.1396	2627.2969	2652.7676	2685.7852	2711.2969	2733.8555	2755.1836	2857.8047	3086.3438	3375.7500	3760.3125
2700	2594.8814	2612.1231	2623.3704	2632.0633	2639.2319	2664.7751	2697.9401	2723.4833	2746.1426	2767.5659	2870.5627	3100.1221	3390.8203	3777.0996
2712	2606.6632	2623.9808	2635.2781	2643.9683	2651.1687	2676.7841	2710.0551	2735.6704	2758.4304	2779.8662	2883.4863	3113.9004	3405.8906	3793.8867
2730	2624.4216	2641.7715	2653.1021	2661.8500	2669.0774	2694.8003	2728.2504	2753.9941	2776.9052	2798.4833	2902.6245	3134.5679	3428.4961	3819.0674
2736	2630.3148	2647.7029	2659.0583	2667.8046	2675.0479	2700.8064	2734.2883	2760.1304	2783.0083	2804.6338	2909.0039	3141.4570	3436.0313	3827.4609
2760	2653.9563	2671.4337	2682.8467	2691.6486	2698.9343	2724.8346	2758.5260	2784.5105	2807.5891	2829.4043	2934.5215	3169.0137	3466.1719	3861.0352
2784	2677.5864	2695.1521	2706.6431	2715.4790	2722.8069	2748.8687	2782.7681	2808.9785	2832.1729	2854.1777	2960.2090	3196.5703	3496.3125	3894.6094
2790	2683.5061	2701.0883	2712.6041	2721.4378	2728.7814	2754.8781	2788.8080	2815.0323	2838.3618	2860.3290	2966.5887	3203.4595	3503.8477	3903.0029
2808	2701.2261	2718.8789	2730.4475	2739.3168	2746.6864	2772.9086	2806.9717	2833.3652	2856.7595	2878.8684	2985.7280	3224.1270	3526.4531	3928.1836
2820	2713.0495	2730.7562	2742.3312	2751.2384	2758.6395	2784.9307	2819.1394	2845.5597	2869.0540	2891.2573	2998.6597	3238.2495	3541.5234	3944.9707
2832	2724.8752	2742.6141	2754.2168	2763.1619	2770.5513	2796.9543	2831.2222	2857.7549	2881.3491	2903.6470	3011.4199	3252.0293	3556.5938	3961.7578
2850	2742.6075	2760.4156	2772.0703	2781.0505	2788.4651	2814.9490	2849.3912	2876.0925	2899.8367	2922.1893	3030.5603	3272.6990	3579.1992	3986.9385
2856	2748.5121	2766.3578	2778.0152	2787.0143	2794.4445	2820.9624	2855.4771	2882.1910	2905.9417	2928.3413	3036.9404	3279.5889	3586.7344	3995.3320
2880	2772.1582	2790.0879	2801.8213	2810.8521	2818.3447	2845.0195	2879.7363	2906.6309	2930.5371	2953.1250	3062.6367	3307.1484	3616.8750	4028.9063
2904	2795.8134	2813.8260	2825.6129	2834.6968	2842.2297	2869.0382	2903.9557	2931.0300	2955.1355	2977.9116	3088.1587	3334.7080	3647.0156	4062.4805
2910	2801.7231	2819.7729	2831.5620	2840.6424	2848.1909	2875.0548	2910.0000	2937.1303	2961.2411	2984.0643	3094.5392	3341.5979	3654.5508	4070.8740
2928	2819.4554	2837.5723	2849.4119	2858.5261	2866.1213	2893.0620	2928.1787	2955.4321	2979.7368	3002.6118	3113.8594	3362.6250	3677.1563	4096.0547
2940	2831.2798	2849.4260	2861.3141	2870.4657	2878.0472	2905.0983	2940.3140	2967.6343	2991.9489	3015.0073	3126.6211	3376.4063	3692.2266	4112.8418
2952	2843.1063	2861.3040	2873.2181	2882.3846	2889.9745	2917.0909	2952.4504	2979.8372	3004.2510	3027.3135	3139.3828	3390.1875	3707.2969	4129.6289
2970	2860.8501	2879.1135	2891.0550	2900.2773	2907.9135	2935.1047	2970.6345	2998.1882	3022.7509	3045.9540	3158.5254	3410.8594	3729.9023	4154.8096
2976	2866.7659	2885.0435	2897.0317	2906.2500	2913.8789	2941.1250	2976.6812	3004.2451	3028.8574	3052.1074	3164.9063	3417.7500	3737.4375	4163.2031
3000	2890.4114	2908.7906	2920.8069	2930.0995	2937.7670	2965.1642	3000.9155	3028.6560	3053.4668	3076.9043	3190.6128	3445.3125	3767.5781	4196.7773
3024	2914.0653	2932.5454	2944.6348	2953.9556	2961.6614	2989.2085	3025.1536	3053.0698	3077.9868	3101.6118	3216.1377	3472.8750	3797.7188	4230.3516
3030	2919.9859	2938.4795	2950.5698	2959.9091	2967.6302	2995.2319	3031.2021	3059.2200	3084.1864	3107.7658	3222.5189	3479.7656	3805.2539	4238.7451
3048	2937.7277	2956.2847	2968.4235	2977.7950	2985.5387	3013.2579	3049.3953	3077.4866	3102.6013	3126.3208	3241.8486	3500.4375	3827.8594	4263.9258
3060	2949.5503	2968.1570	2980.3436	2989.7287	2997.5029	3025.2612	3061.5408	3089.6960	3114.9097	3138.7225	3254.6118	3514.2188	3842.9297	4280.7129

continues

Table B-1 *Extended Erlang B with 40 Percent Retry Possibility (Continued)*

Circuits

	0.001	0.002	0.003	0.004	0.005	0.01	0.02	0.03	0.04	0.05	0.1	0.2	0.3	0.4
3072	2961.3750	2980.0313	2992.2422	3001.6406	3009.4453	3037.2656	3073.6406	3101.9063	3127.2188	3151.1250	3267.3750	3528.0000	3858.0000	4297.5000
3090	2979.1276	2997.8460	3010.1049	3019.5348	3027.3853	3055.2979	3091.8388	3120.2701	3145.6366	3169.6829	3286.5198	3548.6719	3880.6055	4322.6807
3096	2985.0540	3003.7852	3016.0443	3025.5161	3033.3582	3061.3250	3097.8896	3126.3289	3151.7446	3175.8376	3292.9014	3555.5625	3888.1406	4331.0742
3120	3008.7177	3027.5464	3039.8767	3049.3506	3057.2534	3085.3418	3122.1423	3150.7544	3176.3672	3200.5518	3318.6182	3583.1250	3918.2813	4364.6484
3144	3032.3654	3051.2910	3063.6682	3073.2149	3081.1306	3109.4110	3146.3987	3175.1829	3200.9927	3225.3633	3344.1460	3610.6875	3948.4219	4398.2227
3150	3038.2965	3057.2342	3069.6350	3079.2000	3087.1067	3115.3931	3152.4513	3181.2424	3207.1014	3231.5186	3350.5280	3617.5781	3955.9570	4406.6162
3168	3056.0449	3075.0425	3087.4900	3097.0854	3105.0374	3133.4370	3170.6104	3199.6143	3225.5244	3250.0811	3369.6738	3638.2500	3979.3359	4431.7969
3180	3067.8877	3086.9330	3099.4034	3109.0109	3116.9687	3145.4517	3182.7173	3211.8311	3237.8394	3262.4890	3382.6318	3652.0313	3994.4092	4448.5840
3192	3079.7082	3098.8010	3111.2941	3120.9379	3128.9257	3157.4674	3194.8737	3224.0486	3250.1550	3274.8003	3395.3965	3665.8125	4009.4824	4465.3711
3210	3097.4668	3116.6183	3129.1573	3138.8310	3146.8639	3175.5176	3213.0368	3242.3273	3268.5809	3293.3652	3414.5435	3686.4844	4032.0923	4490.5518
3216	3103.3792	3122.5664	3135.1289	3144.7961	3152.8440	3181.5513	3219.1406	3248.4368	3274.6904	3299.6191	3420.9258	3693.3750	4039.6289	4498.9453
3240	3127.0578	3146.3141	3158.9209	3168.6603	3176.7188	3205.5908	3243.3618	3272.8271	3299.3262	3324.3420	3446.4551	3720.9375	4069.7754	4532.5195
3264	3150.7192	3170.0684	3182.7686	3192.5303	3200.6484	3229.6348	3267.5859	3297.2695	3323.8652	3349.0664	3472.1836	3748.5000	4099.9219	4566.0938
3270	3156.6357	3176.0204	3188.7190	3198.4987	3206.6068	3235.6215	3273.6923	3303.3806	3329.9753	3355.2228	3478.5663	3755.3906	4107.4585	4574.4873
3288	3174.4131	3193.8292	3206.5726	3216.4061	3224.5338	3253.6831	3291.8632	3321.7148	3348.4058	3373.8926	3497.7144	3776.0625	4130.0684	4599.6680
3300	3186.2503	3205.7121	3218.4769	3228.3211	3236.5036	3265.7089	3303.9780	3333.9780	3360.7269	3386.2061	3510.4797	3789.8438	4145.1416	4616.4551
3312	3198.0894	3217.5967	3230.3826	3240.2626	3248.4243	3277.6853	3316.0935	3346.1125	3373.0488	3398.5195	3523.4473	3803.6250	4160.2148	4633.2422
3330	3215.8260	3235.4393	3248.2439	3258.1522	3266.3837	3295.7529	3334.2682	3364.4504	3391.4822	3417.1930	3542.5964	3824.7034	4182.8247	4658.4229
3336	3221.7475	3241.3707	3254.1984	3264.1245	3272.3454	3301.7421	3340.3777	3370.5125	3397.5930	3423.3501	3548.9795	3831.5947	4190.3613	4666.8164
3360	3245.4382	3265.1257	3278.0457	3287.9919	3296.2720	3325.8032	3364.6143	3394.9658	3422.2412	3448.0811	3574.5117	3859.1602	4220.5078	4700.3906
3384	3269.1105	3288.8870	3301.8475	3311.8649	3320.1782	3349.8688	3388.8538	3419.3705	3446.7891	3472.8135	3600.0439	3886.7256	4250.6543	4733.9648
3390	3275.0361	3294.8476	3307.8053	3317.8404	3326.1427	3355.8600	3394.9141	3425.4849	3452.9004	3478.9709	3606.4270	3893.6169	4258.1909	4742.3584
3408	3292.8157	3312.6804	3325.6809	3335.7173	3344.0636	3373.8867	3413.0962	3443.7773	3471.3384	3497.5474	3625.7842	3914.2910	4280.8008	4767.5391
3420	3304.6449	3324.5535	3337.5998	3347.6715	3356.0211	3385.9232	3425.2185	3456.0077	3483.6658	3509.9670	3638.5510	3928.0737	4295.8740	4784.3262
3432	3316.4758	3336.4281	3349.5201	3359.6010	3367.9799	3397.9607	3437.3416	3468.2388	3495.9939	3522.2827	3651.3179	3941.8564	4310.9473	4801.1133
3450	3334.2648	3354.2690	3367.3771	3377.5108	3385.9074	3415.9927	3455.5275	3486.5341	3514.4348	3540.8615	3670.4681	3962.5305	4333.5571	4826.2939

Table B-1   *Extended Erlang B with 40 Percent Retry Possibility (Continued)*

Circuits	0.001	0.002	0.003	0.004	0.005	0.01	0.02	0.03	0.04	0.05	0.1	0.2	0.3	0.4
3456	3340.1689	3360.2080	3373.3389	3383.4902	3391.8750	3421.9863	3461.5898	3492.6504	3520.5469	3547.1250	3676.8516	3969.8438	4341.0938	4834.6875
3480	3363.8690	3383.9941	3397.1631	3407.3584	3415.8014	3446.0687	3485.8411	3517.0642	3545.1013	3571.8640	3702.5977	3997.4121	4371.2402	4868.2617
3504	3387.5493	3407.7598	3420.9928	3431.2317	3439.7062	3470.1021	3510.0952	3541.4802	3569.7642	3596.6045	3728.1328	4024.9805	4401.3867	4901.8359
3510	3393.4838	3413.7021	3426.9578	3437.1874	3445.6764	3476.0976	3516.1592	3547.5980	3575.8768	3602.7631	3734.5166	4031.8726	4408.9233	4910.2295
3528	3411.2362	3431.5313	3444.8280	3455.1101	3463.6157	3494.1390	3534.3523	3565.8984	3594.3223	3621.3464	3753.6680	4052.5488	4431.5332	4935.4102
3540	3423.0821	3443.4192	3456.7612	3467.0242	3475.5858	3506.1859	3546.4819	3578.1354	3606.6559	3633.6639	3766.4355	4066.3330	4446.6064	4953.9258
3552	3434.9297	3455.3086	3468.6687	3478.9937	3487.5300	3518.1797	3558.6123	3590.3730	3618.8818	3646.0898	3779.2031	4080.1172	4461.6797	4970.7188
3570	3452.6905	3473.1454	3486.5460	3496.8961	3505.4757	3536.2262	3576.8092	3608.6765	3637.3297	3664.6756	3798.5724	4100.7935	4484.2896	4995.9082
3576	3458.6298	3479.0918	3492.4876	3502.8550	3511.4491	3542.2786	3582.8752	3614.7415	3643.4429	3670.8347	3804.9565	4107.6855	4491.8262	5004.3047
3600	3482.3090	3502.8534	3516.3391	3526.7212	3535.3729	3566.3269	3607.1411	3639.2212	3668.1152	3695.5811	3830.4932	4135.2539	4521.9727	5037.8906
3624	3506.0220	3526.6481	3540.1685	3550.6198	3559.3015	3590.3789	3631.3546	3663.5933	3692.6799	3720.3289	3856.0298	4162.8223	4552.1191	5071.4766
3630	3511.9375	3532.5977	3546.1404	3556.5813	3565.2498	3596.3786	3637.4222	3669.7142	3698.7936	3726.4883	3862.6355	4169.7144	4559.6558	5079.8730
3648	3529.7139	3550.4209	3564.0029	3574.4956	3583.2070	3614.4346	3655.6260	3688.0225	3717.2461	3745.0781	3881.7891	4190.3906	4583.1563	5105.0625
3660	3541.5761	3562.3233	3575.9221	3586.4493	3595.1614	3626.4359	3667.7069	3700.2100	3729.5856	3757.3975	3894.5581	4204.1748	4598.2324	5121.8555
3672	3553.4119	3574.1992	3587.8425	3598.3762	3607.1169	3638.8545	3679.8442	3712.4539	3741.8137	3769.8289	3907.3271	4217.9590	4613.3086	5138.6484
3690	3571.1966	3592.0294	3605.7115	3616.2968	3625.0523	3656.4986	3698.0516	3730.7648	3760.2686	3788.4210	3926.4807	4238.6353	4635.9229	5163.8379
3696	3577.1162	3597.9829	3611.6873	3622.2616	3631.0313	3662.5287	3704.1211	3736.8311	3766.3828	3794.5811	3932.8652	4245.5273	4643.4609	5172.2344
3720	3600.8267	3621.7722	3635.5087	3646.1517	3654.9500	3686.5668	3728.4009	3761.3232	3791.0669	3819.3347	3958.4033	4273.0957	4673.6133	5205.8203
3744	3624.5149	3645.5669	3659.3635	3670.0181	3678.8730	3710.6367	3752.6265	3785.7041	3815.6396	3844.0898	3984.1699	4300.6641	4703.7656	5239.4063
3750	3630.4379	3651.4950	3665.3137	3675.9853	3684.8545	3716.6405	3758.6975	3791.8282	3821.7545	3850.2502	3990.5548	4307.5562	4711.3037	5247.8027
3768	3648.2377	3669.3384	3683.1947	3693.8888	3702.8005	3734.7103	3776.8542	3810.1439	3840.2139	3868.8464	4009.7095	4328.2324	4733.9180	5272.9922
3780	3660.0870	3681.2260	3695.1265	3705.8546	3714.7659	3746.7197	3788.9978	3822.3358	3852.4438	3881.1676	4022.4792	4342.0166	4748.9941	5289.7852
3792	3671.9377	3693.1150	3707.0306	3717.7928	3726.7324	3758.7587	3801.1421	3834.5859	3864.7896	3893.6045	4035.2490	4355.8008	4764.0703	5306.5781
3810	3689.7166	3710.9653	3724.9180	3735.7022	3744.6552	3776.8044	3819.3018	3852.9044	3883.2513	3912.0868	4054.4037	4376.4771	4786.6846	5331.7676
3816	3695.6437	3716.9258	3730.8713	3741.6725	3750.6396	3782.8103	3825.3746	3858.9719	3889.3667	3918.3640	4061.0215	4383.3691	4794.2227	5340.1641
3840	3719.3555	3740.7129	3754.7461	3765.5566	3774.5508	3806.8945	3849.6680	3883.4180	3913.9453	3943.1250	4086.5625	4410.9375	4824.3750	5373.7500

continues

Table B-1 *Extended Erlang B with 40 Percent Retry Possibility (Continued)*

Circuits

	0.001	0.002	0.003	0.004	0.005	0.01	0.02	0.03	0.04	0.05	0.1	0.2	0.3	0.4
3864	3743.0436	3764.5051	3778.5670	3789.4451	3798.4955	3830.9235	3873.9053	3907.8662	3938.5254	3967.7695	4112.1035	4438.5059	4854.5273	5407.3359
3870	3748.9739	3770.4391	3784.5525	3795.4179	3804.4528	3836.9312	3879.9797	3913.9343	3944.6411	3974.0488	4118.4888	4445.3979	4862.0654	5415.7324
3888	3766.7670	3788.3024	3802.4220	3813.3380	3822.4149	3855.0146	3898.1448	3932.2573	3963.1069	3992.5327	4137.6445	4466.0742	4884.6797	5440.9219
3900	3778.6308	3800.2029	3814.3364	3825.2861	3834.3613	3867.0319	3910.2951	3944.5129	3975.4578	4004.9744	4150.4150	4479.8584	4899.7559	5457.7148
3912	3790.4663	3812.0750	3826.2817	3837.2353	3846.3384	3879.0498	3922.3865	3956.6499	3987.6899	4017.2974	4163.1855	4493.6426	4914.8320	5474.5078
3930	3808.2669	3829.9150	3844.1572	3855.1611	3864.2761	3897.0781	3940.6142	3974.9753	4006.1581	4035.9018	4182.3413	4514.3188	4937.4463	5499.6973
3936	3814.2012	3835.8823	3850.1162	3861.1069	3870.2659	3903.1179	3946.6904	3981.1641	4012.2744	4042.0635	4188.7266	4521.2109	4944.9844	5508.0938
3960	3837.9117	3859.6646	3873.9551	3885.0128	3894.1974	3927.1893	3970.9369	4005.5603	4036.8604	4066.8311	4214.5093	4548.7793	4975.1367	5541.6797
3984	3861.6277	3883.4821	3897.7983	3908.9231	3918.1025	3951.2336	3995.1855	4029.9580	4061.4478	4091.6001	4240.0518	4576.3477	5005.2891	5575.2656
3990	3867.5347	3889.4220	3903.7903	3914.8709	3924.1251	3957.2452	4001.2633	4036.0881	4067.6862	4097.7621	4246.4374	4583.2397	5012.8271	5583.6621
4008	3885.3492	3907.2740	3921.6460	3932.7766	3942.0725	3975.2809	4019.4364	4054.3572	4086.0366	4116.3706	4265.5942	4603.9160	5035.4414	5608.8516
4020	3897.1967	3919.1565	3933.5715	3944.7354	3953.9978	3987.3363	4031.5933	4066.6187	4098.3929	4128.6951	4278.6108	4617.7002	5050.5176	5625.6445
4032	3909.0454	3931.0708	3945.4980	3956.6953	3965.9854	3999.3926	4043.6895	4078.8193	4110.6270	4141.0195	4291.3828	4631.9766	5065.5938	5642.4375
4050	3926.8364	3948.8983	3963.4209	3974.6063	3983.9378	4017.4324	4061.8652	4097.1519	4129.1016	4159.6298	4310.5408	4652.6550	5088.2080	5667.6270
4056	3932.7777	3954.8723	3969.3545	3980.5875	3989.9019	4023.4460	4067.9447	4103.2837	4135.2188	4165.7922	4316.9268	4659.5479	5095.7461	5676.0234
4080	3956.4844	3978.6475	3993.2153	4004.4836	4013.8220	4047.5024	4092.2021	4127.6880	4159.8120	4190.5664	4342.4707	4687.1191	5125.8984	5709.6094
4104	3980.2275	4002.4583	4017.0806	4028.3839	4037.7772	4071.5618	4116.4618	4152.0938	4184.4067	4215.3420	4368.0146	4714.6904	5156.0508	5743.1953
4110	3986.1406	4008.4039	4023.0476	4034.3674	4043.7744	4077.5771	4122.5427	4158.1641	4190.5243	4221.5048	4374.4006	4721.5833	5163.5889	5751.5918
4128	4003.9446	4026.2739	4040.9187	4052.2881	4061.7048	4095.6240	4140.7236	4176.5010	4209.0029	4240.1191	4393.5586	4742.2617	5186.2031	5776.7813
4140	4015.8051	4038.1677	4052.8551	4064.2259	4073.6700	4107.6563	4152.8870	4188.7683	4221.3647	4252.4451	4406.3306	4756.0474	5201.2793	5793.5742
4152	4027.6668	4050.0626	4064.7925	4076.1647	4085.6362	4119.6892	4164.9877	4200.9730	4233.6006	4264.7710	4419.1025	4769.8330	5216.3555	5810.3672
4170	4045.4459	4067.9070	4082.6690	4094.0904	4103.5712	4137.7400	4183.1712	4219.2490	4252.0816	4283.3871	4438.5150	4790.5115	5238.9697	5835.5566
4176	4051.3942	4073.8557	4088.6389	4100.0768	4109.5712	4143.7573	4189.2539	4225.3835	4258.1997	4289.5503	4444.9014	4797.7043	5246.5078	5843.9531
4200	4075.1106	4097.6852	4112.4893	4123.9609	4133.5098	4167.8284	4213.5223	4249.8596	4282.8003	4314.3311	4470.4468	4824.9756	5276.6602	5877.5391
4224	4098.8320	4121.4873	4136.3438	4147.8809	4157.4199	4191.9023	4237.7930	4274.2734	4307.4023	4339.1133	4495.9922	4852.5469	5306.8125	5911.1250
4230	4104.7833	4127.4385	4142.3161	4153.8373	4163.4222	4197.9213	4243.8126	4280.3448	4313.5208	4345.2768	4502.3785	4859.4397	5314.3506	5919.5215

Table B-1 *Extended Erlang B with 40 Percent Retry Possibility (Continued)*

Circuits	0.001	0.002	0.003	0.004	0.005	0.01	0.02	0.03	0.04	0.05	0.1	0.2	0.3	0.4
4248	4122.5746	4145.2938	4160.2022	4171.7725	4181.3657	4215.9792	4262.0010	4298.6887	4332.0059	4363.8970	4521.7969	4880.6367	5336.9648	5944.7109
4260	4134.4153	4157.1986	4172.1492	4183.7196	4193.3400	4228.0188	4274.1705	4310.8969	4344.2432	4376.2244	4534.5703	4894.4238	5352.0410	5961.5039
4272	4146.2897	4169.1046	4184.0647	4195.6677	4205.3152	4240.0265	4286.2756	4323.1055	4356.6108	4388.5518	4547.3438	4908.2109	5367.1172	5978.2969
4290	4164.0873	4186.9656	4201.9560	4213.6079	4223.2633	4258.0554	4304.4667	4341.4517	4374.9673	4407.1738	4566.5039	4928.8916	5389.7314	6003.4863
4296	4170.0259	4192.8871	4207.9312	4219.5667	4229.2683	4264.0763	4310.5525	4347.5237	4381.2173	4413.3376	4572.8906	4935.7852	5397.2695	6011.8828
4320	4193.7671	4216.7065	4231.8018	4243.4692	4253.1921	4288.1616	4334.8315	4371.9434	4405.6934	4438.1250	4598.4375	4963.3594	5427.4219	6045.4688
4344	4217.4966	4240.5304	4255.6432	4267.3755	4277.1193	4312.2499	4359.0465	4396.3645	4430.3020	4462.7813	4623.9844	4990.9336	5457.5742	6079.0547
4350	4223.4215	4246.4870	4261.6207	4273.3360	4283.0933	4318.2724	4365.1337	4402.5032	4436.4212	4469.0781	4630.3711	4997.8271	5465.1123	6087.4512
4368	4241.2310	4264.3253	4279.5216	4291.2854	4301.0830	4336.2744	4383.3296	4420.7871	4454.9121	4487.5708	4649.5313	5018.5078	5487.7266	6112.6406
4380	4253.0832	4276.2410	4291.4456	4303.2417	4313.0328	4348.3209	4395.4385	4433.0658	4467.2845	4500.0330	4662.3047	5032.2949	5502.8027	6129.4336
4392	4264.9700	4288.1578	4303.3705	4315.1990	4324.9834	4360.3682	4407.6149	4445.2112	4479.5237	4512.3618	4675.0781	5046.0820	5517.8789	6146.2266
4410	4282.7522	4306.0014	4321.2765	4333.1197	4342.9779	4378.4404	4425.8134	4463.5638	4498.0170	4530.8551	4694.5074	5066.7627	5540.4932	6171.4160
4416	4288.6802	4311.9609	4327.2568	4339.0825	4348.9541	4384.4648	4431.8350	4469.6367	4504.1367	4537.1543	4700.8945	5073.6563	5548.0313	6179.8125
4440	4312.4286	4335.7681	4351.1133	4363.0032	4372.8946	4408.4967	4456.1243	4494.0637	4528.7512	4561.8127	4726.4429	5101.2305	5578.1836	6213.3984
4464	4336.1647	4359.5793	4374.9734	4386.8936	4396.8384	4432.5989	4480.3477	4518.4922	4553.2310	4586.6074	4751.9912	5128.8047	5608.3359	6246.9844
4470	4342.1123	4365.5413	4380.9560	4392.8581	4402.8163	4438.6249	4486.4378	4524.6336	4559.4873	4592.7722	4758.3783	5135.6982	5615.8740	6255.3809
4488	4359.9055	4383.3946	4398.8372	4410.8214	4420.7512	4456.6355	4504.6410	4542.9221	4577.8477	4611.4036	4777.5396	5156.3789	5638.4883	6280.5703
4500	4371.7690	4395.3209	4410.7704	4422.7524	4432.7431	4468.6890	4516.7542	4555.2063	4590.2252	4623.7335	4790.5884	5170.1660	5653.5645	6297.3633
4512	4383.6335	4407.2139	4422.7046	4434.7185	4444.7014	4480.7432	4528.9365	4567.3535	4602.4658	4636.0635	4803.3633	5183.9531	5668.6406	6314.1563
4530	4401.4325	4425.0723	4440.6248	4452.6521	4462.6749	4498.7567	4547.0732	4585.7126	4620.9650	4654.6967	4822.5256	5204.6338	5691.2549	6339.3457
4536	4407.3660	4431.0372	4446.5757	4458.6189	4468.6549	4504.7845	4553.1650	4591.7864	4627.0854	4660.8618	4828.9131	5211.5273	5698.7930	6347.7422
4560	4431.1377	4454.8645	4470.4504	4482.5226	4492.5769	4528.8977	4577.3950	4616.2207	4651.7065	4685.6616	4854.4629	5239.1016	5728.9453	6381.3281
4584	4454.8792	4478.6609	4494.3289	4506.4296	4516.5368	4552.9438	4601.6964	4640.6565	4676.1892	4710.3230	4880.0127	5266.6758	5759.0977	6414.9141
4590	4460.8152	4484.6281	4500.2815	4512.4331	4522.5185	4558.9732	4607.7896	4646.7307	4682.4500	4716.6284	4886.4001	5273.5693	5766.6357	6423.3105
4608	4478.6074	4502.4961	4518.1758	4530.3750	4540.5000	4576.9922	4625.9297	4665.0938	4700.8125	4735.1250	4905.5625	5294.2500	5789.2500	6448.5000
4620	4490.4643	4514.3976	4530.1181	4542.3138	4552.4652	4589.0524	4638.0469	4677.3129	4713.1952	4747.4561	4918.3374	5308.0371	5804.3262	6465.2930

continues

Table B-1 *Extended Erlang B with 40 Percent Retry Possibility (Continued)*

Circuits

	0.001	0.002	0.003	0.004	0.005	0.01	0.02	0.03	0.04	0.05	0.1	0.2	0.3	0.4
4632	4502.3399	4526.3000	4542.0613	4554.2534	4564.4312	4601.1134	4650.2351	4689.5325	4725.4373	4759.7871	4931.1123	5321.8242	5819.4023	6482.0859
4650	4520.1553	4544.1730	4559.9602	4572.1996	4582.3814	4619.1353	4668.4479	4707.8979	4743.8004	4778.4256	4950.2747	5342.5049	5842.0166	6507.2754
4656	4526.0944	4550.1431	4565.9150	4578.1703	4588.3652	4625.1665	4674.4717	4713.9727	4750.0635	4784.5913	4956.6621	5349.3984	5849.5547	6515.6719
4680	4549.8532	4573.9545	4589.8077	4602.0905	4612.3022	4649.2218	4698.7097	4738.4143	4774.5483	4809.3970	4982.4976	5376.9727	5879.7070	6549.2578
4704	4573.5806	4597.7695	4613.6682	4626.0139	4636.2781	4673.3152	4723.0210	4762.8574	4799.1768	4834.0605	5008.0488	5404.5469	5909.8594	6582.8438
4710	4579.5220	4603.7059	4619.6608	4631.9863	4642.2636	4679.3120	4729.1171	4768.9325	4805.2982	4840.3702	5014.4366	5411.4404	5917.3975	6591.2402
4728	4597.3480	4621.5883	4637.5320	4649.9046	4660.2211	4697.4111	4747.2623	4787.3020	4823.8066	4858.8684	5033.6001	5432.1211	5940.0117	6616.4297
4740	4609.1972	4633.4990	4649.4832	4661.8872	4672.1938	4709.4058	4759.3835	4799.4525	4836.0498	4871.3452	5046.3757	5445.9082	5955.0879	6633.2227
4752	4621.0836	4645.4106	4661.4353	4673.8345	4684.1671	4721.4734	4771.5776	4811.6755	4848.4380	4883.6777	5059.1514	5459.6953	5970.1641	6650.0156
4770	4638.8971	4663.2980	4679.3106	4691.7567	4702.1285	4739.5033	4789.7246	4829.9744	4866.8033	4902.1765	5078.3148	5480.3760	5992.7783	6675.2051
4776	4644.8232	4669.2367	4685.3058	4697.7312	4708.1160	4745.5378	4795.8223	4836.1227	4872.9250	4908.3428	5084.9941	5487.2695	6000.3164	6683.6016
4800	4668.5852	4693.0664	4709.1797	4721.6675	4732.0679	4769.6045	4820.0684	4860.4980	4897.5586	4933.1543	5110.5469	5514.8438	6030.4688	6717.1875
4824	4692.3330	4716.8998	4733.0568	4745.5703	4756.0026	4793.6733	4844.3159	4884.9478	4922.1936	4957.9673	5136.0996	5542.4180	6060.6211	6750.7734
4830	4698.2613	4722.8403	4739.0174	4751.5464	4761.9749	4799.7093	4850.4149	4891.0973	4928.3157	4964.1339	5142.4878	5549.3115	6068.1592	6759.1699
4848	4716.0848	4740.6998	4756.9373	4769.5129	4779.9434	4817.7444	4868.5649	4909.3989	4946.6821	4982.6338	5161.6523	5569.9922	6090.7734	6784.3594
4860	4727.9622	4752.6196	4768.8602	4781.4670	4791.9232	4829.8178	4880.7642	4921.6251	4959.0747	4994.9670	5174.4287	5583.7793	6105.8496	6801.1523
4872	4739.8406	4764.5403	4780.7838	4793.4218	4803.9038	4841.8548	4892.8898	4933.8516	4971.3193	5007.4490	5187.2051	5597.5664	6120.9258	6817.9453
4890	4757.6694	4782.4045	4798.7080	4811.3553	4821.8761	4859.9300	4911.0416	4952.1547	4989.8355	5025.9494	5206.3696	5618.2471	6143.5400	6843.1348
4896	4763.5818	4788.3845	4804.6707	4817.3335	4827.8672	4865.9304	4917.1421	4958.3057	4995.9580	5032.1162	5212.7578	5625.1406	6151.0781	6851.5313
4920	4787.3456	4812.1948	4828.5608	4841.2482	4851.8335	4890.0082	4941.3959	4982.6862	5020.5231	5056.9336	5238.3105	5652.7148	6181.2305	6885.1172
4944	4811.1134	4836.0461	4852.4165	4865.1658	4875.7650	4914.0883	4965.6511	5007.1428	5045.0889	5081.6016	5263.8633	5680.2891	6211.3828	6918.7031
4950	4817.0277	4841.9907	4858.4187	4871.1456	4881.7577	4920.0897	4971.7529	5013.2950	5051.2115	5087.7686	5270.2515	5687.1826	6218.9209	6927.0996
4968	4834.8474	4859.8632	4876.3130	4889.0863	4899.6991	4938.1705	4989.9078	5031.5251	5069.7312	5106.4211	5289.4160	5707.8633	6241.5352	6952.2891
4980	4846.7537	4871.7920	4888.2436	4901.0477	4911.6861	4950.2124	5002.0367	5043.8306	5081.9769	5118.7555	5302.4963	5721.6504	6256.6113	6969.0820
4992	4858.6230	4883.6836	4900.2129	4913.0098	4923.6738	4962.2168	5014.1660	5055.9844	5094.3750	5131.2422	5315.2734	5735.4375	6271.6875	6985.8750
5010	4876.4479	4901.5606	4918.1113	4930.9543	4941.6568	4980.3005	5032.3988	5074.3680	5112.7441	5149.7443	5334.4391	5756.1182	6294.3018	7011.0645

Table B-1 *Extended Erlang B with 40 Percent Retry Possibility (Continued)*

Circuits	0.001	0.002	0.003	0.004	0.005	0.01	0.02	0.03	0.04	0.05	0.1	0.2	0.3	0.4
5016	4882.3645	4907.5073	4924.0778	4936.9362	4947.6132	4986.3032	5038.4257	5080.4451	5118.8672	5155.9116	5340.8276	5763.0117	6301.8398	7019.4609
5040	4906.1481	4931.3727	4947.9456	4960.8270	4971.5552	5010.3918	5062.7637	5104.9072	5143.5132	5180.5811	5366.3818	5790.5859	6331.9922	7053.0469
5064	4929.8970	4955.2031	4971.8549	4984.7591	4995.5383	5034.4827	5087.0266	5129.2936	5168.0061	5205.4050	5391.9360	5818.1602	6362.1445	7086.6328
5070	4935.8155	4961.1516	4977.8231	4990.7426	5001.5346	5040.5251	5093.0539	5135.4483	5174.2841	5211.5726	5398.3246	5825.0537	6369.6826	7095.0293
5088	4953.6497	4979.0369	4995.7288	5008.6941	5019.4856	5058.5757	5111.2910	5153.6807	5192.6543	5230.2305	5417.4902	5845.7344	6392.2969	7120.2188
5100	4965.5273	4990.9355	5007.6668	5020.6238	5031.4796	5070.5841	5123.3459	5165.9912	5204.9011	5242.5659	5430.5786	5859.5215	6407.3730	7137.0117
5112	4977.4059	5002.8739	5019.6055	5032.5930	5043.4354	5082.6709	5135.5569	5178.1465	5217.3040	5254.9014	5443.3564	5873.3086	6422.4492	7153.8047
5130	4995.2451	5020.7245	5037.5150	5050.5482	5061.4288	5100.6850	5153.7181	5196.4577	5235.6747	5273.4045	5462.5232	5893.9893	6445.0635	7178.9941
5136	5001.1659	5026.6750	5043.4852	5056.5337	5067.3878	5106.6899	5159.8242	5202.6138	5241.7983	5279.7290	5468.9121	5900.8828	6452.6016	7187.3906
5160	5024.9295	5050.5185	5067.3679	5080.4379	5091.3428	5130.7892	5184.0930	5227.0038	5266.4502	5304.4006	5494.4678	5929.0869	6482.7539	7220.9766
5184	5048.6968	5074.3652	5091.2534	5104.3843	5115.3003	5154.8511	5208.3633	5251.3945	5291.1035	5329.2305	5520.0234	5956.6641	6512.9063	7254.5625
5190	5054.6590	5080.3175	5097.2253	5110.3713	5121.3000	5160.8569	5214.3915	5257.5517	5297.2275	5335.3986	5526.4124	5963.5583	6520.4443	7262.9590
5208	5072.4677	5098.2153	5115.1419	5128.2938	5139.2604	5178.9148	5232.6350	5275.8655	5315.5994	5353.9028	5545.5791	5984.2412	6543.0586	7288.1484
5220	5084.3546	5110.1216	5127.0872	5140.2695	5151.2613	5190.9673	5244.6918	5288.1015	5328.0066	5366.2390	5558.3569	5998.0298	6558.1348	7304.9414
5232	5096.2423	5122.2087	5139.0333	5152.2458	5163.2230	5203.0203	5256.8284	5300.3379	5340.2549	5378.7349	5571.1348	6011.8184	6573.2109	7321.7344
5250	5114.0556	5139.9307	5156.9538	5170.1717	5181.1867	5221.0808	5275.0740	5318.5730	5358.6273	5397.2397	5590.3015	6032.5012	6595.8252	7346.9238
5256	5119.9805	5145.8851	5162.9277	5176.1607	5187.1882	5227.0878	5281.1027	5324.7316	5364.7515	5403.4080	5596.6904	6039.3955	6603.3633	7355.3203
5280	5143.7622	5169.7046	5186.7847	5200.0781	5211.1560	5251.1572	5305.3784	5349.1260	5389.4092	5428.2422	5622.2461	6066.9727	6633.5156	7388.9063
5304	5167.5274	5193.5674	5210.6847	5223.9981	5235.1263	5275.2689	5329.6556	5373.6021	5414.0684	5452.9160	5647.8018	6094.5498	6663.6680	7422.4922
5310	5173.4743	5199.5235	5216.6602	5229.9886	5241.0889	5281.2769	5335.7657	5379.6808	5420.1929	5459.0845	5654.1907	6101.4441	6671.2061	7430.8887
5328	5191.2960	5217.3929	5234.5876	5247.9207	5259.0586	5299.3422	5353.9343	5398.0796	5438.5664	5477.7524	5673.6826	6122.1270	6693.8203	7456.0781
5340	5203.1918	5229.3068	5246.5402	5259.9033	5271.0663	5311.3998	5366.0742	5410.2374	5450.8154	5490.0897	5686.4612	6135.9155	6708.8965	7472.8711
5352	5215.0681	5241.2214	5258.4935	5271.8458	5283.0339	5323.4172	5378.2145	5422.4769	5463.2278	5502.4270	5699.2397	6149.7041	6723.9727	7489.6641
5370	5232.8944	5259.0946	5276.3839	5289.7810	5301.0068	5341.4850	5396.3846	5440.7959	5481.6019	5521.0968	5718.4076	6170.3870	6746.5869	7514.8535
5376	5238.8438	5265.0732	5282.3613	5295.7734	5306.9707	5347.5352	5402.4961	5446.8750	5487.7266	5527.2656	5724.7969	6177.2813	6754.1250	7523.2500
5400	5262.6022	5288.9282	5306.2317	5319.7037	5330.9509	5371.5729	5426.6968	5471.3562	5512.3901	5551.9409	5750.3540	6204.8584	6784.2773	7556.8359

continues

Table B-1 *Extended Erlang B with 40 Percent Retry Possibility (Continued)*

Circuits	0.001	0.002	0.003	0.004	0.005	0.01	0.02	0.03	0.04	0.05	0.1	0.2	0.3	0.4
5424	5286.3640	5312.7656	5330.1460	5343.6365	5354.8923	5395.6948	5450.9810	5495.7561	5536.8896	5576.7817	5775.9111	6232.4355	6814.4297	7590.4219
5430	5292.3360	5318.7254	5336.1250	5349.6304	5360.8987	5401.7049	5457.0937	5501.9183	5543.1802	5582.9507	5782.3004	6239.3298	6821.9678	7598.8184
5448	5310.1499	5336.6060	5354.0217	5367.5718	5378.8775	5419.7358	5475.2666	5520.1567	5561.5554	5601.4578	5801.4683	6260.0127	6844.5820	7624.0078
5460	5322.0337	5348.5272	5365.9813	5379.5197	5390.8502	5431.7986	5487.4100	5532.4823	5573.8055	5613.7958	5814.5801	6273.8013	6859.6582	7640.8008
5472	5333.9183	5360.4492	5377.9417	5391.5098	5402.8235	5443.8618	5499.5537	5544.6416	5586.2227	5626.3008	5827.3594	6287.5898	6874.7344	7657.5938
5490	5351.7364	5378.3336	5395.8417	5409.4544	5420.8054	5461.9368	5517.7281	5562.9643	5604.5984	5644.8083	5846.5283	6308.9429	6897.3486	7682.7832
5496	5357.7111	5384.2954	5401.8226	5415.4083	5426.8136	5467.9061	5523.8423	5569.1279	5610.7236	5650.9775	5852.9180	6315.8379	6904.8867	7691.1797
5520	5381.4651	5408.1445	5425.7062	5439.3512	5450.7642	5492.0361	5548.0481	5593.4473	5635.3931	5675.6543	5878.4766	6343.4180	6935.0391	7724.7656
5544	5405.2435	5431.9966	5449.5923	5463.2966	5474.7169	5516.0837	5572.3392	5617.9358	5659.8948	5700.5002	5904.0352	6370.9980	6965.1914	7758.3516
5550	5411.1992	5437.9601	5455.5748	5469.2940	5480.7266	5522.1382	5578.4546	5624.0158	5666.0202	5706.6696	5910.4248	6377.8931	6972.7295	7766.7480
5568	5429.0039	5455.8091	5473.4810	5487.2021	5498.6719	5540.2178	5596.6318	5642.4258	5684.5664	5725.1777	5929.5938	6398.5781	6995.3438	7791.9375
5580	5440.9172	5467.7376	5485.4475	5499.1983	5510.6502	5552.2430	5608.7787	5654.5862	5696.8176	5737.6868	5942.3730	6412.3682	7010.4199	7808.7305
5592	5452.7888	5479.6668	5497.3722	5511.1525	5522.6290	5564.2687	5620.9259	5666.7466	5709.0688	5750.0259	5955.1523	6426.1582	7025.4961	7825.5234
5610	5470.6403	5497.5620	5515.3244	5529.1063	5540.6197	5582.3506	5639.1046	5685.1584	5727.6169	5768.5345	5974.3213	6446.8433	7048.1104	7850.7129
5616	5476.5769	5503.5275	5521.2660	5535.1055	5546.5884	5588.3639	5645.1357	5691.2388	5733.7427	5774.7041	5980.7109	6453.7383	7055.6484	7859.1094
5640	5500.3468	5527.3480	5545.1624	5559.0179	5570.5499	5612.4609	5669.4324	5715.7324	5758.2458	5799.5544	6006.2695	6481.3184	7085.8008	7892.6953
5664	5524.1199	5551.2144	5569.0613	5582.9326	5594.5569	5636.5166	5693.7305	5740.0547	5782.9219	5824.2334	6031.8281	6508.8984	7115.9531	7926.2813
5670	5530.0582	5557.1814	5575.0472	5588.9333	5600.5266	5642.5740	5699.7620	5746.2218	5789.0479	5830.4031	6038.2178	6515.7935	7123.4912	7934.6777
5688	5547.9177	5575.0619	5592.9628	5606.8929	5618.5230	5660.6171	5717.9432	5764.5505	5807.4258	5849.0859	6057.3867	6536.4785	7146.1055	7959.8672
5700	5559.7961	5586.9759	5604.9362	5618.8522	5630.5069	5672.6898	5730.0934	5776.7120	5819.8517	5861.4258	6070.1660	6550.2686	7161.1816	7976.6602
5712	5571.6753	5598.9122	5616.8668	5630.8121	5642.4478	5684.7195	5742.2439	5788.9607	5832.1040	5873.7656	6083.2939	6564.0586	7176.2578	7993.4531
5730	5589.5173	5616.8182	5634.7856	5648.7749	5660.4472	5702.8084	5760.4266	5807.2906	5850.4825	5892.2754	6102.4640	6584.7437	7198.8721	8018.6426
5736	5595.4796	5622.7434	5640.7734	5654.7773	5666.4181	5708.7799	5766.5460	5813.3716	5856.6086	5898.4453	6108.8540	6591.6387	7206.4102	8027.0391
5760	5619.2432	5646.6211	5664.6387	5678.7012	5690.3906	5732.8857	5790.7617	5837.8711	5881.2891	5923.3008	6134.4141	6619.2188	7236.5625	8060.6250

Table B-2   *Extended Erlang B with 50 Percent Retry Possibility*

Circuits	Grade of Service													
	0.001	**0.002**	**0.003**	**0.004**	**0.005**	**0.01**	**0.02**	**0.03**	**0.04**	**0.05**	**0.1**	**0.2**	**0.3**	**0.4**
1	0.0000	0.0000	0.0000	0.0000	0.0000	0.0100	0.0202	0.0305	0.0408	0.0513	0.1055	0.2249	0.3643	0.5332
2	0.0457	0.0652	0.0805	0.0935	0.1051	0.1518	0.2212	0.2772	0.3267	0.3716	0.5654	0.8994	1.2305	1.5996
3	0.1937	0.2485	0.2880	0.3203	0.3481	0.4532	0.5960	0.7042	0.7958	0.8767	1.2070	1.7366	2.2368	2.7832
4	0.4390	0.5344	0.6011	0.6543	0.6993	0.8650	1.0811	1.2397	1.3711	1.4863	1.9424	2.6504	3.3066	4.0156
5	0.7617	0.8987	0.9927	1.0669	1.1292	1.3538	1.6403	1.8469	2.0160	2.1625	2.7368	3.6084	4.4092	5.2734
6	1.1451	1.3239	1.4443	1.5388	1.6176	1.8992	2.2529	2.5049	2.7092	2.8857	3.5698	4.5967	5.5342	6.5508
7	1.5776	1.7966	1.9431	2.0572	2.1520	2.4883	2.9057	3.2005	3.4385	3.6436	4.4323	5.6055	6.6753	7.8374
8	2.0503	2.3081	2.4800	2.6128	2.7227	3.1113	3.5903	3.9268	4.1973	4.4287	5.3164	6.6309	7.8281	9.1328
9	2.5560	2.8521	3.0476	3.1992	3.3239	3.7634	4.3011	4.6758	4.9779	5.2350	6.2183	7.6685	8.9912	10.4326
10	3.0902	3.4229	3.6423	3.8110	3.9502	4.4385	5.0330	5.4456	5.7764	6.0596	7.1338	8.7158	10.1563	11.7383
11	3.6490	4.0172	4.2593	4.4453	4.5983	5.1334	5.7827	6.2325	6.5917	6.8992	8.0620	9.7700	11.3330	13.0464
12	4.2290	4.6318	4.8962	5.0984	5.2654	5.8462	6.5479	7.0327	7.4209	7.7505	9.0000	10.8311	12.5098	14.3613
13	4.8278	5.2646	5.5502	5.7684	5.9485	6.5738	7.3268	7.8465	8.2607	8.6138	9.9452	11.8987	13.6919	15.6724
14	5.4431	5.9131	6.2190	6.4540	6.6462	7.3145	8.1177	8.6714	9.1106	9.4849	10.8982	12.9678	14.8750	16.9941
15	6.0736	6.5753	6.9022	7.1521	7.3563	8.0667	8.9191	9.5050	9.9701	10.3656	11.8579	14.0442	16.0620	18.3105
16	6.7178	7.2505	7.5977	7.8613	8.0791	8.8301	9.7295	10.3467	10.8379	11.2539	12.8242	15.1250	17.2500	19.6250
17	7.3742	7.9376	8.3039	8.5830	8.8113	9.6030	10.5482	11.1978	11.7124	12.1482	13.7938	16.2073	18.4443	20.9512
18	8.0414	8.6347	9.0198	9.3131	9.5537	10.3843	11.3752	12.0542	12.5925	13.0496	14.7700	17.2925	19.6348	22.2715
19	8.7195	9.3417	9.7458	10.0532	10.3048	11.1734	12.2090	12.9175	13.4800	13.9554	15.7483	18.3784	20.8276	23.5923
20	9.4067	10.0574	10.4797	10.8008	11.0632	11.9702	13.0493	13.7866	14.3701	14.8669	16.7310	19.4678	22.0215	24.9219
21	10.1027	10.7820	11.2216	11.5562	11.8292	12.7725	13.8940	14.6605	15.2681	15.7833	17.7162	20.5591	23.2251	26.2397
22	10.8066	11.5129	11.9708	12.3186	12.6033	13.5822	14.7463	15.5413	16.1697	16.7014	18.7075	21.6563	24.4170	27.5645
23	11.5182	12.2524	12.7269	13.0877	13.3825	14.3975	15.6019	16.4246	17.0759	17.6262	19.6982	22.7473	25.6167	28.8848
24	12.2366	12.9976	13.4897	13.8618	14.1680	15.2183	16.4634	17.3115	17.9854	18.5537	20.6924	23.8477	26.8242	30.2109
25	12.9623	13.7489	14.2578	14.6439	14.9582	16.0431	17.3279	18.2037	18.8965	19.4855	21.6888	24.9451	28.0212	31.5430
26	13.6935	14.5060	15.0313	15.4296	15.7549	16.8737	18.1987	19.1001	19.8142	20.4172	22.6897	26.0444	29.2246	32.8682

continues

Table B-2   *Extended Erlang B with 50 Percent Retry Possibility (Continued)*

Circuits														
							Grade of Service						
	0.001	0.002	0.003	0.004	0.005	0.01	0.02	0.03	0.04	0.05	0.1	0.2	0.3	0.4
27	14.4311	15.2699	15.8104	16.2208	16.5553	17.7072	19.0717	19.9995	20.7345	21.3541	23.6909	27.1450	30.4277	34.1982
28	15.1741	16.0371	16.5942	17.0164	17.3616	18.5459	19.9473	20.9009	21.6563	22.2954	24.6914	28.2461	31.6230	35.5195
29	15.9213	16.8099	17.3834	17.8170	18.1710	19.3888	20.8278	21.8066	22.5819	23.2368	25.6971	29.3469	32.8303	36.8447
30	16.6754	17.5873	18.1760	18.6218	18.9862	20.2350	21.7108	22.7161	23.5071	24.1809	26.7041	30.4541	34.0356	38.1738
31	17.4328	18.3703	18.9729	19.4299	19.8036	21.0836	22.5972	23.6246	24.4382	25.1270	27.7153	31.5601	35.2383	39.5068
32	18.1953	19.1563	19.7734	20.2422	20.6250	21.9375	23.4863	24.5391	25.3711	26.0742	28.7227	32.6641	36.4453	40.8438
33	18.9613	19.9462	20.5787	21.0580	21.4508	22.7922	24.3794	25.4550	26.3049	27.0260	29.7330	33.7654	37.6487	42.1685
34	19.7320	20.7395	21.3870	21.8788	22.2793	23.6531	25.2717	26.3737	27.2432	27.9778	30.7461	34.8716	38.8560	43.4961
35	20.5067	21.5375	22.1997	22.7017	23.1097	24.5132	26.1688	27.2925	28.1812	28.9331	31.7615	35.9827	40.0586	44.8267
36	21.2849	22.3374	23.0142	23.5272	23.9458	25.3784	27.0681	28.2173	29.1226	29.9894	32.7744	37.0898	41.2734	46.1602
37	22.0659	23.1408	23.8330	24.3558	24.7826	26.2460	27.9691	29.1411	30.0648	30.8484	33.7932	38.2014	42.4741	47.4785
38	22.8513	23.9495	24.6545	25.1880	25.6240	27.1154	28.8734	30.0679	31.0095	31.8074	34.8086	39.3081	43.6777	48.8174
39	23.6395	24.7594	25.4783	26.0222	26.4673	27.9860	29.7784	30.9948	31.9541	32.7682	35.8246	40.4187	44.8843	50.1401
40	24.4312	25.5725	26.3062	26.8604	27.3120	28.8623	30.6860	31.9238	32.9004	33.7305	36.8457	41.5283	46.0938	51.4648
41	25.2259	26.3882	27.1352	27.6995	28.1600	29.7365	31.5958	32.8571	33.8505	34.6938	37.8669	42.6416	47.3062	52.8115
42	26.0231	27.2062	27.9675	28.5417	29.0109	30.6156	32.5049	33.7892	34.8018	35.6580	38.8879	43.7534	48.5112	54.1406
43	26.8225	28.0272	28.8014	29.3867	29.8643	31.4968	33.4179	34.7223	35.7511	36.6224	39.9083	44.8582	49.7188	55.4717
44	27.6262	28.8508	29.6390	30.2339	30.7200	32.3796	34.3320	35.6587	36.7061	37.5923	40.9331	45.9766	50.9287	56.8047
45	28.4312	29.6782	30.4788	31.0831	31.5761	33.2639	35.2496	36.5955	37.6611	38.5593	41.9568	47.0874	52.1411	58.1177
46	29.2399	30.5062	31.3190	31.9338	32.4350	34.1490	36.1677	37.5350	38.6160	39.5313	42.9790	48.2012	53.3447	59.4541
47	30.0491	31.3372	32.1633	32.7873	33.2964	35.0377	37.0859	38.4744	39.5702	40.4996	44.0051	49.3121	54.5503	60.7925
48	30.8628	32.1694	33.0088	33.6416	34.1602	35.9268	38.0068	39.4160	40.5293	41.4727	45.0293	50.4258	55.7578	62.1094
49	31.6777	33.0056	33.8565	34.4995	35.0244	36.8188	38.9272	40.3568	41.4873	42.4443	46.0571	51.5361	56.9673	63.4512
50	32.4951	33.8409	34.7046	35.3577	35.8917	37.7106	39.8499	41.3025	42.4469	43.4174	47.0825	52.6489	58.1787	64.7705
51	33.3147	34.6796	35.5574	36.2205	36.7590	38.6049	40.7745	42.2468	43.4079	44.3947	48.1113	53.7642	59.3921	66.1157
52	34.1361	35.5215	36.4102	37.0814	37.6289	39.5015	41.7009	43.1926	44.3701	45.3667	49.1372	54.8818	60.6074	67.4375

Table B-2 *Extended Erlang B with 50 Percent Retry Possibility (Continued)*

Circuits	Grade of Service													
	0.001	0.002	0.003	0.004	0.005	0.01	0.02	0.03	0.04	0.05	0.1	0.2	0.3	0.4
53	34.9592	36.3631	37.2656	37.9449	38.5013	40.3970	42.6290	44.1397	45.3334	46.3427	50.1663	55.9955	61.8118	68.7603
54	35.7836	37.2074	38.1220	38.8125	39.3728	41.2960	43.5553	45.0879	46.2975	47.3225	51.1919	57.1113	63.0176	70.1104
55	36.6107	38.0542	38.9807	39.6790	40.2496	42.1967	44.4861	46.0370	47.2589	48.2996	52.2205	58.2227	64.2383	71.4355
56	37.4404	38.9033	39.8398	40.5474	41.1250	43.0972	45.4146	46.9868	48.2275	49.2769	53.2520	59.3428	65.4336	72.7617
57	38.2708	39.7511	40.7009	41.4175	41.9990	43.9990	46.3473	47.9372	49.1931	50.2577	54.2864	60.4581	66.6577	74.0889
58	39.1033	40.6025	41.5636	42.2893	42.8805	44.9019	47.2772	48.8879	50.1588	51.2385	55.3167	61.5684	67.8555	75.4170
59	39.9377	41.4556	42.4279	43.1625	43.7621	45.8075	48.2112	49.8425	51.1281	52.2156	56.3496	62.6875	69.0830	76.7461
60	40.7739	42.3102	43.2935	44.0369	44.6448	46.7139	49.1455	50.7935	52.0972	53.1995	57.3779	63.8086	70.2832	78.1055
72	50.9172	52.6641	53.7825	54.6284	55.3140	57.6650	60.4248	62.2925	63.7690	65.0215	69.7896	77.2207	84.8145	94.0781
90	66.4508	68.4860	69.7906	70.7739	71.5759	74.3088	77.5195	79.7003	81.4197	82.8864	88.4839	97.3608	106.6333	118.0371
96	71.6924	73.8193	75.1816	76.2100	77.0449	79.9043	83.2559	85.5352	87.3340	88.8633	94.7344	104.0859	113.9063	126.0469
120	92.9169	95.3870	96.9690	98.1592	99.1333	102.4475	106.3403	108.9844	111.0864	112.8735	119.7729	131.0010	143.0273	158.0273
144	114.4556	117.2417	119.0215	120.3662	121.4648	125.2002	129.5947	132.5918	134.9648	136.9951	144.8789	157.9219	172.1250	189.9844
150	119.8792	122.7402	124.5712	125.9491	127.0752	130.9158	135.4340	138.5056	140.9454	143.0328	151.1536	164.6667	179.4067	198.0469
168	136.2283	139.3096	141.2783	142.7651	143.9751	148.1074	152.9780	156.2900	158.9355	161.1914	170.0303	184.8779	201.2637	221.9766
180	147.1893	150.4056	152.4655	154.0228	155.2863	159.6094	164.7070	168.1787	170.9418	173.3093	182.6147	198.3691	215.8154	238.0078
192	158.1855	161.5430	163.6875	165.3105	166.6289	171.1406	176.4492	180.0762	182.9648	185.4492	195.1992	211.8281	230.3906	253.9688
210	174.7522	178.3058	180.5777	182.2952	183.6923	188.4732	194.1064	197.9517	201.0278	203.6682	214.1016	232.0715	252.2461	277.9834
216	180.2922	183.9111	186.2249	187.9717	189.3955	194.2603	200.0017	203.9238	207.0549	209.7510	220.4033	238.8076	259.5059	286.0313
240	202.5220	206.3892	208.8647	210.7324	212.2559	217.4634	223.6084	227.8198	231.1816	234.0820	245.6250	265.7813	288.6328	317.9297
264	224.8528	228.9617	231.5922	233.5781	235.1975	240.7324	247.2744	251.7539	255.3472	258.4490	270.8481	292.7461	317.7539	349.9805
270	230.4533	234.6185	237.2882	239.2987	240.9384	246.5579	253.1909	257.7475	261.3977	264.5453	277.1521	299.4983	325.0415	357.9346
288	247.2759	251.6133	254.3906	256.4912	258.2051	264.0586	270.9756	275.7305	279.5449	282.8408	296.0859	319.7109	346.9219	381.9375
300	258.5175	262.9669	265.8234	267.9749	269.7281	275.7385	282.8430	287.7319	291.6504	295.0378	308.7158	333.2153	361.4502	397.9980
312	269.7770	274.3378	277.2609	279.4746	281.2646	287.4250	294.7185	299.7363	303.7639	307.2583	321.3501	346.7344	376.0605	413.9180
330	286.6956	291.4238	294.4501	296.7361	298.5992	304.9841	312.5473	317.7539	321.9434	325.5688	340.2924	366.9800	397.9175	437.9590

continues

Table B-2 *Extended Erlang B with 50 Percent Retry Possibility (Continued)*

Circuits	Grade of Service													
	0.001	0.002	0.003	0.004	0.005	0.01	0.02	0.03	0.04	0.05	0.1	0.2	0.3	0.4
336	292.3491	297.1274	300.1831	302.5005	304.3872	310.8369	318.4966	323.7568	328.0020	331.6831	346.6230	373.6934	405.1523	445.9219
360	314.9780	319.9658	323.1628	325.5798	327.5464	334.2920	342.3010	347.8162	352.2656	356.1328	371.8872	400.6934	434.3555	477.9492
384	337.6641	342.8555	346.1836	348.7031	350.7480	357.7734	366.1289	371.8828	376.5469	380.5781	397.1719	427.6875	463.5000	510.0000
390	343.3447	348.5815	351.9438	354.4849	356.5558	363.6493	372.0877	377.9077	382.6208	386.7032	403.4729	434.4177	470.7422	517.9688
408	360.3992	365.7905	369.2457	371.8542	373.9834	381.2922	389.9707	395.9722	400.8281	405.0615	422.4434	454.6670	492.5684	541.8750
420	371.7810	377.2668	380.7916	383.4512	385.6238	393.0579	401.9019	408.0286	412.9761	417.2955	435.0732	468.1421	507.1582	557.8125
432	383.1812	388.7578	392.3438	395.0464	397.2612	404.8286	413.8462	420.0820	425.1445	429.5479	447.7148	481.6758	521.7539	573.9609
450	400.2869	406.0135	409.6939	412.4680	414.7339	422.5067	431.7627	438.1760	443.3670	447.9126	466.6992	501.8555	543.6035	597.8760
456	405.9998	411.7749	415.4766	418.2737	420.5559	428.4045	437.7283	444.1992	449.4595	454.0239	473.0054	508.6582	550.8516	605.8477
480	428.8550	434.8169	438.6401	441.5332	443.8916	451.9922	461.6309	468.3398	473.7744	478.5352	498.3105	535.6641	579.9609	637.9688
504	451.7512	457.8882	461.8334	464.8096	467.2397	475.5916	485.5583	492.4797	498.1091	503.0464	523.5952	562.6318	609.0820	669.8672
510	457.4794	463.6661	467.6349	470.6387	473.0823	481.5024	491.5411	498.5138	504.1946	509.1595	529.9219	569.3921	616.4575	677.8418
528	474.6731	480.9976	485.0500	488.1196	490.6252	499.2217	509.4858	516.6401	522.4570	527.5488	548.8828	589.6172	638.3438	701.7656
540	486.1533	492.5555	496.6754	499.7818	502.3196	511.0455	521.4606	528.7115	534.6277	539.8022	561.5552	603.1494	652.8516	717.9785
552	497.6305	504.1245	508.2938	511.4524	514.0214	522.8738	533.4360	540.7976	546.8115	552.0674	574.2026	616.6201	667.3594	733.9336
570	514.8665	521.4853	525.7471	528.9565	531.5831	540.6198	551.4047	558.9368	565.0598	570.4523	593.1702	636.8665	689.2603	757.8662
576	520.6113	527.2822	531.5625	534.7969	537.4424	546.5303	557.4023	564.9785	571.1484	576.5977	599.4844	643.6406	696.5156	765.8438
600	543.6218	550.4608	554.8462	558.1696	560.8795	570.2087	581.3599	589.1602	595.5322	601.1353	624.7925	670.6055	725.6836	797.7539
624	566.6521	573.6599	578.1541	581.5532	584.3335	593.8931	605.3379	613.3359	619.8867	625.6567	650.0889	697.5820	754.8633	829.9688
630	572.4179	579.4643	583.9824	587.4046	590.2020	599.8151	611.3315	619.3872	625.9818	631.8073	656.4166	704.2896	762.1216	837.9492
648	589.7120	596.8806	601.4784	604.9688	607.8065	617.6052	629.3320	637.5388	644.2822	650.1951	675.4087	724.5703	784.0547	861.8906
660	601.2469	608.4979	613.1506	616.6754	619.5557	629.4553	641.3287	649.6472	656.4551	662.4774	688.0371	738.0688	798.5742	877.8516
672	612.7939	620.1152	624.8218	628.3799	631.2920	641.3203	653.3174	661.7461	668.6572	674.7480	700.7109	751.5703	813.0938	893.8125
690	630.1135	637.5572	642.3477	645.9590	648.9175	659.1092	671.3223	679.8926	686.9467	693.1586	719.6906	771.8701	834.8730	917.7539
696	635.8901	643.3773	648.1882	651.8203	654.7939	665.0317	677.3298	685.9534	693.0264	699.2922	726.0337	778.5820	842.1328	925.7344
720	659.0039	666.6504	671.5613	675.2747	678.3179	688.7769	701.3452	710.1563	717.4292	723.8452	751.3330	805.6055	871.3477	957.6563

Table B-2 *Extended Erlang B with 50 Percent Retry Possibility (Continued)*

Circuits	Grade of Service													
	0.001	0.002	0.003	0.004	0.005	0.01	0.02	0.03	0.04	0.05	0.1	0.2	0.3	0.4
744	682.1400	689.9392	694.9457	698.7374	701.8367	712.5308	725.3591	734.3958	741.8203	748.4048	776.6499	832.5498	900.5742	989.9414
750	687.9272	695.7664	700.8018	704.6127	707.7255	718.4601	731.3690	740.4327	747.9172	754.5319	782.9590	839.3555	907.8369	997.9248
768	705.2930	713.2383	718.3594	722.2266	725.3906	736.2891	749.3906	758.6016	766.2188	772.9688	801.9375	859.5000	929.6250	1021.8750
780	716.8785	724.8944	730.0598	733.9636	737.1533	748.1625	761.4093	770.7166	778.4290	785.2368	814.6106	873.0249	944.1504	1037.8418
792	728.4694	736.5663	741.7749	745.7146	748.9292	760.0474	773.4133	782.8396	790.6223	797.5107	827.2881	886.5527	958.6758	1053.8086
810	745.8536	754.0604	759.3379	763.3424	766.6054	777.8773	791.4482	801.0269	808.9124	815.9326	846.2384	906.8005	980.6616	1077.7588
816	751.6523	759.8950	765.1992	769.2085	772.4956	783.8262	797.4478	807.0850	815.0288	822.0762	852.5566	913.5176	987.9258	1085.7422
840	774.8492	783.2446	788.6407	792.7295	796.0748	807.5977	821.4917	831.3098	839.4360	846.6394	877.8882	940.4883	1017.1875	1117.6758
864	798.0688	806.5986	812.0962	816.2490	819.6504	831.3970	845.5430	855.5625	863.8418	871.2246	903.2344	967.5703	1046.2500	1149.6094
870	803.8699	812.4390	817.9614	822.1298	825.5548	837.3431	851.5741	861.6101	869.9469	877.3544	909.5599	974.2896	1053.5156	1157.5928
888	821.2943	829.9662	835.5623	839.7898	843.2585	855.1959	869.5994	879.8159	888.2710	895.7776	928.5410	994.5557	1075.3125	1181.9766
900	832.9147	841.6626	847.2931	851.5640	855.0522	867.0959	881.6254	891.9250	900.4669	908.0750	941.1987	1007.9956	1089.8438	1197.9492
912	844.5352	853.3579	859.0356	863.3357	866.8564	878.9912	893.6587	904.0679	912.6680	920.3496	953.8594	1021.5469	1104.3750	1213.9219
930	861.9699	870.8958	876.6431	880.9996	884.5615	896.8506	911.7224	922.2519	930.9933	938.7982	972.8558	1041.7090	1126.3989	1237.8809
936	867.7881	876.7430	882.5273	886.8834	890.4683	902.8081	917.7330	928.3162	937.0854	944.9121	979.1895	1048.5439	1133.6660	1245.8672
960	891.0498	900.1465	906.0205	910.4590	914.0918	926.6309	941.8066	952.5586	961.5234	969.4922	1004.4727	1075.5469	1162.7344	1277.8125
984	914.3320	923.5660	929.5269	934.0313	937.7098	950.4573	965.8773	976.8230	985.9519	994.0898	1029.8247	1102.4355	1192.0430	1309.7578
990	920.1489	929.4241	935.3911	939.9229	943.6240	956.4189	971.9028	982.9001	992.0544	1000.2118	1036.1646	1109.2786	1199.3115	1317.7441
1008	937.6172	946.9841	953.0288	957.5969	961.3499	974.2852	989.9429	1001.1094	1010.3687	1018.6436	1055.1270	1129.5703	1221.1172	1341.7031
1020	949.2618	958.7091	964.7946	969.4016	973.1680	986.2106	1001.9925	1013.2141	1022.5836	1030.9570	1067.8125	1143.0176	1235.6543	1357.6758
1032	960.9177	970.4290	976.5467	981.1842	984.9950	998.1281	1014.0326	1025.3547	1034.8030	1043.2434	1080.4380	1156.4648	1250.1914	1373.6484
1050	978.3989	988.0119	994.1963	998.8907	1002.7359	1016.0019	1032.0877	1043.5593	1053.1082	1061.6638	1099.4751	1176.7639	1271.9971	1397.6074
1056	984.2314	993.8672	1000.0708	1004.7920	1008.6431	1021.9688	1038.1143	1049.6191	1059.2227	1067.8271	1105.7578	1183.4883	1279.2656	1405.5938
1080	1007.5397	1017.3120	1023.6072	1028.3862	1032.3083	1045.8215	1062.2021	1073.9026	1083.6584	1092.3926	1131.0864	1210.5176	1308.3398	1437.5391
1104	1030.8728	1040.7781	1047.1626	1051.9973	1055.9561	1069.6685	1086.3120	1098.1714	1108.1104	1117.0049	1156.4238	1237.4180	1337.6836	1469.4844
1110	1036.7125	1046.6377	1053.0400	1057.9010	1061.8813	1075.6343	1092.3175	1104.2413	1114.2004	1123.1433	1162.7087	1244.2786	1344.9536	1477.4707

continues

Table B-2   *Extended Erlang B with 50 Percent Retry Possibility (Continued)*

Circuits	Grade of Service													
	0.001	0.002	0.003	0.004	0.005	0.01	0.02	0.03	0.04	0.05	0.1	0.2	0.3	0.4
1128	1054.2125	1064.2471	1070.7015	1075.6241	1079.6345	1093.5245	1110.4094	1122.4578	1132.5439	1141.5630	1181.7012	1264.4561	1366.7637	1501.4297
1140	1065.8798	1075.9863	1082.4921	1087.4323	1091.4679	1105.4535	1122.4484	1134.6075	1144.7314	1153.8812	1194.4116	1278.0469	1381.3037	1517.4023
1152	1077.5566	1087.7168	1094.2734	1099.2305	1103.3086	1117.3887	1134.4922	1146.7266	1156.9570	1166.1680	1207.0547	1291.5000	1395.8438	1533.9375
1170	1095.0719	1105.3372	1111.9427	1116.9594	1121.0655	1135.2942	1152.5757	1164.9298	1175.2844	1184.6036	1226.0577	1311.6797	1417.6538	1557.9053
1176	1100.9209	1111.2030	1117.8245	1122.8668	1126.9940	1141.2598	1158.5940	1171.0115	1181.4192	1190.7502	1232.4170	1318.4063	1424.9238	1565.8945
1200	1124.2767	1134.6863	1141.4063	1146.4966	1150.6714	1165.1184	1182.7148	1195.3125	1205.8594	1215.3442	1257.7148	1345.4590	1454.2969	1597.8516
1224	1147.6494	1158.1924	1164.9814	1170.1549	1174.3759	1188.9998	1206.8174	1219.5923	1230.2754	1239.9500	1283.0186	1372.5176	1483.3828	1629.8086
1230	1153.5004	1164.0669	1170.8798	1176.0599	1180.3015	1194.9783	1212.8458	1225.6458	1236.4188	1246.1032	1289.3829	1379.2456	1490.6543	1637.7979
1248	1171.0283	1181.6924	1188.5669	1193.7847	1198.0693	1212.8848	1230.9185	1243.8677	1254.7412	1264.5293	1308.3281	1399.4297	1512.4688	1661.7656
1260	1182.7208	1193.4489	1200.3607	1205.6190	1209.9161	1224.8163	1242.9657	1256.0010	1266.9598	1276.8420	1320.9851	1412.8857	1527.0117	1677.7441
1272	1194.4215	1205.2130	1212.1615	1217.4408	1221.7690	1236.7529	1255.0364	1268.1570	1279.1814	1289.1189	1333.6436	1426.4971	1541.5547	1693.7227
1290	1211.9634	1222.8387	1229.8659	1235.1805	1239.5503	1254.6872	1273.1113	1286.3782	1297.5192	1307.5580	1352.6733	1446.6833	1563.3691	1717.6904
1296	1217.8081	1228.7241	1235.7642	1241.1035	1245.4937	1260.6416	1279.1514	1292.4404	1303.6333	1313.7188	1358.9648	1453.5703	1570.6406	1725.6797
1320	1241.2061	1252.2437	1259.3536	1264.7717	1269.2029	1284.5508	1303.2623	1316.7371	1328.0566	1338.3289	1384.2920	1480.4883	1599.7266	1757.6367
1344	1264.6245	1275.7705	1282.9688	1288.4443	1292.9150	1308.4395	1327.3887	1341.0469	1352.5313	1362.9082	1409.6250	1507.4063	1628.8125	1789.5938
1350	1270.4762	1281.6513	1288.8714	1294.3611	1298.8518	1314.4043	1333.4175	1347.1161	1358.6517	1369.0750	1416.0004	1514.1357	1636.0840	1797.5830
1368	1288.0316	1299.3036	1306.5886	1312.1098	1316.6290	1332.3263	1351.5095	1365.3281	1376.9758	1387.5381	1434.9639	1534.4912	1658.2324	1821.5508
1380	1299.7513	1311.0800	1318.3868	1323.9459	1328.4943	1344.2871	1363.5754	1377.4731	1389.1809	1399.7937	1447.6355	1547.9517	1672.7783	1837.5293
1392	1311.4570	1322.8524	1330.1909	1335.7877	1340.3650	1356.2314	1375.6450	1389.6211	1401.4307	1412.1357	1460.3086	1561.4121	1687.3242	1853.5078
1410	1329.0287	1340.5069	1347.9080	1353.5449	1358.1706	1374.1562	1393.7347	1407.8485	1419.7678	1430.5682	1479.2780	1581.7749	1709.1431	1877.4756
1416	1334.8894	1346.4056	1353.8167	1359.4775	1364.1013	1380.1333	1399.7520	1413.9258	1425.8958	1436.6990	1485.6592	1588.5059	1716.4160	1885.4648
1440	1358.3276	1369.9512	1377.4438	1383.1567	1387.8369	1404.0527	1423.8940	1438.2422	1450.3271	1461.3135	1510.9277	1615.4297	1745.5078	1917.4219
1464	1381.7706	1393.5097	1401.0938	1406.8572	1411.5707	1427.9451	1448.0054	1462.5256	1474.7673	1485.8921	1536.2886	1642.3535	1774.5996	1949.3789
1470	1387.6243	1399.4003	1406.9930	1412.7800	1417.5128	1433.9319	1454.0520	1468.6093	1480.9012	1492.0715	1542.5848	1649.0845	1781.8726	1957.3682
1488	1405.2173	1417.0693	1424.7209	1430.5448	1435.3242	1451.8762	1472.1519	1486.8193	1499.2617	1510.5234	1561.5645	1669.4590	1803.6914	1981.3359
1500	1416.9388	1428.8521	1436.5425	1442.3904	1447.1970	1463.8367	1484.2072	1498.9929	1511.4899	1522.7966	1574.2493	1682.9224	1818.6035	1997.3145

Table B-2   *Extended Erlang B with 50 Percent Retry Possibility (Continued)*

Circuits	Grade of Service													
	0.001	0.002	0.003	0.004	0.005	0.01	0.02	0.03	0.04	0.05	0.1	0.2	0.3	0.4
1512	1428.6665	1440.6405	1448.3694	1454.2526	1459.0745	1475.7781	1496.2885	1511.1233	1523.7202	1535.1174	1586.9355	1696.3857	1833.1523	2013.2930
1530	1446.2581	1458.3163	1466.1021	1472.0320	1476.8880	1493.7204	1514.4049	1529.3463	1542.0465	1553.5794	1605.9210	1716.7676	1854.9756	2038.0078
1536	1452.1172	1464.2109	1472.0156	1477.9453	1482.8203	1499.7188	1520.4375	1535.4375	1548.1406	1559.7188	1612.2188	1723.5000	1862.2500	2046.0000
1560	1475.5801	1487.7795	1495.6586	1501.6571	1506.5726	1523.6279	1544.5752	1559.7620	1572.6160	1584.3274	1637.6001	1750.4297	1891.3477	2077.9688
1584	1499.0548	1511.3694	1519.3213	1525.3638	1530.3307	1547.5518	1568.7004	1584.0483	1597.0518	1608.9434	1662.8906	1777.3594	1920.4453	2109.9375
1590	1504.9150	1517.2641	1525.2340	1531.2994	1536.2608	1553.5350	1574.7395	1590.1456	1603.1982	1615.0864	1669.2865	1784.0918	1927.7197	2117.9297
1608	1522.5284	1534.9559	1542.9792	1549.0887	1554.0941	1571.4902	1592.8367	1608.3435	1621.5439	1633.5176	1688.2822	1804.4854	1949.5430	2141.9063
1620	1534.2613	1546.7569	1554.8154	1560.9457	1565.9761	1583.4402	1604.9213	1620.5191	1633.7439	1645.8069	1700.8813	1817.9517	1964.0918	2157.8906
1632	1546.0122	1558.5381	1566.6313	1572.8071	1577.8623	1595.4185	1616.9839	1632.6724	1645.9951	1658.1475	1713.5801	1831.4180	1978.6406	2173.8750
1650	1563.6177	1576.2440	1584.3887	1590.5949	1595.6932	1613.3675	1635.0952	1650.9064	1664.3509	1676.5869	1732.5806	1851.6174	2000.4639	2197.8516
1656	1569.4805	1582.1400	1590.3018	1596.5178	1601.6221	1619.3353	1641.1421	1656.9855	1670.4536	1682.7341	1738.8809	1858.5527	2007.7383	2205.8438
1680	1592.9700	1605.7361	1613.9777	1620.2454	1625.3979	1643.2910	1665.2856	1681.2817	1694.9194	1707.3267	1764.1846	1885.4883	2036.8359	2237.8125
1704	1616.4677	1629.3512	1637.6455	1643.9897	1649.1639	1667.2086	1689.4395	1705.6121	1719.3926	1731.9971	1789.5952	1912.4238	2065.9336	2269.7813
1710	1622.3421	1635.2449	1643.5684	1649.9089	1655.1274	1673.1834	1695.4665	1711.6699	1725.4990	1738.0756	1795.8966	1919.1577	2073.2080	2277.7734
1728	1639.9731	1652.9590	1661.3306	1667.7246	1672.9453	1691.1387	1713.5771	1729.9248	1743.8203	1756.5820	1814.9063	1939.3594	2095.0313	2301.7500
1740	1651.7203	1664.7565	1673.1729	1679.5848	1684.8550	1703.1216	1725.6628	1742.0709	1756.0895	1768.8867	1827.5098	1952.8271	2109.5801	2317.7344
1752	1663.4724	1676.5583	1685.0061	1691.4489	1696.7421	1715.0812	1737.7244	1754.2456	1768.3074	1781.1929	1840.2202	1966.2949	2124.1289	2333.7188
1770	1681.1030	1694.2694	1702.7769	1709.2589	1714.5795	1733.0530	1755.8478	1772.4847	1786.6370	1799.6008	1859.2346	1986.7126	2145.9521	2357.6953
1776	1686.9778	1700.1753	1708.6981	1715.1885	1720.5271	1739.0361	1761.8811	1778.5474	1792.8018	1805.7554	1865.5371	1993.4473	2153.2266	2365.6875
1800	1710.4889	1723.7961	1732.3792	1738.9435	1744.2993	1762.9761	1786.0474	1802.8564	1817.2485	1830.3772	1890.8569	2020.3857	2182.7637	2397.6563
1824	1734.0051	1747.4063	1756.0759	1762.6860	1768.0854	1786.9277	1810.1953	1827.1729	1841.7012	1855.0049	1916.1797	2047.5469	2211.8672	2429.6250
1830	1739.8906	1753.3218	1762.0061	1768.6240	1774.0411	1792.9175	1816.2337	1833.2391	1847.8152	1861.1627	1922.4829	2054.2822	2219.1431	2437.6172
1848	1757.5259	1771.0470	1779.7744	1786.4291	1791.8855	1810.8629	1834.3521	1851.4966	1866.1597	1879.5820	1941.5054	2074.4883	2240.9707	2461.5938
1860	1769.2932	1782.8595	1791.6293	1798.2990	1803.7766	1822.8488	1846.4337	1863.6612	1878.3911	1891.9006	1954.2261	2087.9590	2255.5225	2477.5781
1872	1781.0508	1794.6760	1803.4739	1810.1865	1815.6852	1834.8091	1858.5176	1875.8276	1890.6240	1904.2207	1966.8340	2101.4297	2270.0742	2493.5625
1890	1798.6954	1812.3940	1821.2476	1827.9959	1833.5330	1852.7975	1876.6187	1894.0375	1908.9761	1922.6459	1985.8612	2121.6357	2291.9019	2517.5391

continues

Table B-2 *Extended Erlang B with 50 Percent Retry Possibility (Continued)*

Circuits	Grade of Service													
	0.001	0.002	0.003	0.004	0.005	0.01	0.02	0.03	0.04	0.05	0.1	0.2	0.3	0.4
1896	1804.5791	1818.3067	1827.1740	1833.9437	1839.4839	1858.7662	1882.6630	1900.1371	1915.0942	1928.8074	1992.1655	2128.3711	2299.1777	2525.5313
1920	1828.1104	1841.9385	1850.8740	1857.6855	1863.2813	1882.7344	1906.8164	1924.4531	1939.5703	1953.4570	2017.5000	2155.3125	2328.2813	2557.5000
1944	1851.6440	1865.5708	1874.5884	1881.4406	1887.0765	1906.6838	1930.9779	1948.8054	1964.0522	1978.0532	2042.8374	2182.2539	2357.3848	2589.4688
1950	1857.5226	1871.4924	1880.5229	1887.3962	1893.0496	1912.6877	1937.0270	1954.8798	1970.1736	1984.2178	2049.1425	2189.2273	2364.6606	2597.4609
1968	1875.1794	1889.2181	1898.3020	1905.2087	1910.8843	1930.6436	1955.1475	1973.1050	1988.4800	2002.6538	2068.1777	2209.4355	2386.4883	2621.4375
1980	1886.9458	1901.0550	1910.1489	1917.0978	1922.8079	1942.6273	1967.2202	1985.2570	2000.7257	2014.9860	2080.7886	2222.9077	2401.0400	2637.4219
1992	1898.7162	1912.8653	1921.9991	1928.9749	1934.7045	1954.6135	1979.2947	1997.4104	2012.9729	2027.2588	2093.5210	2236.3799	2415.5918	2653.4063
2010	1916.3947	1930.5949	1939.7960	1946.8041	1952.5548	1972.5824	1997.4252	2015.6740	2031.3464	2045.7001	2112.4384	2256.5881	2437.4194	2677.3828
2016	1922.2690	1936.5117	1945.7249	1952.7539	1958.5063	1978.5630	2003.4800	2021.7524	2037.4717	2051.8682	2118.8672	2263.3242	2445.1875	2685.3750
2040	1945.8224	1960.1724	1969.4330	1976.5146	1982.3199	2002.5220	2027.6422	2046.0699	2061.9141	2076.4819	2144.0918	2290.5176	2474.2969	2717.3438
2064	1969.3759	1983.8159	1993.1697	2000.2874	2006.1453	2026.4905	2051.8118	2070.4248	2086.3608	2101.1001	2169.4424	2317.4648	2503.4063	2749.3125
2070	1975.2587	1989.7408	1999.0901	2006.2285	2012.1034	2032.5078	2057.8395	2076.5067	2092.4890	2107.2711	2175.8752	2324.2017	2510.6836	2757.3047
2088	1992.9287	2007.4889	2016.8877	2024.0563	2029.9504	2050.4685	2075.9568	2094.7225	2110.8757	2125.7227	2194.7959	2344.4121	2532.5156	2781.2813
2100	2004.7028	2019.3146	2028.7514	2035.9451	2041.8732	2062.4451	2088.0478	2106.8893	2123.0713	2138.0035	2207.4097	2357.8857	2547.0703	2797.2656
2112	2016.4966	2031.1436	2040.6182	2047.8369	2053.7666	2074.4238	2100.1406	2119.0576	2135.3320	2150.3496	2220.1523	2371.3594	2561.6250	2813.2500
2130	2034.1702	2048.8932	2058.3998	2065.6801	2071.6278	2092.4286	2118.2671	2137.2803	2153.6609	2168.8065	2239.0741	2391.5698	2583.4570	2837.2266
2136	2040.0469	2054.8114	2064.3448	2071.6293	2077.5938	2098.4205	2124.2992	2143.3660	2159.7927	2174.9810	2245.5117	2398.3066	2590.7344	2845.2188
2160	2063.6279	2078.4760	2088.0835	2095.4004	2101.4319	2122.3938	2148.4644	2167.7124	2184.2578	2199.5508	2270.7422	2425.2539	2619.8438	2877.1875
2184	2087.1903	2102.1367	2111.8176	2119.1825	2125.2477	2146.3425	2172.6694	2192.0314	2208.7273	2224.1902	2296.1060	2452.4678	2648.9531	2909.1563
2190	2093.0914	2108.0621	2117.7363	2125.1381	2131.2032	2152.3393	2178.7051	2198.1203	2214.8621	2230.3006	2302.4139	2459.2053	2656.2305	2917.1484
2208	2110.7666	2125.8098	2135.5466	2142.9756	2149.0737	2170.3330	2196.8145	2216.3555	2233.2012	2248.7666	2321.4727	2479.4180	2678.0625	2941.1250
2220	2122.5430	2137.6511	2147.4069	2154.8593	2160.9906	2182.3315	2208.8892	2228.5364	2245.4736	2261.1237	2334.0894	2492.8931	2692.6172	2957.1094
2232	2134.3398	2149.4784	2159.2870	2166.7456	2172.9100	2194.2982	2220.9994	2240.7188	2257.6794	2273.4141	2346.8423	2506.3682	2707.1719	2973.0938
2250	2152.0157	2167.2421	2177.0782	2184.5970	2190.7768	2212.3032	2239.1167	2258.9264	2276.0239	2291.8854	2365.7684	2526.5808	2729.0039	2997.0703
2256	2157.9265	2173.1591	2183.0215	2190.5603	2196.7222	2218.2715	2245.1565	2265.0190	2282.1621	2297.9971	2372.0771	2533.0771	2736.2813	3005.0625
2280	2181.5094	2196.8518	2206.7670	2214.3512	2220.5786	2242.2528	2269.3195	2289.3585	2306.6492	2322.6526	2397.4512	2560.5469	2765.3906	3037.0313

Table B-2 *Extended Erlang B with 50 Percent Retry Possibility (Continued)*

Circuits	Grade of Service													
	0.001	0.002	0.003	0.004	0.005	0.01	0.02	0.03	0.04	0.05	0.1	0.2	0.3	0.4
2304	2205.0879	2220.5215	2230.5234	2238.1348	2244.4102	2266.2422	2293.5234	2313.7031	2331.1406	2347.2422	2422.8281	2587.5000	2794.5000	3069.0000
2310	2210.9889	2226.4451	2236.4378	2244.0866	2250.3607	2272.2496	2299.5667	2319.7636	2337.2113	2353.4253	2429.1376	2594.2383	2801.7773	3076.9922
2328	2228.6792	2244.2025	2254.2554	2261.9282	2268.2512	2290.2396	2317.6985	2338.0173	2355.6010	2371.8347	2448.0659	2614.4531	2823.6094	3100.9688
2340	2240.4707	2256.0562	2266.1252	2273.8376	2280.1575	2302.2235	2329.7882	2350.2118	2367.8503	2384.2035	2460.8276	2627.9297	2838.1641	3116.9531
2352	2252.2654	2267.8949	2277.9976	2285.7316	2292.0659	2314.2092	2341.8435	2362.3359	2380.0649	2396.5020	2473.4473	2641.4063	2852.7188	3132.9375
2370	2269.9541	2285.6671	2295.8290	2303.5680	2309.9689	2332.2093	2359.9828	2380.5959	2398.4244	2414.9149	2492.3767	2661.6211	2874.5508	3156.9141
2376	2275.8640	2291.5805	2301.7500	2309.5448	2315.9257	2338.1862	2366.0299	2386.6589	2404.5688	2421.1011	2498.6865	2668.3594	2881.8281	3164.9063
2400	2299.4568	2315.2771	2325.5127	2333.3313	2339.7583	2362.1704	2390.2222	2411.0229	2429.0039	2445.7031	2524.0723	2695.3125	2910.9375	3196.8750
2424	2323.0616	2338.9662	2349.2672	2357.1270	2363.5997	2386.1620	2414.3833	2435.3551	2453.5159	2470.3081	2549.4609	2722.2656	2940.0469	3228.8438
2430	2328.9601	2344.9040	2355.2119	2363.0912	2369.5615	2392.1796	2420.4337	2441.4203	2459.6260	2476.4969	2555.7715	2729.0039	2947.3242	3236.8359
2448	2346.6599	2362.6659	2373.0315	2380.9504	2387.4500	2410.1609	2438.5869	2459.6917	2477.9575	2494.9160	2574.7031	2749.2188	2969.1563	3260.8125
2460	2358.4634	2374.5103	2384.9080	2392.8470	2399.3784	2422.1631	2450.6534	2471.8616	2490.2545	2507.2961	2587.4744	2762.6953	2983.7109	3276.7969
2472	2370.2510	2386.3762	2396.7869	2404.7457	2411.3090	2434.1671	2462.7587	2483.9949	2502.4775	2519.5269	2600.0962	2776.1719	2998.2656	3292.7813
2490	2387.9661	2404.1327	2414.6191	2422.5980	2429.1710	2452.1576	2480.8813	2502.2722	2520.8514	2538.0249	2619.0289	2796.6907	3020.0977	3316.7578
2496	2393.8535	2410.0591	2420.5518	2428.5498	2435.1387	2458.1426	2486.9355	2508.3398	2526.9258	2544.1406	2625.4922	2803.4297	3027.3750	3324.7500
2520	2417.4673	2433.7711	2444.3262	2452.3627	2458.9957	2482.1246	2511.1176	2532.6892	2551.4539	2568.7573	2650.7373	2830.3857	3056.4844	3356.7188
2544	2441.0925	2457.4739	2468.0713	2476.1843	2482.8611	2506.1133	2535.3047	2557.0430	2575.9087	2593.3770	2676.1377	2857.3418	3085.5938	3388.6875
2550	2446.9860	2463.3865	2474.0089	2482.1411	2488.8142	2512.1407	2541.3620	2563.1126	2581.9839	2599.5712	2682.4493	2864.0808	3092.8711	3396.6797
2568	2464.7095	2481.1670	2491.8448	2499.9952	2506.7153	2530.1085	2559.4578	2581.3619	2600.3665	2617.9995	2701.3843	2884.2979	3114.7031	3420.6563
2580	2476.5024	2493.0368	2503.7251	2511.8939	2518.6258	2542.1283	2571.5753	2593.5425	2612.5964	2630.3119	2714.0076	2897.7759	3129.2578	3436.6406
2592	2488.3176	2504.8894	2515.6274	2523.8145	2530.5579	2554.1104	2583.6548	2605.6846	2624.8271	2642.6250	2726.7891	2911.2539	3144.4453	3452.6250
2610	2506.0357	2522.6628	2533.4555	2541.6795	2548.4498	2572.1260	2601.7960	2623.9389	2643.2144	2661.1359	2745.7251	2931.7896	3166.2817	3476.6016
2616	2511.9364	2528.6017	2539.3993	2547.6222	2554.4081	2578.1188	2607.8569	2630.0508	2649.3706	2667.2534	2752.0371	2938.5293	3173.5605	3484.5938
2640	2535.5457	2552.3035	2563.1598	2571.4581	2578.2458	2602.0935	2632.0239	2654.3811	2673.8379	2691.8848	2777.4463	2965.4883	3202.6758	3516.5625
2664	2559.1855	2576.0347	2586.9287	2595.2618	2602.1113	2626.1147	2656.1953	2678.7151	2698.3081	2716.5190	2802.6958	2992.4473	3231.7910	3549.8320
2670	2565.0920	2581.9588	2592.8773	2601.2292	2608.0737	2632.1109	2662.2592	2684.8297	2704.3854	2722.6373	2809.0082	2999.1870	3239.0698	3557.8271

continues

Table B-2 *Extended Erlang B with 50 Percent Retry Possibility (Continued)*

Circuits	Grade of Service													
	0.001	0.002	0.003	0.004	0.005	0.01	0.02	0.03	0.04	0.05	0.1	0.2	0.3	0.4
2688	2582.7949	2599.7344	2610.7061	2619.0938	2625.9844	2650.1016	2680.4121	2703.0527	2722.7813	2741.1563	2828.1094	3019.4063	3260.9063	3581.8125
2700	2594.6136	2611.6081	2622.5876	2631.0127	2637.9135	2662.0972	2692.5018	2715.2435	2735.0189	2753.3936	2840.7349	3032.8857	3275.4639	3597.8027
2712	2606.4349	2623.4636	2634.4918	2642.9337	2649.8445	2674.0942	2704.5927	2727.3940	2747.2573	2765.7136	2853.3604	3046.3652	3290.0215	3613.7930
2730	2624.1508	2641.2508	2652.3106	2660.7877	2667.7235	2692.0926	2722.7518	2745.6628	2765.6163	2784.1534	2872.2986	3066.5845	3311.8579	3637.7783
2736	2630.0643	2647.1810	2658.2651	2666.7400	2673.7119	2698.0928	2728.7776	2751.7390	2771.7363	2790.3560	2878.7783	3073.3242	3319.1367	3645.5734
2760	2653.6826	2670.9073	2682.0465	2690.5746	2697.5656	2722.0972	2752.9669	2776.0876	2796.2183	2815.0012	2904.0308	3100.2832	3348.2520	3677.7539
2784	2677.3315	2694.6211	2705.8359	2714.4170	2721.4263	2746.1074	2777.1606	2800.3975	2820.7031	2839.5645	2929.4531	3127.2422	3377.3672	3709.7344
2790	2683.2294	2700.5562	2711.7739	2720.3522	2727.3978	2752.1109	2783.1885	2806.5179	2826.7822	2845.7693	2935.7666	3133.9819	3384.6460	3717.7295
2808	2700.9690	2718.3647	2729.6120	2738.2456	2745.3153	2770.1235	2801.3588	2824.7531	2845.1909	2864.2148	2954.7070	3154.2012	3406.4824	3741.7148
2820	2712.7698	2730.2184	2741.5137	2750.1627	2757.2411	2782.1338	2813.4595	2836.9537	2857.4359	2876.5411	2967.3340	3167.6807	3421.0400	3757.7051
2832	2724.5944	2742.0740	2753.3958	2762.0815	2769.1685	2794.1455	2825.5181	2849.1123	2869.6816	2888.8682	2979.9609	3181.1602	3435.5977	3773.6953
2850	2742.3248	2759.8721	2771.2440	2779.9416	2787.0735	2812.1223	2843.6508	2867.3515	2888.0081	2907.3166	2999.0753	3201.3794	3457.4341	3797.6807
2856	2748.2289	2765.8130	2777.1872	2785.9030	2793.0282	2818.1298	2849.7246	2873.4316	2894.1753	2913.4373	3005.3892	3208.1191	3464.7129	3805.6758
2880	2771.8945	2789.5386	2800.9863	2809.7314	2816.9165	2842.1411	2873.9355	2897.7539	2918.6279	2938.0957	3030.6445	3235.4297	3493.8281	3837.6563
2904	2795.5254	2813.2722	2824.7710	2833.5668	2840.7896	2866.1580	2898.1066	2922.1234	2943.0828	2962.6685	3056.0771	3262.3916	3522.9434	3869.6367
2910	2801.4345	2819.1957	2830.7183	2839.5323	2846.7700	2872.1686	2904.1388	2928.2053	2949.2523	2968.8785	3062.3914	3269.1321	3530.2222	3877.6318
2928	2819.1650	2837.0138	2848.5630	2857.4092	2864.6470	2890.1580	2922.2813	2946.4519	2967.5845	2987.3320	3081.3340	3289.3535	3552.0586	3901.6172
2940	2830.9882	2848.8876	2860.4617	2869.3217	2876.6116	2902.1823	2934.3924	2958.6621	2979.8364	2999.5752	3093.9624	3302.8345	3566.6162	3917.6074
2952	2842.8135	2860.7410	2872.3623	2881.2360	2888.5331	2914.1631	2946.5046	2970.8284	2992.0891	3011.9084	3106.7710	3316.3154	3581.1738	3933.5977
2970	2860.5556	2878.5471	2890.1939	2899.1217	2906.4407	2932.1590	2964.6524	2989.0338	3010.4242	3030.3644	3125.7147	3336.5369	3603.0103	3957.5830
2976	2866.4707	2884.4758	2896.1462	2905.0693	2912.4258	2938.1733	2970.6870	2995.1631	3016.5967	3036.5771	3132.0293	3343.2773	3610.2891	3965.5781
3000	2890.1138	2908.2184	2919.9371	2928.9322	2936.2793	2962.1887	2994.8730	3019.5007	3041.0156	3061.1572	3157.2876	3370.2393	3639.4043	3997.5586
3024	2913.7885	2931.9686	2943.7581	2952.7559	2960.1848	2986.2092	3019.0627	3043.8413	3065.5283	3085.8311	3182.7305	3397.2012	3668.5195	4029.5391
3030	2919.6854	2937.9016	2949.6913	2958.7301	2966.1507	2992.2267	3025.0992	3049.9269	3071.6107	3091.9537	3189.0454	3403.9417	3675.7983	4037.5342
3048	2937.4254	2955.7033	2967.5398	2976.6090	2984.0504	3010.2349	3043.2561	3068.1848	3090.0439	3110.4148	3207.9902	3424.5352	3697.6348	4061.5195
3060	2949.2702	2967.5734	2979.4565	2988.5381	2995.9854	3022.2263	3055.3775	3080.3577	3102.2095	3122.7539	3220.6201	3438.0176	3712.1924	4077.5098

Table B-2 *Extended Erlang B with 50 Percent Retry Possibility (Continued)*

Circuits	Grade of Service													
	0.001	0.002	0.003	0.004	0.005	0.01	0.02	0.03	0.04	0.05	0.1	0.2	0.3	0.4
3072	2961.0938	2979.4453	2991.3516	3000.4688	3007.9219	3034.2188	3067.4531	3092.5313	3114.4688	3135.0000	3233.4375	3451.5000	3726.7500	4093.5000
3090	2978.8447	2997.2566	3009.1855	3018.3325	3025.8293	3052.2331	3085.6151	3110.7458	3132.8119	3153.4634	3252.3834	3471.7236	3748.5864	4117.4854
3096	2984.7469	3003.1946	3015.1467	3024.2878	3031.7992	3058.2543	3091.6538	3116.8806	3138.9895	3159.6812	3258.6987	3478.4648	3756.6211	4125.4805
3120	3008.4082	3026.9513	3038.9484	3048.1604	3055.6824	3082.2473	3115.8582	3141.2329	3163.4180	3184.2700	3283.9600	3505.4297	3785.7422	4157.4609
3144	3032.0775	3050.6913	3062.7567	3071.9916	3079.5714	3106.2927	3140.0662	3165.5402	3187.9438	3208.8604	3309.4131	3532.3945	3814.8633	4189.4414
3150	3037.9841	3056.6334	3068.7218	3077.9503	3085.5446	3112.2688	3146.1067	3171.6293	3194.0277	3215.0803	3315.72288	3539.1357	3822.1436	4197.4365
3168	3055.7307	3074.4382	3086.5715	3095.8528	3103.4663	3130.2949	3164.2295	3189.8979	3212.4243	3233.5488	3334.6758	3559.3594	3843.9844	4221.4219
3180	3067.5723	3086.3264	3098.4814	3107.7736	3115.4160	3142.2977	3176.3608	3202.0779	3224.6411	3245.7971	3347.3071	3572.8418	3858.5449	4237.4121
3192	3079.4160	3098.1921	3110.3687	3119.6959	3127.3671	3154.3015	3188.4445	3214.2100	3236.9070	3258.1428	3359.9385	3586.3242	3873.1055	4253.4023
3210	3097.1484	3116.0060	3128.2267	3137.6065	3145.2720	3172.3338	3206.5714	3232.5311	3255.2582	3276.6138	3379.0814	3606.5479	3894.9463	4277.3877
3216	3103.0847	3121.9530	3134.1720	3143.5693	3151.2491	3178.3125	3212.6631	3238.5732	3261.3918	3282.7383	3385.3975	3613.2891	3902.2266	4285.3828
3240	3126.7365	3145.6961	3157.9816	3167.3996	3175.1367	3202.3526	3236.8359	3262.9395	3285.8789	3307.4341	3410.6616	3640.2539	3931.3477	4317.3633
3264	3150.4204	3169.4707	3181.7974	3191.2603	3199.0298	3226.3726	3261.0117	3287.3086	3310.3682	3332.0332	3435.9258	3667.2188	3960.4688	4349.3438
3270	3156.3364	3175.3967	3187.7460	3197.2263	3204.9852	3232.3782	3267.1060	3293.3514	3316.5033	3338.1583	3442.2418	3673.9600	3967.7490	4357.3389
3288	3174.0870	3193.2272	3205.6194	3215.1017	3222.9283	3250.3718	3285.2406	3311.6305	3334.8596	3356.6338	3461.3906	3694.1836	3989.5898	4381.3242
3300	3185.9230	3205.0827	3217.5201	3227.0370	3234.8671	3262.3856	3297.3312	3323.7671	3347.1313	3368.9850	3474.0234	3707.6660	4004.1504	4397.3145
3312	3197.7609	3216.9650	3229.4224	3238.9739	3246.8071	3274.4004	3309.4226	3335.9546	3359.3027	3381.2358	3486.6563	3721.1484	4018.7109	4413.3047
3330	3215.5211	3234.7787	3247.2784	3256.8819	3264.7323	3292.4501	3327.5610	3354.2372	3377.6614	3399.7137	3505.6055	3741.3721	4040.5518	4437.2900
3336	3221.4421	3240.7344	3253.2312	3262.8265	3270.6910	3298.4333	3333.6584	3360.3318	3383.8491	3405.8394	3511.9219	3748.1133	4047.8320	4445.2852
3360	3245.1050	3264.4849	3277.0459	3286.6846	3294.5801	3322.4707	3357.8467	3384.6606	3408.2959	3430.5469	3537.3926	3775.0781	4076.9531	4477.2656
3384	3268.8007	3288.2673	3300.8665	3310.5482	3318.4742	3346.4608	3382.0378	3408.9917	3432.7958	3455.1541	3562.6597	3802.0430	4106.0742	4509.2461
3390	3274.7257	3294.2010	3306.8225	3316.5214	3324.4615	3352.4977	3388.0861	3415.0877	3438.9340	3461.2802	3568.9764	3808.7842	4113.3545	4517.2412
3408	3292.4777	3312.0304	3324.6929	3334.4172	3342.3735	3370.5066	3406.2319	3433.3770	3457.2979	3479.7627	3587.9268	3829.4238	4135.1953	4541.2266
3420	3304.3057	3323.9012	3336.6083	3346.3408	3354.3251	3382.5311	3418.3301	3445.5707	3469.5236	3492.0154	3600.5603	3842.9077	4149.7559	4557.2168
3432	3316.1616	3335.7997	3348.5251	3358.2656	3366.2780	3394.5306	3430.4290	3457.7128	3481.7498	3504.3728	3613.4033	3856.3916	4164.3164	4573.2070
3450	3333.9226	3353.6110	3366.3769	3376.1684	3384.1965	3412.5710	3448.5786	3476.0056	3500.1160	3522.8577	3632.3547	3876.6174	4186.1572	4597.1924

continues

Table B-2 Extended Erlang B with 50 Percent Retry Possibility (Continued)

Circuits	Grade of Service													
	0.001	0.002	0.003	0.004	0.005	0.01	0.02	0.03	0.04	0.05	0.1	0.2	0.3	0.4
3456	3339.8525	3359.5488	3372.3369	3382.1191	3390.1875	3418.5586	3454.6289	3482.0508	3506.2559	3528.9844	3638.6719	3883.3594	4193.4375	4605.1875
3480	3363.5239	3383.3304	3396.1542	3406.0043	3414.0756	3442.5641	3478.8318	3506.3910	3530.7642	3553.5974	3663.9404	3910.3271	4222.5586	4637.1680
3504	3387.2018	3407.0914	3419.9769	3429.8683	3437.9685	3466.6267	3503.0376	3530.7334	3555.2212	3578.2119	3689.2090	3937.2949	4251.6797	4669.1484
3510	3393.1357	3413.0326	3425.9402	3435.8217	3443.9626	3472.6163	3509.0895	3536.8327	3561.3089	3584.3390	3695.5261	3944.0369	4258.9600	4677.1436
3528	3410.9132	3430.8583	3443.8052	3453.7374	3461.8931	3490.6399	3527.2463	3555.1318	3579.6797	3602.8279	3714.6929	3964.2627	4280.8008	4701.1289
3540	3422.7580	3442.7440	3455.7079	3465.6738	3473.8303	3502.6749	3539.3518	3567.2781	3591.9635	3615.1904	3727.3279	3977.7466	4295.3613	4717.1191
3552	3434.6045	3454.6311	3467.6118	3477.5845	3485.7686	3514.6567	3551.4580	3579.4248	3604.2480	3627.4453	3739.9629	3991.2305	4309.9219	4733.1094
3570	3452.3637	3472.4645	3485.5110	3495.4797	3503.7053	3532.6854	3569.5642	3597.7272	3622.5673	3645.9366	3758.9154	4011.4563	4331.7627	4757.0947
3576	3458.2751	3478.4097	3491.4509	3501.4636	3509.6757	3538.6772	3575.6726	3603.8284	3628.7102	3652.0642	3765.2329	4018.1982	4339.0430	4765.0898
3600	3481.9794	3502.1667	3515.2954	3525.3479	3533.5876	3562.7014	3599.8352	3628.1250	3653.1738	3676.6846	3790.7227	4045.1660	4368.1641	4797.0703
3624	3505.6626	3525.9569	3539.1178	3549.2097	3557.4767	3586.7569	3624.0553	3652.5337	3677.6389	3701.3064	3815.9941	4072.1338	4397.2852	4829.0508
3630	3511.6051	3531.9054	3545.0603	3555.1689	3563.4773	3592.7783	3630.1108	3658.5809	3683.7831	3707.5452	3822.3120	4078.8757	4404.5654	4837.0459
3648	3529.3660	3549.7251	3562.9453	3573.0762	3581.3979	3610.7886	3648.2783	3676.8340	3702.1055	3725.9297	3841.2656	4099.5469	4426.4063	4861.0313
3660	3541.2131	3561.6252	3574.8610	3584.9973	3593.3464	3622.8058	3660.3351	3689.0405	3714.3951	3738.2977	3853.9014	4113.0322	4440.9668	4877.0215
3672	3553.0757	3573.4988	3586.7780	3596.9474	3605.2960	3634.7959	3672.4482	3701.1918	3726.6855	3750.5544	3866.5371	4126.5176	4455.5273	4893.0117
3690	3570.8306	3591.3538	3604.6417	3614.8329	3623.2224	3652.8387	3690.6194	3719.4475	3745.0099	3769.0521	3885.7159	4146.7456	4477.3682	4916.9971
3696	3576.7496	3597.2780	3610.6157	3620.8235	3629.1984	3658.8347	3696.6768	3725.5518	3751.1558	3775.1807	3892.0342	4153.4883	4484.6484	4924.9922
3720	3600.4578	3621.0626	3634.4302	3644.6759	3653.1052	3682.8772	3720.8514	3749.9139	3775.6274	3799.8083	3917.3071	4180.4590	4513.7695	4956.9727
3744	3624.1721	3644.8528	3658.2495	3668.5613	3677.0164	3706.9233	3745.0854	3774.2783	3800.1006	3824.4375	3942.5801	4207.4297	4542.8906	4988.9531
3750	3630.0945	3650.7797	3664.2265	3674.5262	3682.9948	3712.9211	3751.1444	3780.3268	3806.1905	3830.6808	3948.8983	4214.1724	4550.1709	4996.9482
3768	3647.8640	3668.6197	3682.1023	3692.4514	3700.9319	3730.9444	3769.2649	3798.5874	3824.5752	3849.0681	3967.8530	4234.4004	4572.0117	5020.9336
3780	3659.7121	3680.5051	3694.0018	3704.3839	3712.8914	3742.9706	3781.3843	3810.8002	3836.8707	3861.4417	3980.7202	4247.8857	4586.5723	5036.9238
3792	3671.5616	3692.4207	3705.9313	3716.3174	3724.8230	3754.9688	3793.5044	3822.9558	3849.0513	3873.7002	3993.3574	4261.3711	4601.1328	5052.9141
3810	3689.3388	3710.2386	3723.8134	3734.2197	3742.7657	3773.0255	3811.6278	3841.2190	3867.4384	3892.2043	4012.3132	4281.5991	4622.9736	5076.8994
3816	3695.2652	3716.1980	3729.7650	3740.1877	3748.7472	3779.0255	3817.6886	3847.3264	3873.5288	3898.3337	4018.6318	4288.3418	4630.2539	5084.8945
3840	3718.9746	3739.9805	3753.6035	3764.0625	3772.6758	3803.0273	3841.8750	3871.6406	3898.0078	3922.9688	4043.9063	4315.3125	4659.3750	5116.8750

Table B-2 *Extended Erlang B with 50 Percent Retry Possibility (Continued)*

Circuits	Grade of Service													
	0.001	0.002	0.003	0.004	0.005	0.01	0.02	0.03	0.04	0.05	0.1	0.2	0.3	0.4
3864	3742.6899	3763.7681	3777.4468	3787.9417	3796.5793	3827.0911	3866.1226	3896.0153	3922.5472	3947.6052	4069.1807	4342.2832	4688.4961	5148.8555
3870	3748.6196	3769.7010	3783.4010	3793.9121	3802.5632	3833.0928	3872.1259	3902.1240	3928.6972	3953.7350	4075.4993	4349.0259	4695.7764	5156.8506
3888	3766.3813	3787.5608	3801.2948	3811.8252	3820.4868	3851.0991	3890.3137	3920.3921	3947.0295	3972.2432	4094.6924	4369.2539	4717.6172	5180.8359
3900	3778.2440	3799.4293	3813.2057	3823.7686	3832.4570	3863.1340	3902.4399	3932.4921	3959.2712	3984.5032	4107.3303	4382.7393	4732.1777	5196.8262
3912	3790.1082	3811.3288	3825.1177	3835.7131	3844.3984	3875.1698	3914.5071	3944.7114	3971.5133	3996.8826	4119.9683	4396.2246	4746.7383	5212.8164
3930	3807.8771	3829.1954	3843.0178	3853.6020	3862.3572	3893.1802	3932.6985	3962.9819	3989.8471	4015.2731	4138.9252	4416.4526	4768.5791	5236.8018
3936	3813.8108	3835.1316	3848.9751	3859.6055	3868.3140	3899.1841	3938.7026	3969.0322	3996.0586	4021.5234	4145.2441	4423.1953	4775.8594	5244.7969
3960	3837.5189	3858.9093	3872.8070	3883.4720	3892.2336	3923.2315	3962.9608	3993.4149	4020.5457	4046.0449	4170.5200	4450.1660	4804.9805	5276.7773
3984	3861.2325	3882.7222	3896.6433	3907.3425	3916.1572	3947.2822	3987.1611	4017.7998	4045.0342	4070.6880	4196.0391	4477.1367	4834.1016	5308.7578
3990	3867.1694	3888.6610	3902.6031	3913.3184	3922.1159	3953.2878	3993.1659	4023.8507	4051.1261	4076.8185	4202.3584	4483.8794	4841.3818	5316.7529
4008	3884.9517	3906.5096	3920.4840	3931.2477	3940.0543	3971.3057	4011.3636	4042.1257	4069.5242	4095.3325	4221.3164	4504.1074	4863.2227	5340.7383
4020	3896.7979	3918.3897	3932.4060	3943.1712	3952.0349	3983.3185	4023.4351	4054.2892	4081.7084	4107.5940	4233.9551	4517.5928	4877.7832	5356.7285
4032	3908.6763	3930.3018	3944.3291	3955.1265	3963.9858	3995.3320	4035.5684	4066.4531	4094.0156	4119.9785	4246.5938	4531.0781	4892.3438	5372.7188
4050	3926.4656	3948.1567	3962.2158	3973.0305	3981.9294	4013.3537	4053.7079	4084.7305	4112.2925	4138.4949	4265.5518	4551.3062	4914.1846	5396.7041
4056	3932.3754	3954.0987	3968.1786	3979.0093	3987.8904	4019.3923	4059.7753	4090.7820	4118.4467	4144.6260	4271.8711	4558.0488	4921.4648	5404.6992
4080	3956.1108	3977.9004	3992.0325	4002.8961	4011.8298	4043.4247	4083.9844	4115.1746	4142.9407	4169.2749	4297.1484	4585.0195	4950.5859	5436.6797
4104	3979.8204	4001.6755	4015.8907	4026.7870	4035.7419	4067.4913	4108.1957	4139.5067	4167.4362	4193.8000	4322.6763	4611.9902	4979.7070	5468.6602
4110	3985.7643	4007.6200	4021.8246	4032.7368	4041.7049	4073.5007	4114.2645	4145.6213	4173.5916	4200.0568	4328.9960	4618.7329	4986.9873	5476.6553
4128	4003.5352	4025.4866	4039.7219	4050.6504	4059.6577	4091.5298	4132.4092	4163.9033	4191.8701	4218.4512	4347.9551	4638.9609	5008.8281	5500.6406
4140	4015.3944	4037.3781	4051.6548	4062.6151	4071.6170	4103.5501	4144.4852	4176.0709	4204.1821	4230.8405	4360.5945	4652.4463	5023.3887	5516.6309
4152	4027.2550	4049.2707	4063.5571	4074.5491	4083.5771	4115.5712	4156.6249	4188.2388	4216.3682	4243.1038	4373.2339	4665.9316	5037.9492	5532.6211
4170	4045.0642	4067.1117	4081.4600	4092.4679	4101.5350	4133.6041	4174.7722	4206.5231	4234.7745	4261.6260	4392.1930	4686.1597	5059.7900	5556.6064
4176	4050.9800	4073.0592	4087.4282	4098.4519	4107.5002	4139.6155	4180.8428	4212.5757	4240.8677	4267.7578	4398.5127	4692.9023	5067.0703	5564.6016
4200	4074.7101	4096.8521	4111.2717	4122.3267	4131.4270	4163.6307	4204.9988	4236.9141	4265.3687	4292.2852	4423.7915	4720.3857	5096.1914	5596.5820
4224	4098.4453	4120.6494	4135.1191	4146.2051	4155.3574	4187.6807	4229.2207	4261.2539	4289.8711	4316.9414	4449.3281	4747.3594	5125.3125	5628.5625
4230	4104.3638	4126.5994	4141.0897	4152.1914	4161.3245	4193.6613	4235.2927	4267.3714	4295.9647	4323.0734	4455.6482	4754.1028	5132.5928	5636.5576

continues

Table B-2   *Extended Erlang B with 50 Percent Retry Possibility (Continued)*

Circuits	Grade of Service													
	0.001	0.002	0.003	0.004	0.005	0.01	0.02	0.03	0.04	0.05	0.1	0.2	0.3	0.4
4248	4122.1533	4144.4511	4158.9706	4170.1196	4179.2591	4211.7012	4253.4448	4285.6600	4314.3750	4341.5991	4474.6084	4774.3330	5154.4336	5660.5430
4260	4134.0253	4156.3536	4170.9142	4182.0621	4191.2274	4223.7286	4265.5902	4297.8314	4326.6275	4353.8635	4487.2485	4787.8198	5168.9941	5676.5332
4272	4145.8986	4168.2572	4182.8262	4194.0055	4203.1967	4235.7568	4277.6711	4310.0032	4338.8804	4366.2583	4499.8887	4801.3066	5183.5547	5692.5234
4290	4163.6945	4186.0819	4200.7123	4211.9387	4221.1359	4253.8005	4295.8260	4328.2288	4357.2276	4384.6555	4518.8489	4821.5369	5205.3955	5716.5088
4296	4169.6162	4192.0349	4206.6857	4217.8951	4227.1051	4259.8154	4301.8997	4334.3478	4363.3872	4390.7878	4525.1689	4828.2803	5212.6758	5724.5039
4320	4193.3386	4215.8496	4230.5493	4241.7883	4251.0498	4283.8770	4326.0645	4358.6938	4387.8955	4415.4492	4550.4492	4855.2539	5241.7969	5756.4844
4344	4217.0658	4239.6687	4254.3838	4265.6852	4274.9650	4307.8751	4350.2970	4383.1077	4412.3390	4440.1121	4575.9946	4882.2275	5270.9180	5788.4648
4350	4222.9900	4245.5910	4260.3596	4271.6766	4280.9692	4313.8916	4356.3721	4389.1617	4418.4998	4446.2448	4582.3151	4888.9709	5278.1982	5796.4600
4368	4240.7977	4263.4589	4278.2552	4289.5858	4298.8835	4331.9421	4374.5317	4407.4570	4436.7832	4464.7764	4601.2764	4909.2012	5300.0391	5820.4453
4380	4252.6822	4275.3722	4290.1758	4301.5375	4310.8607	4343.9767	4386.6165	4419.5654	4449.1058	4477.0422	4613.9172	4922.6880	5314.5996	5836.4355
4392	4264.5344	4287.2531	4302.0972	4313.4565	4322.8389	4356.0121	4398.7017	4431.8079	4461.2952	4489.3081	4626.5581	4936.1748	5329.1602	5852.4258
4410	4282.3317	4305.1266	4319.9979	4331.4038	4340.7573	4373.9992	4416.8637	4450.0383	4479.7137	4507.8415	4645.5194	4956.4050	5351.0010	5876.4111
4416	4288.2759	4311.0850	4325.9766	4337.3643	4346.7305	4380.0176	4422.9404	4456.1602	4485.8086	4513.9746	4651.8398	4963.1484	5358.2813	5884.4063
4440	4311.9882	4334.8874	4349.8260	4361.2756	4370.6927	4404.0930	4447.1814	4480.5139	4510.3235	4538.6426	4677.1216	4990.1221	5387.4023	5916.3867
4464	4335.7390	4358.6938	4373.6792	4385.1566	4394.5906	4428.1033	4471.3564	4504.8691	4534.8398	4563.1758	4702.6758	5017.0957	5416.5234	5948.3672
4470	4341.6689	4364.6546	4379.9260	4391.1530	4400.5996	4434.1232	4477.4345	4510.9241	4540.9351	4569.4455	4708.9966	5023.8391	5423.8037	5956.3623
4488	4359.4603	4382.5043	4397.5360	4409.0751	4418.5256	4452.1842	4495.6014	4529.2258	4559.2207	4587.8459	4727.9590	5044.0693	5445.6445	5980.3477
4500	4371.3398	4394.3939	4409.4658	4421.0014	4430.5115	4464.2258	4507.6904	4541.3361	4571.5485	4600.1129	4740.6006	5057.5562	5460.2051	5996.3379
4512	4383.2205	4406.3188	4421.3965	4432.9629	4442.4639	4476.1992	4519.7798	4553.5840	4583.7393	4612.5176	4753.2422	5071.0430	5474.7656	6012.3281
4530	4401.0178	4424.1737	4439.2770	4450.8895	4460.3938	4494.2638	4537.9491	4571.8190	4602.1637	4630.9186	4772.2046	5091.2732	5496.6064	6036.3135
4536	4406.9507	4430.1374	4445.2606	4456.8539	4466.4055	4500.2856	4544.0288	4577.9436	4608.2593	4637.0522	4778.5254	5098.0166	5503.8867	6044.3086
4560	4430.6854	4453.9252	4469.1284	4480.7483	4490.3503	4524.3054	4568.2104	4602.2351	4632.7808	4661.7261	4803.8086	5125.5469	5533.0078	6076.2891
4584	4454.4245	4477.7516	4492.9649	4504.6809	4514.2635	4548.3624	4592.4635	4626.5973	4657.2338	4686.4014	4829.0918	5152.5234	5562.1289	6108.2695
4590	4460.3600	4483.7176	4498.9508	4510.6471	4520.2423	4554.3858	4598.4746	4632.7231	4663.3997	4692.5354	4835.4126	5159.2676	5569.4092	6116.2646
4608	4478.1680	4501.5469	4516.8398	4528.5469	4538.1797	4572.4219	4616.6484	4650.9609	4681.6875	4710.9375	4854.6563	5179.5000	5591.2500	6140.2500
4620	4490.0414	4513.4811	4528.7787	4540.5162	4550.1389	4584.4350	4628.7415	4663.1433	4694.0204	4723.3466	4867.2986	5192.9883	5605.8105	6156.2402

Table B-2 Extended Erlang B with 50 Percent Retry Possibility (Continued)

Circuits	Grade of Service													
	0.001	0.002	0.003	0.004	0.005	0.01	0.02	0.03	0.04	0.05	0.1	0.2	0.3	0.4
4632	4501.9158	4525.3812	4540.7184	4552.4511	4562.1341	4596.4486	4640.8348	4675.3260	4706.2126	4735.6150	4879.9409	5206.4766	5620.3711	6172.2305
4650	4519.7119	4543.2507	4558.6121	4570.3903	4580.0755	4614.5233	4659.0111	4693.5654	4724.6429	4754.0176	4898.9044	5226.7090	5642.2119	6196.2158
4656	4525.6326	4549.1840	4564.5652	4576.3586	4586.0563	4620.5131	4665.0938	4699.6926	4730.7393	4760.2939	4905.2256	5233.4531	5649.4922	6204.2109
4680	4549.3890	4573.0261	4588.4509	4600.2695	4609.9814	4644.5801	4689.2834	4723.9893	4755.2673	4784.8315	4930.5103	5260.4297	5679.7559	6236.1914
4704	4573.1499	4596.8364	4612.3044	4624.1836	4633.9453	4668.6138	4713.4746	4748.3584	4779.6533	4809.5127	4955.7949	5287.4063	5708.8828	6268.1719
4710	4579.0728	4602.7716	4618.2594	4630.1537	4639.9278	4674.6405	4719.5586	4754.4868	4785.8217	4815.6473	4962.1161	5294.1504	5716.1646	6276.1670
4728	4596.8791	4620.6504	4636.1613	4648.0649	4657.8765	4692.6497	4737.7394	4772.7290	4804.1836	4834.0510	4981.0796	5314.3828	5738.0098	6300.1523
4740	4608.7633	4632.5587	4648.1090	4660.0429	4669.8431	4704.7046	4749.8364	4784.9149	4816.3770	4846.4648	4994.0112	5327.8711	5752.5732	6316.1426
4752	4620.6123	4644.4680	4660.0214	4671.9855	4681.8105	4716.7240	4761.9338	4797.1011	4828.7153	4858.7344	5006.6543	5341.3594	5767.1367	6332.1328
4770	4638.4422	4662.3154	4677.9277	4689.9007	4699.7630	4734.7723	4780.1170	4815.4175	4847.0059	4877.1387	5025.6189	5361.5918	5788.9819	6356.1182
4776	4644.3860	4668.2893	4683.8848	4695.8729	4705.7476	4740.8009	4786.1298	4821.4746	4853.1757	4883.4192	5031.9404	5368.3359	5796.2637	6364.1133
4800	4668.1274	4692.1143	4707.7881	4719.7998	4729.6875	4764.8438	4810.4004	4845.7764	4877.6367	4907.9590	5057.2266	5395.3125	5825.3906	6396.0938
4824	4691.8729	4715.9429	4731.6215	4743.6932	4753.6304	4788.8888	4834.5996	4870.1525	4902.1721	4932.6460	5082.2891	5422.2891	5854.5176	6428.0742
4830	4697.8191	4721.8822	4737.6171	4749.6671	4759.6165	4794.9188	4840.6128	4876.2836	4908.2693	4938.7811	5088.8342	5429.0332	5861.7993	6436.0693
4848	4715.6224	4739.7382	4755.4948	4767.5896	4777.5392	4812.9360	4858.8003	4894.4561	4926.7090	4957.1865	5107.7988	5449.2656	5883.6445	6460.0547
4860	4727.4802	4751.6556	4767.4512	4779.5389	4789.5131	4824.9605	4870.9012	4906.7194	4938.9038	4969.6051	5120.4419	5462.7539	5898.2080	6476.0449
4872	4739.3760	4763.5739	4779.3713	4791.5261	4801.4877	4836.9855	4883.0024	4918.8347	4951.0986	4981.8757	5133.0850	5476.2422	5912.7715	6492.0352
4890	4757.1844	4781.4345	4797.2903	4809.4526	4819.4511	4855.0053	4901.1923	4937.1570	4969.5401	5000.2817	5152.0496	5496.4746	5934.6167	6516.0205
4896	4763.1335	4787.3760	4803.2512	4815.4285	4825.4392	4861.0371	4907.2061	4943.2148	4975.6377	5006.5664	5158.6699	5503.2188	5941.8984	6524.0156
4920	4786.8576	4811.2189	4827.1344	4839.3338	4849.3561	4885.0909	4931.4111	4967.5964	5000.1782	5031.1084	5183.9575	5530.1953	5971.0254	6555.9961
4944	4810.6230	4835.0277	4850.9832	4863.2421	4873.3132	4909.1470	4955.6931	4991.9795	5024.5693	5055.8013	5209.2451	5557.1719	6000.1523	6587.9766
4950	4816.5745	4841.0088	4856.9458	4869.2196	4879.3030	4915.1802	4961.7073	4998.0377	5030.7426	5061.9370	5215.5670	5563.9160	6007.4341	6595.9717
4968	4834.3925	4858.8777	4874.8727	4887.1533	4897.2354	4933.2052	4979.9015	5016.2882	5049.1121	5080.3440	5234.5327	5584.1484	6029.2793	6619.9570
4980	4846.2598	4870.7661	4886.7998	4899.1100	4909.2165	4945.2351	4992.0062	5028.4808	5061.3080	5092.7673	5247.1765	5597.6367	6043.8428	6635.9473
4992	4858.1279	4882.6934	4898.7275	4911.0674	4921.1982	4957.2656	5004.1113	5040.5977	5073.6563	5105.0391	5259.8203	5611.1250	6058.4063	6651.9375
5010	4875.9510	4900.5668	4916.6588	4929.0049	4939.1341	4975.2933	5022.2314	5058.9258	5091.9507	5123.4467	5278.7860	5631.3574	6080.2515	6675.9229

continues

Table B-2   *Extended Erlang B with 50 Percent Retry Possibility (Continued)*

Circuits	0.001	0.002	0.003	0.004	0.005	0.01	0.02	0.03	0.04	0.05	0.1	0.2	0.3	0.4
5016	4881.9053	4906.5123	4922.6235	4934.9844	4945.1257	4981.3282	5028.3226	5064.9844	5098.0488	5129.5825	5285.1079	5638.1016	6087.5332	6683.9180
5040	4905.6482	4930.3345	4946.4844	4958.8660	4969.0558	5005.3931	5052.5354	5089.3726	5122.5952	5154.2798	5310.3955	5665.0781	6116.6602	6715.8984
5064	4929.3948	4954.1600	4970.3481	4982.7887	4993.0270	5029.4214	5076.7496	5113.7622	5147.1431	5178.8240	5335.9922	5692.0547	6145.7871	6747.8789
5070	4935.3513	4960.1459	4976.3145	4988.7698	4998.9816	5035.4192	5082.8421	5119.8212	5153.2416	5185.1147	5342.3145	5698.7988	6153.0688	6755.8740
5088	4953.1644	4977.9888	4994.2537	5006.7144	5016.9624	5053.4517	5100.9653	5138.0757	5171.5371	5203.5234	5361.2813	5719.0313	6174.9141	6779.8594
5100	4965.0410	4989.9239	5006.1882	5018.6783	5028.9116	5065.5258	5113.0737	5150.2716	5183.8120	5215.7959	5373.9258	5732.5195	6189.4775	6795.8496
5112	4976.9184	5001.8209	5018.1235	5030.6039	5040.9003	5077.5227	5125.1825	5162.3899	5196.0872	5228.0684	5386.5703	5746.0078	6204.0410	6811.8398
5130	4994.7363	5019.7069	5036.0278	5048.5522	5058.8457	5095.5579	5143.3855	5180.7239	5214.3832	5246.6336	5405.5371	5766.2402	6225.8862	6835.8252
5136	5000.6957	5025.6563	5041.9962	5054.5353	5064.8408	5101.5959	5149.4011	5186.7832	5220.5603	5252.7700	5411.8594	5772.9844	6233.1680	6843.8203
5160	5024.4571	5049.4949	5065.8719	5078.4302	5088.7839	5125.6714	5173.6212	5211.1780	5245.0342	5277.4731	5437.1484	5799.9609	6262.2949	6875.8008
5184	5048.2024	5073.3369	5089.7505	5102.3672	5112.7295	5149.7095	5197.8428	5235.4951	5269.5879	5302.0195	5462.4375	5826.9375	6291.4219	6907.7813
5190	5054.1442	5079.2880	5095.7206	5108.3519	5118.7262	5155.7094	5203.9380	5241.6339	5275.6870	5308.1561	5468.7598	5833.6816	6298.7036	6915.7764
5208	5071.9512	5097.1425	5113.6320	5126.2674	5136.6777	5173.7494	5222.0658	5259.8130	5293.9841	5326.7249	5487.7266	5853.9141	6320.5488	6939.7617
5220	5083.8368	5109.0862	5125.5739	5138.2384	5148.6328	5185.7899	5234.1779	5272.0917	5306.3416	5338.9984	5500.3711	5867.4023	6335.1123	6955.7520
5232	5095.7234	5120.9908	5137.5165	5150.1702	5160.6284	5197.8311	5246.2903	5284.2114	5318.5400	5351.2720	5513.3350	5880.8906	6349.6758	6971.7422
5250	5113.5349	5138.8493	5155.3917	5168.1290	5178.5831	5215.8737	5264.4196	5302.4712	5336.8378	5369.6823	5532.3029	5901.1230	6371.5210	6995.7275
5256	5119.4993	5144.8024	5161.3638	5174.1156	5184.5817	5221.8748	5270.5162	5308.6113	5343.0172	5375.9795	5538.6255	5907.8672	6378.8027	7003.7227
5280	5143.2385	5168.6572	5185.2539	5198.0237	5208.5376	5245.9204	5294.7437	5332.9321	5367.4951	5400.5273	5563.9160	5934.8438	6407.9297	7035.7031
5304	5167.0215	5192.4749	5209.1470	5221.9343	5232.4556	5270.0083	5318.9725	5357.2537	5392.0547	5425.2371	5589.2065	5961.8203	6437.0566	7067.6836
5310	5172.9476	5198.4297	5215.1207	5227.9225	5238.4557	5276.0104	5324.9895	5363.3949	5398.1543	5431.3742	5595.5292	5968.5645	6444.3384	7075.6787
5328	5190.7676	5216.3361	5233.0430	5245.8475	5256.4164	5294.0577	5343.1216	5381.6572	5416.4531	5449.7856	5614.4971	5988.7969	6466.1836	7099.6641
5340	5202.6622	5228.2475	5244.9513	5257.7949	5268.3774	5306.1035	5355.2371	5393.8596	5428.8153	5462.0599	5627.1423	6002.2852	6480.7471	7115.6543

Table B-2   *Extended Erlang B with 50 Percent Retry Possibility (Continued)*

Circuits	Grade of Service													
	0.001	0.002	0.003	0.004	0.005	0.01	0.02	0.03	0.04	0.05	0.1	0.2	0.3	0.4
5352	5214.5577	5240.1597	5256.9011	5269.7429	5280.3798	5318.1090	5367.3530	5406.0623	5441.0149	5474.3342	5639.7876	6015.7734	6495.3105	7131.6445
5370	5232.3823	5258.0294	5274.8270	5287.6506	5298.3028	5336.1589	5385.5685	5424.2441	5459.3143	5492.9095	5658.7555	6036.0059	6517.1558	7155.6299
5376	5238.3105	5263.9863	5280.8027	5293.6406	5304.3047	5342.2031	5391.5859	5430.3867	5465.4961	5499.0469	5665.0781	6042.7500	6524.4375	7163.6250
5400	5262.0872	5287.8159	5304.6661	5317.5613	5328.2318	5366.2170	5415.8203	5454.7119	5489.9780	5523.5962	5690.3687	6069.7266	6553.5645	7195.6055
5424	5285.8674	5311.6690	5328.5735	5341.4846	5352.2025	5390.3152	5440.0562	5479.1206	5514.5435	5548.3110	5715.9902	6097.3652	6582.6914	7227.5859
5430	5291.7975	5317.6276	5334.5094	5347.4762	5358.2059	5396.3194	5446.0739	5485.1816	5520.6436	5554.4485	5722.3132	6104.1101	6589.9731	7235.5811
5448	5309.6303	5335.5253	5352.4422	5365.4105	5376.1758	5414.3324	5464.2935	5503.4476	5538.9441	5572.8611	5741.2822	6124.3447	6611.8184	7259.5664
5460	5321.4922	5347.4442	5364.3983	5377.3535	5388.1425	5426.3832	5476.3293	5515.6531	5551.2277	5585.3027	5753.9282	6137.8345	6626.3818	7275.5566
5472	5333.3965	5359.3638	5376.3135	5389.3389	5400.1099	5438.4346	5488.4487	5527.7754	5563.5117	5597.5781	5766.5742	6151.3242	6640.9453	7291.5469
5490	5351.2337	5377.2236	5394.2500	5407.2764	5418.0409	5456.4917	5506.6704	5546.1264	5581.8127	5615.9912	5785.5432	6171.5588	6662.7905	7315.5322
5496	5357.1660	5383.1842	5400.2292	5413.2279	5424.0461	5462.4551	5512.6886	5552.1877	5587.9131	5622.1289	5791.8662	6178.3037	6670.0723	7323.5273
5520	5380.9387	5407.0074	5424.1058	5437.1613	5447.9846	5486.5613	5536.9299	5576.5173	5612.4829	5646.8481	5817.1582	6205.2832	6699.1992	7355.5078
5544	5404.7148	5430.8546	5447.9850	5461.0972	5471.9676	5510.5851	5561.1727	5600.8477	5636.8850	5671.3997	5842.4502	6232.2627	6728.3262	7387.4883
5550	5410.6487	5436.8168	5453.9658	5467.0921	5477.9320	5516.6336	5567.1913	5606.9939	5643.0702	5677.5375	5848.7732	6239.0076	6735.6079	7395.4834
5568	5428.4941	5454.7046	5471.8667	5484.9932	5495.9106	5534.6953	5585.3320	5625.2637	5661.4570	5696.1211	5867.7422	6259.2422	6757.4531	7419.4688
5580	5440.3638	5466.6307	5483.8298	5496.9846	5507.8830	5546.7087	5597.4545	5637.3871	5673.6584	5708.3972	5880.3882	6272.7319	6772.0166	7435.4590
5592	5452.2555	5478.5576	5495.7510	5508.9340	5519.8559	5558.7224	5609.5774	5649.5958	5685.9452	5720.6733	5893.0342	6286.2217	6786.5801	7451.4492
5610	5470.0838	5496.4278	5513.6552	5526.8806	5537.8377	5576.7865	5627.7196	5667.8668	5704.3332	5739.0875	5912.0032	6306.4563	6808.4253	7475.4346
5616	5476.0199	5502.3706	5519.6378	5532.8774	5543.8033	5582.7938	5633.8242	5673.9287	5710.4341	5745.3970	5918.3262	6313.2012	6815.7070	7483.4297
5640	5499.8090	5526.2292	5543.5272	5556.7804	5567.7530	5606.8671	5657.9865	5698.3484	5734.9237	5769.9500	5943.9624	6340.1807	6844.8340	7515.4102
5664	5523.5797	5550.0908	5567.4192	5580.6855	5591.7048	5630.8989	5682.2358	5722.6831	5759.4141	5794.5029	5969.2559	6367.1602	6873.9609	7547.3906
5670	5529.5391	5556.0350	5573.4034	5586.6838	5597.7148	5636.9504	5688.3417	5728.7453	5765.5151	5800.8142	5975.5792	6373.9050	6881.2427	7555.3857
5688	5547.3536	5573.9119	5591.3137	5604.6363	5615.6589	5654.9756	5706.4867	5747.0186	5783.9052	5819.2295	5994.5493	6394.1396	6903.0879	7579.3711
5700	5559.2308	5585.8452	5603.2402	5616.5909	5627.6367	5667.0364	5718.6127	5759.2300	5796.1945	5831.5063	6007.1960	6407.6294	6917.6514	7595.3613
5712	5571.1306	5597.7792	5615.2108	5628.5460	5639.6151	5679.0542	5730.6519	5771.4419	5808.3970	5843.7832	6019.8428	6421.1191	6932.2148	7611.3516

continues

Table B-2 *Extended Erlang B with 50 Percent Retry Possibility (Continued)*

Circuits	Grade of Service													
	0.001	0.002	0.003	0.004	0.005	0.01	0.02	0.03	0.04	0.05	0.1	0.2	0.3	0.4
5730	5588.9708	5615.6378	5633.1244	5646.5016	5657.6056	5697.0815	5748.8855	5789.6292	5826.7007	5862.3734	6038.8129	6441.3538	6954.0601	7635.3369
5736	5594.9106	5621.6056	5639.0667	5652.4579	5663.5735	5703.0908	5754.9053	5795.7792	5832.8895	5868.5120	6045.1362	6448.0986	6961.3418	7643.3320
5760	5618.6719	5645.4346	5662.9688	5676.4160	5687.5342	5727.1729	5779.1602	5820.1172	5857.3828	5893.0664	6070.4297	6475.0781	6990.4688	7675.3125

Table B-3 *Extended Erlang B with 60 Percent Retry Possibility*

Circuits	Grade of Service													
	0.001	0.002	0.003	0.004	0.005	0.01	0.02	0.03	0.04	0.05	0.1	0.2	0.3	0.4
1	0.0000	0.0000	0.0000	0.0000	0.0000	0.0100	0.0202	0.0304	0.0406	0.0510	0.1044	0.2200	0.3511	0.5063
2	0.0457	0.0652	0.0805	0.0935	0.1050	0.1516	0.2207	0.2764	0.3252	0.3699	0.5596	0.8799	1.1875	1.5195
3	0.1937	0.2484	0.2879	0.3202	0.3479	0.4526	0.5949	0.7020	0.7925	0.8723	1.1942	1.6978	2.1592	2.6440
4	0.4390	0.5343	0.6008	0.6541	0.6990	0.8640	1.0791	1.2358	1.3657	1.4785	1.9224	2.5908	3.1895	3.8145
5	0.7616	0.8987	0.9924	1.0666	1.1285	1.3525	1.6370	1.8414	2.0074	2.1515	2.7075	3.5278	4.2529	5.0098
6	1.1451	1.3235	1.4440	1.5381	1.6168	1.8973	2.2485	2.4968	2.6982	2.8711	3.5325	4.4941	5.3408	6.2227
7	1.5774	1.7961	1.9427	2.0563	2.1508	2.4857	2.9001	3.1907	3.4248	3.6256	4.3853	5.4824	6.4395	7.4443
8	2.0498	2.3076	2.4790	2.6118	2.7217	3.1084	3.5830	3.9141	4.1797	4.4063	5.2607	6.4844	7.5527	8.6758
9	2.5557	2.8512	3.0471	3.1976	3.3223	3.7595	4.2924	4.6615	4.9570	5.2086	6.1523	7.4971	8.6726	9.9141
10	3.0899	3.4222	3.6414	3.8098	3.9484	4.4342	5.0226	5.4297	5.7532	6.0291	7.0593	8.5205	9.7998	11.1523
11	3.6487	4.0162	4.2579	4.4432	4.5963	5.1287	5.7712	6.2130	6.5648	6.8629	7.9761	9.5525	10.9302	12.3965
12	4.2286	4.6311	4.8948	5.0969	5.2625	5.8403	6.5347	7.0122	7.3901	7.7109	8.9048	10.5908	12.0674	13.6406
13	4.8274	5.2634	5.5486	5.7661	5.9454	6.5667	7.3125	7.8227	8.2266	8.5693	9.8405	11.6353	13.2095	14.8916
14	5.4431	5.9114	6.2173	6.4514	6.6428	7.3068	8.1014	8.6440	9.0739	9.4370	10.7837	12.6807	14.3486	16.1396
15	6.0732	6.5739	6.9003	7.1489	7.3526	8.0585	8.9008	9.4757	9.9298	10.3125	11.7334	13.7329	15.4944	17.3950
16	6.7168	7.2490	7.5947	7.8584	8.0752	8.8213	9.7100	10.3154	10.7930	11.1973	12.6895	14.7891	16.6406	18.6484
17	7.3732	7.9355	8.3008	8.5789	8.8071	9.5936	10.5275	11.1625	11.6647	12.0859	13.6486	15.8462	17.7886	19.9053

Table B-3   *Extended Erlang B with 60 Percent Retry Possibility (Continued)*

Circuits	Grade of Service													
	0.001	0.002	0.003	0.004	0.005	0.01	0.02	0.03	0.04	0.05	0.1	0.2	0.3	0.4
18	8.0409	8.6331	9.0176	9.3098	9.5482	10.3733	11.3522	12.0168	12.5420	12.9836	14.6140	16.9058	18.9404	21.1553
19	8.7184	9.3400	9.7424	10.0485	10.2990	11.1618	12.1846	12.8781	13.4243	13.8835	15.5813	17.9702	20.0947	22.4141
20	9.4055	10.0555	10.4761	10.7959	11.0583	11.9580	13.0225	13.7451	14.3115	14.7900	16.5552	19.0381	21.2500	23.6719
21	10.1014	10.7794	11.2178	11.5510	11.8240	12.7597	13.8658	14.6169	15.2065	15.7013	17.5316	20.1028	22.4048	24.9272
22	10.8053	11.5109	11.9668	12.3132	12.5966	13.5687	14.7168	15.4929	16.1025	16.6182	18.5088	21.1729	23.5576	26.1895
23	11.5168	12.2496	12.7227	13.0821	13.3755	14.3834	15.5710	16.3740	17.0057	17.5364	19.4905	22.2448	24.7183	27.4473
24	12.2358	12.9946	13.4854	13.8574	14.1606	15.2021	16.4297	17.2588	17.9121	18.4585	20.4756	23.3145	25.8750	28.7109
25	12.9608	13.7466	14.2532	14.6378	14.9506	16.0263	17.2943	18.1488	18.8202	19.3848	21.4600	24.3896	27.0325	29.9683
26	13.6919	14.5036	15.0265	15.4232	15.7469	16.8562	18.1606	19.0430	19.7317	20.3125	22.4517	25.4668	28.1899	31.2305
27	14.4294	15.2666	15.8055	16.2142	16.5471	17.6891	19.0322	19.9385	20.6488	21.2454	23.4404	26.5419	29.3533	32.4844
28	15.1724	16.0337	16.5891	17.0095	17.3530	18.5271	19.9080	20.8376	21.5674	22.1792	24.4351	27.6172	30.5156	33.7422
29	15.9204	16.8063	17.3781	17.8099	18.1622	19.3693	20.7853	21.7411	22.4899	23.1165	25.4281	28.6956	31.6763	35.0039
30	16.6736	17.5836	18.1705	18.6145	18.9752	20.2148	21.6669	22.6465	23.4119	24.0564	26.4258	29.7766	32.8345	36.2695
31	17.4309	18.3665	18.9673	19.4223	19.7932	21.0627	22.5518	23.5546	24.3398	24.9983	27.4202	30.8562	33.9971	37.5391
32	18.1934	19.1523	19.7676	20.2344	20.6152	21.9141	23.4395	24.4648	25.2676	25.9414	28.4219	31.9375	35.1563	38.7969
33	18.9593	19.9422	20.5726	21.0500	21.4397	22.7701	24.3290	25.3784	26.1982	26.8890	29.4229	33.0161	36.3193	40.0576
34	19.7299	20.7354	21.3807	21.8705	22.2679	23.6282	25.2219	26.2927	27.1311	27.8367	30.4224	34.0996	37.4863	41.3213
35	20.5046	21.5332	22.1933	22.6921	23.0991	24.4897	26.1176	27.2113	28.0658	28.7836	31.4282	35.1837	38.6487	42.5879
36	21.2827	22.3330	23.0076	23.5173	23.9326	25.3521	27.0132	28.1294	29.0039	29.7356	32.4316	36.2637	39.8145	43.8398
37	22.0636	23.1363	23.8251	24.3467	24.7713	26.2189	27.9126	29.0508	29.9406	30.6903	33.4364	37.3523	40.9746	45.1118
38	22.8489	23.9448	24.6476	25.1787	25.6101	27.0875	28.8154	29.9751	30.8820	31.6427	34.4421	38.4360	42.1377	46.3682
39	23.6371	24.7535	25.4700	26.0127	26.4531	27.9598	29.7189	30.8996	31.8256	32.5992	35.4485	39.5237	43.3037	47.6265
40	24.4287	25.5664	26.2976	26.8494	27.2986	28.8330	30.6250	31.8262	32.7686	33.5547	36.4600	40.6055	44.4727	48.9063
41	25.2234	26.3832	27.1265	27.6895	28.1475	29.7077	31.5308	32.7570	33.7129	34.5137	37.4666	41.6907	45.6345	50.1689
42	26.0206	27.2010	27.9586	28.5315	28.9968	30.5848	32.4408	33.6841	34.6582	35.4734	38.4778	42.7793	46.7988	51.4336
43	26.8199	28.0219	28.7935	29.3762	29.8486	31.4653	33.3523	34.6173	35.6068	36.4361	39.4884	43.8661	47.9656	52.7002

continues

Table B-3 *Extended Erlang B with 60 Percent Retry Possibility (Continued)*

Circuits								Grade of Service						
	0.001	0.002	0.003	0.004	0.005	0.01	0.02	0.03	0.04	0.05	0.1	0.2	0.3	0.4
44	27.6235	28.8455	29.6296	30.2218	30.7039	32.3474	34.2649	35.5513	36.5557	37.3989	40.4980	44.9561	49.1348	53.9473
45	28.4285	29.6713	30.4678	31.0707	31.5610	33.2309	35.1782	36.4856	37.5073	38.3615	41.5118	46.0437	50.2954	55.2173
46	29.2371	30.5005	31.3105	31.9212	32.4196	34.1154	36.0947	37.4199	38.4587	39.3263	42.5242	47.1287	51.4580	56.4893
47	30.0463	31.3314	32.1533	32.7744	33.2792	35.0033	37.0114	38.3568	39.4095	40.2931	43.5404	48.2163	52.6340	57.7402
48	30.8599	32.1636	32.9985	33.6299	34.1426	35.8916	37.9307	39.2959	40.3652	41.2588	44.4547	49.3008	53.8008	59.0156
49	31.6747	32.9981	33.8460	34.4860	35.0064	36.7799	38.8495	40.2372	41.3198	42.2260	45.5726	50.3937	54.9575	60.2690
50	32.4921	33.8348	34.6954	35.3455	35.8734	37.6740	39.7705	41.1774	42.2729	43.1946	46.5881	51.4832	56.1279	61.5479
51	33.3100	34.6734	35.5465	36.2049	36.7403	38.5659	40.6935	42.1192	43.2305	44.1643	47.6008	52.5688	57.3003	62.8037
52	34.1313	35.5151	36.3990	37.0671	37.6099	39.4602	41.6152	43.0625	44.1892	45.1350	48.6167	53.6631	58.4619	64.0605
53	34.9559	36.3566	37.2543	37.9304	38.4819	40.3582	42.5417	44.0038	45.1458	46.1065	49.6357	54.7533	59.6250	65.3442
54	35.7803	37.2008	38.1105	38.7960	39.3530	41.2548	43.4663	44.9495	46.1096	47.0786	50.6580	55.8457	60.8027	66.6035
55	36.6074	38.0475	38.9673	39.6622	40.2295	42.1530	44.3954	45.8960	47.0676	48.0511	51.6766	56.9336	61.9690	67.8638
56	37.4370	38.8948	39.8279	40.5320	41.1045	43.0527	45.3223	46.8433	48.0293	49.0239	52.6914	58.0234	63.1367	69.1250
57	38.2673	39.7441	40.6887	41.4019	41.9811	43.9537	46.2534	47.7911	48.9913	50.0002	53.7158	59.1152	64.3059	70.3872
58	39.0997	40.5954	41.5512	42.2734	42.8593	44.8576	47.1816	48.7393	49.9570	50.9766	54.7325	60.2090	65.4766	71.6504
59	39.9341	41.4484	42.4153	43.1463	43.7404	45.7625	48.1140	49.6876	50.9192	51.9491	55.7518	61.2975	66.6343	72.9146
60	40.7703	42.3010	43.2825	44.0204	44.6210	46.6663	49.0466	50.6396	51.8848	52.9248	56.7773	62.3877	67.8076	74.1797
72	50.9128	52.6531	53.7671	54.6064	55.2876	57.6079	60.3018	62.1035	63.5098	64.6919	69.0557	75.4980	81.8262	89.3672
90	66.4426	68.4723	69.7687	70.7465	71.5375	74.2346	77.3657	79.4586	81.0901	82.4634	87.5500	95.2075	102.8760	112.1484
96	71.6865	73.8047	75.1582	76.1777	77.0068	79.8223	83.0918	85.2715	86.9766	88.4063	93.7383	101.7773	109.8984	119.7656
120	92.9077	95.3687	96.9397	98.1226	99.0820	102.3450	106.1279	108.6548	110.6323	112.2949	118.5132	128.0859	137.9590	150.1172
144	114.4424	117.2153	118.9863	120.3179	121.4033	125.0771	129.3354	132.1875	134.4111	136.2920	143.3496	154.4238	166.0781	180.4922
150	119.8654	122.7127	124.5300	125.9033	127.0111	130.7831	135.1593	138.0798	140.3687	142.3004	149.5697	161.0229	173.0713	188.0859
168	136.2129	139.2788	141.2373	142.7087	143.9033	147.9587	152.6704	155.8184	158.2793	160.3608	168.2358	180.7764	194.1680	210.9023
180	147.1729	150.3754	152.4188	153.9569	155.2094	159.4501	164.3719	167.6624	170.2441	172.4194	180.6812	193.9526	208.2129	226.0986
192	158.1680	161.5078	163.6406	165.2461	166.5469	170.9648	176.0977	179.5313	182.2207	184.4883	193.1484	207.1406	222.2813	241.3125

Table B-3 *Extended Erlang B with 60 Percent Retry Possibility (Continued)*

Circuits														
							Grade of Service							
	0.001	0.002	0.003	0.004	0.005	0.01	0.02	0.03	0.04	0.05	0.1	0.2	0.3	0.4
210	174.7330	178.2706	180.5264	182.2247	183.6026	188.2809	193.7155	197.3492	200.2075	202.6172	211.8457	226.9189	243.3252	264.0894
216	180.2725	183.8716	186.1688	187.8992	189.3032	194.0691	199.5996	203.3042	206.2112	208.6699	218.0830	233.5078	250.3828	271.6875
240	202.5000	206.3452	208.8025	210.6519	212.1497	217.2437	223.1616	227.1240	230.2441	232.8809	243.0322	259.8633	278.4375	302.1094
264	224.8286	228.9133	231.5237	233.4814	235.0767	240.4907	246.7749	250.9966	254.3079	257.1196	267.9961	286.2363	306.5391	332.4492
270	230.4286	234.5691	237.2141	239.2039	240.8231	246.3107	252.6801	256.9647	260.3265	263.1940	274.2517	292.8406	313.5718	340.0708
288	247.2539	251.5649	254.3203	256.3901	258.0732	263.7861	270.4307	274.8867	278.4023	281.3906	292.9922	312.6445	334.6875	362.8125
300	258.4900	262.9166	265.7410	267.8650	269.5953	275.4547	282.2754	286.8530	290.4602	293.5364	305.4749	325.8179	348.7061	378.0762
312	269.7484	274.2854	277.1799	279.3604	281.1266	287.1394	294.1282	298.8223	302.5261	305.6777	317.9795	339.0029	362.8066	393.1992
330	286.6704	291.3634	294.3594	296.6153	298.4482	304.6820	311.9229	316.7871	320.6342	323.9072	336.7273	358.8025	383.8184	416.0449
336	292.3184	297.0659	300.1011	302.3774	304.2334	310.5293	317.8506	322.7725	326.6689	329.9810	342.9727	365.4082	390.8789	423.6094
360	314.9451	319.8999	323.0640	325.4480	327.3816	333.9624	341.6089	346.7505	350.8264	354.3091	367.9761	391.7725	418.9746	454.0430
384	337.6289	342.7852	346.0781	348.5625	350.5723	357.4219	365.3906	370.7578	375.0000	378.6328	392.9766	418.1719	447.0938	484.5000
390	343.3090	348.5161	351.8427	354.3420	356.3773	363.2922	371.3379	376.7651	381.0498	384.7156	399.2358	424.7534	454.1748	492.0703
408	360.3618	365.7158	369.1399	371.7048	373.7966	380.9063	389.1863	394.7769	399.1970	402.9822	417.9858	444.5566	475.2363	514.7813
420	371.7426	377.1964	380.6763	383.2974	385.4315	392.6669	401.0944	406.7853	411.2970	415.1550	430.5103	457.7344	489.3164	530.0244
432	383.1416	388.6853	392.2251	394.8882	397.0635	404.4331	413.0024	418.8032	423.4043	427.3330	443.0215	470.9707	503.2969	545.2734
450	400.2457	405.9380	409.5703	412.3032	414.5279	422.0810	430.8838	436.8439	441.5680	445.6055	461.7828	490.7593	524.3774	567.9932
456	405.9580	411.6914	415.3513	418.1067	420.3472	427.9731	436.8516	442.8494	447.6226	451.7139	468.0234	497.3584	531.4805	575.5664
480	428.8110	434.7290	438.5156	441.3574	443.6719	451.5381	460.7080	466.9043	471.8408	476.0742	493.0664	523.7109	559.5703	606.0938
504	451.7051	457.8036	461.6949	464.6250	467.0090	475.1147	484.5740	490.9878	496.0789	500.4624	518.0889	550.1426	587.6719	636.3984
510	457.4327	463.5727	467.4948	470.4520	472.8488	481.0199	490.5450	497.0041	502.1402	506.5448	524.3500	556.6919	594.6680	643.9746
528	474.6248	480.9009	484.9050	487.9263	490.3755	498.7222	508.4546	515.0610	520.3140	524.8418	543.1143	576.5332	615.7852	666.7031
540	486.1038	492.4567	496.5189	499.5758	502.0642	510.5347	520.4059	527.1130	532.4524	537.0337	555.6226	589.7021	629.7803	681.9873
552	497.5800	504.0234	508.1422	511.2418	513.7687	522.3516	532.3579	539.1467	544.5710	549.2373	568.1382	602.9414	643.9102	697.2773
570	514.8143	521.3809	525.5818	528.7477	531.3222	540.0719	550.2914	557.2321	562.7637	567.5299	586.9427	622.7417	664.9072	720.0146
576	520.5586	527.1768	531.4043	534.5859	537.1699	545.9766	556.2686	563.2559	568.8281	573.6445	593.1914	629.2969	671.9063	727.5938

continues

Table B-3 *Extended Erlang B with 60 Percent Retry Possibility (Continued)*

Circuits	Grade of Service													
	0.001	0.002	0.003	0.004	0.005	0.01	0.02	0.03	0.04	0.05	0.1	0.2	0.3	0.4
600	543.5669	550.3510	554.6814	557.9407	560.5957	569.6411	580.1880	587.3657	593.0969	598.0408	618.2373	655.6641	700.0488	757.9102
624	566.6045	573.5457	577.9827	581.3247	584.0479	593.3027	604.1191	611.4697	617.3730	622.4575	643.2715	682.1191	728.2031	788.3789
630	572.3602	579.3489	583.8094	587.1739	589.9136	599.2191	610.1010	617.5031	623.4247	628.5580	649.5337	688.6780	735.2051	796.1133
648	589.6527	596.7620	601.3004	604.7216	607.5000	616.9823	628.0664	635.6008	641.6323	646.8728	668.2896	708.5127	756.3691	818.8594
660	601.1865	608.3771	612.9593	616.4236	619.2435	628.8208	640.0397	647.6532	653.7762	659.0735	680.8264	721.7139	770.3760	834.0234
672	612.7324	619.9922	624.6372	628.1338	630.9844	640.6641	652.0049	659.7363	665.9297	671.2822	693.3281	734.8359	784.3828	849.1875
690	630.0504	637.4309	642.1477	645.7063	648.6017	658.4459	669.9747	677.8290	684.1461	689.5999	712.1100	754.6875	805.5615	871.9336
696	635.8264	643.2499	647.9865	651.5654	654.4753	664.3733	675.9705	683.8718	690.2014	695.7026	718.3872	761.2500	812.5664	879.5156
720	658.9380	666.5186	671.3525	675.0000	677.9773	688.0957	699.9280	708.0029	714.5068	720.1318	743.4229	787.6758	840.5859	909.8438
744	682.0719	689.8030	694.7413	698.4650	701.4961	711.8042	723.9060	732.1479	738.8005	744.5676	768.4761	814.1133	868.7871	940.3535
750	687.8586	695.6177	700.5844	704.3266	707.3708	717.7505	729.8927	738.1897	744.8730	750.6638	774.7192	820.6787	875.7935	947.9370
768	705.2227	713.0977	718.1367	721.9336	725.0156	735.5391	747.8672	756.3047	763.1016	768.9844	793.5000	840.4688	896.8125	970.8750
780	716.8071	724.7516	729.8337	733.6780	736.7963	747.4127	759.8621	768.3838	775.2393	781.2140	806.0413	853.6963	910.8252	986.0449
792	728.3969	736.4092	741.5453	745.4125	748.5667	759.2739	771.8665	780.4709	787.3835	793.4260	818.5869	866.8301	925.0313	1001.2148
810	745.7794	753.9120	759.1031	763.0334	766.2222	777.0987	789.8538	798.5797	805.6247	811.7551	837.3395	886.6296	946.0547	1023.9697
816	751.5776	759.7456	764.9626	768.9097	772.1221	783.0293	795.8540	804.6196	811.6919	817.8677	843.6167	893.2969	953.0625	1031.5547
840	774.7723	783.0908	788.3972	792.4091	795.6775	806.7902	819.8511	828.7976	836.0010	842.3071	868.6597	919.6729	981.0938	1061.8945
864	797.9897	806.4404	811.8457	815.9326	819.2549	830.5664	843.8423	852.9521	860.3086	866.7422	893.7158	946.0547	1009.3359	1092.2344
870	803.7902	812.2797	817.7092	821.8112	825.1433	836.4935	849.8483	859.0082	866.3892	872.8674	900.0018	952.6245	1016.3452	1099.8193
888	821.2130	829.8036	835.3048	839.4510	842.8250	854.3423	867.8514	877.1331	884.6396	891.1978	918.7852	972.4424	1037.3730	1122.5742
900	832.8323	841.4978	847.0322	851.2207	854.6265	866.2170	879.8676	889.2197	896.7865	903.4058	931.3110	985.6934	1051.3916	1137.7441
912	844.4517	853.1909	858.7712	862.9878	866.4250	878.1145	891.8635	901.3125	908.9663	915.6460	943.8398	998.8359	1065.6328	1152.9141
930	861.8848	870.7256	876.3734	880.6448	884.1216	895.9566	909.8776	919.4421	927.1902	933.9734	962.5818	1018.6633	1086.6650	1175.8960
936	867.7024	876.5717	882.2560	886.5406	890.0255	901.9083	915.8906	925.4883	933.2864	940.0847	968.8491	1025.2354	1093.6758	1183.7109
960	890.9619	899.9707	905.7422	910.0928	913.6377	925.6934	939.9023	949.6729	957.5977	964.5410	993.9258	1051.6406	1121.7188	1214.0625
984	914.2419	923.3859	929.2266	933.6559	937.2444	949.4963	963.9254	973.8501	981.92801	988.9849	1018.9541	1078.0518	1149.7617	1244.4141

Table B-3 *Extended Erlang B with 60 Percent Retry Possibility (Continued)*

Circuits	Grade of Service													
	0.001	0.002	0.003	0.004	0.005	0.01	0.02	0.03	0.04	0.05	0.1	0.2	0.3	0.4
990	920.0583	929.2429	935.1041	939.5453	943.1557	955.4521	969.9390	979.9091	988.0060	995.1059	1025.2277	1084.6252	1156.7725	1252.0020
1008	937.5249	946.7996	952.7366	957.2278	960.8730	973.3008	987.9434	998.0640	1006.2466	1013.4448	1044.0527	1104.4688	1178.0508	1274.7656
1020	949.1684	958.5223	964.4989	969.0125	972.6855	985.2145	999.9692	1010.1480	1018.4125	1025.6653	1056.5442	1117.6172	1192.0752	1289.9414
1032	960.8232	970.2321	976.2554	980.8063	984.5068	997.1202	1011.9855	1022.2368	1030.5828	1037.8894	1069.1001	1130.7656	1206.0996	1305.1172
1050	978.3028	987.8036	993.8919	998.4901	1002.2232	1014.9765	1030.0049	1040.3870	1048.8144	1056.2485	1087.8754	1150.6165	1227.1362	1327.8809
1056	984.1267	993.6738	999.7808	1004.3892	1008.1436	1020.9375	1036.0195	1046.4287	1054.9043	1062.3486	1094.1563	1157.1914	1234.1484	1335.4688
1080	1007.4408	1017.1143	1023.3105	1027.9742	1031.7810	1044.7668	1060.0598	1070.6396	1079.2419	1086.8225	1119.2212	1183.6230	1262.1973	1365.8203
1104	1030.7717	1040.5759	1046.8425	1051.5762	1055.4338	1068.5903	1084.1052	1094.8359	1103.5620	1111.2773	1144.2275	1210.0605	1290.5156	1396.1719
1110	1036.6109	1046.4345	1052.7351	1057.4776	1061.3562	1074.5503	1090.1157	1100.8878	1109.6613	1117.3846	1150.5139	1216.6370	1297.5293	1403.7598
1128	1054.1093	1064.0405	1070.3917	1075.1938	1079.1010	1092.4230	1108.1547	1119.0498	1127.8967	1135.7454	1169.3086	1236.3662	1318.5703	1426.5234
1140	1065.7755	1075.7689	1082.1616	1086.9974	1090.9286	1104.3402	1120.1697	1131.1285	1140.0696	1147.9669	1181.8176	1249.6582	1332.5977	1441.6992
1152	1077.4512	1087.5059	1093.9395	1098.8086	1102.7637	1116.2637	1132.2070	1143.2461	1152.2461	1160.1914	1194.3633	1262.8125	1346.6250	1456.8750
1170	1094.9648	1105.1141	1111.6035	1116.5131	1120.5121	1134.1516	1150.2548	1161.3950	1170.4999	1178.5336	1213.1323	1282.5439	1367.6660	1479.6387
1176	1100.8043	1110.9877	1117.5015	1122.4182	1126.4377	1140.1113	1156.2612	1167.4585	1176.5742	1184.6492	1219.4253	1289.2646	1374.6797	1487.2266
1200	1124.1669	1134.4666	1141.0583	1146.0480	1150.1038	1163.9465	1180.3162	1191.6504	1200.9155	1209.1187	1244.4580	1315.5762	1402.7344	1517.8711
1224	1147.5374	1157.9590	1164.6266	1169.6880	1173.7969	1187.8044	1204.3707	1215.8569	1225.2700	1233.5999	1269.5339	1342.0371	1431.0879	1548.2285
1230	1153.3784	1163.8417	1170.5232	1175.5907	1179.7197	1193.7584	1210.3871	1221.9296	1231.3513	1239.7220	1275.7947	1348.6157	1438.1030	1555.8179
1248	1170.9141	1181.4639	1188.2051	1193.3181	1197.4695	1211.6660	1228.4238	1240.0781	1249.5996	1258.0547	1294.6172	1368.3516	1459.1484	1578.8906
1260	1182.6054	1193.2086	1200.0050	1205.1480	1209.3201	1223.5858	1240.4663	1252.1942	1261.8073	1270.3052	1307.1423	1381.6626	1473.1787	1594.0723
1272	1194.3051	1204.9607	1211.7927	1216.9556	1221.1674	1235.5107	1252.5132	1264.2946	1273.9797	1282.5198	1319.6689	1394.8213	1487.2090	1609.2539
1290	1211.8355	1222.6025	1229.4919	1234.6983	1238.9401	1253.4077	1270.5524	1282.4414	1292.2243	1300.8655	1338.4222	1414.5593	1508.2544	1632.0264
1296	1217.6895	1228.4868	1235.3884	1240.6091	1244.8608	1259.3760	1276.5806	1288.5249	1298.2939	1306.9951	1344.7266	1421.1387	1515.2695	1639.6172
1320	1241.0852	1252.0020	1258.9911	1264.2682	1268.5583	1283.2416	1300.6238	1312.7289	1322.6587	1331.4807	1369.7900	1447.6172	1543.3301	1669.9805
1344	1264.4912	1275.5244	1282.5791	1287.9316	1292.2588	1307.1270	1324.7021	1336.9453	1346.9941	1355.9355	1394.8594	1473.9375	1571.3906	1700.3438
1350	1270.3423	1281.4041	1288.4903	1293.8461	1298.1926	1313.0859	1330.7190	1342.9962	1353.0899	1362.0300	1401.0864	1480.5176	1578.4058	1707.9346
1368	1287.9064	1299.0531	1306.1920	1311.5880	1315.9819	1330.9904	1348.7959	1361.1742	1371.3398	1380.3992	1419.8511	1500.4248	1599.7852	1730.7070

continues

Table B-3 *Extended Erlang B with 60 Percent Retry Possibility (Continued)*

Circuits	Grade of Service													
	0.001	0.002	0.003	0.004	0.005	0.01	0.02	0.03	0.04	0.05	0.1	0.2	0.3	0.4
1380	1299.6249	1310.8273	1317.9868	1323.4195	1327.8310	1342.9395	1360.8170	1373.2828	1383.5376	1392.6343	1432.3901	1513.5864	1613.8184	1745.8887
1392	1311.3296	1322.5869	1329.8086	1335.2567	1339.6853	1354.8721	1372.8625	1385.3943	1395.6958	1404.8716	1444.9307	1526.7480	1627.8516	1761.0703
1410	1328.8996	1340.2487	1347.5208	1353.0070	1357.4821	1372.7792	1390.9163	1403.5670	1413.9587	1423.2532	1463.7012	1546.6626	1648.9014	1783.8428
1416	1334.7598	1346.1356	1353.4169	1358.9374	1363.4099	1378.7505	1396.9431	1409.6045	1420.0620	1429.3528	1470.0161	1553.2441	1655.9180	1791.4336
1440	1358.1848	1369.6875	1377.0483	1382.6074	1387.1338	1402.6245	1421.0156	1433.8477	1444.4165	1453.8428	1495.0195	1579.5703	1683.9844	1821.7969
1464	1381.6254	1393.2305	1400.6693	1406.2987	1410.8558	1426.5154	1445.1013	1458.0579	1468.7805	1478.2969	1520.1152	1605.8965	1712.0508	1852.1602
1470	1387.4897	1399.1199	1406.5668	1412.2192	1416.7950	1432.4963	1451.1136	1464.1232	1474.8450	1484.4003	1526.3452	1612.6575	1719.0674	1859.7510
1488	1405.0697	1416.7969	1424.2896	1429.9772	1434.5977	1450.4004	1469.1775	1482.3010	1493.1313	1502.7583	1545.1714	1632.4043	1740.1172	1882.5234
1500	1416.8015	1428.5660	1436.1191	1441.8182	1446.4645	1462.3489	1481.2317	1494.4153	1505.3101	1515.0146	1557.6782	1645.5688	1754.1504	1897.7051
1512	1428.5281	1440.3636	1447.9310	1453.6758	1458.3362	1474.3015	1493.2661	1506.5321	1517.4910	1527.2271	1570.2319	1658.7334	1768.1836	1912.8867
1530	1446.1180	1458.0244	1465.6586	1471.4484	1476.1409	1492.2263	1511.3232	1524.7005	1535.7431	1545.5951	1589.0186	1678.6670	1789.2334	1935.6592
1536	1451.9766	1463.9297	1471.5703	1477.3594	1482.0703	1498.1953	1517.3438	1530.7500	1541.8594	1551.7031	1595.2969	1685.2500	1796.2500	1943.2500
1560	1475.4373	1487.4939	1495.2063	1501.0620	1505.8109	1522.1045	1541.4331	1555.0012	1566.1890	1576.1865	1620.3662	1711.5820	1824.6973	1973.6133
1584	1498.8977	1511.0793	1518.8621	1524.7595	1529.5573	1546.0049	1565.5342	1579.2144	1590.5742	1600.6772	1645.3916	1737.9141	1852.7695	2003.9766
1590	1504.7694	1516.9730	1524.7852	1530.6807	1535.4845	1551.9580	1571.5613	1585.2933	1596.6476	1606.7889	1651.7212	1744.4971	1859.7876	2011.5674
1608	1522.3689	1534.6615	1542.5131	1548.4753	1553.3090	1569.8954	1589.6224	1603.4608	1614.9192	1625.1753	1670.5181	1764.4424	1880.8418	2034.3398
1620	1534.1130	1546.4479	1554.3457	1560.3278	1565.1851	1581.8582	1601.6830	1615.6000	1627.1191	1637.4023	1682.9846	1777.6099	1894.8779	2049.5215
1632	1545.8503	1558.2393	1566.1707	1572.1846	1577.0654	1593.7998	1613.7217	1627.7168	1639.2715	1649.6309	1695.5508	1790.7773	1908.9141	2064.7031
1650	1563.4666	1575.9293	1583.9104	1589.9654	1594.8875	1611.7310	1631.7970	1645.8710	1657.5531	1667.9764	1714.3524	1810.5286	1929.9683	2087.4756
1656	1569.3289	1581.8368	1589.8343	1595.8861	1600.8135	1617.7181	1637.8066	1651.9318	1663.6311	1674.0923	1720.5864	1817.1123	1936.9863	2095.0664
1680	1592.8162	1605.4285	1613.5034	1619.6045	1624.5776	1641.6248	1661.9275	1676.1804	1687.9980	1698.6108	1745.6250	1843.6523	1965.0586	2125.4297
1704	1616.3117	1629.0262	1637.1645	1643.3397	1648.3319	1665.5446	1686.0073	1700.4119	1712.3723	1723.0847	1770.7185	1869.9902	1993.1309	2155.7930
1710	1622.1856	1634.9318	1643.0727	1649.2566	1654.2924	1671.5135	1692.0483	1706.4775	1718.4540	1729.2041	1777.0056	1876.5747	2000.1489	2163.3838
1728	1639.8018	1652.6162	1660.8428	1667.0522	1672.1016	1689.4512	1710.1230	1724.6514	1736.7539	1747.5645	1795.8164	1896.3281	2021.2031	2186.1563
1740	1651.5610	1664.4379	1672.6685	1678.9078	1683.9922	1701.4224	1722.1582	1736.7609	1748.9209	1759.8065	1808.2874	1909.4971	2035.2393	2201.7627
1752	1663.2986	1676.2375	1684.5115	1690.7805	1695.8866	1713.3702	1734.2223	1748.8989	1761.0894	1772.0500	1820.8652	1922.6660	2049.2754	2216.9473

Table B-3 *Extended Erlang B with 60 Percent Retry Possibility (Continued)*

Circuits	Grade of Service													
	0.001	0.002	0.003	0.004	0.005	0.01	0.02	0.03	0.04	0.05	0.1	0.2	0.3	0.4
1770	1680.9274	1693.9453	1702.2638	1708.5837	1713.7152	1731.2975	1752.3097	1767.0831	1779.3448	1790.4181	1839.6808	1942.6355	2070.3296	2239.7241
1776	1686.8152	1699.8501	1708.1968	1714.5110	1719.6599	1737.3018	1758.3311	1773.1274	1785.4578	1796.5415	1845.9170	1949.2207	2077.3477	2247.3164
1800	1710.3241	1723.4528	1731.8710	1738.2431	1743.4204	1761.2183	1782.4219	1797.3633	1809.8328	1820.9839	1870.9717	1975.5615	2105.8594	2277.6855
1824	1733.8381	1747.0723	1755.5610	1761.9902	1767.1948	1785.1465	1806.5215	1821.6064	1834.1865	1845.4863	1896.0293	2001.9023	2133.9375	2308.5000
1830	1739.7091	1752.9868	1761.4755	1767.9259	1773.1476	1791.1024	1812.5757	1827.6823	1840.2759	1851.6129	1902.2662	2008.4875	2140.9570	2316.0938
1848	1757.3427	1770.6945	1779.2386	1785.7101	1790.9832	1809.0582	1830.6299	1845.8569	1858.5461	1869.9382	1921.0898	2028.2432	2162.0156	2338.8750
1860	1769.1087	1782.5047	1791.0901	1797.5894	1802.8683	1821.0324	1842.6874	1858.0133	1870.7281	1882.1942	1933.6212	2041.6406	2176.0547	2354.0625
1872	1780.8794	1794.3190	1802.9312	1809.4724	1814.7568	1832.9810	1854.7471	1870.1147	1882.9116	1894.4517	1946.1533	2054.8125	2190.0938	2369.2500
1890	1798.5223	1812.0479	1820.6996	1827.2749	1832.6102	1850.9230	1872.8119	1888.2985	1901.1896	1912.7829	1964.9817	2074.5703	2211.1523	2392.0313
1896	1804.4055	1817.9451	1826.6243	1833.2060	1838.5437	1856.9147	1878.8441	1894.3799	1907.2830	1918.9131	1971.2197	2081.1563	2218.1719	2399.6250
1920	1827.9199	1841.5723	1850.3320	1856.9531	1862.3438	1880.8594	1902.9492	1918.5938	1931.6602	1943.4375	1996.2891	2107.5000	2246.2500	2430.0000
1944	1851.4512	1865.2148	1874.0248	1880.6990	1886.1273	1904.7854	1927.0624	1942.8728	1956.0432	1967.9084	2021.3613	2133.8438	2274.3281	2460.3750
1950	1857.3441	1871.1205	1879.9576	1886.6524	1892.0677	1910.7536	1933.0994	1948.9288	1962.1399	1974.0417	2027.6001	2140.4297	2281.3477	2467.9688
1968	1874.9993	1888.8428	1897.7314	1904.4580	1909.9233	1928.7217	1951.1836	1967.0991	1980.3721	1992.3838	2046.4365	2160.4277	2302.4063	2490.7500
1980	1886.7645	1900.6622	1909.5749	1916.3425	1921.8109	1940.6937	1963.2321	1979.2145	1992.5684	2004.6533	2058.9148	2173.6011	2316.4453	2505.9375
1992	1898.5338	1912.4854	1921.4368	1928.2150	1933.7318	1952.6682	1975.3129	1991.3617	2004.7661	2016.8635	2071.5146	2186.7744	2330.4844	2521.1250
2010	1916.1953	1930.2116	1939.2133	1946.0220	1951.5733	1970.6195	1993.3768	2009.5399	2023.0655	2035.2109	2090.2332	2206.5344	2351.5430	2543.9063
2016	1922.0845	1936.1118	1945.1404	1951.9695	1957.5220	1976.5942	1999.4194	2015.6001	2029.1353	2041.3477	2096.4727	2213.1211	2358.5625	2551.5000
2040	1945.6201	1959.7678	1968.8571	1975.7208	1981.3239	2000.5298	2023.5333	2039.8755	2053.5095	2065.8362	2121.5552	2239.4678	2386.6406	2581.8750
2064	1969.1711	1983.4065	1992.5713	1999.5000	2005.1217	2024.4749	2047.6545	2064.1260	2077.8574	2090.3291	2146.6406	2265.8145	2414.7188	2612.2500
2070	1975.0692	1989.3301	1998.4900	2005.4388	2011.0611	2030.4547	2053.6702	2070.1895	2083.9609	2096.4688	2152.8809	2272.6538	2421.7383	2619.8438
2088	1992.7375	2007.0747	2016.2823	2023.2598	2028.9309	2048.4294	2071.7512	2088.3823	2102.2734	2114.8264	2171.7290	2292.4160	2442.7969	2642.6250
2100	2004.5105	2018.8980	2028.1425	2035.1440	2040.8318	2060.3943	2083.8181	2100.4807	2114.4196	2127.0447	2184.2102	2305.5908	2456.8359	2657.8125
2112	2016.2871	2030.7246	2040.0059	2047.0313	2052.7354	2072.3613	2095.8867	2112.6123	2126.6309	2139.3281	2196.8203	2318.7656	2470.8750	2673.0000
2130	2033.9589	2048.4707	2057.7985	2064.8513	2070.5878	2090.3160	2113.9769	2130.8125	2144.8856	2157.6910	2215.5432	2338.5278	2491.9336	2695.7813
2136	2039.8513	2054.3877	2063.7255	2070.7982	2076.5508	2096.3020	2119.9969	2136.8474	2150.9927	2163.7690	2221.7842	2345.1152	2498.9531	2703.3750

continues

Table B-3 *Extended Erlang B with 60 Percent Retry Possibility (Continued)*

Circuits	Grade of Service													
	0.001	0.002	0.003	0.004	0.005	0.01	0.02	0.03	0.04	0.05	0.1	0.2	0.3	0.4
2160	2063.4137	2078.0475	2087.4573	2094.5764	2100.3442	2120.2515	2144.1138	2161.1206	2175.3589	2188.2788	2246.8799	2371.4648	2527.5586	2733.7500
2184	2086.9904	2101.7201	2111.1844	2118.3494	2124.1813	2144.2097	2168.2705	2185.3663	2199.7295	2212.7930	2271.9785	2397.8145	2555.6426	2764.1250
2190	2092.8742	2107.6277	2117.1181	2124.2860	2130.1172	2150.2007	2174.2941	2191.4369	2205.8395	2218.8721	2278.2202	2404.4019	2562.6636	2771.7188
2208	2110.5645	2125.3718	2134.9065	2142.1333	2147.9956	2168.1768	2192.3672	2209.6172	2224.1045	2237.2441	2297.0801	2424.4336	2583.7266	2794.5000
2220	2122.3398	2137.2107	2146.7633	2154.0125	2159.8897	2180.1297	2204.4177	2221.7615	2236.3275	2249.4708	2309.5642	2437.6099	2597.7686	2809.6875
2232	2134.1354	2149.0356	2158.6399	2165.8942	2171.8032	2192.1185	2216.5038	2233.8732	2248.4839	2261.7664	2322.0483	2450.7861	2611.8105	2824.8750
2250	2151.8097	2166.7957	2176.4259	2183.7387	2189.6782	2210.0716	2234.5848	2252.0599	2266.7542	2280.1437	2340.9119	2470.5505	2632.8735	2847.6563
2256	2157.7028	2172.7115	2182.3674	2189.6825	2195.6206	2216.0684	2240.6125	2258.1343	2272.8677	2286.2241	2347.1543	2477.1387	2639.8945	2855.2500
2280	2181.2833	2196.3995	2206.1060	2213.4641	2219.4305	2240.0262	2264.7620	2282.3657	2297.2559	2310.7544	2372.2632	2503.4912	2667.9785	2885.6250
2304	2204.8594	2220.0645	2229.8555	2237.2383	2243.2676	2263.9922	2288.8828	2306.6367	2321.6133	2335.2188	2397.2344	2529.8438	2696.0625	2916.0000
2310	2210.7598	2225.9869	2235.7681	2243.2054	2249.2328	2269.9585	2294.9139	2312.7141	2327.6944	2341.3353	2403.5477	2536.4319	2703.0835	2923.5938
2328	2228.4483	2243.7407	2253.5804	2261.0402	2267.0790	2287.9307	2313.0095	2330.9128	2345.9744	2359.6860	2422.3477	2556.1963	2724.1465	2946.3750
2340	2240.2386	2255.5920	2265.4468	2272.9271	2279.0149	2299.9384	2325.0751	2343.0350	2358.2098	2371.9208	2434.8340	2569.3726	2738.1885	2961.5625
2352	2252.0500	2267.4283	2277.3336	2284.8164	2290.9175	2311.9124	2337.1421	2355.1582	2370.3750	2384.1921	2447.4639	2582.8359	2752.2305	2976.7500
2370	2269.7372	2285.1970	2295.1419	2302.6639	2308.7755	2329.8587	2355.2454	2373.3632	2388.6603	2402.5470	2466.1945	2602.6025	2773.2935	2999.5313
2376	2275.6284	2291.1092	2301.0612	2308.6203	2314.7474	2335.8658	2361.2443	2379.4080	2394.7438	2408.7019	2472.4380	2609.1914	2780.3145	3007.1250
2400	2299.2188	2314.8010	2324.8169	2332.3975	2338.5864	2359.8267	2385.3882	2403.6621	2419.1162	2433.1787	2497.5586	2635.5469	2808.3984	3037.5000
2424	2322.8212	2338.4854	2348.5644	2356.2023	2362.4161	2383.7948	2409.5010	2427.9207	2443.5293	2457.6584	2522.5342	2661.9023	2836.4824	3067.8750
2430	2328.7191	2344.4220	2354.5074	2362.1457	2368.3749	2389.7694	2415.5392	2434.0045	2449.5776	2463.8159	2528.9264	2668.4912	2843.5034	3075.4688
2448	2346.4171	2362.1803	2372.3218	2379.9979	2386.2546	2407.7703	2433.6563	2452.1836	2467.8721	2482.1411	2547.6592	2688.2578	2864.5664	3098.2500
2460	2358.2195	2374.0224	2384.1948	2391.9086	2398.1584	2419.7232	2445.7361	2464.3542	2480.0446	2494.3835	2560.1477	2701.4355	2878.6084	3113.4375
2472	2370.0247	2385.8670	2396.0702	2403.8027	2410.0642	2431.7153	2457.7797	2476.4509	2492.2555	2506.6267	2572.7871	2714.6133	2892.6504	3128.6250
2490	2387.7191	2403.6388	2413.8972	2421.6291	2427.9552	2449.6880	2475.8661	2494.6353	2510.5170	2525.0308	2591.5210	2734.3799	2913.7134	3151.4063
2496	2393.6250	2409.5640	2419.8281	2427.5786	2433.9199	2455.6670	2481.9082	2500.7227	2516.6426	2531.1152	2597.7656	2740.9688	2920.7344	3159.0000
2520	2417.2366	2433.2712	2443.5956	2451.3821	2457.7460	2479.6252	2506.0419	2524.9988	2540.9949	2555.6067	2622.8979	2767.6318	2948.8184	3189.3750
2544	2440.8402	2456.9692	2467.3337	2475.1750	2481.5801	2503.6095	2530.1807	2549.2405	2565.3889	2580.1011	2647.8779	2793.9902	2976.9023	3219.7500

Table B-3 *Extended Erlang B with 60 Percent Retry Possibility (Continued)*

Circuits	Grade of Service													
	0.001	0.002	0.003	0.004	0.005	0.01	0.02	0.03	0.04	0.05	0.1	0.2	0.3	0.4
2550	2446.7525	2462.8807	2473.2697	2481.1295	2487.5496	2509.6115	2536.2259	2555.2917	2571.4783	2586.2640	2654.1229	2800.5798	2983.9233	3227.3438
2568	2464.4548	2480.6576	2491.1003	2498.9960	2505.4222	2527.5615	2554.3246	2573.4858	2589.7866	2604.5984	2673.0146	2820.3486	3004.9863	3250.1250
2580	2476.2662	2492.5250	2502.9968	2510.8900	2517.3660	2539.5694	2566.3788	2585.6296	2601.9672	2616.8481	2685.5054	2833.5278	3019.0283	3265.3125
2592	2488.0605	2504.3752	2514.8760	2522.7861	2529.2725	2551.5396	2578.4341	2597.7744	2614.1484	2629.0986	2697.9961	2846.7070	3033.0703	3280.5000
2610	2505.7768	2522.1451	2532.6988	2540.6639	2547.1555	2569.5374	2596.5390	2615.9738	2632.4615	2647.4757	2716.8915	2866.4758	3054.1333	3303.2813
2616	2511.6769	2528.0828	2538.6409	2546.6043	2553.1307	2575.5242	2602.5879	2622.0275	2638.5132	2653.6018	2723.1372	2873.0654	3061.1543	3310.8750
2640	2535.3040	2551.7798	2562.3944	2570.4108	2576.9568	2599.4952	2626.7065	2646.2842	2662.2809	2678.1079	2748.1201	2899.4238	3089.2383	3341.2500
2664	2558.9213	2575.5062	2586.1564	2594.2253	2600.8308	2623.4725	2650.8702	2670.5852	2687.2921	2702.6169	2773.2656	2925.7822	3117.9727	3371.6250
2670	2564.8272	2581.4291	2592.1033	2600.1700	2606.7700	2629.4627	2656.8814	2676.6408	2693.3853	2708.7039	2779.5117	2932.3718	3124.9951	3379.2188
2688	2582.5488	2599.2012	2609.9268	2618.0273	2624.6719	2647.4355	2674.9980	2694.8086	2711.6660	2727.0469	2798.2500	2952.1406	3146.0625	3402.0000
2700	2594.3665	2611.0519	2621.8048	2629.9416	2636.5952	2659.4193	2687.0636	2706.9626	2723.8953	2739.3036	2810.8246	2965.6494	3160.1074	3417.1875
2712	2606.1660	2622.9256	2633.7056	2641.8578	2648.5203	2671.4044	2699.1302	2719.1177	2736.0842	2751.5610	2823.3999	2978.8301	3174.1523	3432.3750
2730	2623.9009	2640.7093	2651.5400	2659.7255	2666.4114	2689.4057	2717.2531	2737.2899	2754.3274	2769.9069	2842.1393	2998.6011	3195.2197	3455.1563
2736	2629.7930	2646.6383	2657.4719	2665.6754	2672.3760	2695.4000	2723.2668	2743.3477	2760.4644	2776.0781	2848.3857	3005.1914	3202.2422	3462.7500
2760	2653.4299	2670.3598	2681.2463	2689.5007	2696.2180	2719.3597	2747.4078	2767.6227	2784.8474	2800.5560	2873.5400	3031.5527	3230.3320	3493.1250
2784	2677.0554	2694.0688	2705.0288	2713.3125	2720.0669	2743.3462	2771.5532	2791.9014	2809.1909	2825.0361	2898.5273	3057.9141	3258.4219	3523.5000
2790	2682.9739	2700.0027	2710.9650	2719.2666	2726.0568	2749.3437	2777.5690	2797.9610	2815.2878	2831.1671	2904.7742	3064.5044	3265.4443	3531.0938
2808	2700.6905	2717.7863	2728.7979	2737.1316	2743.9442	2767.3385	2795.7030	2816.1409	2833.5795	2849.5613	2923.6860	3084.2754	3286.5117	3553.8750
2820	2712.5116	2729.6590	2740.6961	2749.0439	2755.8641	2779.3369	2807.7795	2828.2617	2845.7748	2861.8250	2936.1804	3097.4561	3300.5566	3569.0625
2832	2724.3351	2741.5122	2752.5747	2760.9580	2767.7856	2791.3367	2819.8140	2840.4265	2857.9709	2874.0029	2948.6748	3110.6367	3314.6016	3584.2500
2850	2742.0639	2759.3067	2770.4178	2778.8109	2785.6819	2809.2957	2837.9539	2858.6105	2876.2665	2892.4438	2967.4164	3130.4077	3335.6689	3607.0313
2856	2747.9674	2765.2465	2776.3592	2784.7700	2791.6555	2815.2971	2843.9722	2864.7158	2882.3218	2898.5332	2973.7507	3136.9980	3342.6914	3614.6250
2880	2771.6089	2788.9673	2800.1514	2808.5889	2815.5103	2839.2847	2868.1348	2888.9648	2906.7188	2923.0225	2998.8281	3163.3594	3370.7813	3645.0000
2904	2795.2595	2812.6961	2823.9291	2832.4369	2839.3716	2863.2777	2892.2574	2913.2168	2931.1187	2947.5139	3023.8184	3189.7207	3398.8711	3675.3750
2910	2801.1681	2818.6185	2829.8746	2838.3778	2845.3491	2869.2824	2898.2776	2919.2802	2937.1747	2953.6038	3030.1547	3196.3110	3405.8936	3682.9688
2928	2818.8970	2836.4106	2847.7141	2856.2476	2863.2396	2887.2539	2916.3838	2937.4717	2955.5215	2972.0076	3048.9873	3216.4395	3426.9609	3705.7500

continues

Table B-3 *Extended Erlang B with 60 Percent Retry Possibility (Continued)*

Circuits	Grade of Service													
	0.001	0.002	0.003	0.004	0.005	0.01	0.02	0.03	0.04	0.05	0.1	0.2	0.3	0.4
2940	2830.7190	2848.2820	2859.6094	2868.1778	2875.1761	2899.2439	2928.4708	2949.6002	2967.6791	2984.2328	3061.4832	3229.6216	3441.0059	3720.9375
2952	2842.5432	2860.1554	2871.5065	2880.0873	2887.0917	2911.2352	2940.5588	2961.7745	2979.8822	2996.5034	3073.9790	3242.8037	3455.0508	3736.1250
2970	2860.2837	2877.9579	2889.3329	2897.9434	2904.9905	2929.2133	2958.6703	2979.9701	2998.1882	3014.8654	3092.8134	3262.5769	3476.1182	3758.9063
2976	2866.1982	2883.8855	2895.2834	2903.9114	2910.9727	2935.2217	2964.6929	2986.0356	3004.2451	3021.0015	3099.0615	3269.1680	3483.1406	3766.5000
3000	2889.8392	2907.6233	2919.0674	2927.7420	2934.8145	2959.2133	2988.8306	3010.2997	3028.6560	3045.5017	3124.1455	3295.5322	3511.2305	3796.8750
3024	2913.4885	2931.3457	2942.8813	2951.5792	2958.7083	2983.2100	3012.9719	3034.5667	3053.0237	3069.9580	3149.1387	3321.8965	3539.3203	3827.2500
3030	2919.4080	2937.3006	2948.8129	2957.5280	2964.6712	2989.1984	3018.9963	3040.6339	3059.1275	3076.1417	3155.3870	3328.4875	3546.3428	3834.8438
3048	2937.1463	2955.0987	2966.6561	2975.3998	2982.5621	3007.1885	3037.1169	3058.8365	3077.3936	3094.5088	3174.3179	3348.2607	3567.4102	3857.6250
3060	2948.9667	2966.9664	2978.5693	2987.3241	2994.4913	3019.1913	3049.2142	3070.9726	3089.6027	3106.6919	3186.8152	3361.4429	3581.4551	3872.8125
3072	2960.7891	2978.8359	2990.4609	2999.2500	3006.4219	3031.1719	3061.2656	3083.1094	3101.8125	3118.9688	3199.3125	3374.6250	3595.5000	3888.0000
3090	2978.5382	2996.6437	3008.2896	3017.1066	3024.3205	3049.1684	3079.3913	3101.3159	3120.0815	3137.3383	3218.0585	3394.3982	3616.5674	3910.7813
3096	2984.4635	3002.5805	3014.2491	3023.0832	3030.3111	3055.1836	3085.4180	3107.3851	3126.1871	3143.4774	3224.4016	3400.9893	3623.5898	3918.3750
3120	3008.1226	3026.3086	3038.0438	3046.9226	3054.1827	3079.1528	3109.5740	3131.6162	3150.5640	3167.9883	3249.4922	3427.3535	3651.6797	3948.7500
3144	3031.7657	3050.0676	3061.8452	3070.7443	3078.0363	3103.1744	3133.7336	3155.8975	3174.9430	3192.4534	3274.4883	3453.7178	3679.7695	3979.8926
3150	3037.6957	3055.9845	3067.8085	3076.7246	3084.0065	3109.1446	3139.7621	3161.9682	3181.0501	3198.5939	3280.7373	3460.3088	3686.7920	3987.4878
3168	3055.4407	3073.8098	3085.6531	3094.5959	3101.9194	3127.1528	3157.8486	3180.1816	3199.3242	3216.9683	3299.5811	3480.0820	3707.8594	4010.2734
3180	3067.2812	3085.6714	3097.5595	3106.5120	3113.8632	3139.1437	3169.9557	3192.3248	3211.5399	3229.2023	3312.1765	3493.6523	3721.9043	4025.4639
3192	3079.0994	3097.5590	3109.4432	3118.4539	3125.8085	3151.1356	3182.0153	3204.4688	3223.7076	3241.4854	3324.6753	3506.8359	3735.9492	4040.6543
3210	3096.8546	3115.3693	3127.2961	3136.3330	3143.7046	3169.1501	3200.1059	3222.6370	3242.0334	3259.8624	3343.4235	3526.6113	3757.0166	4063.4399
3216	3102.7657	3121.2905	3133.2396	3142.2935	3149.6788	3175.1228	3206.1855	3228.7588	3248.0933	3265.9556	3349.6729	3533.2031	3764.0391	4071.0352
3240	3126.4398	3145.0534	3157.0422	3166.1389	3173.5547	3199.1144	3230.3101	3253.0023	3272.4811	3290.4272	3374.7693	3559.5703	3792.1289	4101.4160
3264	3150.0967	3168.7983	3180.8511	3189.9653	3197.4360	3223.1104	3254.4375	3277.2480	3296.8711	3314.9502	3399.8672	3585.9375	3820.2188	4131.7969
3270	3156.0120	3174.7481	3186.7980	3195.9290	3203.3885	3229.1350	3260.5197	3283.3722	3302.9315	3321.0938	3406.1169	3592.5293	3827.2412	4139.3921
3288	3173.7859	3192.5499	3204.6661	3213.8223	3221.3229	3247.1107	3278.6180	3301.5461	3321.2633	3339.4753	3424.8662	3612.3047	3848.3086	4162.1777
3300	3185.6209	3204.4281	3216.5634	3225.7278	3233.2558	3259.1125	3290.6845	3313.6963	3333.4351	3351.6632	3437.3657	3625.4883	3862.3535	4177.3682
3312	3197.4576	3216.3080	3228.4622	3237.6599	3245.1899	3271.1155	3302.7517	3325.8472	3345.6577	3363.9521	3449.9663	3638.6719	3876.3984	4192.5586

Table B-3 *Extended Erlang B with 60 Percent Retry Possibility (Continued)*

Circuits	Grade of Service													
	0.001	0.002	0.003	0.004	0.005	0.01	0.02	0.03	0.04	0.05	0.1	0.2	0.3	0.4
3330	3215.1908	3234.1182	3246.3130	3255.5608	3263.1063	3289.1219	3320.8539	3344.0240	3363.9423	3382.3361	3468.8177	3658.4473	3897.4658	4215.3442
3336	3221.1112	3240.0727	3252.2640	3261.5030	3269.0621	3295.1246	3326.8883	3350.1002	3370.0034	3388.4304	3475.0679	3665.0391	3904.4883	4222.9395
3360	3244.7974	3263.8184	3276.0718	3285.3516	3292.9395	3319.1382	3351.0791	3374.3555	3394.4019	3412.9102	3500.0684	3691.4063	3932.5781	4253.3203
3384	3268.4650	3287.5703	3299.8854	3309.2056	3316.8219	3343.1045	3375.2219	3398.6646	3418.8025	3437.3914	3525.1721	3717.7734	3960.6680	4284.5273
3390	3274.3895	3293.5286	3305.8397	3315.1765	3322.8062	3349.1354	3381.2581	3404.6906	3424.8642	3443.5378	3531.4224	3724.3652	3967.6904	4292.1240
3408	3292.1396	3311.3284	3323.7048	3333.0652	3340.7095	3367.1265	3399.3677	3422.9246	3443.1533	3461.8740	3550.2773	3744.1406	3988.7578	4314.9141
3420	3303.9926	3323.2228	3335.6168	3344.9840	3352.6552	3379.1391	3411.4417	3435.0293	3455.3815	3474.1681	3562.7783	3757.3242	4002.8027	4330.1074
3432	3315.8212	3335.0927	3347.5302	3356.9041	3364.6022	3391.1005	3423.5164	3447.1868	3467.5580	3486.4105	3575.2793	3770.5078	4016.8477	4345.3008
3450	3333.5804	3352.9266	3365.3767	3374.7997	3382.5119	3409.1228	3441.6298	3465.3717	3485.8498	3504.7485	3594.0308	3790.2832	4037.9150	4368.0908
3456	3339.5098	3358.8633	3371.3350	3380.7744	3388.5000	3415.1309	3447.6680	3471.4512	3491.9648	3510.9492	3600.2813	3796.8750	4044.9375	4375.6875
3480	3363.2053	3382.6135	3395.1453	3404.6237	3412.3764	3439.1125	3471.8225	3495.7178	3516.3208	3535.4370	3625.4956	3823.2422	4073.0273	4406.0742
3504	3386.8810	3406.3696	3418.9611	3428.4781	3436.2576	3463.1246	3495.9800	3520.0400	3540.6782	3559.9263	3650.0371	3850.0371	4101.9727	4436.4609
3510	3392.8143	3412.3096	3424.9226	3434.4292	3442.2487	3469.1350	3502.0198	3526.0675	3546.8481	3566.0220	3656.7499	3856.6296	4108.9966	4444.0576
3528	3410.5633	3430.1585	3442.7823	3452.3377	3460.1704	3487.1407	3520.1404	3544.2576	3565.0909	3584.4170	3675.5024	3876.4072	4130.0684	4466.8477
3540	3422.4069	3442.0418	3454.6815	3464.2694	3472.1017	3499.1368	3532.2217	3556.4209	3577.2711	3596.6089	3688.0042	3889.5923	4144.1162	4482.0410
3552	3434.2522	3453.9265	3466.5820	3476.1753	3484.0342	3511.1338	3544.3037	3568.5850	3589.5059	3608.9092	3700.6143	3902.7773	4158.1641	4497.2344
3570	3452.0096	3471.7291	3484.4760	3494.0907	3501.9621	3529.1446	3562.3737	3586.7780	3607.8049	3627.3065	3719.4763	3922.5549	4179.2358	4520.0244
3576	3457.9477	3477.6731	3490.4141	3500.0449	3507.9296	3535.1305	3568.4154	3592.8062	3613.8684	3633.4028	3725.7275	3929.1475	4186.2598	4527.6211
3600	3481.6223	3501.4526	3514.2517	3523.9197	3531.8298	3559.1309	3592.5842	3617.1387	3638.2324	3657.8979	3750.7324	3955.5176	4214.3555	4558.0078
3624	3505.3308	3525.2104	3538.0671	3547.7719	3555.7072	3583.1349	3616.7560	3641.3635	3662.6532	3682.3945	3775.7373	3981.8877	4242.4512	4588.3945
3630	3511.2451	3531.1576	3544.0079	3553.7288	3561.7049	3589.1503	3622.7994	3647.4477	3668.7726	3688.4912	3782.0993	3988.4802	4249.4751	4595.9912
3648	3529.0181	3549.0015	3561.8877	3571.6289	3579.6167	3607.1426	3640.9307	3665.6455	3687.0762	3706.8926	3800.9648	4008.2578	4270.5469	4618.7813
3660	3540.8640	3560.8713	3573.7999	3583.5452	3591.5593	3619.1757	3652.9633	3677.8152	3699.2047	3719.0863	3813.4680	4021.4429	4284.5947	4633.9746
3672	3552.7115	3572.7704	3585.7134	3595.4907	3603.5030	3631.1539	3665.0522	3689.9297	3711.4453	3731.3921	3825.9712	4034.6279	4298.6426	4649.1680
3690	3570.4928	3590.5936	3603.5719	3613.3690	3621.4206	3649.1789	3683.1590	3708.1302	3729.7513	3749.7958	3844.7260	4054.4055	4319.7144	4671.9580
3696	3576.4113	3596.5448	3609.5442	3619.3572	3627.3937	3655.1689	3689.2042	3714.2161	3735.8159	3755.8931	3850.9775	4060.9980	4326.7383	4679.5547

continues

Table B-3 *Extended Erlang B with 60 Percent Retry Possibility (Continued)*

Circuits	Grade of Service													
	0.001	0.002	0.003	0.004	0.005	0.01	0.02	0.03	0.04	0.05	0.1	0.2	0.3	0.4
3720	3600.1172	3620.3247	3633.3517	3643.2001	3651.2888	3679.1876	3713.3588	3738.5046	3760.1880	3780.3955	3875.9839	4087.3682	4354.8340	4709.9414
3744	3623.8008	3644.0815	3657.1641	3667.0759	3675.1882	3703.1814	3737.4873	3762.7383	3784.5615	3804.8994	3901.2188	4113.7383	4382.9297	4740.3281
3750	3629.7226	3650.0359	3663.1393	3673.0385	3681.1638	3709.2018	3743.5341	3768.8255	3790.6837	3810.9970	3907.4707	4120.3308	4389.9536	4747.9248
3768	3647.4902	3667.8723	3681.0099	3690.9565	3699.0921	3727.1785	3761.6755	3787.0309	3808.9940	3829.4048	3926.2266	4140.1084	4411.0254	4770.7148
3780	3659.3660	3679.7552	3692.9059	3702.8842	3711.0457	3739.2215	3773.7708	3799.1492	3821.1823	3841.6003	3938.7305	4153.2935	4425.0732	4785.9082
3792	3671.2145	3691.6395	3704.8319	3714.8130	3722.9714	3751.2078	3785.8088	3811.3257	3833.3708	3853.9116	3951.2344	4166.4785	4439.1211	4801.1016
3810	3688.9899	3709.4829	3722.7088	3732.7082	3740.9054	3769.2176	3803.9539	3829.5337	3851.6254	3872.2055	3969.9902	4186.2561	4460.1929	4823.8916
3816	3694.9158	3715.4119	3728.6587	3738.6738	3746.8839	3775.2116	3810.0026	3835.5645	3857.7491	3878.3617	3976.2422	4192.8486	4467.2168	4831.4883
3840	3718.6084	3739.1895	3752.4902	3762.5391	3770.8008	3799.2188	3834.1406	3859.8633	3882.1875	3902.8711	4001.4844	4219.2188	4495.3125	4861.8750
3864	3742.3066	3762.9721	3776.3265	3786.4087	3794.6926	3823.2587	3858.2809	3884.1643	3906.5691	3927.3230	4026.4937	4245.5889	4523.4082	4892.2617
3870	3748.2358	3768.9333	3782.2790	3792.3768	3800.6735	3829.2545	3864.3311	3890.1956	3912.6352	3933.4804	4032.7460	4252.6538	4530.4321	4899.8584
3888	3766.0254	3786.7599	3800.1676	3810.2827	3818.5884	3847.2429	3882.4530	3908.4082	3930.9521	3951.8350	4051.5029	4272.4336	4551.5039	4922.6484
3900	3777.8870	3798.6557	3812.0750	3822.2214	3830.5527	3859.2361	3894.5251	3920.5902	3943.0847	3964.1510	4064.0076	4285.6201	4565.5518	4937.8418
3912	3789.7202	3810.5528	3823.9836	3834.1611	3842.4882	3871.2599	3906.6277	3932.7133	3955.3367	3976.3484	4076.5122	4298.8066	4579.5996	4953.0352
3930	3807.5173	3828.3858	3841.8484	3852.0428	3860.4082	3889.2824	3924.7229	3950.9285	3973.5960	3994.7644	4095.3891	4318.5864	4600.6714	4975.8252
3936	3813.4354	3834.3208	3847.8340	3858.0439	3866.3921	3895.2803	3930.7749	3956.9604	3979.7227	4000.8633	4101.7617	4325.1797	4607.6953	4983.4219
3960	3837.1564	3858.1238	3871.6589	3881.9009	3890.3000	3919.2737	3954.9243	3981.2695	4004.1101	4025.3796	4126.7725	4351.5527	4635.7910	5013.8086
3984	3860.8678	3881.9015	3895.4883	3905.7620	3914.2119	3943.3004	3979.0759	4005.5200	4028.4990	4049.8975	4151.7832	4377.9258	4663.8867	5044.1953
3990	3866.7737	3887.8391	3901.4463	3911.7355	3920.1677	3949.3000	3985.1294	4011.6133	4034.5660	4055.9967	4158.0359	4384.5190	4670.9106	5051.7920
4008	3884.5541	3905.6840	3919.3220	3929.6576	3938.0973	3967.3304	4003.2297	4029.8331	4052.8894	4074.3556	4176.7939	4404.2988	4691.9824	5074.5820
4020	3896.4299	3917.5923	3931.2405	3941.5764	3950.0720	3979.3314	4015.3381	4041.9598	4065.0238	4086.6156	4189.2993	4417.4854	4706.0303	5089.7754
4032	3908.2764	3929.4712	3943.1602	3953.5269	3962.0171	3991.3330	4027.3857	4054.0869	4077.2813	4098.8145	4201.9277	4430.6719	4720.0781	5104.9688
4050	3926.0639	3947.3225	3961.0416	3971.4237	3979.9210	4009.3369	4045.5505	4072.3091	4095.5452	4117.2363	4220.8099	4450.4517	4741.1499	5127.7588
4056	3932.0041	3953.2632	3967.0027	3977.4001	3985.9100	4015.3385	4051.5439	4078.4041	4101.6746	4123.3359	4227.0630	4457.0449	4748.1738	5135.3555
4080	3955.7062	3977.0599	3990.8496	4001.2775	4009.8376	4039.3469	4075.7043	4102.6611	4126.0693	4147.8589	4252.0752	4483.4180	4776.2695	5165.7422
4104	3979.4134	4000.8615	4014.7009	4025.1588	4033.7380	4063.3583	4099.8669	4126.9197	4150.4656	4172.3833	4277.0874	4509.7910	4804.3652	5196.1289

Table B-3 *Extended Erlang B with 60 Percent Retry Possibility (Continued)*

Circuits	Grade of Service													
	0.001	0.002	0.003	0.004	0.005	0.01	0.02	0.03	0.04	0.05	0.1	0.2	0.3	0.4
4110	3985.3567	4006.8047	4020.6331	4031.1063	4039.6980	4069.3616	4105.9236	4133.0159	4156.5335	4178.4833	4283.3405	4516.3843	4811.3892	5203.7256
4128	4003.1572	4024.6362	4038.5251	4049.0127	4057.6421	4087.4041	4124.0317	4151.1797	4174.8003	4196.8462	4302.0996	4536.1641	4832.4609	5226.5156
4140	4015.0154	4036.5253	4050.4546	4060.9726	4069.5955	4099.4124	4136.1465	4163.3734	4186.9995	4209.1095	4314.7321	4549.3506	4846.5088	5241.7090
4152	4026.8749	4048.4471	4062.3534	4072.9019	4081.5498	4111.3898	4148.1987	4175.5045	4199.1991	4221.3098	4327.2385	4562.5371	4860.5566	5256.9023
4170	4044.6506	4066.2845	4080.2511	4090.8135	4099.4989	4129.4046	4166.3095	4193.6700	4217.4673	4239.7375	4346.1255	4582.3169	4881.6284	5279.6924
4176	4050.5977	4072.2308	4086.2175	4096.7952	4105.4612	4135.4099	4172.3679	4199.7678	4223.5994	4245.8379	4352.3789	4588.9102	4888.6523	5287.2891
4200	4074.2935	4096.0190	4110.0540	4120.6604	4129.3762	4159.4330	4196.5393	4224.0326	4248.0011	4270.3674	4377.3926	4615.2832	4916.7480	5317.6758
4224	4098.0264	4119.8115	4133.8945	4144.5293	4153.2949	4183.4590	4220.7129	4248.2988	4272.3398	4294.8984	4402.4063	4641.6563	4944.8438	5348.0625
4230	4103.9442	4125.7603	4139.8634	4150.5132	4159.2590	4189.4659	4226.7082	4254.3979	4278.4731	4300.9991	4408.6597	4648.2495	4951.8677	5355.6592
4248	4121.7643	4143.6085	4157.7391	4168.4343	4177.1849	4207.4879	4244.8563	4272.5665	4296.7441	4319.3013	4427.4199	4668.0293	4972.9395	5378.4492
4260	4133.6028	4155.5086	4169.6466	4180.3720	4189.1473	4219.5035	4256.9449	4284.7009	4308.9468	4331.6327	4440.0568	4681.2158	4986.9873	5393.6426
4272	4145.4749	4167.4098	4181.5876	4192.3107	4201.1107	4231.5198	4269.0015	4296.9009	4321.1499	4343.8345	4452.5640	4694.4023	5001.0352	5408.8359
4290	4163.2690	4185.2637	4199.4685	4210.2040	4219.0411	4249.5129	4287.1198	4315.0713	4339.4879	4362.2681	4471.4557	4714.1821	5022.1069	5431.6260
4296	4169.1901	4191.2155	4205.4402	4216.1907	4225.0074	4255.5218	4293.1813	4321.1719	4345.5571	4368.3691	4477.7095	4720.7754	5029.1309	5439.2227
4320	4192.9266	4215.0256	4229.2969	4240.0745	4248.9404	4279.5264	4317.3633	4345.4443	4369.9658	4392.8394	4502.7246	4747.1484	5057.2266	5469.6094
4344	4216.6681	4238.8070	4253.1244	4263.9619	4272.8439	4303.5667	4341.4812	4369.7183	4394.3097	4417.3103	4527.7397	4773.5215	5085.3223	5499.9961
4350	4222.5918	4244.7613	4259.0984	4269.9177	4278.8120	4309.5772	4347.5441	4375.7538	4400.4456	4423.4116	4533.3935	4780.1147	5092.3462	5507.5928
4368	4240.3978	4262.6257	4276.9889	4287.8529	4296.7507	4327.6099	4365.6672	4393.9937	4418.7209	4441.8486	4552.7549	4800.4277	5113.4180	5530.3828
4380	4252.2478	4274.5033	4288.9059	4299.7998	4308.7221	4339.5992	4377.7277	4406.1319	4430.9271	4454.0515	4565.2625	4813.6157	5127.4658	5545.5762
4392	4264.0988	4286.4153	4300.8239	4311.7141	4320.6943	4351.5890	4389.8555	4418.2705	4443.0667	4466.3884	4577.9041	4826.8037	5141.5137	5560.7695
4410	4281.9111	4304.2518	4318.7194	4329.6542	4338.6040	4369.6252	4407.9813	4436.4455	4461.4105	4484.6933	4596.8005	4846.5857	5162.5854	5583.5596
4416	4287.8379	4310.2090	4324.6626	4335.6123	4344.5742	4375.6377	4413.9785	4442.5488	4467.4805	4490.7949	4603.0547	4853.1797	5169.6094	5591.1563
4440	4311.5817	4334.0067	4348.5388	4359.5142	4368.5248	4399.6555	4438.1708	4466.8286	4491.8958	4515.3369	4628.0713	4879.5557	5197.7051	5621.5430
4464	4335.2963	4357.8083	4372.3850	4383.3856	4392.4109	4423.6758	4462.2971	4491.1099	4516.3125	4539.8804	4653.0879	4905.9316	5225.8008	5651.9297
4470	4341.2256	4363.7679	4378.3301	4389.3455	4398.3829	4429.6898	4468.3630	4497.1463	4522.3828	4545.9824	4659.3420	4912.5256	5232.8247	5659.5264
4488	4359.0494	4381.6141	4396.2349	4407.2604	4416.3342	4447.6987	4486.4934	4515.3926	4540.6622	4564.2883	4678.1045	4932.3076	5253.8965	5682.3164

continues

Table B-3 *Extended Erlang B with 60 Percent Retry Possibility (Continued)*

Circuits	Grade of Service													
	0.001	0.002	0.003	0.004	0.005	0.01	0.02	0.03	0.04	0.05	0.1	0.2	0.3	0.4
4500	4370.9106	4393.5356	4408.1612	4419.2162	4428.3142	4459.6939	4498.5580	4527.5345	4552.8717	4576.6296	4690.6128	4945.4956	5267.9443	5697.5098
4512	4382.7729	4405.4238	4420.0884	4431.1729	4440.2607	4471.7241	4510.6575	4539.6768	4565.0815	4588.8340	4703.1211	4958.6836	5281.9922	5712.7031
4530	4400.5685	4423.2751	4437.9636	4449.0923	4458.1819	4489.7363	4528.7558	4557.8563	4583.3624	4607.2096	4722.0218	4978.4656	5303.0640	5735.4932
4536	4406.5009	4429.2376	4443.9456	4455.0544	4464.1906	4495.7521	4534.8234	4563.9624	4589.4331	4613.3811	4728.4146	4985.0596	5310.0879	5743.0898
4560	4430.2332	4453.0554	4467.8064	4478.9392	4488.0890	4519.7827	4558.9563	4588.2495	4613.8550	4637.7905	4753.4326	5011.4355	5338.1836	5773.4766
4584	4453.9698	4476.8773	4491.6359	4502.8273	4512.0253	4543.7809	4583.1606	4612.5381	4638.2783	4662.3398	4778.4507	5037.8115	5366.2793	5803.8633
4590	4459.9047	4482.8071	4497.6201	4508.8261	4518.0011	4549.7983	4589.1595	4618.5754	4644.3494	4668.4424	4784.7052	5044.4055	5373.3032	5811.4600
4608	4477.7109	4500.6680	4515.5039	4526.7188	4535.9297	4567.8164	4607.2969	4636.8281	4662.6328	4686.8906	4803.4688	5064.1875	5394.3750	5834.2500
4620	4489.5831	4512.5647	4527.4393	4538.6833	4547.8830	4579.8175	4619.4008	4648.9032	4674.8456	4699.0961	4815.9778	5077.3755	5408.4229	5849.4434
4632	4501.4564	4524.4623	4539.3755	4550.6135	4559.8724	4591.8545	4631.5052	4661.0490	4686.9880	4711.3015	4828.4868	5090.5635	5422.4707	5864.6367
4650	4519.2684	4542.3283	4557.2639	4568.5455	4577.8049	4609.8759	4649.5743	4679.3037	4705.3436	4729.7516	4847.2504	5110.3455	5443.5425	5887.4268
4656	4525.2063	4548.2959	4563.2153	4574.5115	4583.7828	4615.8596	4655.6448	4685.3416	4711.4150	4735.8545	4853.6470	5116.9395	5450.5664	5895.0234
4680	4548.9427	4572.0978	4587.0584	4598.4128	4607.6962	4639.9026	4679.7858	4709.6356	4735.8435	4760.3375	4878.8086	5143.3154	5478.6621	5925.4102
4704	4572.6833	4595.9033	4610.9407	4622.2815	4631.6484	4663.9482	4704.0000	4733.9312	4760.2017	4784.8213	4903.8281	5169.6914	5506.7578	5955.7969
4710	4578.6237	4601.8732	4616.8938	4628.2851	4637.6280	4669.9331	4710.0000	4739.9693	4766.2733	4790.9244	4910.0830	5176.2854	5513.7817	5963.3936
4728	4596.4282	4619.7125	4634.7905	4646.1892	4655.5679	4687.9603	4728.1443	4758.2281	4784.5605	4809.3779	4928.8477	5196.0674	5534.8535	5986.1836
4740	4608.2932	4631.6185	4646.7348	4658.1262	4667.5287	4699.9672	4740.2170	4770.3772	4796.7764	4821.5845	4941.3574	5209.2554	5548.9014	6001.3770
4752	4620.1772	4643.5254	4658.6437	4670.1002	4679.4902	4711.9746	4752.2900	4782.4541	4808.9927	4833.7910	4953.8672	5222.4434	5562.9492	6016.5703
4770	4637.9691	4661.4056	4676.5448	4688.0083	4697.4339	4730.0050	4770.4367	4800.7150	4827.2813	4852.2464	4972.6318	5242.2253	5584.0210	6039.3604
4776	4643.9123	4667.3419	4682.5001	4693.9781	4703.4155	4735.9911	4776.5101	4806.5101	4833.3534	4858.3499	4978.8867	5248.8193	5591.0449	6046.9570
4800	4667.6514	4691.1621	4706.3599	4717.8955	4727.3438	4760.0464	4800.6592	4831.0547	4857.7148	4882.8369	5003.9063	5275.1953	5619.1406	6077.3438
4824	4691.3945	4714.9860	4730.2229	4741.7794	4751.2381	4784.0674	4824.8097	4855.3572	4882.1506	4907.3247	5029.0730	5301.5713	5647.2363	6107.7305
4830	4697.3401	4720.9241	4736.2168	4747.7509	4757.2213	4790.0546	4830.8844	4861.3962	4888.2230	4913.4283	5035.4755	5308.1653	5654.2603	6115.3271
4848	4715.1416	4738.8135	4754.0892	4765.6663	4775.1720	4808.0907	4848.9617	4879.5872	4906.5879	4931.8872	5054.2412	5327.9473	5675.3320	6138.1172
4860	4727.0352	4750.7286	4766.0422	4777.6108	4787.1400	4820.1031	4861.0382	4891.7395	4918.7329	4944.0948	5066.7517	5341.1353	5689.3799	6153.3105
4872	4738.8928	4762.6075	4777.9589	4789.5560	4799.1088	4832.1161	4873.1151	4903.8922	4930.9523	4956.3025	5079.2622	5354.3232	5703.4277	6168.5039

Table B-3 *Extended Erlang B with 60 Percent Retry Possibility (Continued)*

Circuits	Grade of Service													
	0.001	0.002	0.003	0.004	0.005	0.01	0.02	0.03	0.04	0.05	0.1	0.2	0.3	0.4
4890	4756.6994	4780.5018	4795.8726	4807.4753	4817.0634	4850.1553	4891.2685	4922.0847	4949.2447	4974.7632	5098.0280	5374.1052	5724.4995	6191.2939
4896	4762.6479	4786.4421	4801.8318	4813.4487	4823.0112	4856.1438	4897.3447	4928.1987	4955.3174	4980.8672	5104.2832	5380.6992	5731.5234	6198.8906
4920	4786.4072	4810.2429	4825.7080	4837.3819	4846.9537	4880.1736	4921.5015	4952.4316	4979.7583	5005.2832	5129.3042	5407.0752	5759.6191	6229.2773
4944	4810.1516	4834.0847	4849.5498	4861.2806	4870.8992	4904.2057	4945.6597	4976.7407	5004.1252	5029.8501	5154.3252	5434.0547	5787.7148	6259.6641
4950	4816.0835	4840.0269	4855.5107	4867.2558	4876.8860	4910.1952	4951.6617	4982.7805	5010.1982	5035.9543	5160.5804	5440.6494	5794.7388	6267.2607
4968	4833.8998	4857.8923	4873.4324	4885.1444	4894.8096	4928.2399	4969.8193	5001.0513	5028.4929	5054.3427	5179.4978	5460.4336	5815.8105	6290.0508
4980	4845.7658	4869.8163	4885.3560	4897.0963	4906.7848	4940.2579	4981.8997	5013.1311	5040.7150	5066.6272	5192.0087	5473.6230	5829.8584	6305.2441
4992	4857.6709	4881.7031	4897.2803	4909.0488	4918.7227	4952.2764	4993.9805	5025.2871	5052.9375	5078.8359	5204.6719	5486.8125	5843.9063	6320.4375
5010	4875.4732	4899.5730	4915.2063	4926.9791	4936.6878	4970.3242	5012.1405	5043.4836	5071.1572	5097.2255	5223.4387	5506.5967	5864.9780	6343.2275
5016	4881.4078	4905.5555	4921.1693	4932.9562	4942.6765	4976.3150	5018.1431	5049.6002	5077.3070	5103.4065	5229.6943	5513.1914	5872.0020	6350.8242
5040	4905.1483	4929.3732	4945.0232	4956.8665	4966.5948	5000.3174	5042.3071	5073.8379	5101.6772	5127.8247	5254.7168	5539.5703	5900.0977	6381.2109
5064	4928.9312	4953.1941	4968.8800	4980.7797	4990.5157	5024.3602	5066.4727	5098.1536	5126.1255	5152.3975	5279.7393	5565.9492	5929.4297	6411.5977
5070	4934.8485	4959.1402	4974.8447	4986.7584	4996.5060	5030.3906	5072.5529	5104.1940	5132.1991	5158.5022	5285.9949	5572.5439	5936.4551	6419.1943
5088	4952.6792	4977.0183	4992.7397	5004.6570	5014.4780	5048.4053	5090.6396	5122.4707	5150.4199	5176.8164	5304.7617	5592.3281	5957.5313	6441.9844
5100	4964.5546	4988.9122	5004.7096	5016.6161	5026.4214	5060.4286	5102.7237	5134.5520	5162.6450	5189.1037	5317.2729	5605.5176	5971.5820	6457.1777
5112	4976.4309	5000.8458	5016.6414	5028.5759	5038.4042	5072.4525	5114.8081	5146.7113	5174.8704	5201.3914	5329.7842	5618.7070	5985.6328	6472.3711
5130	4994.2471	5018.6893	5034.5405	5046.5170	5056.3408	5090.4698	5132.9745	5164.9118	5193.1700	5219.7061	5348.5510	5638.4912	6006.7090	6495.1611
5136	5000.1863	5024.6766	5040.5072	5052.4585	5062.3330	5096.4628	5138.9780	5171.0310	5199.2439	5225.8110	5354.9634	5645.0859	6013.7344	6502.7578
5160	5023.9453	5048.4714	5064.3759	5076.3831	5086.2643	5120.4749	5163.1494	5195.2734	5223.6182	5250.3882	5379.9866	5671.4648	6041.8359	6533.1445
5184	5047.7080	5072.3086	5088.2476	5100.2710	5110.1982	5144.5283	5187.3223	5219.5957	5248.0723	5274.8086	5405.1680	5697.8438	6069.9375	6563.5313
5190	5053.6295	5078.2585	5094.2159	5106.2533	5116.1920	5150.5618	5193.4053	5225.6369	5254.1464	5280.9137	5411.4240	5704.4385	6076.9629	6571.1279
5208	5071.4744	5096.1491	5112.1221	5124.2012	5134.1347	5168.5840	5211.4966	5243.8400	5272.4484	5299.3879	5430.1919	5724.2227	6098.0391	6593.9180
5220	5083.3589	5108.0507	5124.0605	5136.1276	5146.0840	5180.5728	5223.5843	5256.0022	5284.6765	5311.5985	5442.7039	5737.4121	6112.0898	6609.1113
5232	5095.2244	5119.9530	5135.9996	5148.0945	5158.0737	5192.6019	5235.6724	5268.1648	5296.8252	5323.8091	5455.2158	5750.6016	6126.1406	6624.3047
5250	5113.0543	5137.8479	5153.8696	5166.0461	5176.0197	5210.6266	5253.8052	5286.3693	5315.1283	5342.2852	5473.9838	5770.3857	6147.2168	6647.0947
5256	5118.9780	5143.7999	5159.8400	5171.9903	5181.9752	5216.6217	5259.8496	5292.4109	5321.2028	5348.3906	5480.2397	5776.9805	6154.2422	6654.6914

continues

Table B-3 *Extended Erlang B with 60 Percent Retry Possibility (Continued)*

Circuits	Grade of Service													
	0.001	0.002	0.003	0.004	0.005	0.01	0.02	0.03	0.04	0.05	0.1	0.2	0.3	0.4
5280	5142.7551	5167.6099	5183.7231	5195.9290	5205.9192	5240.6836	5284.0283	5316.7383	5345.5811	5372.8125	5505.2637	5803.3594	6182.3438	6685.0781
5304	5166.4955	5191.4632	5207.6093	5219.8301	5229.8657	5264.7072	5308.2085	5340.9862	5370.0410	5397.3962	5530.2876	5829.7383	6210.4453	6715.4648
5310	5172.4615	5197.4169	5213.5812	5225.8159	5235.8629	5270.7033	5314.2133	5347.1091	5376.1157	5403.5019	5536.5436	5836.3330	6217.4707	6723.0615
5328	5190.2798	5215.2792	5231.4576	5243.7338	5253.8148	5288.7327	5332.3901	5365.3162	5394.4211	5421.8188	5555.4741	5856.1172	6238.5469	6745.8516
5340	5202.1529	5227.1883	5243.4032	5255.6662	5265.7700	5300.7664	5344.4815	5377.4002	5406.5707	5434.1116	5567.9865	5869.3066	6252.5977	6761.0449
5352	5214.0269	5239.0981	5255.3494	5267.6400	5277.7256	5312.8008	5356.5324	5389.5659	5418.8020	5446.4048	5580.6621	5882.4961	6266.6484	6776.2383
5370	5231.8497	5257.0052	5273.2702	5285.5611	5295.6807	5330.7919	5374.6706	5407.7742	5437.1086	5464.7223	5599.4312	5902.2803	6287.7246	6799.0283
5376	5237.8184	5262.9609	5279.2441	5291.5488	5301.6797	5336.7891	5380.6758	5413.8984	5443.1836	5470.8281	5605.6875	5908.8750	6294.7500	6806.6250
5400	5261.5723	5286.7859	5303.1006	5315.4602	5325.5951	5360.8612	5404.8615	5438.1500	5467.5659	5495.4163	5630.7129	5935.2539	6322.8516	6837.0117
5424	5285.3295	5310.6138	5326.9596	5339.3741	5349.5541	5384.8942	5429.0486	5462.4023	5491.9490	5519.8403	5655.7383	5961.6328	6350.9531	6867.3984
5430	5291.2589	5316.5712	5332.9351	5345.3220	5355.5132	5390.8923	5435.0542	5468.5277	5498.1070	5525.9464	5661.9946	5968.2275	6357.9785	6874.9951
5448	5309.0900	5334.4446	5350.8627	5363.2906	5373.4741	5408.9290	5453.2372	5486.7385	5516.3328	5544.4307	5680.7637	5988.0117	6379.0547	6897.7852
5460	5320.9923	5346.3611	5362.7737	5375.2290	5385.4349	5420.9262	5465.3320	5498.8239	5528.5666	5556.6431	5693.2764	6001.2012	6393.1055	6912.9785
5472	5332.8538	5358.2783	5374.7271	5387.1680	5397.4380	5432.9656	5477.3855	5510.9927	5540.8008	5568.8555	5705.7891	6014.3906	6407.1563	6928.1719
5490	5350.6892	5376.1555	5392.6584	5405.0983	5415.3603	5450.9628	5495.5289	5529.2047	5559.0271	5587.1741	5724.5581	6034.1748	6428.2324	6950.9619
5496	5356.6208	5382.1150	5398.5939	5411.0894	5421.3625	5457.0040	5501.5349	5535.2476	5565.1025	5593.3641	5730.8145	6040.7695	6435.2578	6958.5586
5520	5380.3912	5405.9546	5422.5055	5435.0134	5445.2893	5481.0022	5525.7275	5559.5874	5589.5728	5617.8735	5756.0083	6067.1484	6463.3594	6988.9453
5544	5404.1649	5429.7971	5446.3777	5458.8977	5469.2183	5505.0864	5549.9216	5583.8441	5613.9598	5642.2991	5781.0344	6093.5273	6491.4609	7019.3320
5550	5410.1194	5435.7582	5452.3567	5464.8903	5475.2220	5511.0867	5555.9280	5589.8872	5620.0356	5648.4901	5787.4603	6100.1221	6498.4863	7026.9287
5568	5427.9419	5453.6213	5470.2524	5482.8267	5493.1919	5529.0879	5574.0747	5608.1016	5638.3477	5666.8945	5806.2305	6119.9063	6519.5625	7049.7188
5580	5439.8316	5465.5238	5482.1695	5494.7708	5505.1584	5541.1317	5586.1304	5620.2731	5650.4993	5679.1077	5818.7439	6133.0957	6533.6133	7064.9121
5592	5451.7222	5477.4483	5494.1298	5506.7582	5517.1254	5553.1335	5598.2289	5632.4451	5662.7362	5691.3208	5831.2573	6146.2852	6547.6641	7080.1055
5610	5469.5488	5495.3364	5512.0287	5524.6550	5535.0984	5571.1796	5616.3773	5650.6609	5681.0495	5709.8117	5850.0275	6166.0693	6568.7402	7102.8955
5616	5475.5057	5501.2994	5518.0096	5530.6494	5541.0612	5577.1809	5622.4270	5656.7043	5687.1255	5715.9185	5856.2842	6172.6641	6575.7656	7110.4922
5640	5499.2496	5525.1535	5541.8921	5554.5859	5564.9991	5601.2302	5646.6266	5680.9644	5711.5155	5740.3455	5881.3110	6199.0430	6603.8672	7140.8789
5664	5523.0396	5548.9673	5565.7771	5578.4817	5588.9392	5625.2813	5670.7412	5705.3115	5735.9063	5764.9453	5906.3379	6225.4219	6631.9688	7171.2656

Table B-3 *Extended Erlang B with 60 Percent Retry Possibility (Continued)*

Circuits	Grade of Service														
	0.001	0.002	0.003	0.004	0.005	0.01	0.02	0.03	0.04	0.05	0.1	0.2	0.3	0.4
5670	5528.9767	5554.9319	5571.7596	5584.4776	5594.9462	5631.2835	5676.8349	5711.3553	5741.9824	5771.0522	5912.5946	6232.0166	6638.9941	7178.8623
5688	5546.8111	5572.8270	5589.6647	5602.3797	5612.8815	5649.2908	5694.9434	5729.5734	5760.2977	5789.3730	5931.3647	6251.8008	6660.0703	7201.6523
5700	5558.7090	5584.7145	5601.5877	5614.3730	5624.8535	5661.2961	5707.0450	5741.7480	5772.5372	5801.5869	5943.8782	6264.9902	6674.1211	7216.8457
5712	5570.5858	5596.6461	5613.5548	5626.3235	5636.8260	5673.3453	5719.1470	5753.8359	5784.6899	5813.8879	5956.3916	6278.1797	6688.1719	7232.0391
5730	5588.4025	5614.5449	5631.4632	5644.2284	5654.8077	5691.3547	5737.2569	5772.0552	5803.0064	5832.2964	5975.3366	6297.9639	6709.2480	7254.8291
5736	5594.3417	5620.4897	5637.4037	5650.2261	5660.7728	5697.4017	5743.2645	5778.0992	5809.0829	5838.4036	5981.5935	6304.5586	6716.2734	7262.4258
5760	5618.1445	5644.3359	5661.2988	5674.1309	5684.7217	5721.4160	5767.4707	5802.4512	5833.4766	5862.8320	6006.7969	6331.6406	6744.3750	7292.8125

TCL IVR Scripts

Overview of Interactive Voice Response and Tool Command Language

Interactive Voice Response (IVR) applications collect user input in response to recorded messages over telephone lines. User input can take the form of spoken words or, more commonly, dual-tone multi-frequency (DTMF) signaling. For example, when someone makes a call with a debit card, an IVR application (or script) prompts the caller to enter a specific type of information, such as a PIN. After playing a voice prompt, the IVR application collects a predetermined number of touch tones (digit collection), forwards the collected digits to a server for storage and retrieval, and then places the call to the destination phone or system. Call records can be kept and a variety of accounting functions performed.

The prompts used in an IVR script can be either static or dynamic:

- Static prompts are audio files at a static URL. The name of the audio file and its location are specified in the Tool Command Language (TCL) script.

- Dynamic prompts are formed by the underlying system assembling smaller audio prompts and playing them out in sequence. The script uses an API command with a notation form to instruct the system what to play. The underlying system then assembles a sequence of URLs, based on the language selected and the location of the audio file, and plays them in sequence. This provides simple Text-to-Speech (TTS) operations.

For example, dynamic prompts are used to inform the caller of how much time is left in his or her debit account, as in the following:

"You have 15 minutes and 32 seconds of call time remaining in your account."

The preceding prompt is created by using eight individual prompt files. The filenames are youhave.au, 15.au, minutes.au, and.au, 30.au, 2.au, seconds.au, and leftinyouraccount.au. These audio files are assembled dynamically by the underlying system and played as a prompt based on the selected language and prompt file locations.

The Cisco IVR feature, available in Cisco IOS Release 12.0(7)T and later, provides IVR capabilities using TCL 1.0 scripts. These scripts are signature locked and can be modified only by Cisco. The IVR feature allows TCL IVR scripts to be used during call processing. The scripts interact with the IOS software to perform various call-related functions.

Starting with Cisco IOS Release 12.1(3)T, TCL scripts are no longer signature locked, so you can create and change your own TCL scripts. The TCL IVR Version 2.0 feature delivers a new set of TCL verbs and TCL scripts that replace the previous TCL Version 1.0 verbs and scripts. Note that the TCL IVR Version 2.0 feature is not backward compatible with IVR 1.0 scripts.

For a complete list of available TCL software, TCL scripts, and audio files for both Version 1.0 and Version 2.0, refer to the following URL:

http://www.cisco.com/cgi-bin/tablebuild.pl/tclware

For more information about TCL IVR Version 1 scripts, refer to the *TCL IVR API Version 1.0 Programmer's Guide* at the following URL:

http://www.cisco.com/univercd/cc/td/doc/product/access/acs_serv/vapp_dev/ tclivrpg.htm

For more information about TCL IVR Version 2 scripts, refer to *TCL IVR API Version 2.0 Programmer's Guide* at the following URL:

http://www.cisco.com/univercd/cc/td/doc/product/access/acs_serv/vapp_dev/ tclivrv2.htm

For more general information about TCL and how to create scripts using TCL, it's recommended that you read *TCL and the TK Toolkit* by John Ousterhout (published by Addison-Wesley).

TCL IVR Script in Detail

The following is an example of a TCL script—in this case, the TCL code for the clid_authen.tcl TCL Version 1.0 script. This particular TCL script authenticates the call using ANI and DNIS numbers, collects the destination data, and makes the call.

NOTE   You can view the contents of any TCL IVR script by using the **show call application voice** command.

```
Router #show call application voice clid_authen.tcl
Application clid_authen
    The script is compiled into the image
    It has 0 calls active.
```

```
The TCL Script is:
- - - - - - - - - - - - - - - - -
# clid_authen.tcl
#- - - - - - - - - - - - - - - - - - - - - - - - - - - - - - - - -
# September 1998, Development Engineer name
 - -More-
#
# Copyright (c) 1998, 1999 by cisco Systems, Inc.
# All rights reserved.
#- - - - - - - - - - - - - - - - - - - - - - - - - - - - - - - - -
# Mimic the clid_authen script in the SP1.0 release.
#
# It authenticates using (ani, dnis) for (account, password). If
# that fails, play a message and end the call.
#
# If authentication passes, it collects the destination number and
# places the call.
#
# The main routine is at the bottom. Start reading the script there.
#

proc do_get_dest {} {
    global state
    global destination

    playTone Dial
    set prompt(dialPlan) True
    set prompt(terminationKey) #
set event [promptAndCollect prompt info ]

    if {$event == "collect success"} {
        set state place_call
        set destination $info(digits)
        return 0
    }
if {$event == "collect aborted"} {
        set state get_dest
        return 0
    }
set state get_fail
    return 0
}
proc do_authen_pass {} {
    global state
    global destination

    set dnislen [string len [dnis]]

if { [did] && $dnislen } {
        set destination [dnis]
        set state place_call
    } else {
        set state get_dest
    }
    return 0
}
proc do_place_call {} {
    global state
    global destination

    set event [placeCall $destination callInfo info]

    if {$event == "active"} {
```

continues

```
                set state active
                return 0
            }
            if {$event == "call fail"} {
                set state place_fail
                return 0
            }
        set state end
            return 0
    }
    proc do_active_notimer {} {
        global state

        set event [waitEvent]
        while { $event == "digit"} {
            set event [waitEvent]
        }
        set state end
        return 0
    }
    proc do_active_last_timer {} {
        global state

        set event [startTimer [creditTimeLeft] info]
        while { $event == "digit"} {
            set event [startTimer $info(timeLeft) info]
        }
    if { $event == "timeout"} {
            clearOutgoingLeg retInfo
            set state out_of_time
        } else {
            set state end
        }

        return 0
    }
    proc do_active_timer {} {
        global state

        if { [creditTimeLeft] < 10 } {
            do_active_last_timer
            return 0
        }
        set delay [expr [creditTimeLeft] - 10]
        set event [startTimer $delay info]
        while { $event == "digit"} {
            set event [startTimer $info(timeLeft) info]
        }
        if { $event == "timeout"} {
    insertMessage flash:beep.au retInfo
            do_active_last_timer
        } else {
            set state end
        }

        return 0
    }

    proc do_active {} {
        global state

        if { ( [creditTimeLeft] == "unlimited") ||
            ([creditTimeLeft] == "uninitialized") } {
                do_active_notimer
```

```
    } else {
            do_active_timer
    }
    return 0
}

proc do_out_of_time {} {
    global state
 --More--

    set prompt(url) flash:out_of_time.au
    set prompt(playComplete) true
    set event [promptAndCollect prompt info ]
    set state end
    return 0
}

proc do_authen_fail {} {
    global state

    set prompt(url) flash:auth_failed.au
    set prompt(playComplete) true
    set event [promptAndCollect prompt info ]
    set state end
    return 0
}

proc do_get_fail {} {
    global state


    playTone None
 --More--

    set prompt(url) flash:collect_failed.au
    set prompt(playComplete) true
    set event [promptAndCollect prompt info ]
    set state end
    return 0
}

proc do_place_fail {} {
    global state

    playFailureTone 5 retInfo
    set state end
    return 0
}
#---------------------------------------
# And here is the main loop
#

acceptCall

 --More--
set event [authenticate [ani] [dnis] info]

if {$event != "authenticated"} {
    set state authen_fail
} else {
    set state authen_pass
}

while {$state != "end"} {
```

continues

```
    puts "cid([callID]) running state $state"
    if {$state == "get_dest"} {
        do_get_dest
    } elseif {$state == "place_call"} {
        do_place_call
    } elseif {$state == "active"} {
        do_active
    } elseif {$state == "authen_fail"} {
        do_authen_fail
    } elseif {$state == "authen_pass"} {
        do_authen_pass
    } elseif {$state == "place_fail"} {
        do_place_fail
    } elseif {$state == "get_fail"} {
--More--
        do_get_fail
    } elseif {$state == "out_of_time"} {
        do_out_of_time
    } else {
        break
    }end
```

INDEX

Symbols

s variable, 319

Numerics

4-wire transmission, 36

A

AAA (authentication, authorization, and accounting), 312, 413. *See also* security
    debit card applications, 419–423, 425
    prepaid services, 440
    security, 341-343
aaa accounting update command, 420
aaa new-model command, 341
aaa new-model component, 312
AAA RADIUS Security Server, 258
ACB (Agent Communications Broker), 361
access
    dedicated Internet, 393–394
    dial Internet, 385, 390
    services, 359
accounting. *See also* AAA
    debit card applications, 419–420
    MMoIP, 346
    RADIUS, 344–347
    SMTP, 347–352
ACF (admission confirm message), 371
ACL (access control list), 326
ACOM (acombined), 43
adaptation period, 42
adding rate centers, 193
addresses, virtual, 186
administration, dial plan call routing, 197–206
administrators
    faxes, 383
    greeting, 383
    UMSA, 384
AF (Assured Forwarding) PHB, 80
AHT (Average Hold Time), 6
allocation of bandwidth, 157

AltDGK (alternate directory gatekeeper), 263
alternate directory gatekeeper (AltDGK), 263
alternate gatekeepers, 186–187, 216
AMM (agent manager and monitor), 361
analog signals, leak-through, 32
analyzing traffic, 5
    sampling methods, 8
    VoIP networks
        point-to-multipoint links, 24
        RTP header compression, 21
        samples per packet, 20
        VAD, 21
        voice codecs, 19
ANI (automatic number identification), 177, 293, 366
answer-address, 177
answer-address command, 177
application name command, 465
application on-ramp command, 314
application settlement command, 463
applications
    billing, 255
    components, 257–258
    debit cards, 413–425, 426–431
    hosting, 255
    IP telephony, 121
    mediation applications, 255
    prepaid services, 433–434
    servers, 256
    services, 360–361
applying
    Cisco IOS tools, 208–212
    NTP, 457–459
architecture
    OSP, 453, 456
    prepaid services, 432–434
    PV-VPN, 289–290
area codes, zone prefixes, 198–199
ARJ (Admission Reject), 206
ARQ (Admission Request), 173
arq reject-unknown-prefix gatekeeper command, 206
ASP (application service provider), 233-235
ATM (asynchronous transfer mode)
    PVC bundles, 90
    QoS example, 89, 91–92

E

K–L

M

N

U

Train with authorized Cisco Learning Partners.

Discover all that's possible on the Internet.

One of the biggest challenges facing networking professionals is how to stay current with today's ever-changing technologies in the global Internet economy. Nobody understands this better than Cisco Learning Partners, the only companies that deliver training developed by Cisco Systems.

Just go to **www.cisco.com/go/training_ad**. You'll find more than 120 Cisco Learning Partners in over 90 countries worldwide.* Only Cisco Learning Partners have instructors that are certified by Cisco to provide recommended training on Cisco networks and to prepare you for certifications.

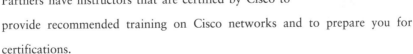

To get ahead in this world, you first have to be able to keep up. Insist on training that is developed and authorized by Cisco, as indicated by the Cisco Learning Partner or Cisco Learning Solutions Partner logo.

Visit **www.cisco.com/go/training_ad** today.

CISCO SYSTEMS

EMPOWERING THE
INTERNET GENERATION℠

CCIE Professional Development

Cisco LAN Switching

Kennedy Clark, CCIE; Kevin Hamilton, CCIE

1-57870-094-9 • AVAILABLE NOW

This volume provides an in-depth analysis of Cisco LAN switching technologies, architectures, and deployments, including unique coverage of Catalyst network design essentials. Network designs and configuration examples are incorporated throughout to demonstrate the principles and enable easy translation of the material into practice in production networks.

Advanced IP Network Design

Alvaro Retana, CCIE; Don Slice, CCIE; and Russ White, CCIE

1-57870-097-3 • AVAILABLE NOW

Network engineers and managers can use these case studies, which highlight various network design goals, to explore issues including protocol choice, network stability, and growth. This book also includes theoretical discussion on advanced design topics.

Large-Scale IP Network Solutions

Khalid Raza, CCIE; and Mark Turner

1-57870-084-1 • AVAILABLE NOW

Network engineers can find solutions as their IP networks grow in size and complexity. Examine all the major IP protocols in-depth and learn about scalability, migration planning, network management, and security for large-scale networks.

Routing TCP/IP, Volume I

Jeff Doyle, CCIE

1-57870-041-8 • AVAILABLE NOW

This book takes the reader from a basic understanding of routers and routing protocols through a detailed examination of each of the IP interior routing protocols. Learn techniques for designing networks that maximize the efficiency of the protocol being used. Exercises and review questions provide core study for the CCIE Routing and Switching exam.

Cisco Press   **www.ciscopress.com**

Cisco Press Solutions

Enhanced IP Services for Cisco Networks

Donald C. Lee, CCIE

1-57870-106-6 • AVAILABLE NOW

This is a guide to improving your network's capabilities by understanding the new enabling and advanced Cisco IOS services that build more scalable, intelligent, and secure networks. Learn the technical details necessary to deploy Quality of Service, VPN technologies, IPsec, the IOS firewall and IOS Intrusion Detection. These services will allow you to extend the network to new frontiers securely, protect your network from attacks, and increase the sophistication of network services.

Developing IP Multicast Networks, Volume I

Beau Williamson, CCIE

1-57870-077-9 • AVAILABLE NOW

This book provides a solid foundation of IP multicast concepts and explains how to design and deploy the networks that will support appplications such as audio and video conferencing, distance-learning, and data replication. Includes an in-depth discussion of the PIM protocol used in Cisco routers and detailed coverage of the rules that control the creation and maintenance of Cisco mroute state entries.

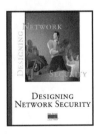

Designing Network Security

Merike Kaeo

1-57870-043-4 • AVAILABLE NOW

Designing Network Security is a practical guide designed to help you understand the fundamentals of securing your corporate infrastructure. This book takes a comprehensive look at underlying security technologies, the process of creating a security policy, and the practical requirements necessary to implement a corporate security policy.

Cisco Press   **www.ciscopress.com**

Cisco Press Solutions

Residential Broadband, Second Edition
George Abe

1-57870-177-5 • **AVAILABLE NOW**

This book will answer basic questions of residential broadband networks such as: Why do we need high speed networks at home? How will high speed residential services be delivered to the home? How do regulatory or commercial factors affect this technology? Explore such networking topics as xDSL, cable, and wireless.

Internetworking Technologies Handbook, Third Edition
Cisco Systems, et al.

1-58705-001-3 • **AVAILABLE NOW**

This comprehensive reference provides a foundation for understanding and implementing contemporary internetworking technologies, providing you with the necessary information needed to make rational networking decisions. Master terms, concepts, technologies, and devices that are used in the internetworking industry today. You also learn how to incorporate networking technologies into a LAN/WAN environment, as well as how to apply the OSI reference model to categorize protocols, technologies, and devices.

OpenCable Architecture
Michael Adams

1-57870-135-X • **AVAILABLE NOW**

Whether you're a television, data communications, or telecommunications professional, or simply an interested business person, this book will help you understand the technical and business issues surrounding interactive television services. It will also provide you with an inside look at the combined efforts of the cable, data, and consumer electronics industries' efforts to develop those new services.

Performance and Fault Management
Paul Della Maggiora, Christopher Elliott, Robert Pavone, Kent Phelps, James Thompson

1-57870-180-5 • **AVAILABLE NOW**

This book is a comprehensive guide to designing and implementing effective strategies for monitoring performance levels and correctng problems in Cisco networks. It provides an overview of router and LAN switch operations to help you understand how to manage such devices, as well as guidance on the essential MIBs, traps, syslog messages, and show commands for managing Cisco routers and switches.

Cisco Press

www.ciscopress.com

Cisco Press Fundamentals

Internet Routing Architectures, Second Edition

Sam Halabi with Danny McPherson

1-57870-233-x • AVAILABLE NOW

This book explores the ins and outs of interdomain routing network design with emphasis on BGP-4 (Border Gateway Protocol Version 4)--the de facto interdomain routing protocol. You will have all the information you need to make knowledgeable routing decisions for Internet connectivity in your environment.

Voice over IP Fundamentals

Jonathan Davidson and James Peters

1-57870-168-6 • AVAILABLE NOW

Voice over IP (VoIP), which integrates voice and data transmission, is quickly becoming an important factor in network communications. It promises lower operational costs, greater flexibility, and a variety of enhanced applications. This book provides a thorough introduction to this new technology to help experts in both the data and telephone industries plan for the new networks.

For the latest on Cisco Press resources and Certification and

Training guides, or for information on publishing opportunities, visit

www.ciscopress.com

Cisco Press

 **CISCO SYSTEMS**

Cisco Press

Committed to being your long-term learning resource while you grow as a Cisco Networking Professional

Help Cisco Press **stay connected** to the issues and challenges you face on a daily basis by registering your product and filling out our brief survey. Complete and mail this form, or better yet ...

Register online and enter to win a FREE book!

Jump to **www.ciscopress.com/register** and register your product online. Each complete entry will be eligible for our monthly drawing to win a FREE book of the winner's choice from the Cisco Press library.

May we contact you via e-mail with information about **new releases, special promotions**, and **customer benefits**?

❒ Yes   ❒ No

E-mail address _____

Name _____

Address _____

City _____ State/Province _____

Country _____ Zip/Post code _____

Where did you buy this product?

❒ Bookstore   ❒ Computer store/Electronics store   ❒ Direct from Cisco Systems
❒ Online retailer   ❒ Direct from Cisco Press   ❒ Office supply store
❒ Mail order   ❒ Class/Seminar   ❒ Discount store
❒ Other _____

When did you buy this product? _____ **Month** _____ **Year**

What price did you pay for this product?

❒ Full retail price   ❒ Discounted price   ❒ Gift

Was this purchase reimbursed as a company expense?

❒ Yes   ❒ No

How did you learn about this product?

❒ Friend   ❒ Store personnel   ❒ In-store ad   ❒ cisco.com
❒ Cisco Press catalog   ❒ Postcard in the mail   ❒ Saw it on the shelf ❒ ciscopress.com
❒ Other catalog   ❒ Magazine ad   ❒ Article or review
❒ School   ❒ Professional organization ❒ Used other products
❒ Other _____

What will this product be used for?

❒ Business use   ❒ School/Education
❒ Certification training ❒ Professional development/Career growth
❒ Other _____

How many years have you been employed in a computer-related industry?

❒ less than 2 years   ❒ 2–5 years   ❒ more than 5 years

Have you purchased a Cisco Press product before?

❒ Yes   ❒ No

Cisco Press

How many computer technology books do you own?
❏ 1 ❏ 2–7 ❏ more than 7

Which best describes your job function? (check all that apply)
❏ Corporate Management ❏ Systems Engineering ❏ IS Management ❏ Cisco Networking
❏ Network Design ❏ Network Support ❏ Webmaster Academy Program
❏ Marketing/Sales ❏ Consultant ❏ Student Instuctor
❏ Professor/Teacher ❏ Other _____

Do you hold any computer certifications? (check all that apply)
❏ MCSE ❏ CCNA ❏ CCDA
❏ CCNP ❏ CCDP ❏ CCIE ❏ Other _____

Are you currently pursuing a certification? (check all that apply)
❏ MCSE ❏ CCNA ❏ CCDA
❏ CCNP ❏ CCDP ❏ CCIE ❏ Other _____

On what topics would you like to see more coverage?
_____
_____

Do you have any additional comments or suggestions?
_____
_____

Thank you for completing this survey and registration. Please fold here, seal, and mail to Cisco Press.

Deploying Cisco Voice over IP Solutions (1-58705-030-7)

Indianapolis, IN 46278-8046
P.O. Box #781046
Customer Registration—CP050227
Cisco Press

ciscopress.com
Indianapolis, IN 46290
201 West 103rd Street
Cisco Press

Place
Stamp
Here